P9-DNU-668

The Age of Impeachment

Herblock, *Washington Post*, August 6, 1974. © The Herb Block Foundation.

The Age of Impeachment
American Constitutional Culture since 1960

David E. Kyvig

 University Press of Kansas

© 2008 by the University Press of Kansas

Published by the University Press of Kansas (Lawrence,
Kansas 66045), which was organized by the Kansas
Board of Regents and is operated and funded by
Emporia State University, Fort Hays State University,
Kansas State University, Pittsburg State University, the
University of Kansas, and Wichita State University

Library of Congress Cataloging-in-Publication Data

Kyvig, David E.
    The age of impeachment : American constitutional
culture since 1960 / David E. Kyvig.
        p.   cm.
    Includes bibliographical references and index.
    ISBN 978-0-7006-1581-0 (cloth : alk. paper)
    1. Impeachments—United States—Cases.
2. Constitutional law—United States. I. Title.
    KF5075.K98 2008
    342.73´068—dc22   2008001345

British Library Cataloguing-in-Publication Data is
available.

Printed in the United States of America
10 9 8 7 6 5 4 3 2 1

The paper used in this publication is recycled and
contains 50 percent postconsumer waste. It is acid free
and meets the minimum requirements of the American
National Standard for Permanence of Paper for Printed
Library Materials Z39.48-1992.

Contents

Preface

The United States Constitution of 1787 stands as unquestionably one of the great achievements of the eighteenth-century Enlightenment. Based on a faith that humans could perceptively observe their environment, come to understand how the social as well as the natural world worked, and rationally devise arrangements for governing a society in which a maximum of individual worth was preserved, the Constitution created a structure for a government that would be responsive and responsible to its citizens, limited in its authority, and exquisitely balanced among its legislative, executive, and judicial branches so that the power of each would be checked by the others. Among its less-often acclaimed but extraordinarily important features were explicit provisions for governmental repair should the Constitution fail to function as its creators intended or should it confront conditions they had not anticipated. The first of these devices was a clearly defined process for constitutional amendment. The second was a mechanism for the formal charging and subsequent removal of individuals holding office who seriously violated its definition of their authority, what has come to be known commonly as the impeachment power.

Having started my career as an American historian sometime after the Enlightenment but still in the grip of optimistic rationalism, I initially focused my attention on the Constitution's first repair device. I began by examining the adoption and subsequent removal from the Constitution by the prescribed amending process of a remarkable provision for social reform, the national prohibition of alcoholic beverages.[1] I then turned my attention to the larger history of constitutional amendment, believing that it was important to look at its overall use rather than focusing on particular amending episodes, even those as important as the ones that produced the Bill of Rights, the Civil War amendments, or the amendments of the Progressive Era, such as those ushering in woman suffrage or national prohibition. I concluded that work with an understanding that amendment had become a very difficult means for achieving constitutional repair in the closely divided and highly contentious political climate of the late twentieth century.[2] However, the framers' other device for protecting the Constitution, impeachment power, had emerged from a long period of disuse to become a prominent weapon in the arsenal of those claiming to defend the integrity of the American system of constitutional self-government.

This book examines the extraordinarily frequent use of the second constitutional repair mechanism in the period since 1960, a period I have chosen to label the age of impeachment. The book seeks to provide answers to the question of why impeachment has been employed so often since 1961 in contrast to its infrequent use between 1789 and 1960. Ultimately, this work returns to the larger question with which I began my studies of U.S. constitutional history: Does our eighteenth-century Constitution still serve us well more than two centuries after it was first constructed? For the reader who persists, the only conclusions I can offer with confidence, as a conscientious historian but unreliable forecaster, are "maybe" and "it is too soon to tell."

Understanding any period in the past poses difficulties, but perhaps no era offers a greater challenge than the recent past. Personal memory based on incomplete evidence and obstructed vision is an inevitable obstacle to full insight. Fewer historians have attempted to digest the mass of existing information, distill its essential qualities, and make sense of it than have attempted over the years to understand eras already a half century or more in the past. Figuring out the enduring characteristics of the New Deal, the Civil War, or the American Revolution is hard enough even with the perspective and distilled knowledge provided by the passage of time and the efforts of generations of thoughtful scholars. Dealing with an era whose latest shifts and new recurrent patterns are too recent to be fully discerned is even more daunting. Yet if the study of the past is to be useful as a means of comprehending our circumstances, needs, opportunities, and likely prospects, an effort needs to be made to come to terms with recent developments that link the present to a more distant past. The first attempts to identify the deeper patterns of historical development may fall well short of the ideal, but they do serve to start us thinking about the meaning of the period through which we have lived.

In 1999, as I was thinking about fresh ways of teaching a course on U.S. history since 1960, I started contemplating impeachment as a recurring phenomenon of recent history. The tumultuous impeachment of President Bill Clinton had just concluded, and in its course I had made various observations. First, the impeachment process had riveted Americans even though most did not appear to understand all its dimensions. Second, many remembered little or nothing of Watergate and related events that had taken place even afterward, much less earlier. For a steadily increasing number of people, those events had occurred before they were born, or at least before they had become aware of events beyond their immediate sphere of consciousness. Third and most important, neither journalists, scholars, politicians, nor the general public were making appropriate linkages between the Clinton impeachment and earlier impeachments. Famed Watergate reporter Bob Woodward's ambitious effort to do so in his 1999 book *Shadow: Five Presidents and the Legacy of Watergate* was unique. As useful as his book was, it proved very consistent with Woodward's usual approach of limiting himself to the presentation of facts uncovered in his own investigations of executive branch conduct. As he would say to me, he thought of himself as a fact seeker who left the larger task of providing context and interpretation to historians whose work would follow.[3]

As I thought about the Clinton impeachment, I harkened back to my high school days when, on the outskirts of my hometown, a billboard had been erected with an exhortation to "Impeach Earl Warren!" I revisited vivid memories of Watergate, including my own attendance at one morning of the Senate hearings. I have since always regretted my failure to return for the afternoon session and its surprise revelation of the White House tape-recording system, though it has ever after given me an effective means to explain historians' limited capacity to predict the future. I recalled thinking at the time of the Iran-Contra revelations in 1986–1987 that they suggested the need for another impeachment, one that for some reason did not take place. Finally, I ruminated on the events of recent months, during which an impeachment and trial had occurred that many Americans clearly felt should not have gone forward. At that moment, however, I did not think about all the ways these episodes connected to and influenced each other. In the beginning, I gave no thought whatsoever to a number of closely related episodes during the same period.

Since those initial 1999 meditations, I have studied impeachment in some detail. I have come to understand the post-1960 impeachment episodes not as isolated incidents but as events interrelated in many respects, each event building on the previous experiences of Congress, the judicial and executive branches, the press, and the public in dealing with impeachment. Furthermore, I have come to believe that calls for impeachment have been a sort of canary in the mine shaft, an early signal of an increasingly toxic political culture. Both the conduct that has provoked such calls and, more recently, the tendency to think of impeachment as a first response to hints of official missteps have become barometers of the American political climate.

This book attempts to explore the political and constitutional culture of impeachment since 1960 as a means of understanding broad patterns of our times. The detailed stories told here seek to be informative and interesting in their own right, but the purpose of presenting them is to shed light on evolving patterns and webs of connections among various episodes. I trust that what follows will illuminate the nature and limits of the constitutional repair mechanism of impeachment in the recent past by showing why some of those cases proceeded and others did not. It is for the reader to decide whether examining this history leads to the conclusion that the Constitution's impeachment mechanism functions well or is itself in need of repair through amendment or less formal and drastic alterations of the American political culture.

Acknowledgments

In pursuing this examination of nearly a half century of impeachments I have had substantial assistance for which I am most grateful. That is not to say that those who aided me in the variety of ways described below are responsible for what has resulted. I bear sole responsibility for the judgments reached in this book.

My first debt of gratitude is to my students at Northern Illinois University. Their questions and observations in undergraduate courses on America since 1960 and on U.S. Constitutional history, in various graduate seminars, and especially in an undergraduate honors seminar on impeachment helped motivate me to go forward with this project. Their interest in the subject and even their occasional blank stares of incomprehension helped me realize how I needed to proceed and why it was worthwhile to do so.

Students were not the only people who helped shape my work. I would like as well to thank all those who talked to me, not only those listed in the bibliography as interviewees but also the larger number, scholars and nonacademics alike, who during informal conversations asked questions, offered insights, suggested contacts, and made helpful observations. Some of these folks, I am sure, did not even know how much they were moving my thinking ahead.

I owe a great debt to several professional colleagues who encouraged and assisted me. I am especially indebted to those who wrote letters of support, approved leaves, listened to various presentations of my ideas, and commented on my evolving manuscript. Thanks are due particularly to Stanley Katz and Linda Kerber, and also to Michael Les Benedict, Peter Hoffer, Mike Marty, James Patterson, and Melvin Urofsky for advice and encouragement at the inception of this project. I may never know the identities of the anonymous readers of various grant applications, but I am grateful to them for providing vital endorsements that allowed me to proceed. Their intellectual support as much as the funding they made possible served to propel me forward.

The contribution of Northern Illinois University (NIU) has been vital to the advancement of this project. NIU has repeatedly demonstrated in a variety of ways its esteem for serious scholarship in the humanities as well as its commitment to sustaining it. In my experience, the university has been noteworthy in its support for research leaves and sabbaticals, its assistance to faculty in the pursuit of external funding, and its understanding that time free of distractions is crucial to the pursuit of scholarship. A semester research leave connected with the award of a presidential research professorship got this project underway.

The willingness of NIU, its College of Liberal Arts and Sciences, deans Frederick Kitterle and Joseph Grush, and my colleagues in the Department of History to allow me to spend two and a half years away from the classroom, two of those years in Washington, D.C., was most generous and absolutely essential to my being able to bring a project of this size to closure as rapidly as I did. Graduate Dean Jerrold Zar and his successor Rathindra Bose were also stalwart supporters of the enterprise.

Other institutions were likewise extraordinarily supportive. The Woodrow Wilson International Center for Scholars in Washington, D.C., provided a year's fellowship, a marvelous working environment, stimulating contact with a wide variety of scholars-in-residence and visitors, and introductions to people whom I was then able to interview. The Wilson Center's president and director, Lee Hamilton; the head of its U.S. Studies Program, Philippa Strum; and the head of its Congress Project, Don Wolfensburger, were all unfailingly generous with their assistance. The American Council of Learned Societies provided additional fellowship support during my first year in Washington. The following year, the Library of Congress gave me a place to work amidst its wonderful resources, and the National Endowment for the Humanities granted most helpful financial support through a "We the People" fellowship. I am exceedingly grateful to each of these institutions and trust that they will regard this book as justification for their generosity.

I would also like the thank the archivists at Brown, Yale, and Central Michigan universities, the University of Maryland, the Everett Dirksen Congressional Research Center, the Howard Baker Center at the University of Tennessee, the Gerald Ford Presidential Library, the National Archives and Records Administration, and the Library of Congress Manuscripts Division. Also due my gratitude are the librarians at the Woodrow Wilson International Center for Scholars, the Library of Congress, and Northern Illinois University. The professional keepers and providers of the unpublished and published records of the past are vital to the success of any research project. I am in awe of their willingness to put themselves out to assist scholars in locating material useful to their work and their often inspired suggestions of additional helpful resources.

Scholars who helped me immeasurably by providing insightful readings of the manuscript included my longtime collaborator Myron "Mike" Marty of Drake University, Lewis Gould of the University of Texas, and Michael Gerhardt of the University of North Carolina School of Law.

As he has done for me before, Michael Briggs, editor in chief at the University Press of Kansas, provided constant encouragement and helpful advice from the early stages of this project. He has been exceptionally tolerant of an author who insists that detailed narratives are necessary to illuminate the complexities of constitutional history. Together with the press's director Fred Woodward and assistant director Susan Schott, Mike has made the University Press of Kansas an extraordinarily congenial outlet for serious scholarly works on American political, legal, and constitutional history.

As has been the case for more than two decades, my greatest debt is to my wife, Christine Worobec. She sets an example with her own estimable scholarship in Russian history, her gentle encouragement to match her high standards, and her shrewd advice as to how I might do so. The two years we spent in Washington, often working side by side, were a particular joy. Christine's Canadian background as well as her knowledge of Russia enables her to make acute observations about the distinctiveness of the political structures and behavior of the United States, thereby helping me appreciate the extraordinary nature of matters easy for an American to take for granted. In countless ways, she enriches my thought as well as my life.

This book is dedicated to our grandson Noah. He was born soon after I began concentrated work on the project and has provided numerous delightful distractions from it. He gives new purpose to my scholarly endeavors. I offer this book in hopes that he will live a life in which impeachment is a curiosity from the past and neither a necessary nor distracting aspect of his adult years.

Introduction

In the first decade of the twenty-first century, Americans were once again discussing Article II, section 4, of the United States Constitution. Such conversations had occurred frequently since 1961, particularly during the second term of every reelected American president of the era. The often feverish talk contrasted sharply with the rare attention paid the article during the first 174 years after it was written in 1787. Article II, section 4, proclaims: "The President, Vice President and all civil Officers of the United States, shall be removed from Office on Impeachment for and Conviction of Treason, Bribery, or other high Crimes and Misdemeanors." Other provisions of the Constitution define treason, set forth Senate guidelines for trying an impeachment, and specify the limits of punishment upon conviction. The whole complicated process had come to be commonly referred to by the legal term for its initial step, assigned by the Constitution's framers to the most democratic body of the federal government. Article I, section 2, specifies: "The House of Representatives . . . shall have the sole Power of Impeachment." Whether or not the Senate by a two-thirds vote were to convict an official and remove him (never yet her) from his position, the mere act of impeachment in a formal vote by a majority of representatives had come to be thought of as disgraceful for the person subjected to it and was thus a powerful constitutional weapon for waging political combat.

For most of American history little attention was paid to the complicated constitutional procedure by which officials could be removed from their positions before the completion of their terms. The Constitution's framers had opted to specify fixed four-year terms for executive officers of their new government and lifetime tenure for federal judges. Removing these officials ahead of schedule would be contrary to the framers' understanding of the principles of democratic selection. As a result, only on rare occasions was normal tenure in office challenged. When specific cases arose—Senator William Blount in 1799, Justice Samuel Chase of the Supreme Court in 1805, President Andrew Johnson in 1868, Secretary of War William W. Belknap in 1876, and nine federal district judges scattered between 1803 and 1936—contemporary comments underscored the troubling nature of the situation. Otherwise, impeachment remained in the constitutional shadows, occasionally called for by isolated voices but little remembered by the general public and seldom given serious consideration by public officials, journalists, or scholars. When Representative Robert Michel of Illinois came to Congress in 1957 to begin what would become a thirty-eight-year career in the House, he recalled that impeachment was not even on the agenda. "Gosh no, we didn't even think about it. All we knew was what we'd read about it in history."[1]

During the last four decades of the twentieth century and the first of the twenty-first, however, the role of impeachment in American political culture expanded substantially. So, too, did public engagement with it. During this period impeachment either occurred or was seriously contemplated nearly as many times as during the previous seventeen decades. Casual suggestion of impeachment, perhaps heartfelt by its proponent but gathering little if any additional support, also seems to have become more frequent, although that is extremely difficult to measure. Described as the nuclear weapon of American politics, impeachment became sufficiently commonplace to be properly regarded as one of the normal challenges of national political life. The roughly fourfold acceleration in its use during the late twentieth century legitimizes labeling this era the age of impeachment.

Discussion of impeachment by public figures, journalists, and the general public grew even more rapidly than the number of formal cases. "He ought to be impeached!" became a commonplace grassroots expression as political divisions grew. It was as much the increased talk of impeachment as its more frequent use that made impeachment seem more a conventional political device than a special constitutional mechanism to be employed only on extraordinary occasions. Understanding why impeachment became far more common in the decades after 1960 and how its place in the constitutional and political culture changed is, therefore, important not only in itself but also to achieve an overall comprehension of public affairs in the United States during this era.

In 2005 unexpected revelations about events a third of a century earlier stirred public memory of what remained perhaps the most noteworthy and widely approved of all twentieth-century impeachment episodes, that involving President Richard M. Nixon. Americans were momentarily reminded of a signal moment in what had become a distinctive era in American constitutional and political culture. In 2005 it was uncertain whether the age of impeachment had passed or was ongoing. While talk of impeachment had become commonplace and at the moment a grassroots campaign to impeach President George W. Bush was generating vocal support, no actual impeachment had occurred since proceedings against President Bill Clinton had concluded early in 1999, the better part of a decade before.

It will no doubt be some years before it becomes evident whether, after the Clinton case, the use of impeachment had permanently receded or whether there was merely a momentary lull in an extended saga. Thus, it is impossible to know whether this book serves as an epilogue to the age of impeachment or as a prologue to an extended era of governmental instability due to political combat using the most deadly of constitutional weapons. As with many important matters of contemporary history, it is too early to tell.

America's familiarity with impeachment, not to mention the widespread sense of its legitimacy, even admirability, manifested itself in striking fashion in 2005. On May 31 news reports concerning a previously obscure ninety-one-year-old California man in failing health jolted American memories of events that had set in motion a presidential impeachment more than thirty years earlier. An article in *Vanity Fair* magazine stirred a journalistic uproar and widespread public reminiscence about events associated with Nixon's agonizing departure from the presidency. The details of Nixon's downfall had remained at the edge of national consciousness and apparently took little reminding to be brought to the fore.[2] The article's title as well as a banner headline in the following day's *Washington Post* identified the man only as "Deep Throat."

The name Deep Throat was instantly recognized by large numbers of Americans who could remember the early 1970s as well as by millions of younger people who knew it in only limited fashion from popular film, literature, and mention by their elders. All could identify Deep Throat as the alias given the anonymous informant who helped young *Washington Post* reporters Bob Woodward and Carl Bernstein pursue the story of a June 1972 break-in at Democratic National Committee offices in the Watergate, a sprawling complex of hotel, office, and apartment buildings on the banks of the Potomac River. Woodward and Bernstein had quickly discovered connections between the Watergate burglars and White House officials. With the help of Deep Throat, they began the process of placing responsibility for the crime and its concealment in the Oval Office. The unfolding story of the Watergate affair, as it came to be known, eventually led Nixon to the brink of impeachment. He resigned in August 1974 rather than face a trial by the U.S. Senate and almost certain removal from office.

Over the years speculation about Deep Throat's identity spawned numerous books and articles, not to mention countless discussions by those fascinated with how someone could point the way to exposing a president's venality, come to be regarded as a national hero, and yet not step forward to claim celebrity and perhaps accompanying riches. Deep Throat's shunning of the spotlight deepened the mystery, motivated many to try to solve the puzzle, and led at least a few to conclude that Deep Throat was either a fiction or a composite of various sources. Woodward and Bernstein steadfastly protected the identity of their famously anonymous informant.

University of Illinois journalism professor William Gaines even structured a graduate seminar on investigative reporting around the hunt for Deep Throat. Gaines's students, asserting the thoroughness and careful nature of their research, nominated one candidate, then another. In the end it turned out that both identifications were off the mark. The failure mattered little, certainly less than the chance their stories provided readers to revisit Watergate and the mystery of Deep Throat.

Perhaps the most remarkable aspect of the Gaines-led investigation was that a thirty-year-old unsolved mystery could sustain exceptional interest and industriousness among the journalists-in-training, most of whom had not yet been born at the time of the original Watergate investigation. In turn, the national media gave their quest the serious attention often dreamed of but almost never attained by student journalists. Gaines's great gift to his students was his recognition that for over three decades Deep Throat's identity, and even the question of whether he really existed, was a beguiling national riddle. Those who answered the question about Deep Throat's identity by naming Hal Holbrook, the actor who played him in the movie *All the President's Men,* had for years provided the only available confirmably correct answer, but not a very satisfying one. The Gaines seminar taught its participants valuable lessons about the techniques of research and the rewards of addressing genuine public curiosity, not to mention the continuing strength of public interest in the unresolved puzzle of the Nixon saga.

When W. Mark Felt, Sr., onetime deputy director of the Federal Bureau of Investigation (FBI), and his family decided to reveal his identify as Deep Throat, Woodward and Bernstein soon confirmed the *Vanity Fair* report. They had conscientiously kept their promise to protect Felt's anonymity, an adherence to principle much praised at the time of the Deep Throat revelations and one that over the years had led other highly placed people in and out of government to share confidences that made their way into Woodward's series of best-selling books. The Felt family's action released Woodward and Bernstein from pledges of confidentiality made and kept.

Most of those responding to the *Vanity Fair* disclosure thought of Deep Throat only as a pivotal character in the story of Watergate. At least one conservative columnist, however, linked his conduct to that of participants in other impeachment episodes in the recent American past, arguing that if Deep Throat had been a hero, so too was Linda Tripp, the woman who exposed Clinton's sexual improprieties with White House intern Monica Lewinsky.[3] The connection offered was that both Deep Throat and Tripp had generated revelations of behavior equivalently loathsome and worthy of impeachment. The fact that one case produced a presidential resignation to avoid almost certain impeachment and conviction while the other resulted in a Senate acquittal did not appear consequential to the writer.

Whether such a view of Tripp was broadly shared is difficult to determine. More apparent was the widespread contemporary American belief it embodied, that all presidents are knaves to one degree or another and thus that to expose their misdeeds, whether large or small, served the nation well. Disdain for political figures, while not new, became especially commonplace in American thought in the late twentieth and early twenty-first centuries, due in no small part to repeated disclosure of misconduct by legislators and due especially to the intense scrutiny of presidential behavior in the course of impeachment inquiries. Even though impeachment remained relatively rare and when it did occur most often involved lower-profile federal judges, its increased frequency after 1960 contributed to the atmosphere of suspicion that enveloped American government. In both its overt manifestations and the way it became entwined in the fabric of American political culture, impeachment became a profoundly important feature of the final four decades of twentieth-century U.S. history.

Starting in the 1960s, impeachment emerged from the recesses of American constitutionalism. Once largely ignored, impeachment became a threat frequently hurled into the midst of rancorous political debates. Each of the four presidents elected to a second term between 1960 and 2008 heard his impeachment seriously proposed. Two of the four, Nixon and Clinton, confronted congressional impeachment proceedings, while another, Ronald Reagan, narrowly escaped a similar fate. The last of the four, George W. Bush, did not even have to wait until his second term for calls for his impeachment to begin. In addition, a vice president facing indictment for taking a bribe, Spiro T. Agnew, argued that the only way he could be forced out of office was through impeachment. Rather than pursuing that argument in light of congressional resistance, however, he resigned once government prosecutors offered a generous plea bargain.

Eight federal judges also contended with demands for their impeachment. Although these cases did not attract as much public notice as did presidential ones, they would prove important in familiarizing Congress with the conduct of an impeachment proceeding. Three judges were impeached by the House, tried by the Senate, and convicted and removed from the bench; three others, including one Supreme Court justice, resigned while their impeachment was under consideration but had yet to be formally initiated. Only two of the eight, both Supreme Court justices, escaped relatively unscathed, if enduring a congressional hearing before charges were dropped (which was Justice William O. Douglas's fate) can be considered escaping relatively unscathed. Yet even these two cases are important for their role in bringing impeachment back into the forefront of constitutional consciousness.

Early-twenty-first-century advocates of impeachment considered it a proper, prompt response to perceptions of executive or judicial misconduct. A half century earlier, even the most outspoken of judicial and presidential critics did not immediately think of impeachment as an appropriate remedy for their discontent. Since the 1960s, however, popular and political attitudes toward impeachment evolved because of a number of specific experiences. Examining each in turn, noting interconnections among various episodes, and considering their cumulative effect is vital to understanding an underlying shift in American constitutional and political practice.

A careful examination of the constitutional role of impeachment, its political practice, and the public response to its repeated use has multiple benefits. First, such a study recalls to mind a number of dramatic and pivotal moments in America's recent past, some of them well known but others much less so. Second, such a review demonstrates that numerous connections exist among the various episodes and that impeachment cases should not be thought of only in isolation. Third, such an appraisal offers reason to believe that as impeachment has been resorted to more frequently, it has lost some of its constitutional luster and capacity to restrain federal officials, especially chief executives. It may be too soon to speak definitively of the end of an era, but certainly a comparison of the two most striking episodes of that era—the resignation in disgrace of Nixon and the failed effort to impeach Clinton—suggests that attitudes toward the use of impeachment have evolved.

For a historian, the most natural and useful manner of considering the disparate episodes of late-twentieth-century impeachment is to trace them chronologically. A detailed narrative of each case in turn provides a sound evidentiary basis for comprehending the political evolution of the impeachment process, appreciating its cultural development, and, finally, drawing analytical conclusions about its constitutional function in recent times. Besides the cases themselves, the way they are subsequently treated by government and remembered in the popular culture shapes evolving thought about impeachment and is, therefore, worthy of attention.

A variety of resources are available for assembling a reliable account of the age of impeachment. The formal record of proceedings preserved in government documents serves as a detailed foundation. Transcripts of congressional hearings, debates, and impeachment trials are particularly illuminating, as are the case records and rulings of relevant judicial proceedings. Newspaper and magazine accounts contain the version of proceedings most readily available to the general public, and newspaper editorial cartoons further reduce the conveyed meaning to its essence. The unpublished contemporary papers of individual participants in various impeachment episodes reveal aspects of the story not found in the public record. Published memoirs and transcripts of oral-history interviews with participants add further detail. Interviews with veterans of one or more episodes reveal their considered reflections and evolving perspectives on events long past. In addition, the extensive bibliography of books and articles on post-1960 impeachment contains a rich variety of observations by journalists, legal scholars, political scientists, and historians. Together, all these sources of information infuse a study of multiple impeachments with insights not available from any one of them and certainly not within reach of contemporary observers.

Past studies of impeachment have taken various forms. Most frequent have been examinations of individual cases, in particular those of President Andrew

Johnson, Supreme Court Justice Samuel Chase, and in the recent era President Richard Nixon and President Bill Clinton. Also common have been more abstract studies of impeachment law, either as it evolved in a specific period, as it applied to a particular class of officials, or in overall terms. Much less commonplace are comparative or collective studies of impeachment cases; those that do exist most often define and analyze the topic narrowly.

What is missing from the literature on impeachment but seems needed is a study that puts individual cases in social and political context and then compares cases over an extended time span. This method should make possible an understanding of what circumstances fostered the use of impeachment, why impeachment came to be resorted to more and more often, and how the political culture evolved in its thinking and practice regarding impeachment. The almost casual attitude toward impeachment manifested in the early twenty-first century clearly represented a far cry from views of the 1950s, not to mention those of the framers of the Constitution in 1787. The new outlook is no doubt a direct result of the accumulation of post-1960 impeachment experiences. Thus, the detailed and contextualized examination of those late-twentieth-century cases offers the best means of understanding the role impeachment has come to play in contemporary American constitutional culture.

1

Impeachment Evolves

As a new millennium dawned for the United States of America in the year 2000, the nation's Constitution, the basic outline of its governmental structures, responsibilities, authority, and restraints, had already endured for more than two centuries. The instrument's extraordinary capacity to accommodate changing geographic, demographic, social, economic, technological, and political circumstances facilitated the remarkable durability of a constitutional system designed in the late eighteenth century for a much smaller and simpler nation and government. The Constitution's capacity to evolve through formal amendment, creative use of its spare outline of requirements, and expansive interpretation of its terse language allowed it to remain vital far beyond its framers' expectations. However, the very qualities that gave the Constitution continued vibrancy also allowed practices unsettling to the American system of government. In the decades immediately preceding the millennium the foremost instance of constitutional mechanisms being used in a fashion both innovative and fraught with peril involved the instrument of impeachment.

Impeachment, a constitutional process for the removal of public officials before the end of their designated term, was for most of the history of the United States rarely employed or even mentioned. Few citizens possessed even the foggiest notion of what it was, much less how it worked. Historians Peter Charles Hoffer and N. E. H. Hull have pointed out that the British American colonies occasionally used impeachment.[1] However, except for a few early and generally discouraging efforts soon after the Constitution began operating in 1789, impeachment of federal officials was not often seriously considered, much less attempted before the 1960s. The mere suggestion of impeachment led a handful of judges to resign. Less frequently, given the great reluctance to overturn a democratic choice made directly by the electorate or through their representatives, the process was actually put into motion. By the turn of the millennium, however, impeachment had become a familiar constitutional device. From the 1960s onward, it developed into a weapon in political arsenals and a commonplace presence in American thought, language, and culture.

Only thirteen times between 1789 and 1960 were impeachment proceedings formally initiated by the House of Representatives. Resolutions for the impeachment of an additional thirty-one judges and nine other federal officials were introduced in the House but failed to move forward for one reason or another, most often resignation of the accused official. Overall these cases involved only a minuscule fraction of the federal officials who held impeachable positions during that lengthy period. Even the thirteen cases that did go ahead, most involving judges, were not always carried through to the prescribed conclusion of a judgment by the Senate. Before 1960, only eleven federal impeachment trials had ever been held by the Senate, and only four resulted in an official of the U.S. government being removed from office. Four other individuals resigned while facing impeachment, leading either to the termination of the proceedings or Senate verdicts of acquittal.[2] The most notable impeachment efforts of all, those involving Justice Samuel Chase of the Supreme Court in 1805 and President Andrew Johnson in 1868, both failed to convict, leaving in their wake serious doubts about impeachment's viability.

The prospects for impeachment seemed so slight that it was hardly ever contemplated even in the most contentious of political disputes. During the nineteenth century the country heard calls for the impeachment of two deeply unpopular presidents—John Tyler and Andrew Johnson—but under circumstances that did not altogether violate the principle of fixed terms for democratically chosen executives. Both had been vice presidents who inherited higher office to which they were not personally elected. Angry Whigs, upset at having won the 1840 election only to lose effective control of the White House when President William Henry Harrison died after a month in office, proposed the impeachment of his successor, John Tyler. In 1843 an impeachment resolution failed in the House by a vote of 127 to 83.[3] The first effort to impeach Abraham Lincoln's successor, Andrew Johnson, failed by an even wider margin.

After Johnson ultimately escaped conviction once he finally was impeached, reluctance to use this constitutional device increased even more. The few exceptions to the pattern merely underscored its near universality. Distraught Republican representative Louis McFadden of Pennsylvania, having lost his chairmanship of the House Banking Committee, introduced two resolutions to impeach President Herbert Hoover following the nation's plunge into the abyss of the Great Depression.[4] Indiana's Senator William Jenner, a staunch anticommunist, growled that President Harry Truman should be impeached for removing Korean War commander General Douglas MacArthur for insubordination, but he did not submit a resolution to that effect. Jenner's California colleague Richard Nixon applauded the idea while himself suggesting that Truman be censured by the Senate and ordered to reinstate MacArthur.[5] Nothing came of either of these cries of frustration because no support could be found for removing even these widely disparaged chief executives. Surely no one at the time could have imagined that more than twenty years later Nixon would again be involved in an impeachment episode with roots in an Asian war, much less that this time there would be an effective use of the instrument with Nixon himself as the target.

The rarity of impeachment's employment before the 1960s appears more in keeping with its designers' expectations than its more frequent use thereafter. The impeachment provisions of the Constitution were crafted not with the sense that they would often need to be put into operation but, rather, in the belief that their mere existence would serve to restrain official conduct. The framers concluded that impeachment must be available in light of some of the other elements of the plan of government. The impeachment mechanism was typical of the intricate structure of checks and balances woven into the Constitution to assure that individual officials of the government serving under its provision of fixed terms of office and broadly defined powers could be removed ahead of schedule if absolutely necessary.

When representatives of twelve of the thirteen states that had recently won independence from Great Britain met in Philadelphia in May 1787 to reconsider their constitutional arrangements for government, impeachment was on their minds though it was certainly not their highest priority. The delegates were well aware that the British Parliament had the previous year begun what would become a protracted, nine-year impeachment trial of Warren Hastings, governor general of the East India Company. They also knew that the first frame of government for the United States, the Articles of Confederation, had not specified a procedure for impeachment.[6] As the Philadelphia convention went about its work of designing a new structure for American government, one in which principal officials would be granted much greater power, the need for an impeachment process as a feature of the new Constitution appeared evident to the framers.

The Constitution's framers could look back on a four-hundred-year history of impeachment in Great Britain. They could also examine a century and a half of adaptation and embellishment of the device to suit the needs of the British American colonies. Over that long period of time, repeated use of impeachment provided the experience to turn an initially loosely defined mechanism into an agreed-upon process with generally understood objectives and requirements.[7]

Beginning during the fourteenth-century reign of Edward III, the British Parliament developed a system whereby its representative legislature, the House of Commons, could ask the highest court in the realm, the House of Lords, to try any individual, private citizen or public official, who allegedly committed an offense, loosely defined as a "high crime or misdemeanor," that posed a danger to the government or the public as a whole. A process was gradually established whereby a formal accusation was followed by a trial in which persuasive evidence needed to be presented that a specified offense had been committed in order to obtain a conviction. This process reflected the growing English commitment to the equal application of regulations to all similarly situated persons, that is, the rule of law. The nature of the purported threat to the common good rather than the position of the alleged offender was what led Parliament to assume jurisdiction in such instances.[8]

The British system of impeachment rested on the recognition that in certain cases, primarily those involving allegedly treasonous or corrupt judges, ministers of the Church of England, or councilors of the monarch, Parliament was in a stronger position to bring charges and render judgment than were ordinary courts of law. The process of lodging accusations—or, put another way, impeaching behavior—was overtly political in that it was devised to deal with disputes over the conduct of government. At the same time it was judicial, demanding the presentation of a specific charge and evidence to support it in order to achieve the requested result, which might include fines, property forfeiture, disqualification from future officeholding, imprisonment, or even execution but invariably involved removal from currently held office.

The tumultuous seventeenth century produced the greatest use and most substantial refinement of the British system of impeachment. As the nation descended into civil war during the reign of Charles I and then sought to reconstruct itself after the Restoration, the houses of Parliament often split over impeachment just as they did on other issues. The House of Commons repeatedly used a broad definition of offensive conduct in voting to impeach private as well as governmental opponents, while the House of Lords demanded evidence of specific and substantial offenses for conviction. Indeed, impeachment was apparently often used by the increasingly assertive lower house of Parliament merely to issue a warning to its critics. Over the course of the seventeenth century very few of the cases initiated by the Commons ever came to trial before the Lords, and only five of fifty-seven cases that did advance resulted in conviction.[9]

For its part, the House of Lords insisted on ever more circumscribed specification of charges and presentation of evidence before it would proceed with the trial of an impeachment, referring cases that did not meet its rising standards to the ordinary courts. The Commons objected to the narrowing of its power, saying, "It is the undoubted right of the Commons, in Parliament assembled, to impeach before the Lords in Parliament, any peer or commoner for treason or any other crime or misdemeanor; and . . . the refusal of the Lords to proceed in Parliament upon such impeachment is a denial of justice, and a violation of the constitution of Parliament."[10] But the Lords made clear that they would only consider cases based upon evidence of serious and willful wrongdoing, negligence, or betrayal of public trust, as they did in convicting the Lord Chancellor Sir Frances Bacon; George Villiers, Duke of Buckingham; and others.

After the Revolution of 1688, the intense political conflict between Whigs and Tories produced a series of closely divided and generally unsatisfying impeachment battles. However, as the cabinet system of government emerged under Robert Walpole and Parliament gained confidence in its capacity to control and even terminate governments under the new system, the use of impeachment as a political weapon declined in Great Britain, occurring only in rare instances. After the acquittal of Lord Melville in 1806, the British abandoned the system altogether. An increasingly robust parliamentary system eliminated dissonance between a majority in the House of Commons and the government. If a Commons majority was no longer confident of a government's capacity to police itself, that government would simply and invariably fall, so there was no need for more elaborate disciplinary procedures.[11]

Able to observe developments in Stuart England but freed by circumstance to operate with a good deal of autonomy, the American colonies in the seventeenth century honed their own set of impeachment procedures. Colonial assemblies increasingly ignored the British assertion that only Parliament had the right of impeachment. Instead they wielded impeachment powers as a means of disciplining officials of the Crown. The first colonial action resembling impeachment occurred in 1635 when the Virginia House of Burgesses accused Governor John Harvey of a variety of crimes against the public trust and sent him to England for judgment. Rhode Island did likewise in 1657 and made the first colonial use of the term "impeach" in charging William Harris with heresy and treason. The Maryland assembly went further and itself judged three cases between 1669 and 1683. A close study of colonial impeachment practices noted that the American colonies employed the British standards of impeachment for violations of public trust, misuse of official power, or felonious conduct by a person in a position of authority. Unlike the British, however, the Americans confined the use of impeachment to public officeholders and limited the penalties for conviction to loss of office. Impeachment represented one of the few means by which prerevolutionary colonial assemblies could check the executive and judicial power of the Crown.[12]

In the first half of the eighteenth century the volume of colonial impeachment efforts declined, but the ones that did take place focused narrowly on removing royal officeholders from their positions. The growing estrangement between Great Britain and its colonial assemblies was reflected in the fact that every colonial impeachment failed to survive its appeal to British authority.[13] After midcentury, colonial impeachments, likewise unsuccessful in removing officials sustained by Britain, became ever-stronger expressions of grievance at the misconduct of British officials and assertions of the supremacy of representative assemblies.

The most noteworthy late-colonial impeachment was the Massachusetts General Assembly's action against Chief Justice Peter Oliver in 1774. Oliver, appointed by Governor Thomas Hutchinson and thrice related to him by marriage, was seen as central to the governor's attempts to bring the Massachusetts judiciary under royal control. Hutchinson not only put a relative on the bench, but he also proposed that judicial salaries be paid out of customs duties rather than through legislative appropriations. The assembly, fearing that judges would do the bidding of their paymasters and be insensitive to local interests, approved its own judicial salaries and prohibited judges from accepting royal salaries. Oliver refused to declare whether he would decline the royal salary, and grand jurors thereafter refused to sit if Oliver was on the bench. With a functioning judicial system in jeopardy, the assembly decided its proper course was to impeach the chief justice and ask for his trial by the governor and council.

The Massachusetts General Assembly charged that Chief Justice Oliver had allowed himself to be bought by a salary unconstitutionally levied and collected and thus had committed "high crimes and misdemeanors." Governor Hutchinson, caught between the wishes of the British government and the council's probable conviction of Oliver, responded by proroguing, in other words terminating, the session of the General Court. Despite having been dismissed by the governor, the assembly and council had won an important public relations victory. The outcome underscored their argument that royal authority was antithetical to representative government and powerfully advanced the case for breaking colonial relations with Great Britain. Whatever the immediate result, the Oliver case and other colonial impeachment efforts conditioned the revolutionary generation to believe that an effective impeachment procedure was important in constructing a government of limited powers respectful of the popular will.[14]

As American ties to Great Britain unraveled in 1776, each colony saw the need for a new state constitution and within it a means for dealing with official misconduct. Frequently scheduled election of public officials was counted upon to eliminate most of the problems associated with potential malfeasance. Nevertheless, eight of the thirteen new state constitutions included specific provisions for impeachment; three more states added impeachment provisions in the 1780s. While the provisions of individual state constitutions varied in detail, they were consistent in limiting their applicability to public officials and confining the penalties for conviction to loss of office and disqualification from holding further positions. The British perception that only Parliament could be counted on to deal with any improper behavior by aristocrats and others close to the monarchy gave way in the new republican states to the view that normal courts should take care of most misconduct. Only high officials conducting the public's business needed the direct restraint that impeachment provided. Narrowly defined impeachment powers in turn served to restrain excessive legislative use of the device. Thus, impeachment came to be seen as a republican instrument for protection against abusive government officials rather than the broader, less-well-defined parliamentary judicial power of the British model.[15]

Nearby a dozen of the delegates who gathered in Philadelphia in the summer of 1787 had experience with impeachment in their home states, either through participation in lawmaking or involvement in actual cases. These men proved to be some of the most influential members of the convention: James Madison, George Mason, and Edmund Randolph of Virginia; Elbridge Gerry and Rufus

King of Massachusetts; James Wilson and Gouverneur Morris of Pennsylvania; William Paterson of New Jersey; Alexander Hamilton of New York; Hugh Williamson of North Carolina; and Charles Cotesworth Pinckney of South Carolina. They understood impeachment law, in both its British and American variants, and believed in its efficacy. Furthermore, they agreed from the outset that a federal constitutional provision should mirror what the states had adopted: impeachment only for public officials who committed serious misconduct in office, with removal and disqualification the sole punishments.[16] What remained to be done was to work out a definition of impeachable offenses and procedures for dealing with them. It did not prove an easy task.

Discussion of an impeachment provision in the proposed constitution went on throughout the entire Philadelphia Convention.[17] Delegates routinely advanced ideas for the new government they were creating based on what they knew best: standing arrangements in their own states. From the outset, consideration of impeachment followed this pattern. Randolph got deliberations started on May 29 by presenting a set of proposals from his delegation for a much stronger central government with legislators and an executive chosen for set terms and a judiciary that would serve during "good behavior." The plan included a provision, modeled on Virginia's own state system, for impeachment of national officers to be tried by the national judiciary.[18] While much debate over the terms of an impeachment provision would follow, the need for such a device was clear at the outset to the Virginians and, as it turned out, to most others.

A good deal of discussion early on in the convention centered on the creation of a chief executive. Most delegates took for granted that such an official would be impeachable, but some wondered whether that would provide sufficient protection against an errant executive. In arguing that the Virginia Plan's seven-year term for a chief executive was too long, Gunning Bedford, Jr., of Delaware worried that some chosen to serve would prove to lack the qualifications ascribed to them during the selection process or would lose them in the course of such a lengthy term. Impeachment, he said, would be no remedy for this problem since it dealt only with misconduct, not ineptitude.[19] Two other delegates joined Bedford in arguing that the executive should be removable at the request of a majority of the state legislatures. Mason contended, "Some mode of displacing an unfit magistrate is rendered indispensable by the fallibility of those who chose, as well as the corruptibility of the man chosen."[20]

Delegates James Madison and John Dickinson were concerned that the legislature's use of simple majority no-confidence votes would render the executive office either invulnerable, when protected by small states with a majority of Senate seats though only a minority of the population, or else weak and vulnerable to political intrigues against him. The convention quickly rejected the proposal for easy removal of the executive by the legislature. Instead, it agreed to Williamson's resolution, again reflective of his home state's practice, that the executive "be removable on impeachment & conviction of mal-practice or neglect of duty."[21] Thus emerged the idea that impeachment should result from improper behavior, though not necessarily criminal acts, and certainly not just political unpopularity.

When Paterson on June 15 presented the New Jersey Plan, a proposal to protect the interests of small states through design of the legislature and other measures, he offered a different approach from that of the Virginia Plan in regard to the removal of federal officials. Paterson's plan called for removal simply upon the request of a majority of state executives as well as by legislative impeachment and trial by the federal judiciary.[22] Some scholars argue that Paterson was merely forgetting his own state's grant of impeachment power to the lower house of its legislature,[23] but it seems more likely that he deliberately chose to expand the possibilities for removing federal officials beyond impeachment for improper conduct. Paterson clearly sought to enhance the power of small states to rein in the potential political dominance of large states such as Virginia.

In offering his own alternative to the Virginia Plan a few days later, Hamilton also addressed impeachment. He proposed a strong executive who, together with senators and federal judges, would continue to serve as long as he exhibited "good behavior" yet would be liable to impeachment, removal, and disqualification from further office holding for "mal- and corrupt conduct." Hamilton's plan reflected his home state's special court of impeachments and errors. His twist was to have impeachments tried before a court composed of the highest judicial officers of each state, figures who would presumably be fairly independent of his proposed executive, whom some regarded as a lifetime republican monarch.[24] With the convention a month old, the delegates seemed to have agreed only on the principle of impeachment. The more complicated determinations of what constituted an impeachable offense and how it should be dealt with remained unsettled.

Following the so-called Connecticut Compromise creating a Congress of two houses, the convention shifted its focus from the design of a legislative body back to the issue of an executive. Some delegates remained unconvinced that the chief executive should be impeachable. The central concern, as expressed by Morris and Pinckney on July 19 and 20, was that the threat of impeachment would render the executive subservient to the Congress. Mason, Wilson, and Gerry responded, arguing vehemently that some check on an executive's power was necessary.[25]

One alternative to impeachment existed, observed the convention's senior member, Benjamin Franklin. When a public official became obnoxious, he could always be assassinated. Franklin's droll comment perhaps startled his fellow delegates but appeared to calm the dispute. He quickly silenced objections to impeachment by proceeding to explain why it was preferable to a violent alternative. After all, assassination deprived its target not only of his life but also of the opportunity to vindicate himself. Impeachment, Franklin declared, "would be the best way therefore to provide in the Constitution for the regular punishment of the Executive when his misconduct should deserve it, and for his honorable acquittal when he should be unjustly accused."[26]

Having contemplated Franklin's unsavory alternative, Gouverneur Morris conceded that corruption and a few other enumerated and defined offenses ought to be impeachable. Some, but not all, other delegates signaled their agreement. Madison immediately declared it "indispensable that some provision should be made for defending the Community against the incapacity, negligence or perfidy of the chief Magistrate. The limitation of the period of his service was not a sufficient security." A corrupt legislator might be kept in check by other members of the body, but a single executive, if corrupt, "might be fatal to the Republic."[27] Elbridge Gerry declared impeachments a necessity, saying, "A good magistrate will not fear them. A bad one ought to be kept in fear of them."[28] After further discussion, the convention on July 20 endorsed the principle, eight states to two, that the executive should be removable through impeachment.[29]

Where and how impeachments should be tried remained at issue. According to various members' notes, the Committee of Detail was appointed on July 26, was given the task of presenting a draft constitution, and considered several formulations of the matter of impeachment during its deliberations.[30] In its report to the full convention on August 6, the committee specified that the executive "shall be removable from his office on impeachment by the House of Representatives, and conviction in the supreme Court, of treason, bribery, or corruption."[31] When it addressed impeachment over two weeks later, the convention itself added, "The Judges of the Supreme Court shall be triable by the Senate, on impeachment by the House of Representatives."[32]

Not until the convention settled the issue of presidential elections less than two weeks before final adjournment was there further progress regarding the impeachment mechanism. Doubts about the Supreme Court's trying impeachments remained evident, as Morris's objections on August 27 attested.[33] When the Committee of Eleven, appointed on August 31 to resolve a variety of unsettled issues, reported on September 4, it resolved basic difficulties concerning impeachment. The committee took the election of the president out of the hands of the Senate and gave it to the Electoral College, thus removing the objection that a body that had chosen a chief executive could hardly be impartial in trying his impeachment. The Senate was granted power to try all impeachments, with a two-thirds supermajority required for conviction. As for other action with long-term consequences that would be difficult to undo, such as the approval of treaties and constitutional amendments, the framers sought a higher degree of consensus than provided by a simple majority.[34]

Even as the trial of impeachments was moved to the Senate, the solemn nature of the process and the desire to keep it from descending into political partisanship was underscored by designating the chief justice to preside over presidential impeachments. The framers perceived a particular need for this unusual blurring of the otherwise clear demarcations they were trying to establish among the legislative, executive, and judiciary functions. The just-created vice president, ordinarily to be the Senate's presiding officer, would be supplanted for presidential impeachment trials since the vice president would be directly affected by the president's removal and thus could not be regarded as impartial. In judicial impeachments, on the other hand, the chief justice might well be conflicted, and so the vice president was not displaced when such cases came before the Senate.[35]

The grounds for impeachment stipulated by the Committee of Eleven only included treason and bribery.[36] After reflection, George Mason declared this to be insufficient and moved to add "maladministration." James Madison objected that "so vague a term [would] be equivalent to a tenure during pleasure of the Senate." Mason saw the merit of his Virginia colleague's argument, immediately withdrawing the term "maladministration" and substituting "other high crimes and misdemeanors against the State." Moments later "State" was replaced with "United States" in a further effort to remove ambiguity.[37] Later, the Committee on Style dropped the "against the United States" phrase. The change did not provoke any delegate to comment at the time, perhaps because the meaning of the old British terminology "high crimes and misdemeanors" was so well understood. Ultimately, however, the removal rendered the definition of impeachable offenses potentially more expansive than just crimes against the state.[38]

Madison continued to object, arguing that the president would be rendered improperly dependent on the legislature, especially if he could be impeached "for any act which might called a misdemeanor." But his effort to remove the process from the Senate drew support only from Virginia and Pennsylvania.[39] The convention then approved the overall provision, with only Pennsylvania dissenting. At the last minute Morris proposed adding the phrase "and every member shall be on oath," presumably to quell fears that senators might otherwise act out of selfish political interest. With this last modification accepted, the drafting of the impeachment provision appeared to be completed, virtually the last act of the delegates before turning their work over to the Committee on Style to put it into final form.[40]

In the convention's final days, as the delegates reviewed the work of the Committee on Style, John Rutledge of South Carolina, along with Gouverneur Morris, raised a question the delegates had not earlier considered: What would be the status of officials in positions of authority who had been impeached but not yet tried? Would they pose a threat? Rutledge and Morris moved that "persons impeached be suspended from their office until they be tried and acquitted." Madison immediately saw a danger in such suspensions. "The President is made too dependent already on the Legislature," he said, "by the power of one branch to try him in consequence of an impeachment by the other." Madison feared that suspension would tilt the balance even further: "The intermediate suspension will put him in the power of one branch only—They can at any moment, in order to make way for the function of another who will be more favorable to their views, vote a temporary removal of the existing magistrate." Rufus King concurred with Madison, as both clearly worried at the moment more about legislative overreaching than about further misconduct by an impeached executive. The convention overwhelmingly agreed, and all delegations except Connecticut, South Carolina, and Georgia rejected the suspension proposal.[41]

Impeachment was firmly implanted in the Constitution that the delegates to the Philadelphia Convention, with a handful of exceptions, endorsed on September 17, 1787. In setting forth the document for approval by the Congress of the Confederation and subsequent ratification by the states, the framers were gambling that their fellow citizens would recognize the need for a stronger central government in light of the deficiencies of the constrained system under which they had all been operating since independence from Britain had been declared. Throughout the compact document, the gamble was hedged with reassurances for the wary. Easily noticed was the division of authority among three balanced branches of government, each having checks on the other two. No less obvious were the two overall checks on the new federal government that had also been provided: a process for amendment so that the structure and authority of government could be reconfigured should that be desired and one for impeachment so that officials who failed to conduct the country's business within the specified bounds could be dealt with in a familiar and effective fashion.

As the country contemplated the proposed new constitution, the impeachment system appeared as one of its strengths. Alexander Hamilton devoted two of his contributions to the *Federalist Papers* to its praise. In *Federalist* 65 he stressed the difficulty of dealing with the offenses of public officials who abuse the public trust. Such offenses, he said, "may with particular propriety be denominated *political,* as they relate chiefly to injuries done immediately to the society itself." He predicted that the prosecution of offenses of this sort would arouse emotions and divide the community. The greatest danger, he said, was that cases would be decided on the basis of the relative strength of factions rather than on demonstrated guilt or innocence. The Senate was the best forum for trying impeachments because of its dignity, deliberative nature, and independence from the passions of the moment. "What other body," Hamilton asked, "would be likely to feel *confidence enough in its own situation* to preserve, unawed and uninfluenced, the necessary impartiality between an *individual* accused, and the *representatives of the people, his accusers?*"[42]

Hamilton thought the Supreme Court inappropriate to try impeachments. He doubted whether it would have the credibility or authority to reconcile the public to a decision contrary to the views of their immediate representatives in the

House. A mistaken judgment could be fatal to the reputation of the accused, on the one hand, or dangerous to public tranquility, on the other, so better not to entrust it to a small body. "The awful discretion which a court of impeachments must necessarily have, to doom to honor or to infamy the most confidential and the most distinguished characters of the community, forbids the commitment of the trust to a small number of persons." Furthermore, Hamilton wrote, officials impeached and removed from office would still be subject to ordinary legal prosecution and punishment. It would not be proper for judges who had already heard and decided an impeachment case that cost a person his public standing to then determine a second case pertaining to the same offense. A predisposed judge should not preside at a trial that could strip the defendant of life or fortune. Hamilton likewise disposed of other alternatives to trial by the Senate.[43]

Hamilton's conclusion that Senate trials of impeachment offered the best, if not a perfect, solution of where to place the responsibility carried over into *Federalist* 66. There he dismissed the charge that the procedure improperly breached the separation of powers, arguing that impeachment would restrain encroachment by executive power and that the legislature itself would be restrained by the apportionment of responsibility for accusation and judging between the two legislative houses. To the complaint that too much power was concentrated in the Senate, Hamilton pointed out that the House of Representatives had the sole power to initiate an impeachment. Hamilton also dismissed the objection that the Senate would be biased toward an official it had confirmed in office, pointing out that it only approved choices made by the president and was not likely to condone malfeasance. Finally, Hamilton addressed the charge that the Senate, once having approved a ruinous treaty, would be disinclined to impeach a president for treachery in connection with it. He argued that security against corruption, whether in approving treaties or conducting impeachments, rested on the distribution of authority throughout a body selected by the collective wisdom of state legislatures. Care in the selection of senators, he concluded, would ensure their fidelity to their responsibilities. In impeachment as in other matters, Hamilton was willing to place his faith in representative government, especially when well insulated from popular passion.[44]

Only limited references to impeachment appear in the rest of the *Federalist Papers*. In *Federalist* 79 Hamilton argued that the Constitution's reference to judges serving "during good behavior" did not threaten judicial independence but meant only that if judges acted with propriety they would enjoy lifetime tenure. Hamilton did not address whether his or the convention's sense of good behavior involved more than avoiding impeachment for treason, bribery, or other high crimes and misdemeanors. He did contend in *Federalist* 81 that the judiciary would enjoy "complete security" against congressional unhappiness with court decisions because of the division between House and Senate of responsibility for impeachment. Hamilton's commentary may have reassured his readers, but it hardly covered the full range of questions that could have been asked about the scope of the impeachment power and the manner in which it would be executed. The framers' original intent could be read in more than one way. For example, what was the scope of "good behavior"? Did the framers intend that judges, who were to serve "during good behavior," would be disqualified for a wider range of offenses than those specified for impeachment, or, alternatively and just as plausibly, that they would continue to serve as long as impeachment was avoided?

The conventions held in each state to consider ratification of the new Constitution repeatedly signaled their comfort with the impeachment provision by devoting relatively little time to its discussion. Some of the same objections voiced at the Philadelphia Convention were heard in the state ratifying conventions. Delegates first in Pennsylvania, later in Virginia, and finally in North Carolina expressed concern about the Senate as the trier of impeachment cases. Was too much power concentrated in the Senate? Would the Senate be too sympathetic to officials whose appointment it had approved? Would it be too much influenced by a wayward president? Meanwhile, delegates in each of these states, as well as in Massachusetts, raised an issue not touched on in Philadelphia: Should the Congress be expected to impeach and try its own members? Would Congress be willing to punish miscreants within its own ranks? The question could not be answered, but both Virginia and North Carolina added it to the list of amendments to the new Constitution, such as a bill of rights, that they asked Congress to propose.[45]

In none of the ratifying conventions was a case made for rejecting the Constitution due to its impeachment mechanism, perhaps because most states had experience with their own imperfect impeachment devices. The risk that impeachment would become a tool of partisan warfare was not even raised, although that would soon become an element in actual cases. As state after state debated the Constitution, trepidation focused on other matters, in particular the absence of a bill of rights. By comparison, the impeachment provisions were accepted with equanimity. As the Constitution won ratification and took effect early in 1789, its still loosely defined impeachment provision stood unchallenged and ready to be put to use.[46]

In the early years of the new federal Republic, it appeared that impeachment might become a frequently employed constitutional provision. In a half dozen states, New Hampshire, Massachusetts, Pennsylvania, Kentucky, South Carolina, and Georgia, officials were impeached and removed from office under the terms of state constitutions that generally followed the federal model.[47] Impeachment had come into use in an era before cohesive and durable political parties appeared. At first impeachment was thought of as a means to remove discredited officials in a nonpartisan fashion. In eighteenth-century theory at least, impeachment offered an alternative to organized parties for the disciplining of government. Despite the rapid rise of cohesive political parties, impeachment remained for a time an attractive means of removing opponents from office. Before long, however, building and maintaining electoral majorities so that opponents could be turned out wholesale rather than in selective cases came to be seen as a more attractive and effective way to achieve or maintain control of government. After scarcely more than a decade and a half, impeachment fell into general disuse, only to be revived briefly nearly two-thirds of a century later in circumstances where a dominant political party found itself otherwise thwarted.[48] Thereafter the mechanism would slumber again for another century.

The first serious federal impeachment case involved William Blount, a U.S. senator from Tennessee, a lifelong self-aggrandizing politician who had represented North Carolina at the 1787 Constitutional Convention before moving west. As the Democratic-Republican Party began to be constructed around Thomas Jefferson, mutterings were heard from within its ranks about impeaching John Jay and even George Washington over the Jay Treaty with Great Britain. These proposals led to nothing, but the Blount case went beyond mere policy disputes or partisanship and generated charges of serious misconduct. Senator Blount had engaged in a complicated and possibly treasonous conspiracy to maneuver Great Britain into an invasion of Spanish-held Louisiana, thereby leaving Spanish territory there and in the Floridas vulnerable to takeover by a small private army organized by Blount and fellow land speculators. Upon learning of the failed plot from a letter sent by Blount to a coconspirator who got cold feet, the Senate promptly expelled the Tennessean in July 1797. The House of Representatives, not satisfied, impeached the ex-senator to disqualify him from further office holding. In January 1798 the House adopted five articles of impeachment. A year later the Senate, after hearing a variety of House arguments, refused jurisdiction. Senators did not wish, in effect, to make impeachment universal by extending it to reach persons who were not currently in office. They were also clearly uncomfortable with the prospect of conducting an impeachment trial of one of their own and, feeling freed of the need to do so because of his expulsion from office, declined to proceed.[49]

The outcome of the Blount case left unresolved most questions about impeachment, including whether legislators fell within the category of "civil officers" of the United States eligible for impeachment. But Blount's removal from the Senate did provide a precedent that has been followed ever since: Congress had exercised its authority to determine the qualifications of its own members, to refuse to seat them without any judicial proceeding if it chose, and to expel them once seated. Since action could be and occasionally was taken by one house more quickly and with fewer restrictions than could be provided by a quasi-judicial process, expulsion rather than impeachment became the method for removing legislators from positions of public trust.

Five years after the Blount case, the next use of the impeachment power proved less complicated. With Jefferson and his Republican supporters solidly in control of the nonjudicial branches of the federal government, the overwhelmingly Federalist judiciary, particularly President John Adams's last-minute appointments, came under close scrutiny. John Pickering, a federal district judge for New Hampshire since 1795, proved especially vulnerable. A man of talent and education, he had served as a state assemblyman, attorney general, and chief justice of New Hampshire before receiving his appointment to the federal bench. Sadly, he also had a long history of mental difficulty, beginning with a phobia about traveling over water that had kept him from attending the Continental Congress when elected a delegate. Although increasingly senile and reportedly presiding over his court while intoxicated, Pickering refused to retire from the bench. Once alerted to the situation, the Republican House wasted little time in impeaching him. Although Judge Pickering's deteriorating mental state kept him from attending his trial, much less mounting an effective defense, and despite the fact that his problems stemmed from madness rather than from a substantial high crime or misdemeanor, the Senate Republican majority, seeing no other way to remove an obviously incompetent judge, proceeded to convict and remove him in March 1804.[50] This fairly easy first successful use of the impeachment power encouraged the belief that it could be turned against others on the bench.

While the Senate was still dealing with the Pickering case, the House undertook to impeach an associate justice of the Supreme Court, Samuel Chase. The heavily Republican House charged Chase with a variety of offenses, all underlain by the fact that he was a staunch and irascible Federalist. A signer of the Declaration of Independence as a Maryland delegate to the Continental Congress, Chase became chief judge of his state's highest court in 1791 and was named to the Supreme Court by George Washington in 1796. On the bench he had become a determined and short-tempered supporter of the Alien and Sedition Acts of 1798. He further infuriated Republicans by openly campaigning for John Adams in 1800. In cases in Philadelphia; New Castle, Delaware; and Richmond while riding circuit in 1800 and in Baltimore in 1803, Chase had repeatedly acted on the bench and ruled in ways that Republicans found offensive, though most later legal authorities, including Chief Justice William Rehnquist, writing about the Chase impeachment in 1992, did not.[51]

Chase's judicial behavior outraged Republicans and made him the prime target of what seemed destined to become a sustained campaign to remove the Court's Federalist majority. Impeached for flagrant judicial misbehavior in multiple trials, Chase defended himself by saying that while he might have erred, he was surely not guilty of any of the impeachable offenses of "treason, bribery, or other high crimes or misdemeanors." Defended by, among others, Maryland's longtime attorney general Luther Martin, himself a delegate to the 1787

Constitutional Convention, Chase was able to persuade several members of the large Republican majority that his conduct, undoubtedly partisan but not criminal, was not impeachable. As a result, though a Senate majority voted to convict, nothing close to the necessary two-thirds margin for removal could be assembled. Ironically, given his own partisanship and that of Senate Federalists who gave him unwavering support, Chase escaped conviction because some Republican senators balked at making partisanship rather than evidence of high crimes or misdemeanors the constitutional standard for impeachment.[52]

The failure to remove Chase brought an end for the time being to the use of impeachment as a partisan tool. Democratic-Republicans and Federalists alike had found the tactic unpalatable. William Cooke, a Republican senator from Tennessee, told John Quincy Adams after the Senate trial concluded that even though he had felt compelled to vote against Chase, he was sorry the charges had been brought and was glad for the acquittal. Adams himself deplored the partisanship involved and wrote in his diary that the verdict "proved that a sense of justice is yet strong enough to overpower the furies of factions."[53] Had Chase been convicted and removed from the Supreme Court, the subsequent history of U.S. government might well have been much different. The two-thirds Senate supermajority necessary for conviction together with the inclination of at least some senators to subordinate partisan appetites to the constitutional definition of impeachable offenses served to produce another outcome.

Vice President Aaron Burr, who presided over both the Pickering and Chase trials in the Senate, made an unlikely but important contribution to the unfolding understanding of impeachment. In July 1804, during the brief period between the end of the Pickering trial in March and the beginning of the Chase trial the following February, Burr killed Alexander Hamilton in a duel. He was promptly indicted for murder in both New Jersey, the site of the duel, and New York, the home of both men and the place where the challenge to a duel was made by Burr and accepted by Hamilton. Staying away from either state, the vice president managed to avoid arrest, extradition, and arraignment, not to mention trial. When Burr presided at the Chase trial, contemporaries observed that in most courts murderers were arraigned before a judge, but in this instance a judge was being arraigned before a murderer.[54]

Burr might conceivably have been impeached for Hamilton's murder. The vice president had been estranged from the large Democratic-Republican majority in Congress ever since he had maneuvered in the Electoral College chosen in 1800 to supplant Jefferson as president. However, facing a national election in a few months, the Democratic-Republicans were clearly not eager to take action against a vice president of their own party, even a highly controversial one they had no intention of keeping on their ticket. Regardless of political considerations, the Democratic-Republican position affirmed the founders' distinction between ordinary crimes against individuals and "high crimes and misdemeanors" by federal officials acting in their public capacity, actions that threatened the society at large. Furthermore, the New Jersey and New York indictments of Burr suggested that, at least in some quarters, impeachment was not thought to insulate an officeholder from criminal charges. The Burr murder case was never resolved, but the indictment and nonimpeachment would be treated as relevant precedents when similar constitutional questions arose nearly 170 years later.

The Blount, Pickering, and Chase cases occurred within a span of six years, but a quarter century elapsed before another impeachment was voted by the House and tried before the Senate. The case of James H. Peck, the first federal district judge in Missouri, was quite unlike any of its predecessors. After Peck issued his ruling in an important case involving Spanish land claims, the losing attorney, who had many similar cases pending, had disparaged Peck's decision in a letter to a St. Louis newspaper. When the letter was published, Peck, in turn, cited his critic for contempt of court and suspended his right to practice for eighteen months. The attorney, whose name, ironically, was Luke Lawless, was politically well connected and persistent. On his third attempt he persuaded the House Judiciary Committee that Peck's contempt citation was a "high misdemeanor" justifying impeachment. The only federal impeachment ever based upon a single complaint by a single individual, the Peck case apparently went forward in part because of general hostility to the federal judiciary at the time. However, without any persuasive evidence of impeachable conduct or, indeed, any improper ruling except possibly Lawless's suspension from legal practice, both the Senate as a whole and the overwhelming Democratic majority in particular divided evenly. The wide margin of Peck's 1831 acquittal reaffirmed high standards for impeachment.[55]

Thirty years later different circumstances produced a dissimilar outcome but further confirmation of the central purpose of impeachment. West H. Humphreys, a federal district judge in Tennessee since 1853, accepted a judicial appointment in the Confederacy without resigning his federal position. The House impeached him for malfeasance for not holding court, for gross misconduct that violated the "good behavior" clause, and for high treason for having advocated and supported secession. In June 1862 the Senate held a three-hour trial at which, not surprisingly, Judge Humphreys failed to appear and presented no defense. A bipartisan Senate quickly found him guilty on all seven specific articles of impeachment, unanimously so on two articles and with near-unanimity on all but one of the others. Not content with removing him from office, the senators took the additional step of unanimously disqualifying Humphreys from further federal officeholding.[56]

The impeachment of President Andrew Johnson represented the greatest nineteenth-century test of the limits of the Constitution's impeachment provision, not to mention the central dramatic moment of the post–Civil War era of Reconstruction. Johnson was a unionist Tennessee Democrat added to

Republican Abraham Lincoln's national unity ticket for the election of 1864. After barely a month in the vice presidency he became the unexpected successor to the assassinated Lincoln and was at odds with Congress from the outset. Stubborn and abrasive, Johnson fought for the lenient and conciliatory treatment of the South that he (and in his perception Lincoln) favored. He considered it the constitutional responsibility of the chief executive to deal with the errant states. An equally feisty Republican congressional majority believed that it held constitutional authority over conquered territory as well as the right to set the terms for readmitting the former Confederate states to the Union. Originating in contrasting views as to whether the Confederate states had left the Union, the clash between Johnson and Congress was fundamentally constitutional in nature.[57]

Had the South been willing to fully acknowledge its defeat and had Johnson been less dogmatic in his views, Congress might not have pursued the president's impeachment. As Johnson took office, northern sentiment inclined toward amicable reunion as long as the South acknowledged its defeat and demonstrated its assent to the sort of union for which the North had fought. A few radicals sought severe punishment of the South, but most of the victors were inclined to leniency as long as the South signaled its intention to provide considerate treatment of former slaves. "Given the strong desire for 'normalcy,'" wrote one respected modern scholar, "it is most likely that the South could have satisfied northern opinion by ratifying the Thirteenth Amendment, repudiating secession, and acquiescing in the exercise by blacks of civil, but not political, rights."[58]

Instead, in the months before the Congress chosen in 1864 first convened in December 1865, the Confederate states, with Johnson's support, merely reconstituted their familiar governments, repealed their ordinances of secession rather than repudiating them as initially wrong, and ratified the Thirteenth Amendment abolishing slavery. Several state legislatures took this last step reluctantly, and Mississippi flatly refused to do so at all. The southern states' grudging concessions of defeat were quickly followed by their establishment of legal codes consigning blacks to nonvoting and restrictive second-class citizenship.

Congress was not immediately ready to impeach Johnson, but it did wish to reverse his reconstruction plans. Defeat, northerners believed, was being snatched from the jaws of victory, notwithstanding the adoption of the Thirteenth Amendment. To assure it would have the political capacity to secure the victory, Congress refused to seat southern representatives and senators until its reconstruction requirements were met. For his part, Johnson continued granting pardons to prominent Confederates, refused to require southern reform, and insisted that the national government had no power to compel state action. Frustrated northerners concluded that both direct congressional action and further constitutional reform were needed.

A series of clashes followed in which Congress approved reconstruction measures and the president opposed them. Congress adopted a bill renewing the

Freedman's Bureau, and Johnson vetoed it. Congress then approved the Civil Rights Act of 1866, defining blacks as citizens and rendering the Black Codes inoperable. Johnson again issued a veto, and this time Congress overrode it. Concerned that its legislative action was insufficient, Congress then approved the Fourteenth Amendment to the Constitution, guaranteeing, among other things, equal protection of the law to all citizens and reducing a state's congressional representation in proportion to its denial of citizens' voting rights. Although the president has no formal role in the amending process, Johnson advised states not to ratify the proposed amendment, a recommendation heeded in the South but not throughout the North. Congress responded with the Military Reconstruction Act, passed over Johnson's veto, placing the southern states under military control until state conventions ratified the Fourteenth Amendment, granted blacks equal suffrage, and met other requirements. Finally, Congress passed, over yet another Johnson veto, the Tenure of Office Act requiring Senate approval of a successor before the dismissal of any official whose appointment required Senate approval. This last measure, of dubious constitutionality, was an obvious attempt either to stifle Johnson or lead him into committing an impeachable offense.

The House, although increasingly unhappy with the president, did not rush to impeach him, even after the 1866 election gave the Republican Party more than three-quarters of all seats. When Representative James Ashley of Ohio called for an impeachment investigation in December 1866, the House declined to take up his resolution. The following month a second Ashley resolution was referred to the House Judiciary Committee, which reported that it did not have enough time to complete an investigation before the Thirty-ninth Congress expired but recommended that the inquiry continue. Ashley's third resolution, at the start of the Fortieth Congress in March 1867, led to a lengthy Judiciary Committee inquiry and an impeachment recommendation the following November. The House heeded a minority report asserting that Johnson had not committed impeachable offenses, and in December it firmly rejected its committee's recommendation, 108–57. Despite widespread hostility toward Johnson, most House members took seriously the Constitution's requirements.

In less than three months the situation changed. Johnson had tried initially to comply with the requirements of the Tenure of Office Act by suspending the secretary of war, Edwin Stanton, and submitting for Senate approval the name of a replacement, General Ulysses S. Grant. When the Senate refused to concur in Stanton's dismissal, Grant departed and Stanton resumed his position. Furious and feeling betrayed by Grant, Johnson formally removed Stanton from office on February 21, 1868. Later the same day, an impeachment resolution was introduced in the House charging Johnson with "high crimes and misdemeanors" for violating the Tenure of Office Act.

The pace of the Johnson impeachment proceedings thereafter was breathtaking. The Reconstruction Committee took one day to return a recommendation of impeachment. After two days listening to speeches denouncing the president, the House voted along strict party lines—126 Republicans voting yes and 47 Democrats voting no—to impeach Johnson. Four days later, the House approved eleven articles of impeachment, nine dealing with Stanton in one way or another, one concerning Johnson's "intemperate, inflammatory, and scandalous harangues" against Congress, and a final one charging the president with repeatedly disregarding acts of Congress. Five days after that, the Senate opened its trial. After preliminaries were out of the way and Johnson's defense team was granted a ten-day recess to prepare, the Senate's forty-two Republicans and twelve Democrats began trial proceedings in earnest on March 23, a mere thirty-one days after Stanton's firing.

House manager Benjamin Butler's opening statement to the Senate addressed the still-unresolved question of what constituted an impeachable offense. Did it necessarily involve an indictable crime? In the Pickering removal, the answer appeared to have been no, but in the Chase and Peck acquittals it seemed to have been yes. Butler now declared that an impeachable offense was any act "in its nature or consequence subversive of some fundamental or essential principle of government, or highly prejudicial to the public interest, and this may consist of a violation of the Constitution, of law, of an official oath, or of duty, by an act committed or omitted, or, without violating a positive law, by the abuse of discretionary powers from improper motives, or for any improper purpose."[59] Johnson's defenders, not surprisingly, objected to Butler's broad view of impeachment, although it appears justified by both American and British precedent. Unfolding events left the issue unresolved.

Much of the trial itself focused on the Stanton affair. The House managers and Johnson's defenders sparred endlessly over the constitutionality of the Tenure of Office Act and over whether it applied to Stanton, who had been appointed by Lincoln well before its adoption. They also differed over whether the president's attacks on Congress were protected free speech under the First Amendment. Impeachment procedures in dispute included whether senators who had expressed hostility to Johnson could give him a fair trial, whether the Senate's president pro tempore, Benjamin Wade, who would become president if Johnson was removed, should have a vote, and whether as presiding officer Chief Justice Salmon Chase should have a tie-breaking vote on procedural matters. (The Senate answered all three of these procedural questions in the affirmative.) Curiously, relatively little time was devoted to the final article of impeachment, which many regarded then and since as having the best chance of adoption.

Testimony and arguments completed, the Senate voted first on the last, most sweeping article of impeachment on May 16. Thirty-five senators, all Republicans, voted for conviction, while nineteen, all twelve Democrats and seven Republicans, voted against. Had one senator in the minority voted with the majority, the president would have been convicted and removed from office. The stunned majority obtained a ten-day recess, hoping to change the mind of at least one of their apostate colleagues, but to no avail. On May 26 votes on other articles produced the exact same result, after which the Senate adjourned the trial.

The outcome of Johnson's impeachment and trial left a lasting impression of failed partisanship. All the votes in the House for impeachment and in the Senate for conviction had come from Republicans, whereas every Democrat in Congress stood opposed. Despite overwhelming congressional majorities of over 70 percent in each house, Republicans had proven unable to meet the Constitution's requirements of a two-thirds vote to remove a president from office. Too often overlooked is the fact that Johnson's narrow escape was due to the abandonment of their party's majority view by seven Republican senators unconvinced that Johnson had committed an impeachable offense. Those same senators were also concerned about the possible succession to the presidency of their radical colleague, Benjamin Wade, and were persuaded that Johnson would cause no further difficulties over Reconstruction if allowed to serve out the remaining ten months of his term as president.[60] Michael Les Benedict's judgment seems appropriate: Honest men came to different conclusions regarding the merits of the particular case brought before them.[61]

The impact of the Johnson impeachment was felt outside of Washington and in ways far more significant than his survival as a lame-duck president. The initiation of impeachment efforts forced the recalcitrant states of the former Confederacy to realize that, whatever the outcome, they would be compelled to comply with the unambiguous requirements of the Reconstruction Acts, including approval of the Fourteenth Amendment, before their representatives would be allowed to take their seats in Congress. Watching Johnson, their strongest supporter in the federal government, being reduced to political impotence, most southern states moved ahead quickly to comply with the terms of military reconstruction. Ratification by the southern states of the proposed Fourteenth Amendment was, arguably, the first and greatest constitutional consequence of impeachment.

Otherwise, the Johnson impeachment appears to have reinforced the American political system's reluctance to resort to impeachment in disputable cases. The failure of a party to win Senate conviction on charges brought by its members in the House, even in the exceptional situation when it held constitutionally sufficient majorities to do so in both houses of Congress, long discouraged further thoughts of partisan use of impeachment. Even exceptional circumstances led to only six impeachments of federal district judges and one of a cabinet official within the span of the subsequent century.

Two of the post-Johnson impeachment cases came during the scandal-ridden Grant presidency. Mark H. Delahay, a federal district judge for Kansas appointed by Lincoln in 1863, was impeached by the House ten years later for "personal habits [that] unfitted him for the judicial office." He was reportedly intoxicated both on and off the bench, including while passing sentences. Delahay quickly resigned even before specific articles were drawn up, much less a trial held. Nevertheless, his impeachment, like that of Judge Pickering, reinforced the principle that an indictable offense was not required, merely egregious official conduct.[62]

Three years later the Senate tried the case of Secretary of War William W. Belknap. He was impeached for corruption by the House in a bipartisan, unanimous vote. On his wife's advice, he had awarded the Fort Sill post tradership to an individual who, in return for not taking up the lucrative position, extracted large payments from the existing trading-post operator and split the payoffs with Mrs. Belknap. The Senate proceeded with the trial despite the secretary's resignation, presumably to deny him the possibility of future federal officeholding. No doubt members also desired to separate themselves from the stench of scandal permeating the Grant administration. Belknap narrowly won acquittal, not because senators thought him innocent but because they doubted their jurisdiction once he had resigned.[63]

For nearly a century thereafter, only federal judges confronted impeachment. Nearly thirty years passed before the procedure of impeachment was even invoked again. This time Charles Swayne, a federal district judge for northern Florida, a Republican appointed by Benjamin Harrison and tenaciously opposed by dominant Florida Democrats, was impeached, at the request of the Florida legislature and upon the recommendation of the judiciary committee, by a House vote of 198 to 61. Judge Swayne was charged with expense-account padding, improper use of a private railcar owned by a bankrupt railroad under his jurisdiction, failure to live in his judicial district as required by Congress, and improper citation of three individuals for contempt of court. After a trial in which Swayne's attorneys disputed all charges on their merits and claimed as well that none rose to the level of an impeachable offense, the judge was acquitted by a Senate that did not come anywhere close to a simple majority, much less a two-thirds supermajority, for any of the four impeachment charges.[64]

After a half century without a successful impeachment, Robert W. Archbald was convicted and removed in 1913 from the U.S. Court of Appeals for the Third Circuit, where he served as an associate judge of the recently created U.S. Commerce Court, which heard appeals from Interstate Commerce Commission rulings. The Commerce Court was widely perceived as favoring the railroads that were its principle litigants; the Archbald case no doubt reinforced this impression. Congress soon abolished the court.

Initially an interim appointee to a Scranton, Pennsylvania, federal district judgeship by William McKinley, Robert Archbald was affirmed in office by Theodore Roosevelt. He was then elevated to his appellate court seat by William Howard Taft. Archbald betrayed the trust of all three presidents by repeatedly engaging in personally profitable business transactions with railroad and coal company litigants before his district and appellate bench. None of the judge's conduct, if carried out by a private businessman, would have been indictable, but his use of judicial influence for personal gain provoked outrage. Among other things, Archbald had written letters on Commerce Court stationary encouraging the sale or lease of property on favorable terms to third parties who, in turn, rewarded the judge, their silent partner. In another instance, Archbald clandestinely corresponded with an appellant's attorney in a railroad case before his court, asked the lawyer his opinion on the case, and then supported the successful appeal, all of which violated judicial ethics. After investigation of complaints by the Justice Department and the House, Archbald was impeached in July 1912 by a bipartisan vote of 223 to 1.

The Senate put off Archbald's trial until after the contentious 1912 election. After hearing evidence and argument from mid-December to mid-January, senators had to choose between the House managers' charge that the judge's conduct violated the Constitution's "good behavior" standard and the defense's contention that Archbald could not legitimately be found guilty since no indictable crime was alleged and no official judicial ruling had been shown to be corrupted. House manager Henry D. Clayton declared that, on the bench, Archbald had been "seized with an abnormal and unjudgelike desire to make money by trading directly and through others with railroads and their subsidiary corporations [having or likely to have] litigation in his court." Once again refusing to limit impeachment to indictable conduct, a large bipartisan Senate majority convicted Archbald on four of six articles involving his appellate court behavior and, by a lesser margin, on one catchall article. The senators failed to convict on six articles relating to Archbald's activities while on the district court, either finding the charges not proven or, more commonly, not believing that the judge could be impeached for a position he no longer held. The Senate then voted 39–35—a simple majority held sufficient for such a determination—to disqualify Archbald from holding future U.S. office.[65]

Before the next actual impeachment in 1926 the House was urged to take action in three separate cases, all involving federal district judges. A judge in the District of Columbia resigned in 1914 after an impeachment investigation was launched, and a Utah counterpart quit the next year as soon as allegations of impropriety with a courtroom "cleaning lady" surfaced. Far more famously, a member of Congress asked in 1921 that Judge Kennesaw Mountain Landis be impeached for taking on a position as the first commissioner of baseball while still serving on the federal bench. Landis resigned his federal post a year thereafter.[66]

Four years later, by a vote of 306 to 62, the House impeached George W. English, a federal judge for the eastern district of Illinois, for various alleged abuses of authority. On one occasion, he had federal marshals round up all sheriffs and state's attorneys in the district to appear for what turned out to be an imaginary case; he then subjected them to a loud, angry, and profane rant in which he threatened to remove all of them from office before dismissing them from his courtroom without further explanation. Judge English was also charged with threatening attorneys and reporters who covered his courtroom and with colluding with bankruptcy referees to place funds in banks in which he had an interest. With a Senate trial scheduled to begin in less than a week, English resigned and the Senate dismissed the charges.[67]

Not every official threatened with impeachment chose resignation, however. Judge Harold Louderback, appointed by Calvin Coolidge to the federal bench for the northern district of California, fought back. A 1932 request by the San Francisco Bar Association led to an investigation of Louderback by a three-member House committee. It recommended that the judge be impeached for repeatedly appointing incompetent bankruptcy receivers, allowing them to charge excessive fees, and remaining indifferent to the interests of those in receivership. The House Judiciary Committee voted 17–5 against the recommendation, concluding that Louderback's conduct, even if as alleged, did not rise to the level of an impeachable offense. The House, after reviewing both majority and minority reports from the Judiciary Committee, voted 183–142 for impeachment. On March 3, 1933, the final day of the Seventy-second Congress, the House sent five articles of impeachment to the Senate.

Called into special session on March 9, 1933, to deal with the national crisis brought on by the Great Depression, the Senate as a body devoted considerable time over the next two and a half months to the Louderback trial. Most senators, however, did not give it a lot of their attention after quickly determining that the charges were insubstantial and the House managers' presentation unpersuasive. Much of the trial took place in a nearly empty Senate chamber. The senators accepted Louderback's protestation of innocence, or at least his reminder that the House Judiciary Committee had recommended against impeachment. Each of the four substantive impeachment articles drew the support of considerably less than a majority, in one case only eleven votes. A final omnibus article produced a 45–34 majority for conviction that was still well below the necessary two-thirds majority. The Louderback case is hard to see as anything more than an intramural quarrel within the San Francisco Bar Association or an outcry against the pain of innumerable bankruptcies in the early 1930s.

Only five days after Louderback's acquittal, similar charges of improprieties in handling bankruptcies caused the House to initiate an investigation of Halsted L. Ritter, a successful Denver attorney who had moved to Florida in 1925 for his wife's health and who four years later had been appointed by Coolidge to be a federal judge for the state's southern district. Unlike Louderback, however, Ritter was convicted and removed from office in 1936 for taking a kickback of fees in a resort-hotel bankruptcy case, for evading income taxes, and for continuing to practice law after going on the bench. All the alleged misconduct dated from the first year of Ritter's judgeship. A three-year investigation by a House Judiciary subcommittee had produced a 2–1 recommendation for impeachment followed by a 10–8 Judiciary Committee confirmation and a 181–146 House impeachment vote.

The case against Judge Ritter that House managers presented to the Senate in March and April 1936 was not impressive. Ritter plausibly contradicted it, claiming that the money he supposedly received improperly was merely money owed him by his former law partner from the settlement of their accounts before Ritter went on the bench. The Senate responded by refusing to convict him on any of the six articles of impeachment containing specific allegations of impeachable conduct. The votes on all six articles were below the two-thirds threshold, some far below.

Having declined to convict on any specific charge, the Senate nevertheless voted 56–28 for an article that collected all the previous charges into one summary article that charged Ritter with bringing his court into "scandal and disrepute, to the prejudice of said court, and public confidence in the administration of justice." By the margin of a single vote, the Senate convicted Ritter and removed him from the federal bench. Notably, Senator Sherman Minton of Indiana, later named to the federal appellate bench by Franklin Roosevelt and elevated to the Supreme Court by Harry Truman, voted to acquit Ritter on all six of the substantive articles and to convict on the omnibus article. With the inexplicable exception of Minton, the senators voting for the seventh article seemed to rest their vote on something they found worthy of impeachment in a previous article. Presumably Minton, while not finding any single charge to be of sufficient weight, perceived a general pattern of bad behavior leading to "scandal and disrepute" that was sufficient to condemn Ritter on the final ballot.[68]

Ritter subsequently challenged his removal on the grounds that the charges against him did not meet the constitutional standards for impeachable offenses and, particularly, that the Senate, after finding him not guilty on six articles, had no right to find him guilty on a seventh that dealt only with matters present in the first six. Ritter's suit in the U.S. Court of Claims to recover his unpaid salary represented the first judicial challenge ever to an impeachment verdict. The Court of Claims ruled, however, that the Constitution gave the Senate sole jurisdiction in an impeachment proceeding. No court had authority to set aside a Senate impeachment verdict. Judicial review simply did not apply.[69]

Halsted Ritter was the last U.S. official to face impeachment before 1960. With the settlement of his Court of Claims case, the framework of U.S. impeachment law seemed well established. It applied only to current holders of federal executive or judicial positions. It pertained to conduct beyond indictable criminal offenses and dealt with official behavior that subverted some fundamental principle of government or betrayed the public trust by violating the Constitution, a law, a formal oath, or an official duty through an act of commission or omission. Impeachment could also result from the willful abuse of discretionary powers. Conviction itself led only to loss of office and, possibly, ineligibility for further federal office, though criminal indictment and conviction could follow.

While both before and after the Ritter case, investigations for the purpose of possible impeachment took place from time to time, impeachment itself was rare and conviction even more so. Resignation repeatedly provided an escape route for the targets of impeachment. Congress either concluded that it lacked jurisdiction over those no longer in office or decided that further proceedings were a waste of its time. Although the courts determined that congressional action in bringing and trying impeachments was judicially unreviewable, Congress continued to regard impeachment as an instrument of last resort.

By 1960, the Constitution's impeachment provision had lain totally dormant for nearly two and a half decades. It was often mistakenly written off as comatose, if not completely dead, but, to the contrary, it was merely slumbering and awaiting the call that would cause it to arise and demonstrate its vitality. Until this point, the history of the impeachment mechanism in the United States had resembled that of its British cousin. Coming to life during a period of political turmoil and uncertain lines of government authority—the seventeenth century in Great Britain, the late eighteenth and very early nineteenth centuries in the United States—impeachment had proven to be little needed once durable political parties emerged to provide order and discipline in the quest for continuing control of government. Whether the creature would continue to hibernate or would once again spring to life depended in large measure on whether the political culture would remain content with waging contests for control of government by customary means. Once the contest was decided for the moment, would the victors respect the constitutional and customary bounds of their authority and would the vanquished accept the electorate's preference for their rivals? If political competition took on a more brutal character or if other restraints on official conduct appeared insufficient, the Constitution's impeachment provision was fully capable of being aroused.

2

Impeachment as Exceptional:

The Case of Earl Warren

In April 1961 billboards began appearing across the United States, from rural Orangeburg, South Carolina, to rapidly urbanizing Orange County, California, bearing a message never seen before by travelers on the nation's highways.[1] As Americans began to adapt to the use of automobiles in the early twentieth century, roadside signs quickly became commonplace. As hard-surfaced roads and higher-speed travel became common in the 1920s and 1930s, highway placards large and small both advertised more and more products and services and conveyed political and public-service messages. By 1960 nearly seventy-four million motor vehicles traversed America's vast networks of thoroughfares. None of the countless signs along those roads, however, resembled what began to appear in the third month of John F. Kennedy's presidency: billboards with a simple but strident demand, usually in bold red letters: "SAVE AMERICA—IMPEACH EARL WARREN."

The billboards varied in design and some also contained a plea to "Get the U.S. Out of the U.N.," but the calls to "Impeach Earl Warren" were ubiquitous. The sign makers obviously felt that they had no need to identify the target of their displeasure as the chief justice of the United States or explain why he should be removed from office. The reasons seemed to them self-evident. Eventually more than eleven hundred of these billboards could be found scattered across the landscape from central New York to south Florida and along highways from North Carolina to California.[2] In Atlanta twenty more went up as Warren arrived under heavy security guard to give speeches at the Georgia Institute of Technology and Emory University.[3]

As the signs became familiar throughout the country, they sometimes provoked intense if divided reactions. The Roman Catholic Diocese of Bridgeport, Connecticut, censured one of its priests for advocating impeachment from his pulpit.[4] A McLean, Virginia, dentist was fined $200 for spray painting "Join the Nuts!" on an "Impeach Earl Warren" sign on his neighbor's front lawn.[5] In Grand Haven, Michigan, an eighteen-year-old student charged with malicious destruction of property for chopping down another such placard was ordered to write an essay on the rights of minority groups or face a five-day jail sentence.[6] Whether they struck a chord or stirred outrage in those who saw them, the signs did manage to raise the nearly buried profile of impeachment.

Eastern Colorado billboard, 1963. *U.S. News & World Report* Magazine Collection, Library of Congress, Prints & Photograph Division.

Members of the John Birch Society (JBS), an organization of ardently anticommunist conservatives, funded the impeachment billboards. Small, only a little more than two years old, and hitherto generally unknown, the John Birch Society sought and captured widespread public attention with its billboards. To some who saw them, the idea of impeaching Earl Warren, the chief justice of the United States, seemed preposterous. To others, uncomfortable with the direction they saw both the Supreme Court and the new administration moving, it seemed inspired. Most Americans, however, lacked any comprehension of impeachment and simply found the notion bewildering.

In 1961 impeachment was a little understood and indeed largely forgotten constitutional instrument. It had not been employed during the lifetime of nearly half the American population; most of their elders had paid scant attention when it had been used against five federal judges between 1905 and 1936. One of the most respected political scientists of the 1950s, Clinton Rossiter of Cornell University, saw impeachment as "the extreme medicine of the Constitution," discredited by being "so brutally administered in the one case in which it was prescribed for a President." Reflecting on the outcome of President Andrew Johnson's 1868 impeachment, Rossiter concluded that the device was "a rusted blunderbuss that will probably never be taken in hand again."[7]

Action to remove a federal officeholder had only been formally taken by the House of Representatives thirteen times since the Constitution took effect in 1788, and those impeachment proceedings had produced only four convictions of federal district judges and three resignations by other judges and a secretary of war. In its most notable usages, it had failed to achieve the objective of removing higher officeholders from their positions. The Senate chose not to convict either Justice Samuel Chase or President Andrew Johnson when they were impeached in 1805 and 1868, respectively. Thereafter the impeachment process had been viewed skeptically, employed sparingly, and, finally, allowed to remain dormant after 1936. The few legal scholars, political scientists, and historians who paid it any attention at all tended to think of impeachment as a relic of a bygone era. Not surprisingly, the John Birch Society's campaign against Earl Warren was regarded by most contemporaries as a quixotic crusade rather than as what it turned out to be: the beginning of a forty-year era in which impeachment of federal officials would become a much more frequent occurrence than ever before.

The target of the first significant post–World War II impeachment effort appeared to most contemporary observers to be an unlikely candidate for such a dubious distinction. During a long political career, Earl Warren had repeatedly won broad and bipartisan political support. After thirteen years as district attorney of Alameda County, California, he won both the Republican and Democratic primaries in the course of his 1938 election as California attorney general. In 1942 he went on to win the first of three terms as governor of California. Nominally a Republican, in 1942 and 1950 he nearly won the Democratic gubernatorial primary as well under California's unusual cross-filing system, and in 1946 he actually did win the nomination of both the Republican and Democratic parties. He came very close to being elected vice president of the United States as the running mate of Republican Thomas Dewey in 1948. After receiving a September 27, 1953, recess appointment as chief justice of the United States from President Dwight Eisenhower, Warren was confirmed on March 1, 1954, on a voice vote by an overwhelming bipartisan majority of the Senate.[8]

Warren himself described the manner of his elevation to the chief justiceship after he retired from the Court:

As for my own appointment, it was a very simple operation from my standpoint. I was Governor of California in September 1953 when Chief Justice Vinson suddenly died. There was public discussion in the press about the possibilities for the vacancy created by his passing, but I had no communication with anyone concerning it although my name was mentioned in the press as one of the prospects. In the last week of September, Attorney General Brownell flew to Sacramento to see me. He said the President was considering appointing me to the Court, and wanted to know if I would be interested in accepting. I told him I would. There was no discussion of the President's views or my views of the law, and he returned to Washington within an hour. There was no mention of whether I would be appointed Chief Justice or an Associate Justice.

On Wednesday of that week, the President phoned me, and said that he was nominating me for the Chief Justiceship. I thanked him, and told him that in accordance with his wishes I would be available on the following Monday to be inducted into office on a recess appointment. There was no discussion of our respective views of the law in that conversation.

I flew to Washington on Sunday, October 4th, and was inducted into office the following day.[9]

Warren's account did not include the information that Eisenhower, after passing him over for a cabinet appointment, had promised to appoint the governor to the first vacancy on the Supreme Court, never expecting that Fred Vinson, the sixty-three-year-old chief justice, would be the first to depart. Nor did he mention the president's hesitation or Warren's insistence to Herbert Brownell, Jr., that Eisenhower honor the pledge.[10]

Eisenhower later famously regretted his appointment of Warren, but at the time the president made the nomination he did so with apparent ease, comfortable with Warren's judicial abilities and judgment. Others who shared Eisenhower's unhappiness with the way the Warren appointment turned out endorsed the closer Senate scrutiny of Court nominees that had become routine by the time Warren himself left the bench.

By April 1961 Warren had served seven and a half years as chief justice and was only a month past his seventieth birthday. He appeared to be in excellent health and likely to remain on the bench for many years under the terms of his lifetime appointment to the foremost position on the nation's highest court. Warren's seemingly secure place on the Supreme Court paradoxically spurred the John Birch Society to call for his impeachment. The constitutional process offered the only authorized means for his removal. The Warren episode, which at the time seemed so eccentric, turned out in retrospect to be the opening shot in a volley of impeachment initiatives over the next four decades. It is, therefore, the appropriate starting point for exploring America's age of impeachment.

Earl Warren had shown himself by 1961 to be a strong leader of a Supreme Court that was asserting its constitutional role in a profoundly important, some would say unprecedented, fashion. Although the Warren Court's role in transforming American government and society would grow during the 1960s, it had already made a substantial mark in the area of civil rights and civil liberties, especially in terms of race relations and treatment of political radicals. Not all were pleased with the changes the Warren Court had wrought.

When Warren arrived in Washington, the Supreme Court was already wrestling with the case of *Oliver Brown v. Board of Education of Topeka, Kansas*. *Brown*, first argued before the Court in 1952, was the consolidated appeal of five cases decided in the district courts of Delaware, the District of Columbia, Kansas, South Carolina, and Virginia, all of them upholding the racial segregation of local public schools. The eight justices whom Warren would join were all to one degree or another uncomfortable with segregation, but some believed strongly in stare decisis, the principle of ensuring the stability of the law by adhering to previous judicial rulings. They were reluctant to overturn the Court's 1896 holding in *Plessy v. Ferguson* that the equal protection of the laws required by the Fourteenth Amendment did not prohibit arrangements that were "separate but equal." Doubts also arose as to whether the federal government possessed the authority to intervene in matters having to do with schools, historically a state and local responsibility. Finally, some justices thought that the legislative branch of government, not the judiciary, should determine racial policy.

All these concerns, amplified in some cases by personal rivalries among the justices, offset or at least complicated a general sense of the injustice of segregation. Four justices, Hugo Black, William O. Douglas, Harold Burton, and Sherman Minton, were ready to ban segregation. Chief Justice Vinson argued for letting the *Plessy* precedent stand, and his colleagues Tom Clark, Robert Jackson, and Stanley Reed seemed prepared to do so. Justice Felix Frankfurter, opposed to segregation but worried about the effect on the nation of a closely divided ruling, appeared undecided about how to proceed. As a delaying tactic, Frankfurter posed questions to be addressed by opposing counsel at a second round of oral argument in December 1953. Vinson's death in September did not alter or resolve the problem of what one observant legal scholar called "the most severely fractured Supreme Court in history." The deadlock remained as Warren joined the Court in the fall of 1953.[11]

Warren's impact on the Court was immediate and profound. Having reflected at length on his own wartime role in incarcerating Americans of Japanese ancestry and concluding that unwarranted racial prejudice had resulted in gross injustice, Warren had become a determined foe of racial discrimination and a committed proponent of the Constitution's guarantee of equal protection of the law. He welcomed the second round of oral arguments on *Brown*, which afforded him some time to work on his new colleagues. Then he used a combination of effective legal reasoning and shrewd concessions on the means of implementing the decision to win over Clark, Frankfurter, and Jackson. The final holdout, Kentuckian Stanley Reed, in the end joined his brethren. Warren achieved remarkable unanimity for the opinion he wrote declaring that the Fourteenth Amendment's equal protection clause bound the states as well as the federal government and in the circumstances of the 1950s required an end to racial segregation of schools. Especially because of its unanimous character, the

Brown v. Board of Education decision, announced May 17, 1954, signaled that separate public schools for black and white children must end but also, by implication, that all other legally sanctioned racial segregation faced the same fate. The *Brown* decision, still widely regarded as the most significant Supreme Court ruling since World War II, bore the unmistakable mark of its chief architect, Earl Warren.[12]

A second *Brown* decision the following year reflected the concessions had Warren made to win the support of his most reluctant colleagues. The second *Brown* decision underscored the Supreme Court's view that time would be required for the transition to a desegregated educational system in the seventeen states (plus the District of Columbia) where segregation persisted. In many of those jurisdictions resistance to change in racial arrangements was as evident as anger with the Supreme Court's ruling that it must take place. In *Brown II* the Court expressed its determination that the defendants make "a prompt and reasonable start" toward ending segregation and proceed toward that goal "with all deliberate speed." Once again the Court was unanimous, and Warren's central role in achieving such an outcome was evident.

American society faced the prospect of sweeping and fundamental changes as the result of the *Brown* decision. A culture that had been based on unequal racial status through more than two centuries of slavery and a subsequent century of discriminatory segregation was being ordered by the Court to reconstitute itself on the basis of racial equality. Little wonder that criticism of the *Brown* decision and the nine men who made it emerged immediately from those quarters that faced a reduction in their prior privileged position.

Southern white politicians, with few exceptions, vigorously denounced the *Brown* rulings. In what came to be known as the Southern Manifesto, ninety-six southern senators and representatives called the Court's decision in the segregation cases "a clear abuse of judicial power" in which the justices "with no legal basis for such action, undertook to exercise their naked judicial power and substituted their personal political and social ideas for the established law of the land." The manifesto's signers vowed to "use all lawful means to bring about a reversal of this decision which is contrary to the Constitution."[13] While the signers were not specific about what those means included, they made clear that they viewed the *Brown* ruling in terms of unconstitutional behavior by each individual justice. The Georgia state legislature demonstrated one means of implementing the manifesto by adopting a resolution advocating the wholesale impeachment of the Supreme Court and calling upon southern sister states to join in the demand. The resolution, introduced by the Georgia House's speaker and the segregationist governor's floor leader, among other things, characterized the National Association for the Advancement of Colored People, the *Brown* plaintiff, with being "a Communist front organization."[14]

Fierce criticism of the directive to alter the customary social order also flowed from many pulpits and newspaper editorial pages throughout the South.

Ordinary citizens deluged the Court with critical mail. By June 1956, just over a year after the *Brown II* ruling was announced, the *New York Times* reported, "Old timers here say they have never seen anything to match in bitterness and vulgarity the mail that has come to members of the Supreme Court from the South since the court's decision outlawing racial segregation in the public schools."[15] Impassioned calls to resist *Brown* were heard in every part of the affected region. Not surprisingly, much resentment focused on the most identifiable messenger of racial reform, the leader of the Court and author of the troubling decision, Chief Justice Warren.

While Supreme Court decisions disallowing other forms of racial discrimination continued to flow from the initial reasoning of *Brown*, rulings on other matters just as controversial were also forthcoming under the leadership of the new chief justice. Warren once more found himself in the center of the storm on the issue of whether civil rights and liberties should be afforded to perceived American enemies. Apprehension about communist infiltration of the United States, ever present since the 1917 Bolshevik Revolution, had been dramatically heightened by the House Un-American Activities Committee (HUAC) in the late 1940s. The so-called Red Scare then reached a peak of sorts with Senator Joseph McCarthy's repeated charges that communists had infiltrated various government agencies. Efforts to expose domestic communists continued to produce legal cases that made their way to Warren's Court.

The issue of whether Fifth Amendment protections against self-incrimination applied to a witness's testimony before HUAC arose during Warren's first term on the Court. Put over by a divided Court for reargument the following term, *Quinn v. United States* and *Emspak v. United States* ultimately resulted in 7–2 and 6–3 opinions, respectively, striking down lower-court rulings denying the witnesses' rights. Warren's majority opinions took a broad view of procedures under which Fifth Amendment rights could be claimed.[16] The *Quinn* and *Emspak* rulings followed by six months the Senate censure of McCarthy's conduct and gave the first solid indication that the Court would strengthen the effort to rein in congressional communist-hunters.

During the 1955–1956 term, in *Pennsylvania v. Nelson,* the Court addressed the question of whether the conviction of an acknowledged communist under the Pennsylvania Sedition Act should give way to a federal prosecution under the 1940 Smith Act outlawing the Communist Party.[17] When Warren's opinion for a 6–3 majority upheld the constitutional supremacy of federal authority and derailed a more expansive state law, Virginia congressman Howard Smith, the Smith Act's author, as well as Senate Judiciary Committee chairman James O. Eastland and Senator McCarthy denounced the ruling for weakening anticommunist efforts.[18] *Pennsylvania v. Nelson* struck the most sparks but was not the only decision of the term that took steps to restrain the anticommunist crusade. In *Slochower v. Board of Higher Education of New York City,* the Court disallowed the firing of a Brooklyn College professor for declining to testify about Communist Party membership before 1942.[19]

The Court's view that even alleged communists deserved constitutional protections was stated more broadly and forcefully near the end of the 1956–1957 term. First, the Court disallowed efforts by New Mexico and California to block alleged and even admitted former communists from entering the legal profession. *Schware v. Board of Bar Examiners of New Mexico* addressed the case of Rudolph Schware, a World War II military veteran seeking admission to the state bar who had been denied because he had been a party member from 1932 to 1940 and had been arrested but never tried for "criminal syndicalism." *Konigsberg v. State Bar of California* confronted the case of Raphael Konigsberg, a candidate for admission to the bar who had refused to answer questions about Communist Party membership. On May 6, 1957, the Court ruled unanimously in favor of Schware on the basis that at the time of his membership, it had not been illegal to belong to the Communist Party.[20] The justices also supported Konigsberg, but by a narrower 5–3 margin because of doubts regarding his refusal to answer bar examiners' questions.[21] Four weeks later, in *Jencks v. United States,* an 8–1 Court ruled that Clinton Jencks, president of a local of the International Union of Mine, Mill, and Smelter Workers convicted of filing a false report to the National Labor Relations Board denying his communist association, had been improperly deprived of access to reports by FBI-paid informants so that witnesses against him could be effectively cross-examined.[22]

The *Jencks* due process decision provoked an immediate hostile response. President Eisenhower, Attorney General Brownell, and FBI director J. Edgar Hoover all expressed outrage at the opening of FBI files required by the ruling. In his dissenting opinion in the case, Justice Clark quoted an agitated Hoover's warning that the *Jencks* ruling would give criminals "a Roman Holiday for rummaging through confidential information as well as vital national secrets." After the decision was announced, the powerful FBI director declared he would favor nonprosecution rather than open his confidential files. He immediately began lobbying for congressional action to thwart *Jencks*. Three months later Congress adopted legislation tightening the rules pertaining to documents demanded by criminal defendants. Perceived as a rebuke to the Court, the bill did not actually overturn the *Jencks* ruling, but it called for striking a witness's testimony rather than declaring a mistrial if pertinent documents were not produced.[23] Despite the outcry against it, however, *Jencks* did not elicit the reaction that would accompany four decisions addressing the rights of alleged communists handed down two weeks later on Monday, June 17, 1957.

The so-called Red Monday cases collectively marked the strongest statement yet from the Warren Court upholding the civil rights of alleged communists. The four separate decisions announced together represented, in the words of one legal scholar, "a once-in-a-generation day."[24] One case, *Service v. Dulles,* involved

John Stewart Service, a senior foreign-service specialist on China charged with being a communist sympathizer and security risk, investigated and exonerated by the State Department Loyalty Review Board and the deputy undersecretary of state, but nevertheless dismissed by Secretary of State Dean Acheson. A unanimous Court found that procedures written to protect state department employees against unfounded accusations of disloyalty had been violated. When it invalidated Service's dismissal, the Court outraged proponents of the view that China had turned to communism in 1949 because of communist sympathizers in the U.S. State Department rather than as a result of the actions of Chiang Kai-shek and the Chinese Nationalists.[25]

Even more disquieting to hardened anticommunists were the Court's rulings against various communist prosecutions. *Watkins v. United States* and *Sweezy v. New Hampshire* challenged federal and state legislative investigations of communism. John T. Watkins, a United Automobile Workers vice president, freely described his own past cooperation with communists but refused to answer HUAC questions about the communist ties of others in the union. Paul M. Sweezy, a state university professor, likewise answered most questions put to him by New Hampshire's attorney general, Louis Wyman, who was conducting an inquiry authorized by a state legislative committee. He freely admitted to being a "classical Marxist" and a "socialist." Sweezy refused, however, to answer questions about the allegedly communist Progressive Party of New Hampshire or its members (forty-three in all according to an FBI count). Both Watkins and Sweezy contended that the questions were not pertinent inquiries within the committees' investigative power and that contempt citations for refusing to answer such questions were invalid. The Court, for the most part, agreed.[26] In *Yates v. United States,* perhaps the most dramatic of the Red Monday rulings, the Court reversed the convictions of fourteen Communist Party leaders under the Smith Act, dismissing five outright and ordering retrials in the other nine cases. By finding that mere party membership did not constitute organizing a conspiracy to overthrow the government by force and violence, the Court in *Yates* effectively overturned its 1951 decision in *Dennis v. United States* that party membership was prima facie evidence of conspiracy and thus punishable.[27]

While the Red Monday decisions had their admirers (a *New York Times* editorial called the Court "courageous"),[28] they were excoriated by outspoken anticommunists. During the 1957 American Bar Association (ABA) convention in London, its Special Committee on Communism issued a scorching report criticizing the Court for aiding the communist cause by its rulings. A year and a half later, the ABA House of Delegates called on Congress to override the Court's decisions. Warren, who attended the London convention, responded by resigning from the ABA.[29] From the floor of the Senate, James Eastland and Joseph McCarthy ridiculed the Red Monday decisions, while Senator Strom Thurmond added a rhetorical flourish by calling for the wholesale impeachment of the

Court. Some members of the House reportedly considered an impeachment resolution but chose not to offer one.[30] While nothing resulted from these efforts, they were harbingers of attacks ahead that would be more substantial.

During subsequent Court terms, Warren and his colleagues continually reinforced the civil rights principles articulated in *Brown* and the Red Monday cases. They would further enrage conservatives with rulings affirming federal power to enforce desegregation,[31] reforming criminal justice procedure,[32] relaxing restraints on pornography,[33] prohibiting prayer and Bible reading in public schools,[34] insisting on "one man, one vote" in federal and state legislative districts and thus reducing the political power of rural conservatives,[35] and, finally, finding a zone of personal privacy regarding sexual matters into which government had no right to intrude.[36] But while these and other Court positions would draw sustained criticism from conservatives into the following century, *Brown* and especially the Red Monday cases were what set off the era's initial effort at judicial impeachment.

Conservative anger with the Supreme Court's decisions was widespread and quickly led to demands that action be taken to thwart the Court. For example, a Boston woman wrote to her senator early in 1958 to say, "I urge that you add your efforts to the impeachment of Earl Warren and the associate justices responsible for the weakening of our national security through the 'Jencks' and 'Watkins' decisions and the invasion of states' rights in the 'Desegregation' decision." She also called for repeal of "the Communist-inspired federal income tax."[37] The writer may not have fully understood impeachment procedures, which the Senate had no power to initiate, but clearly she was ready for drastic measures. She was alarmed about communism and perceived the Warren Court as its abettor. The senator's prompt reply was entirely unsympathetic but likewise betrayed a lack of familiarity with impeachment, declaring, "Impeachment proceedings violates [*sic*] the fundamental integrity of our separation of powers system."[38] The exchange did, however, foreshadow both the growing number of calls soon to come for Supreme Court impeachments and the political resistance those calls would encounter.

Less than a year after the Red Monday decisions, Rosalie M. Gordon lashed out at Warren and his colleagues in *Nine Men against America: The Supreme Court and Its Attack on American Liberties*.[39] Gordon, a regular writer for the conservative organization America's Future, warned in a simplistic gloss on the Red Monday decisions that the Court was protecting communists teaching in the public schools, allowing them to talk about overthrowing the U.S. government as long as they did not discuss specific plans, permitting them admission to the bar, and sheltering them from having to answer congressional questions.[40] The Court, she asserted, had been shaped by "socialist revolutionary" Franklin Roosevelt, whose appointments ranged from "pale pink . . . to just this side of deep red."[41]

Furthermore, the *Brown* decision ignored the tradition of state control of education and constituted a judicial fiat assuring "that the federal government in Washington henceforth would set the standards of admission to their state schools."[42] Finally, on Red Monday the Warren Court had moved to "break down completely all our defenses against the communist conspiracy in our midst."[43] Gordon proposed that the tide be turned by impeaching the current justices, imposing term limits and multiple restrictions on their successors, and eliminating entirely the effects of the post–New Deal Court by adopting a constitutional amendment declaring all post-1937 Court decisions void.[44]

A few months later Robert H. W. Welch, Jr., a candy company executive, wove Gordon's ideas into his plans for the anticommunist organization he was seeking to establish. He intended to call the body the John Birch Society, after a Baptist missionary turned military intelligence officer who was killed in China. Welch alleged that John Birch was the first American casualty of the cold war. Gordon's characterization of the Court fit neatly with Welch's view that a rapidly expanding communist conspiracy was seizing control of American government. He embraced her agenda for thwarting it. Over the next several years, he would use her first priority, impeaching the members of the Supreme Court or at least its chief justice, as an effective identifying and recruiting device for the JBS.

Welch embodied in its most intense form the 1950s American obsession with the threat of communism. Like quite a few Americans, Welch had become convinced that communism was an insidious enemy poised to transform the nation's comfortable way of life. He tended to see deliberate conspiracy as the sole explanation for every unpalatable development and thus repeatedly blamed events on procommunist intentions on the part of American leaders. His apprehension over communism was unrestrained by mounting evidence that the Communist Party of the United States was small, weak, and filled with FBI informants. Welch was willing to devote all his abundant energy, ample resources, and wide contacts in the American business community to battle what he regarded as an already well-advanced communist takeover of the United States.

A sense of alarm about a communist menace gripped many Americans, stirred by politicians such as senators Joseph McCarthy and Richard Nixon and FBI director J. Edgar Hoover, Christian evangelists such as Billy Graham, and a host of business and cultural figures who all found that anticommunist rhetoric served to advance their own agendas.[45] More than a few outspoken anticommunists asserted that the red peril had gained a foothold in the United States through the New Deal of the 1930s. In their eyes, any advocate of extending New Deal social welfare or corporate regulatory programs was a radical socialist in league with Marxism-Leninism. The United Nations, they agreed, would extend the New Deal drive for a collectivist world order.

Welch became one of the most single-minded and fervent anticommunists of an era in which those qualities were not in short supply. He had been born in the last month of the previous century on a North Carolina farm. After graduating from the University of North Carolina and then spending two years each at the U.S. Naval Academy and Harvard Law School, he settled in Boston. For many years he worked as vice president for sales and advertising of the James O. Welch Company, his brother's candy-manufacturing firm. He joined the stridently anti–New Deal National Association of Manufacturers (NAM), serving seven years as a member of its board of directors, three years as its regional vice president, and two years as chairman of its Educational Advisory Committee. Through the committee the NAM spent millions on newspaper advertisements and radio programming to publicize the virtues of unrestrained capitalism. Welch also joined the board of directors of the Foundation for Economic Education, an uncompromising libertarian group founded in 1946 that spread its message through pamphlets, seminars for businessmen, free conservative textbooks for cash-strapped high schools, and a magazine, the *Freeman*, that businessmen could pay to have sent free to employees, vendors, and clients.[46] By the early 1950s Welch began his own publishing ventures, producing two anticommunist tracts[47] as well as a monthly magazine, *American Opinion.* He also supported other conservative undertakings, contributing $1,000 in 1955 to help William F. Buckley, Jr., get his *National Review* off the ground. An ardent supporter of Robert Taft's presidential aspirations and McCarthy's investigations of communist subversion, Welch was disappointed when neither succeeded. In January 1957, five months before Red Monday, he retired from business to dedicate all his time to the anticommunist cause.[48]

Welch devoted 1957 and 1958 to developing his ideas and plans further. His views of the communist menace grew more alarmist as the Supreme Court handed down its decisions and when, a few months later, Senator McCarthy died. During this period, he wrote for private circulation a book-length manuscript, sometimes known as *The Black Book,* that would several years later be revised and published as *The Politician.* In its original version he asserted, "My firm belief that Dwight Eisenhower is a dedicated, conscious agent of the Communist conspiracy is based on an accumulation of detailed evidence so extensive and so palpable that it seems to me to put this conviction beyond a reasonable doubt."[49] If the president was a dedicated communist, then it followed that the man he appointed chief justice of the United States must be as well.

Robert Welch gathered eleven sympathetic men, mainly midwesterners, in Indianapolis on December 9, 1958, to hear him present his ideas and form the John Birch Society. Over the course of two days he set forth an elaborate assessment of problems he saw besetting the United States and what could be done in response. Welch began by asserting that communism was much further advanced and more deeply entrenched in the United States than generally realized. He blamed the Eisenhower administration for undermining the nation's defenses as well as for a "huge and highly organized effort to wear down the morale of both our officers and our men in uniform."[50] Welch attributed to unnamed authorities the claim that "at least thirty huge Communist espionage rings" were operating in the United States unchecked since McCarthy's efforts to expose them had been blocked by the Supreme Court. Echoing Rosalie Gordon, he asserted that "scores of known Communist-sympathizers have been restored, by Supreme Court rulings, to their former jobs within our Federal Government,"[51] a vast exaggeration of John Stewart Service's reemployment with only a low-level security clearance at the State Department.

Welch argued that the conspiracy to undermine the United States extended further. He asserted that communists had long sought to foment civil war within the United States by agitating for black civil rights. It had been their plan, he said, "gradually carried out over a long period with meticulous cunning, to stir up such bitterness between whites and blacks in the South that small flames of civil disorder would inevitably result. They could then fan and coalesce these little flames into one great conflagration of civil war." He regarded civil rights as simply a communist slogan to make trouble in the South.[52] Welch made evident his own lack of sympathy for reform of American race relations.

What most concerned Welch was what he called "the cancerous disease of collectivism," an attitude inherent in communism but extending beyond it and endorsing government doing for people what they should do for themselves.[53] It would be easy to label him a libertarian except for his authoritarian leadership of the John Birch Society, a leadership style whose self-justification was reminiscent of German fascism of the 1930s and 1940s. Welch argued, paradoxically, that only extremely centralized control would allow the society to meet effectively the challenge of collectivism. He insisted that "'so-called democratic processes' could play no part in John Birch Society affairs" and was prepared to exercise authority to prevent communist infiltrators from undermining the effort.[54] The men with whom he met in Indianapolis in December 1958 accepted this approach as they agreed to serve as directors of the society. Thus, it seems fair to say that the John Birch Society was an organization that mirrored the beliefs of Welch himself as it extended his influence.

In order to wage the war against communism in America, wipe out the "Communist Internationale now called the United Nations," reduce government to a necessary minimum, and promote individual responsibility, Welch proposed to the Indianapolis meeting that the JBS be built out of local chapters of ten to twenty members, eventually comprising a total membership of one million.[55] A hierarchy of section leaders for each four to eight chapters, district governors, and a national council would all ultimately report to Welch himself, or as he preferred to be called, "the Founder." The local chapters would be vital, he thought, in winning the battle for public opinion.

Welch told his Indianapolis colleagues that he admired the communist tactic of setting up front organizations focused on various topics to recruit a broad base of support. He proposed to employ the same approach:

With such fronts as A Petition To Impeach Earl Warren (and I think we could get the names of a hundred outstanding leaders from the South and many from the North on the letterhead right now) . . . with these and dozens of new fronts popping up to attack the Communists—or persons, institutions, and movements giving aid and comfort to the Communists—we can certainly keep this whole front operation from being so one-sided, as it has been.[56]

An effort to impeach Warren had clearly taken shape in Welch's mind by December 1958 as not only worthwhile in its own right but also as a device to advance his larger agenda. Whether or not the chief justice's impeachment was a realistic political goal, it would serve as a means of recruiting members who shared Welch's basic premises. Additionally, Welch saw such a campaign as a way to keep the society's grassroots membership engaged. In particular, gathering signatures for impeachment petitions would utilize local workers' time and energy in a profitable fashion.[57]

Even if impeachment of the chief justice did not represent an achievable objective, the crusade against Warren did galvanize the development of the JBS. Welch's original Indianapolis group and before long a paid staff of field coordinators repeated Welch's message to small gatherings across the country. These membership solicitations produced enthusiastic recruits willing to pay monthly dues of two dollars for men, one dollar for women. Within four years, the society claimed to have enrolled forty thousand dues-paying members across the country, although because it insisted on keeping its membership lists confidential that figure was impossible to verify. The society did eventually employ a 220-member staff, including 75 field coordinators, and operated on an annual budget of $5 million. Growth was shrewdly managed. When a chapter reached a membership of twenty, it would be divided so that a strong sense of personal involvement could be maintained. The largest membership clusters appeared in Southern California, Texas, and Florida.[58]

Who joined the John Birch Society? Random interviews of fifty California members not part of the society's leadership found that the group was surprisingly youthful. Most were between thirty and sixty years of age with an overall average age of forty-four. Those surveyed were reasonably well educated by contemporary standards, with a quarter being high school graduates, another quarter having one or two years of college, 30 percent holding B.A. or B.S. degrees, and 16 percent having obtained graduate training or degrees. Most of the women were housewives, while most of the men had white-collar jobs. Family income was comparatively high. Nearly nine out of ten professed a religious affiliation, with half those being Protestant fundamentalists or Catholics. They belonged to few, if any, other secular organizations. Birchers were, in the judgment of the political scientist who conducted the survey, basically well-to-do, apolitical people who felt threatened by civil and international turmoil, opposed any expansion of government, and accepted Welch's conspiracy theories, especially in terms of seeing the United Nations and the U.S. Supreme Court as agents of collectivism.[59]

Once enlisted, society members received Welch's *Bulletin* once a month. Many also attended monthly chapter meetings where speakers and films effectively reinforced Welch's messages, and attendees were encouraged to take personal action to advance the cause. In September 1960 Welch's call was to take over the local parent-teacher association.[60] In January 1961 the *Bulletin* suggested that its readers write to their congressmen urging Earl Warren's impeachment, with Welch declaring that the campaign could succeed in the current congressional session if the demand was sufficiently insistent and that it would send "a mighty warning to all who would destroy our Constitution.[61] The subsequent deluge of letters caught Capitol Hill's attention and first brought the John Birch Society large-scale media attention.[62]

Orange County, California, provided some of the most fertile ground for the society's growth. The area south of Los Angeles had much in common with other areas where the JBS flourished: Phoenix, Arizona; Dallas, Texas; and panhandle Florida. A once sparsely populated area of ranches and farms, Orange County developed rapidly during and after World War II, its booming economy built on military bases, defense contractors, and construction and service industries for a rapidly arriving, largely white, Protestant, midwestern, and newly middle-class population. Rapid and robust growth overwhelmed existing community leadership and gave control to recently arrived people with business and military interests. Orange County in the 1950s became a model of increasingly affluent, baby-boom suburban culture characterized by sprawling developments of single-family homes and a community life centered on schools and conservative Protestant churches.[63]

Staunch individualism, Protestant piety, and resentment of far-off Washington, D.C., with its power-accumulating "collectivism," were all deeply embedded in the culture of Orange County. Domestic communism became a widespread concern, stirred up from pulpits and in the pages of the local press. Anticommunism found outlets in, among other things, a successful 1961 campaign to recall three Anaheim school board members who criticized the House Un-American Activities Committee. The John Birch Society grew rapidly in this environment because it enabled concerned men and women, many of them doctors, engineers, managers, and small-business owners and most recruited by friends and family, to meet in their own homes and neighborhoods with people of similar backgrounds and to feel that they were fighting communism. By the end of 1962 there were eight John Birch Society chapters rooted in Santa Ana, five in Anaheim, five in Costa Mesa, three in Garden Grove, and five in Newport Beach. In all, thirty-eight chapters, with an estimated membership of more than eight hundred people, operated in Orange County. While the JBS only represented the most extreme fringe of the generally conservative Orange County population of seven hundred thousand, its organization and outspokenness made its presence felt beyond its mere numbers.[64]

The society slowly started coming to general public attention during the summer of 1960. Large urban daily newspapers in Chicago, Milwaukee, and Boston all published lengthy reports on the society, which had established chapters in their circulation areas. The stories not only described the society's organization as it was laid out in the easily obtainable *Blue Book,* a print version of Welch's December 1958 Indianapolis presentation, but they also spotlighted Welch's privately circulated manuscript variously known as *The Politician* or *The Black Book*. The reports highlighted the book's charge that President Eisenhower and his brother Milton Eisenhower, as well as the secretary of state, John Foster Dulles, and his brother, CIA director Allen Dulles, were all dedicated and conscious agents of the Communist Party. Relatively little attention was given to the JBS agenda, though Warren's impeachment was listed among its goals.[65]

In January 1961 Welch devoted his entire monthly members' *Bulletin* to launching a public crusade against Chief Justice Warren. The JBS leader argued that impeachment was justified by the constitutional provision that federal judges "shall hold their offices during good behavior." Warren, Welch contended, had violated his oath to support and defend the Constitution and thus had not exhibited good behavior. He urged members to write their congressmen demanding Warren's impeachment.[66] The relative anonymity previously enjoyed by the society abruptly vanished.

Congressional offices began reporting an extraordinary flood of mail calling for action against the chief justice. For example, one New Hampshire congressman received numerous anti-Warren letters, individually composed and often handwritten, from residents of, among other places, California, Illinois, Mississippi, and especially Texas, though his files contained nothing from his own constituents. The correspondents did not identify themselves as members of the John Birch Society, but their messages used arguments that Welch had encouraged members to press on Congress. In generally well-crafted and insistent language the letters repeatedly asserted that Warren had violated the Constitution's judicial "good behavior" requirement by rulings in favor of communist principles and party members. One Texas woman, focusing on the Red Monday and desegregation decisions, declared that those rulings "clear the way for the destruction of our Country and the conquest and enslavement of our people by the Communist Conspiracy." Another stressed the common theme that Warren's impeachment was "not only desirable, but imperative."[67]

Within weeks a wave of negative publicity regarding the John Birch Society erupted. The *Los Angeles Times* ran a five-part series of well-documented articles by investigative reporter Gene Blake on the society in early March, concluding with a sharply condemnatory editorial by Otis Chandler, the unquestionably conservative publisher of the paper. Chandler declared that the society's conspiracy theories and smear tactics "will sow distrust, and aggravate disputes, and they [would] weaken the very strong case for conservatism."[68] *Time* magazine published a highly critical article on March 10, and the *Nation* followed with its own blistering article on March 11 as well as several later pieces.[69] Conservative columnist Walter Trohan of the *Chicago Tribune* tried to mount a defense but mainly succeeded in calling attention to some of Welch's most extreme ideas.[70] On April 1, the august *New York Times* certified the organization's new prominence by running a story on the society on its front page.[71]

The *New Republic* issue of April 10, 1961, treated the society with disdain, but concluded, "Abominable (or silly, if you wish) as the John Birch Society is, it would be a rash man who would claim that it endangers the Republic." The *New Republic* argued against a proposed congressional investigation, saying that a probe into the thoughts and activities of a private organization was no more justified on the right than on the left. The magazine urged that a judgment on the society be left to the press and public opinion.[72] In the next month, it demonstrated what it had in mind by running two disparaging essays on the society.[73] The constant, heavy drumbeat of criticism continued.

The John Birch Society received some attention for its campaigns to repeal the federal income tax and to "Get the U.S. out of the U.N.," but far less than it did for its effort to impeach Earl Warren. Calling attention to the impeachment campaign allowed media and political friends and foes alike to emphasize the society's core beliefs that a communist conspiracy was afoot in the American government and that drastic action was required to thwart it. Neither supporter nor critic was likely to ignore a broadside featuring a mug-shot-style photo of the chief justice and the headline "WANTED for Impeachment—EARL WARREN." The text below contained the usual Welch litany of charges describing Warren as "a dangerous and subversive character, an apparent sympathizer of the Communist Party and . . . a rabid agitator for compulsory racial mongrelization. . . . Persons wishing to aid in bringing him to justice should contact their Congressmen to urge his impeachment for treason."[74]

Two months into the 1961 Warren impeachment campaign Welch admitted to the JBS membership, "Dislodging Warren from Washington could be as difficult as kicking Khrushchev out of the Kremlin."[75] Not even such a sober assessment from their leader, however, daunted the energized faithful. Virginia field coordinator Bryton Barron, a retired U.S. State Department historian, declared a month later that a massive letter-writing campaign for Warren's impeachment was continuing because the chief justice had "voted 92 percent of the time in favor of Communists and subversives since joining the Court."[76]

JBS members continued writing letters, circulating broadsides and petitions, and erecting billboards advocating the chief justice's impeachment. However, these were not the only tactics they employed. When Warren arrived in Los Angeles in July 1961 to give an after-dinner speech, he was met at the airport by forty-five JBS picketers with signs saying "Earl Warren, Socialite or Socialist" and, as always, "Impeach Earl Warren."[77] In August, during a speech in Tulsa, Oklahoma, at a convention of the Christian Crusade (its head, Reverend Billy James Hargis, was a member of the society's board of directors), Welch announced that the society would conduct an essay contest open to all college students in the country. The best essay on grounds for impeaching Chief Justice Warren would win $1,000, and eight other essays would each be given prizes of $500 to $100.[78]

Despite the essays and all the letters and petitions to Congress demanding it, no impeachment resolutions were introduced in the House of Representatives. With media attention focused on the society, California Republican congressmen John Rousselot and Edgar W. Hiestand acknowledged that they were members. Both had been recently elected to Congress in part on the basis of their outspoken anticommunist positions. Although Welch's impeachment campaign would live on for several years, in a practical sense a death knell for the effort was signaled when not even Rousselot or Hiestand proved willing to buck the tide of negative reaction to the impeachment campaign by putting an impeachment resolution into the House hopper.

Members of the society indicated in correspondence with Welch that they were troubled by the difficulties they faced in pursuing the Warren impeachment campaign. Some complained that Rosalie Gordon's book was too long and too expensive to use in winning converts: They sought, unsuccessfully as it turned out, a succinct brochure articulating the JBS argument for impeachment. Some preferred other objectives such as impeaching the whole Court, getting rid of the United Nations, or impeaching the "Socialistic Communist" President Kennedy. Still others were bothered by the negative publicity the campaign was generating; they unhappily reported that as soon as they mentioned impeaching Warren, they were identified as JBS members and were put on the defensive. Doubts about the importance of Warren's impeachment, not to mention the problems of explaining and justifying it, gradually sapped the enthusiasm of even very loyal members.[79] The society appeared to recognize its failure. While it continued to collect Warren impeachment petitions with fifty signatures on each page, they remained in Welch's Belmont, Massachusetts, headquarters, tabulated but with totals unannounced and never forwarded to Congress in a demand for action.[80]

The effort and resources expended by the John Birch Society in its Earl Warren impeachment campaign did not have the effect Welch sought. When made public, the call to impeach the chief justice seemed to most Americans who learned of it to be more than a little bizarre. The society contributed to this view by resting its case on the sweeping and unsubstantiated claim that Warren was part of a communist conspiracy. An argument challenging the *Brown* and Red Monday decisions might have had wider resonance, though those decisions were still far from being high crimes or misdemeanors. Hardly anyone in the mainstream media had even the slightest experience with impeachment and thus the understanding to evaluate the society's impeachment call on its merits. The press quickly labeled impeachment and its proponents as "extremist." The John Birch Society was branded the "lunatic fringe." What ultimately proved fatal to the society and its impeachment campaign, however, was the decision by other politically active conservatives to distance themselves from the society.

The John Birch Society was only one manifestation of a new American conservative activism developing in the 1950s and early 1960s. After the death of Senator Taft and the implosion of Senator McCarthy, a new generation of conservatives began to emerge. Some concentrated on aggressive anticommunism while others focused more on a traditional libertarian agenda of restraining government economic regulation, welfare programs, and social reform. Clashes between different segments of the movement were probably inevitable.[81]

One of the most influential young conservatives to appear on the scene was William F. Buckley, Jr. The eldest son of a multimillionaire oilman, Buckley at twenty-six published *God and Man at Yale,* a book attacking liberalism and indifference to religion at his alma mater. After spending a year working for the CIA in Mexico, writing a book defending McCarthy, and serving as an editor of *American Mercury,* Buckley in 1955, at age thirty, founded his own conservative journal, *National Review.* Under his editorship it soon became an important forum for expressions of conservative political ideas. In 1957 Buckley hired William Rusher, a Harvard-trained lawyer, staff counsel for the Senate Internal Security Committee,[82] and Young Republican leader, to serve as *National Review*'s publisher. The two would work together for more than thirty years to advance the conservative agenda.[83]

Buckley and Rusher devoted themselves to building a political movement that would place conservatives in control of first the Republican Party and then American government. Like many of their conservative contemporaries, they were unhappy with Eisenhower's embrace of New Deal programs and federal authority, and they distrusted his heir apparent, Richard Nixon, as self-serving and unreliable. Buckley and Rusher were among those who saw Senator Barry Goldwater of Arizona as an attractive conservative alternative to Nixon. A group of John Birch Society–affiliated Republicans led by former Notre Dame law school dean Clarence Manion launched a feeble and unsuccessful attempt to gain Goldwater the 1960 Republican presidential nomination.[84] When Nixon then lost the general election, Rusher was among the first to begin serious planning for a Goldwater candidacy in 1964.[85] Rusher and Buckley shared an immediate concern that Republican moderates and the American electorate in general would not distinguish between Goldwater's conservatism and the JBS's far more extreme and conspiratorial views.

Initially, Buckley and Welch supported each other's efforts. The two had been introduced in 1954 by Henry Regnery, both men's publisher. Welch had pledged $1,000 to *National Review* in 1955 and again in 1957, while Buckley wrote Welch in June 1958 after seeing him in Boston, "I have always felt certain that we agree on essentials, and my opinion is now confirmed. Our differences are a matter of emphasis."[86] However, when Welch gave Buckley an early typescript of *The Politician* with its declaration that Eisenhower was a dedicated communist, Buckley sent it back a month later without comment.[87] Subsequently, Buckley told Welch that he found his "assumptions about the root causes of America's difficulties . . . false and misleading."[88] Still, for a time the two remained cordial and drew on some of the same contributors.[89] By 1961, however, Buckley had come to see Welch as a liability to the development of a conservative political movement with broad appeal.

As the John Birch Society burst into the national spotlight in March 1961, Buckley tried to distance himself and his magazine from it. Previously, Buckley had differed with Welch in private, but he had only done so publicly by publishing a Eugene Lyons essay in 1959 that lampooned Welch's conclusion that Boris Pasternak's novel *Doctor Zhivago* was really procommunist trickery. (Buckley himself told Welch that he thought Welch's reading of *Doctor Zhivago* was "preposterous.")[90] The *National Review* editorial board, especially Rusher, worried that Buckley might alienate subscribers and other conservatives who belonged to the John Birch Society but did not fully embrace Welch's views.[91] Nevertheless, in April 1961 Buckley went public with his criticism of Welch, albeit cautiously.

Abandoning more-strident earlier drafts, Buckley devoted a two-and-a-half-page *National Review* editorial to the JBS, setting the piece up as a series of answers to questions from readers concerned about the recent press furor about the society. In the midst of a piece that sought to treat the JBS membership respectfully, Buckley made it clear that he disagreed with Welch's belief, "most sincerely and passionately held, that the government of the United States is under the effective control of the world-wide Communist conspiracy." Buckley distinguished between JBS members, most of whom he characterized as well-meaning anticommunists not even aware of Welch's privately circulated thoughts on Eisenhower, and Welch himself, whose reasoning on conspiracies Buckley disdained. At the same time, Buckley tempered his direct criticism of the JBS leader by concluding that "certain elements of the press are opportunizing on the mistaken conclusions of Robert Welch to anathematize the entire American right wing."[92] Within a few days the *National Review* editor told a St. John's University audience that he hoped the membership, not Welch, would control the John Birch Society.[93]

Five months later, Buckley's magazine addressed the prime JBS initiative in its lead article. "Should We Impeach Earl Warren?" by L. Brent Bozell, Buckley's brother-in-law and an attorney, began, "Earl Warren, by any dispassionate view of the record, is a bad Chief Justice." Nevertheless, Bozell went on, impeachment was both unachievable and inappropriate. Warren had committed no criminal offense, impeachment for political views had been discredited in the Chase and Johnson decisions, and the real problem was the Court majority, not just Warren. Bozell recommended congressional action to limit the Court's jurisdiction as well as censure of the offending justices. The article offered plenty of criticism of the judiciary for conservatives unhappy with the Warren Court, but at the same time it found Welch's reasoning flawed and further undermined the society's impeachment campaign.[94]

The movement to nominate Barry Goldwater as the 1964 Republican candidate for president confronted an ongoing and not entirely inaccurate impression that the candidate was linked to Robert Welch. After excoriating Eisenhower and Nixon at the founding meeting of the John Birch Society, Welch had declared, "I know Barry fairly well" and acknowledged contributing to his recent Senate reelection campaign. Welch considered Goldwater "a great American." Welch went on to say, "I'd love to see him President of the United States, and maybe some day we shall.[95]

Goldwater for his part declined to criticize Welch publicly when the JBS began receiving media attention in early 1961. Privately, he seemed concerned but cautious as he suggested to Buckley that they "allow it to go along for awhile before we take any other steps."[96] Eight months later Goldwater was willing to tell NBC's *Meet the Press* that he was more concerned with extremism on the left than on the right. Trying to separate himself from the John Birch Society but perhaps achieving the opposite effect, the senator said, "I speak—as I have said many, many times—only for one organization of the Birch Society, and that is the group I happen to know in my home town of Phoenix, Arizona."[97] Under national media scrutiny, Goldwater left the impression that he sympathized with the JBS, if he did not actually participate in it.

In January 1962 Buckley spent two days in Palm Beach, Florida, with Goldwater, encouraging him to run for president. The editor tried to convince the Arizona senator that Welch was a menace to the conservative cause.[98] Goldwater held to his long-established belief that, while Welch might personally be a liability, JBS members should be welcomed as part of the conservative cause. He devoutly wished to avoid open confrontation.[99] Buckley nevertheless soon went well beyond his mild April 1961 disparagement in his next condemnation of Welch. The continued high visibility of the JBS was, he felt, casting a shadow over other conservatives and enveloping them in its extremist image. Therefore, in February 1962 Buckley devoted more than five pages of the *National Review* to denouncing Welch and calling "for rejecting, out of a love of truth and country, his false counsels."[100]

Buckley's February 1962 editorial pointed out that Welch himself estimated that the JBS needed a million members to achieve effective political leverage. However, "even after great national publicity, and largely because of Mr. Welch's 'intemperance of utterance' [it has enlisted] less than one-tenth that many members, and is growing no faster than the movement to impeach Earl Warren, who remains as unimpeached today as when Mr. Welch first launched that ill-conceived campaign. Mr. Welch, for all his good intentions, threatens to divert militant conservative action to irrelevance and ineffectuality."[101] The Buckley condemnation of the JBS founder's wild reasoning and conspiracy theories was immediately noticed and reported to a much wider audience by *Time* magazine, which, in its characteristic flippant style, referred to Welch as a "retired Taffy-Puller."[102]

Responding in a letter published in *National Review*, Goldwater echoed Buckley's criticism of Welch and called for the JBS leader to resign.[103] He declined, however, to disassociate himself further from the John Birch Society. This stance contrasted with the general condemnation of the JBS issued by Nixon in the 1962 California gubernatorial primary in which he faced JBS member Joe Shell. Nixon won the primary but lost the subsequent general election, convincing Goldwater of the dangers of alienating the society.[104] Stressing the ongoing bond between Goldwater and the JBS, syndicated columnist Drew Pearson entitled a November 1963 column "Goldwater and His Birch Friends." Pearson called attention to Welch's contribution to Goldwater's 1958 campaign and further connected the two by pointing out that in a 1959 speech in Jackson, Mississippi, Goldwater had called Earl Warren "a socialist unqualified to head the Supreme Court."[105] The distinction that Goldwater and Buckley had attempted to draw between Welch and the JBS membership failed to impress Pearson.

California, the state where the JBS was strongest, became the pivotal battleground in the contest for the 1964 Republican presidential nomination. Withstanding a barrage of criticism from his liberal Republican rival, Governor Nelson Rockefeller of New York, for his refusal to disavow the JBS, Goldwater won a narrow victory, drawing heavy support from the southern part of the state where Birchers were concentrated and active.[106] Goldwater's electoral success no doubt reinforced his view that the JBS was a necessary part of his conservative coalition. Accepting the Republican nomination in San Francisco a month later, the Arizona senator, in what would become the most memorable single sentence of his entire presidential campaign, declared, "I would remind you that extremism in the defense of liberty is no vice!" That statement cemented in the public mind Goldwater's bond with the Birchers and their agenda.

The landslide Democratic victory in the 1964 election reflected, in part, the party's increasing popularity under the leadership of John Kennedy and Lyndon Johnson, but it also indicated the alarm with which much of the electorate viewed Goldwater. The Republican candidate's links to the John Birch Society proved a serious liability, especially as he sought to win over voters beyond his conservative base. As a result, Welch, the JBS, and the most visible aspects of their peculiar agenda soon became anathema to many dispirited conservatives as they surveyed the 1964 election results.

In October 1965 Buckley published a special feature section of *National Review* entitled "The John Birch Society and the Conservative Movement." Setting forth a litany of Welch's extreme statements since *The Politician,* Buckley himself expressed dismay that JBS members continued to defend Welch. He concluded that unless the membership disavowed Welch, they had to be regarded as sanctioning his views. Buckley reached three judgments:

The first is that Mr. Welch's views have not changed, on the contrary they have become more virulent. The second is that there is no effective movement from within the Society to contain Mr. Welch's utterances, or to remove him as the Society's leader. The third is that Mr. Welch succeeded in influencing his membership to believe those surrealisms which he first ventilated in *The Politician;* and that as the membership comes to believe the Welch analysis, it ceases to be effectively anti-Communist.[107]

After two other *National Review* editors joined in decrying Welch's conspiracy theories, Buckley concluded, "The John Birch Society, as headed by Mr. Robert Welch, is a grave liability to the conservative and anti-Communist cause."[108]

Although it was now too late to do him any political good, Goldwater joined in the *National Review*'s condemnation of the JBS in a statement published as part of the special-feature section. Welch, he wrote, had exacerbated the organization's problems "as a leader whose statements have generally been wrong, ill-advised and, at times, ill-tempered."[109] This disparagement of the JBS leader by the unquestioned leader of the 1960s conservative movement diminished the society's stature, though it did not complete its destruction altogether.

For a time, the zealous Welch stubbornly continued his single-minded pursuit of Warren. In late 1965 he announced that the John Birch Society would distribute a set of materials, including Gordon's book *Nine Men against America* and speeches by Senator James Eastland of Mississippi, JBS leader and former Internal Revenue Service (IRS) commissioner T. Coleman Andres, and Welch himself. Welch made available this "Warren Impeachment Packet" for one dollar.[110] More than a year later, he asserted that up to that point the Warren impeachment campaign had been a relatively low-key "educational" effort compared to what he was now contemplating, which would use eighty paid field coordinators. Given conservative gains in the 1966 congressional elections, he estimated the odds of success by 1968 "are perhaps 2-to-1 or maybe 3-to-1 against us, but that's not impossible odds."[111] Nine months later, however, Welch acknowledged that an impeachment petition effort had gained little citizen support, and thus the campaign against Warren was being abandoned.[112]

As the moribund impeachment campaign folded, the John Birch Society itself began its own slower decline. Welch grumbled that Buckley had been "a false leader of conservatism, driven by vanity, ambition, and greed to seek a place in the Establishment which he professes to oppose," but to no avail.[113] Welch had been marginalized even as conservatism flourished after 1968. In retrospect, the effort spearheaded by Buckley and eventually joined by Goldwater to exile Welch to the outer darkness of the conservative movement proved a deathblow to the Warren impeachment effort. As Welch was increasingly portrayed as a luminary of the lunatic fringe, the impeachment campaign he waged and indeed the use of impeachment itself was treated as lunacy as well.

Earl Warren provided few signs that he was affected by the impeachment campaign against him. For the most part, he responded with dry humor. When a California legislator wrote to him about the "Impeach Earl Warren" billboards he was seeing, the Chief Justice replied,

> To see my name again on billboards almost makes me feel that I am back in politics. However, I have not concerned myself about them because, as you know, we have always had the equivalent of the John Birch Society in California, and I became accustomed to their activities through the years. If they were not venting their spleen in this manner, they would be doing it in some other way. Consequently, everyone who has a difficult position in the public service must condition himself to the theory of Mark Twain that a few fleas are good for any dog.[114]

Otherwise, the chief justice simply thanked bar associations and newspaper editorialists who condemned the JBS while expressing support for him. He declined further comment on the society itself.[115]

Warren did keep a reminder of the campaign to unseat him in his chambers at the Supreme Court. Right above his formal commission as chief justice, he hung a framed copy of a *New Yorker* cartoon published in 1964. Modeled after the classic painting known as *Whistler's Mother,* the cartoon depicted an elderly woman in a rocking chair finishing a piece of embroidery with the message "Impeach Earl Warren." A biographer concluded that Warren found the cartoon amusing, but a good case could be made that the sober and earnest justice saw it as a reminder of his responsibilities.[116]

The clearest indication of the negligible effect of the John Birch Society impeachment campaign on Warren himself can be found in his judicial rulings once the campaign began. The justice, whose reputation was anchored in his progressive constitutional interpretations of civil rights and civil liberties during the 1950s, steadfastly defended and steadily extended the reach of that jurisprudence in the 1960s as he came under attack. In a host of cases Warren continued the *Brown* initiative to secure the rights of minorities to equal protection of the laws. He helped extend the rights of the accused to fair judicial treatment, from the alleged communists of the Red Monday verdicts to individuals charged with

Lee Lorenz, *The New Yorker*, September 5, 1964. © *The* New Yorker Collection from cartoonbank.com. All rights reserved.

criminal conduct on the basis of unwarranted search, inadequate legal representation, or improper police interrogation. Warren moved further in the direction of what he regarded as equal protection of the law by championing the reform of legislative redistricting to assure "one man, one vote." He embraced, with some discomfort, equal protection of religious belief and nonbelief in cases banning school prayer and Bible reading. He endorsed the idea that individuals retained a zone of personal privacy, including but not limited to matters of sexual conduct. In none of these decisions, or in any others during Warren's remaining tenure on the high court, was there any appearance of trimming back the thrust of his jurisprudence.

While the John Birch Society impeachment crusade did not alter the course of Supreme Court rulings in the 1960s, it did have an impact. Billboards, broadsides, petitions, letters, and speeches calling for Warren's impeachment brought back into public consciousness the existence of a constitutional device for removing unsatisfactory federal officials. An almost forgotten constitutional term was once again being publicly discussed. Reintroduced into the political vocabulary, it would inevitably be linked with names other than that of the invulnerable chief justice.

Other members of the Supreme Court felt the reverberations of the campaign against Warren. At a November 1973 luncheon honoring his eclipsing the record of Stephen Field as the longest-serving member of the Court, Justice William O. Douglas offered a poignant reminiscence of visiting Texas while doing research on a book. "I saw those great billboards screeching 'Impeach Earl Warren.' They made me sad and I wished they were down," Douglas said. He then ruefully added, "When Chief Justice Warren retired, they came down—and I at once regretted it. For other names took his place and the crunch was on."[117]

At the same time that it began to kindle discomfort among Supreme Court justices, the nature of Welch's campaign fostered a public image of impeachment as little more than a strange and ineffective form of political attack, a constitutional process decidedly eccentric, extreme, and impossible to achieve. More than once the chief justice's critics indicated their lack of faith in the constitutional process of removal by growling, "Earl Warren shouldn't be impeached, he should be hanged."[118] Bringing the word back into public discourse was a modest achievement. Rehabilitating impeachment as a functional constitutional device would require circumstances and advocacy quite different from those that characterized the John Birch Society crusade against Chief Justice Warren.

3

Impeachment as Political:

The Case of Abe Fortas

Ironically, having easily avoided his own impeachment, Earl Warren set off far more serious and substantial efforts at impeachment by deciding to retire after fifteen years in the center seat of the nation's highest court. By the late 1960s the political culture was changing rapidly from what had existed earlier in Warren's tenure. A more aggressive and combative partisanship was beginning to emerge from the turmoil stirred by changing race relations, shifting economic opportunities, altered social patterns, and divisions over the Vietnam War. Accumulated grievances against decisions of the Warren Court manifested themselves in new efforts to discredit and remove some of the Court's members. Warren had proved himself to be invulnerable, but the same could not be said of all his colleagues in the majority that had dominated the Court throughout his term.

The 1950s Supreme Court had angered anti-integrationist social conservatives with *Brown v. Board of Education* and had incensed anticommunist zealots with the Red Monday decisions. The bitter protests of the John Birch Society and its allies merely foreshadowed the more wide-ranging hostile reactions to the rulings of the Court thereafter. As steadfastly liberal Justices William Brennan, Arthur Goldberg, Abe Fortas, and Thurgood Marshall joined the Court, Warren and his senior allies Hugo Black and William O. Douglas were able to maintain steady control of the Court's direction. By the late 1960s, however, criticism of the Court had gained a foothold closer to the political mainstream. Richard Nixon made complaints about the Warren Court one of the centerpieces of his second campaign for the presidency. Subsumed under Nixon's superficially benign call for "law and order" was his rejection of the Court's foundational position on the extent of constitutional protections for civil rights and civil liberties.[1]

Ever since Earl Warren's first months as chief justice, decisions had poured forth from a Court that reflected what most legal historians and social progressives saw as the Fourteenth Amendment's original intent: the provisions of the Bill of Rights as well as the amendment's explicit requirements of equal protection and due process of law should apply to the states just as they did to the federal government. Conservatives had been relatively comfortable with the far more limited view of the Fourteenth Amendment that had generally prevailed since Reconstruction. They became increasingly upset each time the Court extended its understanding of the Constitution's requirements to a new area of jurisprudence.

Warren Court rulings repeatedly enraged many conservatives. For instance, affirmations of federal power to enforce desegregation made states' rights defenders, not to mention white supremacists, furious.[2] So too did decisions reforming criminal justice procedures. Restrictions on police searches and interrogations as well as requirements that legal counsel be provided to criminal suspects and defendants might well have been seen as valuable protections for innocents confronting improper or false accusations but instead were often characterized as changes aimed at coddling criminals.[3] Prohibitions on prayer and Bible reading in public schools along with relaxation of restraints on pornography might have been regarded as guarantees of individual liberty but instead were seen as attacks on bedrock values.[4] The Court's insistence on "one man, one vote" in state as well as federal legislative apportionment could have been viewed as a step forward for fair representative government but instead met resistance because it ended disproportionate political power for rural conservatives.[5] Finally, finding a zone of personal privacy regarding sexual matters into which government had no right to intrude might well have been seen as a commendable restraint on government authority but instead was held to undermine the maintenance of a proper social code.[6] Each time the Warren Court upset some conventional practice, however unfair that custom may have been, it alarmed those content with the status quo.

Most critics of the Warren Court's jurisprudence understood that the Constitution's impeachment provision was not intended as a device for overturning judicial rulings. The framers had quite explicitly provided a means for reversing the Court through amendment of the Constitution. Amendments had toppled Court decisions supporting slavery, disallowing a federal income tax, and preventing woman suffrage. However, to the frustration of conservatives, efforts to reverse the Warren Court's decisions on school prayer and legislative apportionment by constitutional amendment had failed to achieve congressional approval or state ratification.[7]

The Constitution also provided another means of reining in the Court, though one that was far more problematic. Congress could restrict the judiciary's jurisdiction and thus prevent federal courts from ruling on certain types of cases. To do so, however, would eliminate the judiciary as an assured means of resolving disputes in an orderly and equitable fashion. Applied prospectively, it was a very blunt instrument, and yet after a ruling had been made it would not undo the decision already rendered. Congressional restriction of judicial jurisdiction was decidedly fraught with peril for the rule of law. Responsible legislators did not find it an attractive means of dealing with the judiciary, even if they were unhappy with some court rulings.

In theory at least, impeachment offered another, if far less direct, means of disciplining judges whose rulings gave offense. Article IV of the Constitution specified that judges' lifetime appointments continued during "good behavior." Some antifederalists during the initial ratification debates as well as later legal scholars raised the question of whether this language provided a looser standard for judicial impeachment and removal than the other constitutionally specified offenses of "treason, bribery, and other high crimes and misdemeanors."[8] While "good behavior" clearly could not be construed as meaning always making popular judicial rulings, it did provide an opening for critics to engage in close scrutiny of a judge's conduct off the bench as well as in the courtroom.

The timing and manner of the chief justice's departure from the Court provoked an intensely partisan political response. What began as a simple confirmation battle over the person nominated by President Lyndon Johnson to succeed Warren, Associate Justice Abe Fortas, gradually turned into a serious consideration of Fortas's impeachment for violation of the "good behavior" standard as details of his off-the-bench conduct came to light. Shortly after the Fortas case was resolved, the tide of unhappiness with the Warren Court's legacy generated an even more clearly partisan call for the impeachment of another sitting justice on charges of violating "good behavior." This time the target was Associate Justice William O. Douglas, a three-decade veteran of the high court. Notably, the call for impeachment in these two instances originated not in fringe political groups such as the John Birch Society but in the mainstream of the Republican Party.

The efforts to remove two of Warren's closest colleagues, Fortas and Douglas, proceeded well beyond the comparatively feeble earlier attempt to displace Warren himself. Members of Congress engaged in serious investigations of both cases, and in the Douglas case the Judiciary Committee of the House of Representatives held a formal preliminary impeachment hearing. Furthermore, these impeachment efforts precipitated Fortas's departure from office, albeit by resignation rather than removal. The Fortas and Douglas episodes deserve closer attention than they have received. As a result of the two cases, the political culture and to a lesser degree the society as a whole began to grow more familiar with the vocabulary and process of impeachment, not to mention its possible consequences. Less than a decade after the start of the John Birch Society's seemingly eccentric public campaign against Chief Justice Warren, the age of impeachment began to take on a more substantial shape.

In the spring of 1968, Chief Justice Warren decided that it was time for him to retire from the Supreme Court.[9] Although still intellectually and physically vigorous, he had more than one reason for deciding to leave the bench. First and foremost, he had passed his seventy-seventh birthday and was more than a dozen years beyond the age at which most Americans then chose or were compelled to retire. With the notable exceptions of eighty-two-year-old Hugo Black, who would serve until a week before his death three years later, and Felix Frankfurter, who had retired in ill health at age seventy-nine in 1962, all justices who sat on the Court with Warren had either left at an earlier age or, if still serving, was anywhere from seven to twenty-six years younger than their chief. In the long-gone era before judicial pensions were first provided in the late 1930s, as well as after Warren's time when close ideological divisions on the Court encouraged retention of a seat for as long as possible, justices remained on the Court to a very advanced age. In Warren's era, however, retirement from the bench in one's sixties or seventies was typical. Justices did not regard the constitutional provision of a lifetime appointment as the equivalent of a life sentence without parole. At seventy-seven, Warren had stayed on the high bench to a greater age than most.

Warren's 1968 decision to retire understandably also reflected the natural and not uncommon preference of federal judges to be succeeded by someone who would continue to move the Court in the direction he had helped set rather than try to reverse course. Continuity would be much more likely if a judge's replacement was chosen by a president whose views corresponded to the judge's own rather than by a president who was unsympathetic. With the notable exception of the Republican-appointed justices who clung to office during the first five years of Franklin Roosevelt's New Deal, members of the Supreme Court had seldom confronted circumstances where the alternatives appeared as clear-cut and pressing as they did for Warren in the spring of 1968.

Of all the presidents during Warren's tenure as chief justice, Johnson was clearly the one most in tune with the Court's and Warren's own evolving jurisprudence. Although their party affiliations were different, Warren and Johnson shared a vision of social justice, a view of government responsibility for its achievement, and a well-honed political sensibility. Eisenhower had lacked the enthusiasm and Kennedy the political capacity to implement significant enforcement of the racial equality rulings of the Court. Johnson, on the other hand, displayed extraordinary determination and achieved remarkable success in fighting for the adoption of the Civil Rights Act of 1964 and the Voting Rights Act of 1965. Both hard-won measures provided formidable legislative endorsement and effective enforcement of the equal protection principles articulated by the Court beginning with *Brown v. Board of Education.* In a host of other measures as well, not to mention his appointment to the Court of Abe Fortas and Thurgood Marshall, Johnson consistently supported the socially progressive values embraced by Warren and his brethren.[10]

By 1968, however, Johnson had fallen deep into disfavor with much of the American public. Tensions between those who felt that too much had been done to alter race relations in the United States and those who believed that not nearly enough had been accomplished had erupted with increasing frequency into outbursts of urban violence. At the same time, military intervention in Vietnam, tolerated by Americans only as long as its reality and costs were out of sight, was becoming more and more visible and unpopular. In February 1968 a large-scale and unexpected communist offensive erupted at the time of the normally tranquil Vietnamese New Year holiday of Tet. The "Tet offensive" followed months of White House and military assurances to the American people that the war was being won and that there was "light at the end of the tunnel." Unhappiness with Johnson's Vietnam policy, already substantial, quickly escalated after the Tet offensive made it appear that the light in the tunnel was the headlight of an oncoming freight train.

Only three and a half years earlier Johnson had carried more than 61 percent of the national vote when he ran for election against Republican Barry Goldwater. Based on the impressive accomplishment of his first year in office following the death of John Kennedy as well as his electoral triumph, Johnson was being touted at the time of his 1965 inauguration as the most skilled and effective politician of his age. By 1968, however, Johnson faced open opposition within his own Democratic Party as well as from the rival Republicans. Eugene McCarthy, a U.S. senator hitherto little known outside Minnesota, challenged Johnson in the New Hampshire presidential primary, the year's first, and nearly won on a simple platform of opposition to the war. Within a week, a seemingly more substantial opponent with both social reform and antiwar agendas, New York senator Robert Kennedy, declared that he, too, would be a candidate for the Democratic nomination. On the last day of March, Johnson, saying that he wanted to devote himself fully to ending the war in Vietnam, announced that he would neither seek nor accept nomination for another term as president.

Despite these dramatic turns of political fortune in the first months of 1968, the sense of a country falling apart did not end. Less than two weeks after Johnson's withdrawal from the presidential contest, the nation's most prominent civil rights advocate, Martin Luther King, Jr., was assassinated. An unprecedentedly large-scale outburst of rioting and destruction by embittered urban blacks followed immediately in cities across the country. Only a few weeks after a rough and uncertain truce had been achieved, Robert Kennedy, the presidential candidate widely perceived to be best able to bridge the growing racial chasm as well as bring the Vietnam War to an end, was also assassinated. Kennedy, whose brother John had been killed less than five years before, died in Los Angeles on the night he had won the California Democratic presidential primary and become the favorite to win his party's presidential nomination. The chief justice had told his clerks only days before that he expected Kennedy would be elected president.[11]

The elimination of Robert Kennedy from the contest for the presidency, together with the lackluster images of the leading Democratic alternatives, McCarthy and Vice President Hubert Humphrey, immediately boosted the prospects of Warren's long-time California Republican Party rival, Richard Nixon. Warren, a notably progressive California Republican from the northern part of the state, had repeatedly succeeded in bridging partisan divides, whereas Nixon, an intensely anticommunist conservative from Southern California, had, by contrast, emphasized partisan differences. The clash between the two men had reached a peak in 1952 when, as governor, Warren hoped to emerge as a compromise Republican presidential candidate if the two leading contenders, Robert Taft and Dwight Eisenhower, deadlocked. Nixon, though pledged as a California delegate to support Warren on the first convention ballot, surreptitiously undermined Warren's favorite-son control of the large California delegation, winning support for Eisenhower in a crucial struggle over contested delegate seating that ultimately gave Eisenhower victory over Taft. Warren suffered an embarrassing defeat, while Nixon was rewarded with the vice presidential nomination. The two men's mutual distaste for each other continued unabated.[12]

In 1968, when he began to mount his second attempt in eight years to win the presidency, Nixon made criticism of the Supreme Court's recent direction a major theme of his campaign. Should Nixon enter the White House in January 1969, Court appointments for at least the next four years, and most likely the next eight, would almost certainly not be to Warren's liking. Nixon unknowingly nudged Warren toward his retirement decision. His later steps to end the era of the Warren Court would be much more deliberate, though just as much out of the public spotlight.

The repeated blows during the spring of 1968 to the nation's sense of well-being, social progress, and political stability were still reverberating when Warren met with Johnson on June 13 and then sent him a one-sentence letter saying, "Pursuant to the provisions of U.S.C. Section 371 (b), I hereby advise you of my intention to retire as Chief Justice of the United States, effective at your pleasure." Johnson acknowledged Warren's request thirteen days later: "With your agreement, I will accept your decision to retire effective at such time as a successor is qualified." The somewhat unusual language of this exchange indicated the agreement of both men that Warren would continue to serve as chief justice until the Senate had confirmed his successor. Most past justices had either died in office or indicated a specific date for their retirement. Warren had said more than once that he thought it unwise for the country to be without a chief justice to handle the ongoing administrative duties of the Court even when it was in recess. He also clearly wished to spare his aged and ailing colleague Hugo Black, the senior associate justice, from the possibility of having to step in as acting chief justice. Yet such was the popular view of Lyndon Johnson by June 1968 that suspicion quickly spread that the president was improperly maneuvering either to secure a supportive chief justice or, failing that, to allow his friend Warren to keep the seat.[13]

A rumor that Warren intended to retire so that Johnson rather than Nixon would be able to name his replacement first appeared in print as a two-paragraph item buried in the middle of the *Wall Street Journal*'s weekly political gossip column on June 14.[14] Reading it on a flight from Detroit to Washington, Michigan's junior senator, Republican Robert P. Griffin, immediately decided that a president who had already announced that he was leaving the White House should not be allowed to appoint a Supreme Court justice. Griffin, himself a lawyer, certainly knew that a president's constitutional power of appointment, along with his other constitutional authorities and responsibilities, continued unrestricted until his term ended. At the same time, as a shrewd and ambitious politician, he understood that a president's effective power diminished as his term drew to a close. Griffin could see the opportunity and advantage of keeping the chief justiceship from being filled before his own party had a chance to capture the presidency and place one of its own in the seat.

On June 21, before either Warren or Johnson had spoken publicly about the resignation, Griffin told the Senate of "an unconfirmed report" that Warren was leaving the Court "so that President Johnson could designate the next Chief Justice." Griffin scorned the possibility, ignoring the Constitution's provision of unlimited terms for judges and thus their freedom to resign whenever and for whatever reason they chose, not to mention a president's constitutional duty to nominate a replacement whenever a vacancy occurred. With considerable indignation Griffin said, "I want to indicate emphatically, as one U.S. Senator, that I shall not vote to confirm an appointment of the next Chief Justice by a 'lame duck' President." Such an appointment, Griffin asserted, "would be breaking faith with our system" and "an affront to the American people."[15] Republican senators John Tower of Texas, Strom Thurmond of South Carolina, and Hiram Fong of Hawaii rushed to concur. Aided by another Republican colleague, George Murphy of California, Griffin began the same day to circulate a petition to enlist more support.[16]

Griffin's declaration of absolute opposition to a lame-duck nomination came before Johnson had uttered a word on the subject, much less before the identity of a nominee to replace Warren on the Court could be known. Griffin was taking an obviously partisan position, trying to thwart a retiring president of the opposing party from making an appointment so that the most important position on the high court could be filled by a chief executive who, chances seemed good, might come from his own party. The lame-duck argument possessed political appeal because of Johnson's unpopularity. However, it appeared weak on its merits, both constitutionally and historically. John Marshall, generally acknowledged as the greatest chief justice of all, had been appointed by President John Adams and confirmed by the Senate following the Federalists' crushing 1800 election defeat, and not merely in anticipation that a shift in political power might occur. While Griffin's protest might have been predicted to gain some support, at the time there was absolutely no way of anticipating that in the hands of this resolute partisan it might lead to an impeachment.

Undeterred by the statement, no matter how dogmatic, of a minority party senator less than two years in office, Johnson at a press conference five days later announced that Warren had resigned, effective upon his successor's confirmation. The president then revealed that he intended to elevate Fortas to chief justice and nominate Homer Thornberry, a federal appellate court judge from Texas, to fill Fortas's position. Fortas, well known as a prominent New Deal liberal, thereafter a high-profile Washington lawyer, and eventually one of Johnson's closest advisers, had been confirmed as an associate justice by a unanimous Judiciary Committee and an uncontested voice vote of the full Senate only three years earlier. The only question at the moment appeared to be whether Griffin's lame-duck objection would gain currency.[17]

Griffin had been elected to his first term in the Senate in 1966 after spending a decade in the House of Representatives. In the House he had cast himself as a moderate Republican and proved both an effective legislator and a shrewd, aggressive politician. Early in his House career he had helped craft and pass the Landrum-Griffin Act, legislation placing new regulations on labor union leaders at a time when more strident antiunion legislators were thwarted. In 1965 he had helped engineer a coup by younger Republican members to oust minority leader Charles Halleck and replace him with Gerald R. Ford, who represented a Michigan congressional district adjoining Griffin's own. Griffin's reward was appointment to the Senate by Michigan's Republican governor, George Romney, to fill the last few months of the unexpired term of deceased Democrat Patrick McNamara. He then won election in his own right in November 1966. Griffin came to the Senate well schooled in how to achieve his objectives. He had succeeded as a member of a congressional minority and had evident ambition to do so again. The Warren resignation provided him with his first major opportunity.

Two days before Johnson nominated Fortas and Thornberry, Griffin told the Michigan Press Association, "The people are in the process of choosing a new government. For a 'lame duck' President to make such an appointment in the waning months of his term—before the American people have an opportunity to speak in November—would break faith with our system."[18] Amplifying this view the day after the nominations were made, the senator issued a press release saying that "maneuvering to deny the people and the next President their choice in this instance is wrong in principle." Griffin declared that Johnson's choice of two close and longtime friends smacked of "cronyism at its worst."[19] He announced that he was prepared to "talk at length" on the Senate floor against the nominations. By the following day, Griffin's petition had nineteen Republican signatures, giving credibility to his threat of a filibuster.[20]

Senate Republican minority leader Everett Dirksen gave Griffin no encouragement. Dirksen, who had already reached a bargain with Johnson to support the nomination, bluntly told a meeting of Republican senators, "There's nothing about lame ducks in the Constitution."[21] On July 1 he said flatly that he would vote to confirm both nominees and to break any filibuster that developed. At a press conference the next day he predicted confirmation and announced that at least two of the senators who had signed Griffin's petition had experienced a change of heart. Griffin responded that the White House was going all out to win the confirmation battle, clearly implying that the well-known close relationship between Dirksen and the president was being inappropriately brought into play.[22]

As the two Republican senators sparred, each was trying to enlist support. Dirksen got an inkling of the challenge facing him when his own son-in-law, Senator Howard Baker, Jr., of Tennessee, said over dinner that he agreed with Griffin on lame-duck presidential appointments.[23] Half the Republican caucus, mainly its younger members, chose to follow Griffin. Georgia senator Richard Russell, the leader of the conservative southern bloc within the Democratic caucus, privately told the Michigan Republican that he and his southern Democratic allies did not wish to take a public position but would support Griffin in a showdown. Griffin instantly knew that he had a good chance to prevail.[24]

When the Judiciary Committee opened confirmation hearings, the gulf between Dirksen and Griffin became even more apparent. Testifying on the second day of the hearing, Griffin reiterated his argument against lame-duck nominations and spoke disparagingly about Fortas's close relationship with Johnson both before and after going on the Court. Dirksen, a member of the committee, declared that Johnson held constitutional power until the following January and should not be referred to as a lame duck. Furthermore, he said, many presidents, including Lincoln, had placed close associates or "cronies" on the Supreme Court. The minority leader sarcastically dismissed Griffin's arguments as "frivolous, diaphanous and gossamer." A veteran observer commented that Dirksen treated Griffin as roughly verbally as he ever did a Democratic opponent.[25] At that point, if not before, the personal stakes became evident in Griffin's threat to Fortas's confirmation.

Finding himself in a precarious political position with the leader of his own party as well as the majority of Democrats, Griffin set out to demonstrate the validity of his position and slow the confirmation process by raising additional, more substantive objections to Fortas. All would take time to be discussed even if they were ultimately dispelled. He focused attention on Fortas's role as a close adviser to Johnson after as well as before he went on the Court, making effective use of a lengthy article by Fred Graham, "The Many-Sided Justice Fortas," in the *New York Times Sunday Magazine* of June 4, 1967. Ignoring many precedents, such as John Jay counseling George Washington, Roger Taney advising Andrew Jackson, Louis Brandeis consulting with Woodrow Wilson, William Howard Taft advising Warren Harding, and Felix Frankfurter providing frequent counsel to Franklin Roosevelt, Griffin declared that advice by a justice to a president violated the requirements of the separation of powers. Meanwhile he continued to speak out against a lame-duck appointment. Any argument that might extend the examination of the nomination appeared welcome.

Griffin's allies on the Judiciary Committee found ways to extend the scheduled three days of confirmation hearings to an unprecedented nine days.[26] Senator Thurmond in particular stretched out the hearings by giving time and attention to testimony from groups concerned about recent Court rulings on pornography. They criticized Fortas not as an isolated individual but as a member of a majority bloc of justices that repeatedly overturned obscenity convictions.[27] With the national political conventions compelling a long August recess and the demands of a national election providing limited time for congressional deliberation before adjournment, the possibility of blocking Senate action grew brighter each day senators continued to talk. The rules of the Senate give individual members a variety of means to slow the consideration of any matter and, if they can enlist enough allies, to thwart majority action. With nearly twenty Republicans rallying to his cause and an equivalent cadre of conservative southern Democrats opposing Fortas for their own reasons, Griffin had put together enough support to place the nomination in jeopardy.

The controversies stirred by Griffin led Fortas to appear before the Senate Judiciary Committee, the first nominee for chief justice ever to do so. In his testimony Fortas acknowledged that he had conferred with Johnson about Vietnam and urban rioting, but he insisted they never discussed anything that might come before the Court. Four days of questioning by committee members exposed the hostility to Fortas of the committee's three southern Democrats, chairman James Eastland of Mississippi, Sam Ervin of North Carolina, and John McClellan of Arkansas, and also confirmed the similar attitude of Democrat-turned-Republican Thurmond. Senator Thurmond, fuming about rising crime rates that he attributed to recent Court decisions, lectured Fortas at length about a ruling disallowing the conviction of an accused rapist because of irregularities in his arraignment. Fortas did not respond to Thurmond's "Mallory! Mallory! I want that word to ring in your ears" harangue against the Warren Court, perhaps because the case had been decided eight years before he joined the Court.[28] Nevertheless, Griffin had by this time gained enough powerful allies to stretch out a planned three-day committee hearing and keep the nomination from reaching the Senate floor until after the national political conventions.

Griffin continued his high-visibility, high-risk opposition to the Fortas nomination when he spoke at the National Press Club on July 30. In his speech he suggested that there was no vacancy on the Court because Warren had not really resigned and because Johnson had not properly accepted a resignation. He poked fun at Dirksen's earlier characterization of Griffin's arguments as "frivolous, diaphanous and gossamer." The Michigan senator went on to accuse the president of manufacturing a vacancy and selecting Fortas and Thornberry "primarily because they are close personal friends of long standing." Griffin declared it unprecedented that a president would name two cronies at the same time and predicted that the opponents would prevail: "In this battle, we are right. Because we are right, time is on our side."[29]

During the August congressional recess, criticism of the Fortas nomination continued along the lines already laid down. Senator Ervin issued a lengthy statement criticizing Fortas and, by implication, the Warren Court for "an easy willingness to depart from the words and history of the Constitution, and, if necessary to reach a desired result, to cast into the judicial garbage can sound precedents of past courts." Ervin, for more than a dozen years one of the Senate's most steadfast defenders of the South's rapidly eroding segregationist arrangements, focused his wrath on Fortas's liberal votes on a series of Fourteenth Amendment equal protection cases. The North Carolinian also disparaged Fortas's position in *Miranda v. Arizona* and other defendants' rights rulings. To Ervin, the Warren Court had not been applying the Constitution to modern circumstances but, rather, had been departing from age-old precedents.[30]

On the day Fortas finished testifying before the judiciary committee, Griffin acquired a potent new weapon to use against the justice. Lawrence Meyer, a member of Griffin's staff, received a phone call from a man who insisted on anonymity and then claimed that he had learned from a friend that Fortas was teaching a seminar at the American University Law School. The financial arrangements, the friend reported, were highly questionable: Fortas was being paid $15,000 for a nine-week seminar, and the money was being raised by Fortas's former law partner, Paul Porter, from their firm's clients. Meyer immediately took the story to Griffin, who answered a question at his July 30 National Press Club speech by saying cryptically, "I can tell you that all the facts haven't been presented yet."[31] After Meyer tipped off *New York Times* reporter Fred Graham to look into the matter and engaged in further discussions with fellow staff members about how to make public what Griffin himself felt was thin evidence on the American University story, he shared his information with senators Ervin and Thurmond. Thurmond pressured B. J. Tennery, dean of the law school, to be the leadoff witness as the confirmation hearings resumed on September 13. The Tennery testimony revealed the story publicly and provided fresh ammunition for Fortas's determined opponents.[32]

Griffin and Thurmond had been planning to make Fortas's assistance to the president in the preparation of a State of the Union speech and the Court's recent pornography decisions the focus of attention in the September Judiciary Committee hearings.[33] They did not neglect those issues but shifted their attention as Dean Tennery's testimony on the American University seminar captured the attention of the press.[34] No evidence was provided that Fortas had acted illegally or unethically. No one charged that Fortas had failed to recuse himself when contributors to the seminar fund were involved in cases before the Court. Accepting paid speaking and teaching engagements, especially during the summer recess, while not widely known, was not uncommon among the justices. Indeed, Justice William Brennan was teaching a course at the New York University Law School the same summer without causing a stir. While Fortas's $15,000 honorarium was substantial, it was not unprecedented for universities to pay such amounts when enlisting a celebrity for their faculty. Three years earlier, in fact, the New York State Board of Regents had authorized ten professorships at $100,000 per year to recruit notable figures to enhance state university faculties.[35] It was quite common for universities to receive donations to endow professorships as well as to mount all manner of special programs. Yet Griffin thought it was unseemly for a Supreme Court justice to supplement his $39,500 salary in this manner. Political and editorial reaction would soon confirm his judgment.[36]

Senator Griffin quickly called for Fortas's nomination to be withdrawn. He labeled the revelation of the justice's large honorarium and the way it was arranged "the last straw." Since Fortas had declined to return to the Judiciary Committee to testify further regarding his nonjudicial activities, Griffin concluded that senatorial doubts about the propriety of Fortas's conduct should be resolved against him. "So long as we do not have all the facts," he declared, tipping his hand, "I see no reason why the Senate should be in any hurry to vote."[37]

Despite the efforts of Griffin, Thurmond, Eastland, Ervin, and McClellan, the Judiciary Committee voted 11–6 to recommend Fortas's confirmation to the Senate. Opponents of the nomination, however, were able to seize on the various issues that had appeared during the two-month delay their leaders had secured before bringing it to the floor of the Senate. Griffin's initial objection to lame-duck nominations, never very compelling except to determined Republican partisans, had given way to charges of improper conduct by Fortas in functioning as a presidential adviser, in joining a Warren Court majority in some controversial pornography decisions, and in accepting the American University honorarium. Reasonable explanations existed for each of these matters, but they either were not presented or were unavailing. By the time the Fortas nomination got to the floor, it no longer enjoyed enough support to thwart its foes.

The first clear signal that Griffin had prevailed came on September 27, the third day of Senate debate of the nomination, when Dirksen indicated that he had new questions concerning Fortas. The minority leader in an oblique disparaging reference to Griffin said, "The charge of cronyism seems to have vanished." He then scoffed at the American University seminar revelations as "at most an indiscretion." Then, however, Dirksen expressed concern about a recent Court ruling, *Witherspoon v. Illinois,* which overturned a death sentence for the murder of a Chicago policeman because potential jurors who opposed the death penalty had been removed from the jury. Until his concerns were addressed, Dirksen declared, he would favor continued Senate deliberation. By saying that he would oppose cutting off debate, the minority leader, without acknowledging for a moment his upstart junior colleague's victory, signaled that Griffin had won.[38]

Michigan's senior senator, Democrat Philip Hart, a member of the Judiciary Committee and a steadfast liberal so well liked by his colleagues of both parties that, after he retired in 1977, they accorded him the rare honor of naming a new

Senate office building for him, led the effort to defend Fortas. He reminded the Senate that there was nothing unprecedented or legally improper in Warren's resignation, Johnson's appointment, Fortas's extrajudicial conduct, or the justice's rulings. He particularly disparaged Senator Thurmond's characterization of Fortas as a purveyor of pornography. Hart pointed out that the cases Thurmond complained about had been decided on grounds of legal procedure, not content, and that in another case, *Ginsberg v. New York,* Fortas had ruled that the state's police power could, within limits, be used to protect parents and children from obscene material.[39] He could not, however, stem the erosion of support for the Fortas nomination.

On October 1, following final speeches by Hart and Griffin, the Senate voted on a cloture petition to cut off debate on the Fortas nomination. Griffin in his remarks noted that the Senate had only devoted four days to floor debate on the nomination, that at least fifteen of his colleagues still wished to speak, and that no delaying tactics had been employed.[40] He did not acknowledge what all understood: With the election fast approaching and senators eager to go home to campaign, the effort to extend discussion of the nomination after the already extraordinarily protracted committee hearings was, in fact if not in name, a filibuster. Although cloture received a bare 45–43 majority, it fell fourteen votes short of the two-thirds margin required to compel a vote on the nomination. Democratic defections and absences, together with solid Republican opposition, spelled doom for Johnson's choice for chief justice.

Perceiving that continuing the fight would be futile, Fortas asked Johnson to withdraw the nomination. In a letter to the president, he said, "Continued efforts to secure confirmation of that nomination, even if ultimately successful, would result in a continuation of the attacks upon the Court which have characterized the filibuster—attacks which have been sometimes extreme and entirely unrelated to responsible criticism."[41] Johnson complied, and Fortas, assuming that his troubles were behind him, returned to his seat as an associate justice when the Supreme Court began its new term days later on the first Monday in October. In the interim he told a friendly audience at the New York University Law School, "I shall persevere." The crowd showed its approval with a three-minute standing ovation.[42]

Abe Fortas had not escaped the junior senator from Michigan. Within two weeks of the cloture vote, Griffin had entered into discussions about writing a book on the Fortas case. He got detailed suggestions from a knowledgeable literary adviser on how to proceed in a fashion that would call attention to his own central role yet not appear immodest. The book would focus on the whole litany of questions raised about Fortas and the justice's failure to provide satisfactory explanations.[43] The senator had reason to want to bring his version of the story to the attention of the public, particularly his constituents, since he had grounds

"I Don't Get Involved In Senate Matters Like Supreme Court Appointments"

©1968 HERBLOCK

Herblock,
Washington Post,
October 3, 1968.
© The Herb Block
Foundation.

for concern that his conduct in blocking the Fortas nomination had damaged his reputation. Underscoring Fortas's flaws would demonstrate Griffin's rectitude.

Griffin, a Republican in a state with a traditionally Democratic majority, had from the outset been severely criticized by home-state newspapers for helping stymie the Fortas nomination. Even the dependably conservative *Grand Rapids Press* had called him ridiculous for putting forth the lame-duck and cronyism issues in the first place. The *Press* asserted, "Griffin does himself no credit by raising either objection." Observing that Griffin had not challenged Fortas's abilities, the *Press* editorial declared, "This is playing politics with the Supreme Court with a vengeance," and concluded, "To put the position of chief justice up for grabs in the coming presidential campaign, as Sen. Griffin and his cronies apparently want to do, would be degrading of the court and justice and as cynical a political maneuver as any within memory."[44]

Later the *Press* went further, criticizing Griffin for "disservice to his party's cause by throwing in his lot with the reactionary Southern wing of the Democratic party."[45] Michigan's largest newspaper, the *Detroit Free Press,* agreed. It blasted Griffin for joining senators Thurmond and Ervin, "some of the most bigoted and least responsible members of the Senate," to block the majority from acting. "We cannot afford to have a President cease to function six months before he leaves office," the editorial declared, and it scolded Griffin for proceeding even though he had made no case that Fortas was unfit.[46]

William T. Gossett, a Detroit attorney serving that year as president of the American Bar Association, soon added an important voice to the home-state criticism of Griffin. Interviewed by the *Free Press,* he not only endorsed Fortas but also called Griffin's efforts to filibuster the nomination "unworthy of a U.S. Senator."[47] Later, when Fortas asked Johnson to withdraw his nomination, the *Grand Rapids Press* concluded, "We have come to view the filibuster as the last refuge of little men who would thwart the will of the majority for their own selfish political ends and we find no reason to revise that opinion in the light of what has just happened."[48] Griffin had clearly dismayed influential voices in Michigan and now faced the challenge of rebuilding his own credibility with his constituents.

A book laying out a principled case against Fortas would serve Griffin at home plus earn the gratitude of all who had joined him in the confirmation battle. Of course even more helpful to those who had blocked Fortas from assuming the chief justiceship would be an opportunity to make a more conclusive demonstration that the justice was indeed unfit for his position. As he explored the possibility of writing a book, Griffin knew that uncorroborated charges against Fortas remained to be explored, charges that might prove more damaging than anything turned up in the confirmation fight. Indeed, new revelations eventually rendered Griffin's contemplated book unnecessary and ensured that it would never appear. More significant, the disclosures would lead Fortas from the disappointment of not being advanced to the center seat on the Court to the disaster of facing a serious threat of impeachment if he did not immediately resign.

Five weeks after the Fortas nomination was withdrawn, Richard Nixon was elected president and Griffin secured an appreciative ally. Nixon had at the outset subscribed to Griffin's lame-duck argument but then, so as not to appear politically manipulative and underhanded to his own advantage while still only a candidate, deliberately distanced himself from the unfolding Fortas controversy.[49] At the same time he gave confirmation opponents behind-the-scenes encouragement.[50] Furthermore, he continued to campaign in part on a pledge to change the Supreme Court in order to restore "law and order," a clever if obvious term for checking the demands of minority groups and the increased protections for accused criminals that had resulted from Warren Court rulings. Nixon understood that the way to obtain such a result was to change the membership of the Court as much and as quickly as possible.

The president-elect recognized that Johnson, now truly a lame duck, might still attempt to install a new chief justice, though one who was not identified as a close personal friend. Dirksen, still on good terms with Johnson, told some of his Republican minority colleagues that the president was thinking of nominating former Associate Justice Arthur Goldberg. Fortas's predecessor on the Court, Goldberg had reluctantly left the bench at Johnson's request to serve as ambassador to the United Nation. Early on even Griffin had acknowledged that the former justice could be easily confirmed. Dirksen hinted at a January attempt to win Senate confirmation before Johnson left office.[51]

Moving swiftly to squelch any possibility, however slim, of a last-minute appointment, Nixon shrewdly asked Earl Warren to stay on as chief justice through the spring, giving himself time to nominate and the Senate to confirm a new chief justice.[52] The Nixon-Warren agreement finally gave the lie to the always flimsy earlier complaints that Warren had phrased his retirement statement so that he could withdraw it unless a replacement to his liking was installed. In private, the chief justice had made clear that that had never been his intention.[53] With the Warren seat now his to fill, Nixon could direct his attention to the possibility of other Court replacements to advance his "law and order" agenda. Unlike other presidents, however, Nixon was not willing to wait patiently for the inevitable departure of elderly justices from the Court.

Fortas, whose vulnerabilities had been exposed during the battle over his nomination to the chief justiceship, remained a target of opportunity. Indeed, he would become increasingly so after the new Nixon administration took office on January 20, 1969. Within less than four months, the justice's questionable conduct, never demonstrated to be illegal but difficult to explain and easy to condemn, had become the basis of a highly publicized scandal. Members of the House of Representatives began discussing impeachment, and a few readied impeachment resolutions.

Fortas's new round of difficulties revolved around his relationship with Louis Wolfson, a financier and philanthropist. Wolfson, who had made millions in construction, shipbuilding, and diverse investments and was, like Fortas, the self-made son of Jewish immigrants who settled in the American South, became a client of Fortas's law firm in the mid-1960s. Shortly after going on the Supreme Court, Fortas agreed to serve as a consultant to the Wolfson Family Foundation, established to work on issues of civil rights, juvenile delinquency, and social welfare. Fortas agreed to advise the foundation on its charitable efforts in areas where he had considerable expertise for a fee of $20,000 per year for life and, indeed, even longer: His wife was to continue to receive the same annual sum should she outlive Fortas.

Within a few months Wolfson and a business associate were being investigated by the Securities and Exchange Commission (SEC) for failing to register a planned sale of his company's stock. Wolfson was eventually indicted, then convicted in 1967 and imprisoned after the Supreme Court declined to review his case. In June 1966, well before the Wolfson case was litigated, Justice Fortas concluded that it would be inappropriate for him to continue his involvement with the Wolfson Family Foundation. He terminated the arrangement and before the end of the year returned the $20,000 he had received. Neither during nor after his involvement with the foundation did any substantive evidence surface that Fortas ever engaged in legal work for Wolfson or interceded with the government on his behalf. Nor as a judge did he sit on any cases pertaining to Wolfson's affairs. The entire encounter, it would seem, had been inconsequential and forgotten.[54]

In September 1968, at the peak of Griffin's efforts to thwart the Fortas nomination to the chief justiceship, the senator's office received an anonymous tip about Fortas's involvement with Wolfson, by now convicted of securities-sales violations.[55] After an unsuccessful effort to stir an FBI investigation, Griffin made no public use of the Wolfson tip, despite its potential to help seal the still-contested case against confirming Fortas.[56] Within weeks after Fortas's withdrawal, however, the story had somehow reached William Lambert, a reporter for *Life* magazine who specialized in uncovering the financial irregularities of prominent individuals. Lambert, who had long cultivated sources in the IRS, the FBI, and the SEC, tried to find another source to confirm the information he had acquired on Fortas so that he could persuade *Life*'s editors to publish his story. The *Life* reporter made no progress at first and so laid the story aside until the following April.[57]

On April 10, 1969, Lambert met with Will Wilson, newly appointed assistant attorney general in charge of the Justice Department's criminal division. Lambert and Wilson exchanged information regarding Wolfson and Fortas. Wilson then launched a Justice Department investigation, and in little more than two weeks he confirmed Lambert's story of the $20,000 payment. The Justice Department had actually turned up very little substantive evidence, but its endorsement nevertheless gave Lambert license to go forward with a story that would destroy what remained of Fortas's reputation.[58]

According to John Dean, then an associate deputy attorney general, his superiors approached the Fortas case with some caution. They understood the dangers inherent in threatening the independence of the judiciary, not to mention alienating a sitting justice of the Supreme Court, and recognized the Justice Department's traditional hesitancy to do so.[59] Nevertheless, Nixon was giving continued thought to replacing justices. In an April 22 meeting with congressional leaders, the president listened to Dirksen say that if he really wanted some controversial labor legislation limiting common situs picketing, Nixon should also get a new Supreme Court. Nixon responded, "Give us time." He did not give any clues to how little time he was planning to take.[60]

Attorney General Mitchell asked Assistant Attorney General William Rehnquist, who headed the Justice Department Office of Legal Counsel, to determine what the Justice Department should do, assuming that the worst they had learned about Fortas was true. In a May 1 memo to Mitchell, Rehnquist cited precedent for indicting and prosecuting a sitting justice without his first being impeached. He then set forth a plan to prosecute Fortas for having intervened in the government case dealing with Wolfson's stock market activities. Without having any evidence to support such an allegation, Mitchell nevertheless threatened to launch it unless Fortas resigned from the Court. To increase pressure on Fortas, the Justice Department reopened an old case against his wife, Carolyn Agger, and his law partner, Paul Porter, that had been found wanting and dismissed during the Johnson administration.[61]

On May 5, 1969, *Life* published Lambert's article under the headline "Fortas of the Supreme Court: A Question of Ethics; The Justice and the Stock Manipulator." The piece began by acknowledging that the Supreme Court had rejected Wolfson's appeal of his conviction and that Fortas had recused himself from participating in the case of his former law firm's client. Not alleging any specific improper conduct by Fortas, Lambert described Fortas's receipt and later return of the $20,000 fee from the Wolfson Family Foundation as evidence of what he termed a "questionable association" between the justice and a man whose long business career Lambert characterized in sinister terms.[62]

At every turn, the reporter used language and innuendo to cast Fortas in a negative light. After noting that Fortas possessed a quite proper reason for recusing himself without explanation from the Wolfson case, Lambert implied impropriety nevertheless. He wrote, "Actually, quite apart from the actions of his former firm, Justice Fortas had reason to abstain from judging Louis Wolfson." Retreating into impersonal language to give his research and story added weight, Lambert then wrote, "In an investigation over a period of several months, LIFE found evidence of a personal association between the Justice and Wolfson that took place after Fortas was seated as a member of the nation's highest tribunal." He continued in the same vein, for instance, using a cynical modifier to cast doubt on what Fortas had acknowledged: "*Ostensibly*, Justice Fortas was being paid to advise the foundation on ways to use its funds for charitable educational and civil rights projects" (emphasis added).

Lambert then laid out a case that focused on Wolfson's long and frequently litigious business career. Fortas, meanwhile, was described in unflattering terms for his work for Johnson. His unsuccessful attempt in 1964 to help a White House staff member exposed as a homosexual was put in a most sinister light as an effort to suppress news coverage of an unspecified crime "when Johnson aide Walter Jenkins ran afoul of the law." Lambert downplayed the tactics of Fortas's Senate opponents and asserted that a substantive misdeed, Fortas's continuing White House involvement after joining the Court, "finally got him in trouble and cost him the job of Chief Justice."

In the middle of the *Life* article Lambert confessed, "It is not easy to pin down the exact extent of the Wolfson-Fortas relationship, nor has LIFE uncovered evidence making possible a charge that Wolfson hired Fortas to fix his case." After this disclaimer, however, the reporter went on to offer a long list of disconnected details from different sources that could be construed to implicate Fortas in wrongdoing. The fact that Fortas had deposited the Wolfson Foundation's $20,000 retainer in his personal bank account rather than that of his former law firm and then repaid it from the same private account was treated as suspicious. Even more attention was given to a Fortas trip to Wolfson's Florida horse farm; Fortas had said that the two men merely discussed foundation affairs during the brief visit, but Lambert cast doubts on that claim. The reporter used the coincidence of legal proceedings in Wolfson's SEC case and an uncorroborated charge that Fortas had talked of the matter. The claim had been made by a Wolfson associate who bargained for a lesser penalty in return for a guilty plea and testimony against Wolfson. In the end, Lambert rested his case against Fortas on his judgment that the retainer Fortas received was suspiciously large and was belatedly returned and on the fact that Wolfson and his colleagues had claimed at various times that they had friends in high places who would keep them out of trouble. Lambert's insinuations failed to explain either Fortas's complete lack of action on Wolfson's behalf or the financier's failure to avoid conviction.

Given a chance by Lambert to comment on the article's allegations, Fortas responded in a fashion that proved, if anything, more damaging than anything the reporter had uncovered. In a letter to Lambert that the reporter quoted in his article, the justice acknowledged only that Wolfson had told him of the foundation's activities and that he had been present at Wolfson's Florida horse farm when others discussed the foundation's work. Not only did he fail to acknowledge active participation in those conversations, but Fortas said nothing about the contract he had entered into and then terminated, much less that the contract had stipulated a continuing annual payment for his lifetime and that of his wife. Once the article appeared, Fortas continued the obfuscation, telling a reporter that he had been offered a fee but had not accepted it, apparently thinking that it was not necessary to mention that he had held the payment for months before returning it.[63] Fortas obviously felt that, since he had abrogated the contract and ultimately received nothing under its terms, at the time of his letter to Lambert it had ceased to exist. His semantics, clever, precise, and misleading, would come back to harm him.

However problematic Lambert's *Life* magazine story might have been as a legal argument, it became an undoubted political sensation. The day after it appeared it generated discussion during Nixon's regular weekly meeting with Republican congressional leaders at the White House. House minority leader Gerald Ford reported that he had looked into the impeachment process, determined that grounds for impeachment were not limited to indictable offenses, and discovered that a single House member could initiate an impeachment action. Ford's remarks suggested a previous total lack of familiarity with impeachment but a readiness now to proceed with it. Senate minority leader Everett Dirksen, the only person present who had served in Congress during an impeachment, recalled unhappily the 1936 House proceedings against Judge Halsted Ritter. Dirksen declared that he would never care to go through such an experience again and admonished the group to go slow. After other congressional leaders talked about keeping pressure on Fortas, Attorney General Mitchell cryptically advised them "to keep the lid on—more will develop later." Nixon himself then concluded the discussion by referring to Fortas as the Court's wealthiest and perhaps most brilliant member and expressing bewilderment as to why he would consider accepting Wolfson's fee.[64] The president's remarks seem to have been aimed at keeping the congressional leaders focused on Fortas's ethics. Nothing was said about the administration's role in discrediting the justice or pressuring him to resign.

Lambert's *Life* article conveyed an image of questionable behavior that offended many who had supported Fortas the previous year and outraged those who had opposed his elevation to chief justice. Once again Senator Griffin took center stage, and this time his agenda was Fortas's impeachment. On the day Lambert's article was officially published, Griffin and a new ally, Ohio Republican congressman Robert Taft, Jr., the grandson of onetime Chief Justice William Howard Taft and son and namesake of the 1952 presidential aspirant, held a press conference to underscore the story's importance. Griffin suggested that more details on the $20,000 fee remained to be divulged, while Taft predicted that unless a satisfactory explanation of the money was forthcoming, a bill of impeachment would be voted against Fortas. Griffin then concluded that Fortas could best avoid impeachment by resigning.[65] Several other members of Congress followed with similar suggestions, and the public was soon reading headlines reporting "Justice Fortas Faces Threat of Impeachment in Congress."[66]

Three days later Taft and Griffin introduced legislation, clearly aimed at Fortas, requiring federal judges who earned outside annual incomes of $15,000 or more to report such income and its sources to the Judicial Conference of the United States each year. Judges would also be required to report property holdings of $10,000 or more, along with the names of any joint owners.[67] Enlisting the aid of House minority leader Gerald Ford, they pushed for months to have the House Judiciary Committee hold hearings on the bill. They failed to move the committee's Democratic chairman, Emanuel Celler, to do so, but nonetheless they enhanced the notion that for judges to receive outside income was improper, especially after the Judicial Conference in November adopted such a requirement for lower federal judges.[68] Even without being adopted, as it never was, the Griffin-Taft bill increased the impression that what Fortas had done was improper and provided grounds for removal.

While Fortas remained on the Court, Attorney General Mitchell, Richard Nixon's closest cabinet confidant, worked assiduously behind the scenes to force him off the bench. Without revealing what he was doing to Republican congressional leaders at their White House meeting on May 6, Mitchell was using the threat of impeachment to increase pressure on the justice to resign as Griffin had suggested. After Assistant Attorney General Wilson first talked with Lambert about his story and reported to the attorney general on the conversation, Mitchell himself dug into the Fortas-Wolfson connection. He conferred with Wolfson's attorney, William Bittman, apparently offering unspecified considerations to the prison-bound Wolfson in return for his cooperation in an FBI interview once the *Life* story appeared. Wolfson would later be released after serving nine months of an eighteen-month sentence.[69]

Meanwhile, the day after the *Life* story appeared, the IRS obtained subpoenaed documents from the Wolfson Family Foundation, including the Fortas contract. The IRS quickly turned what it had obtained over to the Justice Department. The documents disclosed for the first time that what Lambert had assumed was a onetime payment was indeed the first installment of Fortas's hitherto undisclosed projected lifetime arrangement with Wolfson. While the documents gave no proof of wrongdoing, they did indicate that Fortas had not been fully forthcoming about his aborted relationship with Wolfson. To Mitchell initially and to others later, the previously unrevealed long-term character of the initial contract was a stunning revelation.[70]

On the same day the White House put out the story that President Nixon had urged congressional leaders the day before not to do "something rash" by prematurely instituting impeachment proceedings against Justice Fortas. While the evidence indicates that it was Dirksen, not Nixon, who had made such comments, the president's effort to appear prudent and statesmanlike was characteristic. By asking people to ignore what he vividly inferred was the approach of a menacing monster, Nixon would assure that they would think of nothing else. Impeachment of Fortas quickly became the talk of Washington.[71] Griffin jumped back into the discussion once more, telling the press that he had received threats against his life because of information he had against Fortas and again urging Fortas to resign to avoid impeachment.[72]

Mitchell certainly knew that what the IRS had acquired was not evidence of a crime that the Justice Department could credibly prosecute, or he would have pursued an indictment. He also had to know that he did not possess unquestionable proof of an impeachable offense, or he would have taken steps to turn it over publicly and properly to the House of Representatives. What the attorney general had obtained was information that would, under the circumstances created by the chief justiceship battle and the *Life* story, powerfully embarrass Fortas and the Warren Court.

The attorney general wasted no time embarking on an irregular but effective venture. Having been shown the Wolfson documents following a postmidnight return to Washington after a dinner in New York City, he asked for a confidential appointment the next morning to meet Chief Justice Warren, now in the final weeks of his tenure on the Supreme Court. At 11:30 a.m. on May 7, Mitchell visited Warren at the Court, spending forty minutes showing him the Fortas-Wolfson contract and related documents. Warren, who by all accounts and every measure had a strict sense of judicial ethics that countenanced only a narrow range of extrajudicial activities, was appalled by the Fortas-Wolfson agreement. Fortas's termination of the contract after five months and his return of the money paid while it had been in force, evident from the documents Mitchell provided, failed to assuage the chief justice's sense that the Court's standing with the country would suffer when the information became public, as seemed inevitable.[73]

Warren left it to Hugo Black, the Court's senior member, to talk to Fortas and encourage him to resign. The ongoing fallout from the Lambert story had prompted bipartisan congressional calls for Fortas to step down from the bench. Black, after a two-hour meeting with Fortas, did not join the chorus. Nor did William O. Douglas, once Fortas's teacher at Yale and his colleague in the Roosevelt administration as well as much later on the Court. Finally, Warren called a special conference of all the justices on the morning of Monday, May 13, and shared the documents given him by Mitchell. The Wolfson Family Foundation contract was, of course, the centerpiece. Fortas responded that he had done nothing improper, but he acknowledged the damaging effect on the Court's image. He concluded by announcing that he was prepared to leave the Court. None of the brethren, least of all Chief Justice Warren, sought to dissuade him.[74]

As Fortas got ready to depart, his decision known only to members of the Court, external pressures on him to resign were unrelenting. The information in the *Life* article remained all that was publicly known of the Fortas-Wolfson relationship, and that was enough to generate a steady drumbeat of criticism. Congressman H. R. Gross of Iowa had finally taken the step that he and others had earlier threatened, introducing a bill calling for Fortas's impeachment.[75]

On May 14 Fortas sent a letter of resignation to the president. The White House chose not to make it public immediately so as not to divert attention from a televised Nixon speech on the Vietnam War. Despite the official silence, the president's chief of staff quickly notified Mitchell. The attorney general summoned his closest aides and announced that the occasion called for a drink. Their celebration peaked when the president, not too busy with speech preparations to savor a success, phoned to offer congratulations on a job well done.[76]

By the next morning the *Los Angeles Times* was reporting on the Fortas-Wolfson contract. The story, obviously based on information provided by the Justice Department or the White House, did not include the exculpatory testimony that Wolfson gave under oath that Fortas had not helped at all with his legal problems. No longer willing to wait for the normal protocol of a White House announcement to be followed, Fortas had the Court's press office announce his resignation.[77]

Three weeks later, on June 6, the remaining members of the Court honored Earl Warren on his retirement. Justice Brennan had arranged a dinner for the justices and their wives on board the presidential yacht *Sequoia*. As they cruised down the Potomac River, Justice Douglas presented the chief justice with a farewell gift. The twelve living active and retired members of the Court with whom Warren had served all helped pay for a custom-made Winchester shotgun for their colleague, who loved duck hunting. Fortas had still been on the Court when Brennan had collected funds for the gift.[78]

Warren's last day on the bench came a few days later, on June 23. He received the traditional letter expressing admiration and best wishes from his colleagues who remained on the high court. The letter bore only seven signatures rather than the normal eight because of Fortas's resignation. The man once expected to succeed Warren as chief justice was not able to sign.[79] Even this final act of celebration of Warren's career on the bench served as a reminder of how unceremonious, indeed demeaning, had been Fortas's departure under the threat of impeachment only weeks before.

Abe Fortas's humiliating departure from the Supreme Court certainly could be and generally was attributed to the justice's own imprudent behavior. The arrangements he made to engage in highly compensated extrajudicial work tested the bounds of the relevant canons of judicial ethics. Those canons admonished judges to avoid assuming obligations, financial or otherwise, that interfered or even appeared to interfere with the proper discharge of their official duties. In particular, the canons warned against actions that involved or suggested the possibility of impropriety.

Neither Fortas's American University seminar nor his Wolfson Family Foundation involvement presented a prima facie case of unethical conduct. Many justices gave lectures or courses at law schools and elsewhere for which they were well compensated. Nor was service, paid as well as unpaid, on the boards of nonprofit organizations unheard of for members of the Court. Since Fortas routinely recused himself from cases before the Court involving clients of his former law firm, thus all the donors to the seminar as well as Wolfson, he could not properly be charged with any actual misdeeds.

Fortas remained vulnerable, however, on the basis of appearances. The seminar honorarium seemed unusually large and its origins suspect. The Wolfson contract, when fully revealed, appeared even more questionable because of its magnitude and the identity of its provider. Fortas's failure to explain either arrangement in an immediate, full, and forthright manner when they first came to light, as he might well have done, cast further doubts on their probity.

What sank the Fortas ship, however, was the persistent effort to discredit him that grew out of purely partisan motives to hold open the chief justiceship so that it could be filled by a different president. Robert Griffin's campaign against

Lyndon Johnson's nomination of a chief justice took shape even before the identity of the nominee was known. The effort to find arguments that could be used against Fortas escalated as soon as he was nominated. Attempts to wound the nominee politically led to concocted charges of, first, presidential cronyism and, subsequently, participation in criminal procedure and obscenity rulings. Such transparently partisan allegations appeared to deepen but not broaden opposition to Fortas. The American University seminar story, which erupted late in the battle over the chief justice nomination, was seized on with greater success by politically committed opponents. What followed was not a thoughtful exploration of the subtle and complex parameters of judicial ethics but rather the reduction of a story to its simplest terms to be used as a blunt weapon in an intense political battle.

The partisan contest over who would name the next chief justice came to an end because of the constraints of the political calendar. The victors triumphed not by putting forth an unassailable case but, rather, by maneuvering to ensure that time would run out before confirmation was achieved. Fortas's adversaries were not immune to criticism for their strategy of defeat through delay. Thus, they had a continuing incentive to find more substantial evidence against Fortas. Furthermore, their success in keeping Fortas out of the Court's center seat served to encourage a belief that it might be possible to reshape the Supreme Court more to their liking.

Continued close scrutiny of Justice Fortas brought to light another instance of questionable conduct, his association with Louis Wolfson. Led to believe that the Justice Department had more evidence regarding the Fortas-Wolfson relationship than it indeed possessed, journalist William Lambert and the editors of *Life* magazine published the story that, in turn, brought forth further information unfavorable to Fortas. However dubious the means of constructing the story, when assembled it provided a basis for congressmen to begin proposing impeachment if Justice Fortas did not resign. With the appearance of the *Life* story, the Justice Department was able to acquire the damning contract and present it as new evidence of impropriety rather than as an out-of-date and ultimately unexecuted agreement. At the same time, Wolfson, now in federal prison, was telling Justice Department attorneys that Fortas had not lifted a finger to help him with his legal problems. Wolfson's testimony exonerating Fortas appeared to be of little interest to the Justice Department.

After Attorney General Mitchell presented the damaging but not the exculpatory evidence to Earl Warren, the chief justice shared what he was given with the full Court. Fortas received little sympathy from the shocked brethren. Whether the House of Representatives would have voted impeachment or the Senate convicted is impossible to know, but the prospect no doubt weighed on Fortas's decision to resign. After nearly a year of being battered by accumulating criticism of his relationship with Lyndon Johnson, his judicial rulings, and his personal affairs and facing the likelihood of further damage to his reputation and that of the Court, Fortas decided to abandon his office and accept the public embarrassment that resignation assured. The dispirited justice told *Washington Post* editor Benjamin Bradlee, "If I stayed on the Court, there would be this constitutional confrontation that would go on for months. Hell, I feel there wasn't any choice for a man of conscience."[80]

The Fortas episode demonstrated that impeachment was not quite the "rusted blunderbuss" it had been said to be a decade before or that the abortive campaign to impeach Chief Justice Warren had seemed to confirm. Rather, impeachment stood revealed as a working weapon whose mere threat could achieve the departure of a compromised federal official and advance other political agendas. Persistent investigation of matters that had previously been regarded as outside the realm of public concern could provide the means to drive out a seemingly secure officeholder. The individual who initiated the Fortas inquiry and who at the time was heavily criticized for doing so, Senator Robert Griffin, wound up winning accolades for "principled reasoning and sound judgment."[81] The next year, Griffin, still in his first term, would vault into his party's third-highest leadership position. After the death of Minority Leader Everett Dirksen, his Senate Republican colleagues elected Griffin the party whip.

The newly elected Nixon administration appeared to profit even more from its efforts to build a case against Justice Fortas and turn the Court against him. By raising the possibility of impeachment, the administration had provoked Fortas's resignation. Within four months of taking office, the new president had acquired the opportunity to appoint a second justice in addition to a new chief justice. The replacement of Warren and Fortas, two noted liberals, with two justices more to his liking provided Nixon an unexpectedly early opportunity to reshape the Supreme Court as he had pledged to do. Yet it would soon become evident that a political victory attained by such methods came at a price.

The protracted struggle involving Abe Fortas permanently altered the process of confirming Supreme Court justices. Prior to 1968, most twentieth-century Supreme Court confirmations had been rapid and almost perfunctory ratifications of presidential choices. Fortas's own 1965 confirmation as associate justice was fairly typical, involving a three-hour Senate Judiciary Committee hearing less than two weeks after his nomination and full Senate approval by a voice vote shortly thereafter.[82] The extended hearings and floor debate of the 1968 Fortas battle inaugurated an era of much closer examination of credentials. When the Fortas inquiry did not end with the contest over the chief justiceship but continued until the information regarding his relationship with Wolfson was uncovered and the justice resigned, questions arose about whether the scrutiny of his qualifications, in 1965 as well as 1968, had been sufficient.

Justice Fortas was not alone in suffering humiliation as a result of his ignominious departure from the Supreme Court. The Senate as a whole, and the

Judiciary Committee in particular, had reason to feel that they had somehow failed, and failed badly. The Senate was understandably angry and embarrassed at having a justice face impeachment less than four years after his initial confirmation and less than a year after his consideration for the position of chief justice. The second confirmation process, as strenuous as it was and as close in time to the events that would eventually precipitate Fortas's downfall, had failed to turn up the evidence that would lead to his departure. Henceforth, the Senate would not want again to appear careless in its confirmation deliberations. As a result, it would investigate nominees far more thoroughly and question them much more extensively. Even those who believed, with reason, that Abe Fortas had been the victim of crass political maneuvers had cause to conclude that protracted and even unsuccessful confirmation proceedings in the Senate would be preferable to impeachment trials in the same body. As subsequent events would soon reveal, the shadow of impeachment raised in the Fortas case wrought permanent changes in the process of confirming justices of the Supreme Court.

4

Impeachment as Partisan:
The Case of William O. Douglas

Less than three weeks after Abe Fortas resigned from the Supreme Court to escape the building momentum for his impeachment, an exultant Senator Strom Thurmond bluntly declared, "Douglas is next!"[1] He was referring to Associate Justice William O. Douglas, the Court's second-most-senior member. Thurmond, the veteran South Carolina senator and 1948 Dixiecrat presidential nominee, had been elected to the Senate in 1955 as a Democrat but had later switched his allegiance to the Republican Party when he perceived that it offered greater support for the doctrine of states' rights that he favored. For Thurmond, states' rights had always been, first and foremost, a means to defend traditional southern racial policies.[2] Jubilant over the exodus of Justice Fortas, the South Carolina senator saw an opportunity to advance his segregationist agenda. With liberals reeling from the retirement of Earl Warren and the forced resignation of Fortas, what better time could there ever be to strike another blow against the liberal judiciary Thurmond detested?

Thurmond saw the Fortas episode as a blueprint for eliminating from the Court another justice he absolutely loathed. He was not alone in anticipating an effort to remove Douglas, though others who forecast it did not share Thurmond's enthusiasm. In a conversation with his father and Justice Fortas shortly before the latter announced his resignation, attorney William O. Douglas, Jr., gave both members of the Court a somber warning: "Blood will taste good to this gang," he said, referring to the Nixon administration and its congressional allies. "And having tasted it, they will want more."[3]

During the Wolfson debacle in the spring of 1969 Fortas himself had had a premonition that the forces attacking him might next turn their attention to Justice Douglas. His colleague on the Court had been one of Fortas's principle mentors at Yale Law School before leaving to take a seat on the Securities and Exchange Commission in 1934. Nominated for a seat on the Supreme Court by Franklin Roosevelt in 1939, Douglas at age forty became one of the youngest men ever elevated to the Court. He proceeded to build a reputation as an unwavering liberal over three decades on the bench. Several years after he left the Court, Fortas, perhaps trying to put the best face on his own troubles, would tell a biographer, "I resigned to save Douglas."[4]

Douglas personified the sort of justice that Nixon and Thurmond railed against in the campaign of 1968. He outraged social and legal conservatives with his unwavering support for civil rights, whether for racial minorities, criminal suspects, makers and distributors of books and films they thought obscene, or others he considered victims of abusive government. Furthermore, those same conservatives found reprehensible Douglas's much-publicized personal life. In the summer of 1966 the justice had divorced his young third wife, Joan Martin, who had been a college student when he met her four years earlier. Three weeks later he married the even younger Cathleen Heffernan, a twenty-three-year-old college student forty-five years his junior. The new Mrs. Douglas, who would soon attend law school and who would later have a substantial career as an environmental and public-service attorney, was to the justice's conservative critics nothing more than the symbol of Douglas's dissipated lifestyle. The Republican minority leader of the House of Representatives, Gerald R. Ford of Michigan, conveyed to his staff his disapproval of Douglas's marriages to these young women.[5] Five members of Congress asked that the House Judiciary Committee conduct an investigation into whether Douglas's moral character warranted his impeachment.[6] Their cries soon faded, but the image of "the dirty old man" lingered.

Douglas was as vulnerable as Fortas to charges of inappropriate off-the-bench activities, having in 1966 been identified as the paid director of a private charitable foundation, the Albert Parvin Foundation. The Parvin Foundation had been founded in 1960 with a small but distinguished board of directors. The foundation supported graduate fellowships for students from underdeveloped African, Asian, Middle Eastern, and Latin American nations to attend Princeton University and UCLA. Nevertheless, news stories about Douglas's role as its president focused attention on the source of its income, a mortgage on a Las Vegas hotel and casino that Albert Parvin had sold in 1959. Upon learning about Douglas's involvement with the Parvin Foundation, one senator, Republican John Williams of Delaware, expressed outrage and called for an immediate Senate investigation of the justice's ethics. When Douglas's intimates defended the propriety of his philanthropic activities and none of the senator's colleagues echoed his demand, the story quickly faded.[7] Memories of the Parvin connection, however, would linger in the minds of both Douglas's friends and his foes.

Fortas's remark about resigning to save Douglas suggests that he never fully comprehended that neither the charges levied against his old mentor nor those raised against himself had been in themselves important to the accusers. They merely served as tools for attempts to drive the two liberal justices off the Court. Other grounds for proposing impeachment would have been embraced just as readily, and indeed were. At the time, neither Fortas nor Douglas was in a position to know just how the wheels were turning to hasten their departure.

Only five days after Richard Nixon was sworn in as president, his administration initiated an investigation of Justice Douglas. Eager to advance its goal of remaking the Supreme Court, the White House directed the IRS to audit Douglas's tax returns. Meanwhile the FBI resumed gathering information on Douglas's previously reported involvement with the Parvin Foundation and on his other off-the-Court activities.[8] Furthermore, in one of the earliest instances of what would become a characteristic administration practice, John Ehrlichman, one of Nixon's closest aides, asked Jack Caulfield, a retired New York City detective hired by the White House to conduct its own investigations, to look for compromising information on Douglas. In a June 4, 1969, report Caulfield was only able to inform Ehrlichman that two newspapers were themselves investigating Douglas's Parvin connections.[9]

Ehrlichman later recalled, "From the beginning Nixon was interested in getting rid of William O. Douglas."[10] The thought does not seem to have crossed Nixon's or Ehrlichman's mind, or at least to have bothered either man if it did, that the Constitution's separation of powers design had been intended to restrain the executive branch from such precipitous ideological restructuring of the federal courts. The Constitution established the judiciary as an independent branch of the federal government. The executive branch's judicial authority, other than for the routine enforcement of laws applying to all citizens, was limited to the appointment of judges. The Constitution specified that the legislative branch, not the executive, bore the responsibility for policing and punishing errant judicial behavior. For the moment, the president would bide his time, but Ehrlichman had no doubt that, regardless of the Constitution's directives, Nixon was preparing to launch a campaign to remove Douglas from the Supreme Court. Only the need to fill the two already existing vacancies on the high court postponed a Nixon administration campaign to drive Douglas from the bench.

Nixon moved to fill the high court seats vacated by Warren and Fortas with judges who would help fulfill the president's 1968 campaign pledge to reform the Supreme Court. However, the way Warren and Fortas left the high court had defined a new approach to the process of confirming judicial nominees. Previously the process of examining a nominee's credentials had been quick and cursory: Before the 1940s the process had been assigned to a three-member subcommittee of the Judiciary Committee. Three times during the 1940s the hearings had been dispensed with altogether. Not until after the *Brown v. Board of Education* rulings did asking the nominee to testify become normal, and even then hearings only lasted a day or two, followed by quick approval of the nominee by the full Senate.[11] The conduct of senators Griffin and Thurmond and their colleagues who insisted upon taking much more time to examine Fortas's background established precedents that would prevail thereafter. Likewise, their willingness to probe nonjudicial aspects of a nominee's life in greater detail than had previously been the custom set a new standard. After Griffin demonstrated the effectiveness of the tools available to a minority party in a confirmation battle, the Senate's Democratic majority would have few qualms about using them in turn.

Filling Warren's seat proved to be easy. Scarcely more than a month after hosting a White House dinner in honor of the departing chief justice and only six days after Fortas's resignation, Nixon nominated as Warren's replacement Judge Warren Earl Burger of the United States Court of Appeals for the District of Columbia. As the senior Republican member of the court widely regarded as the second most important in the federal judicial system because so many cases involving the federal government came there, Burger was a logical choice. A politically active Minnesota attorney first named to the bench by Eisenhower, Burger had aggressively sought the appointment.[12] He came bearing a judicial philosophy as well as a name the reverse of his predecessor's, but in the new president's honeymoon period and with no objection to the nominee raised, Senate Democrats did not block Burger's confirmation, as they could have done. Having discovered no reason to question his credentials in an hour-and-forty-minute hearing, at which Burger was the only witness, and after three hours of floor debate, the Senate confirmed him 74–3, only nineteen days after Nixon put his name forward.[13] Yet signs of an altered attitude about the confirmation process came from Senator Gaylord Nelson of Wisconsin, one of the three nay-sayers, who explained that he had not learned enough about the nominee and ruefully declared that he had been mistaken in voting to confirm Fortas.[14]

Nixon waited ten weeks after Burger's confirmation before nominating Clement F. Haynsworth, Jr., chief judge of the U.S. Court of Appeals for the Fourth Circuit, to fill the Fortas seat on the Supreme Court. Nixon chose Haynsworth on the basis of an approving review by an assistant attorney general, William Rehnquist, of the judge's twelve years of conservative appellate rulings. A cursory and unrevealing one-day FBI background check had followed the nomination. Senators and journalists taking further time to investigate the South Carolina judge's background in light of the issues raised about Fortas soon discovered, however, that, unlike the fallen justice, Haynsworth had not recused himself from cases before his court in which he appeared to have a financial interest. Birch Bayh, a Democratic senator from Indiana and leader of the nomination's opponents, brought to light that Haynsworth owned stock in businesses that benefited from his antiunion rulings. The judge's ethical lapses appeared far more clear-cut and egregious than those charged to Fortas.[15]

The Haynsworth nomination fell not to a filibuster preventing a vote but, rather, to a decisively negative 45–55 roll call of the Senate on his confirmation. Since the Democrats controlled the Senate 58–42, Nixon's inner circle attributed the loss to partisan revenge for the ouster of Fortas. That was far too simplistic an explanation for what proved an agonizing vote for many senators, especially the seventeen Republicans, including Fortas's nemesis Robert Griffin, who voted against Haynsworth.[16] Such rationalizations did not take into account either the seriousness of Haynsworth's flaws or the Senate's sense of its own shared responsibility for nominations to the Court, not to mention the raising of the threshold for confirming judicial candidates generated by the threat to impeach Fortas. Nixon himself criticized the Justice Department, in particular John Mitchell, for failing to gather all the facts on Haynsworth.[17] Yet the president, perhaps still not recognizing how the Fortas experience had changed the political culture, went ahead with his next nomination in much the same manner as he had handled Haynsworth.

By the time President Nixon sent another nominee for the Fortas seat to the Senate, the new approach to confirmation had become more firmly entrenched as a result of the Haynsworth revelations. This time, Nixon nominated Judge G. Harrold Carswell of Florida, a twelve-year federal district court judge recently elevated to the U.S. Court of Appeals for the Fifth Circuit. The choice of Carswell was, in John Dean's terms, "a complete screw-up by Nixon's advisors." While some observers cast it as Nixon's angry revenge on the Senate for rejecting Haynsworth or a deliberate effort to reduce the stature of the Supreme Court, Dean persuasively argues otherwise.[18] Burger's recommendation and Mitchell's concurrence had pushed Carswell's name forward. Rehnquist again settled for vetting the judge's opinions and declared him satisfactorily conservative. The FBI background check was so perfunctory that it failed to discover that Carswell was locally known to be both a homosexual and a segregationist. As Dean concludes and as events quickly proved, Carswell's nomination was "a colossal mistake" resulting from the administration's carelessness in examining his credentials.[19]

As legal scholars, civil rights advocates, and Senate staff members probed Carswell's background, it quickly became apparent that he had a stained record. Columbia University law students discovered that while Carswell had been a federal district judge, more than 40 percent of his appealed rulings had been overturned, a reversal rate higher than all but six of the sixty-seven judges in his circuit. Revelations of his racial attitudes were more disturbing. He had advocated white supremacy and racial segregation as a political candidate in 1948. While serving as U.S. attorney in Tallahassee, Florida, in 1956, he had drawn up incorporation documents to convert a local public golf course partially constructed with federal funds into a whites-only private country club. The club's ninety-nine-year dollar-a-year lease from the city, which Carswell helped draw up while serving as the federal government's chief law enforcement officer in the area, appeared to be a blatant effort to circumvent a six-month-old Supreme Court desegregation order for municipally owned recreational facilities.[20]

When these and other features of Carswell's past were brought to light, Senator Bayh, reluctantly once again leading the opposition, told the Senate that the judge's "incredibly undistinguished career as an attorney and jurist is itself an affront to the Supreme Court." In an offhand response that quickly became famous, Republican senator Roman Hruska, of Nebraska, told reporters, "Well, even if he were mediocre, there are a lot of mediocre judges and people and lawyers. They are entitled to a little representation, aren't they, and a little chance?"

After extended consideration focusing on Carswell's competence and his views on civil rights, a majority of senators decided that mediocrity and perceived racial bias should not be rewarded. On April 8, 1970, Carswell's nomination was rejected 51–45, with twelve Republicans as well as thirty-nine Democrats voting against confirmation.[21]

For the first time since Grover Cleveland had occupied the White House, two consecutive efforts by a president to fill a Supreme Court vacancy had been rejected. Nixon had remained outwardly confident that his choices would be confirmed.[22] Dismayed about the twin blows to his image of authority, he made his anger public in a brief press conference.[23] The president tried to explain the two setbacks as Senate prejudice against the South, not acknowledging, and perhaps not fully understanding, that in the aftermath of the Fortas episode the Senate had grown more wary of every Court nominee. The quest for information about prospective justices became more intense and changed the character of the confirmation process. Blemishes that before the Fortas episode might have been excused were thereafter seen as fatal.

The subsequent nomination of Judge Harry Blackmun of the U.S. Court of Appeals for the Eighth Circuit to fill the Fortas seat did not altogether assuage Senate concern. Since one of the first charges leveled against Fortas had been his close relationship with Lyndon Johnson, the issue of cronyism was naturally raised in Blackmun's case as well. As a boyhood friend of Warren Burger and best man at Burger's wedding, Blackmun was inevitably linked to the new chief justice and questioned about whether he would be judicially independent. The soft-spoken and accomplished Harvard-trained appellate judge was able to quell sufficiently the doubts of a Senate admittedly desperate to avoid another confirmation battle. Blackmun might have had a harder time had the Senate known how strenuously Burger had urged Nixon and Mitchell to make the appointment. Burger and Blackmun were immediately labeled the "Minnesota Twins," but any fears that the chief justice would control his colleague's vote gradually faded as their jurisprudential paths diverged.[24]

The Blackmun confirmation process was relatively untroubled in comparison to its two immediate predecessors. By the time it was concluded with a unanimous vote to approve the nomination three days short of a year after Fortas had resigned, senators had become accustomed to subjecting nominees' lives off as well as on the bench to the strictest scrutiny. Clearly, the Nixon administration had not anticipated or prepared for this development. It had not examined its nominees' backgrounds with the attention the Senate gave to Fortas, Haynsworth, Carswell, or Blackmun. Indeed, in the latter two cases the president and the attorney general had for the most part just relied on the advice of Warren Burger.[25] The shadow of impeachment raised in the Fortas case had wrought permanent changes in the Senate's process of confirming justices of the Supreme Court. At the same time it had whetted the Nixon administration's appetite for the additional Court seats that could become available if an impeachment either succeeded or compelled a resignation.

Immediately after Abe Fortas left the Court, House critics of William O. Douglas joined Senator Thurmond in suggesting that he should follow suit.[26] They were well aware of Justice Douglas's receipt of an annual payment for serving on the board of the Parvin Foundation, a relationship that had come to light three years earlier. They also learned that the justice headed the Center for the Study of Democratic Institutions, a small facility for scholars based in Santa Barbara, California, staffed by reform-minded liberal intellectuals and funded in part by the Parvin Foundation. The parallel to Fortas's extrajudicial activity seemed to Douglas's opponents obvious and equally unacceptable. Within a few days Douglas appeared to bow to the criticism by resigning from his Parvin directorship, though he claimed he had decided months earlier because of health reasons and the foundation's increasing workload to give up the position he had held for nine years.[27] Rather than disarming his opponents, however, Douglas's resignation from the Parvin Foundation encouraged them to believe he was vulnerable to an impeachment campaign. Gerald Ford, then House minority leader, quickly asked his aide Robert Hartmann to begin an unpublicized examination of Douglas's conduct.[28]

Opposition to the Haynsworth nomination stirred Nixon to act on his long-contemplated plan to drive Douglas from the Court. In the weeks before the Senate confirmation vote on Haynsworth, the president instructed Ehrlichman to talk to Ford about Douglas. Ehrlichman conveyed the message to Ford "within hours," though he later reported that he obtained no assurance that Ford either understood or accepted the assignment. To prod the minority leader, Ehrlichman himself immediately began to drop hints to journalists that Douglas might face impeachment.[29] Also, White House aide Clark Mollenhoff, a former *Des Moines Register* reporter, began circulating the story that Douglas had gone to the Dominican Republic in 1963 to persuade President Juan Bosch to grant a casino license to Mafia-connected Parvin interests. The story ignored the evidence that Douglas had made the trip on behalf of a Parvin Foundation literacy program in Santo Domingo and had had no contact with Bosch.[30] A *Washington Post* reporter soon asked Ford about his rumored Douglas investigation. Faced with the alternative of having to confirm or deny his efforts well before he was prepared to make them public, Ford acknowledged that he was taking a close look at Justice Douglas's activities. The same professional and ethical standards should be applied to sitting justices as to nominees, the congressman bluntly declared.[31]

Ford and Ehrlichman soon discovered that their message was backfiring. They were seen as attempting to hold Douglas hostage to Haynsworth's confirmation.[32] A *New York Times* editorial called the minority leader's remarks "a poorly veiled threat" against anti-Haynsworth senators that did Ford little credit "either as statesman or tactician."[33] Such comments betrayed a lack of awareness that the anti-Douglas campaign was based on a more substantial agenda than simply helping Haynsworth. In light of the negative response, however, Ford's talk of impeaching Douglas faded for the time being, though his research into the topic continued.[34]

Although the White House–supported Ford investigation of Douglas retreated into the shadows, it did not stop. Late in 1969 or early in 1970, Ford would testify in his 1973 vice presidential confirmation hearings, he was visited in his office by Will Wilson, Mitchell's assistant attorney general for the criminal division. Wilson, who had earlier assisted William Lambert with his May 1969 *Life* magazine story about Fortas, gave Ford leads to pursue in the Douglas investigation. Information about various gamblers supposedly tied to Albert Parvin was typed on eight or nine sheets of plain white paper. Ford considered such unattributed information "unusual," but, he said, "We were conducting a low-level, low-key, low-exposure investigation in my office, so I didn't question it any further." Ford assumed that the information had originated with the FBI. Ford's 1973 interrogator, Representative Jerome Waldie of California, drew attention to Ford's lack of knowledge of the source of the information supplied about Douglas and to the minority leader's subsequent "almost verbatim" use of its questionable claims about Douglas's activities in the Dominican Republic.[35]

Douglas proceeded to give his enemies additional ammunition to use against him. In February 1970 he published a small book with the provocative title *Points of Rebellion*. Really just an extended essay, *Points of Rebellion* offered a long list of situations involving freedom of expression, poverty, and environmental degradation where American practices were falling short of what the Constitution required. Douglas repeatedly expressed admiration for the principles of the U.S. Constitution. Addressed to readers who were disenchanted with the current American government and were advocating radical action against it, of whom there were many at the time, the book could easily be read as an argument to work for change within the system and to consider rebellion only if all else failed. Yet Douglas did indulge in some heated rhetoric, as when he wrote:

> George III was the symbol against which our founders made a revolution now considered bright and glorious. George III had not crossed the sea to fasten a foreign yoke on us. George III and his dynasty had established and nurtured us and all that he did was by no means oppressive. But a vast restructuring of laws and institutions was necessary if the people were to be content. That restructuring was not forthcoming and there was revolution.
>
> We must realize that today's Establishment is the new George III. Whether it will continue to adhere to his tactics, we do not know. If it does, the redress, honored in tradition, is also revolution.[36]

Points of Rebellion infuriated conservatives.[37] Republican Representative Louis Wyman of New Hampshire promptly manifested his anger. Ford's staff had to talk him out of immediately introducing an impeachment resolution. Wyman had been unhappy with Douglas ever since, as attorney general of his state, he had argued the Red Monday case of *Sweezy v. New Hampshire* before the Supreme Court and lost. Now he saw an opportunity to strike back. The Carswell nomination had just gone to the Senate, however, and the minority leader's staff feared a repeat of the Haynsworth debacle.[38]

Two months later, as the Senate continued to wrestle with the Carswell nomination, Douglas ignited further conservative anger. This time the fuse was an article appearing in *Evergreen,* a quarterly journal recently started by publisher Ralph Ginzburg. The piece not only excerpted a substantial portion of *Points of Rebellion,* including some of its most inflammatory passages, but was also accompanied by a caricature of Richard Nixon as George III of England. Furthermore, it was preceded by a collection of nude photographs and followed by an essay by prominent student radical Tom Hayden. As if Douglas's article was not bad enough, its placement seemed almost calculated to offend.

The second defeat of a Nixon Court nominee revived talk of impeaching Douglas. Vice President Spiro T. Agnew captured a large audience with questions about Douglas's fitness for the bench. In a television interview on CBS, he suggested that statements in *Points of Rebellion* justified examination of Douglas's qualifications to remain on the Court. Investigation of the justice's thinking was called for, Agnew said, "particularly in view of the fact that two fine judges have been denied seats on the bench for statements that are much less reprehensible than those made, in my opinion, by Justice Douglas."[39]

Following the vote on Carswell, several angry conservative congressmen approached Ford and said that he must take action or they would do so. Ford could have distanced himself from those ready to retaliate for the Haynsworth and Carswell rejections, but he chose instead to become their champion. His decision was probably bolstered by a massive file of undigested and often uncorroborated information gathered by the FBI and passed on to Ford at the direction of Attorney General Mitchell. In a press conference five days after Carswell's loss, the minority leader once again broached the subject of Douglas's possible impeachment. He proposed that the House of Representatives conduct an investigation to see if impeachment proceedings were warranted.[40]

Two days later, on April 15, 1970, Ford laid out his charges against Justice Douglas in a lengthy address to the House of Representatives. His two-hour speech, developed with the help of aides who had been examining the topic for nearly a year, represented the most substantial discussion of impeachment by a public official since the Halsted Ritter impeachment in the 1930s. It provided insight into one congressional leader's understanding of impeachment nearly a decade after the John Birch Society had reintroduced discussion of the process with its campaign against Earl Warren. Though the speech would be best remembered for one sentence that seemed extreme when taken out of context, overall it was a thoughtful attempt to grapple with the Constitution's impeachment provision, if not the specific case of Justice Douglas.[41]

At the outset of his speech, Ford devoted considerable attention to a detailed explanation of impeachment, distinguishing between its application to presidents and vice presidents, on the one hand, and to judges, on the other. He reminded the Senate that, while the Constitution listed particular offenses for which any federal officer could be removed, it also stipulated that justices served during "good behavior." To Ford, the term implied "a pattern or continuous sequence of action." He assured the House, "The Constitution does not demand that it be 'exemplary' or 'perfect.' But it does have to be good." Determining whether or not a federal judge's behavior qualifies as good, he continued, was a responsibility the Constitution gave to Congress, with the House functioning as prosecutor and grand jury and the Senate as judge and trial jury.

"Impeachment," Ford declared, "is a unique political device, designed explicitly to dislodge from public office those who are patently unfit for it." He reflected on the varying standards that had been applied in past impeachment cases but admitted that there were too few cases to define adequately the limits of what constituted an impeachable offense. Nevertheless, he asserted that the record was sufficient to show that an offense did not need to be indictable in order to be impeachable. In an oversimplified and thereafter much-quoted summary he concluded, "The only honest answer is that an impeachable offense is whatever a majority of the House of Representatives considers [it] to be at a given moment in history; conviction results from whatever offense or offenses two-thirds of the other body considers to be sufficiently serious to require removal of the accused from office. Again, the historical contest and political climax are important; there are few fixed principles among the handful of precedents."

Gerald Ford, a cautious man as well as a Yale Law School–educated lawyer, had obviously given some careful thought to the abstract terms of impeachment. His deliberations led him to conclude that judges needed to be held to a high standard because, unlike legislators and presidents, their constitutional grant of lifetime tenure prevented their removal from office by voters. Justice Douglas, Ford proceeded to argue, had failed to meet this high standard on multiple occasions.

Beginning by suggesting that Douglas had the same sort of conflict of interest that had led Fortas to resign, Ford proceeded to lay out a detailed case against the justice. He noted that Douglas had twice dissented from rulings against publisher Ralph Ginzburg, the first, in 1966, finding his magazine *Eros* obscene and the second, in 1970, sustaining a libel claim by Barry Goldwater against his magazine *Fact*. Meanwhile, Douglas published essays in other Ginzburg magazines,

Ford pointed out, raising the question of whether this violated the judicial obligation to avoid partiality and the appearance of partiality toward those coming before the bench. The first such essay mentioned by Ford, a piece on folksinging, appeared in Ginzburg's *Avant Garde* next to an article titled "The Decline and Fall of the Female Breast" that clearly offended Ford. The second was the piece based on *Points of Rebellion* that appeared in *Evergreen*. Ford acknowledged Douglas's right to publish *Points of Rebellion,* though he found it sophomoric, but the Republican leader considered the *Evergreen* piece different because it was in a magazine he regarded as pornographic.

Ford focused his attention on seven pages of grainy black-and-white photographs by Arthur Freed that immediately preceded the Douglas piece. Most focused on a nude female torso reclining on a rug. Others in the set included a male body as well, and two showed the woman's hand grasping his penis. Artfully cropped, the final photos implied but did not actually display sexual intercourse.[42] "There are nude models of both sexes," Ford declared, "in poses that are perhaps more shocking than the postcards that used to be sold in the back alleys of Paris and Panama City, Panama." Those who knew Ford reported that he was quite straitlaced; this statement reflected his awkwardness in describing the photographs as well as his genuine disapproval. To Ford, this was not simply political opportunism.

Ford went on to discuss at length Douglas's ties to the Parvin Foundation. He focused on Albert Parvin's alleged connections with various Las Vegas gambling figures, implying, though providing no evidence, that Douglas was associated with unsavory individuals. Ford also linked Douglas to the same individuals' allegedly corrupt involvements in the Dominican Republic during the brief ascendancy of Juan Bosch. Suggesting that Douglas had improperly given legal advice to Parvin, Ford characterized Douglas's resignation from his position with the Parvin Foundation as occurring "when things got too hot on the Supreme Court" to continue his affiliation. Noting the ties between the Parvin Foundation and the "leftish" Center for the Study of Democratic Institutions, which he characterized as the incubator for a radical New Left student movement, Ford suggested that Douglas's assumption of the chairmanship of the center's executive committee was, among other things, a guise for continuing his relationship with the Parvin Foundation. The minority leader concluded by linking Douglas to Fortas, paralleling their conduct, and saying that he was ready to vote to impeach Douglas as unfit and needing to be removed. Taking a step backward at the end, he announced that he would "support but not actively sponsor the creation of a select committee" to investigate whether Douglas should be impeached.

Reaction to the Ford speech varied. A bipartisan group of conservative members of Congress, 52 Republicans and 52 southern Democrats, submitted a resolution the following day calling for an investigation of Ford's litany of charges. Within a week their number grew to 112, fully one-fourth of the House.[43] Others assumed that the charges would go nowhere and likened the speech to the John Birch Society's billboard campaign against Earl Warren. They regarded it as revenge for the Haynsworth and Carswell defeats and perceived it as less an attack on Douglas than a disparagement of the integrity and independence of the Court. One unnamed Democratic senator called it "ugly," and explained, "What we seem to be witnessing is McCarthyism directed not at personalities but institutions."[44]

One young Republican congressman, Paul McCloskey of California, soon challenged his party leader's central premise. In a speech to the House less than a week after Ford had spoken, McCloskey, a lawyer and frequently independent-minded legislator, disputed the claim that an impeachable offense was whatever a majority of the House agreed upon at the moment. He regarded that view as a grave threat to the independence of the judiciary that the framers had intended. The provision that judges should serve during good behavior, he told the House, needed to be read with the accompanying language of the article prohibiting judicial salary reduction; it clearly was intended to protect the judiciary from political pressure. The "good behavior" provision must, McCloskey insisted, be read together with the specific provision for impeachment for "treason, bribery, or other high crimes and misdemeanors" and must not be used as an excuse for the House to impeach for any reason it chose. "I can find no precedent," McCloskey said, "for impeachment of a Judge for nonjudicial conduct which falls short of violation of law."[45]

The ABA canons of ethics, McCloskey reminded the House, began by establishing the responsibility of lawyers to uphold respect for the judiciary. Reviewing the charges against Douglas and finding no evidence of criminal conduct in them, the California congressman concluded, "We must balance the disrespect that we may feel that the Justice has brought upon himself against the need to preserve an independent judiciary because long after a personality may have been forgotten, we must have an independent judiciary free to deliberate on the issues of law which is far more desirable than the temporary disappointment we may feel against an individual whom we may feel has brought this upon us."[46] McCloskey's attempt to address the boundaries and implications of impeachment not only engaged the few members who were on the floor and questioned him on various points but also drew the attention of others being forced by Ford's initiative to start thinking seriously for the first time about an actual impeachment.[47]

Ford's call for a select committee to investigate Douglas was an effort to wrest consideration of Douglas's impeachment away from the House Judiciary Committee. Because the committee was controlled by its Democratic majority and chaired by liberal Emanuel Celler of New York, the minority leader viewed it as decidedly unsympathetic. Although Ford enlisted bipartisan cosponsorship for a select committee, he was outmaneuvered by Celler. While the minority leader was still speaking on April 15, Representative Andrew Jacobs, a liberal Democrat from Indiana, submitted an impeachment resolution that by House rules was a privileged motion and allowed Speaker John McCormack to assign jurisdiction to Celler's committee.[48]

Chairman Celler wasted no time in arranging for a Judiciary Committee investigation of Justice Douglas, though not one involving the full committee. In less than a week the chairman organized a special subcommittee composed of experienced senior members of the Judiciary Committee for the purpose of examining Ford's charges. Celler named Democrats Byron Rogers of Colorado and Jack Brooks of Texas as well as Republicans William McCulloch of Ohio and Edward Hutchinson of Michigan to the subcommittee with himself as chairman. McCulloch was the only member with any experience in such an inquiry, having served on the 1953 special subcommittee that had quickly dismissed an earlier effort to impeach Douglas.[49] Celler, who only days before had expressed his view that Ford's charges were "an attack on the integrity and the independence of the United States Supreme Court," promised a subcommittee report within sixty days.

The Nixon administration proved eager to make public its willingness to assist in the investigation of Douglas after earlier surreptitiously providing FBI files to Ford. In sharp contrast to his response later when his own conduct was under investigation, the president announced that the administration would make every effort to provide all the information it could on the justice. Nixon himself wrote to Celler,

> The power of impeachment is, of course, solely entrusted by the
> Constitution to the House of Representatives. However, the executive
> branch is clearly obligated both by precedent and by the necessity of the
> House of Representatives having all the facts before reaching its decision,
> to supply relevant information to the legislative branch, as it does in aid
> of other inquiries being conducted by committees of the Congress, to the
> extent compatible with the public interest.[50]

Celler asked the president for access to tax returns for Douglas and for Albert Parvin, as well as for the latter's foundation and corporation returns.[51] Nixon promptly agreed to provide them.[52] Douglas himself estimated that forty federal agents devoted the equivalent of fifteen man-years to the investigation and turned over hundreds of documents to the House judiciary subcommittee.[53]

The assault by Ford and the White House had the reverse of its intended effect of pushing Douglas to resign to avoid impeachment. The justice, who had undergone three operations in the previous year, including the installation of a heart pacemaker, had been contemplating retirement at the end of the Court's term. But the Fortas experience affected his decision. "I'm not resigning," he told his staff. "That would look too much like a confession of guilt, and I'm not guilty of anything."[54]

Editorial opinion in newspapers around the nation divided over Douglas. Conservative syndicated columnists William F. Buckley, Jr., Ralph de Toledano, Paul Harvey, and James J. Kilpatrick echoed the arguments of the Ford accusations, including the claim that Douglas was involved with gamblers because of his Parvin Foundation activities and the charge that he published radical calls to revolution in pornographic magazines. On the other hand, editorials in newspapers from Lewiston, Idaho, to Hagerstown, Maryland, from Sacramento, California, to Pittsfield, Massachusetts, characterized Ford's charges as partisan and not meriting impeachment.[55]

Douglas made no public acknowledgment of being concerned. He would later joke in his autobiography, *The Court Years,* that people had been trying to get him off the Court for almost as long as he had been on it. The Texas state legislature had called for his impeachment in 1951 because of his majority opinion upholding federal claims to offshore oil fields.[56] When Douglas stayed the execution of convicted atomic spies Julius and Ethel Rosenberg in 1953, Congressman W. M. Wheeler of Georgia had submitted an impeachment resolution to the House and called the justice "a knave unworthy of the high position he holds."[57] After the full Court quickly lifted the stay and the execution was carried out only one day later than originally scheduled, the impeachment resolution received a sixty-five-minute hearing before being killed by the House Judiciary Committee.[58] A similar congressional outcry, though no actual impeachment resolution, had followed Douglas's fourth marriage, in 1966, to Heffernan.[59] Douglas realized, however, that this latest development was of a different order.

Douglas knew, having witnessed the treatment of his former student Fortas, that Ford's effort must be taken more seriously. He recognized that the new Nixon administration intended to reshape the Court and was prepared to go to extraordinary lengths to achieve its goal. The justice worried that he was being set up for even more charges. When he and his wife attended a charity Greek Easter feast in Washington, D.C., and met a Greek dissident politician who was an old friend, a *Washington Post* reporter immediately approached him. She announced, "I understand you are giving Andreas Papandreou legal advice."[60] The increasingly nervous justice also received a report that the FBI had inspected his cabin in Goose Prairie, Washington. "I am told—though I can't prove it," he wrote, "that they planted marijuana on our fields, hoping to have a TV-raid in a few months."[61]

The justice wasted no time in retaining veteran New York attorney Simon H. Rifkind to represent him. Rifkind, a long-time aide to Senator Robert Wagner, a law partner of Adlai Stevenson, and a former federal judge, had been a friend of Douglas's since they entered Columbia Law School together in 1922.[62] A group of other distinguished lawyers, including former secretary of defense Clark Clifford and former attorney general Ramsey Clark, distressed at what they perceived as an attack on the independence of the judiciary, assisted behind the scenes.[63] At the same time, the justice sought to demonstrate that he had nothing to hide by offering the subcommittee complete access to his files "whether it concerns Court records, correspondence files, financial matters or otherwise."[64]

An extraordinary coincidence gave Justice Douglas an unusual opportunity to respond from the bench to the charges against him. The Supreme Court declined to hear the appeal of Stephen S. Chandler, an Oklahoma judge who was objecting to the curtailment of his judicial activities by other members of his court because of alleged improper personal conduct. Douglas dissented, saying that a judge had the right to live his own life off the bench. "Federal judges," he wrote, "are entitled, like other people, to the full freedom of the First Amendment."[65]

Douglas was not the only member of the Court to recognize the gravity of the situation. His longtime staunch ally on the bench, Hugo Black, was apprehensive and agitated. He told a group of southern conservatives, "I have known Bill Douglas for thirty years. He's never knowingly done any improper, unethical or corrupt thing. Tell his detractors that in spite of my age, I think I have one trial left in me. Tell them that if they move against Bill Douglas, I'll resign from the Court and represent him. It will be the biggest, most important case I ever tried."[66] Of course, if the Nixon administration had known of Black's intentions, it would have been thrilled. Yet another liberal justice vacating his seat on the Supreme Court seat as a result of the Douglas impeachment effort would have been an unexpected bonus.

Emanuel Celler's subcommittee proceeded to examine each of Ford's charges of misconduct by Douglas. The subcommittee requested and received information from Gerald Ford and a variety of federal agencies, including the Department of Justice, the IRS, and the SEC, as well as the Parvin Foundation and the Center for the Study of Democratic Institutions. Committee staff visited the Parvin Foundation offices in Los Angeles and the center's headquarters in Santa Barbara and also visited the offices of a small Chicago organization hostile to Douglas that called itself the Citizen's Committee to Clean Up Our Courts.[67] Inundated with material, the subcommittee extended the deadline for its investigation, first by another sixty days and ultimately by an additional month before writing a report.

Whether Chairman Cellar was trying to dampen interest in the inquiry or merely seeking to be thorough, public attention shifted significantly between the time that Congressman Ford made his charges in mid-April and the time the subcommittee announced it was extending its investigation two months later. In the interim, the United States had invaded Cambodia, intense domestic reaction had led to the shooting of students by National Guard troops at Kent State University in Ohio, and continued public debate over the war in Southeast Asia had turned ugly. New York City construction workers used their hard hats to pummel student war protestors as police looked on passively. Six days later Nixon praised the construction workers' patriotism as he accepted a hard hat from their union president. In the face of such events and the contentious 1970 congressional election campaigns that thereafter began to heat up, complaints about an errant Supreme Court justice slipped off center stage.

Rifkind nevertheless responded to Ford's charges with an effective defense of Douglas. He first sent Celler a twelve-page legal memorandum asserting, "There is nothing in the Constitution or in the uniform practice under the Constitution to suggest that federal judges may be impeached for anything short of criminal conduct."[68] Subsequently, pointing out that Douglas had provided voluminous documentation covering every charge against him, Rifkind proceeded to dispute each count in turn. He called the attack on *Points of Rebellion* "not only profoundly subversive of the First Amendment, but . . . based upon an inexcusable distortion of what the Justice actually wrote." The book, Rifkind insisted, was "a patriotic call for our democratic processes to meet the challenges of the day so as to pull the rug from under the small minority advocating violent rebellion.[69]

Rifkind disparaged Ford's complaints about Douglas's magazine articles. He pointed out that Douglas had not authorized *Points of Rebellion*'s publisher, Random House, to reprint excerpts in *Evergreen*. Random House had made those arrangements entirely on its own. Likewise, Douglas had had nothing to do with the location of the article in *Evergreen*, much less its placement next to erotic photographs. Furthermore, Douglas had never had contact with Ginzburg and thus had no reason to recuse himself from cases involving Ginzburg. When he gave his folksinging article to an *Avant Garde* editor, he had no reason to know that the magazine had any connection to Ginzburg.[70]

Charges that Douglas engaged in the practice of law while on the Court lacked any merit, Rifkind declared. Parvin Foundation documents that Douglas was accused of drafting had been prepared by a Los Angeles attorney. Remarks made as a director of a foundation in response to personal attacks or proposals before the board were not "the practice of law" forbidden to judges.[71]

As for Douglas's receipt of compensation for his foundation service, Rifkind pointed out that it had ample precedent. He slyly pointed to the compensated service of the two new Republican-appointed justices, Warren Burger and Harry Blackmun, on the board of the Mayo Clinic Foundation. The Parvin Foundation, he went on to say, spent all its income on worthy causes: fellowship programs at Princeton and UCLA and efforts to improve literacy in the United States and in Latin America. Douglas's associates on the Parvin Foundation board of directors included the president of Princeton University, a former president of the University of Chicago, and a Pulitzer Prize–winning journalist. Rifkind ridiculed allegations of Albert Parvin's connections with "the international gambling fraternity," pointing out that he was a nationally known interior designer and custom furniture supplier who did business in Las Vegas, had temporarily owned a hotel there, and subsequently held a mortgage on it. Furthermore, Douglas had no connection with any of Parvin's Las Vegas interests.[72]

Rifkind characterized the Center for the Study of Democratic Institutions as "one of the free world's great academic institutions." Douglas had participated in its activities, but so had Chief Justices Warren and Burger, Nixon cabinet members, senators, and representatives. Douglas had received the same compensation as had these others for participation in seminars and symposia.[73]

Rifkind dismissed lesser charges against Douglas in similar fashion. He concluded that he found it disquieting that by means of misstatements and illogical insinuations in a major congressional speech Ford had unjustifiably impugned the integrity of an associate justice of the Supreme Court. He suggested that those who had attacked Douglas should heed the ABA ethical canon directing that "a lawyer shall not knowingly make false accusations against a judge."[74]

The response of Douglas's lawyer to the charges upon which a call for his client's impeachment was based drew no direct rebuttal from either Gerald Ford or any of the justice's other congressional critics. Rifkind's letter to Celler made clear that Douglas would not follow Fortas's example and simply retire from the Court. Instead, he would seek to refute the charges against him and would use every opportunity to point out similar conduct by federal officials on the other side of the partisan divide.

Meanwhile, Ford began paying a price for his assault on Douglas. Yale Law School professor Fred Rodell had been one of Ford's teachers as well as a student and then a colleague of Douglas. He remained in contact with both men. Immediately after Ford's congressional speech calling for an impeachment investigation, the *New York Times* published a Rodell letter labeling the impeachment proposal an "obviously vengeful and basically absurd effort." If, as Ford had said, Douglas should be impeached for failing the same ethical test as Haynsworth and Carswell, then it logically followed that Ford should also call for the impeachment of the two failed nominees, who remained on federal appellate courts. "Ford's failure to do so while he badgers Justice Douglas lays bare not only the strictly political motivation of his move but also the blatant and patent intellectual dishonesty of my old student."[75] The *Times* underscored Rodell's caustic remarks by quoting them in a news story on the evolving impeachment controversy.[76]

In the summer of 1970 Rodell wrote to Ford, upset that Billy James Hargis of the Christian Crusade had joined the campaign against Douglas. Hargis, a Tulsa radio evangelist who had earlier embraced Robert Welch's scathing attacks on Earl Warren, was again asserting that a justice was procommunist. Rodell was offended and pleaded to Ford, "Won't you at least disown this sort of garbage and the support of hate-mongers like Hargis—and do it publicly. After all, you started it (or didn't you?—I've long suspected Mitchell goosed you into it)." The Yale professor concluded by expressing concern for the effect of the Douglas impeachment effort on Ford himself. "Politics may be politics," Rodell advised his former student, "but this sort of filth degrades a decent guy like you and ruins your image and reputation forever."[77]

Ford appeared stung by his old professor's remarks. He disavowed any association with Hargis but said he did not want to give him the publicity that a denunciation would provide. As for Douglas, Ford assured Rodell, "I have made my convictions clear. You have the right to disagree but not to question my sincerity, as I do not question yours."[78]

Rodell responded to Ford in his characteristically blunt fashion:

> I really find it hard to believe that you personally think Douglas's outside activities come even close to warranting impeachment. The publication of articles entirely handled by his agent, the few phrases taken way out of context from his new book, and the fact that his activities for an international charitable and useful foundation may in part be subsidized through investments that neither you nor I nor he would make for ourselves—all these add up to an absurdly inadequate ground for kicking off the Court one of the ablest Justices in all our history.

Rodell noted that Douglas had recently gotten a standing ovation at the American Bar Association annual meeting and advised Ford that if that was the reaction of the nation's most conservative lawyers, the attack on Douglas was not likely to get support outside the administration.[79]

Undeterred by evidence that the impeachment campaign against Douglas was exacting a cost, Ford reentered the fray in early August. He criticized what he regarded as the slow pace of Celler's subcommittee investigation, charging it with being a "whitewash" and a "travesty." The minority leader called for the subcommittee to hold public hearings with witnesses testifying under oath. Celler responded by saying that the CIA and the departments of State and Justice had not yet provided information requested six weeks earlier. If the forthcoming information were to show that public hearings were warranted, they would of course be held. Ford tried to characterize the Judiciary Committee chairman's statement as a commitment to public hearings, but of course Cellar had left himself plenty of escape routes, as might be expected. With congressional elections fast approaching, it appeared that both sides were maneuvering for political advantage.[80]

Ford had come to recognize that the outcome of the Douglas investigation would largely hinge on what the subcommittee accepted as its definition of an impeachable offense. On this matter, as on so many others, the language of the Constitution was cryptic and less than crystal clear. Ford's initial venture into defining an impeachable offense in his April 15 speech to Congress had drawn sharp criticism, but no alternative formulation seemed to have won general acceptance either. Therefore the minority leader decided to try again.

Ford gave Celler's subcommittee a legal memorandum prepared by Detroit attorneys Bethel Kelley and Daniel Wyllie buttressing the minority leader's April 15 characterization of an impeachable offense as whatever Congress determined it to be at the moment.[81] Kelley and Wyllie looked at congressional and scholarly debates on the issue as well as at records of the nine congressional impeachment proceedings against federal judges. After dismissing the 1804 case of insane John Pickering as having no value as precedent, Kelley and Wyllie pointed to Luther Martin's successful defense of Samuel Chase as based on the argument that an indictable offense was required to meet the standard of "high crimes and misdemeanors." No indictable offense, no high crime, Martin had maintained. However, Kelley and Wyllie noted, Congress had impeached and removed judges James Peck, Robert Archbald, and Halsted Ritter for offenses that violated "good behavior" but were not indictable crimes. If indictable offenses were required for impeachment, Kelley and Wyllie contended, the founders would have provided an alternative means of removing judges deemed to violate good behavior without committing a criminal offense.

Kelley and Wyllie went on to argue that the design of the impeachment process itself demonstrated that it possessed a broader purpose than just a response to an indictable offense. If violations of criminal law by public officials had been the only concern, they asserted, the framers could have devised much simpler methods for removing the offender. The complexity and cumbersome nature of impeachment suggested that it was intended to guarantee fairness in dealing with conduct outside the purview of the criminal law. Additionally, limiting the consequences of impeachment to removal from office and disqualification from further officeholding indicated that the framers' intentions were primarily protective of the society rather than punitive of the individual. If the aim of judicial impeachment was to maintain public confidence in the courts, as Kelley and Wyllie believed, then it must apply to all misbehavior that cast doubt on the integrity and impartiality of the federal judiciary. They underscored their point by quoting Representative Hatton Summers, a House manager of the 1936 Halsted Ritter impeachment. Summers said, "Where a judge on the bench, by his own conduct, arouses a substantial doubt as to his judicial integrity he commits the highest crime that a judge can commit under the Constitution."[82]

Finally, Kelley and Wyllie found significance in the fact that there was no appeal from the decision of Congress in an impeachment proceeding. It was the conscience of Congress, they said, that determines whether an official's behavior warranted impeachment. Although perhaps stated more elegantly, Kelley's and Wyllie's conclusion was nevertheless the same as Ford's: Grounds for impeachment were whatever Congress at the moment determined them to be.

Simon Rifkind found the argument wanting. Douglas's attorney contended that "Mr. Ford's definition of an 'impeachable offense' means that judges serve at the pleasure of Congress. This is so utterly destructive of the principles of an independent judiciary and the separation of powers that I could not believe that convincing historical support could be found for so radical a proposition." The Kelley and Wyllie memorandum, Rifkind said, only served to convince him that

"Mr. Ford's view is historically and legally as untenable as it is mischievous." Rifkind thought that the Ford proposition had been laid to rest with the unsuccessful attempt to impeach Justice Chase in 1805. "But, the notion persists, and is so radically subversive of cherished American principles—separation of powers, the independence of the judiciary, freedom of speech, and the impermissibility of *ex post facto* determinations—that it must not be allowed to prevail."[83]

The dispute over what constituted an impeachable offense was not settled in the course of the Douglas investigation. The loose definition offered by Ford and the more narrowly drawn standard endorsed by Rifkind continued to be contested years later. Conservatives who embraced the Ford position when applying it to William O. Douglas by and large would find it unpalatable when employed against Richard Nixon. Liberals who disparaged Ford's broad definition in the case of Douglas became more comfortable with it in dealing with Nixon. The positions of both sides would change again years later when Bill Clinton came under scrutiny. The origins of the dispute lay in the uncertain language of the Constitution itself, but partisan applications of the impeachment power were just as responsible for the inconsistent positions of the late twentieth century.

Although Republicans appeared ready in the spring of 1970 to make Douglas a major issue in the autumn congressional elections, they did not proceed to do so. Stymied by the failure of Emanuel Celler's subcommittee to complete its work, Douglas's critics were unable to obtain a vote on impeachment before House members went home to campaign. Perhaps sensing that the issue was lost, Ford never once mentioned the justice as he asked voters in his conservative Grand Rapids, Michigan, district to reelect him.[84]

In early December, Celler's special subcommittee voted 3–1 that no grounds existed for impeaching Justice Douglas. The subcommittee's Democratic majority expressed full agreement point by point with Simon Rifkind's defense of the justice. The two Republicans on the subcommittee divided. Edward Hutchinson, the dissenter in the subcommittee vote, declared that hearings should be held and sworn testimony taken before a decision was reached. William McCulloch chose to abstain, saying that not enough evidence had been presented to conclude whether an impeachable offense had been committed. Chairman Celler, on the other hand, declared it "the most exhaustive inquiry I've known of during my 48 years in Congress." The full Judiciary Committee concurred with the subcommittee recommendations less than two weeks later.[85]

Douglas did not believe his ordeal was over, however. He gloomily predicted that "once a person becomes a target of Nixon he continues to be a target no matter what he does or how many times a jury comes in with a verdict of Not Guilty." He told Rifkind,

> The only good thing I see coming out of it is that not one of the five said I should be impeached. Three exonerated me and the others in effect thought

more should be done. It is the latter which is the ominous part because I am sure Nixon, Agnew, Mitchell and Ford put tremendous pressure on McCulloch and Hutchinson of the subcommittee to leave the matter open. The Administration has its eye on my seat. They want me off, and I am sure they are going to try very hard to get a new committee and get hearings going.[86]

By November 1973, when he surpassed the record of Justice Stephen Field for longest service on the Court, Douglas had mellowed somewhat. He mused, "Government service is not all rosy" and recalled, "Long ago the John Birch Society in Yakima, Washington called me the only known Communist in the country and they dubbed me William Zero Douglas." He then turned more reflective, saying,

I learned long ago the secret of government; the mucilage—the thing that holds us all together—is good will. We are all in a very fragile bark that travels on high and dangerous seas. We have in this country a brave experiment in liberty—an experiment that is unique in history and that lifts the hearts of people everywhere. There are few places in the world where the opposition can denounce the powers-that-be without suffering penalties. For the Republic to survive we must all practice charity.[87]

Ford declared himself "disappointed but not surprised" with the outcome of the Celler investigation that, he said, was not "vigorously pursued or objectively evaluated." He said, "It makes a mockery of the constitutional duty of Congress to attempt to end a matter of such importance to the American people and to the integrity of the Supreme Court of the United States without one public hearing or a single word of sworn testimony." For the moment, he declared, "I can only say that this matter is far from finished." The House minority leader went on to say, "The sentiment of House members, both Democrats and Republicans, is not accurately reflected in the subcommittee's vote."[88] He was unable, however, to offer any concrete evidence that the body actually held views contrary to those expressed by Celler's subcommittee that no grounds existed for impeaching Douglas.

Perhaps a better measure of Ford's understanding of his colleagues' stance on Douglas was his unwillingness to resume the impeachment campaign a few weeks later when the next Congress convened.[89] Congressmen Louis Wyman of New Hampshire, Joe Waggoner, Jr., of Louisiana, Robert Sikes of Florida, and William Scott of Virginia, all of whom had been deeply involved in the previous year's effort, cosponsored a new impeachment resolution in 1971, but this time they went forward without Ford's endorsement.[90] Lacking leadership support, the impeachment effort soon withered. Most members of Congress appeared to agree with Representative Donald Fraser of Minnesota, who declared that the investigation of Douglas had been "exceptionally thorough" and had found no "creditable evidence" warranting impeachment. To proceed further, Fraser concluded, "could impair the independence of the Judiciary."[91]

The effects of the effort to impeach Douglas proved significant, but for the moment at least they were largely invisible. The most consequential effect of the episode may have been the education it provided to members of the House of Representatives about the issues and procedures of impeachment, making them aware of the contentious issue of what constitutes an impeachable offense as well as of the political and constitutional consequences of launching an impeachment effort. In addition, the Douglas impeachment campaign altered the trajectories of Douglas himself, the Nixon administration, Ford, and, perhaps most profoundly, the work of the Court in the years thereafter. The subtle effect on the Court of the attack on Douglas in terms of decisions soon to come still reverberates, testifying to the fact that by 1970 impeachment had assumed an important role in American political culture.

Justice Douglas had been giving serious thought to retirement just prior to the initiation of the impeachment effort against him. On June 3, 1968, he had collapsed while the Court was hearing an oral argument and had been rushed to Walter Reed Army Hospital. Doctors diagnosed a heart arrhythmia and implanted a battery-powered pacemaker in his chest. While he convalesced at Walter Reed, he also underwent prostate surgery. Having passed his seventieth birthday, facing increasingly uncertain health, and from time to time manifesting depression, he told friends, colleagues, and his secretaries early in 1970 that the current term would be his last.[92] By April, however, Douglas had definitely changed his mind. He would remain in office and fight Ford's charges rather than take a step that might give the appearance of acknowledging guilt.

Douglas's feisty, iconoclastic personality led him to conclude that he must remain on the bench to vindicate himself. His acute awareness of the disgrace that had shrouded Abe Fortas upon his departure from the Court the year before no doubt reinforced his determination to stay. Thus the calculations of the Nixon administration that the threat of impeachment could drive justices from the Supreme Court cut both ways. Fortas bowed to the pressure, but Douglas, on the verge of resignation, responded by resolving to remain. He would cling tenaciously to his Court seat even after suffering a debilitating stroke on New Year's Eve, 1974. He did, in fact, outlast the Nixon administration, though, ironically, his eventual reluctant departure from the Court in 1975 after his health deteriorated further gave Douglas's nemesis Gerald Ford the opportunity to name his replacement.

If Ford's 1970 impeachment effort had succeeded or if, alternatively, it had not been undertaken and Douglas had resigned, Richard Nixon would have gained a fifth Supreme Court seat to fill. Nixon, under those circumstances, would have been able to name a majority of the Court during his first term. He would have become the first president to make so many first-term appointments since William Howard Taft named six justices during his single term sixty years earlier and only the second since George Washington nominated the original Court. Nixon would have gained another of the historical bragging rights he seemed to so love and, far more important, an even larger measure of influence with the high court. Assuredly, he would have chosen a justice more conservative than Douglas, as he did in selecting replacements for liberal Hugo Black and moderate John Marshall Harlan when failing health caused them both to resign in September 1971. Nixon's choices for the Court, Lewis Powell and William Rehnquist, turned out to be significantly more conservative than Ford's nominee to succeed Douglas in 1975, John Paul Stevens. If given another chance to reshape the Court, Nixon might well have moved it further to the right.

By using the threat of impeachment against justices Fortas and Douglas, the Nixon administration did more harm to itself than merely achieving a mixed result. In the effort to drive two liberal justices from the Court, the administration had investigated their extrajudicial affairs to an unprecedented degree. In passing along information on Fortas to Chief Justice Warren and on Douglas to Ford, Nixon's subordinates altered both the standards and the practices for evaluating members of the Court. The first two subjects of this expanded scrutiny were both nominees to replace Abe Fortas, and neither Clement Haynsworth nor G. Harrold Carswell stood up well under close examination. Once begun in the attempt to drive Fortas and Douglas from the Court, the more probing examination of judicial nominees, and soon other potentially impeachable officials, would become unceasing.

The charges levied against the two Supreme Court justices early in the Nixon administration may well have had an additional impact. The Fortas and Douglas cases provided the only experiences with the threat of impeachment in their political lifetime for those high in the executive branch. As they considered how the case against the two justices had proceeded, administration officials could understandably conclude that the principal danger from impeachment stemmed from succumbing to demands for resignation. Impeachment seemed a serious threat not to those who, like Douglas, stood up to it but only to those who, like Fortas, fled the prospect of a difficult confrontation. For the resolute, it seemed, impeachment hardly posed a danger.

Ford both gained and lost from his campaign against Douglas. He earned credit with Nixon as a loyal partisan, a considerable advantage when Nixon was compelled to select a replacement for Vice President Agnew in 1973. On the other hand, Ford, perhaps unfairly, carried the burden of being identified as the originator of a misguided and petty attack on Douglas. When Nixon nominated Ford for vice president in 1973 after Agnew's resignation, the House minority leader's judgment was questioned because of his pursuit of Douglas. Finally and ironically, when Ford became president, his only opportunity to make an appointment to the Supreme Court occurred when Douglas was finally forced by illness to resign in 1975. If Douglas had left the Court in 1970 before then House minority leader Ford's impeachment initiative made the justice determined to stay and fight or if, on the other hand, Congressman Ford had been successful in driving Douglas from the Court, President Ford never would have been able to name anyone to the Supreme Court.

Finally, the Douglas impeachment may well have affected the inner workings of the Court in one of the most consequential cases of the Nixon era, *Roe v. Wade*. Even though Justice Douglas eluded those who sought to impeach him, their charges and the uproar they stirred left an impression on the new chief justice, Warren Burger. As a result, Douglas's voice and his bold constitutional views would be muted when the time came to decide and explain *Roe*.

The *Roe* decision grew directly out of the earlier 1965 case of *Griswold v. Connecticut,* a pathbreaking case in the area of sexual privacy rights. Justice Douglas had written the Court's opinion in *Griswold,* overruling Connecticut's statute prohibiting doctors from prescribing and married couples from using condoms or other birth-control devices. Douglas made a strong, simple, and straightforward argument that government had no right to intrude on individual sexual choices. His opinion justifying the Court's decision conceded that the Constitution did not directly mention a right of personal privacy, but he held that emanating from its enumerated guarantees was "a penumbra" of additional rights. Various provisions of the Constitution, he wrote, specifically the First Amendment guarantee of a right of free association, the Third Amendment protection against having to quarter troops in one's home, the Fourth Amendment prohibition of "unreasonable search and seizure," the Fifth Amendment right against "compulsory self-incrimination," the Ninth Amendment's promise that the Constitution's enumeration of certain rights "shall not be construed to deny or disparage others retained by the people," and the Fourteenth Amendment's guarantee of due process of law, collectively implied a right of personal privacy from intrusive government. Such privacy certainly included the most intimate of personal matters.[93] The *Griswold* decision soon became the basis for other Court rulings protecting personal privacy in interracial marriage, premarital use of contraception, and abortion.

When *Roe v. Wade* and its companion case *Doe v. Bolton* came before the Supreme Court, Douglas initially seemed destined to write the opinion. *Roe* and *Doe* were first argued in December 1971 before a reduced Court, Black's and Harlan's recently vacated seats not yet having been filled. In conference, most of the remaining justices agreed that the Texas law being challenged in *Roe* was unconstitutional, with only Byron R. White and Burger arguing otherwise. The justices were more closely divided over the Georgia statute in *Doe*. Only Douglas, Brennan, Potter Stewart, and Marshall, a bare majority of the seven sitting justices, agreed that the Georgia law, which permitted abortion when a woman's life or health was threatened by her pregnancy, should be struck down. Burger, White, and Blackmun either disagreed or did not commit themselves.

By Court custom, when the chief justice was not aligned with the majority, the senior associate justice in the majority, in this case Douglas, would assign someone from the majority to draft an opinion. Though some of his law clerks believed otherwise, Douglas most probably would have assigned the case to himself.[94] Chief Justice Burger nevertheless moved quickly to announce that he was asking Blackmun to write a legal memorandum that would command a majority in both cases, in effect a preliminary opinion. When Douglas angrily objected, Burger claimed that since *Roe* and *Doe* were joined and he was in the majority in *Roe,* he had the right to make the assignment.[95] Believing that Burger had actually been on the other side, Douglas could only mutter, "Burger would never have dared pull that if Hugo [Black] were around."

This was neither the first nor the last time that the chief justice would position himself in the majority not because he shared its view of a case but, rather, in order to gain the opportunity to assign the opinion. In response to Douglas's memo objecting to the assignment, Burger simply pointed out that, as they all knew, with two new justices soon to take their seats a four-member majority could become a minority. Any opinion would stand or fall on its merits. It would be well, he suggested, if each justice put his thoughts on the case in writing.[96] Of course, given the burdens on the justices, the one with the principal assignment was most likely to give the task the most attention, and so the pendulum swung to Blackmun.

The internal Court maneuvering on *Roe v. Wade* was complicated, but it appears that Douglas wanted to write the majority decision and Burger took the opportunity away from him. Burger, who had joined the Court just after the attack on Fortas and shortly before the assault on Douglas, clearly viewed the latter as stained, not vindicated, by the resolution of the impeachment issue. The politically sensitive chief justice was clearly concerned that the *Roe* and *Doe* decisions would be controversial and would probably lead to severe criticism of the Court. Burger indicated to Blackmun that he was concerned with the impact of the abortion decision on the Court's image. He concluded that it would be better not to have the decision closely identified with a justice who had recently been threatened with impeachment, worse yet one charged with, among other things, being a sexual libertine.[97] When Powell and Rehnquist joined the Court and the abortion cases were reargued, Burger reaffirmed the assignment as Blackmun's.

Roe v. Wade was indeed bound to be controversial, and it is easy to imagine the decision turning out very differently if written by Justice Douglas. It would probably have drawn even more heavily on the *Griswold* privacy argument and held that abortion was simply not the government's business. Since Douglas and several other justices in the majority were sensitive to the government's responsibility to protect a fetus when it reached the stage of potential viability, his opinion would have needed to achieve some balance of maternal and fetal rights. However, it might well have struck a sharp contrast to the eventual *Roe v. Wade* opinion with its focus on the right of physicians to employ individual judgment in the practice of medicine. Blackmun's cautious and nuanced approach used medical evidence to devise a rigid formula for allowing increased government intervention with each passing trimester of a pregnancy. A libertarian Douglas opinion in *Roe* might not have secured the seven votes that Blackmun's eventually did, but it certainly would have reshaped the ensuing abortion debate. Burger's action to ensure that Douglas would not write the *Roe v. Wade* decision in light of the effort to impeach him demonstrates that the constitutional process for removing a judge from the bench need not be successful to be influential.

5

Impeachment as Discretionary:
The Case of Spiro Agnew

The Nixon administration's experience with impeachment did not end with the cases it helped advance against Justices Fortas and Douglas. Indeed, those cases of potential judicial impeachment would soon be so overshadowed as to be largely disregarded subsequently: In 1973–1974 the country would experience a singularly concentrated period of impeachment activity—in fact, the most intense such era in American history. The threat of forced removal would provoke two executive resignations within ten months. As a result, the Nixon administration would give a new impeachment-related twist to the old adage that it is better to give than to receive. With the purpose and process of impeachment becoming better understood by legislators, journalists, and the general public, the previous hesitancy to employ it began to evaporate. By the end of the Nixon administration, the age of impeachment would be in full swing.

The first case of possible impeachment to result from the multiple political scandals of the early 1970s did not involve the individual who presided over them, President Richard M. Nixon. Rather, the first impeachment embroiled his vice president, Spiro T. Agnew. Ironically, Agnew was never directly implicated in the complex of misdeeds labeled Watergate that became inextricably linked in the public's mind with justified impeachment. Nevertheless, Watergate shaped the extraordinarily rapid response of all branches of the federal government to the exposure of Agnew's unrelated transgressions.

Vice President Agnew achieved the dubious distinction of being the first federal official to request that the House of Representatives impeach him so that he could stand trial before the Senate. Faced with the threat of indictment, he contended that he was immune from judicial action unless first impeached and removed from office. The refusal of the House of Representatives to accept this argument sped Agnew's downfall. Furthermore, the rejection of Agnew's claim reflected and further shaped Congress's overall understanding of impeachment.

Among other things, the Agnew case brought forth the contention that constitutional differences existed between presidents and other federal officials faced with the possibility of criminal indictment or impeachment. Called upon to resolve the issue, House leaders made a decision based more on political pragmatism than on clear constitutional guidelines. The subtle distinctions that the House decided were embedded in the impeachment mechanism were for the most part overlooked as Agnew abruptly departed the scene and the Watergate story continued inexorably to unfold. Nevertheless, the difference between presidential and nonpresidential impeachment articulated in the Agnew case remained etched in subsequent constitutional understanding.

Certainly the Agnew episode serves as a reminder that impeachment can constitute an untimely and inconvenient distraction from other political agendas. Also, it provides a reminder that Congress's choice of whether or not to pursue an impeachment is discretionary and dependent upon a variety of contemporaneous circumstances. Cases never appear predictably or with advanced warning, much less only one at a time. Likewise uncertain is the possibility of alternative resolutions to a perceived need to remove an errant federal official. Innumerable factors end up being taken into account in the decision to impeach or not. Indeed, during the Nixon era the more impeachment came to be discussed, the more opportunities appeared for its employment—though not always exactly as envisioned by the framers of the Constitution or even by the recent instigators of its use against Supreme Court justices. In any case, threatened as well as actual impeachments arise erratically. They are awkward and unwelcome disruptions of the normal course of United States government.

Spiro Agnew's rise and fall on the American national scene served as a barometer for the political climate of the late 1960s and early 1970s. The close political divisions of the day occasioned his entry into national affairs. During the first five years of the Nixon administration, his career advanced because he offered a strident message that captured a spectrum of resentments festering within the culture against civil rights demands, antiwar protests, and the media that bore unwelcome news of these and other discontents. He ultimately fell because, as the political atmosphere changed, he exposed himself as particularly ill suited for a new set of conditions. A storm that broke nearby though not directly overhead was severe enough to claim him as collateral damage.

When faced with choosing a running mate in 1968, Republican presidential candidate Richard Nixon confronted the unnerving fact that his own public opinion surveys showed that anyone he selected could cost him voter support. Polls revealed that if he ran with the leading Republican moderate, New York's governor, Nelson Rockefeller, he would lose votes among conservatives, who could turn to the independent candidate George Wallace. If, on the other hand, he chose the most popular Republican conservative, California's governor, Ronald Reagan, the ticket would fare less well with the moderate Republican and independent middle-of-the-road voters deemed essential to victory. Nixon would be best off, the polls suggested, with no running mate at all. Since that was not possible, Nixon's chances appeared best with the least well-known running mate, as long as he or she seemed plausible in the vice presidency.[1]

Under the circumstances, Nixon turned to the one-term governor of Maryland, Spiro T. Agnew. The son of Greek immigrant parents, Agnew had served in the army in World War II, worked his way through the University of Baltimore Law School, practiced law briefly, and then entered politics. After serving on a suburban board of zoning appeals and as Baltimore County executive, Agnew had easily won the Republican gubernatorial primary in 1966 and then carried the subsequent general election against a strident racial reactionary. Perceived as a moderate Republican because of the circumstances of his election as governor, he strengthened that image by leading an unsuccessful effort to persuade Nelson Rockefeller to run for the 1968 Republican presidential nomination. However, he first gained national prominence by his strident criticism of black leaders during campus protests and rioting in Baltimore following the assassination of Martin Luther King, Jr. Nixon, attracted to a relatively unknown, apparently moderate Republican governor who was echoing his "law and order" campaign message, named Agnew as his running mate after winning the nomination (with Agnew giving the nominating speech) at the 1968 Republican National Convention in Miami.[2]

The estrangement between Nixon and Agnew that would ultimately contribute to the downfall of both men began almost immediately. As much as Nixon enjoyed springing surprises on the country when it suited his purposes, as with the nomination of Agnew or, likewise, his later diplomatic initiative toward the People's Republic of China, he did not like being caught off guard himself. During the fall of 1968, Agnew repeatedly made off-the-cuff remarks that both took Nixon aback and distracted him from his campaign in a tight race for the presidency. Agnew accused the leaders of youth protests of conspiring with communists, labeled Democratic presidential nominee Hubert Humphrey as "squishy soft" on communism, and explained his failure to campaign in inner-city black ghettos by saying, "If you've see one city slum, you've seen them all." In casual remarks, he referred to Poles as "Polacks" and to a Japanese American reporter as "the fat Jap."[3] Nixon defended Agnew, notably in an election-eve telecast, but privately whatever confidence he had in the governor of Maryland was shaken.[4]

Despite public and personal pledges to give Agnew a substantial role in his administration, Nixon kept his vice president at a distance from the outset.[5] Despite having claimed in nominating him that Agnew brought valuable knowledge of local governments' problems to the Republican ticket, Nixon chose not to involve Agnew in a substantive fashion in urban-affairs policy formation. Nixon did give Agnew responsibility for a new Office of Intergovernmental Relations, essentially delegating to him the task of facilitating communication between the administration and state and local governments. However, he quickly grew dissatisfied with the vice president's lackluster performance and his tendency to bring in state and local complaints rather than promote the administration's programs. A White House perception grew that Agnew was basically lazy and preferred comparatively easy travel and speech making to the hard work of policy making. Agnew's thirteen rounds of golf during a month-long Asian trip in 1971 reinforced the perception. As vice presidents often did, Agnew found himself denied direct access to the president and on the periphery of executive branch operations.[6]

Flamboyant speech making served both Agnew's and the White House's interests. Rising unhappiness with the administration's continuation of the Vietnam War generated protests that reached a peak with the National Moratorium on October 15, 1969. Agnew was encouraged by Nixon and was provided language by speechwriter Patrick Buchanan to speak out against the moratorium and its leaders.[7] At a Republican dinner in New Orleans the vice president declared, "A spirit of national masochism prevails, encouraged by an effete corps of impudent snobs who characterize themselves as intellectuals."[8] Agnew condemned educators and students alike as anti-intellectual and accused the moratorium of making common cause with Hanoi. He repeated his condemnations numerous times in the weeks thereafter, on one occasion calling antiwar spokesmen "merchants of hate" and "parasites of passion."[9] Suddenly Agnew was the focus of media attention and the recipient of considerable public support.

Uncompromising disparagement of opponents of the Vietnam War remained a core element of Agnew's increasingly frequent public statements. In the spring of 1970 Nixon ordered an invasion of Cambodia in an effort to eradicate North Vietnamese camps there. American campuses erupted in protest against the widening war. Agnew responded by speaking out even more harshly. Appearing on CBS television's *Face the Nation,* he labeled the protesters "the dissident and destructive elements in our society" and charged that "they are simply utilizing this as a vehicle to continue their antisocial, outrageous conduct." When the Ohio National Guard shot students at Kent State University, Agnew did not relent. Within hours he called the shootings "a tragedy that was predictable."[10]

The wide notice achieved by Agnew's speeches decrying the administration's antiwar critics helped set him off on a series of similarly strident statements about American mass media. In a speech written by Buchanan, approved by Nixon, and delivered in Des Moines, Iowa, on November 13, 1969, Agnew characterized the nation's leading news commentators as a small, parochial, out-of-touch group of snobs invariably hostile to the administration. He decried their "instant analysis" of Nixon's speeches, asserting that they were "prejudiced" and "hostile" and had "made up their minds in advance." Ironically but properly, the press that was the target of his biting comments and striking phrases regularly reported the vice president's remarks. While Agnew's characterizations were often extreme, unsupported by evidence, and contrary to the reality of most journalism, they gained him an additional following.[11]

In 1970 Agnew became a principal voice for the administration. Speaking invitations rolled in at the rate of fifty per day. At Nixon's direction, Agnew played a major role in the midterm congressional campaign. Among other things, he coined a new term for Democrats. He referred to his partisan opponents as radical liberals or, in his term, "radic-libs." At the same time, he kept up his attacks on the press as "nattering nabobs of negativism," on antiwar protesters, and, especially in the South, on the opponents of Supreme Court nominees Clement Haynsworth and G. Harrold Carswell.[12] On occasion Nixon restrained him but generally did not disapprove.[13]

Defining the political contest as a cultural clash, Agnew contributed to an increasingly bitter political climate. His public statements helped foster the sense that there was little common ground on which to forge compromise solutions to disputes over foreign and domestic policies. Agnew's conduct in the 1970 election campaign stirred hostility to the vice president among partisan Democrats, while the Republicans' failure to make significant advances in the midterm elections limited his capital gains within his own party.

As the vice president became the administration's harshest voice, Nixon privately joked that Agnew was his "insurance policy." As the president explained to John Ehrlichman, "No assassin in his right mind would kill me. They know that if they did they would end up with Agnew."[14] Otherwise, Nixon seemed to have little use for Agnew. Press stories began appearing as early as 1970 that Agnew would be replaced on the 1972 Republican ticket. Throughout 1971 and into 1972, Agnew's political fate remained in limbo.[15]

While Agnew's stock may not have been highly valued within the White House, it certainly had risen within the conservative wing of the Republican Party. The groups around William F. Buckley, Jr., William Rusher, and the *National Review* proved to be great Agnew admirers.[16] Barry Goldwater, the iconic leader of the party's conservative faction, expressed enthusiasm for the vice president's speeches. "If Ted Agnew keeps on expressing the sentiments of the vast, overwhelming majority of the American people," the Arizona senator declared, "he may find himself being boomed for President before it's even his turn."[17] Such conservative support proved crucial to the extension of Agnew's vice presidency.

Nixon long toyed with the idea of replacing Agnew with John Connally, the former Texas governor whom he had appointed secretary of the treasury following the 1970 elections and encouraged thereafter to change his party affiliation from Democrat to Republican. But he heard from Goldwater that conservatives would be most unhappy if Agnew was not retained. Early in 1972, faced with the rebellion of some conservative Republicans in the form of a primary challenge for the presidential nomination by Representative John Ashbrook of Ohio, Nixon declared that he wanted Agnew once again to be his running mate.[18] Though he continued to equivocate somewhat until shortly before the party's national convention, Nixon determined to renew his alliance with Agnew.

Though he had no way of knowing the extent to which he was doing so when he chose Agnew for the 1972 Republican ticket, Nixon was binding his second-term fate to that of his vice president. Even though Agnew remained off the main stage, Nixon's embrace of his running mate for a second time implied approval of his conduct as vice president. With Nixon's own fortunes soon to change as his presidency came under unprecedented scrutiny, the linkage of the two men in the public mind would help seal the fate of both. The irony of Agnew's isolation from the inner workings of Nixon's White House would be ignored.

By 1972 the Nixon administration had wrestled for three years with the problems of trying to govern without perceived sympathetic majorities anywhere in the federal government. The president and his close aides viewed the other two constitutional branches of the federal government as unsupportive. Even the executive branch, dominated by civil service holdovers from previous Democratic administrations, seemed to Nixon to be of doubtful reliability. Operating in an atmosphere it considered akin to a state of siege, the Nixon White House adopted tactics that it regarded as appropriate to a hostile political environment.

The Nixon administration had achieved some success in constructing a more congenial judicial branch with the addition of justices Warren Burger and Harry Blackmun to the Supreme Court. Still, Congress remained solidly Democratic. While Congress manifested substantial cooperation in adopting the administration's progressive environmental and social welfare proposals, at the same time it often resisted the administration, rejecting two Court nominees, contesting budget priorities, and advancing an alternative agenda. The president's vexation increased with the failure of the Republicans to gain much ground in the 1970 election after an unusually aggressive effort to do so. The Republican Party had spent heavily and waged a highly contentious campaign, but to little avail.

To circumvent obstacles they perceived within the existing federal apparatus and gain a stronger leadership position, Nixon and his inner circle began taking actions that overstepped accepted bounds. At least at first, these actions were unconcealed. Although Nixon had endorsed substantial increases in federal spending for social welfare, environmental reform, expanded Social Security benefits, and other programs, he remained at odds with more expensive programs offered by the Democrat-dominated Congress. In 1971 he was willing to spend $6 billion to implement the Clean Water Act, but he vetoed the $24 billion approved by Congress. When Congress overrode his veto by more than 4–1 in the Senate and 10–1 in the House, he still refused to accept the legislative judgment. He asserted that the chief executive possessed the constitutional power not to spend funds appropriated by Congress. He would instead "impound" excessive sums in the interests of restraining federal budgets and taxes. Earlier presidents had declined to spend appropriated funds, but Nixon went much further in both the extent and justification of impoundment. During his first term he impounded a total of nearly 20 percent of discretionary expenditures from more than one hundred federal programs.[19] In doing so, he infuriated many members of Congress, who understood that the power of the purse was a central device for shaping government policy and controlling the executive branch.

In 1971 the administration lost a Supreme Court case that Nixon regarded as crucial to his authority, *New York Times v. United States,* the so-called Pentagon Papers case. The Supreme Court rejected the administration's first-ever attempt, on the grounds of national security, to prevent a newspaper from publishing a story. The Court refused to block publication of a lengthy Defense Department study of the Vietnam War prepared late in the Johnson administration and given to the *New York Times* and *Washington Post* by Daniel Ellsberg, one of its compilers.[20] Several of Nixon's senior staff aides reported that he was terribly upset by loss of the Pentagon Papers case.[21] One considered it the push that "caused Nixon to go over the brink, to lose all sense of balance, to defend his privacy at the expense of everyone else's right to privacy, and to create the climate that led to Watergate."[22]

Having failed to retain absolute control over executive branch secrets, receiving little cooperation from the FBI in investigating the matter, and despairing of sympathy from either the Supreme Court or Congress, Nixon ordered the creation of a White House unit to stop news leaks. Labeling themselves the Plumbers, the members of this group first tried to discredit Ellsberg by obtaining information regarding him from an illegal search of the office of Los Angeles psychiatrist Lewis Fielding, whom Ellsberg was consulting after a divorce. The Plumbers also engaged in wiretapping of National Security Council staff members in an attempt to discover the source of other leaks to the *New York Times*, and they discussed, though they did not carry out, a firebombing of the Brookings Institution to recover White House documents allegedly placed in a vault there. Thus, in mid-1971, nearly a year before the Watergate break-in, the course was set that would eventually lead to Nixon's resignation in the face of impeachment. The White House was engaging in illegal clandestine activity paid for with public funds but unknown to Congress and conducted by individuals accountable to no one but the president.[23]

Even though two more of his appointees, Justices Lewis Powell and William Rehnquist, were subsequently added to the Supreme Court late in 1971, Nixon remained uncertain as to whether the Court would support his administration's assertions of authority. At the same time, Nixon and his inner circle of advisers could look back at repeated instances where their secret actions, unsanctioned by Congress or the Court, had gone undetected and achieved success. The 1969–1970 bombing of Cambodia had not caught the public's attention until acknowledged by Nixon himself. Secret diplomacy by the national security adviser, Henry Kissinger, had made possible a presidential visit to China and proved a triumph when finally revealed. The Plumbers' unproductive search for material to use against Ellsberg remained undiscovered. Therefore surreptitious activity continued to appeal to the White House as a means of circumventing congressional, judicial, and even executive branch obstacles. A paradoxical sense of presidential authority and weakness drove the White House to pursue clandestine enterprises to achieve desired ends that might be impossible to gain otherwise.

The approaching 1972 national elections served to increase Nixon's ever-present sense of insecurity. Despite the success of his efforts to reduce the American troop presence in Vietnam and his steps to curry favor with the Soviet Union and the People's Republic of China so as to undermine their support for North Vietnam, Nixon recognized that the Vietnam War remained a rallying point for his political opponents. His own narrow election victory in 1968 had not dislodged the Democrats as the nation's majority party. Convinced that the nation's media were hostile, Nixon could envision a political contest in 1972 that would be as close as both of his previous runs for the White House. In such circumstances, he and his top aides were predisposed to employ surreptitious measures to assure their continuation in office.

During the first six months of 1972 people working for the Committee to Re-Elect the President (soon to be labeled CREEP by its political opponents) repeatedly sought to hamstring various Democrats' campaigns for the presidency. Some of their clandestine efforts were fairly juvenile attempts at campaign sabotage, such as canceling hotel reservations and requests for the installation of telephone banks. While not exactly in keeping with the ideals of a democratic electoral process, these initial, so-called dirty tricks did not do great damage. Far more serious was the forgery and publicizing of a scurrilous letter denigrating the wife of Democratic front-runner Edmund Muskie, a senator from Maine. When the senator was surprised and upset by the letter in the midst of the New Hampshire primary to the point of shedding a few public tears, his campaign went into a tailspin. Disappointed by the New Hampshire primary results and even more by a dismal fourth-place finish in Florida a week later, Muskie, the Democratic candidate who concerned Nixon the most, withdrew from the race. Interfering in such a manner to affect the rival party's selection of its presidential candidate constituted serious ethical misconduct, to say the least. Even more objectionable behavior—indeed, criminal conduct involving breaking and entering as well as illegal electronic surveillance—soon followed.[24]

In the early hours of June 17, 1972, at the complex of modern riverfront office and apartment buildings next to the Kennedy Center for the Performing Arts in Washington, D.C., security guard Frank Wills discovered an access door taped so as to disable its lock. He removed the tape and continued his rounds. Returning later, Wills found the lock taped open once again. Suspicious, he called for police backup. The guard had no way of knowing that his action would set in motion a series of events that would confer celebrity on a pair of young reporters, generate curiosity about a different sort of tape, and end with a president resigning on the verge of impeachment.

The District of Columbia police summoned to the Watergate arrested five men in the offices of the Democratic National Committee. Those apprehended were dressed in suits, were wearing latex surgical gloves, and carried lock-picking devices, cameras, telephone-bugging equipment, and over $2,300 in cash, including thirteen new hundred-dollar bills with consecutive serial numbers. Because electronic eavesdropping violated federal law and elevated the illegal break-in beyond mere burglary, the police asked FBI agents to join the investigation. It would later turn out that the arrested men had been caught on their second venture into Democratic headquarters to install bugging devices. When the five were taken to police headquarters to be booked, an attorney was there claiming to represent them. This struck the police as curious since none of the five had made a phone call to summon such assistance. Clearly the arrested men had accomplices who had escaped detection. What the security guard and police had interrupted appeared on its face to be far more than what the White House would quickly dismiss as "a third-rate burglary."

The FBI quickly obtained warrants and searched the hotel rooms of the arrested men. The search turned up a sealed envelope containing a check written by E. Howard Hunt. Two address books containing Hunt's name and the notations "W. H." and "W. House" were found as well. When Bob Woodward, a young *Washington Post* reporter assigned to cover the arraignment, learned of the discoveries, he called the White House switchboard and found that E. Howard Hunt was on the staff of presidential assistant Charles Colson. When reached, Hunt was notably upset by Woodward's question as to how his name came to be in the Watergate intruders' address books. The arraignment also revealed that four of the five burglars were Cuban, and the fifth was James McCord, chief of security for the Committee to Re-Elect the President and, like the other four men, a onetime CIA employee.

Within days of their apprehension, a connection between the Watergate intruders and the Nixon administration had been established. It would take further investigation, however, by inquisitive and diligent journalists such as Woodward and his colleague Carl Bernstein to discover the nature of the connection. Politicians would need much longer to determine its implications.

Most politicians and journalists paid remarkably little attention to the Watergate story during the summer and fall of 1972. No more than 15 of the 430 accredited reporters in Washington news bureaus worked full-time on the matter.[25] Most accepted the statement of White House press secretary Ronald Ziegler dismissing it as "a third-rate burglary." Nixon himself, asked about Watergate during an August 29 press conference, declared that there had been a full investigation, not only by the FBI and the Justice Department but also by his own legal counsel. John Dean later acknowledged that this claim was a complete fabrication.[26] Nixon asserted, "I can state categorically that this investigation indicates that no one in the White House staff, no one in this administration, presently employed, was involved in this very bizarre incident." He then went on to say, "We are doing everything we can to take this incident and to investigate it and not to cover it up. What really hurts in matters of this sort is not the fact that they occur, because over zealous people in campaigns do things that are wrong. What really hurts is if you try to cover it up." Even though Nixon's Democratic opponent, George McGovern, called this statement "a whitewash," the president's pronouncement seemed to put the matter to rest, at least for the moment.[27] In time, of course, it would be his undoing.

The Committee to Re-Elect the President remained closemouthed about the Watergate break-in, and the intruders themselves, locked up and waiting trial, were absolutely silent. An attempt by the House Banking and Currency Committee and its chairman, Representative Wright Patman, to investigate the sources of the burglars' cash ended in complete frustration.[28] Without easy access to those clearly involved in the Watergate break-in, reporters and politicians focused their attention on more visible stories: the foundering Democratic campaign, negotiations to end the Vietnam War, and the Nixon-Agnew ticket's apparently serene progress toward reelection.

Almost alone, the *Washington Post* continued to devote substantial resources to pursuit of the Watergate break-in. Having published the initial stories by Woodward and Bernstein, *Post* editor Benjamin Bradlee allowed them to persist in their investigation even though most other journalists abandoned the story. During the summer and fall, Woodward and Bernstein spoke repeatedly to low- and midlevel employees at the White House and the Committee to Re-Elect the President. Woodward also cultivated a confidential source at the FBI whom he would only identify as "Deep Throat." Woodward's source, who more than thirty years later would be revealed as Deputy Director W. Mark Felt, was disturbed by the way the White House had been using his agency as well as by having been passed over for the directorship in favor of White House loyalist L. Patrick Gray following the death of J. Edgar Hoover.[29] Felt pointed Woodward in the right direction on the basis of the FBI's confidential investigations. As a result, the *Post* was able to present fact-laden stories about sources of funding for the Watergate burglars that tied them to the Committee to Re-Elect the President.[30]

Nothing discovered by Woodward and Bernstein or the few other reporters devoting serious attention to Watergate served to derail the reelection of Nixon and Agnew. In fact, judged by Nixon's extraordinary victory with 61.3 percent of the national vote, none of the Watergate journalism appeared to have had any effect on the electorate whatsoever. Nevertheless, when the five burglars, together with Howard Hunt and his deputy, G. Gordon Liddy, were brought before federal district judge John C. Sirica on January 10, 1973, the impact of the stories soon became evident.

Hunt and the four Cuban burglars quickly pled guilty to charges of felonious entry. The trial of McCord and Liddy continued, however, with federal prosecutors

"Miraculous — He Can Walk On Mud"

Herblock,
Washington Post,
October 19, 1972.
© The Herb Block
Foundation.

presenting a case narrowly focused on the burglars themselves, although providing substantial evidence that CREEP had funded the criminal acts. The defendants justified their actions as taken to prevent the greater harm of physical threats to CREEP officials. Unpersuaded, the jury on January 30 convicted both men on all counts. Judge Sirica, believing that there was more to the story and willing to draw on his reputation as "Maximum John," the dispenser of long jail terms, to coax the defendants into talking, scheduled their sentencing for March 23.

Judge Sirica's approach bore fruit. On March 20, McCord delivered a letter to the judge disclosing that the defendants had been pressured to remain silent, that perjury had been committed, and that not the CIA but other government officials were involved. McCord, eager to avoid going to jail, was willing to talk further. An exultant Sirica told his law clerk, "This is going to break this case wide open."[31] He proceeded on March 23 to read McCord's letter in open court and then to sentence the other defendants to lengthy jail terms: six to twenty years for Liddy, thirty-five for Hunt, and forty for the four Cubans. Critics of Sirica regarded these heavy terms as intended to compel self-incrimination in violation of Fifth Amendment protections, but Sirica shrugged them off. He had

Firm Stand On Crime

"EXECUTIVE PRIVILEGE" COVER-UP

ADMINISTRATION CORRUPTION

Herblock,
Washington Post,
March 15, 1973.
© The Herb
Block Foundation.

followed the proscribed sentencing limits and simply would weigh cooperation with investigators in a later review of the sentences.

James McCord's Sirica-induced revelations, together with the progress of investigations by federal prosecutors and Senate staff, did help turn the tide of the Watergate investigation. A month and a half earlier the U.S. Senate had established, with bipartisan support, the Senate Select Committee on Presidential Campaign Activities, chaired by Senator Sam Ervin of North Carolina, to examine the financing and conduct of the 1972 election. The Senate Judiciary Committee was interrogating L. Patrick Gray, whose nomination as permanent FBI director Nixon had submitted in mid-February. As soon as McCord's statement became public on March 23, both committees as well as federal prosecutors began to hear from individuals nervous about being caught up in the spreading scandal. The most notable conversion came from the president's legal counsel John Dean, who only days earlier, just after Sirica had received McCord's letter, had warned Nixon, "We have a cancer within, close to the Presidency, that is growing. It is growing daily. It's compounded, growing geometrically now."[32] Efforts to cover up White House involvement in the initial crime were, as Dean had come to see it, compounding the problem.

All of a sudden, the course of the Watergate affair was changing dramatically. Gray, testifying under oath at his Senate confirmation hearings, had worked with White House counsel Dean to limit the FBI investigation to the Watergate break-in itself. Under sharp questioning from Senator Robert C. Byrd, he described how he had kept the White House informed about the investigation. Within days, Gray asked that his stalled nomination be withdrawn, but its damage had already been done.

John Dean, recognizing that Nixon was looking for scapegoats and that he and former attorney general John Mitchell were at the top of the list of possibilities, decided to throw himself on the mercy of Sam Ervin's Senate Select Committee. On April 5, Dean's attorney approached the committee staff to explore cooperating with the investigation, and three days later Dean himself did likewise. When Jeb Magruder of the Committee to Re-Elect the President acknowledged to the White House that he had reached an agreement with federal prosecutors on April 14 to confess his own involvement and to implicate Mitchell and Dean, the president's legal counsel decided to follow suit.

Alerted to Dean's apostasy and confronted by Gray's admission that he had been given files from Howard Hunt's White House safe along with orders to "deep six" them, Nixon on April 27 fired the still-acting FBI director. On April 30 the president moved to limit further damage by announcing that he was firing Dean and accepting the resignations of his two closest associates, H. R. Haldeman and John Ehrlichman, as well as that of John Mitchell's successor as attorney general, Richard Kleindienst.

In early April Kleindienst had endorsed Nixon's claim that conversations between the president and his aides were covered by the principle of executive privilege. He told the Senate that the Constitution's separation of powers among the three branches of the federal government prevented Congress from compelling executive branch officials to testify or provide documents. Unless the president specified otherwise, the attorney general insisted, internal executive branch communications were confidential. Congress's only constitutionally specified remedies, he declared, were to cut off executive branch appropriations or impeach the president. Now, days later, Nixon expressed a growing realization of what had seemed a remote prospect. "My God!" Nixon exclaimed to Haldeman after his aide had raised the possibility, "What the hell have we done to be impeached?"[33]

Nixon might have relaxed a little after one of his regular talks with Henry Peterson, the assistant attorney general heading the Watergate investigation. Peterson said that he had concluded that investigating the president lay beyond the bounds of his authority. If such an inquiry was to be carried out, he told his staff as well as Nixon, it would have to be done by the House of Representatives, the body with the designated constitutional responsibility for impeachment. Such a probe still seemed most unlikely.[34]

With Attorney General Kleindienst's resignation, however, Peterson would have a new supervisor. Nixon, casting around for someone loyal to the administration who would project an image of integrity, quickly settled on Elliot Richardson, the Boston Brahmin he had only three months before appointed secretary of defense. Richardson had earlier served as secretary of health, education, and welfare. At his confirmation hearings to be attorney general, Richardson faced senators increasingly skeptical about the ability of Justice Department lawyers to conduct an adequate investigation of their White House overlords. Richardson felt compelled to agree to a special Watergate prosecutor who, although within the Justice Department, would function with complete independence. Only the attorney general himself would supervise this special prosecutor. Only the attorney general would be able to dismiss him, and then only for commission of "extraordinary improprieties." Richardson then introduced senators to his choice, Harvard law professor and Kennedy administration solicitor general Archibald Cox.[35]

By the time Senator Ervin called the hearings of the Senate Select Committee to order on May 17, public doubts about the president had risen dramatically. Nixon had been reelected six months earlier with over 61 percent of the vote and had still enjoyed a 59 percent approval rating in an early-April Gallup poll. Now, after the accumulating revelations, the firings of Gray and Dean, and the resignations of his closest aides, Nixon retained only 44 percent approval. Forty-five percent of those polled expressed disapproval of the president. For the first time that number outweighed the tally of those who still approved of Nixon. Worse was soon to come.

During the first five weeks of its hearings, with a two-week recess in the middle, the Senate Select Committee heard from a series of witnesses from the Committee to Re-Elect the President. Chairman Ervin and chief counsel Samuel Dash chose not to call witnesses who they knew in advance would claim Fifth Amendment protection against self-incrimination. Nor would they hector witnesses in the manner of some past Senate investigations. Their strategy was to elicit detailed testimony from cooperative witnesses, among them many who knew that testifying might help them avoid prosecution. Visibly contrite CREEP officials laid out before the senators and an increasingly engaged national television audience a persuasive picture of aggressive fund-raising, secretive transfers of funds, payments to the Watergate burglars, and, most telling, the direction of their activities by White House staff. Sharp questions from the committee's Republican minority members, senators Howard Baker of Tennessee, Edward Gurney of Florida, and Lowell Weicker of Connecticut, focused attention on Dean's

Herblock,
Washington Post,
June 26, 1973.
© The Herb
Block Foundation.

culpability, but the overall effect of the first stage of the hearings was to raise questions about broader and higher White House responsibility.[36]

When Dean appeared before the committee on Monday, June 25, the mood of the hearings for the first time became electric. The former White House counsel proved a compelling witness, not merely because of his position close to the president but also because of his assured and unemotional manner, detailed recall, and vivid descriptions. Dean, reading a 245-page prepared statement, quickly put responsibility on Haldeman and Nixon for direction of a sustained effort to cover up the White House connection to the break-ins at Lewis Fielding's office and the Watergate. Dean described a White House that constantly felt beleaguered, distrusted virtually the entire federal government, was obsessed by secrecy, and believed that the president's authority was beyond the limits of law. Perhaps most important, he identified Nixon as an active and well-informed participant in a September 15, 1972, discussion of the cover-up. Since the president had publicly claimed to know nothing of the cover-up before a March 21, 1973, meeting with Dean, this represented a direct challenge to the president's veracity and was an assertion of his complicity. Dean did not waver during the four full days of hard questioning that followed his opening statement, emerging with his credibility intact and the president's increasingly suspect.[37]

After Dean's week of chilling testimony, the committee took an eleven-day recess and then returned to hear John Mitchell. The former attorney general proved to be a hostile witness but nevertheless added to Dean's menacing picture of the White House. Mitchell confirmed Dean's story of G. Gordon Liddy's March 1972 plan for widespread electronic surveillance as well as disruption of the Democratic campaign. He then went on to talk about what he labeled "the White House horrors." His accounting of improper activities included not only those of the Plumbers but also surreptitious investigations of Senator Edward Kennedy, the forging of documents to fix blame on President Kennedy for the assassination of South Vietnamese president Ngo Dinh Diem, plans to firebomb the Brookings Institution, and other abuses of executive power. In three days of testimony, Mitchell managed to convey both his loyalty to Nixon and an image of administration misdeeds that extended far beyond Watergate.[38]

Turning its attention to the White House itself, the Ervin committee repeated its practice of starting with lower-level staff and working upward. They had barely started with Haldeman aide Gordon Strachen when an astonishing and pivotal revelation occurred. On the afternoon of July 16, the quizzing of Strachen was interrupted so that a surprise witness could testify before the committee and the television cameras. Alexander Butterfield, another Haldeman deputy who only four months earlier had left the White House to become head of the Federal Aviation Administration, had been expected to provide information about the day-to-day operation of the White House. Under questioning by committee staff members three days earlier, however, he had revealed that a tape-recording system had been installed in the president's offices and other locations so that all his private conversations could be recorded. Suddenly an oft-repeated question that committee vice chairman Howard Baker had crafted to defend Nixon and discount stories about what others had done could presumably be answered. The tapes could determine "What did the president know and when did he know it?" What had begun as a device to distance Nixon from the actions of his subordinates now became the central reason for both the Ervin committee and Special Prosecutor Cox to argue that they needed access to the tapes.

After the existence of the White House tapes stood revealed, the committee continued to take testimony, some of which inflicted further damage on the president. A battle over access to the tapes, however, became the central and most contentious issue between Nixon, on the one hand, and the Senate Select Committee and the special prosecutor, on the other. Herbert Kalmbach, the president's personal attorney, and others confirmed the payment of "hush money" to the Watergate burglars. Haldeman and Ehrlichman followed with spirited defenses of their conduct and of the president's, but when Haldeman revealed that he had listened to some of the White House tapes in preparing his testimony, he infuriated the Ervin committee. Its members were offended by the president's willingness to give his ex-assistant access to the tapes but deny the Senate a chance to hear the same recordings.[39]

After the president's closest aides completed their testimony, the committee proceeded through August and September to hear a variety of further but less potent witnesses, ranging from CIA officials to confessed Watergate burglar Howard Hunt to presidential speechwriter Patrick Buchanan. Neither the additional details provided nor the scathing condemnation of the committee unleashed by Buchanan altered the basic picture of substantial illegal conduct painted by earlier witnesses. Nothing could divert attention from the prospect of the tapes resolving the question of Nixon's own involvement in the illegal conduct that had been exposed. As long as the matter of the tapes remained in the background, shocking revelations about Vice President Agnew would only distract the nation momentarily.

As soon as the Republican ticket won its massive 1972 reelection landslide, Spiro Agnew ceased being an asset to Richard Nixon and became a burden. Although not at all a member of the president's inner circle, Agnew was, paradoxically, almost as central to the public image of the administration as the president himself. A week after the polls closed Nixon voiced his disenchantment with Agnew during a protracted conversation at Camp David with Haldeman and Ehrlichman. The president expressed doubts to his aides about Agnew as his successor, disparaging the vice president's energy and leadership. He ordered that Agnew be relieved of responsibility for intergovernmental relations and be put in charge of planning for the U.S. bicentennial celebration, a far less sensitive and substantive responsibility as well as one that would keep the vice president at a distance.[40] Nixon may not have known so at the time, but within a few months he would begin to discover how much of a problem Agnew represented.

On January 15, the day that the trial of the Watergate burglars commenced in Washington, Baltimore businessman Lester Matz conferred with his attorney about a federal grand jury subpoena duces tecum (subpoena of documents) for financial records from his engineering firm. The local U.S. attorney, George Beall, was rumored to be looking into possible kickback schemes involving Baltimore County's executive, Dale Anderson. Matz's attorney advised him to make a clean breast of such payments, certain that Beall would grant his client immunity from prosecution in return for testimony against higher-ups. Matz then explained that his payments had gone not only to Anderson but also to his predecessor as county executive, Spiro Agnew. Matz had continued to hand Agnew envelopes of cash in Annapolis when he moved on to be governor of Maryland and even in his White House office after he became vice president of the United States. Stunned, the attorney advised caution and delay.[41]

Not yet knowing what Matz had to say, Beall continued his pursuit of Dale Anderson, assuring Agnew's former Baltimore law partner George White on February 1 and Attorney General Richard Kleindienst on February 9 that Agnew was not a target of his investigation. White nevertheless reported to Agnew on February 3 that federal prosecutors were examining possible corruption involving some of his associates during the years he served as Baltimore County executive and governor of Maryland. An obviously nervous Agnew soon reacted. On February 12 Kleindienst informed Beall that Agnew was complaining about being investigated and wanted it stopped. Beall began revising his thinking. When he told his three assistants what the attorney general had said, one observed that Agnew was "acting like a guilty man."[42]

As Beall's investigation moved forward, some of its lesser targets began to offer cooperation in return for reduced charges. By mid-May, as the Ervin committee's Watergate hearings were beginning, the Washington Post carried a major story about the Baltimore County corruption probe and "widespread rumors" that Agnew was involved. Within days, Matz and his business partner John Childs decided the time had come to talk to the prosecutors. After a month of negotiations with Beall's staff, they confessed to making cash payments to Agnew as governor and as vice president.[43]

Three weeks later, Jerome Wolff, a lawyer, civil engineer, and former Agnew-appointed director of the Maryland State Road Commission, corroborated and amplified the Matz and Childs story. Wolff also provided explanations and, to the particular delight of the prosecutors, extensive documentation of how the kickback scheme had worked. Together with Matz and Childs, Wolff gave the prosecutors solid evidence of vice presidential corruption.[44]

After his February conversations with Attorney General Kleindienst, Beall had not shared news of the developments in the investigation with the Justice Department in Washington, fearing that he and his colleagues would lose control of the case. Agnew, however, notified Haldeman of Wolff's discussions with Beall, said the information would make him look bad, and sought White House intervention with Beall. By April 14 the information had been shared with Ehrlichman and Nixon.[45] Yet when Elliot Richardson became attorney general, he was not filled in by either Kleindienst or the White House, perhaps because the spreading Watergate scandal had by then cost Haldeman and Ehrlichman their jobs. A conversation with Beall on June 12 first provided Richardson with a general picture of the Baltimore corruption probe and a brief indication that Matz and Childs might somehow implicate Agnew.[46] But after Matz's and Childs's subsequent extraordinary revelations and hints that Wolff would soon come forth to confirm them, Beall and his assistants laid out the full story for the new attorney general on July 3.[47]

After five weeks in office, Elliot Richardson, having heard John Dean's testimony to the Ervin committee and beginning to receive White House complaints about Special Prosecutor Cox's widening investigation, already had plenty on his mind before being jolted by the Agnew story. His immediate reaction, one that would guide him in the weeks ahead, reflected both his political and legal instincts. Before proceeding, he believed, the case against Agnew must be determined to be rock solid. If it was, then the national interest would be best served by pushing the vice president to resign. With Nixon's continuation in office already becoming uncertain, the prospect of an accused felon succeeding him was profoundly unsettling. No such cloud, concluded Richardson, should be allowed to cast its shadow over the government if a necessarily disquieting transition of leadership was required.[48]

A spreading fear of prosecution within the Maryland civil engineering and contracting community prompted several individuals to add to the mountain of evidence of Agnew's corruption piling up before federal prosecutors in Baltimore. One, engineer Allen Green, provided a detailed accounting of $50,000 in payments to Agnew, both as governor and as vice president.[49] Green's testimony provided independent verification of the Matz, Childs, and Wolff stories of payoffs to the vice president.

The White House had long been aware that something was amiss with Agnew. Ehrlichman later claimed that as early as March 1970 there had been warning signs in Agnew's efforts to oversee the General Services Administration's mid-Atlantic region contracts.[50] This had not deterred Nixon from endorsing Agnew as his 1972 running mate once he had decided that Agnew, more than any other prospective nominee, would strengthen the ticket. Agnew repaid Nixon with public expressions of confidence in the president as the Watergate story evolved in the spring of 1973.[51] By April 1973, however, Nixon was saying, according to Ehrlichman, that he definitely would have to get rid of Agnew. "They've got the evidence. Agnew has been on the take all the time he's been here!"[52] The Baltimore investigation, however, had not yet obtained any information from Matz, much less from Wolff or Green, so what was Nixon talking about? Assuming Ehrlichman's veracity, always a risk when either his patron Nixon or his foe Agnew was involved, the most likely explanation is that Nixon was informed by Charles Colson when Agnew retained defense attorney Judah Best, Colson's law partner. Ehrlichman speculated that Nixon was distressed because "as long as Spiro Agnew was Vice President, most Representatives would think twice before voting Articles of Impeachment against Richard Nixon."[53]

Richardson held off telling Nixon about the Agnew case for as long as possible, even after Beall notified Agnew that he was under investigation on August 1.[54] Finally, learning that the *Wall Street Journal* was about to break the story, the attorney general saw the president on the morning of August 6. Richardson noted that Nixon did not seem surprised. The same afternoon, Richardson confronted

Agnew himself, told him what Matz, Wolff, and others were prepared to testify to, and heard the vice president deny all allegations. The next day the public finally became aware of the vice president's situation when the *Wall Street Journal* published its story and a similar account appeared in the *Washington Post*.[55] Agnew issued a press release and three days later held a press conference, declaring in both that he was innocent of any wrongdoing.[56]

As Richardson and Beall pressed forward with plans for indictments based on the evidence they had gathered, they faced a significant constitutional question: Could a constitutional officer of the United States be indicted without first being impeached and removed from office? The issue, potentially critical to setting restraints on the conduct of such officeholders, had never been resolved. The only situations at all comparable dated from the nineteenth century. Vice President Aaron Burr was indicted by the state of New Jersey for the murder of Alexander Hamilton in an 1804 duel, but he was never brought to trial and so the constitutional issue was not put to a test. In 1826 Vice President John C. Calhoun was accused of profiteering from an army contract while he was secretary of war. Calhoun asked the House of Representatives to investigate, asserting that it was the only body constitutionally authorized to inquire into his conduct.[57] The House appointed a select committee, which subpoenaed witnesses and documents, held hearings, and soon exonerated Calhoun. No indictment, much less impeachment, resulted. Finally, Vice President Schuyler Colfax, revealed to have been involved in the Credit Mobilier congressional bribery scandal, escaped unscathed when the House decided that any misdeeds of his occurred before he became vice president. All these cases were revisited in the midst of the Agnew inquiry, but none helped resolve the situation.[58] Even less helpful was the contemporary case of Otto Kerner, a federal appellate judge in Chicago who was appealing a bribery conviction on the grounds that he must first be impeached but whose case remained unresolved.[59] The very fact that Richardson and Beall were asking fundamental questions about the impeachment-indictment issue shows how limited was the understanding of the Constitution's impeachment provision at the time. That such a matter remained unsettled reflected how little impeachment had been considered, much less used, during the previous 184 years of the Constitution's operation.

The attorney general asked Justice Department legal counsel Robert Dixon for a legal opinion on the matter of indictment versus impeachment. Less than a day later Richardson received Dixon's memorandum asserting that since the vice president was not in the position, unique to the president, to direct a prosecution or issue a pardon, he could be indicted.[60] Dixon offered a narrow view of impeachment centering on the executive's potential to corrupt the criminal justice system to protect himself. The legal counsel's memo justified the course the Justice Department was pursuing to deal most quickly with Agnew. It assumed, by implication, that a criminal conviction would compel a vice presidential resignation—a questionable assumption that would be shown to be faulty a few years later as two federal judges, convicted of crimes and imprisoned, refused to resign their offices.

The Dixon memo did not provide a comprehensive assessment of the impeachment process. Its conclusion failed to take into account either the broader constitutional purpose of removing unfit officials or the lower threshold of consensus accepted for doing so. With its penalty limited to removal from office, impeachment placed the public's interest in its government ahead of ordinary concerns for protection of the individual in a criminal process. Impeachment only required the agreement of a simple majority of representatives and conviction only demanded the concurrence of two-thirds of the Senate, whereas conviction for a criminal offense necessitated unanimity from a jury. An 8–4 jury vote following criminal indictment and trial would produce acquittal, while a Senate vote of the same ratio following impeachment and trial would result in removal from office. Put another way, if Agnew were indicted and found guilty by only two-thirds of a jury, he could claim legal vindication. The risks to confidence in government inherent in Dixon's position were, therefore, far from trifling.

A vice presidential resignation would have obviated the need to choose between indictment and impeachment. Therefore throughout August and into September both Richardson and the White House not so subtly nudged Agnew to resign. While the attorney general clearly wanted to get the vice president out of office as quickly as possible, the Nixon White House, given its own situation, may have been equally concerned with not giving Congress experience with impeachment.[61]

As beleaguered as he was, the vice president did not take the resignation bait. He held press conferences on August 8 and 21 to deny steadfastly that he had done anything wrong. News stories contrasted his prompt and forthright denials with Nixon's long silence regarding Watergate. Agnew also complained bitterly about "damnable lies" in news reports that he charged stemmed from information leaked by the Justice Department.[62] Even the devastating news that longtime friend and chief fund-raiser Bud Hammerman had agreed to join the growing list of those willing to testify against him failed to crack Agnew's facade of aggrieved innocence. Meanwhile, the Baltimore prosecutors went about wrapping up their investigation for presentation to the grand jury.

Then, on September 10, Agnew's principal attorney, Judah Best, signaled to Richardson his client's interest in a negotiated settlement. The attorney general, in consultation with the Baltimore prosecutors, formulated a set of conditions and explored them with Agnew's attorneys. They insisted that the vice president must promptly resign his office. They also wanted a demonstration the public would understand that justice had been served. Thus, a guilty plea to at least one felony and a detailed presentation of the full range of charges against the vice president would be required. The negotiations proceeded, with both sides giving ground, until September 22 when a *Washington Post* story revealed that talks were taking place, at which point they stopped.[63]

Unhappy that news had surfaced that he was plea-bargaining, Agnew chose what he perceived as the one path open to him. The vice president boldly asked the House of Representatives to open an impeachment investigation. Attorney General Richardson was distressed by the prospect of Agnew remaining in office while yet another investigation was conducted. It could take months for the House to organize and carry out its inquiry. What if, he speculated to his deputy William Ruckelshaus, at the very moment that the vice president was being cross-examined, Nixon resigned or died and Agnew became president? What would be the consequence in terms of public confidence in government?[64]

The possibility also existed, Richardson knew, that the House might not impeach or the Senate not convict. The Constitution only required a simple majority in the House for impeachment, but it required a two-thirds vote in the Senate for conviction and removal from office. The latter step could only occur with a significant degree of bipartisan consensus, something difficult to achieve on an inherently political matter. Members might perceive a political advantage in keeping a discredited vice president in place. Republicans might do so to protect Nixon from impeachment. Democrats might aspire to improve their electoral prospects. The Nixon White House, agonizing about Agnew's initiative for its own distinct reasons, might also seek to thwart the process.[65] In any case, bipartisan congressional consensus would be difficult to achieve.

Leaders of the House had already begun to discuss the impeachment question. In a meeting in Speaker Carl Albert's office, one member said he spoke for most of his colleagues: "We're for the 'Calhoun precedent.'" The gathering erupted with laughter, because the reference was not to John C. Calhoun but to a joke frequently told by Lyndon Johnson about a football running back named Calhoun: With his team being trounced by the opponent's defense on a messy, muddy field, the coach called, "Give the ball to Calhoun." After three more plays in which other runners ended up facedown in the mud for no gain, the coach called a time-out to ask why Calhoun was not being given a chance. The quarterback replied, "Calhoun says he don't want the ball."[66]

A veteran congressional reporter concluded, "Impeachment is one ball the House does not want either. Its members see a messy, muddy brawl." One member told him, "Our instincts are to hide under the desks." The reporter found that the chairman of the Judiciary Committee, Peter W. Rodino, Jr., of New Jersey, had reluctantly started examining the procedures for conducting an impeachment, but, like other congressmen, seemed in no rush to proceed. Better to let the judicial process deal with Agnew.[67] Much later Rodino would say that the prospect of simultaneous impeachments of Agnew and Nixon concerned him. He feared that the country would be torn apart with neither a president nor a vice president available to pick up the pieces.[68]

In a face-to-face meeting with Speaker Albert on September 25, Agnew formally asked the House of Representatives to undertake a full inquiry. "This request," the vice president explained, "is made in the dual interests of preserving the Constitutional stature of my office and accomplishing my personal vindication." The letter he handed the Speaker went on: "After the most careful study, my counsel have advised me that the Constitution bars a criminal proceeding of any kind—federal or state, county or town—against a President or Vice President while he holds office." He could not "acquiesce" in such a criminal proceeding or look to it for vindication; rather, he believed "it is the right and duty of the Vice President to turn to the House."[69]

Citing the John C. Calhoun case as precedent, Agnew said that he was likewise "the subject of public attacks that may 'assume the character of impeachable offenses,' and thus require urgent investigation by the House as the repository of 'the sole Power of Impeachment.'" No other investigation, he declared, could substitute for one by the House to "lay to rest in a timely and definitive manner the unfounded charges whose currency unavoidably jeopardizes the functions of my Office." Complaining about "an ever-broadening stream of rumors, accusations and speculations" arising from the Baltimore investigation and asserting that in such an atmosphere no jury could fairly consider his case on the merits, Agnew claimed, perhaps implausibly, that the House could do better. "I am confident," he concluded, "that, like Vice President Calhoun, I shall be vindicated by the House."[70]

The White House immediately released a presidential statement reflecting mixed feelings about the vice president's request for an impeachment inquiry. The statement acknowledged that Nixon and Agnew had met and that Agnew had indicated what he planned to seek from the House. While emphasizing that the vice president was entitled to "the same presumption of innocence which is the right of any citizen," the president declined to make any stronger declaration of support. Most significantly, Nixon avoided making any comment on the request for an impeachment inquiry.[71]

Before confronting Albert, the vice president had met with a group of senior House Republicans, including Minority Leader Gerald Ford. Their reaction to his plan was not encouraging. They felt that Albert was not likely to give Agnew the slightest help.[72] Nevertheless, Agnew proceeded to meet with Albert, Majority Leader Thomas P. "Tip" O'Neill, Rodino, and Ford. The vice president took heart in the speaker's promise to consider his request, but Ford sensed that O'Neill's skepticism would, if need be, prevail.[73]

Albert wasted little time dashing Agnew's hopes. By the following day, September 26, he had decided that the House should not intervene in the matter. Whether anticipating that the House might soon have to deal with another impeachment, that of Nixon, or simply unwilling to involve the House in a matter for which a judicial resolution seemed possible, Albert determined that the House should take no action. Four Republican members of the House Judiciary Committee offered a resolution directing the committee to investigate the charges against Agnew, but without the speaker's support the measure went nowhere. Republican Representative Les Arends of Illinois was left to convey the message of failure to Agnew. The House leadership had determined that there would be no impeachment inquiry in the House forestalling federal judicial proceedings.[74]

The following day the Baltimore prosecutors began presenting evidence to a federal grand jury in order to obtain Agnew's indictment. In the midst of the second day of grand jury proceedings, the vice president's lawyers sought a protective order prohibiting the grand jury from proceeding further on the grounds that "the Constitution forbids that the Vice President be indicted or convicted in any criminal court." The impossibility of a fair trial because of press leaks was alleged as well, but the constitutional issue that only impeachment was permissible was the centerpiece of the motion. Judge Walter E. Hoffman, a Virginian assigned to the case after all nine of Maryland's federal judges had recused themselves because of past associations with Agnew, received the request but took no immediate action.

At Attorney General Richardson's request, Solicitor General Robert H. Bork prepared a brief for presentation to Judge Hoffman on the vice president's indictability while in office. In response to the claims of Agnew's lawyer, Bork made a distinction between the president and vice president different from the one drawn earlier by Justice Department legal counsel Robert Dixon. Bork's argument held that while an indictment of the president would immobilize the executive branch, the indictment of the vice president would not do so. The Bork brief spoke directly to Nixon's situation as well as to Agnew's, upholding the president's freedom from indictment but not the vice president's. The stripping away of Agnew's defenses perhaps had more to do with Nixon's parallel circumstances and greater resources for dealing with them than with the inherent weakness of Agnew's position. The constitutional basis for distinguishing presidential and vice presidential preimpeachment legal jeopardy was far from unassailable, but unless Judge Hoffman rejected the Justice Department's argument, which he took no immediate steps to do, the House determination not to proceed appeared likely to stand.[75]

As his situation deteriorated, Agnew took another, more desperate tack, this time seeking to take advantage of the winds of impeachment blowing toward Nixon. In a feisty September 29 speech to two thousand members of the National Federation of Republican Women in Los Angeles, he argued that senior officials in the Justice Department had come after him because they had been embarrassed by revelations, in the Ervin committee hearings, of their weak performance in the Watergate investigation. He was being hounded, Agnew asserted, because the Justice Department was seeking to rehabilitate its own image. Why a Republican-controlled agency would want to destroy an innocent Republican officeholder was not explained to this audience of Republican women.[76] The speech would prove to be Agnew's last serious public effort to extricate himself from his difficulties. By October 4, in a Chicago speech, he was beginning to signal a readiness to surrender, declaring, "A candle is only so long and it eventually burns out."[77]

Having failed to divert the inquiry into his conduct into an impeachment inquiry and facing an impending indictment, Agnew's attorneys resumed discussion of a plea bargain with Richardson and his associates. The attorney general was ever more concerned with obtaining the vice president's prompt resignation in order to eliminate the possibility of his ascension to the presidency. In intense and protracted negotiation between October 5 and 9, the parties explored a deal that would essentially follow the lines of the agreement nearly reached two weeks earlier. Agnew's attorneys focused on avoiding a jail sentence for their client, while the foremost objective of Richardson and the prosecutors was getting a detailed statement of the case against the vice president into the official record. On October 8, Judge Hoffman, whose approval of any bargain would be required, was brought into the discussions. A day later a deal was struck.

Shortly before 2:00 p.m. on October 10, lawyers in a courtroom in the Baltimore federal court building on an unrelated matter were told they could either leave immediately or would have to stay put for an unspecified time during an undisclosed court proceeding. Those who chose to remain watched in stunned silence as first Attorney General Richardson and then Spiro Agnew and his lawyers entered the courtroom and as federal marshals and secret service agents locked the doors. Attorney Judah Best quickly acknowledged that his client had just resigned as vice president, and Judge Hoffman announced that the court was in session to hear a waiver of indictment and a plea from Agnew. After Hoffman ascertained that Agnew had read the prosecutors' bill of particulars and advised him that pleading nolo contendere was equivalent to pleading guilty, Agnew entered his no contest plea to one count of income tax evasion.[78]

Richardson then addressed the court, explaining that the Baltimore prosecutors had accumulated substantial evidence of a pattern of improper cash payments to Agnew. The attorney general hastened to add that no immunity from prosecution had been granted in return for witnesses' testimony. He explained that the government might have moved forward with the case and that, after indictment, Congress might have exercised its power of impeachment. If the Congress had decided not to act, the defendant could have retained office while his case was tried or a court considered whether he was immune as the incumbent vice president. Any of these courses would consume months or years and would produce prolonged anxiety and uncertainty regarding the man next in line of succession to the presidency. The consequences for the United States would be potentially disastrous, and therefore, Richardson said, "I am satisfied that the public interest is better served by this court's acceptance of the defendant's plea of *nolo contendere* to a single count information charging income tax evasion." The attorney general then acknowledged that this settlement could not have been reached without a recommendation for a lenient sentence. To achieve the settlement, he was willing to so recommend.[79]

Agnew responded, saying that he understood that the nation's interest required swift disposition of this case. A legal proceeding that might drag on for several years would be to the country's detriment. He denied that he had acted illegally, except in the one case to which he had pled nolo contendere, and resolutely, if questionably, asserted that none of his actions had harmed the public interest. He concluded his self-serving statement by repeating that his plea was a recognition that a lengthy legal contest would run counter to the national interest.[80]

Judge Hoffman, in passing sentence, acknowledged that removing Agnew from office had been a prime consideration in its determination. Otherwise, he said, his normal practice would have been to impose a much heavier punishment, including imprisonment. But persuaded by the attorney general of the great national interest involved, he would only sentence Agnew to three years of unsupervised probation and the maximum allowable fine of $10,000.[81] Unstated but certainly understood was the fact that Agnew's greater punishment was removal from public office.

Five days later, in a nationally televised "farewell address," Agnew sought for a final time to put his resignation in a more favorable light by correcting "misconceptions." He claimed that he had merely "permitted my fund-raising activities and my contract dispensing activities to overlap" in a way judged unethical and unlawful "by the new, post-Watergate political morality." In his everybody-does-it explanation he made no mention that the envelopes and bags full of cash given him had been concealed in both the contributors' and his own records. Nor did he draw any connection between his own conduct and that of those he called the "bribe brokers, extortionists and conspirators" who gave him money. Instead, he complained that testimony against him had not been subject to cross-examination but had been gained from confessed criminals in exchange for immunity from prosecution (which was not the case) and then leaked to the press "with full knowledge that it was prejudicial to my civil rights" to create an impression of guilt. In these circumstances, he had continued to deny all charges except an unrelated one that he "saw fit not to contest" when he pled nolo contendere but that he now declared "does not represent a confession of any guilt whatever for any other purpose." He resigned to spare the country "a further agonizing period of months without an unclouded successor for the Presidency."[82]

Agnew's "farewell address," like his earlier explanations, attempted to diminish the significance of his conduct or to shift blame rather than clarify why he was allowing himself to be pushed out of office. He skirted the substance of the case that Beall and his colleagues had built and that Richardson called "more complete and convincing testimony than I had ever been able to assemble" in one of his own successful corruption investigations.[83] Nevertheless, judged from the hundreds of letters and telegrams Agnew received, he had persuaded at least some Americans that he had been ill-used. Typical was a Carlisle, Pennsylvania, woman who wrote, "It is frightening to us that our 'System' has reached the point where a man of your caliber is forced from office when we need men like you so badly."[84] However, except among Agnew's most devoted following, the case presented in the Baltimore courtroom was compelling. The nation sighed in relief at Agnew's departure from office.

The resolution of the Agnew case has most often been cast as an alternative to impeachment. In many respects it was. The House of Representatives declined to open a formal impeachment inquiry. The resolution of the case occurred in a courtroom under the supervision of a federal judge and in response to charges brought by the attorney general of the United States rather than in the Senate chamber on articles presented by the House of Representatives. Yet in some respects the Agnew case shared the characteristics of impeachment. Although Vice President Agnew did not go through the formal impeachment inquiry he had requested, the treatment he received had much in common with an impeachment.

Just as the prime concern of the Constitution's framers in constructing its impeachment provisions was to remove unfit officials from positions of authority, Richardson's preoccupation throughout the Agnew case was to get him out of the line of succession to the presidency. Other punishment for Agnew's reprehensible conduct was a decidedly secondary concern. Thus, Richardson was willing to accept a plea bargain involving extremely light punishment for Agnew's offenses. Removing the man from national office and from the exercise of power became the highest priority. Both the framers and Richardson considered that a public humiliation and a punishment of consequence.

The attorney general's insistence that a detailed statement of the charges and evidence against Agnew be included in the public court record served an important purpose. Richardson's desire to get Agnew out of the vice presidency was balanced by his intention to demonstrate conclusively that justice had been done. Agnew was not simply a political victim; he definitely needed to be removed from office. Overturning a democratic choice made only a year previously could only be justified if the electorate was convinced that the person in whom they had placed their trust had betrayed it. The case against Agnew needed to be clear and compelling.

Charges that Agnew had received clandestine payoffs had only been before the public for two months, and at the time the public had been preoccupied with a different, quite unrelated political scandal. Furthermore, the vice president had vehemently denied the accusations throughout almost the entire period.

Newspaper reports of his misdeeds were unavoidably vague and incomplete. Thus, without the further explication and confirmation provided by the Baltimore court proceedings, doubts about the validity of the charges would have lingered and questions about the legitimacy of the removal would have persisted.

The detailed presentation of the case against Agnew and his failure to contest it effectively, either in court or in his subsequent television appearance, made an important contribution to the perception that his removal from office had been appropriate. The American public expressed shock but did not seriously question the outcome of the case or suggest that the vice president had been improperly driven from office. Akin to articles of impeachment and accompanied by Agnew's resignation and nolo contendere plea, the statement crafted by Richardson and the Baltimore prosecutors served as the functional equivalent to a confession of guilt for most observers. The statement and its acceptance gave legitimacy to the view that impeachment would have been appropriate had Agnew not fallen on his sword.

Finally, Agnew's own maneuvering as the noose tightened exposed something of significance. The House of Representatives of the ninety-third Congress, the same body that would have to deal with the case of Nixon in the months ahead, was very reluctant to engage in impeachment. Despite the fact that the vice president himself asked the House to take the first step toward a possible impeachment, the House preferred not to do so. Any expectation that Congress's majority party would relish the opportunity to examine an opposition party leader for possible removal from office proved to be mistaken. Very soon House leaders would find themselves unable to avoid dealing with an impeachment, but as long as they thought they could, they chose not to plunge into the dark and unfamiliar waters that impeachment represented.

6

Impeachment as Essential:
The Case of Richard Nixon

In the space of ten days during mid-October 1973 impeachment moved from the periphery of American constitutional and political consciousness to its absolute center. What had seemed the most remote of constitutional possibilities before 1960 and thereafter a questionable, once successful, twice unsuccessful device to place pressure on Supreme Court justices to resign suddenly acquired new political stature and strength. On October 10 Vice President Spiro Agnew, abandoning hope that he could use impeachment to delay or thwart his indictment for corruption, resigned. He accepted a bargain that functioned much like a successful impeachment, removing him from office but imposing little in the way of other penalties. Only ten days later, an imperious presidential dismissal of the special prosecutor investigating the Watergate affair outraged much of Congress as well as the nation at large. Juxtaposed with the dawning realization that a benign successor had fortuitously become available, President Richard Nixon's conduct caused Congress and the country to consider presidential impeachment as not only possible but also possibly necessary for the first time in more than a century.

Active contemplation of Nixon's impeachment by the political mainstream did not begin with the disclosure that the White House was directly linked to the Watergate break-in. Even revelations that the president's closest associates had impeded the investigation of the original crime did not at first generate a substantial demand for his impeachment, though it did lead to the establishment of a special prosecutor to examine the matter further, free of administration interference. When his distress over reports of the U.S. bombing of Cambodia had impelled Senator Philip Hart of Michigan in April 1973 to suggest a look at the rules for impeachment, his colleague, J. William Fulbright of Arkansas, the Senate's reigning foreign policy authority, had retorted that such a step would be "politically disastrous."[1] *New York Times* columnist James Reston had scoffed that the "eminently rational" Hart had been "smitten by the spring madness."[2]

As late as September 1973, fifteen months after the Watergate break-in was discovered in progress and five months after Nixon's subordinates began appearing before the Ervin committee to confess additional "White House horrors," the House of Representatives still had received only a handful of formal requests for impeachment. The previous May, after Nixon fired John Dean and accepted the resignations of H. R. Haldeman, John Ehrlichman, and Richard Kleindienst, California Democrat John Moss circulated a petition within the House to spur an impeachment inquiry. New Yorker Bella Abzug was one of very few members to join the effort, while Majority Leader Tip O'Neill called it "premature." The first resolution actually proposing that President Nixon be impeached did not appear until after Nixon refused to comply with subpoenas for his recently revealed tapes, and even then the July 31 resolution by Congressman Robert Drinan (who was also a Catholic priest) failed to attract a single cosponsor. The Drinan resolution contained no specific charges but simply stated, "Resolved, that Richard M. Nixon, President of the United States, is impeached of high crimes and misdemeanors." It was referred to the Judiciary Committee, where it languished.[3]

Members of Congress, one shrewd observer noted, "are experts in many things, but one feature of their expertise is that they are knowledgeable about what can safely be said in public."[4] To deviate dramatically from what is acceptable to one's own constituents can quickly terminate a congressional career. Until a considerable portion of the citizens they represented indicated an interest in impeachment, not many legislators would choose to become its advocates. The few impeachment resolutions put forth failed to gain support from other members of the House, much less the body's leadership. However, the events of October 1973, most notably the nomination of Congressman Gerald R. Ford to replace Agnew as vice president followed by the so-called Saturday Night Massacre, Nixon's peremptory dismissal of Special Prosecutor Archibald Cox, caused public and congressional attitudes about impeachment to change dramatically.

Richard Nixon's action precipitating the surge in discussion of his impeachment, not to mention his dismissive response to calls for his resignation or removal, no doubt was shaped by his assessment of the experiences of Earl Warren, Abe Fortas, William O. Douglas, and Spiro Agnew. Conscious at least as early as April 1973 that his own impeachment was a possibility, however remote, Nixon had plenty of time to contemplate the four impeachment episodes of his political lifetime. The president was well aware that in the cases of Fortas and Agnew his own Justice Department had brought forth information and had taken steps to encourage their downfall. If that knowledge had been kept bottled up instead of being made available, Fortas and Agnew might have escaped unscathed. Instead, both the justice and the vice president had quickly wilted under the pressure of the inquiries and resigned to prevent the removal process from advancing.

The other two recent impeachment efforts, those involving Warren and Douglas, had come to nothing. Warren had apparently not taken the John Birch Society campaign seriously, much less contemplated resignation as a result. Douglas faced a somewhat more substantial threat because the Nixon administration was supplying information to his detractors in the House of Representatives.

The justice was forced to retain counsel and endure a House Judiciary subcommittee hearing, but he stood steadfast against his opponents and prevailed. Indeed, Douglas abandoned thoughts of retirement and resolved not to resign as long as Nixon remained in office.

The ever politically observant and calculating Nixon could reasonably conclude from the four cases in recent memory that impeachment and removal from office was not a serious threat to those who stood resolute against them. Such an outcome seemed even more certain for those able to retain control of potentially damaging information about their conduct. The House of Representatives had shown little stomach for impeachment in either the Douglas or Agnew cases, much less for direct challenges to presidential authority. Throughout his career, Nixon had spoken frequently, both in public and in private, about the need to be tough under pressure and unyielding when confronted by adversity. His behavior during and after October 1973 as well as before was certainly shaped by his combative temperament. His conduct was also no doubt conditioned by Nixon's judgment that recent impeachment efforts had failed when met with unflinching resistance.

Despite, or arguably because of, Nixon's recalcitrance, impeachment proceedings moved steadily forward from October 1973 to their ultimate resolution ten months later. In the course of these events, the rationale and process for impeachment came to be better understood both by members of Congress and by the general public. The ever more transparent defiance of the president and the obvious care and caution manifested in the deliberate steps taken by the House of Representatives, special Watergate prosecutor, and Supreme Court combined to produce a widespread sense that impeachment could be a measured and legitimate process—indeed, a necessary and almost unavoidable one under the circumstances. By the summer of 1974 impeachment was no longer regarded as an obsolete, unworkable, or inappropriate constitutional provision. Instead, it had come to be widely appreciated as a vital tool for dealing with a dangerous and otherwise uncontrollable chief executive.

The Nixon impeachment consideration proved to be an important learning experience on many levels. Members and leaders of Congress gained an education in how to conduct an impeachment inquiry in a fashion that would build and sustain broad citizen respect. Some legislators and junior-level executive officers would have the opportunity to employ what they had learned in subsequent attempts to pursue or thwart other impeachments. Special prosecutor and judiciary committee staff attorneys likewise gained valuable experience that they would later put to use in a variety of ways, from providing legal counsel, to presenting radio and television commentary, and even to advising spouses in future impeachment proceedings. Journalists acquired impressions and insights that they would draw upon again and again in assessing political developments thereafter. Last but far from least, the general public gained a sense of impeachment that would long color its views of the operation and character of American government. That all this happened in the midst of one of the most clearly justified impeachment cases ever brought forward helps account for the manner in which impeachment became a more prominent component of American political culture in the decades that followed.

The first step in what would eventually become the march to impeach President Nixon was taken with Vice President Agnew's resignation from office. As John Ehrlichman had noted, Nixon genuinely believed that Agnew was his best insurance policy. As long as Agnew was vice president, most representatives would think twice before voting articles of impeachment against Nixon.[5] Agnew's departure cancelled the president's insurance policy and ironically validated Nixon's original calculation.

The relationship between Nixon and Agnew had always been a complicated one. Nixon had lifted Agnew, whom he knew only slightly, out of the relative obscurity of a one-term governorship of a small state. Agnew repaid his benefactor with repeated public expressions of loyal support, even in his vice presidential "farewell speech."[6] His many harsh and effective rhetorical attacks against Nixon's critics earned the vice president the label "Nixon's Nixon" for taking up the role of partisan warrior that had been his patron's during the Eisenhower administration.

At Washington's annual Gridiron Club dinner in 1970, Nixon and Agnew harmonized, literally as well as figuratively. The president sat at a piano to play favorite songs of his predecessors. At the end of each song, Agnew, at another piano, would break in with a chorus of "Dixie." The bipartisan audience roared with laughter at this self-parody of the successful Republican "southern strategy," and the president left exultant about the convivial evening.[7] Yet Nixon never sought to reprise the duet. Instead, for the most part Nixon kept Agnew at arm's length. Nixon very rarely assigned his running mate substantive responsibilities for the most part, disparaged his vice president to his inner circle, and made no secret of contemplating his replacement on the 1972 Republican ticket. For his part, Agnew complained incessantly, if privately, about his lack of access to the president as well as his lack of involvement in major policy matters.[8]

Although Nixon's own experience as vice president had been similar, perhaps the best explanation of his relationship with Agnew can be found in the president's insurance policy comments. Nixon could welcome talk of Agnew as a presidential aspirant without taking any interest whatsoever in making Agnew look more suitable as a presidential replacement. Agnew served Nixon well as a shield. Indeed, when Agnew's troubles surfaced in August 1973, he continued to perform that function in a different manner, diverting attention from the embattled president for a while. As the vice president faced the prospect of impeachment, Nixon did little to protect or defend his running mate. The president's statements of support for his beleaguered associate were at best measured and on the whole perfunctory. In his memoirs, however, an uncomprehending Agnew looked back gratefully at Nixon's support for his efforts to remain in office. Agnew complained that it had been Nixon's minions, in particular the White House chief of staff, Alexander Haig, who had repeatedly pressed him to resign and become the focus of blame for the ills of the executive branch.[9]

In any case, Agnew's resignation proved costly to Nixon. As anyone who has had an insurance policy canceled knows, finding an adequate replacement can be more difficult than acquiring the original. Agnew's departure left Nixon with such a problem, especially since the circumstances in which he found himself would not permit him to obtain the same type of coverage. The constraints imposed by Agnew's near impeachment and the possibility that he would himself face impeachment dramatically limited Nixon's choices in a situation where he was required to take action.

Throughout most of U.S. history, the vice presidency would simply have stood vacant following a resignation like Agnew's. Indeed, since 1789 the country had operated without a vice president for a total of thirty-eight years: Seven vice presidents died, seven ascended to the presidency, and one other resigned. Finally, after the assassination of John F. Kennedy, Congress decided that it would be best to fill a vice presidential vacancy rather than have the speaker of the House of Representatives stand next in the line of succession. Legislators constructed a constitutional amendment to provide for vice presidential replacement and a means for dealing with presidential disability, which they anticipated would be a more common problem. Adopted by more than the requisite two-thirds vote of the House and Senate in July 1965 and then put into effect in February 1967 after the necessary thirty-eight state ratifications, the Twenty-fifth Amendment had never been used. It specified that whenever a vice presidential vacancy occurred, "the President shall nominate a Vice President who shall take office upon confirmation by a majority vote of both Houses of Congress."[10]

The Twenty-fifth Amendment was not the first constitutional provision that proved to have unintended consequences. Selection of a new vice president at a moment when a president's weakness would shape the choice could, however, scarcely have been predicted. Those who crafted the amendment expected that death or disability would create a vacancy to be filled by a president either new in office or bereft of a close colleague and in either case an object of sympathy. The Twenty-fifth Amendment's framers had acknowledged that they could not foresee every circumstance in which it might need to be employed, but surely they did not anticipate that the first use of the replacement mechanism would fall to a president whose choice would be governed by the threat of his own removal from office.[11]

In October 1973 Nixon could not get away with nominating as vice president someone who would offer him the same insurance against impeachment that he believed Agnew had provided. Given growing speculation that Nixon might himself resign or be forced from office, Congress would simply not approve a vice president it thought would be difficult to work with or ill suited to step into the highest office. Members of Congress might well think it better to reject an unsatisfactory nominee and retain the speaker of the House, Carl Albert, as next in the line of succession. To have his nominee rejected as unsuitable or, alternatively, to decline to make a nomination would inevitably signal Nixon's political weakness and encourage further thoughts of his removal.

At the same time, circumstances did not favor an outstanding candidate. A vice presidential nominee who would be regarded as highly attractive posed risks for Nixon. First, the Democrat-controlled Congress might not wish to confirm someone considered a likely candidate for the presidency in 1976, especially if it perceived that individual as someone who would continue in the path of the Nixon administration. A person who would gain the political advantage of being the sitting vice president, or possibly even the president before the next national election, might be unacceptable to Democrats and even many Republicans. Second, and even more problematic for Nixon, a candidate who was too appealing might encourage thoughts of disposing of the incumbent in the White House. Given the threat of impeachment that hung over Nixon at the moment, either the success or the defeat of his vice presidential nominee carried potential danger.

The various factors Nixon was forced to consider led him to decide that no obscure candidate would do. Likewise unsatisfactory were John Connally, former Texas governor as well as former secretary of the treasury, whom Nixon much admired; Governor Nelson Rockefeller of New York; and Ronald Reagan, former California governor—all likely 1976 presidential candidates. Most likely to curry favor with the Congress and be difficult for members to vote against would be someone from their own ranks. Therefore, Nixon quickly settled on the House minority leader, Gerald R. Ford, who not only possessed a decade of congressional leadership experience but also had already signaled to intimates that he intended to retire after one more term in the House. Ford, well liked on both sides of the congressional aisle and thus presumably easy to confirm, was not, however, viewed as particularly dynamic or charismatic. The Grand Rapids, Michigan, congressman appeared to strike the balance Nixon sought. He was confirmable but not so well known or highly thought of as to be likely to stir national demands that Nixon step aside in his favor. On the evening of October 12, only two and a half days after Agnew resigned, Nixon arranged a nationally televised White House ceremony to announce his nomination of Ford to be the next vice president.

As Nixon had calculated, Ford proved confirmable, but not quite with the ease at first predicted by an enthusiastic congressional leadership. Between the nomination and the confirmation, Nixon's own situation deteriorated dramatically because of his abrupt dismissal of Special Prosecutor Cox, a White House acknowledgment that two of the subpoenaed tapes did not exist and another was blank for eighteen and a half minutes, and, finally, revelations of substantial irregularities in the president's income tax returns. These developments provoked some members of Congress to question whether a Nixon nominee should be confirmed at all. Questions about the nature and extent of Ford's indebtedness to Nixon also arose. The shadow of impeachments past and prospective would hang over the confirmation process.

Never having conducted a Twenty-fifth Amendment confirmation process, Congress lacked precedents on how to proceed. The House chose to have its Committee on the Judiciary hold hearings to question the nominee, while the Senate assigned the task to its Committee on Rules and Administration. Foremost on the minds of the senators and all but a minority of Democratic representatives appeared to be the need to install a vice president as quickly as possible, given the prospect of a presidential impeachment or resignation. Speaker Albert himself, next in line of succession, was particularly eager for Ford's confirmation to avoid any appearance that the Democrats were maneuvering to seize the presidency.[12]

Senator Howard Cannon opened his committee's hearings on November 1 by describing Ford's twenty-five-year congressional record as supportive of big business and indifferent to the disadvantaged. Having made clear that he disagreed with Ford on many matters, Chairman Cannon indicated his belief that current circumstances made imperative the prompt installation of a new vice president. At the same time he called for a thorough inquiry in light of the recent problems of various Nixon appointees.[13]

Ford's longtime friend and colleague, Senator Robert Griffin of Michigan, introduced the nominee at the hearings. In his enthusiastic endorsement of Ford, Griffin made no reference to his 1968 argument against confirming an appointee of a lame-duck president to a continuing office. Nor was the issue raised by senators eager to proceed. The nine committee members instead questioned Ford about his personal finances and campaign contributions and elicited a statement, reiterating ones made earlier, that he had no intention of running for president in 1976.

Committee members asked Ford about his views on many aspects of the presidency, including executive privilege and impeachment. Asked about his future political plans, Ford affirmed that he had no intention of seeking the presidency in 1976 and went on to say, "I can foresee no circumstances where I would change my mind."[14] In answering a pointed question about the authority of a president to block the prosecution of a predecessor who resigned, Fort declared, "I do not think the public would stand for it."[15] Both statements would be quoted in later years to embarrass Ford.

The committee spent more time examining allegations by lobbyist and writer Robert Winter-Berger that Ford had been treated by a New York psychiatrist and had committed financial irregularities. Winter-Berger could substantiate neither charge, and one committee member sneered that Winter-Berger "was about as credible as the White House."[16] The committee seemed most concerned about heeding Chairman Cannon's admonition not to hold up confirmation and expose the Democratic majority to accusations of keeping the speaker of the House in line to become president. Outside witnesses complained about Ford's record on civil rights, his lack of foreign policy experience, and his role in the effort to impeach Justice Douglas, but to little apparent effect. After only four days of hearings, the Rules Committee unanimously endorsed the nomination on November 20, and a week later the Senate approved it 92–3.[17]

When the House hearings began on November 15, they proved to be more probing. Their sharper tone was established at the outset when Representative John Conyers, Jr., of Michigan objected to proceeding before dealing with the question of impeaching Nixon. Ford was questioned about executive privilege, the Winter-Berger allegations, and even the possible impeachment of Nixon. However, committee members, particularly young liberal Democrats, kept returning to Ford's attempt to impeach Douglas, who coincidentally had just weeks earlier become the longest-serving Supreme Court justice ever. Under questioning, Ford made a rather matter-of-fact acknowledgment that John Mitchell's Justice Department had provided him with substantial assistance in his campaign to unseat Douglas. Ford's admission that he had acted at the behest of the administration in a problematic political enterprise raised questions about his judgment, not to mention his loyalties to Nixon.

Ford's definition of an impeachable offense concerned the judiciary committee from the start. The notion that grounds for impeachment could be whatever a majority of Congress chose at the time clearly troubled them. When Ford refused to recant, they lectured him on the importance of restricting impeachment to treason, bribery and other high crimes and misdemeanors.[18] Committee members were obviously concerned to ensure that if they voted to impeach Nixon, their action would be understood as something other than a political assault.

The dramatic high point of the House hearing came as Jerome Waldie of California pressed Ford regarding his charges against Justice Douglas. Ignoring Waldie's request that he desist, Ford held up a copy of *Evergreen,* displaying for television cameras and viewers the erotic photographs adjacent to the Douglas article that served as a central element in Ford's charges that the justice had engaged in inappropriate behavior. Waldie chastised Ford's "lamentable breach of good taste." Don Edwards of California called the nominee "incredibly insensitive," while John Seiberling of Ohio declared the display of the magazine irrelevant to the question asked and "unseemly" for a nominee for vice president.[19]

The House hearing cast Ford's effort to impeach Douglas as intemperate and made it appear to be another of Nixon's "dirty tricks." Given the great and growing sense of an urgent need to install a vice president and the lack of other specific

complaints about Ford's past conduct, questions about the Douglas impeachment campaign were not enough to derail confirmation, though they appeared
to be a major reason for the votes cast against Ford. Concerns about a serious
impeachment proceeding in prospect trumped those about a past impeachment
attempt perceived as misguided but inconsequential. Once the House hearings
were concluded, the committee voted 29–8 to confirm Ford. The House signaled
its approval 387–35, and Ford was sworn in as vice president on December 6.[20]

By the time Ford took the oath of office as vice president, many Republicans in Congress were hoping that he would soon be president, through Nixon's resignation if possible but through a quick impeachment if necessary. "The
President's an albatross around your neck," a Democratic congressman told a
colleague. "At least that," the Republican replied.[21] Despite Nixon's self-inflicted
wounds and declining fortunes, however, he continued to reject calls to resign
and to act as if impeachment was out of the question. His long-established views
of impeachment had not been shaken. What may not have been evident to him,
however, was the reality that Agnew's replacement by Ford had given the American people a vivid example of a smoothly working constitutional process for
substituting one high executive for another following something very much like
impeachment. Apprehension about impeachment was being assuaged just as
public attention was becoming focused on the possibilities and perils of an unconventional change of leadership at the highest level.

The previously almost unthinkable possibility of a presidential impeachment began to appeal to sizable numbers of people across the country and in Congress in
late October, shortly before the Ford confirmation hearings began. While dissatisfaction with Nixon had become commonplace, some of it could be attributed
to a sense that he was not being well served by subordinates. The resistance he
offered to various investigations did not endear him to the public, but at least it
appeared to be based on legitimate questions about constitutional issues of separation of powers and executive privilege. But in the course of one weekend, the
national mood changed decidedly. Actions clearly taken by the president himself, not any subordinate, reneged on an agreement with Congress, thwarted
judicial resolution of issues in dispute, and raised serious doubts about his integrity. Nixon's actions of Saturday, October 20, proved pivotal in transforming
impeachment from an improbability to a possible necessity.

Ever since Alexander Butterfield had revealed the existence of a White House
tape-recording system to the Senate Select Committee on July 16, Special Prosecutor Cox had been persistently seeking access to tapes of various Nixon meetings with his staff. Claims that presidential conversations with advisers were
constitutionally protected by executive privilege had not dissuaded Cox. The
special prosecutor found no justification for executive privilege to conceal evidence of criminal conduct. Judge Sirica found Cox's argument persuasive, but

his August 31 ruling was appealed by the president's attorneys. Increasingly restive, Nixon told Attorney General Richardson during late September discussions regarding Agnew that he was prepared to dismiss Cox. Richardson brushed off the warning.[22]

On Friday, October 12, the same day that Nixon nominated Ford to be vice president, the U.S. Court of Appeals for the District of Columbia, by a 5–2 vote, upheld Sirica's ruling that the president must turn over nine requested tapes to the special prosecutor's office. Cox left no doubt that he expected compliance. The following Monday Chief of Staff Haig told Richardson that the president wanted him to fire Cox. The attorney general reminded Haig that the president had promised him independence when he accepted the position, that he had pledged at his confirmation hearing to dismiss Cox only for "extraordinary improprieties," that none had occurred, and therefore that he would be forced to resign rather than fire Cox.

Over the next few days the president came up with a plan to provide edited transcripts of the tapes verified by elderly Senator John Stennis. Cox rejected the Stennis plan as presented to him by Richardson on the grounds of inadequacy and inadmissibility of such transcripts as evidence. He then refused a direct Nixon order that he accept the arrangement and cease seeking tapes. On Saturday, October 20, in a televised afternoon press conference Cox scorned Nixon's demand that he limit his pursuit of potential evidence of crimes, called for compliance with the court order, and declared that he had no intention of relenting or resigning.

Nixon immediately demanded that Richardson fire Cox. The attorney general refused and instead handed the president his letter of resignation. Deputy Attorney General William Ruckelshaus, given the same order minutes later, resigned as well. Finally the Justice Department's third in command, Solicitor General Robert Bork, conflicted himself but made aware by Richardson and Ruckelshaus of the need to keep the Justice Department from being left entirely leaderless, agreed to dismiss Cox. At 8:30 p.m. a White House spokesman announced that Richardson had resigned, Cox and Ruckleshaus had been fired, the office of special prosecutor had been abolished, and, finally, Bork was now acting attorney general.

Within minutes of the White House statement every television network reported on the Saturday Night Massacre, as the Justice Department housecleaning soon became known. NBC anchorman John Chancellor melodramatically declared, "The country tonight is in the midst of what may be the most serious constitutional crisis in its history." The next day the firings became the lead story in nearly every American newspaper. Banner headlines, reinforcing the grave tones of broadcasters, conveyed the seriousness of the president's defiance of the special prosecutor's quest for evidence. The news coverage, which included pictures of FBI agents sealing off the offices of the special prosecutor and his staff, raised alarms about a president brooking no opposition as he sought to prevent the release of recordings increasingly suspected to contain evidence of crimes. Cox himself underscored the sense of menace by declaring that it was for Congress and ultimately the American people to determine "whether ours shall continue to be a government of laws and not of men."[23]

The Saturday Night Massacre provoked an extraordinary public outcry. Members of Congress received a deluge of phone calls, telegrams, and letters from outraged constituents, a flood that began on Sunday and did not cease. Western Union transmitted a half million telegrams, by far the largest number ever sent on a public issue. Several congressional conservatives reported that their heavy volume of mail, apparently a popular outpouring and not the result of any organized campaign, was running 9–1 in favor of Nixon's impeachment. Among the general public, for the most part not so engaged as to write to a member of Congress, support for impeachment was rising rapidly, but it was still the position of only 37 percent of those polled and was opposed by 54 percent of respondents.[24] The limited enthusiasm for impeachment almost certainly reflected a lack of understanding of the process, since after the Saturday Night Massacre approval of Nixon had evaporated except among a small minority of die-hard supporters.

Public support for Nixon had been bumping downstairs since his 61 percent election victory a year earlier and a late-January peak of 68 percent with the announcement of a U.S. withdrawal from Vietnam. Nixon's approval ratings had dropped to 45 percent by the time the Ervin committee hearings began and fluctuated between 31 and 40 percent in the three months after Dean's testimony. Following the Saturday Night Massacre, however, public support plunged to 27 percent. Thereafter, the percentage of Americans expressing approval of Nixon to poll takers varied no more than four points up or down throughout the rest of his presidency. The dismissal of Richardson, Ruckelshaus, and Cox cost Nixon all but his most stubborn public support.[25]

In addition to the grassroots outburst over the Saturday Night Massacre, a hitherto-silent elite began to be heard. Chesterfield Smith, the president of the American Bar Association, declared that Nixon's action threatened "the rule of law and . . . the administration of justice." One after another, newspapers across the country, most of which had endorsed Nixon's reelection a year previously, printed editorials calling for his resignation or removal. A crescendo of sorts was reached when *Time* magazine in its November 12 issue published the first editorial in its fifty-year history and called for Nixon to resign because he had violated his "compact with the people."[26] The detailed and specific condemnation of the president's conduct by *Time*, the country's leading mass-circulation newsmagazine and one long favorable to Nixon, gave outrage an additional badge of legitimacy.

When Speaker Albert gaveled the House of Representatives into session on Tuesday morning, October 23, Waldie and seven other members each put forth impeachment resolutions, some of which had numerous cosponsors. Ranging from simple one-sentence statements declaring the president impeached to Waldie's six-page list of specific charges, this wave of resolutions signaled that a sizable group of representatives was now ready to go to the mat with Nixon. Albert was prepared to quash suggestions that a special committee be appointed, something he disfavored for the same reason he had done so when a similar proposal was made for the Ford confirmation. As speaker of the House, Albert would have to select the majority membership of a special committee, something he was loath to do lest it appear that he was organizing an effort to open the path to the presidency for himself. Better to have a standing committee with a predetermined membership take charge, so that whatever the outcome, it would not appear to be a politically manipulated result.

The speaker immediately directed that the resolutions be sent to the Committee on the Judiciary, setting in motion a full-scale impeachment inquiry for the first time in decades. Already burdened with the Ford confirmation hearings in the weeks just ahead, the committee would not be able to rush to judgment regarding impeachment. To Albert, eager to avoid any impression of being motivated by partisanship, a deliberate, unhurried approach, responsible and respectful of due process, seemed best under the circumstances. The modest Douglas impeachment inquiry, not to mention the resignation-aborted Fortas and Agnew episodes, would be dwarfed by what the Saturday Night Massacre stirred Congress to pursue.

By December 1973 veteran Capitol Hill reporters became aware of a consensus starting to develop in Congress that the impeachment of Nixon was merited. The seemingly endless stream of revelations of suspicious or blatantly illegal White House conduct appeared to be accelerating, yet Nixon gave no indication of a readiness to resign. "Almost without anybody's noticing," observed Elizabeth Drew of the *New Yorker*, "a bipartisan consensus has grown that the Congress must proceed on the question of impeaching the President."[27] While Congress might be embracing the abstract idea of impeachment, it had yet to address the practical aspects of conducting such an unfamiliar proceeding.

The Judiciary Committee's chairman, Peter Rodino of New Jersey, a twenty-five-year veteran of the committee but only installed as its presiding officer the previous January, had quietly been preparing for months to handle a possible impeachment proceeding. Jerome Zeifman, the committee's chief counsel, had begun in the spring of 1973 to examine the relevant law and precedents, beginning with materials collected at the time of the Douglas inquiry.[28] It was soon evident to Zeifman and Rodino that the magnitude of the task before them would require staff resources far beyond what the Judiciary Committee possessed. They hired Wisconsin attorney Richard Cates, an experienced prosecutor, to start the inquiry, while Rodino began looking for a special counsel to take charge of the overall effort.

By the time Chairman Rodino settled on John H. Doar as the impeachment inquiry's special counsel and announced his selection on December 19, impatient members of Congress were complaining that the time he was taking showed that Rodino was hopelessly out of his depth and incapable of moving the inquiry forward. Nevertheless, Rodino, conscious of the potential for the inquiry to break down into partisan wrangling that would guarantee failure, instinctively moved with caution. Doar, an Eisenhower appointee to the Justice Department who had stayed on to do admirable work in the Civil Rights Division during the Kennedy and Johnson administrations, met Rodino's standard of nonpartisanship and meticulous care in pursuing justice. With the committee's ranking Republican member, Edward Hutchinson of Michigan, appointing Albert Jenner of Chicago as the minority's counsel, the staff was entirely under the direction of nominal Republicans. Although Doar took up his duties immediately and Jenner did so soon thereafter, they soon began to be criticized for moving too slowly, even by Deputy Counsel Cates, who thought sufficient evidence was already in hand to give an experienced prosecutor a compelling case for impeachment. In fact, the Judiciary Committee and its staff faced a task of greater magnitude than that of the previous inquiries into Watergate.[29]

When the Senate had established its Select Committee on Presidential Campaign Activities in February 1973, it had mandated the committee only to explore campaign finance irregularities in the presidential election of 1972 that allowed campaign contributions to be used for the Watergate break-in. Its sponsors understood that a wider investigation risked being called a partisan witch hunt and also faced the danger of being diffuse and thus unproductive. During the floor debate over creating the committee, Senator Ervin had disclaimed any intention of going after the president, calling it "simply inconceivable" that he might be involved. Such politically cagey declarations helped obtain Republican compliance but limited the scope of the Senate probe.[30]

The Select Committee's modest staff had taken some time to assemble. Ervin selected as chief counsel Samuel Dash, a Georgetown University Law School professor, former Philadelphia district attorney, and past president of the National Association of Criminal Defense Lawyers. For his part, Senator Howard Baker had named as chief minority counsel Fred Thompson, a young Nashville attorney. Dash and Thompson in turn had to employ other attorneys, as well as find adequate offices. Although they discovered they could work together, the staff's partisan division remained and it took more than two months to become fully operational. Three more months elapsed before the staff achieved its great breakthrough, the exposure of the White House tapes, and that revelation only complicated the case legally.

Attorney General Richardson had likewise consumed time putting together a legal team. No fewer than six active and retired judges had declined to serve as special prosecutor before Richardson finally approached Harvard Law professor

Archibald Cox. When the two worked out an agreement and Special Prosecutor Cox was installed in May, he in turn had to assemble a staff. Cox understood that his task was different and even at odds with that of the Ervin committee.[31] Cox's charge was to pursue the case of the Watergate cover-up as it stood exposed at the time and to prosecute all those involved. Like Ervin, Cox gathered a cadre of talented lawyers, led by Henry Ruth, James F. Neal, Richard Ben-Veniste, and Philip Lacovara, but once again doing so took time. From its early days the special prosecutor's staff, which grew to more than 150 people, was involved in the legal battle to obtain access to the White House tapes as well as the preparation of numerous cases.[32] The Saturday Night Massacre temporarily put the continuation of those efforts in doubt, but the public uproar compelled Nixon to appoint another special prosecutor, former American Bar Association president Leon Jaworski of Houston. Jaworski did not have to assemble a new staff, but he had to familiarize himself with the case. Meanwhile he and the Cox holdovers needed to continue pursuing the agenda to which they were committed. As the focus of attention shifted to the president himself and grounds for his impeachment, yet another large legal team with a separate agenda had to be constructed. Once again this activity took time.

Doar turned to people he knew in putting together his impeachment inquiry staff. At the advice of a Yale Law School faculty friend, he sought to enlist several young lawyers he had met while judging a Yale mock trial a year earlier. He tracked down the first person on his list, Bill Clinton, at the University of Arkansas Law School, where he had gone to teach. Clinton, having decided to run for Congress in the spring Democratic primary, declined Doar's offer but suggested his Yale Law School girlfriend, Hillary Rodham, who happened to be sitting in his kitchen drinking coffee at the moment. Rodham had also been on Doar's list, and she quickly accepted his invitation.[33] Had Doar been able to recruit Clinton as well as Rodham and the two had become immersed in the Nixon inquiry together, the long-term effect on their careers, not to mention the political culture of impeachment, might have been profound.

Another of Doar's recruits, John Labovitz, reflected on why, in his judgment, the impeachment inquiry staff, which eventually numbered more than one hundred people, including over forty attorneys, proved itself thorough and impartial in building a case for presentation to the Judiciary Committee:

> The staff was bipartisan, so that there were built-in checks against bias in one direction or the other. The staff was isolated from committee members, the press, and the public, so that its professional obligations were constantly reinforced. Finally, the staff was hired for, and committed to, the impeachment inquiry and not the general work of the committee or the House. As a result, it had an organizational single-mindedness not found in previous inquiries or most congressional investigations.[34]

The Judiciary Committee's permanent staff was in some cases disappointed not to be included in impeachment work and understandably jealous of those who were directly involved.[35] Still, the regular work of the committee needed to continue, and the division of responsibility worked well.

The task facing Doar, Jenner, deputy counsels Richard Cates and Bernard Nussbaum, and the rest of the staff spread far beyond what had at the outset confronted Dash or Cox. The House impeachment inquiry needed to determine not simply whether crimes had been committed but whether the president's involvement in improper acts constituted impeachable offenses. If their work was to be perceived as responsible investigation and not just as a transparently political assault, they had to undertake a careful study of the law of impeachment and the facts of the Nixon case so that, one way or the other, a convincing presentation could be made to the Judiciary Committee and the country. The staff divided into a group led by Nussbaum looking at legal and constitutional questions and six others overseen by Cates examining specific allegations against Nixon. The six areas of presidential activity explored included domestic surveillance, clandestine political conduct, the Watergate break-in and cover-up, the president's personal finances, political use of government agencies, and a catchall category of abuses of power from the Cambodian bombing to Nixon's impoundment of funds appropriated by Congress.[36]

The impeachment inquiry staff plunged into its work behind a veil of secrecy. Doar kept staff members at their task at least twelve hours a day, seven days a week, but their progress was neither rapid nor apparent to outsiders. Impatience with Doar's deliberate pace grew in the halls of Congress and throughout the nation, while in the White House spirits began to lift somewhat. After having agreed to a new special prosecutor with undiminished powers in November and eventually turning over nineteen tapes that Cox had sought, Nixon by mid-February was emboldened enough to resist further demands for tapes and documents. The White House let it be known that it thought the demand for impeachment was losing steam.[37] When Democrat Mike Mansfield, the Senate majority leader, declared that he was giving no thought to a Senate impeachment trial, he may have just been trying to dispel notions that the Democrats were conspiring to oust the president. Nevertheless, Mansfield's statement contributed further to a sense of congressional lassitude in dealing with a matter much on the minds of his colleagues and the American public.[38] As Doar's meticulous examination of law and evidence continued, even Judiciary Committee members sensed eroding public enthusiasm for the conduct of the inquiry.[39]

The first public evidence that Doar's staff was making progress appeared in late February when it put forth a memorandum on impeachment law. After a careful examination of English precedents as well as the records of the 1787 Constitutional Convention, state ratifying conventions, and previous impeachments, the staff reached a conclusion that was couched in more temperate language but in substance was not too far from Ford's 1970 observation that an impeachable offense was whatever Congress defined it to be. An impeachable offense, in the staff's view, did not need to be based on a specific crime but could legitimately result from any offense or pattern of offenses against the U.S. system of government that Congress determined to be of such weight as to render the offender unfit to continue in office. "The crucial factor is not the intrinsic quality of behavior but the significance of its effect upon our constitutional system or the functioning of our government." The Constitution explicitly assigns the president the duty, the report noted, to "take care that the laws be faithfully executed." He must swear in his oath of office to "faithfully execute the Office of President of the United States" and to "preserve, protect, and defend the Constitution of the United States." Those obligations involved the duty not to abuse executive powers, transgress their limits, or violate the rights of citizens spelled out in the Bill of Rights. Grievous violations, that is "high crimes and misdemeanors," did not necessarily entail violations of criminal statutes. Likewise, not all misconduct was sufficient to constitute grounds for impeachment. Congress must judge on the basis of all the facts in context whether the alleged offense was substantial enough in its effect upon the conduct of government to constitute impeachable abuse or usurpation of power.[40]

The inquiry staff's analysis, which Bill Clinton's girlfriend Hillary Rodham and just a handful of other lawyers helped craft, distinguished impeachment from a criminal proceeding. It pointed out that impeachment was constructed to deal with damage to the state by high officials and had no roots in ordinary criminal law. The report reminded the Judiciary Committee that the term "high crimes and misdemeanors" was added to the list of impeachable offenses by the framers because they considered treason and bribery too limited grounds and George Mason's suggestion of "maladministration" too vague. The framers drew on English precedent, where they found "high misdemeanor" a term used in William Blackstone's *Commentaries on the Laws of England* to describe an impeachable abuse of the powers of high office. As Alexander Hamilton subsequently explained in the *Federalist Papers,* the framers had chosen to create a single executive so that they would have one person to hold responsible for abuses of power and violations of the public trust. James Madison concurred that the impeachment power was "indispensable" to protect against "the incapacity, negligence, or perfidy of the chief magistrate." The report, which would guide the committee, thus underscored the role of impeachment as a means to thwart the substantial misuse of government.[41]

In a press conference on February 25, Nixon for the first time gave indications that he had been thinking about impeachment. He challenged the Judiciary Committee's definition when Dan Rather of CBS News, alluding to Nixon's training in the law, asked the president to define an impeachable offense. Bristling a bit at a questioner he perceived to be hostile, Nixon said, "Well, Mr. Rather, you don't have to be a constitutional lawyer to know that the Constitution is very precise in defining what is an impeachable offense." He then insisted, contrary to what the Doar staff had said, that "a criminal offense on the part of the president is the requirement for impeachment."[42]

Nixon's legal team, far smaller in number but with a more limited task than its adversaries, merely needed to counter their arguments and demands for information. A week after the inquiry staff released its memorandum, James St. Clair, a distinguished Boston defense attorney who became Nixon's latest counsel at the start of the year, issued a paper setting forth an even more restrictive view of impeachment than Nixon had suggested. St. Clair maintained that impeachment required a criminal offense "of a very serious nature committed in one's governmental capacity." He asserted that this view was supported "by history, logic, legal precedent, and a sound and sensible public policy which demands stability in our form of government." The more flexible and contextualized judgment that the House inquiry staff's paper justified, which had drawn no White House objection when articulated in 1970 by the man just installed as vice president, was decried by St. Clair as "political impeachment." English precedents were altogether inappropriate, his argument continued, because they arose from a quest to establish parliamentary supremacy and thus were contrary to the American constitutional separation of powers.[43]

Concerned that Nixon's political opponents might seek to hold him to account for trivial offenses committed as chief executive, the president's lawyer contended that only "high misdemeanors" were impeachable, arguing that otherwise the framers would have used the term "or" to link crimes with misdemeanors. Indeed, St. Clair held, "high crimes and misdemeanors" must be equivalent in seriousness to treason and bribery to qualify as impeachable offenses. He also pointed out that the Constitution held life-tenure judges to a standard of "good behavior" but applied no such language to executives, who could be defeated for reelection, were limited to two terms, and could be declared incapacitated under the Twenty-fifth Amendment. The almost desperate tone of these contentions underscored the weakness of the argument against the House inquiry staff's position on the nature of impeachment.

Debate between the adversaries quickly shifted from the theoretical to the practical. Disputes over the authority of the House in conducting an impeachment, including its evidence-gathering powers and its procedural obligations to the president, had to be worked out in the absence of clear precedents. Struggles over evidence attracted the most attention, as had been the case ever since the existence of the White House tape recordings had become known the previous July.

Doar's staff began its inquiry into the president's conduct with nothing more to go on than what was already on the public record. It sought further information from the Ervin committee, the special prosecutor, and the president.

"There It Is, Just The Way It Came Off The Founding Fathers' Typewriter"

Herblock,
Washington Post,
March 13, 1974.
© The Herb
Block Foundation.

While the White House proved resistant, the other two cooperated. The Senate Select Committee allowed Doar's staff to photocopy one hundred thousand documents, a task that took six weeks. It also turned over a complete list of the five hundred White House taped conversations the committee had sought for its investigation along with explanations of what each was expected to contain.[44] Once the Watergate grand jury issued indictments of seven individuals involved in the cover-up on March 1, ending worries about the cases being prematurely exposed and compromised, the special prosecutor too cooperated. The grand jury delivered a copy of its report and two large briefcases full of evidence to the House of Representatives.

Close examination of relevant law and history had convinced Special Prosecutor Jaworski that, while in office, a president could only be impeached and not indicted. The disruption to the president's ability to carry out his unique constitutional responsibilities that could occur if he were forced to defend himself in court placed him in a separate category from other impeachable officials, the special prosecutor concluded. Jaworski had to struggle to convince a grand jury very much wanting to indict Nixon that, while an indictment of Vice President Agnew could go forward, one involving the president could not. The prosecutor and the grand jurors eventually reached an accommodation. They agreed that Nixon could be listed as an unindicted coconspirator and that the evidence leading to that conclusion could be placed in the hands of those with the constitutional responsibility for impeaching a sitting president.

The most visible battle between the president and his pursuers continued to be fought over the White House tapes. Momentarily panicked, the president gave seven tapes to the special prosecutor in the aftermath of the Saturday Night Massacre, admitting that one contained an eighteen-and-a-half-minute gap and stating that two others requested did not exist. Even this limited amount of evidence persuaded Jaworski that Nixon was guilty of criminal offenses and convinced him to seek twenty-five more tapes to buttress his case. In his annual State of the Union address in late January, the president sought to deflect the request by saying that the special prosecutor had been given "sufficient material" to complete his investigation. "One year of Watergate," Nixon declared, "is enough."[45]

Unimpressed by Nixon's January 30 declaration, Doar the following month requested forty-two tapes. After two months of negotiations failed to pry them loose, Rodino finally issued a congressional subpoena for these tapes. Five days later Jaworski sought a subpoena for sixty-four tapes, and within two days Judge Sirica approved his request. Ignoring both subpoenas, Nixon announced on April 29 that he would instead make public edited transcripts of the requested tapes, thus demonstrating his innocence. The White House reported that ten of the forty-two requested tapes were missing, while the transcripts it released proved to be incomplete and inaccurate when compared with the few tapes previously obtained by the special prosecutor. Within days, the Judiciary Committee voted to notify Nixon that his transcripts failed to comply with its subpoena.

Perhaps most damaging to the president's cause, however, was what the transcripts did reveal. His conversations were shown to be rambling and disjointed, petty and mean-spirited, and laced with profanity, though it was routinely edited out and replaced by the explanation "expletive deleted." Although the profanity was later revealed to be generally mild and thoroughly unimaginative, "expletive deleted" created an image of coarse presidential language that added to the spreading sense of Nixon's unfitness for his high office.[46]

Reaction to the edited White House transcripts proved devastating to Nixon. Members of Congress, even partisan Republicans, expressed outrage. The Republican leader of the Senate, Hugh Scott of Pennsylvania, called the president's conversations "shabby, disgusting, immoral." Even Ford, Nixon's heretofore loyal and uncritical vice president, declared himself "a little disappointed." Newspaper columnists described the transcripts with terms such as "sleazy" and "repellant." Editorial opinion was, if anything, harsher. The *Los Angeles Times* and the *New York Times,* seldom given to agreeing with each other, both declared that impeachment was now necessary. Even the conservative *Chicago Tribune* found the president's conduct disgraceful. For the second time in six months, an effort to evade apparently legitimate demands for White House tape recordings, first by offering only Stennis-approved summaries and now by substituting edited transcripts, ignited widespread condemnation. By May the country seemed more ready than ever before to listen to legal and constitutional arguments for Nixon's removal.[47]

The longer the battle over the tapes went on, the more Congress and the country became persuaded that, regardless of the president's arguments that he was merely defending the principle of executive privilege, he really had something to hide. The release of the edited transcripts, so damaging to Nixon's image as well-spoken, moralistic, and coldly logical, left the impression that much worse must remain hidden. When the House Judiciary Committee sought more tapes and documents as it began its hearings and Nixon again refused to provide them, the lack of resolution and growth of suspicion remained problems that steadily eroded the president's position.

The House impeachment inquiry was forced to grapple with contentious issues buried beneath the spare language of the Constitution. In granting the House of Representatives the sole power of impeachment, the framers had left fundamental questions unanswered. One was exposed in the tapes struggle: Did the House in pursuing an impeachment inquiry have the authority to compel delivery of executive branch documents? A strong argument could be made that such power was necessary and proper to carrying out the House's constitutional duty. On the other hand, using the impeachment power in such a fashion might be seen as violating the separation of powers and elevating Congress above the other branches. In any case, what could the House do if the president refused to comply with a subpoena to produce documents? Unlike the chief executive, Congress had no police or military force at its disposal. Finally, what rights, if any, did the object of an impeachment inquiry possess in the face of a House proceeding? For instance, did the impeachment power supersede the Fifth Amendment guarantee against self-incrimination? In working out answers to these questions, the House Judiciary Committee demonstrated that in every instance, political as well as constitutional judgments were involved.

The answer to the question of congressional access to executive branch evidence seemed clear, at least to the House of Representatives itself. The Constitution gave the House the specific and unshared duty of impeachment. The House would be hard-pressed to carry out its task responsibly without access to relevant information. Furthermore, the executive branch routinely provided Congress with data on many matters. Nixon's lawyers, however, argued that such transfers were discretionary, and they appealed lower-court decisions on the tapes subpoenas to the contrary. Until the Supreme Court definitively determined the matter, it remained contentious and the House would not have the material it sought. As Doar and Rodino headed into their committee hearings, what they decided was appropriate under the circumstances was to rely on the old English principle of "inference of guilt" widely accepted in U.S. courts. Judges routinely instructed juries that they could reasonably infer guilt when evidence that could presumably exonerate as easily as convict continued to be withheld.[48]

The questions requiring most immediate resolution involved the nature and conduct of the committee's hearing. In dealing with impeachment was the committee, and indeed the House as a whole, acting as a grand jury? Should the committee and the House determine on the basis of a prosecutorial presentation of evidence without defense counsel present whether there was probable cause to proceed to trial in the Senate? Or was the hearing in fact a trial, a judicial proceeding in which the individual in jeopardy should be accorded all the rights to counsel and due process provided in a trial? As Doar and his colleagues prepared for what they assumed should and would follow the grand jury model, James St. Clair began insisting that they were going to conduct a trial. Therefore, he, as the president's attorney, ought to have the right to be present, cross-examine witnesses, call and even subpoena rebuttal witnesses, and make an argument for the defense.[49]

Rodino, Doar, and Jenner immediately worried that a skilled defense attorney, which St. Clair unquestionably was, could throw the hearings into turmoil and perhaps even derail them completely. But they were also well aware that they were dealing with a committee and a larger audience unfamiliar with impeachment and eager for the appearance of fairness at every stage of the process. Soon they found the committee dividing along partisan lines over the issue. Democratic resistance to St. Clair's demands crumbled when veteran Judiciary Committee staff members pointed out that William O. Douglas's counsel Simon Rifkind had been involved in the justice's impeachment hearing before a judiciary subcommittee in 1970. That, of course, had been a situation in which the House Judiciary Committee had little interest in going ahead and gave no particular thought to the precedent it was setting.

The Douglas hearing may have been very different in character, but given the otherwise total unfamiliarity of the current committee members with impeachment hearings, it exerted a powerful influence. Rodino was prepared to bend over backward to show that his committee was free of partisanship. He admitted St. Clair to the hearings and empowered him to question witnesses, suggest additional witnesses, address the committee, and raise objections to questions posed by the inquiry staff and committee members themselves. Rodino did make clear, however, that he retained the power to overrule and silence St. Clair if he felt it necessary to do so. As it turned out, St. Clair was not contentious and did not confirm the committee leaders' worst fears.[50]

Once the rules were agreed upon, the thirty-eight members of the House Judiciary Committee began their long-anticipated hearings on May 9. Unlike the Ervin committee hearings in the Senate nearly a year earlier, these hearings were not open to the public, much less televised. Ostensibly the hearings were closed because confidential grand jury testimony was in use. But in addition Doar believed and persuaded Rodino that the members of the committee ought to make up their minds regarding impeachment on the basis of their own evaluation of the evidence presented, not public pressure, partisan posturing, or the pleas of the inquiry staff. Therefore he thought it best to present the accumulated evidence without emotion, immediate analysis, or the glare of the media spotlight. In a closed hearing room Doar began laying out the results of his investigation in a flat, emotion-free voice that droned on hour after hour. Committee members found Doar's chronological presentation exceedingly dull. More than once more than one nodded off. Even St. Clair occasionally dozed.[51] The tedious presentation continued for six weeks, interrupted at times as the committee members listened to conversations from the few tapes obtained through the special prosecutor.

Doar began by describing the structure and tightly controlled operation of the White House with Nixon and the now-indicted Haldeman at its center. Evidence of the Watergate break-in and steps to conceal White House involvement in it followed in turn. Within days, even Nixon's defenders on the committee began to perceive his direct engagement in reprehensible behavior, especially as they listened to evidence in the president's own voice. Once the Watergate story had been fully covered, the committee voted to subpoena forty-five more tapes. At the same time it decided against seeking to have Nixon declared to be in contempt of Congress for failing to comply with previous subpoenas. Doar then turned to other matters, including the Ellsberg case, corrupt practices involving the International Telephone and Telegraph Company and the dairy industry, the identification and harassment of political enemies, and Nixon's income tax violations. June was nearly at an end before Doar completed his evidentiary presentation, and St. Clair spent two days seeking to refute the mountain of evidence of wrongdoing.

The penultimate stage of the closed hearings involved the examination of nine witnesses, beginning with Alexander Butterfield, including Haldeman and Mitchell, and concluding with John Dean. The committee agreed to limit to one day the testimony, cross-examination, and committee members' questioning of each witness. What committee members heard from the witnesses confirmed in virtually every respect what Doar's lengthy presentation had laid out.

James St. Clair staked his defense of the president on demolishing Dean's credibility but failed to do so. In fact, he inadvertently underscored the quality of Dean's memory, the very thing he was seeking to impugn, by forgetting a question he had asked before a lengthy interruption and standing by helplessly as Dean repeated the long question verbatim.[52] St. Clair further damaged himself with the committee by citing in Nixon's defense a portion of a conversation contained on a tape the committee had subpoenaed but not received. The committee erupted in fury at this manipulative use of withheld evidence.[53]

Doar had taken care to avoid passing judgment on the evidence throughout his lengthy presentation. As an experienced prosecutor, he simply laid out a string of facts that would lead a jury to an inevitable conclusion. In his final summation, after the witnesses had all been heard, however, he reluctantly shifted gears. Pressed to do so by Peter Rodino, Doar made an effective argument that the evidence added up to proof of Nixon's repeated abuses of power. The president had directed his staff and agencies of the federal government in acts demanding "perjury, destruction of evidence, obstruction of justice, all crimes," said Doar. "But most important, it required deliberate, contrived, continued and continuing deception of the American people."[54] In his hastily prepared argument on Friday, July 19, all the more compelling to committee members because Doar had taken such a long and methodical route to reach his conclusion, the special counsel left no doubt that he believed impeachment to be warranted. Having given his undivided attention to the case for so long while they were less thoroughly engaged in it, the special counsel's judgment carried great weight with the members of the House Judiciary Committee as they prepared to debate the question of impeachment before what was expected to be an attentive national television audience.

While attention was focused on the House Judiciary Committee hearings, the battle over the special prosecutor's subpoena of White House tapes finally reached the Supreme Court. The process had been speeded by Jaworski, who sought immediate Supreme Court review, bypassing the appellate court, when Nixon's lawyers had appealed Judge Sirica's initial ruling. The justices agreed to delay their usual summer recess in order to hear an extended three-hour argument of *United States v. Nixon* on July 8.

Although *United States v. Nixon* hinged on the issue of executive privilege, the right of the president to withhold information from Congress and the courts, St. Clair opened by arguing that the case should be dismissed because it involved a "political question," that is, impeachment. The Court traditionally avoided intruding into political questions, leaving them to the other branches to decide. The deputy special prosecutor, Philip Lacovara, responded that neither history nor "sound constitutional law" supported the claim that the Court must give way to the president in resolving the executive privilege issue or defer to Congress and its power of impeachment. Instead, he argued, the Court had both the right and the responsibility to decide this dispute.

St. Clair proceeded to assert an absolute right of secrecy for executive communications. Several justices became frustrated with the circular argument that only impeachment could rein in a president but a president did not need to share information that might provoke impeachment. "How are you going to impeach him," an exasperated Justice Marshall asked from the bench, "if you don't know about it?"[55] The impression given by the justices' questions during oral argument was confirmed the following day when they gathered in conference: No support existed for Nixon's position.

Former Chief Justice Earl Warren, who himself knew the discomfort of a proposed impeachment, was especially interested in the pending decision of *United States v. Nixon*. Warren had been undermined by fellow Californian Nixon as he sought the 1952 Republican presidential nomination and later had been obliged to suffer in silence during Nixon's 1968 presidential campaign calling for restoration of "law and order" by reversing decisions of Warren's Court. On the afternoon of July 9, immediately following the Court's conference, his old colleague and friend William Brennan visited Warren at Walter Reed Army Hospital, where the eighty-two-year-old retired justice was being treated for heart problems. Brennan told the former chief that the Court's forthcoming decision against Nixon would be unanimous. The Nixon appointees would join the Court veterans of Warren's era. Warren smiled and registered his approval. The same evening he succumbed to another heart attack.[56]

Warren's funeral at the Washington National Cathedral and his burial at Arlington Cemetery slowed the drafting of the *United States v. Nixon* opinion only slightly. Achieving the unanimity that the justices considered vital to a decision pitting judicial against executive power proved more time consuming. Conscious of Nixon's earlier declaration that he would obey a "definitive" declaration of the Court, they did not want to leave him with leeway to evade a divided decision and thus weaken the overall standing of the Court. Strengthening Burger's initial lackluster draft and sharpening his points required the same sort of negotiation among the justices that an important opinion normally involved, though in this instance compressed into a much shorter time period than usual.[57] In the end, the effort produced a clear ruling: Executive confidentiality was a legitimate interest, but priority must be given to producing evidence in cases of alleged criminal conduct to ensure due process of law. Not even the president was exempt from equal treatment of the law.

The Supreme Court delivered its answer in the case of *United States v. Nixon* only sixteen days after oral argument. The junior justice, Rehnquist, did not participate because of his previous association in the Nixon administration with three of the defendants in the case.[58] Justices Burger, Blackmun, and Powell, the other Nixon appointees on the Court, chose not to recuse themselves, and indeed, all ended up voting against the president's position. Chief Justice Burger, appointed by Nixon and in his seat only because of the success of the 1968 campaign against Abe Fortas, was the listed author of the opinion, though his more liberal colleagues had collectively made his arguments and his prose more forceful.[59]

"How Can They Say He Hasn't Faithfully Executed The Laws?"

Herblock,
Washington Post,
July 21, 1974. ©
The Herb Block
Foundation.

The ruling in *United States v. Nixon* began by stoutly rejecting St. Clair's claim that the case concerned a political question into which the Court should not intrude. Rather, the chief justice asserted that the case involved exactly the sort of dispute that the Court existed to resolve. Citing a line of decisions reaching back to the 1803 judgment in *Marbury v. Madison,* Justice Burger quoted John Marshall's famous statement that "it is emphatically the province and duty of the judicial department to say what the law is." The rest of St. Clair's argument faired only marginally better.

The Court conceded that the legitimacy of government confidentiality could be traced back to the secret sessions of the Constitutional Convention itself. Furthermore, the concept of executive privilege could be presumed from the provisions of the Constitution regarding separation of powers and executive responsibilities. However, the justices agreed, these considerations could not sustain "an absolute, unqualified Presidential privilege of immunity from judicial process under all circumstances." The value of confidentiality needed to be balanced with other values, in this instance the "primary constitutional duty of the Judicial Branch to do justice in criminal prosecutions." In this case, considerations of confidentiality were superseded by the need for balance among the separate branches when necessary to ensure "a workable government." Nixon's general claim of absolute executive privilege "to withhold evidence that is demonstrably relevant in a criminal trial would cut deeply into the guarantee of due process of law and gravely impair the basic function of the courts." The president must, the Court concluded, provide the requested tapes to the special prosecutor.[60]

The ruling was crafted in such a way as to apply as well to a congressional quest for evidence of criminal activity in an impeachment proceeding. Though the case heard by the Court had been brought by the special prosecutor and not the House Judiciary Committee, the justices clearly understood the connections between indicted Watergate defendants and their unindicted coconspirator facing impeachment. *United States v. Nixon* made a powerful statement in support of the constitutionally privileged status of Congress's authority to pursue an impeachment investigation.

When the House Judiciary Committee began public hearings on the impeachment of Richard Nixon at 7:45 p.m. on July 24, 1974, the first televised House hearings in twenty years, the Republican minority soon sought to stall the proceedings because of the Supreme Court's ruling in *United States v. Nixon* earlier the same day. Ranking minority member Edward Hutchinson suggested a postponement to give the president time to produce the tapes ordered released and the committee time to study them. Two days later, Illinois Republican Robert McClory formally moved to give the president ten days to produce the sixty-three tapes covered by the Court's ruling. A bipartisan majority, however, determined to move ahead, recognizing that McClory's motion, if adopted, could lead to prolonged delay. Most committee members concluded that they had ample evidence to reach an impeachment decision without all or even any of the 147 tapes the committee had by then requested.[61]

In light of all the attention that the tapes had received to that point and would garner once they did become public, the Judiciary Committee made a noteworthy decision. The committee concluded that it possessed sufficient evidence to carry out its task without the tapes themselves. The existence of the tapes had played a great role in creating an image of presidential concealment during the previous year, and the tapes themselves would soon cement the understanding that Nixon was guilty as charged. But in the impeachment deliberations of the House Judiciary Committee the evidence on the tapes played no part.

The House Judiciary Committee hearings were timed, quite successfully as it turned out, to attract a nationwide television audience. An estimated forty million viewers watched all or substantial parts of the hearings, four times the audience for the first weeks of the previous summer's Senate Watergate hearings.[62] After introductory remarks by the chairman and the ranking minority member and submission of an impeachment resolution, each of the thirty-eight members of the committee was given fifteen minutes to make opening remarks. Some spoke with passion, others without betraying much emotion, but all with a sense of the weight they bore. Many, a few Republicans as well as most Democrats, laid out the reasons they believed, after examining the evidence, that Nixon's impeachment was justified. The more circumspect of both parties described serious concerns that had been stirred in the course of their consideration of the evidence but suggested that they would have to listen to the coming debate before reaching a conclusion as to how to vote. Nevertheless, the remarks of more than two-thirds of the committee members laid out a fuller case for Nixon's impeachment than had ever been presented at any one time to an attentive national audience.

Only a hard core of Republicans, most notably Charles Sandman of New Jersey and Charles Wiggins of California, were willing from the outset to criticize the conduct of the hearings and declare that they found no grounds for impeachment.[63] Sandman was particularly scornful, asserting that Andrew Johnson had been wrongly impeached during a fit of hysteria in "one of the darkest moments" in the nation's history. "I do not propose," Sandman declared, "to be any part of a second blotch on the history of this great nation."[64]

Republicans Lawrence Hogan of Maryland and M. Caldwell Butler of Virginia were first to break party ranks and declare that they would support impeachment. Hogan drew attention to his decision by announcing it in advance at a press conference, but Butler caught the committee by surprise, both by his decision and by his manner of expressing it. "There are frightening implications for the future of our country if we do not impeach the President of the United States," Butler said, "because we will, by this impeachment proceeding, be establishing a standard of conduct for the President of the United States which will for all time be a matter of public record." The positive as well as negative consequences of impeachment were much on Butler's mind. "If we fail to impeach, we have condoned and left unpunished a course of conduct totally inconsistent with the reasonable expectations of the American people; we will have condoned and left unpunished a Presidential course of conduct designed to interfere with and obstruct the very process which he is sworn to uphold; and we will have condoned and left unpunished an abuse of power totally without justification. And," he concluded, "we will have said to the American people: 'These misdeeds are inconsequential and unimportant.'" Butler's eloquence helped focus attention on the function of impeachment in sustaining public trust in government.[65]

Barbara Jordan, a black freshman representative from Texas, speaking in an unusually rich and dramatic voice, riveted the attention of the prime-time television audience even more than had Butler. When the Constitution was written, Jordan said, people like her, black and female, were not part of "We the people." Now empowered, she was not prepared to be "an idle spectator to the diminution, the subversion, the destruction of the Constitution." Spelling out the Constitution's terms, she cautioned members that it was the Senate's responsibility to determine whether the president should be removed from office. Their own duty was simply to determine whether the president should be called to account for what Woodrow Wilson had said should be "nothing short of the grossest offenses against the plain law of the land." Stripping the case to its barest bones, Jordan then pointed to undisputed evidence that Nixon had known almost immediately that money found in the burglars' possession had come from his reelection committee. Yet he had engaged in a series of knowingly false public statements and actions designed to thwart the lawful investigation by government prosecutors. In a forceful manner that brought the issues into sharper focus for all who heard her, Jordan concluded that these acts were impeachable offenses in that they betrayed the public trust in their government and attempted to subvert the Constitution.[66]

The ranking minority member, Edward Hutchinson, who had missed most of Doar's presentation due to emergency gallbladder surgery, wrapped up opening arguments for the Republicans. He remained unconvinced of the merits of the case against Nixon. He argued that impeachment required a criminal act with significant impact on government and criticized his colleagues who were, he said, abandoning that standard as well as the highest standards of proof. Hutchinson scorned what he said was the stacking of inference upon inference and concluded, "I do not believe that any crimes by the President have been proved beyond a reasonable doubt."[67]

Rodino, as chairman, spoke last. He abandoned his prior neutrality and spoke forcefully. By the tests that needed to be applied, he declared, he found the president wanting. Stressing his reluctance to do so, Rodino said he would urge impeachment. His sense of regret slightly tinged with anger at having to carry out an unpleasant but unavoidable responsibility summed up the tenor of the committee discussion that had just unfolded. "I shall do so with a heavy heart," the chairman concluded, "because no man seeks to accuse or to find wanting the Chief Executive of this great country."[68]

Drawing up articles of impeachment proved a challenge to the members of the judiciary committee. This was a crucial step in the impeachment process, both constitutionally and politically. The formal charges against Nixon, the articulation of what presidential conduct justified impeachment, needed to present a compelling case that the acts in question amounted to "treason, bribery, or other high crimes and misdemeanors." Accusations viewed as petty or based on political disputes would probably not be persuasive and thus might undermine support for more substantive charges. If the allegations were to lead to a decision by the House to impeach the president and a determination by two-thirds of the Senate that he should be removed from office, the articles must be substantial and overwhelmingly convincing. They would have to persuade a House majority and a bipartisan Senate supermajority that they possessed sufficient merit to override Republican party loyalties as well as the responsibility felt by members of both parties to respect the better than 60 percent preference for Nixon in the most recent national election.

Small groups of committee members, most often but not always all of the same party, began meeting together after hours during the weeks of Doar's evidentiary presentation to go over and bring into focus the evidence before them. Often they invited one or more of the staff counsels, commonly Richard Cates or his minority counterpart Samuel Garrison, to assist them. In the process Democrats and some Republicans began to identify what they regarded as impeachable offenses.[69] Father Drinan, nearly a year earlier, had proposed four distinct grounds for impeachment. Now Jack Brooks of Texas came forth with a list of seven, and Don Edwards of California boiled down a list of twenty-nine individual offenses into five separate packages. Rodino and Doar, advised by Cates as to what would be acceptable to various groups within the committee, produced their own package of four articles with detailed lists of offenses regarding Watergate, the Ellsberg break-in, refusal to comply with the committee's subpoenas, and tax fraud.

During these informal conversations, even those committee members most furious about Nixon's conduct came to appreciate that some of his most egregious behavior would have difficulty passing either the constitutional test of an impeachable offense or the political test of a simple-to-understand, difficult-to-dispute justification for a vote to impeach or convict. Consequently, the bombing of Cambodia, which Father Drinan and a few others saw as a crime against a neutral country and one of Nixon's earliest, most egregious offenses but which others saw as a defensible use of the president's wartime discretionary authority, was set aside as a difficult-to-prove and therefore distracting ground for impeachment. What was not evident at the moment but would become so in later decades was that the failure to charge Nixon with misconduct over Cambodia would encourage some subsequent presidents to believe that aggressive and secretive foreign policy initiatives remained within constitutional bounds. Likewise, the hesitation over Cambodia would reinforce congressional caution in later years when problematic and arguably impeachable presidential conduct of foreign affairs came to light.

Likewise falling by the roadside was the impoundment of appropriated funds, which some regarded as violating Congress's constitutional powers but others considered a traditional and appropriate executive practice. Similarly, the Ellsberg break-in divided a majority who thought it a violation of civil rights from a conservative minority who viewed Ellsberg as a traitor. Nixon's recently exposed failure to pay nearly $500,000 in income taxes, the result of a fraudulently claimed deduction for the misrepresented gift of his prepresidential papers to the National Archives as well as of unreported income derived from government improvements to his private homes in Florida and California, was deemed improper but questionable as an impeachable offense. As their discussions proceeded, committee members were limiting what they considered impeachable offenses not merely to crimes but to those that specifically threatened the overall integrity of the U.S. government.

Gradually, consensus began to develop among the previously most undecided members of the committee, a group of southern Democrats and moderate Republicans, that a strong case could be made that Nixon had abused the powers of his office and obstructed justice. Even after the public, televised committee hearings on Nixon's impeachment began, the group continued to struggle to draft appropriate language. They also negotiated with a Democrat task force seeking to draft articles. In the hours before the debate on an initial article was scheduled to begin, the two groups reached agreement on an article to be presented, on their behalf, by Representative Paul Sarbanes of Maryland.[70]

When the Judiciary Committee convened at noon on July 26, Sarbanes offered his substitute for the brief resolution used to initiate the hearings. It began:

Article I. In his conduct of the office of President of the United States, Richard M. Nixon, in violation of his constitutional oath faithfully to execute the office of President of the United States and, to the best of his ability, preserve, protect, and defend the Constitution of the United States, and in violation of his constitutional duty to take care that the laws be faithfully executed, has prevented, obstructed, and impeded the administration of justice in that:

On June 17, 1972, and prior thereto, agents of the Committee for the Re-Election of the President committed illegal entry of the headquarters of the Democratic National Committee in Washington, District of Columbia, for the purpose of securing political intelligence. Subsequent thereto, Richard M. Nixon, using the power of his high office, made it his policy, and in furtherance of such policy did act directly and personally and through his close subordinates and agents, to delay, impede, and obstruct the investigation of such illegal entry; to cover up, conceal, and protect those responsible; and to conceal the existence and scope of other unlawful covert activities.

Thereafter the proposed article listed nine specific means by which Nixon had obstructed justice. Making false or misleading statements to investigators, withholding evidence, encouraging false testimony, bribing witnesses, and interfering with the FBI were among the offenses charged. The article concluded:

In all of this, Richard M. Nixon has acted in a manner contrary to his trust as President and subversive of constitutional government, to the great prejudice of the cause of law and justice and to the manifest injury of the people of the United States.

Wherefore Richard M. Nixon, by such conduct, warrants impeachment and trial and removal from office.[71]

Republican critics immediately confronted Sarbanes with complaints that the article offered only generalities and that its charges lacked specificity. They tried to convey the impression that the charges against Nixon had no evidence to support them yet were so vague that the president would be unable to defend himself against them. Charles Sandman, in one exchange, complained that the article failed to indicate the date of an alleged misdeed. "The President," he insisted, "is entitled to know in the articles of impeachment specifically, on what day he did that thing for which you say he should be removed from office."[72] Caught off guard, Sarbanes tried to explain that plenty of specific evidence backing up each of the charges would be included in an accompanying report but was not appropriate in the articles themselves. Sandman was not satisfied and belligerently increased his complaints about lack of specificity. Debate dragged on until after 11:00 p.m., with some members trying to demonstrate the sufficiency of the evidence while others disputed the contention that an article must describe offenses precisely. Finally, the committee defeated Sandman's motion to strike the first of the nine charges, 27–11, and adjourned for the night.

The efforts of the Republican critics diminished in force and effectiveness during the following day as the committee moved steadily toward a vote on the first article of impeachment. Overnight, impeachment proponents had decided to make an evidentiary case for each of the eight remaining charges. They did so effectively and defeated in turn each motion to strike a charge. At the same time they agreed to several small textual amendments to tighten language. Sandman's remarks in rebuttal became progressively more acerbic as he grew to understand that his specificity complaints had provoked the proponents into making a comprehensive and effective case for the first article to their colleagues and a national television audience.[73]

Shortly before 7:00 p.m. on Saturday evening, July 26, the Judiciary Committee finally reached the point of being ready to vote on an article of impeachment charging Nixon with obstruction of justice. Though the outcome could easily be predicted from the preliminary votes on changes to the article, the members of the committee were notably tense and somber. Their constitutional responsibility appeared to weigh heavily on them. As the committee clerk called the role, twenty-seven members announced that they supported substituting the revised Sarbanes article for the original resolution. Eleven members opposed the language. Chairman Rodino immediately called for a vote on adopting the impeachment article itself and sending it to the full House. Once again the vote was 27–11.[74] Less than two decades after impeachment had been dismissed as a "rusted blunderbuss," a congressional committee by well over a two-thirds majority had taken an important formal step toward impeaching an American president.

The Judiciary Committee reconvened at midday the following Monday to consider a proposed second article of impeachment focusing on a series of acts termed "abuses of power." As submitted it began:

> Article II. Using the powers of the office of President of the United States, Richard M. Nixon, in violation of his constitutional oath faithfully to execute the office of President of the United States and, to the best of his ability, preserve, protect, and defend the Constitution of the United States, and in violation of his constitutional duty to take care that the laws be faithfully executed, has repeatedly engaged in conduct violating the constitutional rights of citizens, impairing the due and proper administration of justice and the conduct of lawful inquiries, or contravening the laws governing agencies of the executive branch and the purposes of these agencies.

Specific allegations of abuses of power followed—the improper obtaining and use of IRS information in a manner that violated law and constitutional rights, illegal misuse of the FBI and other agencies for improper electronic surveillance, authorization and maintenance of a secret investigative unit (the Plumbers) that engaged in unlawful activities, and the impeding and frustrating of lawful inquiries of the Watergate break-in and other matters in violation of his duty to see that laws were faithfully executed.[75]

Again negotiations had gone on behind the scenes to assure the broadest possible support. In this instance, Illinois Republican Robert McClory, insistent that the president could only be impeached for criminal offenses, was won over by the elimination of allegations that were not overtly criminal and the addition of language that the president had acted "personally and through his subordinates and agents" to commit the offenses specified. Eager to acquire additional Republican support and seeing merit in McClory's narrowing of the article's charges, the majority Democrats had no difficulty embracing his changes.[76]

California Republican Charles Wiggins objected that abuse of power was not worthy of consideration as an impeachable offense. Abuse of power was subject to congressional definition and was not necessarily within the meaning of "high crimes and misdemeanors." He worried that Congress could call anything an abuse of power and use impeachment as a parliamentary vote of no confidence. His fellow Californian, Democrat George Danielson, rejected Wiggins's argument, calling this "certainly the most important article that the committee may pass out." He considered abuses of power true high crimes because only the president could commit them. Danielson termed these "offenses against the very structure of the state, against the system of government." He concluded, "This is uniquely a presidential offense, Mr. Chairman, and the most important subject of this hearing."[77]

Extended discussion of the terms of Article II ensued. Having learned the importance of doing so during debate over the previous article, supporters of impeachment spoke in detail about the specific incidents of wiretapping, illegal entry, improper income tax audits, and other illegal actions that provided the basis for this article. A recurring theme was the president's repeated violation of his oath of office by knowingly acting contrary to his positive duty to take care that the law was faithfully executed. At the end of a long day and evening of debate, the second article of impeachment was approved 28–10, with McClory joining an otherwise stable majority.[78]

Nixon's refusal to comply with the committee's four subpoenas for a total of 147 tapes had initially been included among the charges of abuse of power. It was split off into a separate article at the insistence of McClory, who believed that it related specifically to the House's authority to conduct an impeachment investigation and thus deserved to stand alone.[79] The president had provided none of the tapes sought by the committee, although the special prosecutor had cooperated by passing along the ones he had obtained. McClory applauded the Supreme Court ruling against absolute executive privilege in *United States v. Nixon*. Such privilege, he said, had no application in an impeachment case, and then cited, as would several others, Lord Edward Coke's observation that a person cannot be the judge of his own cause. The Illinois Republican thought the resolution of this issue would set a defining precedent for future impeachments.

When McClory introduced the article as the committee resumed its deliberations on July 30, it drew less support than the two articles already adopted. Some committee members thought the House had not taken all steps necessary to compel compliance with its subpoena. Others thought the article raised Fifth Amendment issues of compelled self-incrimination. Yet representatives John Seiberling of Ohio and Lawrence Hogan of Maryland, among others, reiterated McClory's point that without the authority to compel the delivery of evidence, the House's impeachment power was meaningless. Don Edwards of California asserted that without such power "we will diminish or destroy this only safety valve in the Constitution. . . . to protect ourselves from a President who misbehaves so badly that he becomes a threat to the country." At the end of a two-hour debate, the committee remained closely divided. Article III was adopted by only a 21–17 majority, a much narrower margin than on the two preceding articles.[80]

The committee's enthusiasm for additional articles of impeachment was fast diminishing. Whether the members had exhausted the pool of issues on which a consensus could be reached for impeachment or whether they had merely exhausted themselves is unclear. But when John Conyers of Michigan, a ten-year veteran on the committee, proposed a fourth article, he was able to enlist little support. Conyers had contended in his opening remarks at the hearing that much of Nixon's reprehensible behavior was rooted in the Vietnam War. Nixon had begun his concealed bombing of Cambodia in the spring of 1969 and almost immediately started illegal wiretapping of journalists and Pentagon officials when news of the bombing leaked out. Shortly thereafter Nixon began lying in public statements to conceal a campaign that eventually mounted to 150,000 air strikes dropping 500,000 tons of bombs on a neutral nation.[81] To Representative Conyers this represented a simple-to-explain and easy-to-prove war-related impeachable offense. "The president unilaterally undertook major military action against another sovereign nation and then consistently denied that he had done so to both the Congress and the American people," Conyers declared as he argued for Article IV. Supported by a half dozen Democratic colleagues, Conyers asserted that Nixon had violated Congress's constitutional power to participate in decisions to wage war when he secretly initiated the bombing and thereafter deceived Congress by claiming the United States was respecting Cambodian sovereignty. Congress needed to reclaim its war powers through impeaching Nixon on this account.[82]

Numerous committee members from both parties were troubled by the Conyers proposal. A series of speakers accused Congress of complicity in the conduct of the Vietnam War from at least the time of the Tonkin Gulf resolution of 1965 to the adoption in 1973 of the resolution to halt the Cambodian bombing. William Cohen of Maine blamed "the sloth and default on the part of Congress," and Trent Lott of Mississippi concurred. Others pointed out that presidents other than Nixon had prosecuted the war in dubious ways. Believing that illegal wiretaps and deliberate lying had already been addressed as abuses of power in Article II, even strong critics of the war could not place all the blame for it on Nixon and thus were unwilling to vote for impeachment on such grounds. Conyers's article gained only twelve votes, while twenty-six opposed it.[83] Notwithstanding the defeat of his proposal, Conyers had staked out a broad position on the use of impeachment to discipline official misconduct that he would return to again and again over more than three decades of further service on the House Judiciary Committee. At the same time, the failure of Congress to pursue Nixon's impeachment on the grounds of his foreign policy conduct would long continue to reverberate.

What would turn out to be the last article of impeachment to be proposed was introduced by Representative Edward Mezvinsky of Iowa. He called for Nixon to be impeached for improper self-enrichment through unacknowledged government expenditures for his private benefit at his homes in San Clemente, California, and Key Biscayne, Florida, as well as for willful income tax evasion. Mezvinsky, as well as Rodino, had been particularly upset by Nixon's attempt to claim a $576,000 tax deduction for the gift of his prepresidential papers to the National Archives. The tax code provision permitting such gifts had been terminated, and an alert archivist had spotted that to qualify for the deduction Nixon's deed of gift had been backdated to a year before the papers were even appraised. Mezvinsky concluded that illegitimate deductions together with unreported income meant that Nixon had underpaid his income taxes by three-quarters of a million dollars during his presidency.[84]

A contentious debate followed. Some members of the committee deplored the president's tax fraud as use of presidential power for corrupt purposes, while others, not denying that fraud had occurred, blamed subordinates for the erroneous tax returns. Still others characterized the charge as excessive. Jerome Waldie spoke for many when he called Nixon's conduct shabby and disgraceful but less than impeachable. Nixon's tax avoidance may have been venal, he said, but it did not rise to the level of threatening the integrity of government, the inquiry staff's standard for an impeachable offense. In the end, the Mezvinsky article failed 12–26.[85] With that decision reached, Chairman Rodino declared the impeachment hearings complete, and the committee adjourned.

After the House Judiciary Committee publicly discussed and approved three articles of impeachment, Nixon's downfall came swiftly. Not waiting for the full House to act, the Senate Rules Committee had secretly begun to plan for a trial. Despite what he had said in March, Senator Mansfield was well prepared with suggestions for conducting the trial and carrying out the routine business of the Senate at the same time. The Senate parliamentarian, Floyd Riddick, and an assistant had been devoting their full time for weeks to researching procedures for a trial as well as working out the necessary but mundane details of security, gallery seating, and office space for the House managers. All but one member of the committee agreed with Mansfield's proposal that the Senate should break with tradition to allow the proceedings in its chamber to be broadcast on radio and television. Except for Robert Griffin, the senators felt that the public, which had watched the investigation unfold in the Ervin committee hearings and the impeachment articles being debated in the House Judiciary Committee, needed to see the resolution of the case. While the committee's updating of the Senate rules for an impeachment trial was completed amicably by August 8, it never went further. Unfolding events removed the need for the Senate to put its careful plans into effect.[86]

Nixon had pledged to obey a definitive ruling of the Supreme Court on his tapes. Now one of the articles of impeachment being sent to the House focused on his failure to deliver subpoenaed evidence. As a result, the president found himself with little choice but to surrender the tapes demanded by the special prosecutor. On the day the Judiciary Committee hearing concluded, James St. Clair began delivering the subpoenaed tapes to Judge Sirica.

As soon as he handed over the June 23, 1973, recording of Nixon's conversation with H. R. Haldeman, St. Clair also provided it to Charles Wiggins, Nixon's stalwart defender at the just-concluded hearings. Wiggins read a transcript and immediately recognized its meaning: It was proof that Nixon was guilty beyond reasonable doubt of obstruction of justice and abuse of power. He told his friend Robert Michel, "Well, Bob, we've just had the ground cut out from underneath us in supporting Nixon. . . . Our case is blown. We just don't have any grounds for it anymore." The tape, which was immediately dubbed "the smoking gun," demonstrated conclusively not only that Nixon had known, six days after the Watergate arrests, that his subordinates were involved but also that he had taken active direction of efforts to frustrate the investigation of the crime. His statement that he knew nothing of White House involvement in the cover-up had been a conscious and deliberate lie.[87]

With this incontrovertible evidence of obstruction of justice and abuse of presidential power before them, Wiggins and the other members of the House Judiciary Committee who only days earlier had voted against impeachment began to recant. One after another they all announced that they would now, sadly, have to vote to impeach the president.[88] Even more devastating to Nixon's cause, the hitherto unswervingly loyal vice president issued a press release saying he had concluded, "The public interest is no longer served by repetition of my previously expressed belief that on the basis of all the evidence known to me and to the American people the President is not guilty of an impeachable offense." Though he refused to say so directly, Ford had abandoned Nixon's fast-sinking ship.[89]

Journalists taking quick surveys of members of Congress reported that there was now no doubt that the House would overwhelmingly approve at least the first two articles of impeachment. Thereafter, they predicted, the Senate would vote by well over the required two-thirds to convict and remove the president. Speaker Albert announced that the starting date for floor debate on impeachment would remain August 19 but that floor consideration would be reduced from two weeks to one.[90]

A morose and disconsolate president apparently gave only momentary thought to waging a fight in a Senate trial, as Andrew Johnson had done 107 years earlier and Bill Clinton would do twenty-five years in the future. One of his principal antagonists, John Dean, would look back through the prism of the Clinton trial and speculate that if he had chosen to do battle, Nixon might very well have eked out a Johnsonian escape in the Senate.[91] But lacking the Clinton example and having foremost in his memory only the recent examples of dismissal of charges by House committees or resignation, Nixon was not of a mind to fight on. He knew well the evidence arrayed against him. Any thoughts of struggling on crumbled when Republican congressional leaders Hugh Scott, John Rhodes, and Barry Goldwater came to the White House on August 7 and told him that he could count on no more than fifteen votes in the Senate and probably fewer. They urged him to resign.

The following day, the White House made arrangements for a televised presidential address to the nation that evening and then invited a group of congressional leaders to meet with Nixon in advance. Conservative Democratic senators James Eastland and John Stennis, both of Mississippi, along with the Republican National Chairman, Dean Burch, and the Republican leadership from both houses met in the cabinet room. Apprehensive, somber, and unsure of what to do in this unprecedented situation, they sat as a stiff and tense Nixon walked in, stood behind his usual chair, talked nostalgically about his parents, and then said, "Well fellows, I just hope you won't feel that I've let you down." With no one willing to point out that he had done just that, the all-male group, many of them longtime allies and admirers, was acutely distressed. House Republican whip Robert Michel remembered it as "a room full of tears," an anguished occasion for professional politicians witnessing the public shaming of one of their own. It was a moment that would remain vivid in memories and that none of those present had any desire to repeat.[92]

Without admitting the validity of any of the impeachment charges or taking responsibility for any of the "White House horrors," Nixon told a national television audience later the same evening of August 8, 1974, that he was resigning as president. He had lost, he said, the confidence of Congress, a tacit recognition perhaps that he had not merely squandered popularity but had reached the verge of congressional action to remove him. The following morning, after a maudlin farewell speech to White House staff and guests, he departed. The new president, Gerald Ford, after taking his oath of office, stepped to the microphones and announced, "Our long national nightmare is over."

Ford's declaration hardly made it so. After the two-year-long Watergate trauma came to an end, many politicians and pundits were quick to declare that the impeachment-induced resignation of a president, the first in the nation's history, demonstrated that the constitutional system worked. Yet the impeachment process had proceeded at an agonizingly slow pace, leaving the government largely paralyzed for at least a year and a half. Furthermore, the cautiously drawn articles of impeachment may in the end have increased the latitude of presidential power, especially in foreign affairs, because of their narrow delineations of impeachable offenses. Whatever the impact on the presidency, the Nixon episode had provided the American public with an exposure to the process of impeachment and a sense that it offered a constitutional solution to intractable political problems. As a result, a more frequent reliance on impeachment would follow, in itself producing a political culture that would, at least in some minds, become another long national nightmare.

7

Impeachment as Routine: Pardons, Powers, Prosecutors, and Judicial Self-Policing

Americans breathed a collective sigh of relief as Richard Nixon left Washington on August 9, 1974. His critics and even many who admired certain of his accomplishments had grown more and more uncomfortable with Nixon's assertions of presidential power. Whether taking military initiatives in Cambodia without informing Congress or the country, trying to prevent publication of records of Vietnam policy making, impounding congressionally appropriated funds, carrying out the multitudinous abuses of power revealed in the Watergate affair, or refusing to disclose White House tapes and documents that could shed light on alleged crimes, Nixon had increasingly frightened alert citizens with the prospect of an unchecked "imperial presidency." His departure encouraged prospects that executive office restraint could be reimposed.

Avoiding the uncertainties of carrying out an impeachment heightened the sense of relief. The growing likelihood of Nixon's impeachment by the House of Representatives and the prospect of a protracted period of political uncertainty and executive paralysis before and during a Senate trial of unpredictable duration had generated much apprehension. A multitude of anxieties, either articulated or unspoken, were present as the United States moved slowly but seemingly inexorably toward the use of impeachment to wrest power from a discredited executive. The gradual accumulation of tension during the lengthy struggle between the White House and its adversaries in Congress and the special prosecutor's office had finally and mercifully been broken. Fears could at last dissipate that Nixon would defy judicial rulings, concoct a foreign crisis, employ the military in some way to secure his position, or engage in some unimaginable maneuver to hold on to power. Throughout American society an enormous burden of worry and doubt lifted as it became clear that the unfamiliar impeachment system would not have to be carried to its end and that the irregular transfer of power would take place without being contested.

The immediate reaction to Nixon's departure, first articulated by the new president, Gerald Ford, was that the American constitutional system and its impeachment mechanism had functioned well. Taking the oath of office as president, Ford declared, "Our Constitution works. Our great republic is a government of laws and not of men." Politicians across the spectrum quickly agreed. Senator Edward

Kennedy declared, "The nightmare of Watergate is over, the Constitution is safe, and America can become whole again." Chief Justice Warren Burger, after giving Ford the oath of office, gripped the hand of Hugh Scott, Senate minority leader, and effused about the Constitution, "Hugh, it worked. Thank God it worked."[1]

Each of them was wrong. Ford glossed over the fact that Nixon's personal decision to resign, not the completion of the stipulated legal process of impeachment, trial, and removal, had brought the ordeal to its end. Burger only weeks earlier had expressed doubts as to whether the president would obey the ruling the justices had crafted ordering Nixon to turn his tapes over to Judge John Sirica. Now the chief justice avoided the unpleasant truth that for more than two years the official designated by the Constitution to see that the nation's laws were faithfully executed had consistently done the contrary. He ignored the fact that Nixon had defied constitutional requirements for as long as politically possible and had only capitulated in the end under the enormous weight of public opinion together with intense pressure from frightened political peers. A Constitution designed to provide instant clarity about the responsibilities of government officials had been tied in knots and rendered almost nonfunctional for an extended period.

While Ford and Burger erred in their descriptions of what had just transpired, Kennedy failed as a prophet. The legacy of Watergate was, to some extent, continued turmoil. Challenges to the Constitution's restraints on the presidency would be ongoing. Presidents and their aides would become more sensitive to methods for avoiding scrutiny and pursuit. At the same time, the device for disciplining officials who offended the Constitution would be called upon more frequently. Perhaps most significant, divisions would reemerge and even increase in what had been at least briefly a fairly united body politic.

The upbeat judgments so readily offered as Nixon flew off to San Clemente, his California version of Napoleon's St. Helena, soon began to unravel. Almost immediately Nixon asserted that the official papers of his presidency and the notorious tapes were solely his private property. With both Attorney General William Saxbe and Administrator of General Services Arthur Sampson, the overseer of the National Archives, acquiescing to his claim to control access, evidence of Nixon's misconduct threatened to disappear.[2]

Then, within a month, the disgraced ex-president's successor shook confidence that the constitutional system had indeed worked well as he exercised his authority to grant Nixon a full pardon. *Washington Post* cartoonist Herblock immediately drew Ford and Nixon sitting together on a garbage can overflowing with cash and tapes. A caption declared, "The long national nightmare goes on."[3] Before long, criminal trials of Nixon's closest associates in the Watergate affair provided a more detailed picture of the extent to which the operation of the federal government had been corrupted. Yet the pardon left Nixon immune from any sort of further ordeal of court scrutiny and disclosure of the inner workings of his presidency. He was also spared any of the punishments that might have resulted from further legal proceedings and that many citizens believed he richly deserved. The pardon left in its wake shock, some relief, and more than a little cynicism about American professions of "equal justice."

Over the next several years, Congress responded to the jolts of the Watergate disclosures, the impeachment proceedings, and the pardon with various measures to recapture lost authority, rebuild public confidence in government, and refashion the mechanisms of impeachment to make them more effective. Such efforts had begun even while Nixon was fighting to retain the presidency, but they accelerated after his demise. The brush with impeachment led Congress to adopt an assortment of measures suggested by the Watergate experience that would institutionalize approaches to maintaining discipline among constitutional officers. Congress invested what it had learned in the course of dealing with Nixon in attempts to bureaucratize the impeachment process should it be needed again. Legislation incorporating the lessons of Watergate did not prove effective in every case, but enough of it influenced subsequent government conduct to mark it as a notable result of the uneasy national rediscovery of impeachment.

What to do with a president put out of office through impeachment or prompted to resign because it had become inevitable? The Constitution explicitly prohibits use of the power of pardon in cases of impeachment, but what about in its aftermath for acts that provoked impeachment? Should the impeachment and removal process be considered an end in itself or merely a way station on the road to justice? Should the elected members of Congress be considered the final arbiters of the fate of the impeached or merely office cleaners who give way to a conventional criminal jury of ordinary citizens for ultimate decisions on guilt and punishment?

These questions had begun to be discussed long before Richard Nixon appeared on the scene, much less left the White House. The Constitution's framers chose to limit the direct consequences of impeachment and conviction to loss of official position and further eligibility to hold office. In 1787, however, they did not rule out the possibility that someone so displaced could subsequently be criminally prosecuted for their actions in office. As they saw it, the purpose of impeachment was to ensure the welfare of the society by separating from government an official who had demonstrated serious dereliction of duty. The framers took no steps to limit such an official's further criminal liability. Since impeachment was an overtly political proceeding rather than a criminal one, the Constitution's guarantee against double jeopardy did not apply. Because of impeachment's infrequent use, philosophical questions as well as practical political and judicial ones concerning postimpeachment practices had remained unsettled. Nor would the manner in which Nixon's fate was dealt with resolve them.

At his vice presidential confirmation hearings less than a year before Nixon's resignation, Ford had said he expected the Watergate prosecutions to run their course. Asked if a new president might terminate the prosecution of his predecessor, Ford had said, "I do not think the American people would stand for it."[4] Intervening events and his move from Capitol Hill to the White House caused Ford's perspective to shift and led him to reconsider his confirmation statement.

The Watergate grand jury, told that it could not go further against a sitting president, had in March named Nixon an unindicted coconspirator. As soon as Nixon's resignation removed the obstacle to his indictment, the special prosecutor's staff began considering whether or not to put him in the dock. It did not prove to be an easy decision.

Prosecuting Nixon, either along with the seven Watergate defendants awaiting trial or separately, might appear excessive and partisan in light of the public humiliation he had already suffered. Obtaining an impartial jury, a fair trial, and, ultimately, a conviction might be difficult. Failure to convict could in turn seriously undermine public confidence that Nixon had been legitimately turned out of office. On the other hand, declining to prosecute would raise similar questions as well as others about equal justice. Put another way, would Nixon appear, like Agnew, to have escaped punishment by making a deal to resign? Would he also, like his vice president, subsequently profess to have done nothing wrong? Neither option would be anywhere close to universally popular. A Gallup poll showed 56 percent of Americans favored prosecution, 37 percent opposed it, and a mere 7 percent lacked an opinion. For the moment Special Prosecutor Leon Jaworski delayed a decision.[5]

Before Nixon's resignation Congress considered and rejected the idea of granting him immunity from prosecution in return for stepping down. Compassion for the president remained widespread among his fellow politicians, who presumably could envision themselves in similar circumstances. At the same time, without Nixon's acknowledging the validity of the formal charges, an immunity-resignation bargain might look like an ugly political deal to depose a president. Yet with such a confession, the same arrangement might be seen as excusing a malefactor. Congressmen were wary of either perception. Senator Robert Griffin found that in the end no one in Congress wanted to be identified with a grant of immunity. Given Nixon's sullied image once the House Judiciary Committee had voted for impeachment, immunity from prosecution at that point was thought to send a message that Congress was willing to turn a blind eye toward executive malfeasance. Immunity would amount to letting Nixon off the hook and signaling tolerance of future presidential misconduct.[6]

With the special prosecutor for the moment undecided about how to proceed and with Congress unwilling to take action, the question of Nixon's fate rested in the hands of the new president. In his first days in the White House, Ford confronted a myriad of daunting problems. For a man with no executive, much less presidential, experience, quickly eliminating the ongoing distraction of Nixon possessed appeal. Furthermore, with only a small cadre of his own aides in place, the new chief executive was surrounded by a staff that had worked for Nixon and reflexively protected his interests. Alexander Haig, who served both Nixon and Ford as chief of staff, began urging a pardon when he first notified Ford on August 1 about the incriminating tape of June 23, 1972. Ford discreetly said nothing, either then or over the following days, but the seed had been planted.[7] Soon Leonard Garment, another member of Nixon's senior staff, took up the argument for a pardon, saying that he had discussed the matter with John Osborne of the *New Republic,* Eric Sevareid of CBS News, and even Abe Fortas. Garment reported that they all agreed it was the thing to do.[8] Shortly thereafter Senator J. William Fulbright and Nelson Rockefeller joined Haig and Garment in suggesting that a pardon would be a means of bringing closure to the Watergate affair.

Ford wasted little time before addressing the issue of whether to pardon his predecessor. His first press conference on August 28 convinced him that journalists would focus on little else until the question of Nixon was resolved and that the issue would continue to intrude on his own efforts. Ford was mindful of an observation made by one of his military aides about what two years of scandal had done to the American culture: "We're all Watergate junkies. Some of us are mainlining, some are sniffing, some are lacing it with something else, but all of us are addicted. This will go on and on unless someone steps in and says that we, as a nation, must go cold turkey. Otherwise, we'll die of an overdose." Ford himself imagined that the drama of the former president fighting to stay out of jail would overshadow all other national news as long as the case went on, anywhere from two to six years.[9]

After his August 28 press conference Ford asked his legal counsel, Philip Buchen, to explore the question, and by September 3 the new president was taking steps to arrange a pardon. Ford understood from Buchen's research that a 1915 Supreme Court ruling on pardons still stood. The Court had held that a president possessed the power to grant a pardon for a crime of which the individual had not been convicted and to which he did not admit. Equally important, the offer of a pardon "carries an imputation of guilt, acceptance, a confession of it." Believing on that basis that the offer and acceptance of a pardon would resolve any questions about Nixon's acknowledgment of culpability, Ford decided to proceed.[10]

Ford hoped that a statement of contrition from Nixon in return for the pardon would bring resolution to the whole episode, but he was not prepared to insist on a quid pro quo. He put the matter in the hands of a trusted attorney, Benton Becker, who had previously worked for Ford on the attempt to impeach Justice Douglas. Becker flew to California to work out arrangements with Nixon regarding the pardon and its acceptance as well as the unsettled issue of Nixon's presidential papers and tapes. Negotiating through Nixon aide Ronald Ziegler, Becker found it difficult to wrest concessions from the ex-president. He settled for a loophole-filled agreement leaving Nixon in control of access to his papers and a statement accepting the pardon that, even after four drafts, offered little of the contrition that Ford and Becker sought. Finding Nixon in bad shape both physically and emotionally and suspecting that he might not live out the year, Becker settled for arrangements that in the end served Nixon's interests but not Ford's.[11]

Nixon agreed to issue a statement if a pardon was given. In it, he said his perspective on Watergate had changed since his move to California. "Looking back on what is still in my mind a complex and confusing maze of events, decisions, pressures and personalities, one thing I can see clearly now is that I was wrong in not acting more decisively and more forthrightly in dealing with Watergate, particularly when it reached the stage of judicial proceedings and grew from a political scandal into a national tragedy." Implying that he had merely failed to take sufficient steps to enforce the law once Watergate came to light, Nixon ignored the evidence that he had concealed the crime from the outset. Nor did he make any reference to the other abuses of power listed in the articles of impeachment. The statement expressed "regret and pain at the anguish my mistakes over Watergate have caused the nation," but it offered no apology for his acts themselves. The conclusion of Nixon's statement dodged the substance of the situation even more and strongly implied that he had simply failed to communicate effectively with the American people. "I know that many fair-minded people believe that my motivations and actions in the Watergate affair were intentionally self-serving and illegal. I now understand how my own mistakes and misjudgments have contributed to that belief and seemed to support it. This burden is the heaviest one of all to bear." Nixon ended his curious testament to avoidance and self-pity by declaring, "That the way I tried to deal with Watergate was the wrong way is a burden I shall bear for every day of the life that is left to me."[12]

Having failed to elicit much, if any, contrition from the former president, Ford nevertheless went ahead with his plan to pardon Nixon. In doing so his political instincts failed him. The new chief executive made no effort to find out what congressional leaders thought of the idea and only notified them of his action at the last moment. Sharing his plan with only a handful of staff members, he accepted the endorsements of it by Nixon holdovers Alexander Haig and Henry Kissinger while ignoring the vehement opposition of trusted press secretary Jerald terHorst, who immediately resigned. Ford chose not to wait until after the Watergate trial or even until a grand jury determined whether to indict Nixon, but instead broadcast his decision in a hastily arranged television statement at 11:00 a.m. on Sunday morning, September 8. The announcement came exactly one month after Nixon had revealed his intention to resign. Declaring that he was acting to avoid a continued national preoccupation and polarization, Ford granted a "full, free, and absolute pardon unto Richard Nixon for all offenses against the United States which he, Richard Nixon, had committed or may have committed or taken part in during the period from January 20, 1969, through August 9, 1974." Ford failed to say that both he and the Supreme Court viewed acceptance of a pardon as an admission of guilt. This oversight and others in explaining his decision provided indications that Ford had failed to anticipate the hostile response that followed.[13]

Ford had enjoyed widespread popularity during his first month in office simply for being "not Nixon." But by pardoning his predecessor, he instantly came to be suspected of being a Nixon ally. The following day's announcement that Ford had agreed that Nixon could take his papers and tapes to California and destroy them in five years compounded that impression. Ford's standing in public opinion polls dropped precipitously. Before he granted the pardon, 71 percent of Americans approved of his handling of the presidency, only 3 percent disapproved, and 26 percent had no opinion.[14] Within days that positive image disappeared. Immediately after the pardon, only 32 percent of respondents thought Ford was doing a good job, while 33 percent gave him fair marks, 25 percent a poor grade, and those with no opinion dropped to 10 percent. Sixty-two percent of those polled disapproved of the pardon itself.[15] A month later Ford's overall approval rating stood at 50 percent, while disapproval had jumped sharply to 28 percent, and 22 percent expressed no opinion.[16] The marked resentment at the pardon revealed the deep distaste for Nixon that had built up during the impeachment process and the accompanying desire to see him punished. Ford's effort to bring closure to the Nixon impeachment not only failed but also stirred new anger.

Attempting to repair the damage, Ford took the bold step of offering to go to Capitol Hill to answer questions about the pardon. On October 17 he became the first president since Washington to testify before Congress. Peppered with questions from the Subcommittee on Criminal Justice of the House Judiciary Committee about how the pardon had been negotiated, he said simply, "There was no deal, period, under no circumstances." Lacking any evidence to the contrary and finding it difficult to pursue the investigation by questioning anyone else in the White House once the president had testified, the subcommittee voted 6–2 to terminate its inquiry. Representative Elizabeth Holtzman wanted to continue, asserting that a pardon was invalid if given under fraudulent conditions. She garnered little support, either then or when she tried to revive the issue a year later. The pardon of Nixon would stand, as would the implicit signal of guilt in his acceptance of it, but suspicions about the motives behind it would remain.[17]

The sense that Nixon had escaped conviction and punishment only because of Ford's pardon was reinforced by the guilty pleas or trials and convictions of many of his aides. In a series of cases even before Nixon left office, at

The Long National Nightmare Goes On

Herblock,
Washington Post,
September 12,
1974. © The Herb
Block Foundation.

least a dozen White House and CREEP staff members had been sentenced for crimes committed working for the president. In a highly publicized trial that began October 1, 1974, and lasted nearly five months, Nixon's closest associates, John Mitchell, H. R. Haldeman, and John Ehrlichman, were all found guilty of Watergate-related offenses and sentenced to prison for two and a half to eight years. Ford's failure to pardon any of these men underscored the impression that Nixon himself had eluded justice thanks only to Ford.

Unable to contest the pardon of the ex-president, Congress was, however, in a position to take legislative steps to counteract Nixon's legacy. Deprived of the chance to focus on Nixon himself, federal legislators turned their attention to broader issues of policy and power raised by his administration. With Nixon's near impeachment raising the specter of a government gone seriously off course, the Congress took numerous steps to rein in future executives and assure that mechanisms would be in place to deal with misconduct. It is little wonder that legislative measures were inspired by specific acts of the Nixon administration that met with congressional disapproval. Better to prevent the problems of Watergate from happening again than to have to agonize over proper punishment when they did.

Congress spent a great deal of time over several years devising legislative solutions to the problems exposed by Watergate. In the War Powers Act of 1973, the Federal Election Campaign Act Amendments of 1974, the Freedom of Information Act of 1974, the Presidential Recordings and Materials Preservation Act of 1974, the Ethics in Government Act of 1978 with its provisions for the creation of independent counsels, and, finally, the Judicial Councils Reform and Judicial Conduct and Disability Act of 1980, the Congresses of the 1970s constructed an enduring legacy from their experience with impeachment. A level of scrutiny well beyond anything previously known was brought to bear on impeachable officials and those who served them. In its legislative actions, Congress, for the best of reasons, assured the continuation of the age of impeachment. Suspicion of officialdom, particularly presidents, became institutionalized.

Well before the Nixon administration was finally dispatched, the first Watergate disclosures had rendered it politically vulnerable in ways that it had not been earlier. During his first term Nixon had claimed and exercised presidential authority that Congress and the courts had only occasionally and in limited ways been able to check. Historian Arthur M. Schlesinger, Jr., declared that under Nixon the "imperial presidency" had reached a zenith.[18] The public's disgust at the revelations before the Ervin committee encouraged Congress's first effective challenges to the extraordinary power that Nixon had been able to accumulate. Nevertheless, Congress confronted ongoing claims of independent presidential authority, especially in instances where such power was exercised to thwart inquiries into the chief executive's conduct. Nixon's increasing uncooperativeness, together with his declining political influence, encouraged Congress to assert itself. The struggle over Nixon's impeachment shaped the legislative-executive relationship in various ways.

Nixon was not the first president to assert his authority to carry out acts of war without prior congressional approval or even full disclosure. Lyndon Johnson, himself not the first, had made this a particularly sensitive issue with the 1965 Gulf of Tonkin Resolution and the long buildup of the Vietnam War that followed. Still, Nixon raised presidential independence in war making to new heights with his secretive bombing and sudden ground invasion of Vietnam's neutral neighbor to the west, Cambodia. Once agreement was reached in January 1973 for U.S. withdrawal from Vietnam, Congress moved toward a long-contemplated step to put at least some modest restraints on presidential action without hampering the president's ability to respond immediately to a crisis.

After the summer-long hearings of the Ervin committee tarnished the image of presidential judgment, a large bipartisan congressional majority summoned the determination to rein in the president, passing the War Powers Act over Nixon's objections in October 1973. This legislation called upon a president to consult with Congress before committing troops whenever possible. More forcefully, it required the chief executive to notify Congress within forty-eight hours of committing U.S. troops to combat and mandated that congressional permission be obtained in order to maintain troops in that situation beyond sixty days. Nixon's promised veto of the measure came four days after the Saturday Night Massacre had further undermined his political standing. Congress, no doubt emboldened by the outpouring of criticism of Nixon, voted to override the veto two weeks later.

Passage of the War Powers Act was the first substantive effort to curtail the military authority of the president since the onset of the cold war. Its adoption in the face of vehement presidential opposition is hard to imagine under any other circumstances than a substantial threat of impeachment. As it turned out, the War Powers Act soon showed itself to be weaker than anticipated in compelling presidential consultation with Congress. Gerald Ford in May 1975 only notified Congress after he had committed forces to rescue the crew of the *Mayaguez* after the U.S. merchant ship had been seized by Cambodian forces. The apparent success of the mission undercut congressional grumbling that after-the-fact briefing was hardly meaningful consultation. After the *Mayaguez* incident the War Powers Act never recaptured the image its adoption had projected of a forceful Congress asserting power in foreign affairs.[19] The relationship between the creation of the War Powers Act and the Nixon impeachment was perceived as being at best tangential. Thus, it did not prove to be a lasting restraint on presidential war making.

With the Nixon presidency entering its death throes early in the summer of 1974, Congress adopted a less confrontational but more effective measure to reassert its own authority over government spending while confining that of the president. The Budget and Impoundment Control Act resulted from a discussion of the budget-making process that had been going on in several congressional committees since the start of Nixon's second term. Most of the act was devoted to establishing a consolidated procedure and regimented schedule for Congress to construct the annual federal budget. In its one significant departure from this focus, the act severely restricted presidential power to overturn congressional decisions by impounding funds. The legislation required the president to notify Congress of any proposed impoundment. This budgetary alteration could then only go ahead if, within forty-five days, Congress gave its approval. Either house, in other words, could block a presidential impoundment.

This recapture of full congressional control of spending was approved 75–0 in the Senate and 401–6 in the House. The impeachment-threatened president did not approve of the restriction on impoundment, but in the midst of his struggle to hold on to his office he chose to offer no resistance to a nearly unanimous Congress. On July 12, dressed to attend Earl Warren's funeral, Nixon signed the bill reducing his own power. The weakened president thereby put in place the basic framework of congressional budget making still in use.[20]

Nixon's fall further emboldened Congress. It took significant steps to reform campaign financing practices exposed by Watergate. It also sought to reduce the executive branch's ability to conceal records of its activities. The march toward impeachment, even if not completed, proved a strong catalyst for efforts to restrict presidential power and restore what Congress saw as a proper constitutional balance of power.

The use of political contributions to pay for the Watergate break-in and other clandestine activities, as well as to buy the perpetrators' silence, heightened awareness of campaign financing improprieties. Nixon seemed the embodiment of the perennial American problem of political finance. His entanglement with questionable campaign contributions went back to the secret fund created for him by California supporters when he was in Congress. That fund, when revealed, almost cost him his place on the 1952 Republican ticket and led to the so-called Checkers speech by which he rescued his career. The $17,000 Nixon Fund of 1952 seemed like small change when compared to the millions secretly raised and surreptitiously spent on his behalf twenty years later. Restrictions on contributions and requirements of public disclosure adopted by Congress in the Federal Election Campaign Act of 1971 motivated CREEP to engage in an orgy of fund-raising in the weeks before the act took effect. Bob Woodward and Carl Bernstein traced some of these contributions to the Watergate burglars, providing the justification for the Senate to establish Sam Ervin's select committee to look into irregularities in the 1972 election.

The revelations that poured forth from the Ervin committee led Congress to begin considering further campaign finance legislation. Subsequent steps in Nixon's downfall pushed reform ahead. With the Ervin committee hearings still ongoing, the Senate took a first vote to limit individual contributions. In September 1973 hearings followed on establishing public financing of presidential and congressional elections, and the Senate approved the plan a month after the Saturday Night Massacre, attaching it to a measure to raise the federal debt ceiling that senators thought Nixon would not dare veto. Resistance from the House prevented campaign finance reform from advancing any further in 1973. House members simply lacked enthusiasm for facing publicly funded opponents every two years.[21]

Senate liberals kept pressing for the reshaping of the campaign finance system. In April 1974 they won passage of a bill that incorporated contribution limits and a revised public financing plan as well as created a bipartisan Federal Election Commission to supervise campaigns. By this time, Nixon's opposition to the plan as a raid on the national treasury was no hindrance and perhaps even a help to its adoption.[22] The House, however, remained reluctant to embrace the Senate bill. After three months of consideration by the House Administration Committee and after remarks by its chairman, Democrat Wayne Hays of Ohio, that problems had only arisen in presidential campaigns, the House version of the bill eliminated public financing for congressional elections.[23] Hays's committee finally endorsed the modified measure on July 24, the day the Judiciary Committee began its public impeachment debate, and the House adopted it on August 8, the day Nixon resigned.[24]

Reconciliation of the House and Senate versions of the campaign finance reform bill appeared a difficult task because of their contrasting positions on public financing of congressional elections. In the end, however, House opposition proved to be stronger than Senate support. Desire to achieve a substantial reform of presidential campaign financing with congressional elections looming and memories of Watergate still fresh in voters' minds determined the outcome. A compromise that set contribution limits of $1,000 per candidate per election, severely restricted untraceable cash gifts, compelled public reports of political donations by recipients, provided public funding for presidential campaigns, and established oversight and enforcement through a Federal Election Commission was agreed to and adopted by both houses in early October.[25] Signing the Federal Election Campaign Act Amendments into law on October 15, President Ford acknowledged the impact of the Watergate scandal and Nixon's near impeachment. While he had reservations about the use of federal funds to finance elections, Ford admitted, "The times demand this legislation."[26]

The Federal Election Campaign Act Amendments of 1974 had many loopholes. Opportunities provided for proliferating political action committees and lobbying organizations were the most obvious. The law's constitutionality was soon challenged on First Amendment grounds by an unlikely coalition of conservatives, socialists, labor leaders, and Vietnam War protestors. In a 1976 ruling in *Buckley v. Valeo,* the Supreme Court upheld requirements for record keeping and public disclosure of campaign contributions. Public financing of presidential elections received validation as well. The Court, however, struck down as improper limitations on free speech many of the provisions limiting political contributions, such as what a candidate could spend of his or her own personal wealth and what an individual could donate independently of a candidate or campaign.[27] Nevertheless, the shadow cast by Watergate proved to be a powerful incentive for the significant changes in campaign finance law that were achieved.

A quite different but nonetheless significant reform stirred by Watergate and advanced in the course of Nixon's decline involved easier outside access to government records. According to the report of the Ervin committee, executive branch withholding of records of its activities not only was one of the characteristics of an excessive centralization of power, but also helped conceal abuse of that power.[28] The federal Freedom of Information Act (FOIA) had been adopted in 1966, but the subsequent effective resistance by the executive branch to requests for documents had made clear the law's ineffectiveness. A 1973 Supreme Court ruling that courts could not question bureaucratic decisions to withhold documents set off efforts to amend FOIA. In March 1974, with White House resistance to subpoenas duces tecum reaching a peak, the House of Representatives took the first step toward FOIA reform. By a vote of 383 to 8, the House approved revisions to the original act to provide for quicker responses to information requests as well as for in camera court review of documents that the government claimed should not be released for national security or other reasons.[29] In May the Senate passed a somewhat stronger bill by a vote of 64 to 17 despite rumors that Nixon would veto it.[30]

The House-Senate conference to resolve differences in the two FOIA bills had not completed its work when Ford became president. Ford, urged on by holdover members of Nixon's cabinet, requested further delay. The conferees softened some of the measure's features in response to Ford's objections.[31] Nevertheless, after the resulting bill was approved by acclamation in the Senate and a vote of 349–2 in the House, Ford vetoed it as "unconstitutional and unworkable" and a threat to military, intelligence, and diplomatic secrets by allowing inexperienced federal judges to declassify secret documents.[32] Newspaper editorials across the country, their lingering suspicions of unjustified claims to executive secrecy overriding their usual deference to assertions of threats to national security, reminded Ford of his promise of an "open administration" and scorned his veto as "alarmist," "regrettable," and "wrong."[33]

When Congress returned to wrap up end-of-session business following the 1974 elections, members were acutely aware of the consequences for them of Nixon's conduct. The election campaign had centered on Watergate, the crippled government's failure to accomplish much over the previous two years, and the economic tailspin into which the country had slid, partly as a result. As a consequence, the Republicans had lost forty-three seats in the House and three in the Senate. Neither they nor the Democrats were in any mood to continue policies identified in the slightest with Nixon's misdeeds. With not one member speaking in defense of Ford but several talking of the lessons of Watergate, the House overrode the FOIA veto by 371 to 31. A day later the Senate voted likewise by 65 to 27, and the FOIA amendments took effect. Shortly before the vote, Senator Howard Baker, a Republican, expressed an apparently widespread sentiment that Watergate and the war in Vietnam might not have occurred "if presidents had not been able to mask their actions in secrecy."[34]

Nixon's efforts to take his presidential papers with him when he left office posed distinct questions but ones closely related to those raised in the FOIA reform. Once again a dispute between Nixon and Congress over control of information was involved. An impeachment-heightened sense of the public's right and need to know how their highest official conducted their government led to a fundamental change in the way presidential records were regarded. Though the issue had never before received much attention, the belief now emerged that a former chief executive's papers belonged to the country and not simply to the president himself.

The papers of the president, including those of his executive office, had always been regarded as his property. Since the time of George Washington, presidential papers had always been considered beyond congressional control because of the constitutional separation of powers. Before the 1930s most presidents gave or sold their papers to libraries, most often the Library of Congress. Beginning with Franklin Roosevelt, the volume of White House records expanded tremendously, and other arrangements needed to be made. FDR, his successor Harry Truman, and even, retroactively, his predecessor Herbert Hoover entered into agreements whereby friends would pay for a library building, which together with the papers would be donated to the government in return for its pledge to maintain the structure and the holdings in perpetuity. The growth of this system of presidential libraries administered by the National Archives innocently obscured the reality that a president's papers still remained legally his to dispose of as he saw fit.

Nixon had not made the usual arrangements for a presidential library before his sudden departure from office. Nevertheless, the disposition of his papers, an estimated thirteen thousand cubic feet of documents, tapes, and other materials, clearly weighed on his mind. The day he announced his resignation, he sent a letter to Arthur Sampson of the General Services Administration, the parent agency of the National Archives, directing that before 1985 no access be granted without his personal permission to any of his prepresidential papers already donated to the archives. Although Congress immediately expressed objections, neither Sampson nor the Justice Department believed they had any alternative but to honor Nixon's directive, as well as to treat his White House files as under his control. Ford embraced this view the day after pardoning Nixon. The Nixon papers, however, remained in the physical custody of the National Archives pending the outcome of various legal proceedings. The papers also continued in a legal limbo.[35]

Six months earlier, Senator Birch Bayh of Indiana had proposed legislation declaring all papers of federal officials to be public property. The resolution did not move forward until after Nixon's resignation. Serious consideration began after Nixon negotiated an arrangement with Sampson to take his presidential papers with him to California, control access to them, and eventually have power to destroy them if he wished. Congressional unhappiness escalated after Ford pardoned his predecessor and accepted the Nixon-Sampson agreement. Especially upset by the prospect that Nixon might destroy the notorious tapes without the full grounds for his impeachment ever coming to light, Congress started sorting out the complicated issue of presidential papers.[36]

Ownership of presidential papers proved a difficult issue to settle, especially for a Congress in the midst of a most unusual biennial election campaign. Instead, Senator Gaylord Nelson of Wisconsin offered an aggressive solution to the immediate problem of the Nixon-Sampson agreement, a solution that Congress quickly embraced. Nelson proposed that Congress, without resolving the ultimate ownership issue, simply assert custody rights to the Nixon materials under the principle of eminent domain, require their retention in the Washington area, bar any destruction, and establish a commission to study the issue of ownership of presidential records. In other words, Congress overturned the Nixon-Sampson agreement, passed over the question of ownership, and at a time of presidential weakness boldly insisted upon control of the material in order to ensure its preservation for the public's benefit. The Senate, by a 56–7 vote in early October, and the House, unanimously in its postelection session, accepted this solution, and Ford agreed to it.[37]

The Presidential Recordings and Materials Preservation Act of 1974, like the War Powers Act and the Budget and Impoundment Control Act that had preceded it, marked a significant assertion of congressional authority against the gradual accretion of president power over the course of the previous four decades. Such a bold and successful assertion of legislative power except in circumstances when the presidency was under substantial challenge from a pending or just-concluded impeachment is hard to imagine. Three years later Nixon would mount a legal challenge to the Presidential Recordings and Materials Preservation Act before the Supreme Court. Nixon's counsel argued that the act unconstitutionally violated the principle of separation of powers and intruded on the presumed confidentiality of presidential communications. The Court, however, ruled in *Nixon v. Administrator of General Services* that the separation of powers was not airtight, that appropriate safeguards to protect executive branch communications were in place, and that the public interest eventually overrode legitimate confidentiality.[38]

As a result of *Nixon v. Administrator of General Services*, the Nixon papers and tapes remained in the custody of the National Archives in Washington for more than a decade after the 1994 death of the former president while the contest over ownership and access continued. The Court ruling also encouraged further congressional action. Recognizing that the United States still lacked a clear policy with respect to the papers of other presidents, Congress in 1978 adopted the Presidential Records Act. This legislation established "the public ownership of records created by future Presidents . . . in the course of discharging their official duties." It also provided for preservation, a limited period of confidentiality, and eventual public availability of presidential records. Congress's actions in 1974 and 1978 flowed directly from the impeachment experience and proved to be the crucial steps in securing the public's enduring interest in every post-Watergate president's official records.[39]

Other legislative initiatives growing out of the Nixon removal experience would take considerably longer to bear fruit. Yet the impact of Nixon's impeachment on the evolving political culture is demonstrated by the continued legislative concern for ensuring the capacity of Congress to conduct impeachment effectively. By the end of the decade, two major pieces of impeachment-related legislation had been adopted. The first, the independent counsel provision of the 1978 Ethics in Government Act, was tied very closely to the peculiar circumstances of Watergate. The other, the Judicial Councils Reform and Judicial Conduct and Disability Act of 1980, reflected a heightened sense that Congress should be better prepared to deal with impeachments, even those quite different from what the country had just gone through with Nixon.

In the immediate aftermath of the Saturday Night Massacre, Congress had briefly considered creating a permanent special prosecutor, but the rapid appointment of Leon Jaworski to continue the Watergate prosecution blunted the legislative initiative.[40] Later, as Ervin's Senate Select Committee on Presidential Campaign Activities wrapped up its work in December 1974, it proposed, among other reforms, the creation of a permanent office of public attorney. Congress had established a temporary special prosecutor during the Teapot Dome scandal of the 1920s as well as during Watergate but had never institutionalized such an office. In 1975 Senator Abraham Ribicoff of Connecticut reintroduced the idea, and the Ervin committee's proposal called for a public attorney to be appointed for a five-year term by a panel of three retired federal court of appeals judges and confirmed by the Senate. This public attorney would be independent of the Justice Department and would have jurisdiction over cases in which executive branch corruption or malfeasance was charged, cases referred to it by the attorney general because of potential conflicts of interest, and cases in which federal campaign or election law violations were alleged. The narrow list of matters to be addressed by the public attorney was notably similar to the sorts of offenses that surfaced during the investigation of the Watergate affair. All involved investigations that might raise questions of divided loyalties if pursued by the Justice Department. Senator Lowell Weicker, a Republican member of the Ervin committee who wanted lasting reform to come out of the Watergate experience, became a prime advocate of the plan in hearings conducted between July 1975 and March 1976 and subsequently reported in revised form to the Senate.[41]

Attorney General Edward Levi raised doubts about the constitutionality of the evolving plan because of its intermingling of executive responsibility and judicial appointment authority. When the measure reached the Senate floor, the Ford administration proposed a substitute that would create a permanent independent prosecutor within the Justice Department to be appointed by the president for a three-year term. The Senate embraced this plan, added Congress to the office's jurisdiction, and adopted the act by 91 to 5.[42]

Members of the House remained uncertain about the Senate's plan when it came to them in late July 1976. They proved less willing to bow to the administration's preferences. Memories of the Saturday Night Massacre, one of the central events in Nixon's efforts to stave off the investigation that was boring in on him, kept alive the interest of House Democrats such as Holtzman in establishing truly independent special prosecutors. Ervin committee counsel Samuel Dash reinforced this view in testimony before a House judiciary subcommittee. On the other hand, Republican Watergate veteran Charles Wiggins and freshman Judiciary Committee member Henry J. Hyde defended the adequacy of the Justice Department and warned about overreacting to Watergate by creating a dangerous permanent special prosecutor. Such divisions kept the House from acting in 1976, despite a widespread preelection desire to demonstrate that Congress would ensure there could not be another Watergate.[43]

In 1977 a larger Democratic congressional majority, now aided by a White House friendly to the enforcement of ethics in government, made another effort to arrange for a special prosecutor, now calling it an independent counsel. Senator Ribicoff introduced a modified bill, designed with the help of the American Bar Association, that provided for judicial appointment of a temporary counsel, independent of the Justice Department, to investigate and if necessary prosecute when circumstances warranted. This time the Justice Department supported the plan, and it went quickly forward in the Senate, passing by 74 to 5 on June 27. The House again proved more of a stumbling block, largely because of a dispute over whether to include Congress in the independent counsel's jurisdiction. More than a year elapsed before the House adopted an ethics bill, one lacking any independent counsel provision and in other ways as well different from the Senate's measure. A conference reconciled differences, choosing to adopt the Senate's independent counsel mechanism. When the Senate adopted the conference committee report by voice vote on October 7, 1978, and the House followed suit by a vote of 370 to 23 five days later, a significant legacy of the Saturday Night Massacre had been achieved after almost exactly five years.[44]

Another ten years would elapse before the Supreme Court considered and confirmed the constitutionality of the independent counsel statute. In a 1988 ruling in *Morrison v. Olson* the Court decided that the mechanism did not violate the separation of powers principle or other constitutional provisions. The case itself raised a variety of questions and so tested the law in a host of respects. Alexia Morrison replaced a previous independent counsel appointed in 1982 to look into charges of false testimony to Congress by an assistant attorney general, Theodore Olson, regarding Reagan administration conduct within the Environmental Protection Agency (EPA). Morrison broadened her investigation to include two other Justice Department officials who were alleged to have conspired with Olson to wrongfully withhold EPA documents from Congress. The U.S. District Court for the District of Columbia rejected the contention of Olson and his colleagues that the independent counsel's appointment process, subpoena power, and independence from executive branch control all abridged provisions of the Constitution. The U.S. Court of Appeals for the District of Columbia overturned the district court's opinion. The final determination of *Morrison v. Olson* followed as the Supreme Court sided with the district court and reversed the court of appeals in a 7–1 opinion.

Chief Justice William Rehnquist's opinion for the Court held that there was nothing wrong with the independent counsel appointment process. The independent counsel was not a "principal" federal official but an "inferior" official of limited jurisdiction. Thus, the position did not require Senate confirmation as Olson's lawyers contended. Furthermore, Rehnquist pointed out, the Constitution explicitly gave Congress the power to authorize interbranch appointments. The Court also accepted Congress's limitation of the president's or attorney general's authority to remove an independent counsel to cases where "good cause" for the dismissal could be shown and confirmed by judicial review. Finally, the Court held that the independent counsel law did not violate the separation of powers because in adopting it Congress had not sought to increase its own power. Under the terms of the law the attorney general retained the power to decide whether or not to ask the designated three-judge panel to appoint an independent counsel, and that decision was not reviewable. In the chief justice's view the executive branch retained "sufficient control over the independent Counsel to ensure that the President is able to perform his constitutionally assigned duties."[45]

Only Justice Antonin Scalia dissented from the opinion of the Court in *Morrison v. Olson*. Unlike his fellow justices, he seemed indifferent to the realities of executive behavior during Watergate and treated the case before the Court as an entirely abstract constitutional matter. Taking an absolutist position on the assignment of executive power to the president as well as on the separation of legislative, executive, and judicial powers, he warned that to do otherwise would jeopardize the Bill of Rights. He scornfully rejected each of the majority's findings in favor of the appointment of independent counsels and their subsequent freedom from virtually all executive control. Scalia decried the removal from the president and his subordinates of the power to decide whether an investigation or prosecution would be in the national interest and worth the diversion of resources from other activities. He posed a hypothetical situation in which continuing a prosecution might jeopardize a national security interest, yet the president would have no power to stop it. He expressed alarm at the triggering mechanism for the appointment of an independent counsel, a process that, once initiated, could be stopped by the attorney general only if he found "no reasonable grounds to believe" further investigation was warranted.

Scalia held that legitimate executive power to choose among competing government interests would be breached if neither the attorney general nor the president could stop an independent counsel from proceeding. He went so far as to conjecture that a future Congress might find it easy to shift responsibility to an independent counsel for commencing politically inspired impeachment proceedings against a president on trivial grounds. "How frightening it must be," Scalia mused, "to have your own independent counsel and staff appointed, with nothing else to do but to investigate you until investigation is no longer worthwhile—with whether it is worthwhile not depending upon what such judgments usually hinge on, competing responsibilities."[46] Ten years later, the justice's grim prophecy regarding the dangers of an uncontrolled independent counsel would seem more plausible than it did at the time it was written.

Scalia's dissent in *Morrison v. Olson* may have forecast a future independent counsel's behavior, but it failed to look back. It did not take into account the possibility that a corrupt executive might seek to block an inquiry into its conduct. Scalia brushed aside the reality of the Nixon administration's efforts to stymie investigation of the Watergate cover-up. Had it prevailed, the justice's argument would have validated presidential authority to carry out an action like the Saturday Night Massacre. By contrast, the other justices appeared to be strongly influenced by the Watergate experience. Because of what the country had already been through, they were willing to find constitutional sanction for an independent counsel with authority to go forward unhindered by a defensive executive.

As the Rehnquist and Scalia opinions in *Morrison v. Olson* showed, the legacy of the Watergate experience was paradoxical. Ready justification for an independent counsel was at hand, but reason for apprehension also existed. A sizable majority of the Supreme Court found constitutional support for a prosecutorial office of the sort that had dealt effectively with the Nixon case. At the same time, the justices were willing to ignore what turned out to be realistic warnings about the creation of a durable device that might facilitate less responsible impeachment. As Richard Ben-Veniste, a veteran of the Watergate special prosecution staff, later reflected, "If all you have are hammers, a lot of stuff starts to look like nails."[47] As with other legislative measures of the 1970s, the independent counsel statute was powerfully shaped by the sense that Nixon's removal from office provided a reasonable model for any impeachment possibility that the United States was likely to confront in years ahead.

The Judicial Councils Reform and Judicial Conduct and Disability Act of 1980 effectively demonstrated that, after Watergate, Congress and the federal judiciary achieved a higher level of consciousness and displayed a greater concern about the overall process of impeachment. The federal judiciary established procedures and Congress enacted legislation that dealt with more than just the peculiar circumstances brought to light in the Nixon and Agnew cases. Congress had not altogether forgotten the proposed impeachments of Earl Warren, Abe Fortas, and William O. Douglas, as shown by the sharp questioning of Gerald Ford during his vice presidential confirmation hearing. Furthermore, two other cases, one just predating the Watergate episode and one in its midst, reminded both Congress and the federal judiciary through unrelated scandals involving federal district and appellate court judges that the prospects of having to deal with a judicial impeachment remained ever present. Indeed, as the federal judiciary continued to expand, the likelihood of allegations of judicial misbehavior increased as well. The desire to be prepared for the peculiarities of impeaching federal judges added one more item to the post-Watergate governmental agenda.

In December 1965 the Judicial Council of the U.S. Court of Appeals for the Tenth Circuit had, without notice or grant of a hearing, suspended Stephen S. Chandler, chief judge of the Western District of Oklahoma, from hearing cases, declaring him unable or unwilling to discharge his judicial duties efficiently. Judicial councils are the administrative bodies composed of an appellate circuit's active judges; Congress had established them in 1939 to coordinate and manage more efficiently the work of the district courts under them. Two months after its original unprecedented action, the Tenth Circuit's council reduced Chandler's suspension to a prohibition on taking on any new cases. He could continue to adjudicate his backlog of two hundred cases and assign new cases to the other three judges in his district. No suggestion was made that he should be impeached.

The action against Chandler grew out of his more than two-decade-long feud with the circuit's chief judge, Alfred P. Murrah. Chandler and Murrah, both appointed to the bench by Franklin Roosevelt (in 1943 and 1937, respectively), were members of rival Oklahoma political factions. The conflict had generated intemperate statements on both sides, delayed the construction of a federal courthouse in Oklahoma City where both resided, and led to complaints about Chandler's strenuous efforts to negotiate compromise settlements rather than adjudicate cases as well as about his outside business interests that had left him with substantial debts. Chandler had been indicted in a corruption case that was later dismissed for lack of evidence and was also the defendant in two libel suits by the same complainant, one dismissed and the other unsettled. He had refused to recuse himself from two cases in which his impartiality was challenged. And, finally, he did not appear to be dealing expeditiously with cases before him. His backlog of cases was four times that of the other judges in his district. Chandler challenged his suspension from new case assignments on the grounds that he had, in effect, been removed from the bench, with the judicial council usurping the impeachment power granted to Congress alone.[48]

A Senate judiciary subcommittee immediately began looking at what its chairman, Senator Joseph Tydings of Maryland, described as "wranglings and recriminations" between Chandler and his foes that "have exposed our entire federal judicial system to disrepute and even ridicule." Tydings expressed interest in finding a mechanism other than impeachment for removing judges who failed to meet the constitutional requirement that they serve "during good behavior." Judges who were unfit because of "senility, insanity, physical disability, alcoholism, or laziness" should be removable, he said, without having to resort to the cumbersome process of impeachment. Uncertain about how best to proceed, he signaled his hope that a way could be found for the judiciary to police its own ranks.[49]

During Tydings's 1966 hearing a spokesman for the American Bar Association declared that something needed to be done to make possible easier removal of unfit judges. Impeachment, he said, was "virtually worthless" as a solution. Taking a contrary position, Senator Ervin called the Tenth Circuit's action against Chandler "presumptuous" and said that it "denied Judge Chambers even elementary due process in defending himself." Furthermore, Ervin bristled against any attempt to reduce the independence of the judiciary other than through the constitutionally prescribed method.[50] Neither the Senate hearings nor a 1969 House Judiciary Committee report finding that the Tenth Circuit council had erred in its action toward Judge Chandler produced any legislative remedies. Tydings's 1968 proposal to establish a commission on judicial disabilities and tenure that would be empowered to investigate, try, and recommend removal of federal judges for "willful misconduct in office or willful and persistent failure to perform" went nowhere because of doubts about its constitutionality. Each of these developments did serve to raise consciousness of a problem with the judiciary.[51]

The complicated Chandler case was not argued before the Supreme Court until December 1969, and a ruling was not forthcoming for another six months. In June 1970 the Court refused Chandler's request for a writ of mandamus to order the Tenth Circuit council to assign him new cases. The Court found that acceptable and reasonable practices of judicial administration had been followed and decided that the case had become moot because Chandler had subsequently been restored to normal status. Justice John Harlan sought in a concurrence to stress the necessary and proper role of circuit judicial councils in the overall management and policing of courts.[52] In his opinion for the Court, Chief Justice Burger commented that courts must operate by "reasonable, proper, and necessary rules" and must enforce them. "If one judge in any system refuses to abide by such reasonable procedures it can hardly be that the extraordinary machinery of impeachment is the only recourse."[53] Both Burger and Harlan were strong voices for the spreading belief that the judiciary should be able to police its ranks without the impeachment process being invoked.

Justices Black and Douglas dissented in *Chandler v. Judicial Council,* saying that in dealing with Chandler his fellow judges had exceeded their constitutional authority and compromised the important principle of judicial independence. "Judge Chandler, duly appointed, duly confirmed, and never impeached by the Congress, has been barred from doing his work by other judges," observed Hugo Black. Noting a pattern of treatment of Chandler as a "second-class judge," Black was "unable to find in our Constitution or in any statute any authority whatever for judges to arrogate to themselves and to exercise such powers."[54] With Murrah retired, Chandler remained active on his district bench for another five years and retired voluntarily when he reached seventy-five.[55] The issues he had raised regarding judicial administration and discipline short of impeachment and that neither the Supreme Court nor Congress had resolved remained unsettled.

A second case soon added to the dilemma of how to deal with wayward adjudicators. Judge Otto Kerner of the U.S. Court of Appeals for the Seventh Circuit, a former governor of Illinois and the chair of an important presidential commission on civil disorders during the 1960s, was convicted in February 1973 of accepting a bribe, evading income tax, and committing perjury in a case involving an Illinois horse-racing track. As Vice President Agnew would soon likewise argue, Kerner contended that his indictment was unconstitutional unless he was first impeached and removed from his federal office. In contrast to the vice president, however, the convicted judge chose not to resign and instead pursued an appeal. After his own Seventh Circuit Court of Appeals rejected his argument, the Supreme Court declined to hear his further appeal. Facing imminent impeachment, Kerner finally resigned from the bench on the day that the House Judiciary Committee began its final debate on the fate of Richard Nixon and only two weeks before the president himself stepped down.[56]

Judge Kerner, by strenuously fighting to stay on the bench even after his conviction on multiple criminal charges, again raised the question of whether impeachment was the only way to remove a federal judge from his position, not to mention prevent him from continuing to draw the federal salary that the Constitution stipulated could not be reduced while he remained in office. Kerner's fall, roughly contemporaneous with the disgrace and leave-taking of Agnew and Nixon, drew far less notice from the American public than theirs. Nevertheless, to attentive members of Congress, the bench, and the bar at least, the Kerner case served as a reminder that impeachment had most frequently in the American past involved judges. Stirred by the individually distinctive Fortas, Douglas, Chandler, and Kerner cases as well as by Watergate, Congress and the federal judiciary combined later in the 1970s to prepare for the eventuality of judicial impeachments that, the assumption continued to grow, were inevitable.

A sense of need for a system to supervise and discipline the federal judiciary had long been developing. During his years as a Yale law professor between serving as president and as chief justice, William Howard Taft had suggested that some system be established both to standardize and coordinate administrative practices in the hitherto completely independent federal district courts and to monitor judicial behavior. As soon as he became the nation's highest judge, Taft encouraged Congress to create the Judicial Conference of the United States, to consist of the chief justice of the Supreme Court and the senior judge of each federal circuit. Among other things, the conference was empowered to adjust judicial assignments when a judge's capabilities or conduct warranted. In 1939 the Administrative Office Act supplemented the Judicial Conference with judicial councils of the circuits, giving them power to prevent "any stigma, disrepute, or other element of loss of public confidence occurring as to the Federal courts or to the administration of justice by them, from any nature of action by an individual judge." This authority, made more explicit in the Judicial Code revisions of 1948 and upheld in *Chandler v. Judicial Council*, gave the circuit councils the power to retire a mentally or physically disabled judge. It did not, however, grant them authority to discipline judges who did not comply voluntarily with judicial council directives.[57]

The post-Watergate reexamination of standards and policing of judicial conduct began in 1974 with the introduction by Senator Sam Nunn of Georgia of a Judicial Tenure Act. Like Tydings six years earlier, Nunn had in mind a small body of federal judges to oversee the conduct of their colleagues. His intricate proposal included three distinct new bodies: a Judicial Conduct and Disability Commission for determining standards, a three-judge panel in each circuit to conduct initial review of cases as needed, and a Court on Judicial Conduct and Disability to make final determinations on the censure, involuntary retirement, or removal of judges. Senator Ervin condemned the Nunn plan as "a hazing commission."[58] Nevertheless, at a time when concern remained strong for restoring an image of a government committed to ethical performance, Nunn's measure gained significant bipartisan support in Congress as well as early approval in principle by the Judicial Conference.

Nunn's bill underwent substantial revision, was repeatedly reintroduced, and twice passed the Senate. The principal obstacle to its adoption was resistance by the House of Representatives to the idea of the judiciary rather than the House exercising the power to remove a judge from office. Involuntary removal from the bench by other judges for whatever reason appeared to risk compromising judicial independence. It also intruded on authority given exclusively to the House by the Constitution. The Judicial Conference reconsidered and eventually withdrew its support from the Nunn plan. Finally a compromise was struck that kept the power to investigate and discipline with the judicial councils (to which district court judges were added) and the Judicial Conference but eliminated the power to remove judges.

Under the measure finally agreed upon, written complaints from any source about the misconduct or mental or physical disability of any federal judge would be referred to the chief judge of the circuit. The chief judge's decision to dismiss or pursue the matter was appealable by either the complainant or the target to the circuit council. The chief judge could then appoint an investigating committee of judges within the circuit to make recommendations to the council for appropriate disposition of the matter, short of removal from office. Decisions could be appealed to the Judicial Conference for its own investigation, review, and limited disciplinary measures. If deemed necessary, the confidentiality that bound the entire proceeding to this point could be waved and the case referred to the House of Representatives for possible impeachment action. The compromise measure, the Judicial Councils Reform and Judicial Conduct and Disability Act, was finally adopted in 1980. Jimmy Carter, an advocate of government ethics enforcement throughout his presidency, signed the measure into law on October 15, 1980.[59]

With the enactment of the Judicial Councils Reform and Judicial Conduct and Disability Act, mechanisms were in place, ranging from an independent counsel to a process of judicial self-policing, to accomplish the investigatory phase of the impeachment process. The lingering uneasiness in the wake of the anxious times of Watergate appeared finally to be assuaged by legislation that reassured the polity, perhaps mistakenly, that the Constitution's near meltdown would not recur. The need to rein in the imperial presidency and strengthen the impeachment system had coincided. As a result, Congress had constructed an enduring legacy from its experience with impeachment. Legislators had not merely adopted plans for fighting the last war, but by adopting procedures for dealing with cases that might arise within the judiciary they had endeavored to anticipate other possibilities. Congress had managed to erect a fairly comprehensive structure for carrying out its constitutional responsibilities in the area of impeachment. Only time would tell whether their labors had been prudent as well as vigorous.

As a result of continuing post-Watergate anxieties, Congress had effectively bureaucratized impeachment. As a consequence, impeachable officials and those who served them would become subject to a level of scrutiny well beyond anything such individuals had previously experienced. Accordingly, high-level White House personnel, regardless of party, became accustomed to engaging legal counsel.[60] Not only did this increase their costs for serving a president, but it also encouraged them to have a heightened distrust of the Washington environment and to be obsessively secretive about an administration's activities. Between the staffing of independent counsel inquiries and the representation of persons under scrutiny, a new cottage industry for attorneys grew out of the bureaucratization of impeachment. The cost of this continuing source of distractions for presidential administrations of both parties was incalculable but was part of the price paid for the deeds of the Nixon administration and the desire to discourage their repetition.

The impact of the Watergate trauma was even more widespread than its effect on the operation of the federal government. Endemic suspicion of officialdom, particularly presidents, flourished in the aftermath of the Nixon scandals. The very measures adopted to avoid a repeat of the problem served to institutionalize a regular revisitation of it in the American political culture. In creating a web of legislation restricting the president and especially by adopting the Independent Counsel Act and the Judicial Councils Reform and Judicial Conduct and Disability Act, Congress, for the best of reasons, assured the continuation of the age of impeachment.

Congress could not deal with the most distinctive element of the immediate post-Watergate period, Ford's pardon of Nixon. The Constitution specifically gave the president the power to grant pardons, save in the case of impeachment itself. Ford's use of the pardoning power was beyond the capacity of Congress to overturn, though not for lack of trying, as the hearings at which Ford testified served to demonstrate. But Ford was nevertheless called to account for pardoning Nixon. After testifying in his vice presidential confirmation hearings that he had no intention to run for president in 1976, he decided, once in the White House, to do just that. In 1976 he lost a close contest for the presidency against a previously little-known one-term governor of Georgia, Jimmy Carter. Opinion polls showed that one of Ford's biggest liabilities was public hostility toward the Nixon pardon. Except for the pardon, Ford would probably have been president for another term.[61] But the deep engagement of an electorally significant portion of the public in the impeachment experience of the previous four years and their sense of dissatisfaction with its concluding chapter sent Ford into retirement. The results of the election of 1976 demonstrated that at least some of the American public had come to care deeply about the process of impeachment and were prepared to express dissatisfaction with its resolution at the ballot box.

8

Impeachment as Cultural:

Shaping Public Conclusions

Between the early 1960s and the mid-1970s public understanding of impeachment went from nearly nil to merely nebulous. Neither the John Birch Society's calls to impeach Earl Warren nor the brushes of Abe Fortas, William O. Douglas, and Spiro T. Agnew with possible impeachment gained a great deal of serious attention outside the ranks of right-wing zealots and a few affected officials. To Americans in general and even hard-core conservatives such as William F. Buckley, Jr., the "Impeach Earl Warren" billboard campaign served mainly to brand the Birchers as unrealistic political extremists. Understanding of impeachment as a useful device to maintain discipline among high federal officials and remove those whose conduct overstepped constitutional bounds did not increase noticeably. The Watergate drama made the constitutional instrument much better known and more widely approved. The availability of radio and television broadcasts allowed a much larger audience to follow developments closely than had been the case in the era of Samuel Chase or Andrew Johnson, when even mass-circulation newspapers had yet to appear. From the start of the Ervin committee hearings through the completion of the House Judiciary Committee's deliberations and Richard Nixon's resignation speech, millions of Americans watched or listened closely. The decision of the commercial networks to rotate coverage so that all but one could maintain regular programming and advertising revenues and the choice of the two-and-a-half-year-old Public Broadcasting Service (PBS) to provide complete coverage first drew a large audience to PBS for something other than its children's educational program *Sesame Street*. Yet because the impeachment procedure fell far short of completion, not even Watergate provided a thorough civic education on how the process was carried out and what properly constituted an impeachable offense.

During the years following Nixon's departure from the White House, Americans digested the political and constitutional experience they had gone through. They displayed a voracious appetite for further information about what had happened. Nixon had retreated to his home in California leaving many unanswered questions about Watergate. Had he ordered the break-in or just acted to cover it up? Had he erased eighteen and a half minutes of a taped conversation with Haldeman? Did he accept responsibility for the commission of impeachable offenses? Or did he feel abused by the constitutional system?

Public curiosity about the nearly impeached president fueled a market for participant memoirs and other sorts of explanations. Books, films, plays, and television programs would retrace Watergate from a variety of perspectives. The views of impeachment that politicians, journalists, scholars, and the broader citizenry came to hold were shaped not only by personal memories of watching the complex and often confusing drama unfold—before their eyes in a few cases and on television and radio for millions more—but also by the ways participants subsequently sought to interpret what had taken place. In the first few years after Nixon's resignation, a wave of books, a dramatic film about the initial journalistic investigation of the break-in, an extraordinary television interview with the former president, and a flood of memoirs, including Nixon's own, all contributed significantly to the perceptions of impeachment taking shape in American minds. In later years, images drawn from the Watergate episode would contend and blend with other impeachment experiences to further mold Americans attitudes regarding impeachment.

As the Watergate episode was assimilated and judgments about it found their place in the minds of Americans, the underlying nature of historical knowledge once again became evident. History represents the sum of selected developments and interpretations that are chosen to be remembered. The distilled memory of the past does not always add up the same way for everyone who makes the attempt to remember their own time, much less what preceded it. Furthermore, sums are constantly being recalculated as direct perceptions fade, additional information about original events increases, scholars or creative artists offer new constructions of meaning, and intervening experience alters perspectives.

In the case of Watergate, the protracted drama of a president falling from grace so riveted observers that it erased most memories of the impeachment episodes that had not long preceded it but had followed different courses. Watergate, though it was a single case involving a unique set of characters and circumstances, quickly came to be thought of as the standard model of impeachment. It was perceived to contain a variety of elements essential to justifying impeachment: concealment of outrageous conduct, belligerently uncooperative responses to inquiries about the misconduct, widespread loss of public confidence, and incontrovertible evidence of an official's direct involvement in illegal acts, even if carried out by subordinates. Nixon himself, as well as various of his antagonists, helped shape what would be remembered as the history of Watergate and thus as generic impeachment. The dazzling memory of Watergate thus created helped blot out more dimly recalled episodes and set the standard for how impeachment would thereafter be regarded.

Tracking the cultural shifts that resulted from the Nixon impeachment is more difficult than following the narrative of the Watergate break-in, cover-up, and revelations or even the broader story of Nixon administration misdeeds. It requires examining the ways information diffuses throughout the culture as

"Sir, He Says He Has An Appointment With You"

Herblock,
Washington Post,
July 30, 1974.
© The Herb
Block Foundation.

well as the manner in which that knowledge is retained, reshaped, and put to use. Measuring and evaluating the evolution of political and constitutional culture, much less ascertaining its exact location in the even broader landscape of overall American culture, defies precision and certitude. If there are other ways of expressing caution when reaching conclusions about as slippery a subject as national culture, they should all be invoked. Nevertheless, attempting to determine the characteristics of impeachment as an aspect of American culture during the post-1960 period is worthwhile as a means to better understand the consequences of the increasing resort during these years to this constitutional device.

"Watergate was like having sex three times a day!" Washington Post editor Benjamin Bradlee exclaimed to some of his reporters when it was all over.[1] The excitement of pursuing an important story that brought new revelations and unexpected twists at a rapid and accelerating pace for more than two years stimulated the journalists who covered it. That it was a story involving the highest officials of the federal government, including both the president and the vice president, added to the thrill as well as to the sense of risk in its pursuit. There was regular satisfaction as each new report drew a larger readership and an ever more vast television audience. Then came the climax of seeing one's reporting efforts validated by Congress, a special prosecutor, and the Supreme Court in constitutional actions that led a president to resign in disgrace. Finally, with the story itself at an end, the afterglow included the most diligent of the journalists involved in the drama becoming national celebrities themselves and the heroes of a suspenseful Hollywood blockbuster film. To use Bradlee's coarse but telling metaphor, Watergate produced multiple orgasms for the press, the memories of which would not only linger but shape subsequent quests to repeat the experience. Reporters would look closely at every political scandal, major or minor, that came along thereafter and attach to it the suffix "-gate" to emphasize its significance.

A president's brush with impeachment affected more than the media and the officials, bureaucrats, and attorneys directly involved in it one way or another. The jarring encounter with official misdeeds and their treatment influenced popular belief, language, and memory. The manner in which journalists, government officials, and lawyers presented the Watergate episode to a broader audience exerted a lasting influence on public understanding of what had transpired. Dramatic recountings of Watergate and commentaries on it exercised a wide and lasting impact on attitudes about the conduct of government, the nature of politics, and the instrument of impeachment. The fashion in which the Nixon story was presented and perceived reoriented American political and constitutional culture.

One small sign of how the impeachment experience pervaded the public's consciousness could be found in the many Watergate-related phrases that entered the American language. "What did he know and when did he know it?" "dirty tricks," "stonewall it," "modified, limited hangout," "twisting slowly in the wind," "expletive deleted," "eighteen-and-a-half-minute gap," and "smoking gun" became recognizable expressions with implicit meanings not evident from the words themselves. However, "-gate," as a suffix meaning scandal, may have become the longest-lasting and most ubiquitous term of all. It was applied not only to major improprieties but also to many minor ones for the rest of the century. "Billygate," Irangate," "Koreagate," "travelgate," and "Monicagate" followed one after another. Additions to the language reflected changed notions about government by those using these new words and expecting to be understood.

By the time Nixon announced his resignation, a revised perception of impeachment was already taking shape. Journalists who had covered the story played a major role in molding a new belief that presidential removal might be justified. None exerted a greater impact than the young *Washington Post* reporters who had pursued the Watergate story with extraordinary tenacity. Not only did Bob Woodward and Carl Bernstein eagerly seize the investigative opportunity, but they also later recounted their exploits in a fashion that made them seem both singular and heroic. Woodward and Bernstein, or as some came to refer to them, Woodstein, provided the prism through which many Americans viewed what had taken place in the death spiral of the Nixon administration.

In the summer and fall of 1972, most of Woodward's and Bernstein's journalistic elders believed they had more important stories to follow. Reporters covering national politics riveted their attention on the struggle for the Democratic presidential nomination, the debacle of the Democrats' convention, the contrasting triumphalism of the Republican convention, and thereafter the spectacle of a contentious contest for the presidency. Nixon, safely ahead and buoyed by Henry Kissinger's October announcement that negotiations in Paris to end the Vietnam War were nearing success, did not make himself available to the press, much less for confrontational debates with his Democratic rival, George McGovern. He thus avoided questions about Watergate, should reporters or McGovern ask them. Since it was standard journalistic practice only to report on what presidential candidates actually said and not what they avoided saying, Nixon's silence regarding Watergate was scarcely addressed by the national political press. With their colleagues seemingly uninterested, few in the journalistic pack following the national campaign saw fit to raise the issue.[2]

Woodward and Bernstein stood outside the circle of national political journalism. The two were junior reporters at the *Post* and were assigned to the metropolitan, not the national, desk.[3] They were given the task of covering the Watergate break-in because it at first seemed merely a routine local crime story. Aided at crucial points by *Post* police-beat reporters, they pursued the story with vigor but, especially at the outset, without much knowledge of the cast of White House and CREEP characters whose names began to turn up. Their energy, together with their sense that there was more to the story than was initially evident, drove them forward. Their August and September discoveries linking Republican campaign contributions to money in the burglars' possession made the *Post*'s front page but drew limited notice elsewhere. In October they exposed a wider pattern of campaign sabotage traceable to the office of White House chief of staff H. R. Haldeman. Still, by November 4, election day, a Gallup poll found that 48 percent of the electorate had never heard of Watergate.[4]

Not until the Watergate burglars went on trial before Judge John Sirica on January 8, 1973, did the tide of public awareness start to rise appreciably. The revelations of James McCord in Sirica's courtroom two and a half months later, FBI director-designate Patrick Gray's admissions during his Senate confirmation hearings of complicity in a cover-up, and John Dean's disclosures as he spoke to

Justice Department prosecutors lifted interest in the investigation into a higher gear. By then the contributions of Woodward and Bernstein in bringing the Watergate affair to center stage were largely completed. The questions they had raised stirred the Senate to create a committee of inquiry and led a hard-nosed judge to press the burglars for information. In turn those efforts caused senators to interrogate a presidential nominee and frightened a White House counsel who thought he might be made a scapegoat into cooperating with the investigation. Although the Ervin committee hearings, the special prosecutor's quest for White House tapes, the Saturday Night Massacre, and the House impeachment inquiry all still lay in the future, Woodward's and Bernstein's role in bringing to light the Nixon administration's machinations was primarily over. Thereafter their contribution would lie in shaping how the complex matter would be remembered.

As the Watergate story unfolded, other journalists, including Seymour Hersh of the *New York Times,* Jack Nelson and Ronald Ostrow of the *Los Angeles Times*, and several of Woodward's and Bernstein's colleagues at the *Post,* began to bring forth important information. When the Ervin committee hearings got underway and detailed accounts began emerging from participants such as Dean, Woodward and Bernstein shifted their efforts to describing their own experiences. They spent the later months of 1973 assembling a memoir of their investigation. In their book's final pages they could report that they had learned of the Ervin committee's discovery of the White House taping system the day after it occurred but before it was made public. While this demonstrated their continuing diligence, it also showed that the investigation had acquired a momentum independent of their reports. As they wrapped up their manuscript, they were able to add references to the Saturday Night Massacre and to the initiation of impeachment proceedings against President Nixon, thereby indicating that the story had grown beyond them. The most their account could do was to renew attention to the early stages of the Watergate story and the methods they had employed to assure the reliability of their reports.[5] Even before they wrote their memoir, actor and filmmaker Robert Redford had approached Woodward about buying the rights to their story as the basis for a realistic movie about investigative journalism. As soon as their manuscript was finished, the reporters agreed to let Redford proceed.[6]

As the American people wrestled with unprecedented and increasing doubts about their chief executive in the spring of 1974, the New York publisher Simon and Schuster raced to get Woodward and Bernstein's manuscript, *All the President's Men,* into print and marketed it aggressively. *Playboy* bought excerpts for its May and June issues, the Book of the Month Club chose the book as its July selection, and *Reader's Digest* arranged to publish a condensed version. Even before the book appeared, Simon and Schuster boosted its hardback print run from 35,000 to over 200,000 copies and sold the paperback rights for $1 million, a then unheard-of price for a yet-to-appear nonfiction book. *All the President's*

Men arrived in bookstores in June 1974 as public concern about Nixon's conduct was reaching a peak. The book immediately moved onto the *New York Times* best-seller list, where it remained for nearly a year.[7]

Readers of *All the President's Men* obtained virtually no information on the stealthy conduct of the Nixon administration during the three and a half years before the Watergate arrests but gained a strong impression of how difficult it was thereafter to penetrate a federal government bent on maintaining secrets. For those relying on Woodward and Bernstein to help them assess what was wrong with the federal government, the effect of the book was to narrow the range of offenses charged to the Nixon White House. The *Post* reporters' book conveyed their diligent and careful manner in pursuing the Watergate story and their insistence on having at least two independent confirming sources for every assertion of fact. Their account made clear that they were pursuing leads in a mystery rather than attempting from the outset to assemble a case against a predetermined target against whom they carried a grudge. At the same time, the narrative confined itself to a narrow list of questionable White House activities. Concealment of illegal surveillance activities, improper campaign conduct, misuse of funds, and obstruction of criminal investigations received attention, as did the sense of peril the two young journalists felt at every step of their long investigation.

On the other hand, Woodward and Bernstein quite understandably gave no attention to aspects of the Nixon presidency beyond their immediate and rather narrow area of concern. They paid no heed to the bombing and invasion of Cambodia, the impoundment of appropriated funds, or the concerted efforts against the media that many members of Congress considered alarming and constitutionally dubious expansions of presidential power. As a result, readers who leaned heavily on their account to get a sense of what had been subsumed under the rubric of Watergate acquired a rather narrow view of what was disturbing and potentially impeachable about Nixon's conduct of the presidency. Notably, in adopting impeachment articles a few weeks after the Woodward and Bernstein book appeared, the House Judiciary Committee chose to limit its allegations to those the volume reinforced. The committee dropped counts on Cambodia and tax evasion, which the book did not address.

The success of *All the President's Men,* combined with the termination of the Nixon presidency two months after its publication, gave Woodward and Bernstein ample incentive to undertake a follow-up volume. Armed with another contract from Simon and Schuster and a leave of absence from the *Washington Post,* they undertook to chronicle the collapse of the Nixon presidency. In *The Final Days* their focus shifted away from their own efforts as reporters to an unraveling of the puzzle of Watergate in the year after the break-in. The second book sought to describe the inner workings of the Nixon administration as the existence of the White House taping system was revealed, the Saturday

Night Massacre occurred, and thereafter the president's grip on power slowly but steadily weakened. Woodward and Bernstein once again sought informants among prominent figures on the White House staff, as well as among their deputies and secretaries. They then cross-checked what they were told and wrote from the intersecting perspectives of their sources.[8]

The Final Days only recounted those elements of Nixon's fight against impeachment about which Woodward and Bernstein obtained information. The first half of the book focused on the yearlong battle of White House lawyers to keep the tapes from the special prosecutor and the House Judiciary Committee. The detailed account revealed how little information Nixon made available to his staff and his defenders and yet how unquestioningly, if not always effectively, they continued to fight on his behalf.

For the period after the Supreme Court ruled in *United States v. Nixon* that the tapes must be surrendered, Woodward and Bernstein further narrowed their focus to Nixon himself and those people with whom he had direct contact during the last ten days of his presidency. The second half of their book in particular conveyed a sense of close observation and extraordinary drama as it told of Nixon coming to terms with a series of devastating blows. The loss in his court battle was followed by the vote in the House Judiciary Committee, the revelation of the June 23, 1972, tape that made clear that he had directed the cover-up from the outset, and, ultimately, the irresistible pressure to resign. The two reporters employed sources able to describe the activities and attitudes of Chief of Staff Alexander Haig; White House attorneys Fred Buzhardt, Leonard Garment, and James St. Clair; the president's speechwriters and media spokesmen Ronald Ziegler, Patrick Buchanan, and David Gergen; Senator Barry Goldwater; and even members of the Nixon family.

Woodward and Bernstein conveyed a picture of aides struggling to protect an elusive and erratic president as he drank heavily and plunged into a depression that rendered him largely nonfunctional. In the days before Nixon left office, Chief of Staff Haig came to doubt the president's ability to make sound judgments. Thus, when H. R. Haldeman and John Ehrlichman sought pardons, Haig took it upon himself to refuse them and block their access to Nixon.

The journalists portrayed heated discussions within Nixon's family and the growing exhaustion and demoralization of the White House staff. The visit of senators Barry Goldwater and Hugh Scott and the House minority leader, John Rhodes, to the Oval Office to tell Nixon that his support in Congress had evaporated was described in detail, as was a final maudlin encounter on the eve of his resignation between Nixon and Secretary of State Henry Kissinger. The result was a depiction of a president whose misconduct had become overwhelmingly evident to almost all but himself and a few of his closest associates. Also clear was the fact that Nixon was virtually paralyzed during his last months, not to mention final days in office, leaving the ship of state rudderless.

Appropriate to its title, *The Final Days* captured the waning hours of the Nixon presidency with particular vividness. In so doing, Woodward and Bernstein shed light on how precarious and ineffectual the nation's leadership could be rendered during the slow-moving process of impeachment. Nixon wrestled nearly to the end with the decision over whether to fight through an impeachment trial or instead resign. As he did so, he apparently consulted only with his emotionally distraught family, a chief of staff who possessed military but no political or congressional experience, and three members of Congress, all of whom came from the minority party. Even after deciding to leave office, Nixon did not give any indication of understanding that he had overstepped the Constitution's bounds. "What have I done? What has happened?" he reportedly wailed to the secretary of state the night before resigning.[9]

Neither Kissinger nor anyone else told Nixon more than that he had lost the political support necessary to continue, Woodward and Bernstein noted. That became Nixon's message as he announced his resignation in a televised address from the Oval Office on the evening of August 8 and as he said farewell to the White House staff the following morning. Sidestepping the fact that presidents Truman and Johnson had sunk just as low in public opinion polls but only he was charged with high crimes and misdemeanors, Nixon avoided the central issue of impeachment. He told the nation, "I no longer have a strong enough political base in Congress." He inched closer to an acknowledgment of error the next day but still placed the onus on his foes as he told his staff, "Always remember, others may hate you—but those who hate you don't win unless you hate them, and then you destroy yourself."[10] He thus departed the presidency without providing closure to many of the issues raised by Watergate. Therefore, despite Woodward and Bernstein's title, these would not prove to be Nixon's final days.

Within a week of the publication of *The Final Days*, a much larger audience than existed for nonfiction books began to gain exposure to the work of Woodward and Bernstein. Redford's efforts to turn *All the President's Men* into a film had borne fruit. Starting with a glittery premiere for eleven hundred people at the Kennedy Center, next door to the Watergate complex in Washington, the film would draw immense audiences. Redford, who from the start wanted to play Woodward himself, had enlisted experienced Hollywood screenwriter William Goldman, who had written *Butch Cassidy and the Sundance Kid,* in which Redford had starred, to prepare a script. He also recruited Alan J. Pakula to direct the film, stars Dustin Hoffman and Jason Robards to play Bernstein and *Washington Post* editor Bradlee, and a highly talented roster of other actors to play secondary characters. Eventually Goldman's script was largely discarded in favor of a more factually accurate version on which Woodward, Bernstein, Bernstein's new wife Nora Ephron, and Redford collaborated.[11]

Together Redford and his colleagues turned a story whose ending was well known to everyone walking into the theater into a dramatic thriller of such quality that it gained eight Academy Award nominations and won four Oscars. More remarkable for a Hollywood production, the film was quite faithful to Woodward and Bernstein's account. Publisher Katharine Graham and key *Post* editors Barry Sussman and Howard Simons were either left out or downplayed so that the story could be compressed into a two-hour movie, but neither the tedious process of investigative reporting nor the limits of the Woodward and Bernstein contribution to Nixon's eventual downfall was distorted.[12] In a small but meaningful gesture to their concern for accuracy, the filmmakers arranged for Frank Wills, the Watergate security guard who first discovered the break-in, to play himself in the film's opening scene. Woodward's secret informant, Deep Throat, remained shrouded in mystery, with actor Hal Holbrook's face only partially seen and then in deep shadow.

The film of *All the President's Men* left no doubt of its creators' view of Nixon. Though the president only appeared in a few television clips, the White House was shown repeatedly, always at night and in shadows. In contrast to those dark and foreboding images, the newsroom of the *Post,* where much of the action was set, was uniformly light and bright. The image of a sinister presidency was reinforced by the nighttime settings for the reporters' interviews of CREEP workers and Woodward's meetings with Deep Throat. A mood of threat and fear was subtly conveyed, often without words, in scene after scene. At the end of a film totally without direct confrontation between the protagonists and not one moment of violence, the viewer was left with no doubt that the defenders of justice had survived a perilous undertaking and triumphed over the forces of evil.

All the President's Men drew large audiences to movie theaters in 1976. No doubt the millions who saw it were reminded, though it was not shown on screen, that Nixon had, as a result of the events described, resigned on the eve of his impeachment. Unfortunately for Gerald Ford, who was in the midst of a campaign to be elected president in his own right, moviegoers were also presumably reminded of Ford's pardon of Nixon. Resentment of the pardon proved to be a pivotal factor in Ford's narrow loss to Jimmy Carter, and there can be little question that the film reignited memories of Nixon's fate.

For years thereafter, *All the President's Men* remained a staple of American film culture. In addition to the millions who first saw it on theater screens, countless numbers subsequently viewed it on television. The film reappeared regularly on late-night reruns and soon began to be carried by the infant cable television industry. As videotape recorders and later digital videodiscs became popular, *All the President's Men* remained a best seller. Vastly more people saw the film at home than initially saw it in theaters, and for a steadily growing number of people too young to remember the Watergate period themselves, it provided their principle avenue to understanding what had happened in the early 1970s. Thirty years after the film first appeared, Woodward and Bernstein still ranked twenty-seventh on the American Film Institute's list of cinematic heroes of the past century, just behind Lou Gehrig and Superman and ahead of luminaries such as General George Patton, Tarzan, Mr. Chips, Moses, Zorro, and Batman.[13] Woodward and Bernstein, through their two books and especially through the film in which they were the heroes, may have done more than anyone else to cement in place the historical image of Watergate and what impeachment involved.

After resigning, Richard Nixon retreated to his home in San Clemente and immediately began thinking about ways to redeem his impeachment-clouded reputation, as well as to assure his financial security. On September 27, only seven weeks after leaving Washington and less than three weeks after being pardoned by Ford, he signaled that he intended to offer the public his own view of his presidency. He signed a $2 million contract, negotiated by his literary agent Irving "Swifty" Lazar with Warner Books, to publish his memoirs.[14]

British television personality and producer David Frost had made a successful career of interviewing celebrities, including candidate Nixon in 1968. He noticed the announcement of Nixon's publishing contract and contacted Lazar. Would Nixon, for a substantial fee, be willing to film an extended and exclusive interview with Frost? Nixon's desire for rehabilitation was obvious. Frost understood that "a political comeback was, of course, out of the question to the extent that it implied yet another quest for elective office. But a comeback in the sense that it implied a hoped-for revision of the immediate judgments made about his presidency, a return to political respectability, was something else again."[15] Frost knew that Nixon could not resurrect his public standing simply by writing his memoirs and eliciting support from friends. In order "to regain any semblance of credibility," the former president, Frost reasoned, "would have to subject himself to searching inquiry, to have his account of events tested in something akin to an adversary proceeding."[16] By providing Nixon a forum in which to be questioned by someone completely outside American politics, Frost could give him the chance to explain himself while at the same time attracting an enormous audience to a program he himself would produce. If the interview was probing and newsworthy, it would advance his own career.[17] The circumstances of Watergate thus provided a unique opportunity for two quite different but similarly ambitious men.

Through Lazar, Nixon welcomed Frost's interest in an interview, understandably viewing it as a situation in which he would have the upper hand over a charming but apparently lightweight British entertainer whose knowledge of American politics and government appeared to be limited. Frost, eager to be taken seriously as a journalist, saw the matter differently. In the end, the two negotiated a contract that appealed to them both. For a fee of $600,000 Nixon agreed that, once the Watergate trial of Haldeman, Ehrlichman, and Mitchell was concluded, he would talk to Frost on camera for a total of twenty-eight hours. Frost could extract four ninety-minute programs for broadcast before the ex-president's memoirs were published. Nixon would be able to talk about his overall presidency, but Frost would have editorial control over the questions asked and the editing of the responses to be broadcast. The two men met at Nixon's home to sign the contract on August 9, 1975, the first anniversary of Nixon's resignation.[18]

Because of the Watergate trial and the appeals of the guilty verdicts, the interviews were delayed for more than a year and a half. The delay served Frost well. He soon discovered that none of the American television networks with which he had anticipated dealing would accept an interview conducted by Frost instead of one of their own people. As a result, he was forced to spend months making his own financing and distribution arrangements with 145 television stations in the United States and fourteen other countries.[19]

Recognizing his own limitations, Frost hired a team of researchers to spend nearly a year examining the entire Nixon presidency and help him construct fresh and effective questions to ask. Robert Zelnick, a former lawyer and Washington bureau chief for National Public Radio; James Reston, Jr., a writer, University of North Carolina English professor, and son of the *New York Times* chief Washington columnist; and Philip Stanford, a freelance investigative reporter, plunged into their labors determined to go beyond the well-known public record, particularly when it came to Watergate. Frost and his colleagues also worked on a strategy for the interviews so that the former president would have to be forthcoming in his responses to well-researched and carefully documented questions. By the time the interviews began in March 1977, Frost was well equipped to engage Nixon.[20]

Frost and Nixon agreed to discuss Vietnam first, then other foreign and domestic policy matters, and finally Watergate. Nixon wanted to be sure that attention was given to aspects of his presidency that he desired to have remembered. He also clearly sought to limit as much as possible the time devoted to questions about Watergate. Frost, knowing that Watergate would be the critical topic in establishing the legitimacy of the interviews, negotiated tenaciously to prevent Nixon from evading the issue altogether.[21] At the same time, he wanted Nixon as relaxed as possible before facing Watergate questions. As a consequence, during the first days of filming he allowed Nixon to give long, self-serving answers to queries about his resignation, Vietnam, and other matters. Frost barely challenged Nixon's claims or cut his statements short. This approach elicited from Nixon a remarkably defiant assertion about White House surveillance activities, "When the president does it that means that it is not illegal," he declared. Otherwise the early hours of taping produced few new insights into Nixon's thought.[22]

The mood immediately shifted when the interview turned to Watergate with only a few hours of filming time remaining. Reston in his research had probed the court records of the Watergate trial. He found that some of the prosecution evidence submitted to the court in advance had not been used in the trial itself and thus had been overlooked by reporters covering the proceedings in the courtroom. Among this evidence were transcripts of taped conversations between Charles Colson and Nixon three days after the break-in and again weeks before the president's March 21, 1973, conversation with Dean that Nixon publicly claimed was the first he knew of a Watergate cover-up. In the June 20, 1972, conversation Nixon had mentioned "stonewalling" any investigation. In the February 13, 1973, exchange he impressed upon Colson the need to maintain the cover-up.[23] These tapes had never become public. They were smoking guns of larger caliber than the June 23, 1973, tape that had precipitated Nixon's resignation. Reston suggested to Frost that he use them to start the discussion of Nixon's role in Watergate.[24]

Frost began his questions about Watergate by asking what Haldeman had told the president on the morning of June 23, 1972, during the famous eighteen-and-a-half-minute gap in the tape of their meeting. Nixon replied that he did not remember, and Haldeman's notes provided no clue. Frost then referred to the conversation Reston had discovered of Nixon's exchange with Colson three days earlier, in which there had been references to doing "the right things to date" and to the burglars being "pretty hard-line guys." In the midst of that discussion, Nixon had said, "If we didn't know better we would have thought the whole thing was deliberately botched."[25] Frost's mention of these remarks caught Nixon off guard. He appeared immediately aware that he had underestimated Frost's preparation and knowledge. The former president instantly realized that his interviewer knew much more than he had anticipated and might challenge with supporting evidence any misstatement. Frost observed that Nixon became nervous and began perspiring.[26]

In response to Frost's probing questions, Nixon talked about having been concerned with containing political damage. The former president also conceded that when he had tried to get the CIA to warn the FBI against pursuing the investigation on June 23, he had known that Gordon Liddy of CREEP was involved in the break-in. Nixon defended himself by pointing out that on July 6 he had told FBI director Pat Gray to proceed with an investigation. Frost recognized this as an acknowledgment that justice had been obstructed by the two-week delay.[27] He pressed Nixon with further questions, most dealing with payments to E. Howard Hunt. Nixon finally admitted, "It's a mistake that I didn't stop it."[28]

Frost bored in with questions about the Oval Office encounter with Dean on March 21, 1973. Eventually Nixon acknowledged, "There's plenty of bad. I'm not proud of this period. Ah . . . I didn't handle it well. I messed it up." The ex-president went on to characterize his mistakes as "a disaster," but then he sought to extricate himself somewhat:

I recognize that it was mistake. I made plenty of them. Ah, but . . . ah . . . I also insist that as far as my mistakes were concerned, ah . . . they were mistakes frankly of the head and they weren't mistakes of the heart. They were not mistakes that had what I call an improper, illegal motive, ah . . . in terms of obstructing justice.[29]

Frost's reaction was that this was a statement that Nixon had prepared in advance as a way to acknowledge error but at the same time to make a counterpoint. He understood that Nixon sought to argue that, seen in context, his behavior did not involve criminal conspiracy to obstruct justice. Frost concluded, "While there was genuine emotion in his voice and a trace of sincerity on his countenance, I felt far less than fully satisfied by what I had heard. I wanted him to come to grips far more specifically with his conduct."[30]

Frost continued his sharp questioning of the former president, focusing on his support of Haldeman and Ehrlichman for six weeks after Dean's March 21, 1973, identification of their complicity in the cover-up.[31] During a break, one of Nixon's aides urged Frost to give Nixon an opportunity to explain himself and "give a full accounting." Frost replied that unless Nixon was more forthcoming about the extent of his misdeeds, the cross-examination would continue.[32] The discussion between Frost and the aide continued for some time, and Reston later complained at a press conference that it amounted to negotiating the extent of Nixon's apology.[33]

When the interview resumed, Frost pressed Nixon to go beyond admitting mistakes.[34] Nixon finally responded, "I brought myself down. I gave them a sword. And they stuck it in. And they turned it with relish. And, I guess if I'd been in their place, I'd have done the same thing."[35]

As colorful and quotable as Nixon's statement was, Frost did not think it recognized Nixon's culpability for impeachable offenses. After again claiming that his missteps were not impeachable offenses, Nixon referred to the post–March 21 period, saying,

I will admit that I started acting as a lawyer for [Haldeman's and Ehrlichman's] defense. I will admit that acting as a lawyer for their defense, I was not prosecuting the case. I will admit that during that period, rather than acting primarily in my role as the chief law-enforcement officer in the United States of America, or at least with responsibility for law enforcement—because the Attorney General is the chief law-enforcement officer—but as the one with the chief responsibility for seeing that the laws of the United States are enforced, that I did not meet that responsibility.

And, to the extent that I did not meet that responsibility, to the extent that within the law, and in some cases going right to the edge of the law in trying to advise Ehrlichman and Haldeman and all the rest as to how best to present their cases, because I thought they were legally innocent, that I came to the edge. And under the circumstances, I would have to say that a reasonable person could call that a cover-up.[36]

Confessing failure in his constitutional responsibility for law enforcement meant that Nixon was in effect admitting to an impeachable offense. He did not use any such term, but neither was he finished with his mea culpa. He went on to describe his last meeting with party leaders at the White House, which he left saying, "I'm sorry. I just hope I haven't let you down." Now he acknowledged,

Well, when I said, "I just hope I haven't let you down," that said it all. I had.

I let down my friends.

I let down the country.

I let down our system of government and the dreams of all those young people that ought to get into government, but think it's all too corrupt and the rest.

Always alert to opportunities to boost his image, even in the midst of an acknowledgment of misdeeds, Nixon went on to talk about losing the opportunity to foster peace in the two and a half years remaining in his term. He then, however, repeated, "I let the American people down. And I have to carry that burden with me for the rest of my life."[37]

Continuing to the end to contend that while what he had admitted to was wrong, it was nevertheless not an offense for which the Constitution compelled his removal, Nixon concluded,

While technically, I did not commit a crime, an impeachable offense . . . these are legalisms. As far as the handling of this matter is concerned, it was so botched. I made so many bad judgments, the worst ones, mistakes of the heart rather than the head, as I pointed out. But, let me say, a man in that top judge . . . top job, he's gotta have a heart. But his head must always rule his heart.[38]

Frost and his associates believed that in the course of the interview Nixon had exposed his impeachable conduct. The anguish his face betrayed in the television close-ups underscored the reluctance of Nixon's confession.[39] The former president had admitted ignoring Congress (not to mention the courts) in conducting warrantless covert searches. He had acknowledged participation in a cover-up of illegal activity as well as the failure to carry out the law enforcement responsibilities he had sworn an oath to discharge. Some, such as House Judiciary Committee chairman Peter Rodino, scoffed at Nixon's performance, called it an attempt to rewrite history, and reminded people of the need to examine his committee's report.[40] Frost was more generous but at the same time more damning, saying, "The man whose pride would not permit him to say, 'I broke the law; I violated my constitutional duty,' had come as close to admitting both as it was in his pathology to do."[41] Frost's aide Robert Zelnick agreed, saying immediately after the interview, "The President was as honest today as God has given him the capacity to be honest."[42]

Knowing that the program containing Nixon's comments on Watergate, the final portion of the interviews, would attract the largest audience, Frost chose to air it first, on May 4, 1977. In issues published only days earlier, *Time, Newsweek,* and *TV Guide* all devoted their covers as well as feature stories to the program. All three major television networks broke a prebroadcast embargo and ran excerpts on their nightly news shows just prior to the broadcast. Such publicity helped generate a U.S. audience estimated at forty-five million as well as a large foreign audience. It was an extraordinary television audience, the largest ever for a public affairs program. Forty-two percent of all American televisions switched on at that time were tuned in to the Nixon interview.[43] For those who watched and listened as Nixon talked, it would be difficult not to fix in their minds an image of him confessing guilt for Watergate.

Nixon's comments to Frost did nothing to enhance his image. One poll taken for *Newsweek* magazine revealed that 30 percent of viewers thought less of him afterward, while 48 percent maintained their (largely negative) perception and only 22 percent raised their estimate of him.[44] Looking back on the program nearly thirty years later, Frost's assistant Reston judged that the program had cemented in place the public's understanding of Nixon's role in the Watergate affair:

Nobody has ever said that as a result of the Watergate show that he rehabilitated his reputation on Watergate. He certainly went on to be a sort of senior statesman. He did write a lot of books. But I don't think anybody ever said after that Watergate interrogation, well, the nation made a mistake and he really should have stayed on as president. He was a disgraced, impeached, and convicted American president, and I think the Watergate show confirmed that the American people had made the right decision.[45]

Nixon later sought to recover from the impression left by his encounter with Frost by granting a much briefer interview to Diane Sawyer of CBS News. Sawyer had launched her Washington career in Nixon's White House press office. She continued working for the ex-president in California on press relations and the memoirs project until after the Frost interviews. No wonder Nixon assumed that the former Texas beauty queen would be a gentler interrogator. Yet she asked numerous hard questions about Watergate. His evasive responses suggested he would never move beyond what he had admitted to Frost. Subsequent interviews, while infrequent, confirmed this expectation.[46]

Scholars who studied the evolution of Nixon's image, most notably sociologist Michael Schudson and historian David Greenberg, marked a mellowing of public opinion about the thirty-seventh president in later years. In particular,

Nixon's improvement of relations with the Soviet Union and the People's Republic of China came to be understood as important and commendable accomplishments. Nevertheless, views of Watergate as a serious constitutional offense justifying impeachment remained firmly in place, in no small part due to what so many saw and heard from Nixon in the course of his comments to David Frost.[47]

By the time of the Frost interviews in the spring of 1977, books on the Nixon presidency and Watergate had already started to appear. They would continue rolling off the presses at a steady pace for years. At first, a series of participant memoirs simply added detail and a personal perspective to the outlines of a well-known, generally agreed-upon narrative.[48] Before long Nixon loyalist Victor Lasky began the construction of a conspiracy theory that, amplified by later writers, would blame Watergate on the CIA, Dean, or others, but they failed to persuade many of Nixon's innocence.[49] A few writers offered speculative analyses of Nixon's psychological makeup and apparently self-destructive behavior.[50] A number of scholars sought to shift the focus to aspects of the Nixon presidency that they felt were being obscured by an excessive concentration on Watergate. However, as one shrewd observer noted, "the White House horrors persisted as the central, even if sometimes submerged, issue in considerations of the former president.[51] "Above all," David Greenberg wrote, "Nixon remained a symbol of thrusting ambition gone amok."[52] He echoed Nixon biographer Stephen Ambrose, who, summoning a Macbethian image, described Watergate as "the spot that will not out."[53]

A year after the Frost interviews, Nixon took advantage of another chance to explain himself. In *RN: The Memoirs of Richard Nixon*, the former president had much more control over the way he presented his presidency. He used the opportunity to full advantage in a book of almost eleven hundred printed pages, a third of which dealt with his fifty-six years of life before the presidency. In contrast, more than 42 percent of the text was devoted to the twenty-six months from the Watergate break-in to his resignation. Still, he was unable to erase entirely the mea culpa to Frost. So for the most part he tried to place his acknowledged misbehavior in the most favorable context and turn attention, as he had in the interviews, to the achievements of his administration.

At one level *RN* proved remarkably forthright. Nixon had denied involvement in a cover-up in the Watergate affair from the immediate aftermath of the burglary until the release of the "smoking gun" tape following the Supreme Court decision in *United States v. Nixon*, a span of over two years. In contrast, it only took him until the second page of *RN*'s preface to acknowledge the evidence of his participation in the cover-up that led to an article of impeachment for obstruction of justice. Explaining how he used the White House tapes in writing the memoir, Nixon described having a secretary transcribe all his conversations with Haldeman, Ehrlichman, and Colson during the first month after the break-in, including the June 23, 1972, discussion "when I authorized the meeting in which the CIA was asked to limit the FBI's investigation of Watergate."[54]

When, however, Nixon reached the point 625 pages into his narrative where he began to address Watergate, he was no longer so economical with words. He described in detail his varied activities on the weekend of June 17, 1972, and his surprise at receiving news of the break-in at the offices of the Democratic National Committee. Lengthy expressions of bewilderment at the stupidity of the break-in and descriptions of a quest for information about it were interspersed with comments about how commonplace political espionage, dirty tricks, and vote fraud had long been in American politics. A tone of bitterness permeated his observation that Truman, Kennedy, and Johnson had gotten away with acts similar to those for which he was punished. Nixon then described the exploration of various ways of dealing with the matter. First discussed was having Liddy confess to masterminding the break-in and assert that no one higher up in CREEP or the White House was involved. Later came the plan to have Vernon Walters of the CIA warn the FBI not to pursue the investigation on the grounds that national security issues were involved. Strikingly, Nixon presented all this at length without the least suggestion that he was describing contemplated suborning of perjury or actual aggressive interference with a criminal investigation.[55]

Nixon's concluding comments in this section of his memoir sought to trivialize what had taken place. While acknowledging that these measures had led to the downfall of his presidency, he clearly implied that the matter was too petty and his role in it too tangential for it to have properly produced that result. He wrote:

> I did nothing to discourage the various stories that were being considered to explain the break-in, and I approved efforts to encourage the CIA to intervene and limit the FBI investigation. Later my actions and inactions during this period would appear to many as part of a widespread and conscious cover-up. I did not see them as such. I was handling in a pragmatic way what I perceived as an annoying and strictly political problem. I was looking for a way to deal with Watergate that would minimize the damage to me, my friends, and my campaign, while giving the least advantage to my political opposition. I saw Watergate as politics pure and simple. We were going to play it tough. I never doubted that that was exactly how the other side would have played it.[56]

In the balance of his memoir Nixon dealt with Watergate as something that happened to him rather than something for which he bore responsibility. He treated members of his staff as independent actors rather than as aides acting on his behalf under orders or with a sense that they were carrying out his wishes. Describing the forced resignation of his two top deputies in the spring of 1973 when their participation in the cover-up was exposed, he quoted a bitter Ehrlich-man as saying, "I still feel I have done nothing that was without your implied or direct approval." He remained silent, however, on the validity of Ehrlichman's observation.[57]

In his memoir, as had been the case during his downfall, Nixon blamed his difficulties on partisan opposition and media hostility. Devoting little attention to the improprieties of the break-in itself, the cover-up, the attempt to thwart the investigation by removing Archibald Cox, or other steps he had taken, he avoided accepting full responsibility for his fate. Given this attitude, it was no wonder that he expressed surprise at the "ferocious intensity" of the "almost hysterical reaction" to the Saturday Night Massacre. "For the first time," he wrote, "I rec-ognized the depth of the impact Watergate had been having on America. I sud-denly realized how deeply its acid had eaten into the nation's grain."[58] After that point, he dwelt on his loss of political support rather than on the reasons behind the decline. The memoir, much like his earlier remarks to Frost, briefly acknowl-edged errors but sought to diminish their importance and impeachability. Still, with reviews of the book focusing on his admission of participation in the Water-gate cover-up, the notion spread further, even among those who never read the book, that Nixon accepted responsibility for his own demise.[59] Two young Wash-ingtonians quickly indicated their conclusions that a guilty Nixon was seeking to profit from crimes for which he was responsible but had escaped punishment. They organized a Committee to Boycott Nixon's Memoirs. Within a month they appeared at the American Booksellers Convention in Atlanta with posters and T-shirts urging, "Don't Buy Books by Crooks!"[60]

After publishing RN, Nixon continued his effort to rebuild his reputation through writing. The former president sought to focus attention on his experi-ence and expertise in foreign affairs in a series of five volumes published during the 1980s. All these books, *The Real War* (1980), *Leaders* (1982), *Real Peace: A Strategy for the West* (1983), *No More Vietnams* (1985), and *1999: Victory with-out War* (1988), revolved around his well-regarded diplomatic achievements and his advice on American foreign policy. Not surprisingly, none of these books called attention to aspects of his administration's foreign policy that were draw-ing increasing criticism from historians: the bombing and invasion of Cambodia, support for a right-wing coup in Chile, and prolongation of the war in Vietnam before settling on terms available much earlier. Each of Nixon's 1980s books car-ried the implicit message that he should be thought of, first and foremost, as a thoughtful and skilled international peacemaker, not primarily as the perpetra-tor of Watergate.

In 1990 Nixon sought to further diminish the importance of Watergate and enhance the impression that he had achieved rehabilitation. In another volume of memoirs, entitled *In the Arena: A Memoir of Victory, Defeat, and Renewal,* he combined advice, reminiscence, and more than a few platitudes. Before turning

to stories of his postpresidential life, travels, and encounters with people of prominence, accounts that he obviously hoped would secure him the status of a senior
statesman, Nixon returned once again to the subject of Watergate. He showed less
remorse and more bitterness than he had to Frost or in *RN*. His acknowledgment
of responsibility for the cover-up that led to the obstruction of justice impeachment article was far more muted than it had been in those earlier forums.

Writing a decade and a half after the fact, Nixon used *In the Arena* to repeat
his characterization of Watergate as a matter of little importance in itself but an
opportunity for enemies in politics and the press to torment him. He noted a list
of charges leveled against him that had not been proven, including that he had
personally ordered the Watergate break-in and payments to silence Hunt, without acknowledging that these were not the charges embodied in the articles of
impeachment.[61] He recited many examples of alleged misconduct in other administrations and expressed a sense of unfairness that he had been punished
while others had not. Pointing out that he was not the first president secretly
to tape-record White House conversations, he omitted the crucial fact that it
was not the recording itself but the refusal to provide the tapes in furtherance
of a criminal investigation that got him into trouble.[62] After further bitter complaints about unjust allegations and a vendetta by his political opponents, Nixon
claimed, finally, that he had been forced into the Frost interviews out of financial necessity and then treated badly by hostile interviewers and editors.[63] Falling back on the posture he had struck in accepting Ford's pardon, he reiterated,
"I was wrong in not acting more decisively and more forthrightly in dealing with
Watergate, particularly when it reached the stage of judicial proceedings and
grew from a political scandal into a national tragedy."[64]

After *In the Arena*, Nixon returned to writing about foreign affairs. Before
his death in 1994 he published two more books on the subject: *Seize the Moment* (1992) and *Beyond Peace* (1994). He did not, however, abandon his effort
to expunge the stain of Watergate, an attempt that even reached beyond the
grave. In June 1990 he hired a young woman, Monica Crowley, to assist on his
later books, accompany him on travels, and listen to him talk. Crowley had been
five at the time Nixon left the White House and had just finished a B.A. at Col-
gate University when she went to work for him. He obviously calculated that
she would project his unfiltered message beyond the grave, since he encouraged
her to take copious notes on all that he said. Nixon's explanations to her of his
presidency and his subsequent actions thus fell on the ears of someone unbur-
dened by substantive personal memories of those years. She was not exactly the
well-prepared and skeptical interrogator that David Frost or even the more sympathetic Diane Sawyer had been. Crowley became a willing conduit for Nixon's
efforts to explain himself to the post-Watergate generations, to reshape historical interpretations of his presidency, and to rehabilitate his standing.[65] In two
books published after the former president's death, *Nixon Off the Record* (1996)

and *Nixon in Winter* (1998), the credulous Crowley demonstrated that for his purposes he had chosen well.

Crowley's books focused on foreign affairs, but *Nixon in Winter* also contained a section dealing with Watergate. In it, Crowley provided Nixon one more opportunity to offer his version of the Watergate story. Again, he held that he had been the victim of mistakes he had made in connection with a minor matter seized on by his foes to discredit him. He once more offered his claim of knowing nothing of the cover-up before March 1973. Crowley accepted his explanation of the "smoking gun" tape as merely mistaken discussion of alternative strategies rather than as the actual beginning of his effort to cover up White House culpability. She also accepted without question his description of media and partisan enemies out to get him from the time of the Alger Hiss case onward. They had held him to a higher standard than other politicians. Crowley cast Nixon's minor legal victory in August 1993 in a suit against the National Archives over some of his tapes as a measure of vindication after nineteen years. Nixon continued talking to Crowley until nine days before his fatal stroke, lamenting in their last conversation that Watergate had cost him the opportunity to speak credibly in later years about America's moral decline. Ever admiring, Crowley concluded by declaring that in accepting responsibility for increasing distrust in government, Nixon had provided "a final lesson in repentance, humility, defiance, and ultimately recovery."[66]

Nixon's post-1978 writing, not to mention his posthumous message conveyed by Crowley, for the most part focused attention on the successful aspects of his foreign policy as president and his observations from the sidelines thereafter. Nevertheless, an image of Watergate had become fixed in American minds, an image that would change only slightly and at the margins over succeeding decades. Nixon could distract some notice and impress those unable to comprehend the constitutional implications of his presidency, but he could not entirely erase impressions created in the course of his downfall. Nor could he wipe away the admissions of the Frost interviews and, more grudgingly, his 1978 memoir. Finally, he could not control the references to him that continued to appear in American popular culture.

Treatments of Nixon in a series of films and plays appearing occasionally in the years after his resignation offered images of the disgraced president that, however hard he worked, he could not escape. The first was a sardonic reminder that his reputation rested in the hands of historians and, more precariously, creative writers. Woody Allen's 1974 film *Sleeper* made light of the contemporary preoccupation with Watergate. A comedy set a century in the future, the film included an exchange about Nixon as a forgotten man, a mysterious presence on old videotapes but unmentioned in history books. Allen's time-traveling character explains that Nixon was actually president but comments, "Whenever he used to leave the White House, the Secret Service would count the silverware."[67]

Appearing in 1976, Alan Pakula's *All the President's Men* was the first film fully focused on Nixon and was ultimately the most widely seen. Its evocation of presidential menace throughout the early stages of the journalistic investigation of the Watergate break-in set a tone that subsequent films would, in one way or another, play off of. Woodward's and Bernstein's second book, *The Final Days,* became the basis of a made-for-television movie fifteen years after Nixon's resignation. Less well made and less highly promoted than *All the President's Men,* this film did not reach as broad an audience. However, it too would seek to follow closely the text on which it was based, though in this case the final few days and not the full final year received most of the attention. The film affirmed the core Woodward and Bernstein image of a broken and unstable president choosing to resign from office rather than face inevitable removal for impeachable offenses of which he was definitely guilty.

After the Frost interviews were broadcast, Los Angeles playwright Donald Freed began thinking about creating a play in which Nixon would provide a fuller and, indeed, an alternative explanation of his actions and motivations. *Secret Honor: The Last Testament of Richard Nixon,* the play that Freed eventually wrote with Arnold Stone, was performed first at the small Los Angeles Actor's Theatre in 1982, later in New York and Boston, and finally at the University of Michigan in Ann Arbor. After about a hundred live performances, director Robert Altman made it into a film.[68]

Secret Honor presented Nixon alone in his study reminiscing about his life on audio- and videotape. Portrayed in all performances by veteran stage and screen actor Philip Baker Hall, Nixon gradually descends into a drunken rant. In turn, he takes swipes at his mother, Dwight Eisenhower, Henry Kissinger, and the American press. The core of his gradually revealed explanation of his career, however, is that the Committee of 100, a powerful group of wealthy and powerful men who met every year at Bohemian Grove north of San Francisco, had controlled his entire political life. They recruited him to run for Congress, directed his campaigns, provided the financing partially exposed in the 1952 Nixon Fund scandal and later during Watergate, and were already planning to keep him in office for a third term. Their motives were to reap profits from the China market he was to open and, by keeping the Vietnam War going, the Southeast Asian heroin trade. Nixon's only escape was through a secret act of honor. "I had to find a way to destroy the great 1972 mandate," he explains, and he thus created and then exposed the White House tapes that would force his resignation. At the climax, Nixon, brandishing a revolver, claims that the Committee of 100 wishes he would kill himself, but after holding the weapon to his temple, he declares that he is no quitter and will no longer do their bidding. Instead, in a dramatic ending to the play, he shouts over and over "Fuck'um," "Fuck'um," "Fuck'um!" against a soundtrack of a crowd repeatedly chanting "Four more years!"[69]

In an introductory statement that crawled down the screen, the filmmakers described their work as a "fictional meditation, concerning the character of and events in the history of Richard M. Nixon" but noted that it was "not a work of history or a historical recreation." They acknowledged that it was a work of fiction "in an attempt to understand" and then gave the movie *Secret Honor* the subtitle *A Political Myth*. The conspiracy-driven portrayal they offered might not have offered well-grounded history, but it was riveting drama for those who saw it. Both the *New York Times* and the *Washington Post* declared the film one of 1984's ten best. Although it did not draw large audiences, *Secret Honor* only reinforced what had become the dominant image of the Nixon presidency as improperly conducted and properly ended.

While there were no more theatrical or cinematic efforts to characterize Nixon before his death, three films and two plays in the dozen years thereafter demonstrated that a deeply unflattering view of the thirty-seventh president had become solidly entrenched in the popular culture. An image persisted of Nixon as unscrupulous if not unbalanced, responsible for the Watergate cover-up and perhaps for ordering the initial burglary, and probably guilty of other crimes as well. Nixon's own efforts may have generated some appreciation for his diplomacy, but the sense that Watergate provided a window into his character did not waver.

The year after Nixon's death the prominent and controversial filmmaker Oliver Stone released his film *Nixon*. Not unlike the makers of *Secret Honor*, Stone presented Nixon as shaped by stern parents, marked by two brothers' deaths, and propelled into the presidency by a shadowy group of rich men, this time Texans with ties to Cuba with whom Nixon meets on the eve of John Kennedy's assassination. As much as in his earlier film, *JFK*, an advocate of a conspiracy theory of Kennedy's death, Stone portrayed the Watergate cover-up as an effort to conceal Nixon's earlier connections with CIA agent Howard Hunt. Nixon is portrayed as not wanting to reveal his vice presidential approval of a CIA effort involving Hunt to assassinate Fidel Castro, an enterprise that continued unknown into the Kennedy administration and inspired retaliation against JFK.[70]

Although Stone wove a great deal of known information and photographic record into his narrative to give it historical verisimilitude, he acknowledged at the film's outset that his was an interpretation built on "an incomplete historical record." Stone's disclaimer was followed immediately by an epigram conveying his judgment of Nixon in the form of a biblical verse from the book of Matthew: "For what is a man profited if he shall gain the whole world and loose his own soul." More complex and faster paced than the equally conspiratorial *Secret Honor,* employing the *Secret Honor* and *The Final Days* trope of Nixon talking to the White House portraits, and as dark in its visual treatment of the White House as *All the President's Men,* the three-hour-and-ten-minute *Nixon* reinforced the notion for another large audience of a president richly deserving of removal from office. Whatever the historical merits of these films, they gave more and more strength to a popular image.[71]

By 1999 the tragedy depicted by Stone was being replayed as farce. Andrew Fleming's film *Dick* made fun of Watergate and portrayed Nixon as a bumbler, though still a foul-mouthed malevolent figure guilty as charged. A comedy aimed at teenagers, the script revolved around Arlene and Betsy, two silly fifteen-year-old girls who stumble into the midst of the Watergate burglary, later meet Nixon, who asks them to call him Dick and walk his dog, unwittingly discover the cover-up, and finally, as Woodward's and Bernstein's "Deep Throat," drive him from office. Marketed to an audience too young to remember the 1970s, *Dick* relied, instead, on their remembering images from *All the President's Men* for many of its laughs. Other gags having to do with Nixon's dogs, his negotiating a treaty with Leonid Brezhnev while both are high on marijuana cookies, and the eighteen-and-a-half-minute tape gap seemed more appropriate to an older audience. The satire also depended heavily on contemporary public discussions of presidential sexuality and the looser language of 1999 as the ditzy teenagers Arleen and Betsy squeal, "I love Dick," later "I hate Dick," and finally "You suck, Dick."[72]

A far more sober treatment of the Nixon saga, a two-man play by Russell Lee titled *Nixon's Nixon,* opened on Broadway in March 1996. It took as its point of departure Woodward's and Bernstein's description of Nixon's meeting with Kissinger in the Lincoln Sitting Room on the evening before he resigned. The secretary of state, concerned about his own future and historical reputation, is urging an undecided president to quit. Throughout the fictional account of a night of drink and talk compressed into an eighty-minute one-act play, Nixon is characterized as baffled by his situation. At one point the playwright has Nixon say, "I fell like Satan tossed from heaven." Kissinger, realizing that the White House tapes can ruin him as well, alternates between obsequiousness and assertiveness toward Nixon. The play descends into farce as the two men contemplate creating an international incident, a clash on the Soviet-Chinese border, to create a demand for Nixon to remain in office. *New York Times* critic Vincent Canby preferred *Nixon's Nixon* to Stone's "flatulent" film, writing, "The play doesn't cut deep but it cuts true." For Canby, Lee's play reinforced his vision of Nixon (and Kissinger) as unprincipled and ever grasping for power.[73]

Dramatic interest in Nixon shifted but did not cease once his image and that of his impeachment became firmly lodged in the public culture. A 2004 film *The Assassination of Richard Nixon* employed Nixon as a device to explore the complex nature of anger and terrorism against targets perceived as powerful and corrupt. The film, starring Academy Award–winning actor Sean Penn, offered a fictionalized account of Samuel Byck, a failed salesman, husband, and father, who actually made an unsuccessful attempt to hijack a Delta Airlines jet at Baltimore-Washington International Airport on February 22, 1974, in order to crash it into the White House. Byck never got off the ground, and the bleak film did not do much better, receiving tepid reviews and having limited appeal to a public still traumatized by memories of planes flying into landmark buildings in Washington and New York. Nevertheless, its central metaphor of Nixon as a justifiable target of rage was a measure of the manner in which the American culture had come to regard him. The film's view of Nixon is perhaps best expressed by Byck's boss, who calls him "the greatest salesman in the world." The store manager points out to a puzzled Byck that Nixon pledged in two election campaigns to end the Vietnam War. "He made a promise and he didn't deliver, and then he sold us on the exact same promise all over again." Short television clips of the Watergate investigation are then inserted throughout the rest of the film to symbolize the abusive power Byck perceives himself rebelling against, encouraging viewers to understand that the troubled man's unhappiness was not altogether illegitimate.[74]

Not only Nixon's presidency but also his subsequent attempts to explain himself became the stuff of drama. British playwright and screenwriter Peter Morgan, who had written scripts based on events in the lives of Tony Blair, Queen Elizabeth II, and Ugandan dictator Idi Amin, became fascinated with the encounter between two forceful personalities, each trying to rehabilitate a tarnished image. In August 2006 Morgan's play *Frost/Nixon* opened in London in the small experimental Donmar Warehouse theater. Before long it moved to the West End, and then in April 2007 to New York. Morgan also signed a contract for an American film production. *Frost/Nixon* recounted, in compressed form and with some dramatic embellishment, the 1977 confrontation between the disgraced president and the insecure television performer. The script made use of actual statements by both men as well as imagined exchanges, such as a fictitious late-night telephone conversation in which Nixon mused about his situation. Frost's assistant Jim Reston, Jr., served as the play's narrator as well as its hero for pushing Frost to confront Nixon. Morgan built the drama around Reston's research discovery of documents that provided the means to extract an apology for Watergate from Nixon in the play's climactic scene. The narrator subsequently reflects on what the audience has just seen on a huge screen at the back of the stage:

> David had succeeded, on that final day, in getting, for a fleeting moment, what no investigative journalist, no State Prosecutor, nor Judiciary Committee, nor political enemy had managed to get—Richard Nixon's face, swollen and ravaged by loneliness, self-loathing and defeat—filling every television screen in the country.[75]

Morgan gave the Reston character the play's last triumphant speech, an assessment of the lasting impact of the broadcast:

Despite being buried with full honours in 1994, Richard Nixon never again held public office of any kind, nor achieved the rehabilitation he so desperately craved. Today, his name continues to be synonymous with corruption and disgrace, and his most lasting legacy is that any political wrongdoing is immediately given the suffix "gate."[76]

Declared "riveting theater" by reviewers of its initial London performance and winning three 2007 Tony Award nominations (and the Best Actor award for Frank Langella's remarkable portrayal of Nixon) for the New York production, *Frost/Nixon* further cemented and perhaps exaggerated the spreading image of Nixon as having ultimately confessed to the offenses for which he faced impeachment.[77]

Perhaps understandably, nearly all the testimony, interviews, and memoirs by the former president and his associates sought to place the blame for misjudgment and misconduct on others.[78] Yet even while he gained credit for some other successes, Nixon remained the focus of what was regarded as an exceptionally dark chapter of the American story. As participants, journalists, scholars, and creative artists illuminated the inner workings of the Nixon administration, the American public's political attitudes evolved. Those who lived through the Watergate episode, particularly as adults, revised their views of the presidency and government, generally in a negative direction. In particular, views of impeachment as suitable in Nixon's case became more pronounced. A decade after Watergate began to unravel, two separate panels of professional historians ranked Nixon as only exceeded by the long-condemned Warren Harding and Ulysses Grant as a presidential failure.[79]

Meanwhile a younger generation of Americans was forming its opinions on such matters for the first time. The earlier shift in adult perceptions of the nation's governance had had an impact on the political environment. Most notably, electoral participation steadily declined for the two decades after Nixon's resignation. Nevertheless, the effect upon the young would have even longer-term consequences. The negative atmosphere surrounding their political socialization would extend the impact of Watergate upon the country's fundamental political culture.

Young people do not normally acquire much knowledge of government and politics before very late childhood or early adolescence, if then. Something so abstract, complex, and distant from their own situation does not normally receive much attention, much less comprehension, during early life. Studies in the early 1960s showed that children in the lower grades knew at most that there was a president and that he was both a powerful and admirable figure. While they almost universally learned to esteem the president, the thousands of children under ten who were interviewed by various political scientists otherwise paid scant attention to the political culture in which they lived. Until their early teenage years, children had little idea of how the president was chosen or what he did, much less that his power was confined by the Constitution, Congress, and Supreme Court.[80]

Only an extraordinary event such as the Kennedy assassination could alter this situation, and even then only at the margins. Children who were as young as three or four at that time would in later years identify Kennedy's death as their first memory of a historical event, but largely because parents, teachers, and caregivers were upset in ways the children had never before experienced and because normal television programming was disrupted for several days devoted to extolling his merits. The extended mourning for Kennedy introduced or reinforced the simple idea of the president as a great figure, but for the very young any more-sophisticated understanding of government was beyond reach. For the young, as well as for many of their elders, the Kennedy assassination imprinted an image of a heroic figure tragically removed. As a consequence, Kennedy achieved an enduring status as one of the greatest of all presidents even though the brevity of his administration and its limited achievements would persuade most professional historians otherwise.

Watergate proved to be another event of which children were generally conscious. The preemption of 325 hours of television programming for the thirty-seven days of the Ervin committee hearings, the concern of many adults with the Saturday Night Massacre, and the grim atmosphere of the House Judiciary Committee impeachment hearing broadcasts inevitably penetrated their world, even if they did not fully understand what was taking place. These events and their elders' discussion of them had a pronounced impact on many children in the upper elementary grades as well as a larger proportion of older students. Studies of Massachusetts public school students in the third, fourth, and fifth grades in December 1973 and January 1975 made this evident. In the first survey, taken six weeks after the Saturday Night Massacre, the children showed little esteem for the president. In fact, by a 2–1 ratio third-graders thought Nixon should be impeached. The ratio increased with each grade and reached 3–1 among fifth-graders.[81]

Whereas in a 1962 study of children's knowledge and attitudes two-thirds of students had identified the president as a favorite figure, now less than one-quarter did so. "The once benevolent leader has been transformed into the malevolent leader," the researchers concluded. The president was still perceived as powerful, but was no longer seen as compassionate or trustworthy. Children had become cynical about a figure they viewed as dishonest and selfish. The number who viewed government as too powerful, fewer than one in five in 1962, had nearly doubled.[82] By the time of a second survey in January 1975, children's attitudes had moderated somewhat, but they remained clearly negative about the president.

Especially because of its prolonged duration, the Watergate affair and the near impeachment of Nixon appear to have had a lasting effect on the political socialization of the young. Serious doubts about the integrity and appeal of the nation's political system became embedded in their minds. The substitution of political alienation for the previous generation's positive introduction to government and in particular the presidency would create persistent beliefs. The negative views of Nixon that continued to be conveyed through histories, films, and theater assured that a positive perception of impeachment as the device that brought his presidency to an end would persist beyond one generation. Cynicism about presidents and government, once established, would endure. For young people of an age at which their knowledge of politics and government was rudimentary, the vivid impression left by a single memorable experience, whether it led to the conclusion that the president was estimable or that he ought to be viewed with suspicion, would linger until another extraordinary event occurred to reorient or reinforce their beliefs.[83] The impact of Watergate in shaping thinking favorable to impeachment was both formative and formidable.

9

Impeachment as Distasteful:
The Case of Ronald Reagan

A dog that did not bark gave Sherlock Holmes the vital clue to unraveling a perplexing mystery in Arthur Conan Doyle's short story "Silver Blaze." Noticing that a reliable watchdog had declined to sound the alarm when it would have been possible and appropriate to do so, Holmes concluded that the villain must have been someone with whom the dog was very familiar. Ever since it appeared, the story of the dog that did not bark has served as a metaphor for finding clues in what could have been expected to happen but did not. Even the study of impeachment can benefit from an inquiry as to why a situation that might well have provoked congressional action did not.

When the dogs of impeachment did not bark at President Ronald Reagan in the mid-1980s under circumstances in which they might well have done so, the silence was noteworthy. The nonimpeachment of Ronald Reagan reveals a good bit about how politicians in power at the time as well as an onlooking public viewed the formal requirements of the Constitution, whose two-hundredth anniversary they were in the midst of celebrating with great pride. Examined closely, the incident says a great deal about why impeachment does not always go forward even when a strong or at least plausible case can be made for it. The Reagan episode demonstrates that even in an era in which Watergate had embedded consciousness of impeachment in American political thought, it was not always seen as a palatable solution to perceived problems of serious misconduct at the highest levels of government.

The silence of the impeachment dogs also suggests a good deal about the political temperament of the 1980s. The political culture responded not only to immediate circumstances but also to appraisals of the impeachment experiences of the previous decade. Democratic congressional leaders, used since the 1930s to their party being in the legislative majority and thus responsible for national well-being even when they did not control the executive branch, shied away from impeachment, however legitimate, because of its perceived overall effect of destabilizing and discrediting government. Meanwhile, Reagan and his staff moved to cope with the threat of impeachment in a fashion notably different from that of Richard Nixon and his minions scarcely more than a dozen years earlier. The quintessential nature of the offenses committed varied less than did the approaches of both Congress and the White House to dealing with the re-sulting uproar when improper conduct was revealed. As a result, the contrast between their brushes with impeachment exposes the self-inflicted nature of Nixon's fatal wounds to his presidency and Reagan's avoidance of such a fate by appearing contrite, cooperative, and more than a little inept.

At the same time, the mere whimpering of the congressional impeachment dogs in 1986 and 1987 compared to their loud barking a dozen years earlier and their great howls a dozen years later provides an audible gauge of shifts in po-litical tolerance. Whereas Nixon had eventually pushed Washington's prevailing culture of restraint beyond its limits with his constantly combative manner, Rea-gan benefited from the resurgence of congressional forbearance. Restless young conservatives, many of them Reagan acolytes who failed to appreciate the nar-rowness of their hero's escape, would reshape the political culture over the next decade. When they gained control of Congress, they would not display any re-luctance equivalent to their predecessors' regarding the use of impeachment. Post-Reagan events would thus further illuminate the combination of skills, cir-cumstances, and good fortune that characterized the president for whom the impeachment dogs remained, remarkably, at bay.

Ronald Reagan proved to be an extraordinary phenomenon in late-twentieth-century American politics: a leader who remained popular even when his poli-cies and actions proved otherwise. His personal appeal sheltered him from two impeachment efforts, the first largely inconsequential but the second quite seri-ous. Having first achieved fame well outside the realm of civic affairs, Reagan's celebrity helped him gain attention for his political views and then obtain elec-toral success. The same prominence far from government also insulated Reagan from his own missteps in asserting a position or conducting the public's busi-ness. When confronted with circumstances that might have damaged the public standing of someone with no identity other than as a government leader, a fig-ure such as Nixon, for instance, Reagan proved remarkably impervious to criti-cism. Time and again, never more so than when impeachment loomed, Reagan demonstrated the validity of his characterization as "the Teflon president," be-cause nothing ever stuck to him to mar his image.

Reagan became accustomed to the power of celebrity while still a teenager. Born in 1911 in Tampico, Illinois, into a family that struggled economically and moved often, Reagan knew little stability until his parents settled in nearby Dixon, Illinois, when he was ten. Becoming an excellent swimmer, he began at age sixteen to work during the summers as the lifeguard at a nearby park on the Rock River. The rescues he accomplished (he himself claimed there were seventy-seven) made him something of a local hero.[1]

Reagan managed to achieve a college education at nearby Eureka Col-lege, a tiny and unpretentious Disciples of Christ Church school with much to be unpretentious about. Graduating in 1932 in the midst of the Great Depression, Reagan soon had the good fortune to obtain a position as a radio sports announcer in Davenport, Iowa. A warm, rich speaking voice and an easy manner that conveyed enthusiasm and sincerity even when reading advertising copy soon earned him a move to his employer's flagship station, WHO in Des Moines.

Reagan first tasted wider celebrity during four years of broadcasting the games of the Chicago Cubs, no small feat for someone located in the middle of Iowa three hundred miles from Wrigley Field. Sitting in WHO's Des Moines studio and reaching a statewide audience, he described the action as reported on ticker tape. Occasionally he was forced to invent a lengthy series of foul balls or a sudden rain shower if the ticker tape fell silent and he had to fill dead air without changing the ball-and-strike count. Reagan built a loyal following of listeners who enjoyed his vivid descriptions that would correspond to the next day's newspaper box score. Even knowing that he was not providing an eyewitness account, baseball fans across Iowa esteemed the young man who brought the excitement of Cubs games into their homes. It must have been hard for him to avoid the sense that the public craved absolute truth less than it did plausible, well-told tales.

The line between reality and fantasy blurred further as Reagan moved from radio to film. Offered a Warner Brothers studio contract in 1937, he made the transition to Hollywood easily and found himself cast in dozens of second-tier films and occasionally in an A-level one, usually as a secondary character such as the hero's best friend. His career flourished to the point that he gained his first big contract a month before the United States entered World War II. He neither fully understood nor ever forgot the heavy income taxes imposed to finance the war. His military duty mainly involved making war movies in north Los Angeles County, though later in life he often appeared to confuse the heroic triumphs of the scripts for the realities of combat.

Soon after the war, Reagan first experienced a sort of political success. He was chosen by his peers in 1947 as president of the Screen Actors Guild and was reelected four times. His movie career, however, was fading. Like several other minor movie stars, he made the transition to the new medium of television and became host of *G.E. Theater,* a weekly series of television dramas. The few moments he spent on screen each week introducing the program kept him in the public eye but less than fully occupied. The show's sponsor, General Electric, capitalized on his celebrity status by sending Reagan around the country to talk to employees and civic groups about the threat of communism, the importance of limiting business regulation and taxation by the federal government, and the need for stronger national defenses, which, of course, G.E. could help supply. By the late 1950s Reagan's well-practiced patriotic speech was already attracting attention from the growing conservative movement, of which he was becoming very much a part. He signaled his location on the political spectrum in a 1960 letter to Nixon in which he wrote, "Shouldn't someone tag Mr. Kennedy's bold new imaginative program with its proper age? Under the tousled boyish cut it is still old Karl Marx."[2]

The growing Southern California conservative culture gave Reagan plenty of opportunities to express himself both in public and in political organizations. He gave over two hundred speeches for Nixon in 1960. In California's 1962 Republican senatorial primary, Reagan, after turning down suggestions that he run himself, chaired the campaign of Loyd Wright, an advocate of a preemptive nuclear strike against the Soviet Union. In the spring of 1964 Reagan was prominent and active in Barry Goldwater's presidential campaign, speaking at rallies and narrating a half-hour television advertisement. Then in September he became cochairman of California Citizens for Goldwater. Late in the campaign, Reagan gave a rousing nationally televised version of his standard G.E. speech on behalf of the floundering candidate. It caused some Republicans to conclude that it had not been a mistake to nominate a conservative spokesman. They had just chosen the wrong one, a fumble-tongued senator instead of a polished television performer with an impeccably conservative viewpoint.[3]

Ronald Reagan moved into the mainstream of Republican politics in 1966, elected to the first of two terms as governor of California on a conservative platform of tax and budget cutting, law enforcement, and reform of the state's liberal higher education system. Two years later, conservative Republicans were talking of him as their presidential candidate, as they would for three of the following four presidential elections. Losing the party's presidential nomination by a wide margin at the 1968 Republican National Convention to the ultimately disastrous Nixon, Reagan came close to wresting the nomination from incumbent President Gerald Ford in 1976 before overwhelming all opponents, both within his party and outside of it, in 1980 and 1984. Reagan's ascension to power was facilitated by the ineffectual and often gloomy presidency of Jimmy Carter, whose memory would buoy Republican prospects for a decade. The celebrity Reagan had been accumulating within the Republican Party since 1964, together with his cheerful confidence at the prospects for national rejuvenation through reduced taxation and a more assertive foreign policy, brought him to the pinnacle of American politics and helped him remain there.

Running for president against Carter in 1980, Reagan was highly critical of his opponent's foreign policies, especially those concerning the Soviet Union, the Middle East, and Central America. Democrat Carter had committed errors, he said, in making concessions to the Soviet Union in order to obtain arms limitation agreements and in turning over control of the Panama Canal to the Panamanians. Most grievous, Reagan complained, Carter had permitted the United States to be humiliated by allowing its embassy staff in Tehran, Iran, to be held hostage. There should be no dealing with hostage takers, the Republican candidate insisted, vigorously asserting that his administration would be unyielding in such situations. After a U.S. election that was most notably a measure of voter unhappiness with Carter, Iranian revolutionary leaders chose to bring their growing headache with the embassy hostages to an end. By releasing the hostages just as the new American president was being inaugurated, the Iranian foes of the United States, ironically, bore much of the responsibility for Reagan's initial appearance of presidential strength.

The continuation of unusual circumstances early in his presidency further separated Reagan from Carter and other recent predecessors. Except for Lyndon Johnson, every president since Franklin Roosevelt had entered the White House with limited congressional support and thus little capacity to achieve initial legislative goals. Even with the hostage release, Reagan actually began the same way. After two months of political stalemate, however, he narrowly avoided assassination while leaving a Washington hotel. Astonishingly, the oldest man ever to take the presidential oath survived the murderous attack, whereas less than twenty years earlier a much younger man had succumbed to another gunshot wound. Reagan's escape and recovery, together with his reported good humor throughout the ordeal, gave his image a heroic cast and made him a virtually unstoppable political force for a time. He was able to achieve legislative results that had previously been beyond his reach and also to implement a foreign policy that had earlier been questioned by the military, the State Department, and Congress. This surge of success encouraged the president and those close to him to assume that his authority was and would remain unchecked.

The empowered president gave early notice that a central theme of his administration would be the menace of communism. A perception of peril had gripped Reagan ever since his days leading the Screen Actors Guild. While speaking publicly at that time about his union members' rights of free expression of ideas, he quietly informed the FBI of those he perceived to be communist sympathizers. Later his General Electric speeches stressed the threat from the Soviet Union, a message that would be a mainstay of his various runs for the presidency. He then brought the harshest anti-Soviet presidential rhetoric in years into his first White House press conference; Reagan spoke of Soviet leaders who "reserve unto themselves the right to commit any crime, to lie, to cheat."[4] After the failed assassination attempt had enhanced his stature, Reagan continued speaking forcefully about the need to strengthen American defenses and assume a more aggressive posture vis-à-vis the Soviets. His description of the Soviet Union in a March 1983 speech as "an evil empire" epitomized his viewpoint. So too did his unexpected call two weeks later for the Strategic Defense Initiative, the formal name for a space-based missile defense system often given the Hollywood-inspired label "the Star Wars plan." He underscored his anticommunist mind-set when, unaware that his words were being recorded during a sound check prior to a radio broadcast, he joked that he had signed documents outlawing the Soviet Union and that bombing would start in five minutes. Reagan's repeated and insistent requests for substantial increases in an already swollen defense budget confirmed his posture as an aggressive cold warrior.

At the time Reagan took office, the situation across the Middle East was, even by the region's own dismal standards, exceptionally unsettled. Soviet forces were struggling to occupy Afghanistan, Iran and Iraq were waging war on each other, and the Israeli-Palestinian conflict had boiled over into Lebanon, which was itself riven by civil war between pro-Israeli Christian and Syrian-backed Islamic factions. All these situations seemed to the new American president to offer opportunities for the Soviet Union to expand its influence in the area. In response, he took the first steps into a morass that would eventually provoke more than one call for his impeachment.

Lebanon remained tense but relatively quiet until Israel invaded in June 1982 seeking to dislodge the Palestine Liberation Organization from its foothold there. After the Israeli army drove all the way to Beirut, the United States sought to broker its withdrawal in return for a PLO departure and a U.S. Marine presence to restore calm. A subsequent series of events—the assassination of the Lebanese president-elect, Israel's invitation of the fallen leader's partisans into the Palestinian refugee camps of Sabra and Shatila, where they took murderous revenge, and the arrival of U.S. Marines in Beirut to facilitate the departure of both the PLO and the Israelis—put the United States in the midst of a volatile situation. A tenuous truce was disrupted in April 1983 by the bombing of the U.S. embassy in Beirut, an attack that killed sixty-three people. Six months later, with peacekeeping diplomacy crumbling, an insurgent on a suicide mission detonated a truck bomb in the Marine compound, killing 241 American troops. Reagan ordered U.S. forces withdrawn to ships offshore, after which the sixteen-inch guns of the *U.S.S. New Jersey* pounded villages in the mountains overlooking Beirut.

In the aftermath of the fiasco of U.S. intervention in Lebanon and ignominious "redeployment offshore," Lebanese anti-Israeli Hezbollah insurgents took hostage seven Americans still in Beirut. The Beirut hostages, however, did not rivet American public attention as had the Tehran embassy hostages four years earlier. Not only were they far fewer in number, but also their seizure was overshadowed by simultaneous developments elsewhere. Nevertheless, their plight remained a Reagan concern. He was eager to obtain their release, but he steadfastly maintained, as he would say at a June 18, 1985, press conference, "America will never make concessions to terrorists—to do so would only invite more terrorism."[5] He reiterated this resolve fourteen months later in signing legislation to prohibit arms sales to nations that supported terrorism, specifically Iran among others. The law supplemented the Arms Export Control Act of 1976 that specifically prohibited the transfer of arms by countries purchasing them from the United States to third parties to which the U.S. would not itself sell.

Just as the U.S. position in Lebanon was falling apart, the small eastern-Caribbean nation of Grenada erupted into civil strife. On October 12, 1983,

Grenada's Cuba-friendly government was overthrown and its leaders executed by another Marxist faction on the island. Citing the danger to several hundred American medical students as justification, the Reagan administration intervened three days later. U.S. forces quickly overwhelmed the tiny Grenadan army and also, two days later, a Cuban cadre defending an airstrip. Justifying the action and its handful of casualties, Reagan claimed to have foiled a major Soviet-Cuban effort to establish a base for exporting revolution. Although Reagan's assertions that Grenada represented a threat lacked either supporting evidence or credibility, U.S. intervention did stir an outburst of national self-congratulation that, fortuitously for the administration, obscured the Lebanese debacle that had just occurred.

Roundly criticized in some quarters as unnecessary or worse, within two weeks Reagan's action against Grenada brought the first calls for a presidential impeachment since the resignation of Nixon. Seven Democratic members of the House of Representatives, led by Ted Weiss of New York and including Watergate Judiciary Committee veteran John Conyers, Jr., of Michigan, introduced a resolution calling for the president's impeachment on the grounds that Reagan had violated multiple provisions of the Constitution. The president, they charged, had usurped Congress's power to declare war and had ignored U.S. treaty obligations. He had also, they asserted, violated the First Amendment by preventing news coverage of the invasion itself.[6]

Sent to the House Judiciary Committee, the 1983 impeachment resolution received no consideration. The quick and, in the eyes of most Americans, positive outcome of the Grenada situation crushed what little interest the resolution generated. The will did not exist to condemn, on grounds of constitutional impropriety, a successful military venture. Representative Weiss persisted, however, sending out twenty-four thousand packets of information to peace organizations, schools, political groups, and newspapers, calling for Reagan's impeachment. While Weiss did not expect ultimate success, he said, "It is my hope that one of the constructive outcomes of the impeachment resolution is that it engenders a debate of the issues and strengthens the public's understanding of the constitutional principles upon which our nation is founded."[7] By Representative Weiss's own measure, his effort failed completely. Nevertheless, it demonstrated both the currency and inadequacy of impeachment as a means of raising a challenge to the constitutionality of ever-expanding presidential power.

Well before the Grenada incident, much of Reagan's concern about the advance of communism had focused on the small republics of Central America where poverty and dissatisfaction with self-serving authoritarian regimes had created social and political unrest. The socialist Sandinista government of Nicaragua, having come to power in mid-1979 after forcing the brutally repressive dictator Anastasio Somoza into exile, initially received pledges of $90 million in emergency food aid and other economic support from the Carter administration. As its most militant Marxist-Leninist elements gained control, the Sandinista government drove moderates from its ranks, alienated progressive western European governments that had offered help, and in March 1980 signed economic and cultural agreements with the Soviets. The fledgling government became increasingly heavy-handed as it punished Somoza-era officials while at the same time it pursued large-scale economic redistribution and social reform. The Sandinistas further aroused American ire by supporting guerrilla forces seeking to topple another reactionary regime next door in El Salvador. During its final months, the Carter administration ceased financial assistance to Nicaragua and enlarged its military support of El Salvador. The Reagan administration went further by immediately suspending payment of previously pledged U.S. aid to Nicaragua.[8]

With U.S. hostility to his struggling young government becoming ever more evident, Nicaraguan president Daniel Ortega drew closer to the Soviet Union. It made sense to Ortega, much as it had to Fidel Castro in Cuba more than twenty years earlier, to enlist the support of a sympathetic nation powerful enough to fend off growing pressure from the North American colossus. Rather than responding by intervening directly in what could become another Vietnam for U.S. troops, the Reagan administration within weeks of taking office in January 1981 began to pursue covert action against the Salvadoran rebels and their Nicaraguan allies. By November Reagan had agreed to allocate $20 million in secret funds to supply and train the Contras, an insurgency being formed with CIA assistance and intended to topple the Nicaraguan government. A 1980 law stipulated that such CIA covert action was permissible only if the president found it important to national security and reported such a "finding" in writing to the House and Senate intelligence committees "in a timely fashion."

Reagan administration spokesmen, as well as the president himself, publicly asserted that authoritarian capitalist governments were preferable to totalitarian communist ones. They alleged that the former type of government, such as the ones in El Salvador and pre-Sandinista Nicaragua, were, despite their corruption and brutality, sometimes capable of evolving into democracies. In contrast, they said, totalitarian communist states built on rigid ideologies were unable to change and would only become more repressive. The president and the U.S. ambassador to the United Nations, Jeane Kirkpatrick, repeated these unproven and questionable assertions to justify alliances with autocracies as the lesser of two evils. As had been the case time after time, this would prove an unwise as well as an unprincipled calculation for a nation of professed high ideals. The flawed choice led the Reagan administration into questionable "findings" and clandestine actions that proved not only futile but also constitutionally suspect.

By November 1982 reports began circulating within Washington that the administration was providing clandestine support for the Contras as they sought to topple Nicaragua's government. Questioned by the House Permanent Select Committee on Intelligence, CIA director William Casey denied the reports. He failed to convince the representatives. The House decided to send the administration a strong message of disapproval. Representative Edward Boland, a Democrat from Massachusetts, chairman of the Intelligence Committee as well as House Speaker Tip O'Neill's apartment mate and confidant, proposed an amendment to the annual defense appropriation bill to prohibit the spending of federal funds "for the purpose of overthrowing the government of Nicaragua."[9] The House approved the measure 411–0 on December 8, the Senate concurred, and President Reagan signed the measure into law on December 21. The 1982 Boland Amendment did not deny all funding for all clandestine activity; rather, it took the administration at its word that its support of the Contras was only for the purpose of stopping the flow of weapons from the Sandinistas to El Salvador.[10]

Despite Congress's directive in the Boland Amendment, the Reagan administration continued its efforts to unseat the Sandinista government of Nicaragua. In January 1984 U.S. mines were laid in Nicaraguan harbors, an act of war by virtually any definition. In March a Soviet ship struck one of the mines and sank. Despite Casey's repeated assurances to Congress that his agency had not been helping the Contras, the mining of the harbor clearly involved the CIA and revealed Casey's dissembling. The *Wall Street Journal* soon reported that the CIA had acted with explicit presidential approval.

The ignoring of Congress's directives deeply angered many of its members, even staunch anticommunist conservatives inclined to sympathize with Reagan's views. Senator Barry Goldwater wrote to Casey, "I am pissed off! . . . This is an act violating international law. It is an act of war. For the life of me, I don't see how we are going to explain it."[11] The Senate sent the administration clear notice of its disapproval by voting for a halt to all mine laying. Both Reagan and Casey acknowledged that they had received the message, vowing to keep the Senate Intelligence Committee informed of all future covert actions. Signaling that such communication was necessary but not sufficient, both houses of Congress soon rejected an administration request for further funds to support the Contras.

Despite the administration's reassurances about the narrow focus of its covert undertakings, Congress had learned by fall of 1984 that the CIA was still supporting Contra actions against the Nicaraguan government. Without informing Congress, the CIA had distributed a manual to instruct the Contras on assassination and terrorism tactics. A furious Congress attached a second Boland Amendment to another Defense Appropriation Act, leaving no doubt that it wanted an end to all assistance to the Nicaraguan rebels. The amendment barred the CIA, the military, and "any other agency or entity of the United States involved in intelligence activities" from "supporting, directly or indirectly, military and paramilitary operations in Nicaragua by any nation, group, organization or individual."

The plain language of the legislation admitted of no exceptions to its directive against further aid to the Contras. On October 12, President Reagan once again signed the measure, completing the constitutional process of making it law.[12]

Once safely reelected, however, Reagan reasserted his desire to support the Nicaraguan Contras. He declared in his 1985 State of the Union address that the United States "must not break faith with those who are risking their lives—on every continent, from Afghanistan to Nicaragua—to defy Soviet-supported aggression and secure rights which have been ours from birth." A month later on March 1 he called the Contras "the moral equivalent of our Founding Fathers." Reagan's rhetoric and his apparent public support helped persuade Congress by August 1985 to restore $27 million of aid to the Contras, to be used specifically for nonlethal purposes. This measure marked relaxation by Congress of the most severe version of the Boland Amendment.[13] In June 1986 Congress went further, approving $100 million for the Contras, including $70 million in military aid beginning in the next fiscal year.[14]

More important than his public statements were Reagan's private directives to his staff. His national security adviser, Robert McFarlane, later recounted that during the period that Congress eliminated or restricted funds for the Nicaraguan insurgents, Reagan told him to keep the Contras together "body and soul." McFarlane's deputy and successor, Admiral John Poindexter, would eventually testify that the message was clear. Reagan "wanted to be sure that the Contras were supported."[15]

The president's defenders would claim that Reagan drew a distinction between the National Security Council (NSC) and the intelligence agencies specifically forbidden by the Boland Amendment from assisting the Contras. Reagan also, they contended, differentiated between the Boland prohibition on using U.S. government funds for Contra aid and the solicitation and utilization of private or foreign funds for the same purpose. In either case, the president parsed the words of the Boland Amendment in a creative manner while ignoring Congress's clear intention to forbid all covert U.S. government participation in efforts to overthrow the Nicaraguan government.

McFarlane proceeded to seek funding for the Contras from two important U.S. allies, Israel and Saudi Arabia. The Israelis put him off, but the Saudis agreed to provide the Contras $1 million a month and later doubled the amount. McFarlane's assistant, Marine Lieutenant Colonel Oliver North, set up a Swiss bank account identified only by number into which the Saudis could make deposits and from which untraceable payments could be sent to the Contra bank account in Miami. Once these arrangements were completed, McFarlane slipped the president a note describing the Saudi deal. The note was returned with a handwritten expression of presidential satisfaction. McFarlane also notified other senior administration officials, but he said nothing to the congressional intelligence committees that the White House had promised would be kept informed.[16]

Reagan and his inner circle were well aware that what was being done risked the president's impeachment. At a June 25, 1984, meeting with Reagan, McFarlane, Casey, Secretary of Defense Caspar Weinberger, and Presidential Councilor Edwin Meese, Secretary of State George Schultz warned that if the government acted as a conduit for such secret funding it would be "an impeachable offense." Reagan acknowledged the point, saying that if word got out that they had discussed third-country funding for the Contras, "we'll all be hanging by our thumbs in front of the White House."[17]

The June 25 statements by the president and the secretary of state indicated that they understood that raising private funds abroad to carry out a foreign initiative contrary to a congressional directive was at odds with the law. Congress and the courts would not look favorably on "the Enterprise," as those involved labeled the Contra-aid scheme. From the outset the Enterprise would violate bedrock constitutional principles of executive branch responsibility to observe the law and adhere to the indisputable specific directives of legislative enactments. It nevertheless went forward, with every effort being made to maintain the secrecy of the steps taken. After an August 1985 *New York Times* story that an unidentified military officer on the NSC had been giving the Contras direct military advice and telling people how they might give money to the rebels, the White House issued a nondenial denial. "No member of the National Security Council staff has, at any time, acted in violation of either the spirit or the letter of existing legislation dealing with the U.S. assistance to the democratic resistance in Nicaragua." No mention was made of the narrow interpretation of legislation being used to reach such a conclusion.[18]

The extent to which the Boland Amendment was ignored by the Reagan administration would not become evident until late 1986. By that time, Poindexter had replaced McFarlane as the president's national security adviser and the Enterprise had become much more elaborate. On October 5, 1986, Sandinista troops using a portable Russian missile launcher shot down a C-123 cargo plane flying low over Nicaragua, thirty miles inside the Costa Rican border. Crew member Eugene Hasenfus parachuted to safety as the plane crashed, killing the other three men aboard. Captured by the Sandinistas, Hasenfus confessed that the plane was carrying ammunition and weapons to the Contras. Documents recovered from the wreckage revealed that Southern Air Transport, a well-known CIA front, had operated the plane. The Sandinista government broadcast their discoveries to the world.

The Sandinista capture of Hasenfus was not the only thread unraveling in the blanket of secrecy covering aid to the Contras. A month later, on November 3, a Lebanese newspaper, *Al-Shiraa,* reported that the United States had been surreptitiously shipping arms to Iran, its recent tormenter and a nation with which it did not even have formal diplomatic relations. The revelation compromised not only the United States but also Iran's revolutionary government, which was exposed as making deals with the nation its leaders called the "Great Satan." Within a day, an Iranian minister told his parliament that the United States had initiated the contacts. McFarlane had secretly gone to Tehran seeking Iran's help in freeing the hostages in Lebanon and had been told that Iran would expect gestures of friendship in return.

Over the course of the two weeks after the *Al-Shiraa* story appeared, the Reagan administration wrestled with what to do about the revelations and the growing controversy they stirred. Some senior officials struggled to discover what had been going on that they did not know about, while those most deeply involved in the NSC's Iran and Contra operations concentrated on covering their tracks. On November 12 Reagan himself wrote in the daily diary he maintained throughout his presidency, "This whole irresponsible press bilge about hostages & Iran has gotten totally out of hand. The media looks like it's trying to create another Watergate. I laid down the law in the morning meetings—I want to go public personally & tell the people the truth."[19] He passed over the fact that the previous January 7 he had written in the same diary about giving Israel missiles to replace ones they had given to Iran in exchange for Hezbollah-held U.S. hostages in Lebanon, concluding, "We sit quietly by & never reveal how we got them back."[20]

In a televised speech the following day, Reagan acknowledged U.S. arms sales to Iran, though he did not admit that in November 1985 he had signed a finding for this to be done or that the finding had not been properly reported to the congressional intelligence committees. "The charge has been made that the United States has shipped weapons to Iran as ransom payment for the return of American hostages in Lebanon, that the United States undercut its allies and secretly violated American policy against trafficking with terrorists. These charges are utterly false," he insisted.[21] Privately he drew a fine distinction between dealing with Iranian middlemen and engaging directly with the people holding the hostages in Lebanon. He held to that dubious position at a November 19 press conference, but his statements generated considerable skepticism, especially after the White House quickly released a correction to Reagan's assertion that no third country had taken part in the arms transfer. Israel had been involved, the press release attested.[22]

Finally, as uproar continued to build in Congress and the press, Attorney General Meese, a longtime confidante and loyal friend of the president, decided to conduct a hasty inquiry. Meese later explained that he was concerned that an appearance of covering up misdeeds posed the greatest risk to the administration. If so, his investigation was either incompetent or designed to assure that evidence damaging to the president would not come to light. Meese interviewed the principle administration figures involved in the matter but took no notes of his discussions with the president; the vice president, George H. W. Bush; the White House chief of staff, Donald Regan; William Casey; or John Poindexter.

Although he took extensive and damning notes of his interview with Oliver North, he made no effort to prevent North from subsequently destroying vital documents. Some of the participants in the later congressional investigation would conclude that Meese had not covered up North's or Poindexter's misdeeds but had made it impossible to trace responsibility for them to President Reagan.[23]

The specter of Watergate appeared very much on Meese's mind, as well it might. As he learned that profits from arms sales to Iran had been used to fund the Nicaraguan Contras, Meese became alarmed that the revelation of these intersecting activities could cause Reagan's downfall. The attorney general would acknowledge at North's 1989 trial that he had seen the prospect of impeachment looming. He had worried, he said, "that political opponents might try that kind of tactic."[24] His deputy in the inquiry, Charles J. Cooper, testified at the same trial, "We recognized the sensitivity of this information, the fact that it was information that had to be made public by the President and nobody else, that if the *Washington Post* made this fact public prior to the time that the President did, it would be very calamitous."[25] Avoiding the appearance of parallels with Watergate became a priority for White House communications director Patrick Buchanan and press secretary Larry Speakes as well as for Meese. Buchanan, a close Nixon aide, and Speakes, James St. Clair's press secretary, both knew firsthand the perils of presidential impeachment.[26]

Chief of Staff Regan shared the same worries. He warned the president's wife that Reagan's situation was similar to Nixon's in Watergate and that his presidency was at risk. Nancy Reagan unhappily agreed. Recalling the conversation later, Regan acknowledged that he did not use the term "impeachment." He explained, "It was a no-no word. . . . You never used the word impeachment except to yourself, because that was something no one wanted to even think about, but, as chief of staff, I felt I should at least look that beast in the eye to see, you know, if we were going up here to another Watergate." For the moment, Regan was fearful.[27]

"Meese was right to worry about the possibility of impeachment," the knowledgeable and careful journalist Lou Cannon observed. "The idea of taking such action seemed in the early 1970s a drastic adventure into uncharted territory. But in 1986 impeachment no longer seemed an unthinkable remedy for presidential excess."[28] By moving quickly to preempt other inquiries and alert those involved as to what was coming, Meese successfully anticipated problems threatening the administration in a way that his Nixon-era predecessors as attorney general, John Mitchell and Richard Kleindienst, never had.

On November 25, Reagan, giving the impression of being shaken after receiving Meese's initial report, told a televised press conference that he had not been kept informed about NSC activities. He would therefore now appoint a special commission to thoroughly examine the situation. In the meantime, the president said, John Poindexter had resigned and his aide Oliver North had been relieved of his duties. After Reagan's not-very-illuminating statement, Meese took the podium to announce his findings. Rather than seeking to blunt speculation, he laid out a shocking tale that seemed the very antithesis of a cover-up. The attorney general reported that officials of the NSC had arranged the clandestine sale of TOW missiles to Iran in return for Iran's assistance in negotiating the release of the American hostages in Lebanon. The missiles had passed through Israel so that the United States would merely appear to be replenishing an ally's arsenal. After the $12 million cost of replacing Israel's missiles had been deducted from the $30 million sale to Iran, an extraordinary $18 million profit had been placed in a Swiss bank account, from which funds were being sent to the Contras. In essence, through a series of secret transfers, U.S. military hardware, bought and paid for by American taxpayers, was converted, indeed leveraged, into military aid for the Nicaraguan Contras, which Congress had explicitly prohibited.

The actions carried out by the Reagan administration had clearly violated multiple laws. The transfer of weapons to Iran transgressed the 1976 Arms Export Control Act and its 1980 amendments as well as the embargo Congress had placed on trade with the former ally but foe since 1979. The supplying of weapons to the Contras defied the directives of the first and second Boland Amendments and even those of their weaker replacement. The failure to inform Congress about these transactions, not to mention lying when asked pointed questions about them, represented further offenses. The creation of the Enterprise as a presidentially controlled military force completely outside of congressional oversight may have represented the most alarming breach of constitutional bounds of all. The central question being asked quickly became "What did the President know and when did he know it?" Depending on the answer to these familiar Watergate questions, Reagan could be charged with high crimes and misdemeanors for his own acts or, if subordinates had taken these actions, for violating his oath of office to see that the laws were faithfully executed.

Meese and other members of Reagan's inner circle addressed their leader's situation with tactics learned from the Watergate episode. Although the actions taken vis-à-vis Iran and Nicaragua may have been just as illegal as anything undertaken by the Nixon administration, the response, once secrets were revealed and impeachment became a possibility, could not have contrasted more sharply. The preemptive Reagan-Meese press conference admitting that wrongdoing had occurred before it could be fully exposed by others was a crucial first step. The appointment the very next day of an investigatory panel offered a further demonstration by the Reagan White House that it was not engaging in a Nixon-style cover-up. The same day Meese announced that he had ordered Assistant Attorney General William Weld to undertake a criminal investigation of the diversion of funds from the Iran arms sales to the Contras. Less than a week later, he urged Reagan to call for the appointment of an independent counsel to pursue the matter further. Reagan complied by putting in motion a December 19 judicial selection of Lawrence E. Walsh as independent counsel. The distinguished Walsh, a Republican, had served as a federal judge, deputy attorney general under President Dwight Eisenhower, and president of the American Bar Association. Meese eventually acknowledged, "The actions were taken because they were the appropriate actions under any circumstances but one of the concerns was to prevent this situation from being used by policy opponents of the President."[29] In other words, the threat of impeachment lay heavy on Meese's mind.

Reagan comprehended that he was in trouble, but at least at first he seemed not to understand why. He blamed media revelations of the arms-for-hostages deal, rather than the arrangement itself, or the diversion of funds to the Contras as being the source of the problem. "I've never seen the sharks circling like they are now with blood in the water," the president told *Time* magazine correspondent Hugh Sidey during a November 26 interview. Dodging acknowledgment of the most serious misdeeds, he nevertheless moved adroitly to embrace what would become his core defense. Reagan called North "a national hero" while saying, "My only criticism is that I wasn't told everything."[30] Relying on the public to approve of North and what he had done while hedging that bet by asserting that he was uninformed himself proved to be an effective strategy for the president.

By spotlighting the diversion of funds from one clandestine activity to another rather than the statutory and constitutional violations inherent in supplying Iran and the Contras, Attorney General Meese focused attention on NSC and CIA activities and shifted it away from other aspects of what had happened. The diversion, though spectacularly duplicitous, was arguably a less fundamental violation of law and constitutional authority than were other aspects of what had taken place. The administration had failed to keep Congress informed of its actions as required by law. A parade of administration officials had repeatedly and knowingly given untrue testimony to Congress. Finally, and most egregiously, executive branch officers had acted in direct violation of congressional directives specifically barring arms transfers and military activities. Any of these offenses was arguably a basis for the president's impeachment; his apparent indifference to a systematic pattern of misconduct within his administration fell within the parameters of "high crimes and misdemeanors," at least as had been defined during Watergate by Raoul Berger and Charles Black, legal scholars of impeachment.[31]

The special review board appointed by Reagan to look into what rapidly became known as the Iran-Contra affair in the end deflected the initial storm of criticism of the president prompted by the Meese revelations. Given the task of providing a prompt assessment rather than a necessarily exhaustive one, the commission preempted the long period of uncertainty and speculation that had helped the Watergate episode become focused on the central role of President

Nixon. The review panel did more to deflect charges that the president had committed misdeeds than it did to explain what had actually happened. The commission's three members, Texas Republican senator John Tower, former Democratic senator and secretary of state Edmund Muskie, and former national security adviser Brent Scowcroft, were all experienced and respected figures. At the same time, they were all cautious and conservative men who had long specialized in military and diplomatic affairs. Tower, in fact, had employed McFarlane on his Senate staff for nearly three years. The commission members no doubt wanted to limit as much as possible damage to the institutions of government with which they identified.[32]

Asked to complete their inquiry within forty-five days with a staff of fewer than a dozen members and without the legal power to subpoena documents, compel witnesses to appear, or grant immunity from prosecution in return for testimony, the Tower Commission lacked the muscle to dig much deeper than Meese had already done. Assembling evidence proved exceedingly difficult. Central figures, such as Oliver North, had received sufficient advanced warning from the initial Meese inquiry to be able to destroy critical files documenting their activities. Key witnesses proved unavailable. William Casey suffered a stroke days before the commission's appointment, and Robert McFarlane attempted suicide hours before he was to testify a second time.[33] Moreover, the cooperation Tower, Muskie, and Scowcroft did receive muddied the waters further.

Having declared that he wanted the truth known about Iran-Contra, President Reagan agreed to talk to the Tower Commission. After postponing the interview because of prostate surgery, a slowly recuperating Reagan met with the board on January 26, 1987, and told them that he had approved the initial Israeli arms transfers to Iran in August 1985 as well as U.S. replenishment of Israel's weapons stocks. This contradicted earlier testimony by White House Chief of Staff Regan. After the commission members departed, Regan suggested to Reagan that the president had been upset when McFarlane reported that the arms transfer had taken place. Moments later, Reagan said, "Yes, I guess I was surprised." When the president met with the board a second time two weeks later, Reagan read a statement: "If the question comes up at the Tower Board meeting, you might want to say that you were surprised." The commissioners were dumbfounded that the president was cluelessly treating a staff memo as if it were a script he could read as his own recollection. Then, on February 20, he disavowed in writing the unpersuasive recantation and offered his third different explanation in less than a month: "I'm afraid that I let myself be influenced by others' recollections, not my own. . . . My answer, therefore, and the simple truth is, I don't remember—period." The Tower Commission was aghast at Reagan's limited memory and obvious mental confusion.[34]

Racing to meet the deadline to complete its work, the Tower Commission less than a week later issued a 304-page report that was damning in its revelations yet forgiving in its assessment of the president. The board admitted that, even given two weeks extra time for its investigation, it had been unable to unravel the Iran-Contra affair because those interviewed were either not forthcoming or gave contradictory answers. Nevertheless, the board found White House decision making "too informal" and the National Security Council "very unprofessional." Reagan, it declared, had been motivated by "intense compassion for the hostages" but was unaware of how his subordinates were dealing with the matter. Although he "must bear primary responsibility" for the outcome, the president was principally faulted for a "management style" that gave too much authority to his staff. Offering the most lenient possible interpretation of presidential behavior, the Tower Report generously cast Reagan as the somewhat bewildered and out-of-touch victim of an irresponsible and undisciplined staff rather than as an official constitutionally responsible for actions taken in his name and with at least his tacit encouragement.

The Tower Commission tolerated Reagan's manner of conducting his presidency and absolved him of responsibility for acts of underlings who believed they were carrying out his wishes. The board's report, which a *New York Times* editorial characterized as "Fair, Respectful—and Humiliating" and the *Washington Post* declared "devastating," determined to a great extent the way the public and Congress would thereafter regard Reagan.[35] The Constitution's framers, after considering alternatives, had given all executive duties to a single official, the president. One of the framers, Alexander Hamilton, wrote in the *Federalist Papers,* "Every magistrate ought to be personally responsible for his behavior in office." The Tower panel did not hold Reagan to that standard.[36] In the weeks following the release of the Tower Report, its view of the president as out of touch with what his subordinates were doing became widely accepted. Without compelling evidence at hand that Reagan had himself directed the improper activities in Iran and Nicaragua, discussion of impeachment declined though the president's public stature was severely diminished.

The initial Iran-Contra revelations had caused a plunge in the president's public standing from 67 percent approval in early November to 46 percent by month's end, the sharpest drop in presidential approval ratings since such polls began to be taken in the mid-1930s. An overwhelming majority of respondents, 90 percent in an initial *Newsweek* poll, judged that the president was not telling the truth about what he knew about the Iran-Contra affair. Perhaps most alarming to the White House, a *New York Times*/CBS News poll at the end of November revealed that 57 percent of those surveyed found the matter was "at least as serious as Watergate."[37] With the release of the Tower Report, with its picture of a president who was inattentive and passive rather than engaged and active, Reagan's standing plunged further. Days after the report became public, only 42 percent of respondents to another *Times*/CBS poll approved of his performance, while 46 percent disapproved. A month later, after many newspaper stories reported that the president had been unaware of the details of the arms transfers, his approval ratings improved slightly to 45 percent while disapproval slipped to 43 percent.[38] It appeared that the public was more tolerant of a president, at least one previously popular, who was asleep at the controls than of one clearly in command but deliberately devious.

As soon as the Tower Report was released, Reagan made a change in his White House staff of great symbolic as well as substantive importance. Donald Regan, the chief of staff since the start of the president's second term, was asked to resign. In his place, Reagan installed former Tennessee senator Howard Baker. The onetime Senate Republican majority leader, Baker was best known to the public as the ranking Republican on the Ervin committee investigating Watergate. In that role he had appeared willing to probe the conduct of a president of his own party, skeptical of what he was told, and ultimately prepared to condemn improper presidential conduct. Those qualities earned his appointment widespread bipartisan praise both within Congress and outside of Washington. The chairman of the National Governor's Association, Arkansas Democrat Bill Clinton, said of the president, "It's plain now he's got the kind of White House staff that will minimize the possibility of error."[39]

Baker immediately launched another and this time much more rigorous internal investigation of the Iran-Contra affair. His deputies A. B. Culvahouse and Bill Lytton assembled a staff of over sixty to examine twelve thousand documents. With Baker they interviewed Reagan himself at length on more than a dozen occasions. While they could not entirely disprove the possibility of Reagan's knowledge of or participation in the diversion of arms-sales funds to the Contras, they satisfied themselves that no evidence existed—no document, no tape recording, no "smoking gun" of any sort—that could tie the president to illegal acts. The evidence to dispute Reagan's claims of noninvolvement simply did not exist.[40]

Within three days of Baker's arrival, Reagan offered the public a more forthcoming, if not altogether forthright, explanation of his administration's dealings with Iran. Both Baker and Tower had made clear to the president that he faced a very real threat of impeachment if he did not in some way acknowledge responsibility for the Iranian fiasco. In a thirteen-minute televised speech to the nation, Reagan said, "A few months ago, I told the American people I did not trade arms for hostages. My heart and my best intentions still tell me that is true, but the facts and the evidence tell me it is not." Going on to acknowledge that "what began as a strategic opening to Iran deteriorated in its implementation into trading arms for hostages," Reagan skirted the issue of the illegality of the transaction and the transfer of its proceeds to the Contras. Instead, he asserted that he had not intended a direct trade of arms for hostages and blamed his staff for acting without his knowledge. Insisting that his loose management approach had worked during his eight years as California governor and most of his time

Herblock,
Washington Post,
March 5, 1987.
© The Herb
Block Foundation.

as president, he cast the Iran case as an exception "counter to my own beliefs, to administration policy, and to the original strategy we had in mind."[41]

Reagan treated the Tower Report as the turning point in the Iran-Contra scandal and in terms of the threat of his impeachment he was probably correct, though not for the reasons he would cite. In a March 30 speech to a gathering of senior administration officials, Reagan called the preceding four months of scandal "difficult" and "frustrating" but put them behind him, saying that the Tower Report had presented a "clear account of what took place." Ignoring the many unanswered questions remaining about his own conduct and those of his aides, he treated the matter as resolved. Thereafter, he proclaimed, "We can go on with the business that brought us here and institutionalize the improvements that we've made."[42]

His highly selective explanation of his conduct in the Iran-Contra affair aided Reagan in fending off calls for his impeachment, but at a price. Two-thirds of those responding to a mid-April national poll, although they regarded the president as generally honest, by the same proportion believed that he was not telling the truth about the Iran-Contra affair.[43] The Tower Commission's conclusion that Reagan was an unobservant and detached president who allowed unscrupulous subordinates to do as they pleased appeared to be widely shared. For most of the rest of his term in office, a slight majority of respondents to polling questions would indicate approval of Reagan's conduct as president. Such levels of public support, which increased after he concluded disarmament agreements with the Soviet premier, Mikhail Gorbachev, were respectable for a second-term chief executive but well below his attainments prior to the disclosure of the Iran and Contra transgressions. Although Reagan remained personally popular, confidence in his leadership was severely weakened. At the same time, he never became broadly and deeply disliked, as had Nixon by the summer of 1974. Nixon set a standard of personal disapproval that went far beyond anything reached by Reagan. As Congress addressed the Iran-Contra affair, Reagan's comparatively good public standing became an important factor in the calculus of impeachability.

As soon as revelations of the Iran-Contra affair started to surface in November 1986, Congress began its own investigation. In December the House and Senate select committees on intelligence conducted hearings. Closed to the public because of the national security issues involved, these hearings proved frustrating to committee members because Lieutenant Colonel North and Admiral Poindexter refused to testify, claiming their Fifth Amendment rights against self-incrimination. The Senate committee eventually voted not to release an incomplete staff report.[44] The transition taking place from Republican domination of the Senate to control by the just-elected Democratic majority complicated the situation. The Republican majority leader, Robert Dole, and the incoming Democratic leader, Robert Byrd, agreed to remove the investigation from the Intelligence Committee's hands and establish a special select committee to investigate Iran-Contra. For the moment, this seemed to echo the creation of the Ervin committee to probe Watergate. That image was strengthened by Byrd's choice of Daniel Inouye, the only Democratic member of Ervin's committee still serving in the Senate, as chairman of the select committee. Furthermore, two senators who as members of the House Judiciary Committee had voted to impeach Nixon, Maryland Democrat Paul Sarbanes and Maine Republican William Cohen, were also named to the eleven-member committee. Yet these were careful, cautious senators, and most of the other members of the committee were decidedly sympathetic to Reagan policies, with three of the Democrats as well as all the Republican members having supported aid to the Contras.

Senator Inouye's experience as a member of the Ervin committee probing Watergate would shape his approach to the Iran-Contra investigation. A decorated World War II veteran, he thought of himself foremost as a patriot. He had been profoundly troubled by Watergate, seeing it as damaging not merely to Nixon but to the presidency:

> It was not my proudest moment. . . . As I sat there day after day, it became obvious that we were becoming, well, the attraction of the world. People were reading about us and what they were getting was not positive. It was all negative. This sounds corny but, you know, I'm proud of this country. I love this country, and I saw my activities on the committee as being party to an activity that was demeaning our nation. . . . The committee by doing its work—and I say properly, I don't think we did anything improper, in fact we were very careful—couldn't help but put the presidency in some jeopardy in the eyes of Americans and in the eyes of those abroad that something was wrong with us. . . . I was a little fearful. It had an effect on me.[45]

Less concerned about the temporary occupant of the White House than about the enduring office, Inouye was loath to inflict further damage on the presidency if he could avoid it. The Hawaiian senator went out of his way to demonstrate that the Senate investigation would be bipartisan. He designated the ranking Republican, Warren Rudman of New Hampshire, as the committee's vice chairman, an unusual and generous step under Senate rules, which normally afford the minority party very little power. Likewise, Inouye chose and guided the committee staff to function in a nonpartisan fashion.[46]

By the time the Senate Select Committee on Secret Military Assistance to Iran and the Nicaraguan Opposition was formally established on the first day of the One Hundredth Congress, January 6, 1987, the House of Representatives was only a day away from creating its own select committee to conduct a parallel investigation. The need for a second investigation was questionable. Two separate bodies dealing with witnesses would create profound complications, but the desire of the House to share the spotlight was compelling. So the House broke with the Watergate precedent of allowing the Senate to take the initial risk of investigating an apparently popular president. House Democratic leaders enlisted two veteran members, Lee Hamilton of Indiana, chair of the House Intelligence Committee, and Dante Fascell of Florida, chair of the Foreign Affairs Committee, to serve as the fifteen-member select committee's chair and vice chair, respectively. The House minority leader, Robert Michel, appointed his party's whip, Representative Richard Cheney of Wyoming, to serve as the committee's ranking Republican.

Senators Dole and Byrd soon agreed with Speaker Jim Wright and Minority Leader Michel to combine the Senate and House committees. This raised the prospect of an unwieldy process. None of the eleven senators and fifteen representatives already appointed indicated a willingness to step aside. The merged committee seemed less designed to ensure the thoroughness of the inquiry than to assure that every investigative step taken and conclusion reached would require bipartisan backing in each house of Congress. John Dean, who had worked on the Republican staff of the House Judiciary Committee during the Abe Fortas and William O. Douglas investigations and had then himself been in the spotlight during Watergate, scoffed at the arrangement. "A joint committee is the least effective mechanism for conducting a serious inquiry," he concluded.[47] However, it had faded from memory that most House Republicans had steadfastly refused to acknowledge Nixon's high crimes and misdemeanors until the "smoking gun" tape made that conclusion inescapable. In a congressional investigation with the potential to produce an impeachment resolution, bipartisanship may well have been necessary in the end to assemble the majorities required to complete the process, but along the way it would slow and restrain the proceeding considerably.

Before the joint committee could hold hearings, it needed to do extensive investigation, preparation, and procedural negotiation. Constructing a staff and conducting an investigation took time, even or perhaps especially with an experienced and skilled prosecutor, New York attorney Arthur Liman, as chief counsel. Agreement on hearing procedures was more difficult to achieve. Senator Inouye, eager to move the hearings ahead with dispatch, wanted to limit opening statements to the four committee leaders and interrogation to a pair of designated senators for each witness. House members objected, wanting what for them would be a rare moment in the national spotlight. The committee finally settled on allowing each of its twenty-six members a five-minute opening statement, an arrangement that assured that the televised hearings would start with a series of largely uninformative and repetitive presentations.

As the hearings approached, the committee's leaders came, each by his own path, to reject the possibility of Reagan's impeachment. Representative Cheney was a Reagan loyalist who viewed the very proposition with disdain. At the opening session of the hearings, he took the narrowest possible view of offenses committed and declared that Congress bore a measure of blame for what had happened because, he charged, it had failed to set clear policies.[48] Senator Rudman, more inclined to conduct a thorough investigation, nevertheless judged impeachment inappropriate even before the hearings opened. On the Democratic side, Representative Hamilton concluded,

> We did not hang Reagan because we could not find proof that Reagan knew what he was doing. There were plenty of suspicions and the people around him protected him very carefully, Ollie North and all the others. If you are going to impeach a president you've got to have very direct proof and we just

didn't have it. . . . We couldn't tie it down. Now we worked awfully hard at it and our counsel worked hard at it, but we couldn't come up with the proof. . . .

In the committee's analysis of it, the most important thing at the time was not to prosecute individuals but to get the story out. We really felt that the Reagan presidency was on the brink, and the whole process of government could collapse, literally. We felt the most important thing was to tell the story of Iran-Contra. Part of the thinking back of that—I can't speak for all of the committee, but my thinking anyway—the principle actors on carrying out Iran-Contra, people like Ollie North, Poindexter, Elliott Abrams, and others, I never looked upon them as bad people, criminals. I looked upon them as people who were put in a very, very difficult position by government and by the Reagan administration. I think they did a lot of things they shouldn't have done but they did them out of patriotism and out of loyalty to the president. In other words, I was a little less concerned about criminal prosecution—all of us were on the committee—than with getting the story out and making the government viable again. The Reagan administration really almost came to a halt while Iran-Contra was on. They were not functioning as a government, basically, and it really was a constitutional crisis for us at that point.[49]

Meanwhile, Senator Inouye saw no reason to change his view that, absent overwhelming evidence of personal malfeasance, defending the presidency took priority over punishing an individual president. With such a mind-set among committee leaders, either the hearings had to produce solid proof of Reagan's direct and active involvement in the Iran-Contra fiasco or they would lead nowhere.

As had the House and Senate intelligence committees, the special joint committee found it difficult to obtain testimony from participants in the Iran-Contra affair, since they risked criminal prosecution on the basis of information they provided. Congress could require testimony by granting immunity from prosecution based on any disclosure, but to do so raised the politically embarrassing possibility that admitted wrongdoers would escape punishment. The fact that the independent counsel, Lawrence Walsh, was conducting a separate investigation and might issue indictments further complicated the situation. Walsh could only make use of information gathered before a grant of immunity and so wanted Congress to delay taking action as long as possible.[50] The immunity question caused the joint committee hearings to be delayed until mid-May and the testimony of the key witnesses, Poindexter and North, to be put off even further. Liman eventually explained that immunity was granted because Congress had only two choices: dispel the cloud over the White House or impeach the president. Successful criminal prosecution of North and Poindexter was secondary to the resolution of a constitutional crisis.[51]

The joint committee alternated its Iran-Contra hearings between the Senate and House office buildings, a week at a time in each. The media, not privy to the thinking of Senator Inouye and his committee colleagues, treated the story as the second coming of Watergate. Broadcast networks that had at first been reluctant to give up advertising revenue to cover the Ervin committee proceedings in 1973 now hastened to announce that they would provide gavel-to-gavel coverage of the Iran-Contra hearings. Those that could enlisted commentators prominent during Watergate. Anchorman Tom Brokaw recruited Archibald Cox's principle deputy, Richard Ben-Veniste, to share airtime with him on NBC.[52] Even the Public Broadcasting System, which always operated on a tighter budget than the commercial networks, was able to bring forth a noted participant in Watergate, Daniel Schorr, who as a prominent reporter for CBS at the time had been on Nixon's enemies list.[53]

The opening of the Iran-Contra hearings attracted a television audience that no doubt anticipated a series of revelations about the inner workings of the White House, as had occurred during the Ervin hearings fourteen years earlier. Instead, what they got at the outset was a series of rather dull, detailed descriptions of the intricacies of clandestine arms and fund transfers. Richard Secord, a retired Air Force general, and his business partner Albert Hakim, the arms dealers at the heart of the Enterprise, began by characterizing their activities in bland, matter-of-fact fashion. Robert McFarlane, in the course of extended testimony that added details to the Secord account, suggested early and significant presidential involvement in both the Nicaraguan and Iranian situations but mainly painted a picture of independent action by North. Some members of the committee bemoaned the failure to start with witnesses who would address the public's outrage at the arms-for-hostage deals by clarifying the illegality of what had taken place and the damage done to national interests, much less clarifying the ultimate executive responsibility for what had occurred. No sense of public outrage built, even at the arrogant and evasive testimony of Elliott Abrams, an assistant secretary of state for Latin America (later convicted of perjury), and the testimony of two junior White House lawyers who ineptly revealed the shoddiness of the administration's assessment of the Boland Amendment and the initial Meese inquiry into the Iran-Contra affair.[54]

The hearings continued down a path leading away from Reagan and toward Oliver North. Evidence came to light that North had personally profited from various Enterprise-connected transactions and that with his secretary, Fawn Hall, he had destroyed compromising documents. Hall defended North by saying, "Sometimes you have to go above the written law, I believe." No member of the committee leapt to challenge this defense of illegality. The disjointed questioning of the committee's twenty-six members, who were constantly being called away for floor votes in the House or Senate and who when present had to confine their questions to a few minutes, fragmented the picture being created and caused some parts of it to disappear altogether.[55]

Herblock,
Washington Post,
May 17, 1987.
© The Herb
Block Foundation.

When North and Poindexter finally testified in July, they presented their actions guiding the Iranian arms sales and profit diversion to the Contras as reasonable, indeed heroic, acts that were perhaps technically illegal but served a noble purpose. The committee was caught off guard by an aggressive North, who launched into a speech at every opportunity. He asserted that his actions were patriotic and necessary to overcome congressional weakness. He ducked the issue of funds put to personal use by alleging dangers to his wife and daughter. He admitted lying to Congress because "Congress can't keep a secret, and I had to choose between lies and lives." The committee, nonplussed by North's audacity, did not challenge his extravagant claims to justify illegal acts or call attention to the fact that the leaks in question came not from Congress but from the executive branch and, at least once, from North himself. Many viewers, unfamiliar with the facts, concluded that he was speaking truths instead of offering self-serving fabrications. That North's statements were distortions would be proven too late to stem the tide of public opinion that inundated the committee. Buried in North's testimony was his claim that he thought he was proceeding with the president's knowledge and approval. Only after North had been in the spotlight for a week and had gained widespread public support did members of the committee begin to challenge his statements. By then the Iran-Contra debate had shifted to whether North was a hero or a scoundrel and away from Reagan's responsibility for overseeing his conduct.[56]

John Poindexter, former national security adviser and North's superior, followed him before the committee and repeatedly declared himself unable to remember details about the Iran-Contra affair. He answered 184 questions with some variation of "I don't remember," a striking mental lapse for someone who had graduated first in his class from the U.S. Naval Academy, obtained a Ph.D. in nuclear physics, and received repeated commendations for attention to detail and excellent recall. His alleged memory lapses strained the committee's credulity, yet they accepted his claim that he had made "a very deliberate decision not to ask the President" about diversion of funds to the Contras in order to insulate him "and provide some future deniability for the President if it ever leaked out." Though Poindexter's account sometimes clashed with North's, in the end neither of them produced what the committee considered a "smoking gun" to document Reagan's knowledge or endorsement of their activities.[57]

The next witness was Secretary of State George Schultz, who testified that he had opposed the Iranian arms deal since he first heard of it from Poindexter in December 1985. On multiple occasions Schultz had spoken against any arms-for-hostages agreement in meetings with the president, Poindexter, and others. As the secretary of state presented his story, it became evident that each of these meetings took place within a day or two after Reagan had signed findings allowing the arms transfers to proceed. Reagan's willingness to keep Schultz in the dark raised questions in the minds of at least some committee members about the veracity of the president's other denials of involvement in the affair.[58] The testimony of Defense Secretary Weinberger, who followed Schultz, confirmed the picture of senior cabinet officers being ignored by a president stubbornly committed to proceeding with something they advised against doing.[59] With the hearings drawing to a close, the Schultz and Weinberger accounts strengthened the circumstantial case against Reagan but did not produce irrefutable evidence of the willful presidential misdeed that even the most critical committee members believed was necessary to recommend impeachment.

After the hearings concluded, the bulk of the select committee drew a harsh assessment of Reagan's conduct. In part, the committee declared:

> The ultimate responsibility for the events in the Iran-Contra Affair must rest with the President. If the President did not know what his National Security

Advisers were doing, he should have. It is his responsibility to communicate unambiguously to his subordinates that they must keep him advised of important actions they take for the Administration. The Constitution requires the President to "take care that the laws be faithfully executed." This charge encompasses a responsibility to leave the members of his Administration in no doubt that the rule of law governs.[60]

The report went on to conclude:

In modern government, with its hundreds of thousands of employees, a President obviously cannot personally supervise the acts of all who act in his name. But if the "take care" clause has any vitality, it invests in a President the responsibility for cultivating a respect for the Constitution and the law by his staff and closest associates. When the President's National Security Adviser, who had daily contact with the President, can assume that he is carrying out the President's wishes and policy in authorizing the diversion; when NSC staff members believe that the destruction of official documents is appropriate and the deception of Congress is proper; and when laws like the Boland Amendment can be treated as if they do not exist, then clearly there has been a failure in the leadership and supervision that the "take care" clause contemplated.[61]

It is hard to imagine a more severe condemnation of the president absent a direct call for his impeachment. Nevertheless, those who approved the report, all the committee's Democrats and three of its five Republican senators, were loath to take that additional step. Inouye's concern to avoid institutionally weakening the presidency and Hamilton's reluctance to proceed without absolutely indisputable evidence of active involvement in illegal activity weighed on their colleagues. Despite their comments about presidential responsibility to take care that the laws were faithfully executed, they were unwilling to propose Reagan's impeachment on the basis of failures in that respect. Some members of the majority may have been cowed by Reagan's perceived popularity or intimidated by public enthusiasm for Oliver North. Others did not regard Reagan's own conduct as having crossed constitutional bounds. In any case, the majority report settled for charging a failure to carry out a constitutional responsibility but did not follow through with any mention of impeachment as a censure of that behavior.

Significantly, the committee majority believed that impeachment was too severe a punishment for the offense committed. "A foreign-policy mistake did not demand a political beheading," Maine senators George Mitchell, a Democrat, and William Cohen, a Republican, jointly declared subsequently. "Although the American people will not tolerate a president's flouting the law, neither will they accept a punishment greater than the perceived transgression."[62] While they spoke of what the public would accept, they were no doubt reflecting the long-standing congressional inclination to defer to the president in foreign affairs. They seemed to be suggesting their own doubts about mounting a case against Reagan. They declined to characterize Reagan's offenses as calamitous and the president as constitutionally responsible even if not operationally involved.[63] The editorial staff of the *New York Times* found their position too forgiving: "These were reasonable considerations. But they argued for care, not abdication."[64]

Arthur Liman, the Senate committee counsel, later explained the committee's decision to forego any suggestion that impeachment was warranted: "Even if you concluded that the President was involved in the diversion, an impeachment process had a huge price in a nuclear age at a time that Mr. Reagan was seeking negotiations with the Soviet Union. We were mindful that this country would have been paralyzed." Liman's caution stands in sharp contrast to that of Kenneth W. Starr, an independent counsel investigating presidential conduct a decade later. Starr claimed that, having found some evidence of wrongdoing, he had an obligation to present a case for impeachment for Congress to evaluate.

A minority report filed by Cheney for his House Republican colleagues William Broomfield, Henry Hyde, Jim Courter, Bill McCollum, and Michael Dewine as well as for Republican senators James McClure and Orrin Hatch further dampened the impact of the majority's critical conclusions. Throughout the hearings, Cheney, Hyde, and Hatch in particular had defended the Enterprise as justified and had criticized Congress for having sent mixed signals with shifting positions on Contra aid. Given their overall political conservatism, their vigorous defense of presidential autonomy in foreign affairs was noteworthy. The minority report acknowledged that Reagan and his staff had made mistakes:

> The bottom line, however, is that the mistakes of the Iran-Contra Affair were just that—mistakes in judgment, and nothing more. There was no constitutional crisis, no systematic disrespect for "the rule of law," no grand conspiracy, and no Administration-wide dishonesty or coverup. In fact, the evidence will not support any of the more hysterical conclusions the Committees' Report tries to reach.[65]

The minority report accused the majority of seeking improperly to aggrandize congressional power in foreign policy, an adroit diversion of attention from the most significant assertion of executive independence in the conduct of foreign affairs since the height of the Nixon administration. Cheney and his colleagues went on to assert, "The Administration decided to work within the letter of the law covertly, instead of forcing a public and principled confrontation that would have been healthier in the long run." The minority dismissed the Boland Amendments and the reporting requirements of the Arms Export Control Act of 1976 as either unconstitutional or of no consequence. Selectively employing evidence that had been brought to light, Cheney's report accused the majority of selectively employing evidence that had been brought to light. The minority report labeled the Democratic majority as excessively partisan while itself taking a stridently partisan position. Perhaps the starkest contrast between the two reports was represented by their determination as to what could be said about Reagan's claim to have had no knowledge of the diversion: The majority report concluded that the lack of documentation meant the claim could not be proven, while the minority report concluded that the same lack of documentation meant it could not be *dis*proven. The minority report, however shaky its logic, was, at least for the moment, an effective political rebuttal. Much later, when more evidence surfaced to suggest that Reagan was directly accountable for the misdeeds of Iran-Contra, the possibility of impeachment had long evaporated.

The lingering memory of Watergate in many ways contributed to the determination as to whether the Iran-Contra affair justified another impeachment. The decision was shaped by the failure to find a "smoking gun" tying Reagan to the illegalities committed together with the administration's evident rejection of stonewalling by its prompt, if selective, admissions of improprieties once events abroad exposed their existence. An iconic Watergate figure reinforced the judgment not to hold Reagan accountable. In September 1987 *Washington Post* reporter Bob Woodward published the results of his three-year investigation of CIA director William Casey. *Veil: The Secret Wars of the CIA, 1981–1987,* focused attention on the now-deceased agency head's exceptional power. Woodward's characterization of Casey as an independent operator placed him at the center of the administration's clandestine activities rather than pointing to Reagan's ultimate responsibility for constitutional conduct of executive branch activities. *Veil,* a best seller and Book of the Month Club main selection, strengthened perceptions that subordinates rather than the president bore responsibility for Iran-Contra. Woodward, together with Carl Bernstein, had traced Watergate to Nixon's doorstep, but he was not now making a similar connection. As the *New York Times* book reviewer concluded, despite his failure to reveal his sources other than the problematic Casey himself, Woodward's past record gave his new account extraordinary credibility.[66]

By the time the congressional Iran-Contra report was released on November 18, 1987, intervening events had distracted the American public, though lingering doubts about Reagan remained evident. Three major developments in the autumn of 1987 showed, each in a different way, how the Iran-Contra affair had diminished Reagan's standing even though he had escaped impeachment. A Supreme Court nomination, a stock market plunge, and a turn in U.S. relations with the Soviet Union evoked public responses much different from what might have been the case without Iran-Contra.

Five weeks after the Iran-Contra hearings concluded, the same Senate caucus room where half the sessions had been held became the scene of a hearing on the nomination of Robert Bork to a seat on the Supreme Court. When nominated by Reagan on July 1 to replace Justice Lewis Powell, who was retiring, Bork had spent five years as a judge on the U.S. Circuit Court of Appeals for the District of Columbia, often regarded as the second-most-important federal court because it hears so many cases involving the federal government. But Bork remained best known to the public as the Justice Department solicitor general who had carried out Nixon's order to fire Archibald Cox in the 1973 Saturday Night Massacre after Attorney General Elliot Richardson and Associate Attorney General William Ruckelshaus had refused to do so and resigned. Bork's image as a willing tool of an unscrupulous president may have been unfair. He had, after all, kept the Justice Department and the independent counsel's office functioning at a time when both could have easily fallen apart. Nevertheless, at a time when the Iran-Contra affair had once again raised the prospect of an out-of-control president possibly committing impeachable offenses, the thought of adding someone to the Supreme Court who had abetted Nixon stoked resistance to the nomination. Bork wounded himself with his long list of publications and statements decrying Court decisions on civil rights, which most Americans regarded as advances for minorities and women. He also projected an aura of intellectual arrogance during his confirmation hearings that put off many observers. While staunch conservatives complained that opponents of his confirmation treated him unfairly, his place in the public memory of Watergate long predated the hearings and raised doubts about his suitability for the Court. As it became obvious that his nomination would fail, Bork considered withdrawing. He declined to do so, however, after his son urged him to show the same fortitude he had displayed during the Saturday Night Massacre. The Senate then rejected his nomination 58–42 on October 23.[67] The first defeat of a Supreme Court nomination since the Haynsworth-Carswell fiasco of Nixon's first term showed how much the Iran-Contra affair had diminished regard for Reagan's judgment and respect for his political strength.

On October 19, only days before the Bork nomination crashed, the U.S. stock market did likewise. An improving economy had been an important element in Reagan's popularity for several years. In a single day, however, the Dow Jones average fell by 508 points, or over 22 percent of its value at the time. The plunge in stock prices was the largest one-day drop since the Great Depression. Prompt action by the Federal Reserve Bank to reduce interest rates soon stabilized the market, but gone was the sense that, whatever else, Reagan could be counted on to maintain a healthy environment for business investment. His image as an economic savior, a view that had helped preserve his public standing in the face of Iran-Contra, evaporated overnight.

Reagan's fortunes turned at the end of the month. On October 30, 1987, the

Soviet foreign minister, Eduard Shevardnadze, announced on a visit to Washington that Premier Mikhail Gorbachev would come in December so that he and Reagan could sign a treaty for verifiable reduction of intermediate-range nuclear weapons. Disarmament negotiations between the two leaders had begun in 1985 but had seemed to be completely stalled following their meeting in Reykjavik, Iceland, a week after Eugene Hasenfus had been shot down in Nicaragua. The Iran-Contra revelations served to take the spotlight away from U.S.-Soviet relations, but in February, while the Tower Commission was conducting its examination of the embattled White House, renewed negotiations began to move steadily forward. Both sides made substantial concessions in the course of reaching an agreement. Reagan in particular was notably less belligerent than he had been at any time since entering office. Gorbachev's interest in reducing the cost of the arms race to the Soviet Union was matched by Reagan's desire to recapture the popular approval he had lost as a result of Iran-Contra scandals. The Intermediate-Range Nuclear Forces (INF) treaty had great symbolic value in reducing international friction, even though it involved only about 4 percent of the aggregate nuclear strength of the two nations. The public enthusiasm for the accord displayed by the friendly crowds that greeted Gorbachev everywhere he went in Washington manifested the sense of relief that tensions between the two superpowers were ebbing. The Iran-Contra episode had served as a strong reminder of how independent and unrestrained the president had become in conducting foreign affairs. The INF treaty offered some reassurance that a chastened Reagan would not now propel the United States into a confrontation with the Soviet Union.

After the release of the joint congressional committee's Iran-Contra report, Reagan was able to finish his presidential term and retire without any further threat of impeachment. He told himself that the majority report was a partisan attack "aimed at discrediting me," and he disregarded the support the report had drawn from Republicans. Instead, Reagan read Cheney's minority report as a Republican repudiation of the majority giving him "a clean bill of health."[68] Congress and the country refused to dwell further on his responsibility for Iran-Contra absent a convincing argument of direct involvement. Instead, Reagan's subordinates were treated as having acted independently. Still, confidence in Reagan's leadership had been sorely shaken, and he would never recover the level of public support he had enjoyed prior to the initial Iran-Contra revelations. However, by the time Independent Counsel Walsh completed proceedings against North and others whom he was able to indict, gained access to evidence long denied him, and submitted a report suggesting that Reagan's impeachment indeed merited consideration, the time for congressional action had long since passed.

Not until well after Reagan had left office did additional information regarding Iran-Contra emerge. Complaints arose about the length and cost of the methodical Walsh investigation. Nevertheless, the experienced prosecutor, convinced that a case existed that he was obligated to pursue, was only able to move ahead by pursuing lower-level defendants, slowly assembling evidence about their supervisors, and continuing to search for missing documents thought likely to exist. Eventually, as long-concealed evidence surfaced, the persistent independent counsel prosecuted fourteen individuals, won eleven guilty pleas or jury verdicts, and built a compelling picture of what had happened.[69]

In Robert McFarlane's guilty plea and in the trials of Oliver North and John Poindexter, a clearer picture emerged of individuals seeking to carry out their president's wishes. North's and Poindexter's convictions, however, even though eventually overturned on appeal for procedural reasons, demonstrated that juries exposed to an elaborate presentation of substantive evidence placed responsibility for misdeeds very close to the president. After a four-month trial in 1989, a District of Columbia jury found North guilty of three charges involving personal conduct (preparing false chronologies to disguise how early the Iran-Contra affair had begun, destroying evidence, and accepting illegal gratuities) but acquitted him on nine other counts in which the defense had contended that North believed that in deceiving Congress and other actions he was merely carrying out the president's wishes.[70]

The following year Poindexter defended himself at his trial by asserting that Reagan had authorized his actions and that neither thought they were violating the law. Reagan himself testified in his former national security adviser's behalf. In a lengthy videotaped deposition, Reagan insisted that he told aides, "We don't break the law." He then returned to his original story of not trading arms for hostages or knowing that arms-sales profits went to the Contras, but he claimed over 120 times that he did not remember aspects of the Iran-Contra episode.[71] Whether or not he was merely reflecting a lack of original engagement or was displaying signs of his later-diagnosed Alzheimer's disease, the former president did his aide no good. Poindexter was found guilty of five counts of false testimony to Congress.[72]

Walsh and his staff eventually located evidence that Secretary of State Schultz and Defense Secretary Weinberger had not been fully forthcoming about their knowledge of Iranian arms sales or their possession of evidence about what had occurred. Weinberger in particular had concealed voluminous private notes of White House meetings. These notes, first requested in 1987, were finally found by a Walsh associate in November 1991 hidden among Weinberger family papers in the Library of Congress. The notes showed that the defense secretary, although he disagreed with the policy, had definitely known of Reagan's explicit advanced approval of the November 1985 arms shipment to Iran. Weinberger had specifically denied such knowledge to the Tower Commission, the Congress, and the independent counsel. The notes also revealed Weinberger's subsequent involvement in the ongoing arms transfers as well as efforts to protect the president after the November 1986 revelations. The discoveries from the Weinberger notes focused new attention on the innermost circle of the Reagan administration, including both President Reagan and Vice President Bush.[73]

In June 1992 Walsh, concluding that Weinberger had engaged in a corrupt cover-up, obtained his indictment for obstructing Congress's investigations by withholding his notes. A federal judge, Thomas F. Hogan, dismissed the obstruction charge as imprecise on September 27. Walsh recast and refiled the charge on Friday, October 30, four days before the presidential election. The revised indictment cited evidence from Weinberger's notes that George H. W. Bush had been a knowing participant in critical Iran-Contra decisions and that at a January 7, 1986, meeting he had favored an arms sale to Iran in return for hostages, a sale that Schultz and Weinberger had opposed.[74]

As Walsh and his staff prepared to try Weinberger, Bush was losing his race for reelection to the presidency. Revelation of his dissembling about Iran-Contra did him no good. After the results were in, Bush blamed the charging of Weinberger as a primary cause of his defeat at the polls. The outgoing president had reason to worry that the upcoming trial of Weinberger would further expose the fact that Bush had not been "out of the loop," as he had repeatedly claimed, but rather had been much involved in the Iran-Contra affair. He had dictated more than two hundred pages of notes about meetings he had attended regarding Iran-Contra, put them in his office safe, and declined to disclose their existence when Walsh in 1987 requested any records he might have bearing on Iran-Contra. The notes, which at the very least cast doubt on Bush's public statements regarding Iran-Contra, came to the attention of his White House counsel, C. Boyden Gray, two months before the 1992 election but were not surrendered to Walsh until December 11, 1992.[75]

Late on the afternoon of Christmas Eve 1992, a day when traditionally little notice is paid to news from Washington, the White House issued a press release announcing that President Bush had granted pardons to Weinberger as well as to Robert McFarlane, Elliot Abrams, and others already convicted of Iran-Contra offenses. Less than a month before he was to leave office, Bush thus assured that no trial would be held at which evidence of his own conduct or misrepresentations would be set forth. Asserting that the Iran-Contra affair had already been exhaustively investigated, Bush made certain that it never would be.[76] "In effect," the *New York Times* editorialized, Bush "pardoned himself."[77]

Observers quickly distinguished Bush's actions from Gerald Ford's pardon of Richard Nixon. The Ford pardon, however questionable, had shown mercy to a thoroughly disgraced ex-president who, though not yet indicted, had had his misdeeds fully exposed. Furthermore, it preceded Ford's campaign for the presidency and was therefore subject to assessment by the voters. Bush, by contrast, waited to act until after what he knew would be the last electoral judgment he would ever face. By his pardons the lame-duck president prevented a trial from proceeding that might have revealed his own culpability for concealing evidence of the Iran-Contra affair. Neither Reagan nor even Nixon had pardoned his indicted associates, much less himself. Bush, with his pardons, had foreclosed further investigation of what he himself had done. The price he paid was to leave both his vice presidency and his presidency permanently under a cloud of suspicion.[78]

The Bush pardons provoked an immediate response. President-elect Bill Clinton told a press conference, "I am concerned about any action which sends a signal that if you work for the government, you are above the law, or that not telling the truth to Congress under oath is somehow less serious than not telling the truth to some other body under oath."[79] Similar language poured forth from an angry and frustrated Lawrence Walsh. The pardon, he said, "demonstrates that powerful people with powerful allies can commit serious crimes in high office—deliberately abusing the public trust—without consequence." Underscoring the significance of what Bush had chosen to forgive, Walsh declared, "Weinberger's early and deliberate decision to conceal and withhold extensive contemporaneous notes of the Iran-Contra matter radically altered the official investigation and possibly frustrated timely impeachment proceedings against President Reagan and other officials."[80] Walsh contemptuously described the pardons to a television interviewer as "the last card in the cover-up" and later compared them to Nixon's attempt to shut down the Watergate investigation with the Saturday Night Massacre.[81] Anthony Lewis of the *New York Times* wrote that Bush's action was "the more troubling because the underlying governmental wrongdoing, Iran-contra, was so serious. It was a calculated assault on the constitutional balance of power, far worse than Watergate's cover-up of a political burglary."[82]

Independent Counsel Walsh's final report underscored the same message. The report, filed on August 4, 1993, was finally made public January 18, 1994, following six months of efforts by attorneys for Reagan, North, and Meese to suppress it.[83] The information he eventually managed to pry out of the uncooperative Bush administration proved, Walsh said, Reagan's and Bush's direct involvement in illegal behavior and the subsequent cover-up thereof. McFarlane, North, and Poindexter had served as scapegoats for their cabinet superiors and, above all, for Reagan. Walsh once again implied that he would have been justified in bringing before Congress a case for the president's impeachment. "The Iran/contra affair," he concluded, "was not an aberrational scheme carried out by a 'cabal of zealots' on the National Security Council staff, as the congressional Select Committees concluded in their majority report. Instead, it was the product of two foreign policy directives by President Reagan which skirted the law and which were executed by the NSC staff with the knowledge and support of high officials in the CIA, State and Defense departments."[84]

Walsh, in the end, was not alone. Various journalists and politicians concluded, in retrospect, that Reagan had deserved impeachment. *Washington Post* columnist

Edwin Yoder neatly summed up their views as well in reflecting on why impeachment did not prevail. "Reagan," Yoder wrote, "even if complicit in the affair, was seen as too close to important arms agreements with the Soviet Union; or too old and confused or too near the end of his term; or too popular with the American public to be impeached." But the columnist hastened to point out, however, that such judgments "took a thoroughly mistaken view of the constitutional doctrine of impeachment." Yoder explained why he had drawn such a conclusion:

> Congress seems, in fact, to have silently amended the Constitution to suit its comfort and political convenience. It is almost universally believed on Capitol Hill that without a strong probability that the president had committed a criminal act, an "act of commission," . . . impeachment proceedings would be unwarranted. Before impeaching a president, in other words, you must be satisfied that he is likely to be what Richard Nixon claimed not to be, a "crook."[85]

Yoder considered the congressional judgment politically expedient and possibly wise, but he emphasized that it was not the law of the land. The framers of the Constitution had stipulated impeachment for gross neglect or dereliction of duty. Furthermore, he wrote:

> Negligence and maladministration of the most serious sort were the least of Reagan's derelictions in the Iran-contra affair, assuming he had no knowledge of, or hand in, the "diversion." The Tower Commission politely referred to these derelictions as the president's "management style," but the defects were worse than stylistic. Reagan, by indifference or ignorance, allowed a conspiracy to operate under his nose, usurping the prerogatives of foreign policy. This would be enough to sustain impeachment under any "original intent" reading of that power.
>
> Politicians, however, are practical. Their desire to spare Reagan and the nation the distraction of an impeachment proceeding late in the president's term was by some lights defensible. As Arthur Liman, the chief counsel of the Senate committee, has said, an impeachment process in the nuclear age "has a huge price."
>
> But the continuing silent dilution of the impeachment power, restricting its reach to acts only of gross criminality, carries a price too. Congress must resort more and more to petty legalism to try to enforce its will in disputes with the president. And unless the president is imagined to be a blatant lawbreaker, caught with a "smoking gun" in his hand, he becomes immune to any real standard of constitutional accountability.[86]

Linda Greenhouse, the *New York Times* Washington correspondent who focused on the Supreme Court, underscored what Yoder was suggesting. "The

Iran-contra affair was, at its core, an offense against the political system," she reflected, and "the question that remains is whether the criminal justice system is the best vehicle for arriving at what was and what remains the missing ingredient in the whole six-year-long saga: political accountability." She reminded readers that impeachment was designed to serve as a judgment on the responsible discharge of the duties of high office. It properly encompassed a political determination as to whether official conduct was constitutionally allowable. To limit prosecutions to provable criminal offenses was to risk focusing on comparatively trivial matters and overlook impeachment's separate and more vital purpose of placing bounds on the noncriminal behavior of the nation's leaders. Had Reagan been impeached, Greenhouse concluded, he might not have been convicted and removed, "but the process itself might at least have placed a political judgment on the political offenses carried out in his name. Instead, from whatever combination of institutional exhaustion, timidity, failure of will or lack of evidence, Congress allowed the moment to pass."[87]

Ronald Reagan was able to ride off into the sunset without any impeachment dogs barking behind him. So, too, was his faithful sidekick, George H. W. Bush. In part as a result of their success and that of those around them in shaping the inquiry into their affairs, deflecting requests for information, and stalling on compliance with obligations to deliver documents they possessed, the moment passed when impeachment might have been used to set stricter limits to presidential power in foreign affairs. Congress gave priority to a concern that it not weaken the presidency through the spectacle of impeachment.

In excusing Reagan of responsibility for what occurred while he was president, Congress took a narrow view of the impeachment power granted by the framers of the Constitution. In doing so, Congress ignored the consequences of tolerating unlawful executive conduct. As a result, future presidents were encouraged to believe that they would not face impeachment for ignoring congressional foreign policy strictures. In effect, the outcome of the Iran-Contra affair gave renewed sanction to the imperial presidency that the removal of Nixon had seemed to check over a decade earlier. The failure of the impeachment dog to bark in the 1980s strengthened the imperial presidency and weakened what had been the original intent of the Constitution's framers regarding the balance of legislative and executive powers.

10

Impeachment as Inexorable:
The Cases of Harry Claiborne and Walter Nixon

In a series of little-publicized and widely overlooked cases involving alleged misbehavior by federal judges, the United States Congress grew increasingly familiar with the process of impeachment during the 1980s. The House Judiciary Committee became comfortable with confirming federal court judgments on judicial misconduct. Furthermore, it built a staff familiar with and skilled at conducting impeachment proceedings. The House of Representatives, in turn, became accustomed to relying on the Judiciary Committee's recommendations to adopt articles of impeachment. Just as important, in 1986 the Senate, for the first time since the 1930s, gained experience in conducting an impeachment trial. The upper body then reinforced its newly acquired knowledge in the course of two more trials in 1989. In the process, the Senate embraced and gained Supreme Court approval for methods to avoid legislative paralysis while carrying out a trial. Critics complained that the Senate deprived defendants of the chance to present their entire case to the full body. Nevertheless, the procedures gained Senate acceptance and facilitated convictions.

Collectively, the judicial impeachments of the 1980s demonstrated that impeachment was preeminently a political process rather than a conventional judicial proceeding. The driving force behind these impeachments proved to be the concern of legislators to bolster public confidence in government. Doubts about overreaching prosecution or standards of proof of guilt beyond reasonable doubt that normally serve to protect individuals in the American justice system failed utterly to derail these impeachments and removals from the bench. Close examination of the cases suggests that they went forward to avoid political embarrassment and, above all, to safeguard public faith in government. Judgments were not sharply partisan, but at the same time they could not be characterized as judicial in terms of placing priority on protection of the rights of the accused. These impeachments were political in the sense that above all else they represented the will of a congressional majority as to the best interests of government.

Learning to carry out impeachments made the prospect of dealing with such matters much less daunting for Congress than had earlier been the case. This was true for the House, which was required to take initial action. The House

Judiciary Committee had dealt with each of the cases that had arisen in the 1960s and 1970s, but none of those had reached the floor and required action by the full membership. Representatives who had previously been able to leave such issues in the hands of the less than 10 percent of the body who served on the Judiciary Committee now had to address impeachment motions and determine how to cast their votes. In customary House fashion, they almost always followed the lead of the committee they regarded as most knowledgeable. Nevertheless, every sitting member gained at least some experience with an unfamiliar constitutional undertaking.

The acquisition of impeachment experience was even more transforming for the membership of the Senate. The trials of three federal judges, Harry E. Claiborne of Nevada in 1986 and Walter L. Nixon, Jr., of Mississippi and Alcee L. Hastings of Florida in 1989, were the first carried out by the Senate since the trial of Halsted Ritter a half century earlier in 1936. By means of their participation in this trio of judicial trials, senators became accustomed to conducting a hitherto completely unfamiliar proceeding. The senior house found itself fully integrated into a political culture increasingly conversant with impeachment.

The surge of judicial impeachment cases coming before the Congress in the 1980s and 1990s can be attributed, at least in part, to three circumstances: First, the number of federal judges more than doubled from 313 district and appellate judges in 1960 to 648 in 1980 (and would more than double again to 1,370 by 2000). The enlargement of the federal judiciary increased the likelihood that a few bad apples would get into the barrel or at least that more occasions would arise to question the quality of the harvest. The traditional mechanism for picking and quality-checking nominees for the bench was hard-pressed to accommodate the vastly larger number of appointees undergoing confirmation. Second, the adoption of the Judicial Councils Reform and Judicial Conduct and Disability Act of 1980 simplified and encouraged the bringing of cases once a complaint was made about a judge's conduct. Third, the federal judges who faced impeachment in the 1980s and 1990s themselves possessed increased knowledge and sophistication. The two discussed in this chapter, Claiborne and Nixon, approached impeachment with the view that acquittal could cast doubt on and mitigate the effects of a felony conviction. Hastings, discussed in the next chapter, was in many ways anomalous. Acquitted in a criminal trial but unable to avoid conviction and removal from office, he raised enough doubts about the process to resurrect his political career and win election to Congress.

At the same time, the cases eventually resolved by Congress involved troubling elements. All featured aggressive prosecutions based on allegations by informants of questionable probity with something to gain from persuading the Justice Department to go after the judges. Each originated with criminal proceedings in which the principle offenses initially charged failed to be proven. Each prosecution continued, often with subsidiary, if still significant, allegations of wrongdoing. It may be coincidental that all the judges impeached and removed were appointed by Democratic presidents and prosecuted by a Republican-led federal Justice Department, but in light of the aggressive prosecutions, partisanship cannot be ruled out altogether. Each of the three impeachments gained bipartisan congressional support, but that may reflect rising national suspicion of public officials and endorsement of impeachment more than the merits of the individual cases. Some of the questions surrounding the judicial impeachments of the 1980s defy definitive resolution, but their very existence suggests the need to look at them carefully.

Repeated judicial impeachments and trials at least demystified matters of process for Congress. Thereafter, two judicial resignations on the cusp of impeachment in the early 1990s reinforced the sense that the Constitution provided a workable device for cleansing government of officials who had failed to discharge properly their civic responsibilities and had become public embarrassments. Perhaps more so than with higher-profile and nationally paralyzing presidential cases, judicial impeachments served to humanize the constitutional process for removing unfit federal officials before the expiration of their terms. In various ways, therefore, the multiple judicial incidents brought the age of impeachment to full flower.

Harry E. Claiborne came from the American city synonymous with taking a chance, Las Vegas, Nevada. His encounter with impeachment fully lived up to his hometown's image as a place for sex, shady activities, and, above all, risk taking. He made a high-stakes wager against the impeachment process being carried through to completion. The bet, unfortunately for him, did not pay off, costing him both his reputation and his federal pension. The odds may have favored him, judging from the historical precedents. However, each impeachment, like every flip of a coin, is a unique event, and he lost his gamble. At the moment, Lady Luck seemed to be directing her smiles toward the White House and not the bench in the game of impeachment. Judge Claiborne was left with a weak hand that he played badly.

A native of Arkansas and a graduate of a Tennessee law school, Claiborne served in the Air Force during World War II, which brought him to Nevada. After two years working as a policeman while establishing residence and passing the bar, three years acting as an assistant district attorney and a single term in the state assembly, he built a lucrative criminal defense practice in Las Vegas. Among his clients were Joseph and Sally Conforte, the owners of the Mustang Ranch, Nevada's first legal brothel. In 1978, on the recommendation of both of Nevada's U.S. senators, Jimmy Carter named the sixty-one-year-old Claiborne to the federal district bench. The appointment was cleared by the Justice Department after the usual FBI background investigation, and the Senate promptly confirmed him.[1]

Within two years federal prosecutors in Las Vegas brought the results of an FBI investigation of Judge Claiborne before a grand jury. The judge would later claim that this happened because Nevada federal prosecutors and FBI officials were unhappy with several of his rulings. He had dismissed some of their cases and repeatedly thwarted their applications for wiretaps based on claims by unnamed sources. Moreover, Judge Claiborne had been vocally scornful of the federal strike force on organized crime, the investigators and prosecutors concentrating their efforts on his jurisdiction, publicly calling them "rotten bastards who think everybody in Nevada is a crook."[2] In any case, prosecutors alleged to the grand jury that Claiborne, while a practicing attorney, had hired a private investigator to conduct illegal wiretaps. The grand jury declined to indict Claiborne, and the investigator involved in the case was later found not guilty of the charges brought against him.

Undaunted, prosecutors twice came back to other grand juries with claims that Judge Claiborne had taken bribes. These allegations had been made by brothel operator Joe Conforte on the eve of his flight to avoid a likely tax evasion sentence of five years in jail and a $19.5 million fine. The two grand juries again refused to indict Claiborne, perhaps because of the questionable credibility of his accuser. The notorious Conforte remained a fugitive, living in Brazil. Frustrated again, the prosecutors finally presented a case alleging that in addition to receiving bribes Claiborne had evaded income taxes. Joe Conforte finally agreed to return from South America to testify against Claiborne in exchange for a sentence reduced to fifteen months in jail and a $7.3 million fine. After Conforte's December 1983 testimony, a fourth grand jury to hear charges against the judge indicted him the same day on counts of bribe taking, obstruction of justice, and tax evasion.

Judge Claiborne immediately tried the same argument that had failed Spiro Agnew in the House and Otto Kerner in the U.S. Court of Appeals for the Seventh Circuit. He filed a motion in January 1984 to quash the indictment against him on the grounds that the Constitution allowed only impeachment and not criminal indictment of a sitting judge. The trial court promptly denied the motion as frivolous. A three-judge panel of the U.S. Court of Appeals for the Ninth Circuit nevertheless heard Claiborne's appeal of the initial ruling. The panel concluded that the Constitution did not specifically preclude prosecution and indeed made no exceptions for judges in calling upon the executive branch to enforce the laws. The Ninth Circuit decision denied that indictment was preemptive impeachment or, in what would later prove crucial, that criminal conviction amounted to removal from office. The Supreme Court refused to grant a further appeal, allowing Claiborne's trial to move forward.

Since none of the judges from his own circuit wished to conduct Claiborne's trial, a senior federal district judge from Norfolk, Virginia, Walter E. Hoffman, was assigned to hear the case. Hoffman had, coincidentally, presided in a Baltimore courtroom eleven years earlier when Agnew pled nolo contendere and resigned to avoid impeachment. Nearly a month of contentious testimony pitted Conforte's claims of bribing Claiborne against the accused judge's refutation of multiple details of the story. Hoffman declared a mistrial in April 1984 after a jury declared itself hopelessly deadlocked over the case. The jury had found itself unable to discern from Claiborne and Conforte's contrasting testimony who was telling the truth.

At the start of a second trial before Judge Hoffman in late July, the prosecutors made clear their determination to convict Claiborne of something even if it had little to do with the charges originally leveled against him. They moved to drop all the charges against Claiborne except two counts of making false statements on his 1979 and 1980 income tax returns, the accusations to which the judge was most vulnerable. The tax evasion charges finally produced a guilty verdict for the dogged prosecutors. The court heard testimony that during and after his transition from private practice to the bench, the judge had failed to report $108,000 of income in attorney fees, had repeatedly cashed large checks at casinos making the funds untraceable, had inexplicably switched from the accountant who had handled his affairs for thirty years to an unlicensed tax preparer of questionable competence, and could not produce documents to substantiate various dubious claims. His 1979 and 1980 tax returns appeared not only to have underreported income in attorney fees but also to have made questionable capital gain claims regarding the sale of his law practice and a home. Claiborne had filed these returns at a time when he was financially strapped because his income as a judge was so much less than what he had earned as a private attorney. On August 10, 1984, a jury, after brief deliberations, found him guilty on both tax evasion counts.[3]

Assessed a $10,000 fine and sentenced to a two-year prison term, Claiborne told the court of his remorse at having been sloppy in his personal affairs and embarrassing the judiciary. He pointed out, however, that he had not been afforded the opportunity normally given taxpayers for an IRS audit hearing and a chance to correct mistakes in his returns. He denied he was guilty of a crime and alleged a pattern of government harassment.

Judge Claiborne obtained no relief when he appealed his conviction to the Ninth Circuit. His claims of prosecutorial error, perjury by Conforte, and the unconstitutionality of imprisonment without impeachment were all rejected. Still maintaining that he had been selectively and unfairly prosecuted and had yet to receive a fair hearing, Claiborne entered the federal minimum-security prison at Maxwell Air Force Base in Alabama on May 16, 1986. The first sitting federal judge ever incarcerated, he refused to resign. As a consequence, he continued to draw his $78,700 federal salary, as he had since ceasing to handle cases upon his indictment in 1983. National newspapers that had not covered his trial now reported his incarceration and noted that, barring impeachment, he would be eligible to return to the bench following his release from prison and would not long thereafter be eligible to retire at full pay. The image of a judge convicted of a crime yet drawing his salary reverberated powerfully in the press, while his extraordinary prosecution had little political resonance.[4]

Claiborne calculated that impeachment proceedings would finally give him the proper hearing that he believed he had been denied. He declared that he would welcome an impeachment trial and a chance to tell "my side of the story."[5] His refusal to resign upon entering prison soon provoked a member of the House, Republican James Sensenbrenner of Wisconsin, to threaten to initiate impeachment proceedings unless a resignation was forthcoming by June 4.[6] The day before Sensenbrenner's deadline, the chairman of the House Judiciary Committee, Peter Rodino, reluctantly introduced an impeachment resolution himself. Although he viewed impeachment as cumbersome and time-consuming, Rodino declared, "Conviction of a federal judge is obviously a very serious matter that must be looked into in order to preserve the integrity of the federal judiciary."[7] His resolution was referred to the Subcommittee on Courts, Civil Liberties, and the Administration of Justice chaired by Robert Kastenmeier, like Rodino a veteran of the impeachment hearings for President Richard Nixon.

The House Judiciary Subcommittee disappointed Claiborne's hopes for a full reconsideration of his case. Rather, it treated his conviction as unquestionable evidence of bad behavior and the question before it as a political decision concerning the proper operation of government. The subcommittee wasted no time conducting its own preliminary investigation, instead opting for a one-day formal hearing on June 19 largely restricted to the single question of whether Claiborne's conviction and incarceration constituted behavior incompatible with the duties and responsibilities of a federal judicial officer.[8]

Chairman Kastenmeier and Representative Hamilton Fish, also a member of the Judiciary Committee during the Nixon proceedings, made clear during their opening remarks that they assumed Claiborne was guilty as charged and that they had no interest in revisiting his trial. On that basis the subcommittee special counsel, Richard Cates, John Doar's deputy during the Nixon investigation, presented a single Justice Department witness to summarize the case against Claiborne. Judge Charles Wiggins of the Ninth Circuit Court of Appeals, himself a prominent member of the House Judiciary Committee in its 1974 impeachment deliberations, told the representatives that he believed the facts of the Claiborne case had been proven at trial in a process that had afforded the defendant his full due process rights. Wiggins and his judicial colleagues had taken no action under the 1980 Judicial Councils Reform and Judicial Conduct and Disability Act because they believed it was intended merely for lawyer and litigant complaints. With a criminal conviction, Wiggins continued, the Constitution left impeachment as the only proper course of action. The Ninth Circuit's judicial council had belatedly begun preparing a recommendation to that effect, but Wiggins said that the House need not await judicial action. Wiggins urged the House to immediately exercise its sole responsibility for impeachment on the basis of the conviction in hand. Although Claiborne's attorney argued that the prosecution of his client deserved closer scrutiny, he was unable to persuade the committee to redirect its course.[9]

By the following week the subcommittee had drafted four articles of impeachment, two dealing with filing false income tax returns, the third declaring that the failure to resign following conviction and exhaustion of appeals itself represented misconduct, and the fourth asserting that Claiborne had violated his oath of office and thus brought disrepute upon the federal courts. When the subcommittee met to deliberate, Chairman Kastenmeier reiterated that the conviction represented a prima facie case for impeachment and said that, even were the conviction to be overturned, Claiborne would still be in violation of the good behavior standard for judges. Other members of the committee spoke contemptuously of Claiborne's refusal to resign following conviction, calling it arrogant and improper. None credited it as a proper device to gain a further hearing.[10]

The whole Judiciary Committee met on June 26 to consider the four articles. Kastenmeier observed that eight members of the assembled committee had participated twelve years earlier in the Nixon impeachment hearings. He proudly contrasted the rapid progress of the Claiborne case to the long-drawn-out earlier proceeding and then reiterated that Claiborne had been convicted by a jury of his peers, exhausted all available appeals, and then dishonorably refused to resign, bringing discredit upon the federal judiciary. Other committee members voiced their agreement and applauded the rapid progress toward impeachment. After some discussion of whether the fourth article was necessary, the committee voted unanimously to adopt all four articles against Judge Claiborne.[11]

The House of Representatives took up the articles impeaching Judge Claiborne four weeks later on July 22. After an hour's debate, the House voted 406–0 to send all four articles to the Senate. It then adopted the necessary procedural resolutions to notify the upper chamber officially and to appoint House managers for the impeachment presentation. The nine all-male managers would be led by Rodino and Kastenmeier and would include several who had been elected since Nixon's resignation. Notable among them was Republican Henry Hyde of Illinois, who would eventually rise to the committee's chairmanship and then take a much more prominent role in a later impeachment. The next day the managers walked through the Capitol from the House to the Senate to deliver the formal notice of Judge Claiborne's impeachment.[12]

Senators had long expressed concern that if they were called on to conduct an impeachment trial, their other work on the floor and in committees, not to mention away from Washington, would grind to a halt. Given the Senate's responsibilities to confirm executive and judicial appointments as well as to legislate, a prolonged impeachment trial that required the full attention of all the members could paralyze much of the federal government. Because of such concerns when preparing for Ritter's trial in 1936, the Senate had adopted a standing rule, Rule XI, allowing a committee to act for the full Senate in conducting an impeachment inquiry, taking testimony, and preparing a record on which the Senate could act. Rule XI would allow most of the work of the Senate to go forward with minimal disruption. Ironically, the committee provision was not used in the Ritter case, but it was seized upon as a means of dealing expeditiously with Judge Claiborne.[13]

Following the guidelines of Rule XI, twelve senators, six Democrats and six Republicans, were appointed by the body's majority and minority leaders to conduct the Claiborne hearing. They first met on August 15 to organize their work. Republican Charles Mathias of Maryland was chosen as chairman of the special committee, and Democrat Paul Sarbanes of Maryland was vice chairman. Notably, given the usual Senate practice of considering a single committee member a quorum for hearing testimony, the senators agreed that for the purpose of this unusual impeachment inquiry a majority of the members would be required for a quorum. Gently urged to do so by Senator Sarbanes, the only member of the committee who had served on the House Judiciary Committee during the Nixon impeachment hearings, the senators were willing to tinker with their normal practice in order to foster an image that they were according Claiborne due process.[14] The committee met again on September 10 to dismiss motions by the managers to treat Claiborne's conviction as sufficient grounds for impeachment without further examination. The committee proved equally unwilling to honor Claiborne's continuing requests that the whole history of his prosecutions from 1980 be reexamined.[15]

Substantive hearings by the Senate special committee into the impeachment of Harry Claiborne began on September 15, 1986. The hearings were held in the largest space in the oldest Senate office building, the Senate Caucus Room in the recently renamed Russell Building, where the Ervin committee had conducted the first Watergate hearings thirteen years earlier. With the nine House managers facing the twelve senators of the committee and with Claiborne and his counsel also present, the proceedings for the most part simply retraced the charges and defenses in Claiborne's second trial. During seven days of testimony, the House managers and Claiborne's defense attorney, Oscar Goodman, went over every bit of evidence that had led to the judge's conviction for willfully filing false income tax returns for 1979 and 1980, arguing over its validity at every step. The questioning began with James Wright, Claiborne's original accountant, and proceeded to examine Jerry D. Watson, his subsequent tax preparer, and virtually all the witnesses who had appeared at Claiborne's second trial. In addition Goodman brought forth testimony regarding burglaries of Wright's office, suggesting the destruction of evidence that would exonerate Claiborne.[16] Members of the committee looked closely at the claims of prosecutorial misconduct, with

Senator Orrin Hatch in particular worrying about whether prosecutors had conducted a vendetta against the judge.[17]

Claiborne himself took the stand, testifying in his own defense for most of the final two and a half days of the hearing. His assertions of innocent errors and misplaced confidence in his tax preparer did not explain major elements of the charges against him, including failure to report $88,500 of his 1980 income. Nor did the judge account for such suspicious behavior as cashing a $37,000 check in a casino and carrying it away in thousand-dollar bills. Near the end of his testimony, he asserted again that he had been the victim of selective prosecution designed to drive him from the bench, but he failed once again to explain away the irregularities in his tax returns.[18]

On October 7, 1986, the Senate began considering how to conduct its trial of Claiborne. A week earlier the Impeachment Trial Committee had made available to every senator an 1,185-page transcript of its hearings, together with an additional 2,316 pages of reproduced documents from Claiborne's August 1984 trial, his subsequent appeals, and his financial records. At the same time, Claiborne had submitted various motions to dismiss the charges, delay the proceedings, demand a full trial with witnesses before the entire Senate, and define the standard of proof required for conviction in the most legally demanding fashion.

The Senate turned down all the judge's pretrial motions. Senators, regardless of party or political persuasion, appeared comfortable with the committee arrangement and unsympathetic to Claiborne's assertion that all testimony needed to be heard by the entire body. They rejected by a 61–32 vote efforts to require witness testimony and to prevent their proceeding to judgment on the basis of the special committee's report.[19] The defense of the Rule XI committee arrangement not only suggested that senators believed the record in Claiborne's case to be sufficient to make a decision but also signaled that they were quite willing to set a time-saving precedent for future impeachment trials.

Rejection of another ploy proved equally significant to the outcome of the proceedings and to the larger issue of how impeachments would be handled in the future. Claiborne moved to set the standard for his removal from office at proof beyond a reasonable doubt, the legal standard in criminal proceedings. Representative Kastenmeier for the managers opposed the motion, pointing out that impeachment was not a criminal proceeding and that therefore a lower standard of proof should be applied. "Since we believe the fundamental purpose of an impeachment proceeding is to preserve the confidence of the people in public officials and institutions," Kastenmeier said, "we believe it proper that the House of Representatives establishes by a preponderance of the evidence that Judge Claiborne has committed an impeachable offense." He went on to say that Claiborne had already faced the highest legal standards in being judged guilty beyond reasonable doubt in his criminal trial. In an impeachment the public interest needed to be balanced against individual protections. Thus, the standard of preponderance of evidence should suffice for removing a corrupt official from office.[20] In a crucial vote at the end of the day, the Senate adopted the Kastenmeier view 75–17. Preponderance of evidence was articulated as the legal standard to justify removal of an impeached official.[21]

Claiborne launched a final flurry of motions to block the Senate from proceeding, but he found no support in federal district court, the U.S. Court of Appeals for the District of Columbia Circuit, or an ultimate plea to Chief Justice William Rehnquist. At 10:00 a.m. on October 9, the Senate met in closed session to complete its deliberations. The substance of the case on both sides had been put forth during the procedural discussions of the previous two days. Additionally, the House managers had submitted a brief asserting that Claiborne had willfully understated his income to a massive degree and thus evaded proper taxation in 1979 and 1980. The managers' judgment was severe: "[Judge Claiborne's] vigorous protestations of innocence are not worthy of belief. Indeed, the evidence reveals that Judge Claiborne's testimony has been totally self-serving, largely manufactured, and simply false."[22] Statements made by senators during the closed session and released once the proceedings were completed made evident that the managers' argument had carried the day.[23] When the Senate returned to open session after nearly five hours of discussion, members were ready for an immediate vote on the articles of impeachment.

Though impeachment had been a subject of discussion on repeated occasions during the previous two decades, the articles against Claiborne were the first to be voted upon by the Senate in half a century. Three of the four articles carried overwhelmingly. On Article I, alleging misbehavior and high crimes and misdemeanors by willfully falsifying his 1979 federal income tax return, senators voted 87–10 to find Claiborne guilty. On Article II, the same charge applied to his 1980 return, the vote went against the judge 90–7. On the final article, charging betrayal of the public trust in the judiciary by falsifying his taxes, the Senate voted 89–8 for conviction.[24] Only three senators, Republicans Daniel Evans of Washington and Orrin Hatch of Utah and Democrat David Pryor of Arkansas, voted to acquit Claiborne on all the articles against him.[25]

Only Article III presented difficulty for the Senate. This article charged that Claiborne's district court conviction was itself proof of misbehavior and a high crime. Senator Mathias and several colleagues argued that approval of this article would essentially take the impeachment power out of the hands of the Senate by saying that a judicial branch conviction made impeachment and removal of a federal official mandatory.[26] A majority of senators, including nearly half of those who had already found Claiborne guilty on the tax charges, were unwilling to establish such a precedent. Seventeen voted not guilty, and thirty-five declined to cast a ballot, simply acknowledging that they were present when the roll was called; thus, fifty-two senators failed to support the article, as opposed to forty-six who declared Claiborne guilty. The Constitution's requirement that two-thirds of the senators present must vote for conviction in order to remove an impeached official was not met. This curious division left the Senate's prerogatives intact without according Claiborne, guilty on three other articles, any sense of vindication.

After three days of floor proceedings and a little more than an hour spent on four roll call votes, the Senate brought the judicial career of Harry Claiborne to an ignominious end. In comments made during the previous closed session or filed afterward, several senators expressed concern about the questionable prosecutorial treatment of Claiborne and called for its investigation. They were not dissuaded, however, from finding Claiborne responsible for filing improper tax returns. Indeed, several contended that since the judge knew he was under close scrutiny, his failure to report all his income appeared even more egregious and compromising of his duties as a federal official.[27]

Stripped of his judgeship, Claiborne returned to prison in Alabama for another year before being paroled. He then went back to Nevada to try to rebuild his life. In May 1988 the Nevada Supreme Court readmitted him to practice in the state courts, a locally controversial decision seen as second-guessing the impeachment verdict. The Nevada Supreme Court declared, "Questionable investigations and prosecutorial motivations, as well as anomalous and arguably unfair practices and procedures pervade the record of this matter from its inception." The court called special attention to the problematic use of Joseph Conforte's testimony against Claiborne, the absence of any hearing on Claiborne's claims of prosecutorial misconduct, and, finally, the failure to prove that the judge had engaged in any willful tax evasion. A year and a half later, after one rejection, Claiborne was also readmitted to practice in the federal courts. Claiborne became associated with a Las Vegas firm, engaged in a limited practice, and lived until January 2004. At age eighty-six, suffering from cancer and Alzheimer's disease, he took his own life after carefully completing his tax return. His fourth wife and widow wryly observed, "He did his income taxes early, and he never did them early."[28] Perhaps it was a sign of lessons learned from the impeachment that had cost him so dearly.

Walter L. Nixon, Jr., experienced impeachment much as had Claiborne and rather unlike the president with whom he shared a surname. Whereas President Nixon had resigned to avoid impeachment, Judge Nixon was impeached once he refused to resign. Two similarly named Supreme Court cases involving the two men in important impeachment issues sharpened the contrast. *United States v. Nixon* in 1974 involved a suit by the government against the president to gain access to tape recordings revealing his conduct in office. *Nixon v. United States* in 1993 involved the judge's suit against the government over the manner in which the litigation against him was conducted. Despite dissimilarities in their cases, as well as in their party affiliations, professions, and individual situations, the pair would forever be linked in impeachment history because of the curious coincidence of their uncommon name.

Judge Nixon's impeachment actually shared a great deal with that of Claiborne. Both judges had made rulings unfavorable to the government, Claiborne in a series of cases, Nixon in a federal land-acquisition case. Both were charged with a series of offenses on the basis of initial testimony by witnesses with suspect motives. Subsequently each judge was convicted on peripheral allegations. Both protested what they considered a miscarriage of justice. Both balked at resigning and thereupon faced impeachment by the House and trial by the Senate. Both jurists' removal from office amounted to a political judgment that, despite questions about their convictions, their continued presence on the bench would jeopardize confidence in the federal judiciary.

Walter Nixon came from the Mississippi gentry.[29] Born in 1928 into an economically modest but politically prominent Biloxi family, the son and namesake of a well-known Harrison County supervisor, he graduated from Tulane University Law School in 1951. He then built a successful and lucrative civil practice specializing in personal injury cases. When a third federal judgeship was created for the Biloxi district, Nixon was nominated by President Lyndon Johnson in May 1968 to fill the new seat. Confirmed by the Senate only nine days later with strong backing from old family friend James Eastland, chairman of the Senate Judiciary Committee, Nixon ascended the bench at the age of thirty-nine, young for a federal judge of his era.[30]

Nixon spent an uneventful first decade on the bench. During that time he and his wife of twenty-five years divorced, and he later remarried. With three children, two from his first marriage and one from his second, as well as four stepchildren, and substantial alimony payments until his first wife remarried, Nixon found himself in what he described as bleak financial circumstances. With a salary well below what he had previously earned in private practice and facing the prospect of sending five daughters to college, he began, like many of his peers, looking for appropriate investment opportunities. In 1979 he told his friend attorney Carroll Ingram that he would be interested in an oil or gas venture with Ingram's cousin and legal client, multimillionaire Hattiesburg entrepreneur Wiley Fairchild. Such an investment would, he thought, lie well within the boundaries of the canons of judicial ethics and would probably generate an excellent return.[31]

Ingram, according to later testimony, dawdled several months before bringing Nixon's request to Fairchild's attention in early 1980. Fairchild, who liked to forge business relationships with prominent Mississippians, was amenable to selling Nixon leases on three oil properties that had not yet begun to produce. He was also willing to loan the judge, at 10 percent interest, the $9,500 he sought for the properties. Because of these arrangements Nixon would be able to pay for his investment from revenues it generated and make a tidy profit (eventually about $51,000) at virtually no cost. Fairchild would likewise profit from the deal, since he had bought the land for only a few hundred dollars. Although Fairchild did not have contracts drawn up until 1982, he had them backdated to February 1980, which was according to Nixon the time of their verbal agreement. Later Ingram would date the deal as having been struck in 1981, and Fairchild would claim 1982. The timing of the transaction would eventually contribute to questions about whether it was a normal business deal or a bribe. Undisputed, however, was Nixon's statement to Fairchild in thanking him for the investment deal: "If I can help you, I will. If I can't, I'll just tell you I can't."[32]

In August 1980 Wiley Fairchild's son, Drew, was managing the Hattiesburg airport when three men were arrested there for smuggling more than a ton of marijuana. Only the pilot of the small plane they were using evaded arrest, and he fled the state. Drew Fairchild was implicated in the crime, and his lawyer soon negotiated a plea bargain with federal prosecutors. When Fairchild failed to pay his sizable legal fee, however, the unhappy lawyer encouraged District Attorney Paul H. "Bud" Holmes to begin a state prosecution. The elder Fairchild began to suspect that this was blackmail to get him to pay his son's attorney fees, in part because the airport comanager, also culpable, was not charged. Holmes agreed to a reduced sentence for Drew Fairchild in return for a guilty plea and testimony against the others. The plea and sentencing were to be held in abeyance until the trials were completed. The case dragged on until 1982 as the pilot eluded capture and twice, when arrested, jumped bail. In December 1982 Holmes directed that Fairchild's case be passed to the files, a Mississippi practice that placed the case on inactive status and in essence relegated it to limbo. The case was eventually restored to the active list but remained unresolved. Nixon was not involved in any of the state court proceedings, but Holmes would claim that the judge had discussed the case with him and in his presence informed Wiley Fairchild that the case would be favorably resolved for his son.

In an unrelated matter in March 1982, Judge Nixon had decided a land condemnation case involving a 700-acre barrier island in the Gulf of Mexico. The federal government had used condemnation proceedings to acquire Petit Bois Island and had placed a $330,000 value on it. Ruling in favor of the island's private owners, however, Nixon set its value at $6.2 million. The Justice Department found no grounds to appeal, and the judge rejected posttrial motions for reconsideration as having been filed too late. The Petit Bois case was, according to Nixon's lawyers, "an embarrassing and costly litigation" for the government and an incentive to demonstrate that the judge was corrupt. The Justice Department's Public Integrity Section spent three years investigating the Petit Bois case and presented evidence to two grand juries, neither of which found reason to return any indictments. Nixon's attorneys concluded, "The government was already gunning for Judge Nixon" when, unexpectedly, other allegations surfaced.[33]

Wiley Fairchild's administrative assistant Robert Jarvis, his grandniece's husband, came to believe that the oil leases he had drafted for his employer were evidence of an improper arrangement with Nixon to aid Drew Fairchild. Fired by the elder Fairchild in May 1983, Jarvis also became convinced that his former employer had sought to have him killed by sabotaging the brakes of a car loaned to him. First in anonymous phone calls and later in interviews, Jarvis relayed his various undocumented suspicions to the FBI, which launched an investigation that ultimately resulted in the indictments of the elder Fairchild, Holmes, and Nixon.

In July 1984 Nixon was called before a grand jury looking into whether he had sought to thwart the younger Fairchild's prosecution as the result of a bribe from the elder Fairchild. Asked whether he had ever discussed Drew Fairchild's case with either Wiley Fairchild or Bud Holmes, Nixon said that, to the best of his recollection, he had not. Asked whether Fairchild had ever asked him to do anything regarding his son's case, Nixon emphatically declared, "Absolutely not."

In 1984 interviews with the FBI and testimony to the grand jury, Wiley Fairchild confirmed Nixon's testimony that their business deal was an ordinary transaction that had nothing to do with Drew Fairchild's case. Shortly thereafter federal prosecutors indicted him for perjury and for giving an illegal gratuity to Nixon. Prosecutor Reid Weingarten would later tell the House of Representatives that taking a gratuity involved "a sweetheart deal that was given to a public official only because of his office in anticipation of future favors." He acknowledged that with a potential two-year sentence it ranked well below a charge of bribery, which carried a fifteen-year sentence. Fairchild, seventy-three years old and in failing health, on the advice of his attorney quickly began plea-bargaining to avoid a prison sentence. He admitted to confusion about the dates of various encounters and confessed to making payoffs to Holmes and Nixon. He escaped his legal troubles with a $10,000 fine, two months in a halfway house, and three years of unsupervised probation.

In 1985 Holmes and Nixon were both indicted, Holmes on five counts of perjury and Nixon for accepting an illegal gift and three counts of perjury. Like Fairchild, Holmes saw his legal liability sharply reduced by prosecutors once he agreed to cooperate in the case against Nixon and testify that Nixon had told him that Wiley Fairchild had asked Nixon to "put in a good word for his boy" with Prosecutor Holmes, which was done. At the same time, Holmes acknowledged, the judge had not requested that the prosecutor do anything. A federal probation officer who carried out a detailed examination of the case later observed that Holmes had proceeded to handle the Fairchild case essentially as he would have without ever having any contact with Nixon.[34]

Nixon was tried early in 1986. His case revolved around the conflicting testimony of Ingram, Fairchild, Jarvis, Holmes, and Nixon himself. Weingarten contended that the various accounts added up to evidence of an illegal gift to the judge in anticipation of a quid pro quo and thereafter Nixon's improper intervention in the Drew Fairchild case prior to its records being passed to the files. In rejoinder, Nixon's attorney denied any impropriety on his client's part and challenged what he characterized as an overzealous prosecution. He called particular attention to the questionable credibility of the government's witnesses, who benefited from plea bargains and grants of immunity in return for their testimony. The jury deliberated for eighteen hours before acquitting Nixon of receiving an illegal gratuity and one count of perjury but convicting him on two other perjury counts involving the Drew Fairchild case. The jury's conclusion that Nixon was innocent of the substantial offense but guilty of lying about it was, to say the least, convoluted. Nevertheless, on March 31, 1986, Nixon was sentenced to two concurrent five-year terms in the federal prison camp at Eglin Air Force Base.

Like Harry Claiborne, Walter Nixon refused to resign his judgeship upon conviction and even after appeals failed. "I have committed no crime," he told a press conference the day after the Supreme Court denied certiorari in January 1988, "and I will continue to seek justice."[35] Nixon received considerable support from his home community. Biloxi's mayor, Gerald Blessey, told reporters, "I think there was a heavy presumption of innocence in this community. And I think there still is."[36] But, again like Claiborne, Nixon would discover that the fact of his conviction rather than the issue of its legitimacy would determine his fate in the impeachment proceedings, which he wrongly assumed would provide an unprejudiced reconsideration of his case.

Nixon's appeals to the U.S. Court of Appeals for the Fifth Circuit were rejected on April 30, 1987, and the Supreme Court denied his petition for certiorari on January 19, 1988. Less than two months thereafter, the Judicial Conference of the United States, following the provisions of the Judicial Councils Reform and Judicial Conduct and Disability Act of 1980, recommended to the House of Representatives that Nixon be impeached. Two days later the chairman of the Judiciary Committee, Peter Rodino, introduced an impeachment resolution for himself, Don Edwards of California, Hamilton Fish of New York, and James Sensenbrenner of Wisconsin.[37] Within a week he referred it to the Judiciary Subcommittee on Civil and Constitutional Rights. The subcommittee was replete with Watergate veterans, including its chairman, Edwards, as well as Robert Kastenmeier of Wisconsin and John Conyers of Michigan. On June 9, 1988, the subcommittee began six days of hearings spread over the next month.[38]

The Subcommittee on Civil and Constitutional Rights hearing on Nixon was not prolonged, but it was less cursory than the one afforded Claiborne. After reviewing Nixon's trial, taking its own testimony, and allowing questioning of witnesses, in contrast to the Claiborne hearings, the judiciary subcommittee voted unanimously on July 12 to recommend his impeachment. The full Judiciary Committee soon did likewise. The House of Representatives, not assigning a high priority to Nixon's impeachment as it rushed to adjourn in an election year, postponed the matter until the following session. The subcommittee re-convened on March 2, 1989, and heard two law professors, specialists in judicial ethics, criticize Nixon's judicial conduct. In addition to the previous charges, he had been discovered to have heard two civil cases involving Fairchild's company while the two were financially involved.[39] The subcommittee then reaffirmed its conclusion that Judge Nixon should be impeached. On May 10, 1989, the House finally responded to the committee's recommendation with a 417–0 vote for three articles of impeachment, one for each of Judge Nixon's two perjury convictions and a third for having made a series of fourteen other false statement that "raised substantial doubts as to his judicial integrity, undermined confidence in the integrity and impartiality of the judiciary, betrayed the trust of the people of the United States, disobeyed the laws of the United States, and brought disrepute on the federal courts and the administration of justice."[40]

The day after the House voted to impeach Nixon, the Senate established another twelve-member bipartisan committee to conduct an evidentiary hearing. Two of the members, Howell Heflin, Democrat of Alabama, and Orrin Hatch, Republican of Utah, had taken part in the Senate committee investigation of Harry Claiborne. When the Nixon inquiry committee met to organize on May 15, it chose Georgia Democrat Wyche Fowler as its chairman.[41]

In July the Senate committee met again to consider various motions by the defendant. Most significant was Nixon's effort to have the third impeachment article dismissed. Article III, complained David Stewart, Nixon's attorney, was "the lazy man's impeachment article," piling five standards of misconduct upon fourteen alleged misdeeds, including the perjuries charged in articles I and II. "It is designed to be virtually acquittal-proof," Stewart pointed out, since the wide variety of allegations produced seventy different possible reasons to justify a guilty vote, any one of which would be sufficient. He considered it unfair and impossible to defend against. Furthermore, except for the claim that Nixon disobeyed the law, the charges were subjective allegations, not impeachable offenses. "His conduct is not impeachable simply because it might look bad to someone. That's not what the framers intended." Stewart then asked, "Could the same Constitutional Convention that rejected 'maladministration' as too vague have possibly adopted the impeachable offense of raising substantial doubt as to his integrity?"[42] It would prove to be a telling argument against Article III.

Stewart also objected to the use of a twelve-member committee, rather than the full Senate, for hearing testimony. He found the language of the Constitution that "the Senate shall try all impeachments" to be unequivocal. The eighty-eight senators not on the committee would lack a fair exposure to the case. Rather, they would have to reach a decision based on the printed hearing transcripts and documents, a mass of material he estimated at 6,000 pages, or seventy pounds, and which he doubted that most senators would read. "This is trial by forklift," he exclaimed. "This is not trial by evidence." He reminded the committee that the one impeachment article against Harry Claiborne not based on evidence but on the mere fact of his court conviction had failed.[43] The committee, however, rejected the motion for a full Senate trial along with the motion to quash Article III.[44]

The Senate committee hearings on the Nixon case occupied four days between September 7 and September 13. In addition to a full transcript being provided for members of the Senate, new technology and Senate rules allowed the proceedings to be viewed live on television or later on videotape in every Senate office.[45] Whether any members of the Senate not on the committee would follow the hearings closely was uncertain but, given their heavy workload, unlikely.

Lead House manager Don Edwards presented the charges that Nixon had lied repeatedly in denying involvement in the Drew Fairchild case. Edwards also asserted that Nixon's conduct could not be excused by prosecutorial misconduct, a claim that two courts had examined and rejected. Nixon's actions compelled his removal from the bench, Edwards concluded. Nixon's attorney David Stewart responded for him by disparaging the initial Jarvis accusations as unfounded and arguing that no evidence had surfaced that Nixon had influenced Drew Fairchild's case. Any errors in the judge's initial voluntary FBI interview and later grand jury testimony were forgetful omissions rather than erroneous statements; they did not involve the cover-up of crimes. In sum, Stewart concluded, "a terrible wrong" had been done to Judge Nixon.[46]

After the principal figures in the case had testified, been cross-examined by counsel, and questioned by members of the committee, spokesmen for both sides reviewed the case. Representative Edwards, observing that this was his fourth involvement in an impeachment, described his House subcommittee's initial skepticism about the charges because of recent experiences with prosecutorial excesses. A thorough examination of this case, however, had convinced the subcommittee that Judge Nixon had lied to the FBI and a grand jury and therefore deserved impeachment and removal. The ranking Republican manager, James Sensenbrenner, followed Edwards and called attention to Senate complaints that the House had not thoroughly examined the Claiborne case. This time, he assured the senators, both the judiciary subcommittee and the full House had engaged in a substantial review of the evidence on which the judge had been convicted. They had come to the unanimous conclusion that Nixon had lied repeatedly about his role in the Drew Fairchild case and was unfit for the federal bench.

In his summation, Stewart observed that the case against Nixon was built on the premise that he had fixed the Drew Fairchild case, but in the end that was not even charged, much less proven. Instead, the prosecutor had focused on various allegations of perjury. None, he asserted, involved the cover-up of a crime. "He is in essence," Stewart declared, "accused of having lied to conceal his innocence."[47] With his acknowledgment that the case involved contradictory images, unclear motives, and disputed testimony, Stewart's remark provided a fair summary of the record that the committee would pass on to the Senate for resolution.

The impeachment inquiry committee turned over to the full Senate, without further comment, an 11,245-page printed report including the transcript of its proceedings together with all the exhibited evidence. Separately it also provided 324 pages containing the House brief in support of impeachment and a Nixon rebuttal. The brief made a forceful and seamless case for impeachment with no mention of doubts raised in the House's own proceedings or in the Senate committee. Nixon's rejoinder reiterated the points his attorneys made at the hearings, but no more effectively. Senators were far more likely to read this compact submission than the full record before the Senate trial commenced at 2:00 p.m. on November 1, 1989.[48]

The Senate made clear from the outset that it intended to rely on the evidentiary proceeding of its committee rather than enter into its own detailed examination of the evidence, much less call witnesses to testify before it. Each side was allotted a mere ninety minutes to present its case to the Senate. Representatives Edwards and Sensenbrenner used their time to make arguments virtually identical to those they had presented to the committee. A third House manager, Benjamin Cardin, followed with a detailed and accusatory critique of Nixon's testimony and the blunt conclusion that Nixon had helped a drug smuggler, a charge not made in the impeachment articles, and then lied to cover up his involvement, which the articles did allege.

Nixon, speaking for himself to the Senate, responded, "The investigation of my case was begun on false premises, and pursued for the wrong reasons. From the very beginning, the goal of the federal prosecutors was to get the federal judge, no matter what it took." The balance of his argument and that of his counsel, Stewart, who spoke last, repeated claims made before the committee. Senators, submitting almost two dozen written questions to be asked by the presiding officer, Robert Byrd, the Senate president pro tempore, sought clarification of various points and received brief answers. The testimonial portion of the trial concluded after six hours on the same day it began.[49]

The next day the Senate deliberated in closed session for another six hours. The following morning it reconvened and immediately voted 90–7 to reject Nixon's motion for a full trial in the presence of the entire Senate. By a closer margin of 66–34 the senators then defeated his motion to dismiss Article III on the grounds that its allegations did not represent impeachable offenses. Turning to the articles of impeachment themselves, the Senate voted 90–8 to convict Nixon on Article I involving lying to a grand jury when he said he had not discussed the Drew Fairchild case with District Attorney Holmes. On Article II regarding perjury in denying saying or doing anything to influence the Fairchild case, the Senate voted 78–19 to convict, a less overwhelming but still substantial verdict.

The controversial Article III, however, proved not to be the acquittal-proof lazy man's impeachment article Stewart had called it. While fifty-seven senators voted to convict Nixon on its long list of charges, forty senators disagreed. Article III thus fell well short of the two-thirds necessary for adoption. With Nixon already convicted and removed from office on the first two articles, voting no on Article III may have been easier. Nevertheless, the forty not guilty votes demonstrated senatorial concern to hew to a strict standard of "high crimes and misdemeanors."[50]

In comments printed in the trial record, several senators explained their thinking. Nixon's perjury convictions had inclined them toward his removal, though senators Terry Sanford of North Carolina and Herbert Kohl of Wisconsin expressed reservations about the Justice Department's pursuit of the case in the first place. As Senator Carl Levin of Michigan observed, there was a benign explanation of Judge Nixon's statements, but the fact that a jury found him guilty of perjury beyond a reasonable doubt was compelling. Still, he believed that House and Senate examinations of the case provided independent confirmation of Nixon's misconduct and of the need to take him off the bench. Senator Sanford and Senator Charles Grassley of Iowa both observed that it would be difficult to restore to the bench a judge convicted of perjury. At the same time, more than one senator criticized the way the House had framed the articles of impeachment. In particular, they disliked Article III, Senator Kohl likening it to a Chinese menu of selections from column A and column B and urging the House to do better.[51] Taken together, the comments suggested that senators were becoming more discerning and sophisticated in dealing with impeachment as well as increasingly unwilling to simply endorse the judgments of the House.

Although Nixon's judicial career had come to an end, litigation concerning his impeachment had not. The former judge, returning to private law practice in Biloxi, pressed ahead with a motion to have the Senate proceedings against him declared unconstitutional on the grounds that Senate Rule XI, the provision delegating a committee to hear the case, denied him the full Senate trial the Constitution stipulated in decreeing, "The Senate shall have the sole power to try all impeachments." Claiborne had also objected to Rule XI but had not carried his complaint beyond the Senate. Yet if Nixon were to succeed in convincing the Supreme Court to overturn the use of Senate impeachment trial committees, Claiborne's impeachment and that of Judge Alcee Hastings in 1989 could also be invalidated.

Nixon's attorney, David Stewart, persisted in his claim that by definition a trial must give a defendant the opportunity to confront and cross-examine the witnesses against him in the presence of those passing judgment, in this case the full Senate. Lower courts found Nixon's complaint nonjusticiable. However, a parallel claim filed by Judge Hastings was endorsed by D.C. District Judge Stanley Sporkin in September 1992, leaving the ultimate resolution of the issue in the hands of the Supreme Court.[52] The high court heard Nixon's appeal argued on October 14, 1992. Defending the Senate's action, U.S. Solicitor General Kenneth Starr argued that the Constitution's grant to the Senate of sole power to try impeachments carried with it the authority to determine the procedures to be employed. Stewart responded that it would be "most pernicious for the courts simply to avert their eyes from an unconstitutional impeachment."[53] Ruling three months later, the Court agreed with Starr that the issue involved a political question that could not be resolved by the courts.[54]

Writing for a unanimous Court in *Nixon v. United States,* Chief Justice Rehnquist affirmed the lower court's judgment in Nixon's suit and invalidated the contrary Sporkin ruling. Rehnquist's ruling in *Nixon v. United States* underscored congressional independence in conducting impeachments. Only a year earlier the chief justice had indulged his off-the-bench proclivity for writing about the Court's history when he published *Grand Inquests: The Historic Impeachments of Justice Samuel Chase and President Andrew Johnson.* His book's admiration for the Senate's conduct and decisions in the nineteenth century's two most important impeachment trials would be echoed in his opinion on the Nixon appeal.

In his *Nixon* opinion, Rehnquist began by quoting an earlier Court ruling, in *Baker v. Carr,* that "a textually demonstrable constitutional commitment of the issue to a coordinate political department" takes a controversy out of the judiciary's hands. In other words, a specific delegation of constitutional power left the Court powerless to intrude. Still, the Court must determine the limits of the Constitution's commitment of authority. In this case the Court had no doubts. The Senate had been given "sole power to try all impeachments," just as the House of Representatives had been granted "sole power" to impeach. Indeed those were the only two clauses in the Constitution where the term "sole power" was even used. The requirement that the Senate "try" impeachments did not restrict that body in deciding how to gather evidence or conduct deliberations. In fact, the flexibility of the trial authority was underscored by the impeachment clause's broad language in describing it compared to other provisions specifying that senators must take a special oath, that the chief justice was to preside over a presidential impeachment trial, and that conviction required a two-thirds majority.

Rehnquist concluded that there were also other reasons that the power of judicial review had not been extended to Senate impeachment trials. The first was to assure that unbiased independent judgments would be rendered in the criminal proceedings likely to flow from impeachment. The other and more important was to assure finality to impeachment proceedings. Allowing judicial review would, he feared, "expose the political life of the country to months, or perhaps years, of chaos." Perhaps thinking of how fiercely Richard Nixon had fought impeachment, Rehnquist feared that the finality problem "would manifest itself most dramatically if the president were impeached." The chief justice conjured up the specter of possible impairment of a successor's legitimacy and effectiveness if a removed president were to seek judicial relief, much less if the ex-president were to obtain a measure of it by a judicially imposed second Senate trial. Better there be no judicial review of impeachment.[55]

Justice John Paul Stevens, in a brief concurrence, went further than Rehnquist, asserting that the impeachment power rested entirely with the Congress. Conversely, Justice Byron White and Justice David Souter concurred with the chief justice's opinion but retreated from the holding that the Court had no judicial review authority over an impeachment proceeding. White, joined by Justice Harry Blackmun, emphasized the Constitution's positive grants of power over impeachment to the House and Senate so that the judiciary would not be involved in adjudicating political intrigues, would not be required to try both impeachments and associated criminal cases, and would not be involved in trying impeachments of its own members. Still, he worried about Congress's power in impeachment being unchecked. Souter was likewise concerned, comfortable with the judgment in the Nixon case but "envision[ing] different and unusual circumstances that might justify a more searching review of impeachment proceedings." The justices, not wishing to cede all power of judicial review over impeachment, could not articulate a formula for when it should apply, much less win a Court majority to their view.[56]

With the resolution of *Nixon v. United States,* the second-longest impeachment episode in the nation's history was at last concluded. Measured from Judge Nixon's initial indictment in August 1985 to the final Supreme Court rejection of his procedural appeal in January 1993, seven and a half years had elapsed. During that time, congressional, and particularly Senate, experience with impeachment had ripened noticeably.

Having failed at his final slender possibility of overturning his removal from the federal bench, Nixon returned to the practice of law in Biloxi. He eventually resumed a public career, albeit in a far more modest position. In 2001 the D'Iberville, Mississippi, city council chose him to serve as city attorney for the seven-thousand-resident Biloxi suburb.[57] Six years later, he remained in that office.

The Claiborne and Nixon cases were not the only means by which Congress gained impeachment experience in the 1980s. The case of Judge Alcee Hastings of the Southern District of Florida provided national legislators an additional but quite distinctive experience. The Hastings case began well ahead of Nixon's and resulted in his removal only two weeks before the Biloxi judge was stripped of his office. It proved to be not only the longest but also the most extraordinary judicial impeachment of the era both in its origins and in its ultimate impact upon the man impeached.

11

Impeachment as Irreversible but Not Fatal:

The Case of Alcee Hastings

If questions arose about the circumstances that led to the impeachments of Judges Harry Claiborne and Walter Nixon, they were modest compared to those that surfaced in the case of Judge Alcee L. Hastings of Florida. While Claiborne and Nixon could, with reason, complain about overly zealous prosecution, juries had found both of them guilty of multiple felonies beyond a reasonable doubt. In contrast, Hastings, charged with the crime of conspiracy to obtain a bribe for reducing the sentences of defendants before him, had been acquitted by a Miami jury. Nevertheless, the same allegations of felonious conduct that failed to persuade the jury provoked subsequent judicial calls for his impeachment, a House investigation, a Senate trial, and Hastings's removal from office.

The unique circumstances of the Hastings case raised any number of troubling questions. Did the impeachment of Judge Hastings after his acquittal violate the Constitution's ban on double jeopardy? In a case built entirely on circumstantial evidence, was his impeachment and removal just? In a related vein, did the only impeachment of a black federal official during this period, or indeed at any time in United States history, suggest racism at work, as Hastings charged throughout his ordeal? Looming over all else was the perennial question: What constituted sufficient grounds for impeachment?

The Hastings case demonstrated with particular vividness the distinction between a criminal prosecution and an impeachment process. The case highlighted the differing standards of proof employed in a courtroom proceeding and in the political practice of impeachment. It further illuminated the increasing self-assurance with which both houses of Congress dealt with impeachment by the late 1980s. The outcome of the Hastings case appeared to affect the calculations of other federal judges contemplating the possibility of escaping impeachment if faced with criminal prosecution. Finally, by virtue of Hastings's subsequent successful career in seeking and winning elective federal office, the case cast light on evolving public attitudes toward impeachment.

Alcee Hastings was the first black person ever appointed to the federal bench in the state of Florida. Raised largely by his grandmother while his parents worked out of state as domestic servants for a wealthy white family, he was educated in the segregated schools of central Florida. Hastings then attended predominately black Fisk and Howard universities before completing his education at all-black Florida A&M University Law School in 1963. Thereafter he built what he called a "y'all come" general legal practice in Fort Lauderdale. In addition to run-of-the-mill civil and criminal cases, he took on pro bono civil rights litigation. The young attorney also became active in the National Association for the Advancement of Colored People as well as the local Democratic party. He repeatedly ran unsuccessfully for public office and then worked in the 1976 presidential campaign of Jimmy Carter. After Governor Reubin Askew appointed him a state circuit court judge in 1977, Carter raised him to the federal bench as part of an effort to expand the ranks of minorities in the federal courts. In 1979 the president named the forty-two-year-old Hastings to the U.S. District Court for the Southern District of Florida. After the normal background and credentials review, the Senate confirmed the appointment in October of the same year.[1]

Two years after Hastings ascended the federal bench, he first gained national attention by barring the federal government from deporting Haitian boat people seeking political asylum. Only days later federal prosecutors accused him of taking bribes to reduce criminal sentences. William Dredge, a Miami antiques dealer with a nearly forty-year criminal history, had approached FBI agents offering to tell them about a corrupt judge in return for their dropping drug charges he faced in Maryland. Dredge related a story of payoffs to Judge Hastings channeled through William Borders, a politically well-connected Washington attorney. Borders was a former president of the predominately black National Bar Association and a Carter appointee to the District of Columbia Judicial Nominations Commission. After FBI agents, acting on information provided by Dredge, observed a meeting between Borders and Santos Trafficante, a notorious organized crime figure, the U.S. attorney decided to pursue their informant's allegation.[2]

Dredge claimed to have been approached by Borders with a claim that for $150,000 he could arrange to fix the case of Frank and Thomas Romano, who already stood convicted of racketeering in Judge Hastings's court but still faced the final disposition of their sentences and property forfeiture under the Racketeering and Corrupt Organizations (RICO) Act. According to Dredge, Borders said he did not know the Romanos and wanted Dredge to serve as a go-between. Intrigued, the U.S. Attorney's Office agreed to Dredge's terms. Together with Paul Rico, a retired FBI agent impersonating Frank Romano and wired to record conversations, Dredge met with Borders, who set forth payment arrangements and said that Hastings would signal his agreement by appearing at the restaurant of Miami's Hotel Fontainebleau at 8:00 p.m. four days later.

Hastings appeared at the Fontainebleau on schedule to have dinner with a girlfriend. Rico then delivered $25,000 to Borders as a first payment in their bribery scheme. At that point, Borders indicated that Hastings would hand down a favorable ruling in the Romano case within ten days. Nearly three weeks later, in accordance with recently issued more restrictive appellate court guidelines on RICO forfeitures, the judge issued a ruling rescinding his preliminary sentencing order and restoring $800,000 in RICO-forfeited funds to the Romanos. Rico then delivered the balance of the bribe to Borders in Washington. As soon as the attorney accepted the money, the FBI arrested him.

Hastings learned of the arrest soon after his arrival in Washington for a long-planned National Bar Association party to honor Borders. The judge immediately left the capital by an unconventional route, flying home from Baltimore-Washington International Airport, an hour's taxi ride away, rather than from Washington National Airport, ten minutes from his hotel. While at the airport, he made a number of suspicious calls from various pay phones. Prosecutors would later accuse the judge of having fled to evade the FBI.

Two months later a federal grand jury indicted Borders and Hastings on bribery and related charges. Attorneys for Hasting filed a successful motion to separate the two men's cases. However, as had lawyers for Claiborne and Nixon, they failed to win dismissal of the case against their client on grounds that impeachment must precede indictment. Meanwhile, Borders stood trial in Atlanta in March 1982 on charges of soliciting a bribe, corrupting the judicial process, and interstate travel to carry out these crimes. Prosecutors maintained that he could not have provided the information passed on to Rico without the cooperation of Hastings. A jury found Borders guilty on all counts, and he drew a five-year prison sentence.

Ten months after Borders's conviction, Hastings went on trial in Miami. He claimed that he had gone to the Fontainebleau in response to a prior invitation from Borders (who had not showed up and proved to be in Las Vegas watching a boxing match that day). Hastings maintained that his allegedly coded message to Borders about signing the Romano court papers was, instead, just what it appeared to be, a report that he had signed letters on behalf of his law school roommate and their down-on-his-luck mutual friend, Hemphill Pride. The judge claimed that his abrupt and erratic departure from Washington on the day of Borders's arrest simply involved his desire to return to Florida to calm his hysterical semi-invalid mother and that once there he had willingly submitted to an FBI interview the same evening. Finally, Hastings asserted that his actions in the Romano case were entirely proper. His revision of the Romanos' sentence was required by changes in guidelines just adopted by the U.S. Court of Appeals for the Fifth Circuit.

The federal prosecutor, Reid Weingarten, disputed Hastings on virtually ever point. Weingarten, who the following year would successfully prosecute Walter Nixon, used Paul Rico's testimony concerning his dealings with Borders and a complex web of circumstantial evidence regarding meetings and messages between Borders and Hastings to construct an elaborate picture of conspiratorial activity. After seventeen hours of weighing the evidence and arguments on both sides, a jury returned a verdict of not guilty.[3]

Although he exulted in his victory, Judge Hastings's difficulties were not behind him. At a meeting of the Eleventh Circuit Judicial Council the following month, Chief Judge John Godbold of Alabama reported that Hasting would resume his duties since no complaint had been filed about his conduct. Responding to Godbold's implied invitation, two members of the council decided over dinner the same evening to file a complaint. Neither Judge Terrell Hodges of Florida nor Judge Anthony Alaimo of Georgia had any personal knowledge of Hastings's case, but they relied on the review of Borders's conviction by an appellate judge they both respected, Judge Frank Johnson of Alabama. Johnson had denied Borders's appeal, dismissing his contention that he could not be convicted of a conspiracy all by himself and noting that the prosecution had presented evidence of Hastings's involvement. Alaimo and Hodges deduced that, regardless of the jury's verdict, Hastings must have conspired with Borders. Furthermore, they objected to Hastings's public statements that he had been the victim of a racial and political vendetta. They were also offended by Hastings's judicial conduct as testified to at his trial, and, finally, they disapproved of his use of his position to raise money for his disbarred friend Hemphill Pride. Hastings, they concluded, had repeatedly violated the code of judicial conduct.[4]

Under the terms of the 1980 Judicial Councils Reform and Judicial Conduct and Disability Act, the U.S. Court of Appeals for the Eleventh Circuit moved to investigate the Hodges and Alaimo complaint. Chief Judge Godbold appointed a five-judge committee, including himself, Frank Johnson, and three district judges. The committee in turn hired John Doar of Watergate fame to conduct its inquiry. Ignoring the confidentiality requirement governing the entire process prior to any decision to recommend impeachment to the House of Representatives, Godbold on April 15, 1983, issued a press release outlining the steps he had taken. The notice to the press, followed by Godbold's rejection of Hastings's request to make public other details of the case, details more favorable to him, gave plausibility to the accused judge's complaint that the conservative white jurists of the circuit were hostile to him.[5]

Apparently unknown to Godbold, one of the members of his committee, District Judge Sam Pointer of Alabama, had had previous contact with Hastings. According to Hastings, he and his mother were riding in an elevator at the first judicial conference he attended when Pointer got on and complained to another judge about President Carter that day appointing "a nigger" to the federal bench in Alabama. Hastings, upset, had admonished Pointer, "If you ever make such a comment in my presence again, I'll put my foot in your ass!" Reflecting years later on whether he thought race had entered into his treatment, Hastings exclaimed, "You bet your bottom dollar I do!"[6]

The Eleventh Circuit investigation of Hastings took more than three years and cost $2 million. John Doar's methodical assembly and examination of every piece of evidence took even longer to complete without the pressures so evident in the House Watergate investigation. Objections by Hastings to the inquiry and the way it was being conducted also slowed it considerably. When Doar sought the records of the grand jury that had indicted Borders and the judge, Hastings opposed the violation of grand jury confidentiality. An out-of-circuit judge allowed the use of grand jury materials on the basis that the confidentiality requirement could be breached "in those rare instances where disclosure is necessary to prevent injustice" and where "public interest in the integrity and independence of the judiciary" overrode considerations of double jeopardy. Subsequently, when Hastings objected to subpoenas of his law clerks and staff members as violating the confidentiality of judicial chambers, a three-judge panel, also from outside the circuit, ruled that the Judicial Conduct Act explicitly authorized such subpoenas. Determination to ensure judicial integrity trumped every complaint that due process was being violated.[7]

The Eleventh Circuit's five-judge investigating committee took testimony sporadically over twenty-seven days from the summer of 1985 until the summer of 1986. The panel pursued a range of topics far beyond Hastings's original prosecution. Borders refused to testify, while Dredge spoke scornfully to the committee. He pointed out, "Whatever Hastings did, you guys had a fair shot at him. You took him to trial. He got found not guilty."[8] The committee pressed on, however, eventually hearing from more than one hundred witnesses. Concluding their investigation in August 1986, the five judges, in effect, reversed the jury verdict on Hastings. Although they rejected five of the six charges made by Alaimo and Hodges, the committee endorsed the central allegation of a conspiracy with Borders to secure a bribe. Thereafter, it charged, Hastings had lied at his trial when he denied involvement.[9]

Before making their final recommendations, the investigating committee considered whether further action against Hastings would constitute double jeopardy. The committee concluded that had the jury found Hastings guilty there would be no question of impeachment being in order. His acquittal, therefore, should be no bar to the consideration of impeachment. In itself this might have seemed a dubious claim, but the committee went on to distinguish impeachment from criminal prosecution. "Impeachment is remedial and designed to protect the institution of government from corrupt conduct: conduct that subverts the foundations upon which such institutions rest, namely, the trust of the people in the integrity of the constitutional officers of the United States Government." That being the case, the committee continued, there should be no bar to continued investigation once a criminal proceeding ended.[10]

The investigating committee proceeded to declare that their inquiries suggested that Hastings had not testified truthfully at his trial. The total body of evidence established to their satisfaction that he and Borders had conspired to obtain a bribe and then lied to conceal it. The five judges recommended that the Eleventh Circuit Judicial Council certify to its national counterpart that the judge's conduct warranted impeachment. The council wasted little time before acting favorably on this recommendation.[11]

The Judicial Conference of the United States, on receiving the report submitted by the Eleventh Circuit, chose not to conduct its own separate investigation. At its regular meeting on March 17, 1987, the conference asked the House of Representatives to consider impeaching Hastings.[12] Six days later two Republican members of the Judiciary Committee, James Sensenbrenner and Henry Hyde, independently introduced an impeachment resolution in the House. As the case moved to the Judiciary Committee, Hastings filed more court motions to thwart the proceedings, in particular to block committee access to grand jury records from the original Borders and Hastings trials. Nothing that Hastings attempted worked, however, and the case moved forward.[13]

Appeals for public sympathy brought Hastings national attention. He claimed to be the victim of racism. Conservative white southern jurists, he alleged, were seeking to push the one black federal judge in Florida off the bench. He further charged that, having been acquitted by a jury, he was now being subjected to double jeopardy by unrelenting foes. These were potentially explosive charges only two decades after the racial upheavals of the 1960s, especially in a locality where racial attitudes remained strained.

House Judiciary Committee chairman Peter Rodino referred the Hastings matter to the Subcommittee on Criminal Justice, chaired by John Conyers of Michigan, rather than to the Subcommittee on Civil and Constitutional Rights, to which the Claiborne case had earlier been assigned and Walter Nixon's case would soon be sent. Rodino's decision appears to have been influenced by the fact that Conyers, a founding member of the Congressional Black Caucus, would be sensitive to the allegations that racism was involved in the charges against Hastings and would be certain to give the judge a full and fair hearing. Conyers, a twelve-term representative from Detroit and a veteran of the impeachment hearings on Richard Nixon, possessed the stature and experience to terminate the proceedings if he found the charges stemmed solely from racism. Likewise, he would be able to carry them forward if he deemed them well founded. A wide range of representatives would respect Conyers's judgment either way, and no doubt he would influence their decision on whether or not to vote against a black judge.

Conyers's subcommittee and staff spent two months on a thorough review of the voluminous record of the Hastings case. The investigation covered FBI reports, grand jury proceedings, the trials of Borders and Hastings, and the case of *United States v. Romano,* over which Judge Hastings had presided. The subcommittee also examined material submitted by Hastings and the inquiry conducted by Doar for the Eleventh Circuit. In addition to scouring the written record, the subcommittee interviewed more than sixty witnesses on its own. Thereafter it conducted seven days of hearings from May 18 to June 9, 1988. Both Hastings and Borders were invited to testify, but both declined. Hastings's decision not to cooperate in any way with the committee's investigation and thus his failure to speak in his own behalf appeared to weigh heavily on the committee.[14]

In the end, the subcommittee decided on July 7 to recommend seventeen articles of impeachment against Judge Hastings. The first alleged a conspiracy with Borders to obtain a bribe from the Romanos. The next fourteen alleged a series of false statements during Hastings's 1983 trial. Article XVI involved an unrelated charge that in 1985 Hastings had, in violation of his judicial obligations, disclosed confidential information about an FBI wiretap to Miami's mayor, Stephen Clark, warning him that he was under surveillance and thwarting an investigation into his activities. The final article was the usual omnibus compilation of all previous charges. With little dissent, the Judiciary Committee endorsed the subcommittee recommendations on July 26.[15]

Representative Conyers presented the report of the Judiciary Committee on the floor of the House on August 3, 1988. In an emotional speech, he explained that he had originally been quite skeptical of the charges brought by the Eleventh Circuit against Hastings, a progressive black judge acquitted by a jury. He had suspected, he said, that the complaints against the judge were racially motivated. However, in the course of the subcommittee investigation, he had become increasingly convinced that Hastings was guilty as charged. It was especially difficult for him, Conyers acknowledged, to find fault with one of the nation's handful of black judges, especially one who was, like himself, a civil rights activist and an outspoken liberal. However, he continued,

> We did not wage that civil rights struggle merely to replace one form of judicial corruption for another. And we can no more close our eyes to acts that constitute high crimes and misdemeanors when practiced by judges whose view we approve than we could against judges whose views we detested. . . . The principle of equality requires that a black public official be held to the same standard that other public officials are held to. A lower standard would be patronizing, a higher standard, racist. Just as race should never disqualify a person from office, race should never insulate a person from the consequences of wrongful conduct.[16]

The House was silent when Conyers finished, recalled Alan Baron, the Judiciary Committee's special counsel for both the Hastings and Nixon impeachments. Then the widely respected senior member of the body, Representative Claude Pepper, a Democrat from Florida who had first come to the Senate fifty years earlier, rose slowly and turned to stare squarely at Conyers. After a hushed moment, he began to applaud. The other members present quickly jumped up to join Pepper in a rare standing ovation for what they all recognized as an act of principle and political courage. Conyers's compelling speech seemed to resolve virtually every doubt and bury the issue of racism. Within the hour, the House voted to impeach Hastings by a margin of 413 to 3.[17]

The Senate now had two impeachments simultaneously before it for the first time ever. The House of Representatives had exhibited articles of impeachment against Walter Nixon only three months earlier, and the special inquiry committee assigned to his case was preparing for September hearings. Having to cope with two cases at the same time put a strain on both houses of Congress. The House Judiciary Committee had to enlist two sets of managers to present the cases to the Senate. Each set, as it turned out, contained three Watergate veterans. The five-member Nixon team included Democrats Jack Brooks of Texas and Don Edwards of California as well as Republican William E. Dannemeyer of California and the more junior representatives Democrat Benjamin Cardin of Maryland and Republican James Sensenbrenner of Wisconsin. Brooks, as the ranking member of the Judiciary Committee, was also assigned to the Hastings case, though he scarcely participated. The other managers in the Hastings case were Conyers, Republican Hamilton Fish of New York, and two Republican members also too junior to have served during Watergate, John Bryant of Texas and George Gekas of Pennsylvania. The House Judiciary Committee staff, headed by special counsel Alan Baron, had to stretch to prepare and support both sets of managers.[18] The Senate was hard-pressed as well. It required two twelve-member special committees to conduct evidentiary hearings, a substantial time commitment for nearly one-fourth of the upper body.

The two cases had traveled by different routes and at a different pace from trial court through initial congressional consideration, demonstrating once again that impeachments do not unfold according to any set schedule. Nixon, convicted in a criminal trial in 1986, had his case taken up by a House Judiciary Subcommittee two years later in June 1988, but the case was not considered by the full committee until March 1989. The House voted to impeach Nixon and send his case to the Senate in early May. Acquitted in his criminal trial in 1983, Hastings endured four years of further judicial investigation and review before his case was placed before Congress in March 1987, more than a year ahead of Nixon's. Delayed by the Conyers subcommittee's own investigation, formal hearings on Hastings did not began until May 1988. After the subcommittee voted to recommend impeachment on June 9, the full committee voted likewise the following month, and the House complied on August 3, 1988. Thereafter the Hastings proceedings were slowed again, in part because of congressional elections and in part by the judge's various motions. Among other things, Hasting renewed his assertion that some, though now not all, of the charges against him represented double jeopardy. Once the Senate began to move forward, however, action in the two cases occurred close in time. The Senate evidentiary committee hearings on Hastings took place on eighteen days between July 10 and August 3, 1989, and those on Nixon soon followed on four days from September 7 through 13. The final Senate floor debate and decision on Hastings took place on October 18–20, only two weeks before the Nixon case was finally resolved on November 1–3.[19]

Before the Hastings case reached a Senate impeachment trial committee, however, it took a detour through the Rules Committee and to the floor of the Senate for consideration of the judge's persistent claim that he was being subjected to double jeopardy. His assertion was important not only to the resolution of his case but also to the larger issue of overall limitations on impeachment. On May 15, 1989, the Senate heard the matter debated for two hours. It heard first from Hastings himself, who pointed to jury comments after his acquittal that "it wasn't even close" and "there wasn't enough evidence to convict anybody of anything." He went on to point out that the government had pursued the case with unlimited resources for an additional five years without turning up any evidence not available at the original trial.[20]

Hastings's attorney, Terence Anderson, then painted the prosecution as relentless despite neither initial nor subsequent evidence of wrongdoing by the judge. Anderson tied the decision to allow prior indictment and trial of constitutional officers with the binding effect of such a choice upon impeachment. He reminded the senators that Hastings had initially sought to have impeachment considered before his criminal trial but that the House had deferred to the courts. Respect should, therefore, be given to the jury's verdict, just as the House had contended should be done in the Claiborne case. To take Hastings's acquittal less seriously, he suggested, would be unfair and inconsistent.[21]

The House managers disparaged the double jeopardy claim. At first brushing it aside to run once again through the circumstantial case against Hastings, lead House manager John Bryant argued that fairness and the public interest required the judge's conviction. Only then did he address the constitutional argument. He reminded senators that the Constitution distinguished between judicial actions to punish and impeachment to protect government against errant officials. Sole and unlimited power to impeach rested with the House, and the sole power to try impeachments fell to the Senate. Bryant bluntly contended that to accept Hastings's claims would seriously undermine constitutional checks and balances and weaken the separation of powers. In the Claiborne case, he argued somewhat disingenuously, Congress had not relied on the judicial verdict but had come to its own conclusion about the Nevada judge's guilt; in this case, he said, it should do likewise. Finally, Bryant warned that Hastings's position, if followed to its conclusion, meant that no federal official who had been indicted could ever be impeached.[22]

The next day the Senate deliberated over Hastings's motions for two and a half hours behind closed doors. A day later it rejected his requests by a vote of 92 to 1.[23] The lone dissenter, Ohio Democrat Howard Metzenbaum, had expressed concern during the open questioning of the House managers that the continued investigation of Hastings for perjury after his acquittal had dire implications. He apparently was not satisfied with Bryant's reply that, yes, perjury charges could follow acquittal.[24] Yet the double jeopardy issue had finally been disposed of, and the Senate could proceed to a substantive examination of the case.

Hastings's case before the Senate Impeachment Trial Committee, chaired by Democrat Jeff Bingaman of New Mexico, traversed the same uneven ground covered before in the Eleventh Circuit and the House. The lead House manager, John Bryant, began the hearing by presenting the familiar account involving Dredge, Trafficante, Borders, and the Romanos as well as Hastings's appearance at the Fontainebleau, his conversations with Borders, and his sudden departure from Washington, asserting that it added up to a bribery conspiracy. The judge and his counsel Terence Anderson responded forcefully to what they characterized as selective marshaling of information. They offered alternative explanations of the major pieces of circumstantial evidence, and both insisted that Hastings had done nothing wrong.[25]

After the opening statements, the Senate committee listened for eighteen days as House managers, as well as Anderson and Hastings, examined William Dredge and a series of fifty-four other witnesses. One person who had not testified before the case reached Congress but who had impressed the House subcommittee was Robert W. Shuy, a professor of linguistics at Georgetown University and an experienced expert witness on the interpretation of conversations. Shuy spoke at length and then answered questions regarding his examination of a wiretapped half-minute telephone conversation between Borders and Hastings on October 5, 1981. Shuy concluded that the two men had spoken in a prearranged code to conceal that Hastings was reporting that he had filed the papers reducing the Romanos' penalties, for which Borders was obtaining the bribe. Anderson in his cross-examination expressed considerable skepticism about Shuy's methods and observed that another linguist had characterized his judgments as "plausible speculation."[26]

Throughout the hearing Hastings steadfastly maintained that his October 5 conversation with Borders was just what it appeared to be: a brief, colloquial chat between two friends regarding aid to a third. The judge was merely letting Borders know that he had written letters in support of Hemphill Pride, seeking to get his suspended law license reinstated. He offered drafts of the letters on a yellow legal pad, asserting that he had written them on the bench while hearing a case. The House managers responded by calling the drafts fraudulent, perfectly written without a single error or correction and not produced by the defense until years after they had allegedly been composed. Furthermore, the managers pointed out, the letters had never been typed up by Hastings's secretary nor sent. More damaging to Hastings's claim was Pride's testimony that he had neither sought nor discussed such letters with either Hastings or Borders, though they had talked about his reinstatement. Pride also said that he was not eligible to seek restoration of his law license until 1983, and thus at the time the letters from Hastings were allegedly written they would have had no purpose. Coming from an old friend rather than an expert witness, Pride's testimony perhaps undermined a significant aspect of Hastings's defense more than did Shuy's.[27] When the managers presented their case to the full Senate, Pride's testimony became a central feature of their argument for conviction.[28]

The trial committee devoted a day and a half of its hearing to the late-developing charge that Hastings had tipped off Miami's Mayor Clark that his phone was being tapped as part of an FBI investigation. Hastings's counsel presented compelling testimony that the alleged conversation could not have occurred after a Hastings speech when Clark claimed it had and that at any other time it would have been inconsequential. As the House completed presenting its case on Article XVI, one of the senators on the committee, Slade Gorton of Washington, said bluntly that even if the charge was true, it did not rise to the level of an impeachable offense. The Justice Department had declined to prosecute on the allegations, the Eleventh Circuit Judicial Council had declined to include the charge in its list of offenses warranting impeachment, and yet, he complained, the House had added it to the articles of impeachment it exhibited against Judge Hastings. Gorton implied that the only effect of the Article XVI charge was to undermine his support for the other, more serious charges.[29]

William Borders, several senators observed, was the only person, other than Judge Hastings, who knew definitively whether the two had conspired in the Romano case. The Senate committee repeatedly tried to get Borders to testify, but as had been the case at Hastings's original trial, the Eleventh Circuit hearing, and the House hearing, he refused, asserting Fifth Amendment rights against self-incrimination. Senators tried to explain that an impeachment inquiry imposed a special duty to give the highest priority to the overall integrity of government. Neither offers of immunity nor threats of criminal contempt charges could budge Borders, however. Thus, the senators were obliged to reach a judgment without hearing from the one person who could have resolved their uncertainties.[30]

Borders could have attested to Hastings's innocence by assuming full responsibility himself for the scheme to extract payment from the Romanos for a ruling that Hastings would make legitimately. Borders's failure to take the entire burden upon himself did not necessarily mean, of course, that he had not in fact acted on his own. Situated as he was with a host of Washington contacts, other judicial and legal acquaintances, and access to Hastings, he could plausibly have put together information he had gleaned along with his own shrewd legal guesswork to predict an outcome that he could market to the Romanos as the product of his influence and contacts. Hastings's defenders suggested such a scenario, pointing out that no evidence was ever presented that the judge had received any money. However, neither the Eleventh Circuit investigators nor the House subcommittee nor senators could be persuaded that Borders would take the risk of securing an organized crime payoff without being able to deliver the promised result. At each stage, those sitting in judgment felt more inclined to believe that Hastings was involved than that he was not. Absent Borders's testimony to the contrary, the circumstantial case against Hastings, shaky as it might be, could not be budged.

When the Senate Impeachment Trial Committee adjourned on August 22, it had compiled an evidentiary hearing record of 3,283 pages for senators to consider along with an even lengthier record from the House investigation, the Eleventh Circuit inquiry, and the original 1983 Hastings district court trial. Although the Senate's rules treated all the material presented by its committee as, in effect, trial testimony and evidence made available to the whole Senate, most senators no doubt confined their attention to the trial committee's final report filed on October 2 and to the statements made during the two hours each granted the House managers and Hastings's defense team when the impeachment trial opened on October 20.

House managers John Bryant and George Gekas laid out the case against Judge Hastings persuasively and in detail. John Conyers followed with oratory similar to that which had brought the House to its feet. The three House managers all stressed that careful examination of the case led them to conclude that Hastings was guilty, that his alibis were unconvincing, and that other testimony undermined his defense. In his rebuttal, Hastings rambled on at length about his background, his ruling on the Haitian boat people, his initial jury acquittal, and the double jeopardy he had since experienced. He did not speak directly to the conclusions the managers had drawn. His associate counsel, Patricia Williams, focused on the peripheral charge of tipping off Miami's mayor to an FBI wiretap. She made a strong case that no such thing had happened and implied that the rest of the case against Hastings was equally suspect. Anderson, the judge's principal attorney, disparaged some of the managers' main points, suggested that Borders's conviction could not be used to infer Hastings's guilt, and contended that even without his acquittal Hastings, absent convincing proof of his involvement in a crime, would be entitled to the presumption of innocence. Anderson concluded by calling the Senate to a duty to protect public officials from the fear that in carrying out their duties they could be victims of false accusations and a residue of circumstantial evidence.[31]

On October 19 the Senate deliberated over the Hastings case for seven hours. The chair of the trial committee, Jeff Bingaman, began the discussion by announcing that he intended to vote no on all seventeen articles. He explained, "The evidence, although furnishing grounds for investigation and trial, does not provide a sound basis upon which I can vote for conviction." Senator Bingaman went on to say that he found the evidence presented to be circumstantial and unconvincing. He stressed the lack of any witness testimony or physical evidence of the alleged conspiracy. He found himself unpersuaded by the claims of coded telephone conversations and regarded much of the other evidence as ambiguous. Coming from the man who had presided over eighteen days of testimony, cross-examination by opposing counsel, and questioning by senators, Bingaman's declaration represented a serious blow to the House managers.[32]

The trial committee's vice chair, Senator Arlen Specter of Pennsylvania, a former prosecuting attorney, next declared that he too would vote against conviction. He accorded great deference to the original jury decision acquitting Judge Hastings. Then he pointed out that no evidence of Hastings's receipt of a bribe had ever been presented. In light of the acquittal he stressed the need for proof of an impeachable offense "beyond a reasonable doubt." Though he did not use the familiar term from a previous impeachment episode, Specter suggested that in this case there was no "smoking gun." Finally, he noted that the forfeiture ruling in the Romano case was obligatory for Hastings. Specter, like Bingaman, found much of the circumstantial evidence—such as the dinner at the Fontainebleau, the abrupt departure from Washington after Borders's arrest, and the extensive use of pay telephones—to have alternative innocent explanations.[33]

Few other senators spoke with the certitude of Bingaman and Specter. Charles Grassley of Iowa acknowledged that much of the evidence was ambiguous. Still, he concluded that the mass of assembled information, together with his skepticism that Borders could have or would have acted alone, led him to conclude that Hastings was guilty.[34] Democrat Carl Levin of Michigan agreed with Republican Grassley, while Republicans Slade Gorton and David Durenberger of Minnesota and Democrat Herbert Kohl of Wisconsin, all members of the Impeachment Trial Committee, picked through the articles, finding Hastings guilty of conspiracy with Borders but rejecting many of the other articles.[35] Republican Senate leaders Robert Dole of Kansas and Alan Simpson of Wyoming were among the few who expressed unequivocal support for a guilty verdict.[36]

One senator who was prepared to vote not guilty, Democrat Terry Sanford of North Carolina, argued that the FBI had failed to prove its case. After setting up a sting operation to bribe Borders, it arrested him before the money could be passed along to Hastings and thus establish proof of his involvement. Thereafter the FBI had gone to great lengths to build a circumstantial case against Hastings. However, Sanford concluded, "They did not obtain real evidence." He advised the FBI, "If you are going to carry out a sting operation, you had better leave the stinger in the victim."[37]

Orrin Hatch of Utah explained that he found the case against Hastings circumstantial and the judge's alternative explanations plausible. The House presentation did not rise to the standard of proof he found necessary for conviction.[38] Republican Hatch's skepticism was echoed by Democrat Brock Adams of Washington and by both of Connecticut's Democratic senators, Christopher Dodd and Joseph Lieberman.[39] The latter, a member of the Impeachment Trial Committee, explained at length why he found the evidence unpersuasive. He said, however, that he had no quarrel with senators who reached a contrary conclusion, finding the deliberations "among the most thoughtful and impressive moments of this my first year in the Senate." He concluded, "Put simply, this is a case upon which reasonable men and women can and did differ."[40] Senator Joseph Biden of Delaware, like Lieberman a former state attorney general, also said that he found the evidence wanting. Biden announced that he found nothing of substance had been brought forth since a jury had voted to acquit the judge.[41]

By the time senators had finished speaking, the House managers believed they lacked the votes for conviction and removal. The realization that they had failed to persuade either the chairman or the vice chairman of the Impeachment Trial Committee, not to mention several of its other members, of the merits of their case deeply concerned the managers and their staff. They calculated from what had been said that they would muster a majority but not the two-thirds needed to remove the judge from the bench. Yet two respected members of the trial committee, Democrat Bob Kerrey of Nebraska and Republican Warren Rudman of New Hampshire, were rumored to be lobbying hard for conviction. A third senator, Paul Sarbanes of Maryland, who had taken part in the House Judiciary Committee deliberations over Richard Nixon in 1974, was also calling for Hastings's conviction. Sarbanes explained to his colleagues that impeachment involved issues and standards other than those reached in a criminal trial. Since many senators had still not publicly declared their intentions, the outcome remained uncertain.[42]

The following day President Pro Tempore Robert Byrd called the Senate to order to vote on Hastings's case. Four freshmen senators who had been members of the House during the previous Congress and had voted there to impeach the judge had asked to be excused from participating in the Senate trial to assure the perception of fairness in the proceedings.[43] As the balloting began, the outcome remained uncertain. It would continue to be so until close to the end of the initial roll call. On the critical first article, alleging a conspiracy between Hastings and Borders to obtain a $150,000 bribe from the Romano brothers, the Senate voted 69–26 to convict, four votes more than the necessary sixty-five of those present and voting. Seven of the next eight articles, involving false statements in his criminal trial, were adopted in similar votes, while one minor article, charging that Hastings had lied when he said that he had not expected Borders to show up at his hotel on one occasion, was defeated on a 48–47 vote. The Senate then decided not to cast ballots on six more false statement articles. It resoundingly rejected by a 95–0 vote the unrelated article involving the questionable claim of disclosure of wiretapping to Miami's mayor. The final omnibus article was then rejected on a 60–35 vote, a majority for conviction but less than the required two-thirds. Hastings had been convicted on eight of the seventeen articles impeaching him, and with only one such conviction necessary, he was thereby removed from his judicial position.[44]

The distribution of final votes in the Senate was markedly nonpartisan, both among those favoring conviction and those opposed. On the critical first article and most of those that followed, liberal Democrats Edward Kennedy and John Kerry of Massachusetts lined up with conservative Republicans such as Phil Gramm of Texas and Strom Thurmond of South Carolina as well as moderates from both parties in voting to convict. Those opposing Hastings's removal were, on balance, more liberal but still diverse. The bulk of these naysayers were northeastern Democrats, but they were joined by notably conservative Republican senators such as Alfonse D'Amato of New York, Orrin Hatch, and Richard Shelby of Alabama. The leaders of both parties, Democrat George Mitchell of Maine and Republican Robert Dole, voted for the judge's removal but made no effort to impose party discipline.

Voting on the impeachment of Judge Hastings was clearly treated by the Senate as a matter of individual conscience. Senators divided not along party or ideological lines but very much as jurors. They appeared to base their assessment on the weight they gave the initial jury verdict versus Doar's Eleventh Circuit investigation, Conyers's House Judiciary subcommittee judgment, and the testimony before the Senate Impeachment Trial Committee. The conclusions they reached followed neither the House managers' predictions nor the patterns of previous reviews of the case.

The House of Representatives had followed the lead of its investigating subcommittee almost exactly. After Conyers's subcommittee made a unanimous recommendation for impeachment, the Judiciary Committee did likewise, and the House came only three votes short of following suit. With little debate, the House was ready to accept the recommendations made to it. The Senate, however, behaved in a different manner. It did not follow the lead of its investigating committee so closely. Rule XI required that the trial committee present a record of its investigation without drawing conclusions, which may explain what happened subsequently. Yet it is worth noting that when votes were finally cast, five of the twelve members of the trial committee, including both the chairman and vice chairman, declared Hastings not guilty. If the margin in the committee had been mirrored in the full Senate, there would have been at least nine fewer votes for Hastings's removal, and the two-thirds requirement would not have been met.

The reason that the Senate failed to follow its committee's lead and fulfill the dire expectations of the House managers is difficult to determine, especially since most senators never explained their votes on the record. But perhaps the views of Senator Alan Simpson, one who did reveal himself and who during the alphabetical roll call cast the vote on Article I that assured Hastings's removal, offer some guidance. After admitting that he would not have had the patience to sit on the trial committee, Simpson reduced the issues to the simple one of lying. Known in the Senate for his sarcastic sense of humor, Simpson began by saying, "One of the things that make us uniquely qualified to decide this case is our ability—every one of us—to know when someone is shooting straight or trying to sell us a bill of goods." Having claimed infallibility as a lie detector, Simpson proceeded to assert, "It does not take much sense at all—common sense or horse sense—to know what this guy was doing. When you read about how he left Washington for Miami, his conduct with pay phones, the codes, and the relationship between his conduct and critical junctures in the *Romano* case, it is clear that he was a clever and duplicitous man." Without hesitation, question, or qualification, Simpson accepted the House judgment on Hastings. He was quickly convinced by the circumstantial case put together by prosecutors, the Eleventh Circuit, and the House, and he concluded that Hastings's alternative explanations represented untruths.[45] He was far from alone on the Senate floor.

The Senate vote to convict Hastings, together with the ones finding Harry Claiborne guilty three years earlier and Walter Nixon so two weeks later, necessarily left an impression on the House managers. The Senate's Claiborne and Nixon verdicts were predictable because of the judges' prior felony convictions and imprisonments. The less certain outcome of the Hastings case, however, may have produced a greater impact. The managers inevitably carried back to their Judiciary Committee colleagues an impression that defeat was looming before vindication was achieved. No doubt they were reassured that senators supported their articles of impeachment, even ones on subsidiary charges derivative of the principal alleged offense, well beyond initial expectations. Overcoming the normal skepticism of the upper body, the House spokesmen had been able to win over enough initially uncertain senators to fashion the needed constitutional supermajority. The members of the upper body had accepted their House colleagues' judgment on the assembled evidence, for the most part without any expression of doubt. When the House had brought an impeachment to the Senate, it received a respectful hearing and a favorable nonpartisan resolution. As observations of the only Senate impeachment trials in congressional memory, these perceptions would no doubt constitute a powerful encouragement to the House the next time impeachment was contemplated.

On May 19, 1993, Representative James Sensenbrenner, once again willing to initiate proceedings against off-the-track judges, introduced resolutions calling for the impeachment of two U.S. district judges, Robert F. Collins of Louisiana and Robert P. Aguilar of California.[46] Sensenbrenner submitted his resolutions six days after the Fifth Circuit Judicial Council completed a review of Collins's case and recommended his impeachment. Scripts from the 1980s seemed about to be replayed. Sensenbrenner was once again in the forefront of accusers, and the two cases bore some striking resemblances to those of Claiborne, Nixon, and Hastings. Nevertheless, despite the eagerness of a few representatives such as

Sensenbrenner to proceed, Congress again deferred action until all conventional criminal proceedings, including appeals, had been completed and the Judicial Conference of the United States had considered the cases. Congress did not regard its intervention as appropriate until all other steps had been completed and its participation was absolutely necessary. As a consequence, both judges continued to receive their judicial salaries while their cases moved at a glacial pace toward final resolution.

Robert Collins was, like Hastings, a member of the cadre of black judges put on the federal bench in the late 1970s by President Carter. Like Walter Nixon, Collins had served for a dozen years when he was accused of taking a $100,000 bribe to give favorable sentencing treatment to a man convicted of smuggling twenty-five hundred pounds of marijuana into Louisiana from Belize. Gary Young, already twice convicted of drug smuggling and facing a long prison term and large fine, claimed that he had been approached by Collins's good friend John Ross, who said that for a $100,000 payment the judge would reduce his sentence from the eight years recommended by a probation officer to three and a half years. Young agreed to cooperate with the FBI and delivered marked bills to Ross. The cash was subsequently found in Collins's chambers. When he was indicted along with Ross, the judge denounced "a blatant attempt by a twice-convicted dope dealer, aided and abetted by Government agents, to set up a black federal judge," echoing statements by a number of civil rights leaders accusing the federal government of targeting black officials around the country in an effort to discredit them.[47]

Judge Collins's defense attorney complained of "racial selectivity" in the prosecution of his client but was unable to offer a plausible alternative explanation for the evidence presented. At his trial Collins declined to testify in his own behalf. The defense only offered Ross's assertion that the money in Collins's possession was a down payment on property he was buying from the judge. The jury was evidently unimpressed. It convicted both Collins and Ross on all counts of their indictment. Two months later Collins was sentenced to nearly seven years imprisonment but remained free and on the federal payroll while his conviction was appealed.[48]

Appeals denied, Collins went to prison in 1991. Nevertheless, he did not immediately resign his judgeship and continued to receive his federal salary. In July 1993 the Judicial Conference of the United States, having completed its own review of the case, recommended that the House of Representatives undertake impeachment proceedings against the judge. At long last, with congressional action appearing imminent, Judge Collins departed from the model of Claiborne and Nixon. In August 1993 he decided to give up his seat rather than go through the congressional process to its seemingly inevitably conclusion.[49]

The other judge proposed for impeachment by Sensenbrenner in 1993, Robert Aguilar of the Northern District of California, fared better. He was also a Carter minority appointee. Aguilar, the son of Mexican immigrants with less than a year's state court judicial experience when he ascended to the federal bench in 1980, was no stranger to judicial controversy. Sitting in San Jose, he presided over multiple cases involving the area's computer and software industry. At first, he stubbornly refused to recuse himself from cases involving the Hewlett Packard Company even though his son was a longtime employee of the firm. Eventually, however, he reassigned a major case pitting Apple Computer and Microsoft against Hewlett Packard after Apple formally complained. His action, which he attributed to an unusually heavy caseload, came a month after federal investigators began looking into a $12,000 loan to the judge from a former casino operator who had been convicted of bank fraud.[50]

In 1989 Judge Aguilar was indicted on allegations of corruption and racketeering arising from his involvement with a Teamsters Union official convicted of embezzlement. Among other things, the judge was accused of unlawfully disclosing the existence of a wiretap and, as a result, obstructing justice. The charges against Aguilar rested primarily on evidence collected during eighteen months of wiretaps on his phones.

Aguilar was tried on eight felony charges in March 1990. A jury acquitted him on one count and deadlocked on the others. Retried in August, Aguilar was convicted on the wiretap disclosure and obstruction of justice allegations. The U.S. Court of Appeals for the Ninth Circuit eventually overturned the convictions. The government appealed that judgment, and in 1995 the Supreme Court reinstated the verdict on the wiretap disclosure, sending the case back to the Ninth Circuit for further proceedings.[51] Justice Department pursuit of Aguilar continued until June 1996 when the two sides finally struck a bargain. The department allowed Aguilar to retire immediately from the federal bench with a full pension. In return the judge acknowledged that in 1987 he had improperly divulged the existence of a wiretap. For its part, the Justice Department dismissed the single felony charge still pending.[52]

With their judicial appeals exhausted and the prospect of impeachment looming, both Collins and Aguilar chose to leave the bench. Collins, convicted of a felony, had no choice but to resign, while Aguilar, more successful at holding prosecutors at bay, was able to negotiate a comfortable retirement. In its post-1980 actions involving judges, Congress had made it clear that it would not tolerate blots on the image of the judiciary, whether or not proven beyond a reasonable doubt. Claiborne's and Nixon's impeachments following conviction foreshadowed Collins's certain fate, and the outcome of the Hastings case suggested that Aguilar was wise to negotiate favorable terms to leave the bench. The prospect of impeachment and conviction led both men to choose to bring down the curtain on their judicial careers.

At the same time, the cases of the five judges all took years to settle. The slow resolution of their cases resulted from a combination of protracted prosecutions, defenses that frequently involved procedural appeals, the deliberate pace of actions by the Judicial Conference of the United States, and, finally, Congress's reluctance to proceed unless absolutely necessary. The prolonged process for removing a judge certainly kept impeachment from becoming attractive as a means for dealing with any but the most egregious cases of judicial misconduct.

When the Senate completed voting on the first article of his impeachment, Alcee Hastings patted his counsel, Terence Anderson, on the arm and then wept.[53] After senators approved the second article, Senate Majority Leader George Mitchell moved that Hastings and Anderson be allowed to leave the Senate chamber. The two men did so immediately. It appeared that for all practical purposes Hastings's public career was over, buried in disgrace. But when F. Scott Fitzgerald wrote, "There are no second acts in American lives," he failed to anticipate the career resurrection of one impeached judge. By the time he had walked out of the building and stood on the Capitol steps to talk to reporters, Hastings had recovered his composure. He declared his trial unfair but announced that he was "upbeat" and would return to Florida to run for governor.[54]

Congress did not prohibit further officeholding by any of the judges impeached and convicted in the 1980s. Its failure to take such action was neither unusual nor surprising. Only twice, in 1862 with Confederacy-sympathizing Judge West Humphreys and in 1913 with influence-peddling Judge Robert W. Archbald, did Congress impose the ban on further officeholding that the Constitution stipulated as a consequence of conviction on articles of impeachment. The Senate had always treated the Constitution's reference to disqualification as discretionary. It could be imposed after conviction if a majority of senators wished, but it was not mandatory. In practice, senators seemed to feel that the disgrace of being removed from office was sufficient and thus rarely even suggested the additional penalty. For either the House or Senate to revisit the decision once it had been made would smack of double jeopardy and be legally and politically difficult.

In the 1980s the established pattern continued. As convicted felons, judges Claiborne and Nixon would have faced other obstacles to office seeking had they been so inclined. Hastings, on the other hand, had been acquitted in his criminal trial and therefore remained free of such impediment.

Hastings wasted no time before seeking the vindication that election to public office would provide. He promptly filed to run in the Democratic primary for governor of Florida in 1990, though he later shifted to a race for secretary of state when it became evident that his gubernatorial campaign was foundering. He did no better in the secretary of state contest.[55]

A more promising opportunity presented itself to Hastings in 1992. Following the 1990 U.S. census, Florida gained an additional congressional seat, and the state legislature decided to carve out a majority black district north of Miami, the impeached judge's home base. Hastings found that for once his impeachment served him well. "It certainly ratcheted up my profile," he believed. People in south Florida had paid close attention to the extensive media coverage of his case during the previous decade. "There was elation, horns honking on I-95, when I was found not guilty," he recalled about his initial trial. In the midst of his campaign for the House, a federal district court decision invalidating his Senate trial on procedural grounds, even though overturned a year later in *Nixon v. United States*, reinforced local feeling that he had been unfairly treated. A Democratic competitor's effort to use the impeachment against him backfired. A telephone campaign calling Hastings a crook led one uncommitted voter to respond, "He's my crook. You've got yours, I've got mine!" She then became a big Hastings supporter.[56] With impeachment as his distinguishing characteristic, the former judge narrowly won a multicandidate Democratic primary and then easily prevailed in the general election to become Florida's first black congressman since Reconstruction. The irony of Hastings winning a seat in the body that had impeached him did not go unnoticed.

Some members of Congress found the prospect of having in their midst a man whom they had voted to impeach to be disquieting.[57] Others professed to have no qualms about serving with someone who had been impeached. They pointed to his election by citizens who knew the story of the impeachment. Bryant, the lead House manager for Hastings's Senate trial, told the new congressman the day he was sworn in, "The people elected you. I respect that. If you can wipe the slate clean, I can wipe the slate clean." Soon thereafter Bryant and Hastings cosponsored a piece of legislation. Brooks inquired whether Hastings wished to serve on the Judiciary Committee and laughed when the former judge declined, saying that he thought he had reached the apex of his judicial career.[58] As they came to know him, members of Congress from both sides of the aisle, veterans and newcomers alike, accepted Hastings as a hardworking, genial, and satisfactory colleague.[59]

The resurrection of Alcee Hastings steadily continued. Choosing to devote attention to international relations, he became a member of the House Permanent Select Committee on Intelligence. By 2006 he was the ranking minority member on the Subcommittee on Terrorism and Homeland Security of the Permanent Select Committee as well as a congressional delegate to the Organization for Security and Cooperation in Europe. Perhaps an even greater measure of his acceptance by his peers was his selection as a Democratic party whip and a member of the influential House Rules Committee. With a shrinking minority of his colleagues in the House remaining from the Congress that had impeached him in 1989, Hastings appeared to have emerged from the darkness into which he had then been cast. Perhaps the greatest burden that he continued to bear as his congressional career ripened was the financial cost of his unsuccessful legal defense against impeachment. As late as 2005 Hastings, according to his annual congressional financial disclosure, still carried al $2.1 million debt for legal fees.[60]

More important to Hastings, in 1997 John Conyers publicly expressed doubts about the judge's impeachment. The longtime representative had come to know Hastings in the House and had recently been exposed to revelations of repeated missteps by the FBI crime laboratory, including misleading testimony about a piece of evidence from the Hastings case.[61] As a result, Conyers had come to have second thoughts about his original judgment about Hastings. He subsequently wrote a character reference when Hastings was nominated for an honor in the fraternity to which both men belonged.[62]

Still, Hastings proved unable to escape the stigma of impeachment altogether. This became evident when his party regained control of the House of Representatives in 2006 and he appeared poised to become chair of the Permanent Select Committee on Intelligence. Democrats had made unethical conduct a centerpiece in their campaign to oust Republicans from the House leadership. The incoming speaker, Nancy Pelosi, shied away from elevating Hastings to a particularly sensitive position after influential colleagues warned that his selection would provide too much ammunition for Republicans. Hastings expressed disappointment but characteristically predicted that his rehabilitation would continue, saying, "Sorry, haters, God is not finished with me yet."[63] As if to underscore that point, on the second working day of the first Democratic-controlled House in a dozen years, the speaker invited him to take the gavel and preside over the body that had once impeached him.[64]

Alcee Hastings dented the notion of impeachment as the ultimate political disgrace, although he certainly did not shatter it altogether. Impeachment's function as a public shaming ritual seemed inherent in practice as well as theory. The framers' preference for fixed legislative and executive terms and lifetime appointments for judges involved a conscious choice to diverge from the British parliamentary model of a government serving at the pleasure of a majority and officials losing authority as soon as that majority dissolved. Instead, the framers believed that republican government would be most stable and responsible with fixed terms of office. Removal from office before the completion of one's term represented more than just the acknowledgment of a general shift of political fortune. The framers intended it as a severe negative judgment on an individual's conduct, the utmost censure by a disapproving majority of the people's elected representatives and a supermajority of the body presumed to reflect the mature political wisdom of the nation. That impeachment and conviction imposed no mandatory punishment other than the loss of office itself underscored the seriousness the framers attributed to this public shaming. They regarded not being able to finish a term of office with which one had been entrusted to be a resounding humiliation for a citizen of a democratic republic.

Until the 1990s no federal official impeached and convicted had ever resumed a public career. Impeachees who escaped conviction finished their term in office, as, for example, did both Justice Samuel Chase and President Andrew

Alcee Hastings presiding over the House of Representatives, January 10, 2007.
Public domain image courtesy of C-SPAN.

Johnson. Johnson even sought office again and was elected by the Tennessee legislature to a term in the U.S. Senate. Before Hastings, however, no official removed through impeachment had subsequently secured a position of public trust at the hands of voters.

Hastings, an effervescent personality, continued to maintain his innocence while claiming that he bore no grudges against those who had voted against him. "I learned a long time ago that success is the best revenge," he said. "That is my motto and my mantra, and it is my mind-set. Vengeance serves no useful purpose and bitterness causes you to go after people and to consume yourself when you could be on about your business. I've had a very good career; it was damaged by those events."[65] In 1998 a few colleagues consulted him about his impeachment experience, and he took the House floor to argue against the impeachment of President Bill Clinton. The speech may not have altered any votes, but merely giving it reminded Congress that there could be political life after impeachment.

Hastings's ongoing political career since 1992, even if somewhat hampered by his removal from the bench, is both a testament to the abilities of an individual to overcome a stigma and a suggestion of shifting public attitudes toward impeachment. His repeated elections to the House of Representatives signaled his constituents' indifference to his impeachment, perhaps because of continuing suspicion that it was racially motivated and unjustified. The Hastings story reverberated in a subsequent impeachment and suggested that the culture of impeachment continued to evolve even as Congress developed routines for dealing with calls for it.

12

Impeachment as Consensual:

The Case of Bill Clinton

Alcee Hastings was the first but not the last federal officeholder to endure and outlive the stigma of impeachment in the 1990s. While the United States Congress had since the mid-1980s added considerably to its limited experience in carrying the impeachment process through to conclusion in dealing with Judges Claiborne, Nixon, and, finally, Hastings, the general public paid little notice to these cases or to the subsequent resignation of two other judges on the verge of being impeached. Few beyond residents of their judicial districts and Capitol Hill were even aware of what had transpired. Grassroots America would, however, give far more attention to efforts to impeach President Bill Clinton than to proceedings against federal judges or even the remarkable political resurrection of Alcee Hastings.

The Clinton case provided a vivid reminder of the founders' intention that a federal official should not be removed during his assigned term unless an unusually high degree of consensus was reached as to the necessity of such an action. Only agreement among two-thirds or more of the elected representatives most insulated from the passions of the moment, the members of the Senate, could legitimize an action so contrary to the normal practices of democratic choice. The framers believed that such a consensus would reach beyond the normal bounds of partisanship and meet the high standards of democratic selection of leaders that they sought to assure.

As the campaign to remove Clinton from the presidency went forward, it ignored the constitutional requirements of consensus the founders had established. As a result, the effort to drive Clinton from office would mark a turning point in the evolution of American political and constitutional culture. The infrequently used constitutional device would, ironically, come to be thought of as a more commonplace aspect of political rhetoric and partisan combat.

Bill Clinton's impeachment attracted far more scrutiny than any threatened or actual impeachment since the case of Richard Nixon. Not only did it go further than any formal congressional action against a president in over a century, but it also did so in a manner and with a result that challenged prevailing perceptions of the validity and integrity of the constitutional removal process. For the first time since the era of Andrew Johnson, foes of a president actively engaged in constructing an arguably impeachable offense rather than merely reacting to discovered misconduct of major consequence. The least attractive dimensions of impeachment as political process became evident in the lengthy investigation of Clinton: the pouncing on a tawdry personal misstep after fruitless years of looking for malfeasance in governance and, finally, the inexorable pursuit of impeachment even after the electorate had registered disapproval of the effort. The ability of Clinton to survive impeachment with a remarkably positive public image under the circumstances became a hallmark of his administration. At the same time, the episode demonstrated how unrelentingly impeachment-minded partisan opponents could politically cripple a president and prevent him from advancing his agenda. As a consequence, the Clinton episode affected the political culture of the United States at every level, increasing talk of impeachment as a response to ordinary political differences and yet weakening the threat of impeachment as a restraint upon the American presidency.

The formal charges against President Clinton involved obstructing justice and committing perjury before a grand jury. Nevertheless, to most Americans the Clinton impeachment was about private sexual misconduct and lying about it under oath. To some this was heinous behavior, while to others it was understandable, excusable, and certainly not reason to remove from office an otherwise satisfactory president. Seen in that light, the episode reflected a cultural division regarding sexual behavior that had been growing in the United States since the 1960s. A fractious debate over the proper bounds of personal behavior and the private rights of individuals to deviate from social norms had deeply riven the society. The conflict had evolved from comparatively mild though often deeply felt positions on issues of provocative fashion, literature, and film and the use of artificial birth control to far more emotionally charged disputes over acceptable sexual practices, gender equality, abortion, and the nature of marriage. Uncompromisable differences over standards of sexual conduct played an increasingly important role in the definition of a political conservative or liberal. With beliefs about sexuality serving as a powerful polarizing force in late-twentieth-century America, the political arena inevitably became a battleground on which competing ideologies sought victory.

Profound changes in the methods of political communication since the simple days of "Impeach Earl Warren" billboards played a significant role in the Clinton episode. An extraordinary expansion of the number and variety of outlets for political news and commentary provided media access to a multitude of voices, not all of them well informed, temperate, or even minimally responsible about matters on which they held forth. Post-Watergate journalists confronted increased incentives to investigate the private as well as public conduct of public figures in far greater depth and detail than previously. Changing technology that speeded and diversified the distribution of information also intensified journalistic competition, increased opportunities for ideologically driven commentary, and accelerated the dispersal of the results of closer scrutiny of political figures. These developments took place at the very time that the changing culture of sexuality first made it socially permissible to discuss and debate openly matters that had not previously been a part of general public discourse. While a human tendency to gossip may be ages old, the capacity and eagerness of Americans in the 1990s to document, spread, and reinforce rumor, turning it into public scandal, appeared unprecedented.

A loud and rancorous debate over sexual proprieties, carried out in the most public of forums and employing language never before audible in American political discourse, was only possible in an extremely contentious partisan environment. Verbally vicious and ideologically uncompromising postures had long been struck on the fringes of the American political scene. However, in the hands of strong-willed individuals who felt themselves unfairly denied their proper leadership role in conducting government, a slash-and-burn style of politics had evolved to new heights and by the 1990s had entered the mainstream. Ironically, a resurgent conservatism proved to be less concerned with the maintenance of traditional standards of taste and social as well as constitutional stability than with the acquisition of power to direct the nation's affairs. In such a political culture, impeachment came to be thought of not as a last resort against an otherwise uncontrollable abuser of official power but, rather, as an extension of the ordinary contest for control of the reins of government.

The outcome was the constitutional and political equivalent of a train wreck. A determined effort to impeach President Clinton managed to besmirch his reputation but fell far short of its goal of driving him from office. He survived due to widespread public support for his overall approach to government and belief that his impeachment was being improperly sought on the basis of private rather than official conduct. At the same time, the campaign led his accusers to be widely viewed as rigid, grasping partisans indifferent to finding a means for registering disapproval of unseemly conduct that would be broadly embraced by the American people. The overall result was to raise the profile of impeachment as a political device for challenging a president. At the same time, the episode increased doubts about the efficacy of this constitutional instrument for effectively disciplining federal officials.

In the end, the Clinton impeachment revolved around the distinction between private and official conduct always present in the disciplinary mechanism created in 1787. The founders had devised impeachment at least in part to shelter the nation's chief executive from lesser distractions while serving as the people's chosen tribune. As much as the framers thought they had made their intention evident by limiting the grounds for impeachment to "treason, bribery, and other high crimes and misdemeanors," the Clinton episode made clear that defining such an offense and carrying out such a proceeding was ultimately a political rather than a judicial act. Decisions concerning the impeachment of

Clinton, whether pro or con, were ultimately grounded in political preferences rather than clear legal principles.

The roots of the Clinton impeachment lay buried in the changing culture of Congress. From the beginning of the New Deal through the 1960s, Congress, with two brief exceptions following the elections of 1946 and 1952, remained firmly in Democratic hands. The Democrats' majority in those years, however, included both a large contingent of northern urban progressives and a substantial group of southern conservatives. The influence of the southerners was exaggerated by the fact that after winning a seat in the House or Senate from this heavily Democratic region, they seldom faced significant opposition to their reelection. As a consequence they steadily acquired power in a congressional committee system in which seniority determined leadership. Not only were the two wings of the Democratic majority forced to compromise with each other to assemble a majority for a legislative measure, but both also found it advantageous from time to time to make alliances with the minority Republicans in order to get their way. Depending on the issue, alliances would shift, but legislative success customarily required finding acceptable compromise positions that would bridge partisan or ideological divisions.[1]

Loyalty to the body in which one served and respect for the process of legislative compromise was enhanced by the character of congressional life during these decades. Given the nature of travel in the era before jet airplanes became ubiquitous, members of Congress, especially those whose constituencies were far distant, tended to spend the bulk of their time in Washington. The legislative schedule called for full weeks of committee hearings and meetings, party caucuses, and legislative floor debates, with only occasional extended recesses during a congressional session so that members could travel to the states and districts they represented.

Under such circumstances, most members moved their families to the Washington area. They commonly lived in the same neighborhoods as counterparts in the other party. Their spouses shopped in the same stores and joined the same parent-teacher associations. Their children not only attended the same schools but also played on the same Little League baseball teams and went to the same summer camps. Their families attended the same churches, visited the same museums, and went to the same concerts, plays, and sporting events. Opportunities frequently arose for members, as well as their spouses and children, to become acquainted socially with similarly placed individuals on the other side of the congressional aisle. They could develop an understanding for each other in an environment in which their living situations had much in common even if they were affiliated with different parties. Partisan differences could be sharp, and occasionally rhetorical extremists appeared in their midst. However, the respect and sympathy for adversaries and the faith in their integrity that developed among most members of Congress under these circumstances served to encourage a political climate of accommodation and compromise.

The culture of Capitol Hill changed during the last third of the twentieth century, at first gradually and then at an accelerating pace. The moderate middle of America's complex two-party system began to shrink. Fundamental differences over civil rights legislation and the Vietnam War strained some relationships. Moderation and the incentives to compromise eroded during the Nixon administration. Republican conservatism grew stronger as the party began to win seats in the South, and Democrats such as South Carolina's Senator Strom Thurmond began to switch over to a more ideologically compatible party. Conversely, the Democratic Party started to lose the restraining influence of its southern wing. The huge Democratic congressional victories of 1964 and 1974, the smaller but still quite significant Republican gains of 1966 and 1972, and the simple passage of time had the cumulative effect of removing many of those members on both sides of the aisle accustomed to working across party lines. The Democratic surge in 1974 brought in a large class of new members whose victory could be attributed to Watergate. The perceived need to accommodate the remaining Republicans flagged while the sense of the desirability and even the propriety of doing so waned.

Republican advances in subsequent elections introduced to Congress additional members less inclined than their predecessors to work across the partisan divide. Party gains in the South in particular brought representatives to Washington who believed that accommodation was unprincipled and would render the party forever a powerless minority in the House. Congressman Newt Gingrich, first elected from Georgia in 1978, began to advocate and demonstrate a more adversarial approach, challenging the accommodating practices of House Republican leaders such as John Rhodes and Robert Michel.

Just as Gingrich arrived, the House of Representatives decided to start televising its sessions. At first most members gave the potential of the new technology little thought. Gingrich, however, seized the opportunity to make speech after speech castigating the Democratic majority. With the camera tightly focused on him by House rules, the fact that he often spoke to an empty chamber was not evident to the cable television audience. Democrats seldom thought the angry rhetoric of a minority of the minority party worth an immediate response, leaving viewers with only Gingrich's unchallenged explanation of House actions. On the rare occasions when Gingrich did provoke a response, as from an angered Speaker Thomas P. "Tip" O'Neill in May 1984, it merely served to call attention to the backbench Republican congressman.[2] As other like-minded Republicans first elected in the 1980s and early 1990s joined him in the House, and especially after he mounted an attack on Speaker Jim Wright's ethics, which led to the Democratic leader's resignation in 1989, Gingrich found himself in the vanguard of a Republican insurgency admiring of his aggressive and confrontational approach.

Congressional practices gradually changed along with the personnel. Improvements in air travel made possible easier and thus more frequent trips between Washington and members' home states or districts. A combination of the need to maintain a residence in one's district, the high cost of a second domicile in Washington, and the limitations of salary caused a growing number of members to choose not to uproot their families. The steadily rising populations of most states and districts, leading to increasingly costly television-based campaigns, added substantially to demands on legislators to devote time to fund-raising. The desire of members to spend more time away from Capitol Hill for both personal and political reasons encouraged leaders to compress the congressional workweek. In 1998 sixty-five Republican members of the House signed a formal petition to their speaker-elect demanding that the three-day legislative workweek be maintained.[3] As Friday and Monday committee and floor sessions became ever rarer, the possibility of casual social contact across party lines receded.

Many of the more subtle changes taking place did not become evident, much less reach their apex, until the 1994 election brought a more rapid than usual turnover of seats. In that election the Republicans gained control of both houses for the first time in forty years. Republicans replaced nine Democrats in the Senate and fifty-two in the House. Robert Dole, a longtime Kansas Republican senator and an acerbic partisan, moved from minority to majority leader of the upper body. With the House's minority leader, Robert Michel, retiring, the far more combative Gingrich was chosen speaker by the new House majority.

Elected on a wave of anti-incumbent public sentiment, many of the new members taking office in January 1995 arrived with a hostile attitude toward the customs of the institution they were joining. As a result, they were inclined to absorb as little of the culture of the capital city as possible. For the two or three nights a week they planned to spend there they rented rooms, shared apartments, or, in the case of Representative Bob Barr of Georgia, slept on an office couch and showered in the House gymnasium. In this environment the opportunity for casual social encounters, especially with members of the other party, shriveled. Indeed, the chilly atmosphere was reflected in the collapse of a bipartisan effort by Republican Ray LaHood of Illinois and Democrats David Skaggs of Colorado and Tom Sawyer of Ohio to build a more civil culture through a weekend social retreat for members and their families near the start of each Congress. The first such retreat drew over two hundred members to a resort near Hershey, Pennsylvania, in 1997. However, rapidly declining attendance led to the event's abandonment after 2002.[4] The increasingly combative attitudes toward the opposing party stirred by ever more brutal and negative election campaigns were not assuaged when contact was largely limited to the highly partisan environment of committee hearings, legislation markups, floor sessions, and a few formal occasions where one was expected to applaud for one's party and register silent disapproval of the other side.

As the comity of Congress evaporated, the once-common camaraderie across party lines became rare. Such friendships attracted notice when they did occur, as when Senator William Cohen, a Republican from Maine, relaxed by writing an espionage novel with his Democrat counterpart Gary Hart of Colorado or collaborated on an account of the Iran-Contra investigation with fellow Maine senator, Democrat George Mitchell.[5] Even the social bond maintained by two fellow Rhodes Scholars, Republican Richard Lugar of Indiana and Democrat Paul Sarbanes of Maryland, was considered noteworthy.[6] Interestingly, both Cohen and Sarbanes had learned to cooperate across party lines, if not for the first time at least under the most intense pressure, as they served on the House Judiciary Committee during the 1974 impeachment hearings. In the absence of such cross-partisan relationships, old patterns of accommodation and compromise, neglected in the period following Watergate when the Democrats held large majorities, disappeared, superseded in the 1990s by a far more belligerent and opportunistic partisanship.

The election of Bill Clinton as president in 1992 unsettled Republicans in Washington. After holding the White House for twelve years and twenty of the last twenty-four, they had become accustomed to controlling the executive branch. This had provided a means of blunting the initiatives of the Democratic congressional majority and advancing a conservative agenda embraced by Richard Nixon, Ronald Reagan, and George H. W. Bush. But Bush's ineffective handling of a weak economy together with third-party candidate Ross Perot's persistent warnings about growing federal deficits helped Clinton gain the presidency. Clinton's opponents were very conscious that the new president had received only 43 percent of the popular vote even though his total was well ahead of Bush's 38 percent and Perot's 19 percent. The loss of the presidency challenged the Republicans to find new means to thwart Democratic policy initiatives. Attention quickly focused on the new president, whom they already viewed with disdain as he entered office.

At first glance, Clinton appeared to represent the classic American success story. Rising from very modest origins in a small Arkansas town, he had gone to Washington as an undergraduate student at Georgetown University, then earned a prestigious Rhodes Scholarship for two years of study at Oxford University, and finally completed his formal education at Yale Law School. He returned to Arkansas to teach law at the state university and soon plunged into an ambitious but unsuccessful 1974 race for Congress against an entrenched Republican, who was narrowly able to withstand the reaction against Watergate. Two years later, however, Clinton was elected Arkansas attorney general. Two years after that the thirty-two-year-old Democrat won his first term as governor and, with the exception of the 1981–1982 term, had held onto the office until he entered the White House.[7]

Along the way, Clinton did a variety of things that his political opponents would later hold against him. Together with many contemporaries he received a series of student deferments that allowed him to avoid the military draft. Midway through his Rhodes Scholarship, he pledged that if his deferment was extended, he would enter the Reserve Officers Training Corps (ROTC) program once he finished at Oxford. However, when the Selective Service established a draft lottery system and he drew a high enough number to avoid the draft, Clinton withdrew his ROTC pledge. Meanwhile, he participated in anti–Vietnam War demonstrations in England. Later, while attending law school, he helped manage George McGovern's campaign for president in the state of Texas. During his long service as Arkansas governor, he and his wife, Hillary Rodham, whom he had met at Yale and who practiced law in Little Rock after their 1975 marriage, accepted offers to make some lucrative investments. In the same years rumors began to circulate that Clinton repeatedly engaged in extramarital relationships. None of these behaviors was unique. Indeed, draft avoidance, antiwar efforts, financial opportunism, and even sexual infidelities were not altogether uncommon among his peers in and out of politics. Yet Clinton's extraordinary political rise made him more of a target for complaints about all these deeds.

From the moment of his inauguration as president, Clinton faced determined opposition from Republicans, elements of the press, and even a few members of his own party. He hurt his own cause by several early missteps in staff hiring and firing. He did not adequately check the background of his two initial choices for attorney general, and, to his chagrin, discrediting revelations ultimately forced both to withdraw. A similar fate befell his first candidate to head the Justice Department's Civil Rights Division after she was eviscerated by the *Wall Street Journal* for some of her legal writings. Likewise, the clumsy firing of seven holdover employees of the White House Travel Office proved embarrassing. Those dismissed made travel arrangements for the presidential press corps, which reacted by casting the terminations in an unfavorable light.

Most important, at the outset the young president gave the appearance of being a weak legislative leader. To fulfill a campaign pledge, Clinton first requested that Congress adopt a controversial measure to secure full rights for homosexuals in the military. Solid Republican opposition together with Democratic defections forced him to retreat and settle for a "Don't ask, don't tell" executive order that satisfied no one. Then, having inherited a large and growing federal budget deficit, Clinton proposed a package of economic reforms that would ultimately help generate sustained prosperity. However, with congressional Republicans not willing to give tax increases a single vote and with several conservative Democrats defecting, the economic recovery package proved hard to adopt. A $30 billion public works program to stimulate employment soon fell to a Republican filibuster. Increases in income taxes on the wealthiest 1 percent of the population and a federal gasoline tax increase also failed to pass. The rest of the plan, involving deficit reduction and an Earned Income Tax Credit to reduce taxes on the working poor, finally squeaked through the House on a 218–216 vote and the Senate by the margin of Vice President Al Gore's tie-breaking vote. The truncated economic recovery package, although beneficial in the long run, was far less than what Clinton had sought. The narrow victory (which the switch of one vote in either house could have turned into defeat) exposed the limits of his political leadership. The image of weakness would be confirmed during the next year as his proposed North American Free Trade Agreement (NAFTA) was approved by Congress with more Republican than Democratic support and his foremost legislative initiative, a substantial reform of the nation's health care system, suffered a resounding defeat.[8]

With Clinton's vulnerabilities exposed, his opponents pursued him relentlessly. They made much of the May 1993 death of deputy White House counsel Vincent Foster, formerly one of Hillary Clinton's Little Rock law partners, only four months into the new administration. On its surface the suicide of a man confronting unaccustomed pressure and suffering from clinical depression, Foster's death spawned numerous conspiracy theories, some involving his role in Clinton investments that themselves remained under suspicion.

Since at least 1989, political opponents had been thoroughly exploring the Clintons' activities during the 1970s and 1980s. A few frustrated Arkansas political rivals whom Governor Clinton had regularly outwitted and outpolled as well as a handful of disgruntled state workers became the visible face of the opposition. Their effectiveness in publicizing their complaints was significantly enhanced by substantial financial support they quietly received from outside the state. As early as 1989 Republican National Committee chairman Lee Atwater had started exploring ways to undercut the potential future opponent. By the time Clinton ran for and won the presidency, several enormously wealthy individuals who detested him started to pour funds into an effort to discredit him. They called their effort "the Arkansas Project." Various early foes of the governor contributed stories of sexual peccadilloes and financial chicanery that would surface to wound but not destroy him in the 1992 presidential campaign. Then and later, many of the tales of sexual liaisons turned out to be undocumented, questionable, or outright spurious, spread by enemies or paid for and published by the sensationalist tabloid press that had also reported on George H. W. Bush's meetings with space aliens. As the Clinton-haters moved forward, they enlisted allies, some of whom were or aspired to be high-visibility media figures and others of whom were content to keep a lower profile in law firms, government agencies, and elsewhere. None of this was altogether unusual among efforts to influence American politics, but it was distinctive in the degree of its unrestrained animus toward Clinton.[9]

Much of the attention of their critics focused on the Clintons' investment in the development of riverfront vacation property in northwest Arkansas by the Whitewater Land Company. This speculative venture had been initiated by James McDougal, a contributor to Bill Clinton's political campaigns and, as president of Madison Guaranty Savings and Loan of Little Rock, a legal client of Hillary Clinton. McDougal's Madison savings and loan, whose affairs were entangled with the unsuccessful Whitewater venture, failed as part of the nationwide savings and loan collapse of the middle 1980s. Thanks to McDougal's many missteps, the Clintons ended up losing most of their investment and being saddled with Whitewater debts, perhaps the clearest evidence that they were duped by McDougal rather than conspiring with him.

The complicated affairs of Madison and Whitewater were, however, seized upon by Clinton critics as evidence of failed regulatory oversight by the governor and improper influence on the part of his wife. Charges of corruption in connection with Whitewater and Madison surfaced during the 1992 election campaign and reappeared in the awkward early months of the Clinton presidency. From his exile in New Jersey Nixon analyzed the situation and concluded that the young president might be attempting to cover up something. In 1993 he began telling his aide Monica Crowley he wanted to see as vigorous an investigation by Republicans as the Democrats had conducted of Watergate.[10] No hard evidence of impropriety by the Clintons was ever presented, nor was any "smoking gun" ever found, but McDougal's conviction on various counts and the Clintons' undoubted former friendship with him fueled ongoing suspicions.[11]

The preoccupation of the president's political foes with his prepresidential conduct was unprecedented. Although John Kennedy's private life, Lyndon Johnson's investments, and other presidents' activities prior to their becoming chief executive had raised questions during election campaigns, they never became the subject of congressional investigations once the public had cast its votes. Even the intense scrutiny of Nixon in 1973 and 1974 had been confined to his conduct as president. The decision of Republicans early on in the Clinton administration to break from the pattern of the past signaled their disdain for a president some of them regarded as illegitimate from the start. Launching an inquiry that strongly implied suspicion of criminal conduct and threatened a subpoena of the chief executive's private prepresidential papers as well as of the records of his staff also marked an increasingly combative and negative political atmosphere. Finally, investigating Clinton's earlier history served as a measure of indifference to the limits on political challenges to chief executives implied by the impeachment instrument itself. Extending the reach of presidential examination ignored the long-term impact such a precedent might set, encouraging defensive and secretive conduct of the presidency as well as poisoning congressional relations with executives of the other party.[12]

In the fall of 1993, Republicans, joined by a few congressional Democrats, began calling for the appointment of an independent counsel to investigate the Clintons' possible wrongdoing in connection with their Whitewater investments.

The demand drew on the standard claims since Watergate that administrations should not be relied on to police themselves and on the Supreme Court's 1988 *Morrison v. Olson* ruling that prosecutors independent of executive branch oversight were constitutional. At the White House a debate raged between political advisers who advocated disclosure of financial records and the appointment of a special prosecutor since the Clintons had nothing to hide and legal advisers who objected to such an appointment. White House legal counsel Bernard Nussbaum, who had been Hillary Rodham's superior when she worked on the House Judiciary Committee impeachment staff in 1974, made an impassioned argument against a special prosecutor. Once appointed, Nussbaum contended, such a figure could range without oversight, restraint, or time limit across the Clintons' affairs. Furthermore, he said, some charge would inevitably be filed to justify the investigation. Better to disclose all pertinent documents immediately and watch the story soon fade rather than allow such an "evil" prosecutor to get started. Clinton, however, days after his mother's death and in the midst of a European trip, wearily agreed to request appointment of an independent counsel to examine the Whitewater and Vince Foster matters.[13]

On the first anniversary of Clinton's inauguration, Attorney General Janet Reno named Republican Robert Fiske, a respected New York attorney and former federal prosecutor, as special counsel to investigate Whitewater and the Foster incident. The 1978 independent counsel law had expired near the end of the Bush administration; the still-unconcluded investigation of Iran-Contra by Independent Counsel Lawrence Walsh had soured many, especially Republicans, on the office. When Walsh had indicted Defense Secretary Caspar Weinberger, then Senate minority leader Robert Dole had called the independent counsel and his aides "assassins."[14] Theodore Olson, the Reagan administration assistant attorney general who had unsuccessfully challenged the independent counsel statute in *Morrison v. Olson*, complained, "It results in substantial injustice to individuals and cost to the taxpayers."[15] With the independent counsel law no longer in effect and its restoration uncertain, Reno was under no obligation to follow its guidelines. So she acted on her own in choosing Fiske.

Fiske promptly proceeded with an inquiry into the Whitewater matter, setting up an office in Little Rock within days.[16] After five months, he issued two preliminary reports. The first determined that Vince Foster had been a suicide, a victim of untreated clinical depression, and that no further investigation of his death was warranted. The second found insufficient evidence to establish that there had been any White House or Treasury Department effort to influence the probes of Whitewater or Madison Guaranty. No indictments were justified, Fiske concluded. For a few hours, it appeared that the Whitewater controversy was at an end.[17]

While Fiske was at work, however, Republicans withdrew their objections and Congress finally agreed to renew the 1978 independent counsel law. Ironically, on the very day that Fiske issued his report, President Clinton signed the measure. Thereupon supervisory responsibility for the Whitewater inquiry devolved upon a panel of three federal judges appointed by Chief Justice William Rehnquist. Instead of simply confirming Reno's appointment of Fiske and allowing him to wrap up his work, as the attorney general suggested, the panel of judges selected a counsel who, they decided, would be more independent.[18]

The new Whitewater investigator, Kenneth W. Starr, possessed a contrasting background and, it would turn out, a very different approach from his predecessor. Whereas Fiske had been a largely apolitical moderate Republican and a veteran prosecutor, his replacement was a decidedly partisan veteran of the Reagan and Bush administrations. A highly regarded constitutional lawyer who had clerked for Chief Justice Warren Burger, been appointed to the federal bench at age thirty-seven by Reagan, and then served as Bush's solicitor general, Starr, it was thought, would have been a likely Supreme Court nominee had Bush won a second term. Despite an impressive résumé, however, Starr had no experience whatsoever in conducting a prosecution.

Furthermore, Starr found it difficult to avoid questions about his impartiality. Only weeks before his appointment he had appeared on a Public Television program to criticize the Clinton White House for claiming immunity from a civil suit against the president by an Arkansas woman named Paula Corbin Jones.[19] He subsequently worked for a conservative group on a brief opposing the White House position on the Jones suit, raising questions as to whether he was as unbiased and could be as fair as his sponsors contended. Years later, such concerns would reappear when his undercover collaboration with Jones's attorneys proved to be a turning point in the case against the president.[20] Harry Edwards, a federal appellate judge, dismissed charges that Starr's appointment had resulted from improper influence on David Santelle, chair of the three-judge panel, by North Carolina Republican senators Jesse Helms and Lauch Faircloth, both outspoken Clinton critics, but doubts lingered.[21]

Rather than proceeding on the basis of the work Fiske had done, Starr decided to start the investigation over at the beginning. Unlike Fiske, who had been intent on concluding the work as rapidly as possible, Starr was determined to take as much time as necessary to assure that he and his staff of attorneys and investigators could explore the matter fully. The two men appeared equally committed to punishing those guilty of misconduct, but they had divergent attitudes about a prosecutor's obligation to remove the shadow of suspicion from the innocent as quickly as possible. Whereas Fiske had devoted full time to the Whitewater assignment, Starr gave it only partial attention while he continued to draw a salary at the Washington law firm he had joined after the 1992 election.[22]

Within a year of beginning his work, Starr secured indictments against Jim and Susan McDougal and Jim Guy Tucker, Clinton's successor as Arkansas governor, in connection with the affairs of Madison Guaranty. A year later they would be found guilty, but no connection between Clinton and their complex financial schemes was proven. Only uncorroborated testimony about an alleged 1986 telephone conversation by coconspirator David Hale, who testified for the prosecution in exchange for lenient treatment, sought to tie Clinton to the scheme. Clinton denied the conversation had occurred, and prosecutors presented no evidence in support of Hale's self-serving and suspect claim.[23]

With the McDougal and Tucker convictions in May 1996, the Whitewater prosecution had, except for appeals, run its course. Remaining investigations of the Travel Office firings, the Foster suicide, misuse of FBI records by the White House personnel office, and the disappearance of Hillary Clinton's law office billing records had only the loosest of ties to the president. The ominous "-gate" labels they acquired, "Travelgate" and "Filegate," linking them to the recent history of impeachment, obscured their modest importance. Thereafter, as Starr pressed on and on with dogged investigation of matters of minor consequence, speculation increased as to whether he was displaying his lack of prosecutorial experience or fulfilling a partisan agenda in maintaining a cloud over Clinton for as long as possible. In any case, appreciation grew within the White House for the departed Bernard Nussbaum's warnings about a special prosecutor.

Over the next several years, political life in Washington continued on its contentious course while Starr pursued his inquiry. Congress had changed dramatically in November 1994 as the Republicans gained a majority of seats and Newt Gingrich became speaker of the House. Clinton's fortunes appeared for the moment to have suffered a sharp setback. Not for the last time, however, the newly empowered Republicans underestimated his political skill and resiliency. In a fierce 1995 partisan battle over the federal budget, neither side was willing to compromise. Clinton adroitly placed the blame for a temporary shutdown of the government and delay in payment of Social Security and veterans' benefits on intransigent Gingrich-led Republicans. He also emerged victorious in a partisan fight over welfare reform the following year. In 1996 an acrimonious contest for the presidency confirmed Clinton's popularity with the electorate as he handily defeated his Republican rival, Robert Dole.

Throughout all these political battles the energetic Starr investigation moved forward. With Clinton's second inauguration, however, the probe appeared near collapse. Starr announced his resignation as independent counsel effective August 1. He intended to become dean of the Pepperdine University Law School and School of Public Policy in Malibu, California, a conservative institution that, like the Arkansas Project, received its largest donations from the Scaife family of Pittsburgh. Conservatives were aghast at this abandonment of the pursuit of Clinton. William Safire of the *New York Times,* a former Nixon speechwriter, excoriated Starr for having "a warped sense of duty" and for bringing "shame on the legal profession by walking out on his client—the people of the United States."[24] Safire, who often used Watergate terms such as "cover-up," "stonewalling," and "obstruction of justice" in writing about the Clintons, called Starr "craven."[25] Reportedly shocked by the angry reactions of colleagues and staff as well as opinion shapers such as Safire, Starr reconsidered, withdrew his resignation, and threw himself into even more vigorous probing of the president.[26]

Nevertheless, by the end of 1997 Starr's three-and-a-half-year inquiry had failed to announce a single conclusion about the president. Evidently Starr was loath to admit that he had failed to find any basis for legal action against the president even though his investigation was stalled.[27] A year later the Office of Independent Counsel would finally acknowledge that no grounds had been found to bring any charges relating to Whitewater or Vince Foster's death. In the meantime, Democrats continued to complain about a needless expenditure, approaching $40 million, that served no purpose other than to harass the White House. Soon even the Republican Senate majority leader, Trent Lott, was growing impatient, momentarily calling on Starr to "show his cards" or close down his operation.[28] Yet an unrelated legal matter was about to breathe new life into Starr's moribund inquiry and confirm Bernard Nussbaum's worst fears.

The campaign undertaken by Bill Clinton's political foes to discredit him benefited from chance circumstances. Never was this more true than in the case of Paula Corbin Jones. Using Jones, Clinton's opponents were able to keep alive questions about his gubernatorial conduct and repeatedly accuse him of possessing reprehensible qualities. Then, abetted by a questionable Supreme Court ruling and Clinton's own foolishness, they were able to transform an event from his prepresidential past into a justification for presidential impeachment. Actions that, if they did occur as alleged, were improper but not at all within the realm of what the Constitution's framers had considered the basis for impeachment provided an opportunity to entangle the president in a situation that offered him a choice between immediate and profound public embarrassment and undoubted political damage, on the one hand, and a less likely but still significant risk of arguably valid impeachment, on the other.

In May 1991 Paula Corbin was a twenty-three-year-old state worker. As she later told the story, Arkansas state trooper Danny Ferguson brought her to the governor's suite at the Excelsior Hotel in Little Rock. As soon as she and Clinton were alone, she alleged, Clinton made unwelcome sexual advances that she rebuffed. She left the room but for the moment told no one about the incident. Instead, according to Ferguson, she announced to him that she would like to become the governor's regular girlfriend. Ferguson's fellow trooper, Larry Patterson, conveyed the story to the Arkansas Project. In a 1993 interview published in the *American Spectator*, he claimed that members of the governor's security detail procured women for trysts with Clinton, one of whom Patterson referred to as "Paula." Although unidentifiable from this limited description, Corbin, who by then had married, assumed her husband's name, and moved to

California and thus was even more untraceable, emerged to announce herself as the abused woman in a speech to the February 1994 Washington convention of the Conservative Political Action Committee. Jones offered up a lurid account of Clinton's sexual overtures, saying that she only wanted an acknowledgment of misconduct and an apology. Three months later, when no such self-immolating statement was forthcoming from the president, she filed a $700,000 civil suit for sexual harassment in federal district court in Little Rock.[29]

The Jones suit, coming so soon after the start of the independent counsel's Whitewater investigation, further embarrassed Clinton but for the moment did not draw him into court. Attorneys for the president quickly filed a dismissal motion based on the flip side of the impeachment provision: While in office a chief executive is constitutionally immune from civil as well as criminal suits even if they involve matters that precede his presidency. The purpose was not to immunize a president from responsibility for his conduct but rather to assure the citizenry that their chosen executive would not be distracted from his constitutionally assigned tasks.

The president's attorneys contended that Paula Jones at least needed to wait until Clinton left the White House for a court to hear her complaint. Agreeing in a lengthy opinion, Susan Webber Wright, the Little Rock federal district judge to whom the case was assigned, ruled on December 28, 1994, that the Constitution clearly specified that the overriding interest of the nation required that a sitting president not be diverted from carrying out his public duties. Allowing civil damage actions such as the one filed by Jones, Wright suggested, might permit harassment of the chief executive. Therefore, trial of a civil suit must be postponed until the defendant was no longer president.[30]

Wright underscored that presidential immunity was temporary, a function of public interest and constitutional design. It did not require dismissal of Jones's suit, but only postponement until after Clinton left office in 1997 or 2001. "There would seem to be no reason why," the judge wrote, "the discovery and deposition process could not proceed as to all persons including the President himself. This approach eliminates the problem that witnesses may die, disappear, become incapacitated, or become forgetful due to the passage of time."[31] This ruling, an aside to the main judgment, appeared to be almost an afterthought. It would nevertheless prove fateful, opening a door for the ongoing effort to bring down President Clinton.

Attorneys for both sides immediately appealed Judge Wright's ruling halting substantive proceedings for the moment.[32] The U.S. Court of Appeals for the Eighth Circuit narrowly adopted a contrary view of the extent of constitutional protection for an incumbent president. It took a confined view of executive immunity, holding that a suit arising out of activities prior to assumption of the presidency and not related to official duties was entitled to proceed. It pointed to three comparatively minor civil suits filed against presidents Theodore

Roosevelt, Harry Truman, and John Kennedy before they took office that had gone forward. The appeals court made only one concession to the executive office. It directed the court responsible for the case to schedule it with sensitivity to the president's need to perform official duties.

The Eighth Circuit, in a judgment that ignored the nation's increasingly poisonous political atmosphere, dismissed the possibility that this ruling opened the door to "the unfettered filing of numerous vexatious or frivolous civil lawsuits against sitting presidents for their unofficial acts" as "not only speculative, but historically unsupported." The court majority maintained that only the few people who dealt with the president personally and independently of his official role would have standing to launch a civil suit. Two judges held that the right to redress should not be denied or delayed. A lone dissenter argued that the nature of the suit did not make dealing with it any less of a burden on the president and thus less of a distraction from his constitutional responsibilities. Forcing him to divert energy and attention while in office to protect himself against personal liability would disserve the public interest in his unhindered execution of the role assigned him by the Constitution. Nevertheless, by a 2–1 vote the court overturned the stay granted to Clinton and ordered Judge Wright to proceed with the Jones suit.[33]

Clinton's attorneys appealed the Eighth Circuit's ruling to the U.S. Supreme Court, which heard arguments in January 1997. On May 27, 1997, the high court unanimously affirmed the judgment of the appellate court. It turned the usual separation of powers argument on its head, ruling that executive independence was no basis for blocking the functioning of the judiciary or deferring an individual's access to resolution of a suit against the president. In concluding that this case did not represent the diversion of presidential time and energy that the framers had sought to avoid, both courts demonstrated either ignorance or indifference to the nature of the modern presidency, not to mention the extent of the political assault Clinton faced. The justices assumed, as had the Eighth Circuit, that the Jones suit would not absorb much of the president's time and would only minimally divert him from other activities. Even Justice Stephen Breyer, whose concurring opinion was most sympathetic to the claim of immunity, pointed out that no specific evidence was offered that Clinton would be substantially distracted from other matters. The Jones case appeared to the high court to be a minor matter of little consequence to the operation of the presidency, especially in comparison to the all-consuming presidential distractions of Watergate and Iran-Contra.[34]

Had Jones's suit proceeded as the judges of the Eighth Circuit and the justices of the Supreme Court naively anticipated, it might perhaps have proven only a limited distraction for Clinton. In their narrow reading of constitutional protections for the presidential office, however, the jurists failed to understand the magnitude of the campaign already underway to discredit the president.

Discussions between his lawyers and hers shortly after *Clinton v. Jones* was handed down explored a possible settlement. Three years earlier similar discussions of a resolution had broken down; now even the prospect of a $700,000 payment and a carefully worded statement not specifically acknowledging misconduct but saying that Jones had done nothing improper could not keep negotiations from collapsing again. Paula and Steve Jones had already attracted at least $300,000 in donations to their Paula Jones Legal Fund. The cash flow appeared likely to continue as long as the case remained alive, and thus there was hardly an incentive to settle. Their attorneys resigned in frustration after the Joneses rejected what they viewed as an excellent settlement in a suit based on little evidence and less likelihood that Jones would prevail at trial. The lawyers observed, "Your focus has . . . changed from proving that you are a good person to proving that Clinton is a bad person."[35]

A group of Dallas attorneys soon stepped forward to take over the Jones case. They enjoyed financial underwriting from the Rutherford Institute, a Virginia foundation that had been involved in conservative Christian movements. The Dallas lawyers were also plugged into a loose network of intense Clinton antagonists who collaborated in gathering and passing along negative information about the president. This network, which came to be known as "the elves," included, among others, several University of Chicago Law School graduates working in top law firms in New York, Philadelphia, and Chicago, as well as their classmate Paul Rosenzweig, just hired by Kenneth Starr's Office of Independent Counsel. Theodore Olson, who in 1989 had challenged the validity of the independent counsel law before the Supreme Court but now was prepared to make use of it, was also involved. Other attorneys associated with the elves were rising conservative media figures Ann Coulter and Laura Ingraham. Information passed from the elves to Jones's new advocates made it possible for *Clinton v. Jones* to become a vehicle to confound the president.[36]

As Jones's attorneys prepared to depose Clinton about his dealings with her, Rosenzweig alerted them to ask the president about his relationship with another woman: Monica Lewinsky. Her name had not previously come up in discussions of Clinton's alleged promiscuity, but the independent counsel's office had just received a tip from Pentagon secretary Linda Tripp that Lewinsky was involved with Clinton. Astonishingly, Tripp possessed tape recordings of her telephone conversations with Lewinsky that seemed to carry the potential of the famous Nixon Watergate tapes for exposure and documentation of presidential misconduct. This striking parallel to the iconic "smoking gun" of a quarter century earlier drove the Starr inquiry into new territory.

Tripp, a presidential staff holdover from the Bush administration until being eased out of the executive offices, had become friendly at the White House with Lewinsky, a former intern who also ended up working at the Pentagon. Lewinsky had confided in Tripp, vividly describing her romantic and physical involvement with the president. Tripp promptly betrayed the younger woman's confidence by passing on the story to sometime literary agent Lucianne Goldberg, with whom she shared an eagerness to expose and discredit Clinton. Goldberg, excited by the news of discreditable White House activities and eager to equate them with the Watergate scandals, would identify Tripp to a potential ghostwriter as "Joan Dean."[37] In September 1997 Goldberg advised Tripp to begin taping her conversations with Lewinsky. Although the Lewinsky story had no apparent connection to matters Starr was authorized to explore, it offered, in conjunction with the Jones suit, an opportunity to put Clinton in an uncomfortable situation.

Tripp also made contact with Michael Isikoff, a journalist who had joined the *Washington Post* in 1981 as one of a legion of investigative reporters at that paper and elsewhere who admired and sought to emulate Bob Woodward and Carl Bernstein. Since 1992 Isikoff had pursued stories of Clinton's sexual escapades. He found Paula Jones's 1994 allegations credible and expended considerable effort trying to corroborate them. His editors' skepticism about his early submissions prompted his move to the *Post*'s sister publication *Newsweek*. In 1997, guided by tips from Jones's attorneys, he located Kathleen Willey, another alleged Clinton victim, who led him to Tripp, who, after consulting with Goldberg, pointed him toward Lewinsky. Isikoff does not seem to have been aware that Goldberg was also passing on the story to the elves, who in turn forwarded it to Jones's lawyers. The *Newsweek* reporter would continue, perhaps unintentionally, to serve as a conduit of information that served the various foes of Clinton.[38] Furthermore, when his sex scandal story eventually appeared in print, it would give the crusade against Clinton the post-Watergate patina of a story brought to light by a *Washington Post*–connected investigative reporter.

The appearance of Monica Lewinsky's name on a list of individuals that Jones's lawyers wished to depose gave Clinton a strong signal on December 6, 1997, that his personal conduct might cause him further legal and political problems. In response he advised her to file a technically defensible but decidedly unrevealing affidavit. Clinton differentiated between the sexual intercourse they had not had and the fellatio she had performed on him; the former he defined as sexual relations, the latter not. This distinction was not unknown among sexually liberal elements of the culture, especially younger people and southern males. Relying on though not acknowledging this definition, both Lewinsky and Clinton proceeded to deny that they had had sexual relations. While the president and his paramour parsed language, his personal secretary, Betty Currie, worked to get out of sight gifts that Lewinsky and Clinton had exchanged, and Clinton's close friend, attorney Vernon Jordan, increased ongoing efforts to find Lewinsky a job in New York, well away from the Washington spotlight. These actions, though not inherently illegal since they did not involve defiance of a subpoena, would all come to be labeled by Clinton critics and a media accustomed to Watergate jargon as a "cover-up" and obstruction of justice.

After the Lewinsky affair came to his attention, Kenneth Starr quickly asked Attorney General Janet Reno for permission to expand his inquiry to include possible obstruction of justice in the Jones and Lewinsky matters. He did not disclose to Reno his prior contacts with Jones's attorneys, which might well have given her pause. Lacking such knowledge, Reno and the independent counsel's three-judge supervisory panel promptly granted Starr's request.[39]

On the eve of Clinton's January 17, 1998, deposition in the Jones case, the independent counsel's staff, aided by Tripp, swooped down on Lewinsky. She was persuaded to cooperate with them through what she later described as frightening warnings, bullying methods, and denial of access to an attorney. The next day Jones's lawyers asked Clinton about his relationship with Lewinsky. Choosing his words with deliberation and precision, he denied it was sexual.

Within days, stories of the Clinton-Lewinsky liaison began to appear, first on a notorious Internet political gossip site, the Drudge Report, and on January 21 in the icon of reliable Watergate-era investigative reporting, the *Washington Post*. Isikoff's more detailed and better-documented account then appeared in *Newsweek*. Clinton emphatically repeated his denials at a January 26 press conference. Emphasizing his words by jabbing his finger at the television cameras, he declared, "I did not have sexual relations with that woman, Ms. Lewinsky. I never told anybody to lie, not a single time, never."[40] Clinton once again chose his words carefully and did not elaborate on the definition of sexual relations he was employing. He was, however, addressing a public that had become highly skeptical of such claims as a result of Watergate and Iran-Contra. He also faced a special prosecutor with a different understanding of sexual relations, not to mention what constituted a president's official duties.

The rapidly circulating, if unproven, stories of Clinton's infidelities led to a firestorm of criticism of the president. Disapproving politicians and editorial writers called for him to resign. He responded with a State of the Union address on January 27 that demonstrated his undiminished attention to his public duties and outlined a program that renewed confidence in his conduct of his office. The president's speech highlighted the achievement of a balanced federal budget for the first time in over thirty years, a measure of the health of the American economy that would not go unnoticed. The public's view of his presidential performance, as measured by opinion polls, which had only fallen to 57 percent approval with the original reports of a sexual liaison with a White House intern, rebounded after the speech to 73 percent, suggesting that the general public was differentiating between the president's private conduct of his personal affairs and his discharging of the constitutional responsibilities of his office. The Washington media, relying on what they considered the relevant comparison to Nixon's final days but ignoring the dramatic differences in the two men's standing, widely predicted that the president would be forced to resign, vastly misjudging both Clinton and the public mood.[41]

STATE OF THE PRESIDENT

Herblock,
Washington Post,
January 22, 1998.
© The Herb Block
Foundation.

Throughout the spring, Kenneth Starr sought to build a case against Clinton for perjury in his Jones deposition and for obstruction of justice for his dealing with Monica Lewinsky prior to her public exposure. Starr's efforts to negotiate an agreement whereby Lewinsky would testify against the president moved ahead slowly. Finally, in late July, Lewinsky agreed to testify and to produce a blue dress stained with semen in return for immunity from prosecution herself. Starr immediately tipped his hand as to the sort of evidence he had acquired by seeking a presidential blood sample for DNA testing. In exchange for giving blood, Clinton gained vital notice that he could no longer rely on semantic maneuvers about sexual activities.

The next month Starr compelled Clinton to testify to a grand jury regarding his statements concerning Lewinsky in connection with the Jones case. Judge Wright had dismissed Paula Jones's suit in April as lacking sufficient merit to proceed to trial, but that did not block the independent counsel's pursuit of evidence of presidential perjury in the case. Jones's complaint against Clinton had come to naught, though in November he would agree to pay her $850,000 in return for an end to her continued litigation. Nevertheless, Jones had inflicted enormous damage on the president.

On August 17 Clinton felt himself obliged to tell the grand jury in videotaped testimony that, contrary to what he had disclosed in his Jones deposition and as the DNA test confirmed, he had indeed engaged in an "inappropriate" relationship with Lewinsky. He sought to dodge charges of perjury by pointing out that in his January deposition he had consciously attempted to give answers that were literally truthful but not helpful. "If the deponent is the person who has oral sex performed on him," he explained, "then contact is not with anything on that list [of portions of the body specified by the Jones lawyers], but with the lips of another person."[42] Later, when questioned about his own attorney's claim that "there is no sex of any kind in any manner, shape, or form" between the president and Lewinsky, Clinton seized on the questioner's use of verb tense. "It depends on what the meaning of the word *is* is," he pointed out. "If *is* means is and never has been, that is one thing. If it means there is none, that was a completely true statement."[43] Such semantic precision was legitimate but subject to political ridicule when made public. It was not part of his presentation when he repeated his grand jury admission of an inappropriate relationship with Lewinsky to a national television audience the same evening.

In Clinton's pained acknowledgment of improprieties, he managed to undercut public perceptions that he had been obstructing justice. Instead, an image emerged of clever, disingenuous, but arguably truthful sidestepping of unskillfully posed questions. The fact that his earlier statements had come in a since-dismissed private suit and that he had been forthcoming when facing a federal grand jury earned him some credit. Technically, his delayed admission was just as much an obstruction of justice as Nixon's delay of two weeks in telling the FBI to proceed with its investigation of the Watergate break-in, and furthermore, Starr would determine that Clinton was still failing to acknowledge specific unquestionably sexual conduct that Lewinsky had described under oath. Clinton's public contrition, however, did alter the dynamics of his case. The fact that he testified as to his conduct, however incompletely, rather than exercise his constitutional right not to do so conveyed an important message: He viewed his behavior as embarrassing, not criminal.

In his televised statement on the evening of August 17, Clinton was not satisfied merely to confess and apologize for his actions. He also railed at Starr for his unrelenting pursuit even after the Whitewater investigation itself had found nothing amiss in the president's or first lady's conduct. "It is time to stop the pursuit of personal destruction," Clinton said, "and the prying into private lives and get on with our national life."[44] At the time it was uncertain whether his plea would be accepted or, instead, categorized as the equivalent of Nixon's ineffectual claim, "One year of Watergate is enough." Though their leanings were not readily apparent, the majority of Americans outside the circle of his partisan foes would soon adopt Clinton's view. At the moment, however, his statements stemming from the Jones case and Lewinsky affair threatened to pull down his presidency.

The Lewinsky revelations brought Republican calls for Clinton's impeachment but no immediate action in the House of Representatives. Even prominent Democrats were appalled. As soon as the Senate reconvened in September, Senator Joseph Lieberman of Connecticut took the floor to rebuke his own party's standard-bearer. The House Republican leadership, rather than launching its own inquiry, chose to await the report of Independent Counsel Starr. Speaker Gingrich and the chair of the Judiciary Committee, Henry Hyde, had been discussing impeachment proceedings since at least March, when they increased the committee's budget by $1.3 million and Hyde proceeded to hire Chicago attorney David Schippers, an experienced prosecutor, to head an impeachment staff. Gingrich and Hyde were concerned, however, especially with midterm elections only months away, that any precipitous move on their part would be seen as partisan politics. Better to wait, they concluded, for a report from the independent counsel, who was charged to notify the House if he found "any substantial and credible evidence" that might constitute grounds for impeachment. If the ostensibly nonpartisan independent counsel plunged the dagger, they calculated, House Republicans would not be regarded as partisan assassins.

The House, which had waited four years for Starr to reach a conclusion, did not face much further delay after he had taken Lewinsky's and Clinton's testimonies. Having already started drafting a report before those interviews, the independent counsel and his staff moved quickly to hone and further document their case. Starr had determined that Clinton was guilty of multiple lies under oath in his Jones deposition and subsequent grand jury testimony as well as guilty of encouraging others to lie under oath on his behalf. These acts amounted to perjury, suborning of perjury, and obstruction of justice, all to Starr's mind impeachable offenses. Thus, his report took the form of a referral to the House of charges and evidentiary support for impeachment. On September 9, the day Congress returned from its summer recess, the independent counsel delivered his referral along with supporting documentation to the House.[45]

Unlike John Doar's restrained and low-key presentation of evidence to the Judiciary Committee in 1974, the Starr Report castigated the president in severe and inflammatory language. Both Doar and Starr began by saying that it was up to the House to determine whether impeachment was warranted. Thereafter Doar continued in that vein, hesitating to give an opinion until, at the end of his presentation, he was directly asked to do so. Only then did he say that he thought Nixon deserved impeachment. In contrast, Starr made a most forceful case for impeachment from the outset of his referral.

Following an introduction that merely listed legal offenses, the referral set forth in vivid and explicit fashion a detailed account of Clinton's tawdry behavior. Foregoing delicate summaries of presidential conduct, the report quoted at length and at times more than once Lewinsky's frank descriptions during eight days of interviews with Starr's staff of her sexual encounters with the president. The independent counsel believed that he needed to demonstrate beyond question that Clinton had gone beyond parsing words into outright lies about sexual activities in his Jones deposition and grand jury testimony. Only by doing so, Starr concluded, could he construct a solid foundation on which to erect subsequent charges of deliberate obstruction of justice.[46]

Starr and his staff proceeded to load the text of the report with Lewinsky's graphic descriptions of her multiple encounters with Clinton. Deciding that a single account of a sexual dalliance was not enough to make the case for perjury, though in legal terms it might well have been, the independent counsel's report set forth Lewinsky's reconstruction of her every sexual experience with the president.[47] Among the most graphic was her account of an encounter following the president's Saturday radio address on February 28, 1997:

> We went back over by the bathroom in the hallway, and we kissed. We were kissing and he unbuttoned my dress and fondled my breasts with my bra on, and then took them out of my bra and was kissing them and touching them with his hands and with his mouth.
>
> And then I think I was touching him in his genital area through his pants, and I think I unbuttoned his shirt and was kissing his chest. And then . . . I wanted to perform oral sex on him . . . and so I did. And then . . . I think he heard something, or he heard someone in the office. So, we moved into the bathroom.
>
> And I continued to perform oral sex and then he pushed me away, kind of as he always did before he came, and then I stood up and I said . . . I care about you so much; . . . I don't understand why you won't let me . . . make you come; it's important to me; I mean, it just doesn't feel complete, it doesn't seem right.
>
> Ms. Lewinsky testified that she and the president hugged, and "he said he didn't want to get addicted to me, and he didn't want me to get addicted to him." They looked at each other for a moment. Then, saying that "I don't want to disappoint you," the president consented. For the first time, she performed oral sex through completion.[48]

Not only did Starr's referral elaborately depict the physical encounters that Clinton had denied, but also it described telephone conversations that dwelt on sexual fantasy and a chance Lewinsky glimpse of the president masturbating following one of their meetings. These latter incidents did not bear directly on the conduct the president had denied, but they amplified an unflattering picture of his sexuality.

Building on the graphic account of the president's sexual behavior, the referral fashioned a strong argument that he had gone to great lengths to conceal what had taken place between him and Lewinsky. He had arranged the concealment of their numerous small gifts to each other. He had coached her and his secretary Betty Currie about how to dissemble in testimony. He had enlisted his friend Vernon Jordan to find Lewinsky a New York job, not in itself inappropriate or uncommon but an action that Starr chose to characterize as a corrupt maneuver to buy her silence. Having laid out a sensational narrative, Starr then summarized its most salacious elements in setting forth grounds for impeachment. In all, the referral presented a forceful case for impeachment, one lacking in any mitigating arguments for the House to consider.

As soon as Starr delivered his report advocating impeachment, House Republican leaders moved to make the referral public. Uncertain as to whether the public would react to it as a partisan election season attack or a lesson learned from Watergate, Republican leaders thought it best to release the damning referral immediately when it would be most closely tied to Starr. If held until the Judiciary Committee reviewed its contents, they reasoned, it would come to be thought of as the work of the House instead of the independent counsel. Within two days, therefore, Starr's report was put before the American public without any prior review or editing. In a strict party-line vote, the House Rules Committee refused a request from the president's lawyers for forty-eight hours to review Starr's report and prepare a reply. Instead, the committee decided to put the referral on the Internet as quickly as possible, speeding its distribution before the White House could respond. The House Judiciary Committee's senior Democrat, John Conyers, complained, "We are not a delivery system for Kenneth W. Starr." His Republican counterpart, Chairman Hyde, insisted, "It is important that the American people learn the facts."[49]

The House dissemination decision provided clear evidence of Republican unity in a cause they perceived as not only just but also helpful to their party. Democrats, meanwhile, stood divided in their views of Clinton. Every Republican ballot endorsed the plan and every vote against it came from a Democrat. The 364–63 decision to make public the Starr referral without delay demonstrated that the Gingrich-led Republicans were marching in step while a majority of Democrats were unwilling, weeks before a congressional election, to take a position that might afford Clinton some shelter but that could be characterized as covering up misdeeds by a president of their own party. Only the all-Democratic Congressional Black Caucus stood solidly opposed to immediate release of the Starr referral.[50]

The Starr Report became available on the Internet late Friday afternoon, September 11, 1998. Over the following weekend it was reprinted in major newspapers, described on radio and television, and discussed at county fairs and church services. Within days paperback book editions became available and shot to the top of best-seller lists. Even if they chose not to read the intimate descriptions themselves, few Americans remained unaware that the president's consensual sexual encounters with Monica Lewinsky were vividly described in the report.[51]

The immediate political, media, and public reaction was shock and revulsion at the president's conduct. Still, feelings were mixed as to whether his impeachment was warranted. A fifty-five-year-old Boeing Company worker found Clinton's behavior "wrong but not impeachable," while across the country a retired naval officer declared, "I want him out of there!" They both spoke for many others. Campaigning in their districts for reelection, members of Congress found their constituents appalled but divided about removing the president. Americans carried with them vivid memories of the Watergate ordeal. They mulled over the value of impeachment proceedings against Clinton that could be expected to consume six months or more and immobilize the federal government for the duration.[52]

The House release of the videotape of Clinton's August grand jury testimony provoked additional disagreement. Representative Zoe Lofgren, a Democrat from California, raised a key issue. Significantly, she had served on the staff of the House Judiciary Committee during Watergate and understood the founders' intentions for impeachment better than most. She quoted for her constituents the 1974 judiciary staff conclusion that

> not all Presidential misconduct is sufficient to constitute grounds for an impeachment. Because impeachment of a President is a grave step for the nation, it is predicated only upon conduct seriously incompatible with either the constitutional form and principles of our government or the proper performance of constitutional duties of Presidential office.[53]

Lofgren's Republican colleague, Charles Canady of Florida, countered by pointing out that Judge Walter Nixon had less than a decade before being impeached for precisely the offense with which Clinton was now charged: perjury in testimony before a grand jury.[54] By implication Canady was asking whether the constitutional duties of presidents were any different than those of judges. The outcome of debate on that question would go a long way toward determining Clinton's fate.

By the end of September it was already becoming evident that many Americans were drawing a distinction between the incumbent president's personal behavior, however disgraceful some thought it, and a job-related impeachable offense. Lying about an unrelated sexual matter in a civil suit that had subsequently been dismissed seemed to them understandable and forgivable, if not particularly admirable. Most citizens did not regard removal from office as warranted for such prevarication about intimate personal matters by a president who was perceived as doing a satisfactory job in his official duties. Outside a solid core of committed Republicans, the humiliation of Clinton through release of the sexually explicit Starr Report and the videotaped grand jury interrogation of the president had backfired. A Gallup poll found that 78 percent of the overall population and even 65 percent of Republicans disapproved of the release of the videotape. More notably, 65 percent of Americans thought congressional Republicans were unfairly attacking the president over a purely private matter, and 39 percent of Republicans agreed. This significant majority sensed that a partisan effort to topple a president was under way and clearly disapproved of such a political maneuver.[55]

Not heeding such warning signs, determined House Republican leaders chose to ignore suggestions that a compromise be struck to chastise rather than remove the president. Experience-hardened Gerald Ford, the man who had proposed impeaching William O. Douglas, defined grounds for impeachment loosely, entered the White House upon Nixon's departure, and pardoned his predecessor, broke his public silence on Clinton to suggest that he be censured by Congress but not impeached. Nearly two out of three Americans polled agreed, and the White House signaled that it could accept such a solution. Unwilling to compromise, however, House Republican leaders pushed for a full-blown impeachment inquiry by the Judiciary Committee, one without any time limits as proposed by committee Democrats and without any agreement as to what in the circumstances would constitute an impeachable offense. With Clinton indicating that Democrats should feel free to cast a vote of "principle and conscience" on such a motion, the House adopted the Republican measure 258–176 on October 9. Thirty-one Democrats, mostly from their party's most conservative ranks, joined all 227 members of the unified Republican majority in approving the measure. Shortly thereafter the House recessed until after the November elections.[56]

Republicans made the 1998 election a referendum on President Clinton. House Republican Whip Tom DeLay was the prime advocate of this strategy. Late in the campaign Speaker Gingrich embraced the notion as well. DeLay and Gingrich saw the election as similar to the successful "Contract with America" campaign of 1994, an opportunity to bring national issues to the fore at a time when local concerns usually predominated. They believed that targeting Clinton would enhance Republican prospects. In this they misjudged the reaction of the electorate to the Clinton scandals and miscalculated public support for impeachment. Watergate veteran John Dean, in Washington to serve as a television commentator on the Clinton proceedings, concluded that a transformed Republican Party dominated by "conservatives without conscience" was seeking revenge for the downfall of Nixon. With their political judgment blinded by

"THE GARBAGE MAN IS HERE"
"TELL HIM WE DON'T WANT ANY"
— Marx Brothers routine

Herblock,
Washington Post,
October 14, 1998.
© The Herb Block
Foundation.

hatred for Clinton and a desire to satisfy their right-wing social and religious core of support, they misjudged the nation's mood.[57]

The results of the congressional election of 1998 were extraordinary. Since the time of Ulysses S. Grant, not one chief executive in the sixth year of his presidency had seen his party gain seats in Congress. It mattered not whether the party held a majority or a minority of seats. Winning the presidency twice was in itself rare, and of those who accomplished the feat, two, William McKinley and Richard Nixon, did not last six years. Of the few who did, not only Grant but also Grover Cleveland, Woodrow Wilson, Franklin Roosevelt, Dwight Eisenhower, and Ronald Reagan saw their ranks in Congress diminish in their sixth year. Even Theodore Roosevelt, Calvin Coolidge, and Harry Truman, elevated from the vice presidency and then elected in their own right, saw their party's hold on Congress reduced in their second-term midterm election. Thus, the Democratic

Party's gain of five seats in the House in 1998 and its maintenance of the existing division of the Senate was truly remarkable.

Representative Martin Frost of Texas, the head of the Democratic Congressional Campaign Committee in 1998, later expressed amazement at his opponents' political misjudgment. He thought, and believed most Democrats agreed, that impeachment was going nowhere and that there was no chance that Clinton would be removed from office. While congressional censure of Clinton was possible, he guessed that most Americans did not want the president impeached. The DeLay-Gingrich approach was, Frost concluded, "an enormous mistake [that] harmed the Republicans." At the same time, he conceded, "We got a real assist from the Republicans." In September Frost had trouble getting some traditional volunteers, particularly older women, to come to work on the campaign since they were embarrassed by Clinton and did not want to be seen entering Democratic offices. That attitude seemed to have passed by October. Frost recalled the reaction of his congressional colleagues: "Most Democrats thought Republicans had lost their minds in pushing for impeachment of Clinton." He attributed the Republican strategy to right-wing zealotry, widespread hatred of Clinton, willingness to engage in the politics of personal destruction, and the absence of senior party leaders willing to stand up to their junior colleagues and insist that they stop such self-defeating craziness.[58] Frost's views may have been partisan, but they were not lacking in insight.

The November 3 electoral setback led within days to Newt Gingrich's resignation as speaker of the House, a mere four years after he had attained the position. The election results, however, did not derail the Republican commitment to impeaching Clinton. Two days after the balloting, House Judiciary Committee chairman Henry Hyde announced that the public hearings phase of the Clinton inquiry would begin on November 19 with testimony by Independent Counsel Kenneth Starr.

Hyde had served on the Judiciary Committee since his arrival in Congress in 1975 and had participated in the Iran-Contra hearings as well as the Claiborne, Nixon, and Hastings impeachment proceedings. Save for the senior Democrat, Conyers, Hyde was the committee member most experienced with impeachment. Although announcing his intention to follow precedents established in the judiciary committee's 1974 proceedings, Hyde was, in fact, poised to depart from then chairman Peter Rodino's approach. While Rodino had been reluctant to embark on an impeachment inquiry, insisted on having the committee first examine evidence in seven weeks of closed hearings, and delayed public hearings as long as possible, Hyde chose to speed and compress the process dramatically. With the inquiry's authorization due to expire at the end of the year and with renewal uncertain once the newly elected Congress convened in January, Hyde wanted to bring the issue to a House vote during the lame-duck session of the expiring 105th Congress.

Only weeks before Hyde had been publicly humiliated by a less vividly described but still embarrassing revelation of personal sexual misconduct not unlike that of the president. A cuckolded husband disclosed that, years earlier, the married Hyde had engaged in an extended extramarital affair with his wife. The congressman admitted the affair, describing it as "a youthful indiscretion" when he was forty-one years old. Sexual impropriety between consenting adults, long considered an inappropriate matter for political comment, was becoming a commonplace revelation in the poisonous partisan atmosphere of the late 1990s. Precipitated by the effort to disgrace Clinton, its stain spread rapidly, assisted by a scandal-loving media culture. Hyde was the third Republican member of Congress exposed as an adulterer in 1998 but not the final one. Gingrich's own extramarital affair with a young congressional staff member would soon come to light, and even he was not the last philandering member of the 105th Congress to be exposed. The politics of sexual disgrace, once unleashed, would prove indiscriminate.

After Speaker Gingrich rejected Hyde's offer to step aside and his Republican colleagues on the House Judiciary Committee determined that, despite the election results, they wished to persevere, a grim Hyde pressed ahead with impeachment hearings. He steadfastly maintained that perjury and obstruction of justice, not sexual misconduct, was his concern. When Hyde gaveled the hearings to order on November 19, Starr repeated, though without the salacious details, the strenuous argument for Clinton's removal from office he had made in his referral. The independent counsel spent twelve hours testifying and responding to questions, hostile and probing ones from Clinton's attorney David Kendall and, in sharp contrast, friendly and encouraging ones from the committee's staff counsel David Schippers. At the end of his testimony, Starr's friends and aides in the hearing room and almost every Republican member of the committee stood and applauded him. Democrats remained silent and did not move from their chairs. The moment graphically demonstrated how partisan the proceedings had become.[59]

Whatever impact Starr's appearance before the Judiciary Committee had was sharply diminished the following day by a discordant echo from Watergate, the public's gold standard of impeachment inquiries. When he accepted the position of independent counsel, Starr had hired Georgetown University law professor Samuel Dash to be his ethics adviser. Dash, an experienced prosecutor, had served as counsel to the Ervin committee. He became a national celebrity through his effective questioning of John Dean and other witnesses as a national television audience watched in fascination. Enlisting the nonpartisan Dash, an icon of courage, skill, and integrity in pursing presidential misdeeds, served Starr well by conveying an image of his investigation's probity. However, when Dash suddenly resigned on November 20, declaring that Starr had abandoned prosecutorial objectivity for partisan advocacy, the impact was devastating. Longstanding White House claims and journalistic observations that Starr was engaging in a political witch hunt gained a credibility they had previously lacked.[60]

Throughout the autumn, discussions had continued across party lines within Congress as well as between Congress and the White House about the possibility of a formal censure of the president as an alternative to either impeaching him or doing nothing. Although the Constitution did not mention censure, it had been employed by the House and Senate to register strong disapproval of presidents, most notably in response to Andrew Jackson's attack on the Bank of the United States but also in cases involving John Tyler and James K. Polk. Clinton had, perhaps too readily, signaled his willingness to accept censure for his conduct, and many members of Congress saw it as an appropriate and measured way to condemn the president's bad conduct. Censure ultimately failed, however, because true believers in the criminality of what Clinton had done could not accept what they considered a meaningless reprimand.[61]

As the Judiciary Committee moved forward, it held a one-day hearing on December 1 to explore the issue of whether perjury was a sufficiently serious offense to justify impeachment. Two convicted perjurers insisted that a president abide by the same rules as others. But Charles Wiggins, a federal appellate judge and memorable as one of Nixon's most ardent defenders on the same committee in 1974, testified that Clinton's conduct, while reprehensible and deserving of censure, was "not of the gravity to remove him from office."[62] Once again a voice from Watergate undercut the drive to impeach Clinton.

In drafting articles of impeachment against Clinton, Hyde's staff consciously copied the format of the articles adopted for Nixon by the 1974 Judiciary Committee. They did, however, ratchet up a bit the language of disapproval and punishment. Also, they declined to pare down the list of charges as had been done in the earlier case.[63] Brief statements of specific offenses—perjury in his August grand jury testimony, perjury in his Paula Jones deposition, various acts obstructing justice, and abuse of power in lying to the public and impeding the investigation—were followed by broad claims that the Constitution had been violated by obstruction of justice or abuse of power. Finally, each article reached the same ritual conclusion:

In doing this, William Jefferson Clinton has undermined the integrity of his office, has brought disrepute on the Presidency, has betrayed his trust as President, and has acted in a manner subversive of the rule of law and justice, to the manifest injury of the people of the United States.

Whereas, William Jefferson Clinton, by such conduct, warrants impeachment and trial and removal from office and disqualification to hold and enjoy any office of honor, trust or profit under the United States.[64]

The disqualification on future officeholding had not been contained in the Nixon articles or any others since the early twentieth century. Its inclusion no doubt reflected Alcee Hastings's resurrection and nightmares that Clinton might try to do likewise. What was more noticeable, however, in the terminology of the proposed articles was the parallel drawn between Clinton's sexual behavior and Nixon's conduct of political espionage. Even though both involved presidential concealment, such equivalence would prove difficult for many to accept.

The Judiciary Committee hearings on impeachment made evident the continuing shadow of Watergate. After an opening statement by Clinton attorney Gregory Craig, a series of Watergate veterans paraded before the committee. Leon Jaworski's deputy, Richard Ben-Veniste, and three 1974 Judiciary Committee members, Father Robert Drinan, Elizabeth Holtzman, and Wayne Owens, all made the point that Clinton's offenses did not threaten the U.S. government in the manner that Nixon's had and thus did not justify impeachment. William Weld, the Republican governor of Massachusetts and a member of the committee's impeachment staff in 1974, concurred, though he advocated a strong censure of the president. Finally, Charles Ruff, Jaworski's successor as Watergate special prosecutor, underscored the same point. He warned Republicans not to overturn the popular will as expressed in election results.

In the midst of a series of presentations that might well have given committee members pause was testimony by a young historian who made some of them furious. Princeton history professor Sean Wilentz hectored the committee on what it was preparing to do. Referring to those who would vote for impeachment as "zealots and fanatics," he further inflamed an already testy atmosphere and doused the few remaining hopes that compromise could be reached for presidential censure rather than impeachment. Wilentz stridently warned that future generations would disapprove of the committee's actions as though he knew for certain what would be the perspective of historians to come. He later reinforced the message by enlisting four hundred historians to cosponsor and sign a full-page anti-impeachment advertisement in the *New York Times*. Whatever the merits of his analysis, his political judgment of the situation was questionable. Wilentz did nothing to stall and may have stiffened the drive to condemn the president.

The committee's majority counsel David Schippers then presented the case for impeachment in a similarly injudicious fashion. Besides reviewing the argument for the draft articles, he suggested that other episodes of Clinton misbehavior could be presented if more time were available. Such a vague, impossible-to-counter claim grew out of Schippers's zeal to remove Clinton from office and his growing frustration with Hyde's preference for wrapping up the case quickly instead of pursuing every lead.[65] Schippers managed to enrage Democrats and disquiet some Republicans but did not derail the committee's majority in its determination to vote for impeachment.[66]

On December 12 the Judiciary Committee began two days of voting on the four articles of impeachment. It divided 21–16, precisely along party lines, except when a lone Republican, Lindsey Graham of South Carolina, declined to support the article charging perjury in Clinton's grand jury testimony. The only division in the majority's ranks occurred over a proposal to drop the final article's assertion of improper use of executive privilege. Once the amendment had been agreed to, Republicans once again voted unanimously for the article's passage. The committee then rejected a Democratic motion for censure and adjourned.[67]

As the articles of impeachment headed to the floor of the House, neither the outgoing speaker, Gingrich, nor the man the Republicans had chosen to replace him, Representative Robert Livingston of Louisiana, relished presiding over the proceedings. Despite his role in advancing the matter, Gingrich preferred not to announce the vote on impeachment in his last act as speaker. Nor did Livingston desire to begin his speakership on what was sure to be a bitter partisan note. So both turned to a junior colleague, Representative Ray LaHood of Illinois, to take the gavel. The calm, deliberate LaHood had studied parliamentary procedure closely as chief of staff to Minority Leader Robert Michel. After succeeding to Michel's House seat in 1995, LaHood had frequently substituted for Gingrich in chairing House proceedings. He took pride in treating all members fairly. He accepted the assignment determined to be evenhanded and not knowing what lay ahead.[68]

Shortly before the House debate was to begin on December 18, another case of congressional sexual misconduct was exposed. This time the misconduct, one more extramarital affair, involved Livingston, the Republicans' choice to replace Gingrich. Acutely embarrassed, Livingston also recognized how awkward the revelation of infidelity made his position as party leader under the circumstances. He confessed to House Republican leaders and soon thereafter to the caucus, then remained silent throughout the first day of debate. With the story spreading in the press, Livingston claimed the floor shortly after LaHood called the House to order on the morning of December 19. He spoke briefly about Clinton's misconduct and said that it would be in the nation's interest for the president to resign. Livingston then stood silent as Democrats hooted in derision. As the tumult subsided, he said that he would set an example by resigning himself.[69] LaHood later remembered the moment when Livingston announced that he would not stand for speaker as "sucking all the air out of the House chamber."[70]

A stunning announcement from someone on the cusp of great political power, Livingston's statement brought the House to a momentary standstill. A sobering realization swept the body of the cost of the political storms that had been unleashed. Among the few members immediately able to turn his focus to the future was the chief architect of the House impeachment push, Republican Whip DeLay. Within hours he was able to line up enough support to assure that his close ally and chief deputy whip, Dennis Hastert of Illinois, would be chosen as the next speaker. A leadership crisis was thereby averted, one that might have unhinged the impeachment crusade that DeLay championed.

With House debate about to begin, Clinton declared that the United States was facing a crisis with Iraq. Following the Persian Gulf War of 1991, Iraqi leader

Saddam Hussein had pledged to allow international inspections of facilities in his country that might be used to build chemical, biological, and nuclear weapons of mass destruction. Clinton had repeatedly called attention to Iraq's failure to comply with those agreements, most recently just as the Lewinsky scandal was breaking. Now, after further diplomatic failures and concerned to take action before the beginning of the Muslim holy month of Ramadan, Clinton ordered rocket attacks on Iraqi facilities. Cynics remembered that during Watergate Nixon had placed the military on alert because of an alleged Russian threat and suggested that an attempt to divert the country's attention, not a genuine threat to national security, was again involved. A recent satiric film, *Wag the Dog*, about a fictional president starting a war with Albania to direct attention away from his molesting of a Girl Scout, led to questions as to whether Clinton too was "wagging the dog." Such suspicions had also been aroused in August, just before Clinton's grand jury testimony, when he ordered missile strikes on sites in Afghanistan and Sudan that were alleged to be operated by the perpetrator of the bombings of U.S. embassies in Kenya and Tanzania, a little-known terrorist by the name of Osama bin Laden. On each of these occasions, those obsessed with the crisis of the presidency seemed unwilling to concede that world affairs were continuing to unfold and American interests abroad were affected. Distrustful of presidential motives and unwilling to countenance a long delay, the House Republican leadership agreed to postpone impeachment hearings twenty-four hours but no longer. Air strikes on Iraq would continue for three more days, and thereafter U.S. difficulties with Saddam Hussein would prove real and intractable, but for the moment the problems he posed were dismissed as not sufficient to derail determined efforts to cast out the promiscuous president.[71]

LaHood presided over two days of House debate that changed few minds but allowed members to explain their positions for the record. A *New York Times/ CBS News* public opinion poll was showing that 62 percent of those surveyed opposed impeachment, raising a caution to its Republican proponents.[72] Leading off, Henry Hyde insisted that the issue before the House was not sexual misconduct or even lying about sex but rather lying under oath by the only person with a constitutional obligation to take care that the law be faithfully executed. Hyde, who had been one of the members of the Iran-Contra committee voting to exonerate Ronald Reagan and later twice served as a House manager for the Senate trial of impeached judges, clearly believed that Clinton's offense was constitutionally unacceptable. "Let us declare, unmistakably," he implored, "that perjury and obstruction of justice disqualify a man from retaining the presidency of the United States."[73]

Hyde's Democratic counterparts on the Judiciary Committee saw things otherwise. Barney Frank reminded the House that when a perjury indictment had been brought against Secretary of Defense Caspar Weinberger in the Iran-Contra investigation, President George Bush had pardoned him.[74] John Conyers followed by calling the Republican effort against Clinton an attempted coup d'état. "Impeachment was designed to rid this nation of traitors and tyrants, not attempts to cover up extramarital affairs," he said. "This resolution trivializes our most important tool to maintain democracy. It downgrades the impeachment power into a partisan weapon that can be used with future presidents."[75]

An extraordinary moment came when Representative Alcee Hastings took the floor to remind the House of his own experience and to urge them not to proceed against Clinton. During his tenure in Congress Hastings had earned the regard of at least some members on both sides of the aisle. As much as he sought to discourage members from voting for impeachment, Hastings may have eased minds about doing so by demonstrating through his mere presence that there could indeed be political life after impeachment. In his case, at least, impeachment had not amounted to capital punishment.[76]

The Democratic minority leader, Richard Gephardt, one of the last to speak, brought the focus of the debate back to the question of whether Clinton's offenses justified impeachment. He tied his remarks to the downfall only a few hours earlier of the man he had expected to be his Republican counterpart, calling Livingston's departure "a terrible capitulation to the negative forces that are consuming our political system and our country." Gephardt went on to say,

> We need to stop destroying imperfect people at the altar of an unobtainable morality. We need to start living up to the standards which the public in its infinite wisdom understands, that imperfect people must strive towards, but too often fall short. We are now rapidly descending into a politics where life imitates farce, fratricide dominates our public debate and America is held hostage to tactics of smear and fear.

He concluded by describing the nation as poised on an abyss: "The only way we can stop this insanity . . . is for all of us to finally say, 'Enough.'"[77]

Democrats gave Gephardt's remarks a sustained standing ovation while Republicans sat in stony silence. The pattern of applause prefigured the votes to come. First, the House rejected, on a party-line vote, Gephardt's last-ditch effort to gain a vote on censure. LaHood then called for the yeas and nays on the first article of impeachment, dealing with grand jury perjury. The tally was 228 in favor and 206 opposed, with only five members on each side defecting from their party ranks. Balloting on the second article, perjury in the Paula Jones deposition, followed immediately. With over two dozen Republicans unwilling to support this article, it was rejected 229–205. With eight exceptions, Republicans returned to party lines on the third article, a broader charge of obstruction of justice, which was adopted 221–212. Finally, the most sweeping article, charging abuse of power, failed to win the support of nearly a third of the Republicans and fell 285–148. With very few exceptions, the Democrats had stood firm throughout in their opposition to impeachment. Yet as LaHood brought down his gavel to end the session, two articles of impeachment had been adopted.[78]

Nearly half the House Democrats immediately traveled down Pennsylvania Avenue to stand with Clinton in a show of solidarity. Minority Leader Gephardt told the president and the television audience, "We will stay with you and fight with you until this madness is over." Vice President Gore responded by telling the congressmen, "History will judge you as heroes."[79] But neither such remarks nor Clinton's vow to fight on could conceal the fact that the constitutional role of the House had concluded in Clinton's defeat. His fate now rested elsewhere. For the first time in 130 years an American president faced trial by the Senate.

The partisan division of the House over impeachment made it appear from the outset that the Senate was not likely to produce the bipartisan two-thirds majority vote necessary to remove Clinton from office.[80] However, such an outcome was by no means assured. In the previous decade senators had taken their responsibilities very seriously in conducting the trials of federal judges Harry Claiborne, Walter Nixon, and Alcee Hastings. All had been the appointees of Democratic presidents and had been confirmed with strong Democratic Senate support. Yet each had been removed from office in overwhelming votes as Democratic as well as Republican senators concluded that the judges had violated their constitutional duties. Among the senators a sense of constitutional responsibility had outweighed party loyalty; that could well happen again if a strong case for conviction was presented.

A Senate with so much recent experience in carrying out these extraordinary trials was unique in the history of federal impeachment. As a result the body's judgment was impossible to predict with certainty. Republican Majority Leader Trent Lott, while a member of the House Judiciary Committee when it voted to impeach Richard Nixon, had watched partisanship fall by the wayside. At the same time he understood that his party alone did not command enough votes to win Clinton's conviction. On the other side of the aisle the Democratic minority leader, Tom Daschle, after polling his own colleagues, thought it possible, though not likely, that as many as twenty Democrats could turn on the president. Neither leader felt assured of the outcome.[81]

Efforts to avoid a Senate trial continued after the House impeachment vote. A number of senators from both parties engaged in discussion of censure as a way to resolve the issue short of a trial. The White House signaled its ongoing interest in such a solution and at the same time expressed interest in another escape route. During the House Judiciary Committee hearings, Yale law professor Bruce Ackerman had argued that a lame-duck Congress lacked the constitutional authority to conduct an impeachment. Ackerman's reading of the Twentieth Amendment led him to conclude that the country had chosen to minimize the powers of lame-duck Congresses and that an impeachment under such circumstances was inappropriate. Furthermore, if a lame-duck Congress proceeded anyway, its impeachment resolution would expire at the end of its term.[82] It was a shaky argument, especially since Walter Nixon had been impeached by one Congress and tried by the next, but one that Clinton's defenders seized upon, hoping at least to delay House action until the next Congress convened with a shift of seats that might reverse the close vote on the obstruction of justice article. But the House was not forestalled, and the Senate would not be either.[83]

The House sent a dozen Republicans to accompany Hyde as managers to present the case to the Senate. No Democrats were willing to serve. Of those who did enlist, both Hyde and James Sensenbrenner had significant experience with impeachment. They had jointly introduced a resolution for the impeachment of Alcee Hastings, and Sensenbrenner had submitted four other judicial impeachment resolutions. Both men had served as House managers, Hyde in the proceedings against Harry Claiborne and Sensenbrenner in those against Walter Nixon. In addition, Hyde and Manager Bill McCollum of Florida had sat on the Iran-Contra Committee when the question of impeaching Ronald Reagan was an unspoken agenda item. The ten colleagues of these three had all come to the Judiciary Committee more recently and had no experience of any sort with impeachment discussions across party lines.

In many respects, the most critical Senate discussions were those preceding the trial itself. With Senate leaders of both parties convinced that there was little prospect of a conviction and hoping to avoid the rancorous battle that had appeared to cast the House in an unfavorable light, the critical question was what shape the trial should take. The Senate needed to demonstrate that it was taking its constitutional obligations seriously and yet not expend a great deal of its time to no effect, in essence flogging a dead horse. Should a full vetting of all evidence of Clinton's sexual misbehavior be conducted, as the House managers wished? Complete with live testimony from every witness the managers chose to call, this process might consume several months. Or, as Democrat Joseph Lieberman and Republican Slade Gorton initially proposed in late December, should presentations of evidence and argument be circumscribed and the matter quickly brought to a vote? A variety of elaborate plans were eventually put forth for discussion.[84] In the end what prevailed was rooted in the Senate's recent experience with judicial impeachment trials. In all three of those the Senate had relied heavily on the record of prior evidentiary hearings by the House and its own select committees, followed by relatively brief consideration on the floor involving the entire membership.

The issue of procedure had still not been settled on January 7, 1999, when the House managers appeared in the Senate to exhibit the articles of impeachment and when Chief Justice William Rehnquist, followed by all one hundred senators, swore the requisite oaths to do impartial justice. The next morning senators of both parties met in an unusual joint caucus in the Old Senate Chamber on the Capitol's ground floor, informally discussed how to conduct the trial, and with surprising cordiality reached basic agreement. Details hammered out that afternoon granted each side up to twenty-four hours over three days to make opening arguments. Thereafter the senators would have two days to ask questions, submitted in writing and posed by the chief justice. At that point motions would be in order to dismiss the case or, alternatively, to call witnesses. At the end of the day, the Senate adopted this plan 100–0.[85]

When the trial began at 1:00 p.m. on January 14, senators sat silently as Hyde reminded them of their solemn duty. Then Sensenbrenner and three other managers, Ed Bryant of Tennessee, Asa Hutchinson of Arkansas, and James Rogan of California, began laying out the case against the president. They cogently presented an argument that efforts to find Lewinsky a job in New York and to advise her and presidential secretary Betty Currie on how to testify amounted to obstruction of justice. They followed by showing on large screens video clips of Clinton's statements that, taken together, they felt demonstrated perjury. The managers continued until 7:00 p.m. and presented a clear and coherent statement of their case, which many senators were hearing in its entirety for the first time.

The impact of the managers' initial presentation appeared to be lessened the next day as five other managers spoke in turn. They often repeated what had already been said, and the effect on senators not used to sitting still in the chamber unable to speak was soporific. The growing tedium was suddenly interrupted late in the day as Senator Tom Harkin, a Democrat from Iowa, rose to object to Manager Bob Barr's reference to the senators as jurors. Harkin asserted that in an impeachment trial he and his colleagues had a greater obligation than merely to rule on guilt or innocence. They were, in fact, a court with a duty to evaluate the legitimacy of the charges as "high crimes and misdemeanors" and the consequences of any judgment on the nation. When Chief Justice Rehnquist ruled in Harkin's favor and admonished the managers not to use the term "juror" again, he called attention to the fact that impeachment involved more than the demonstration of personal misconduct.[86]

On the third and final day of their presentation the managers tried to repair the damage Harkin had inflicted on their case. The last four House managers talked about Clinton's misdeeds as constitutional offenses. Lindsey Graham made perhaps the most effective argument by referring to the impeachment only nine years earlier of Judge Walter Nixon and the trial at which most of the senators sitting before him had voted for his removal:

> The question becomes, if a federal judge could be thrown out of office for lying and trying to fix a friend's son's case, can the president of the United States be removed from office for trying to fix his case? You could not live with yourself, knowing that you were going to leave a perjurer as a judge on

the bench. Ladies and gentlemen, as hard as it may be, for the same reasons, cleanse this office.

Hyde wrapped up the managers' case with a florid call to patriotic duty, a responsibility that he defined as requiring Clinton's ouster from office.[87]

After a long weekend recess, Charles Ruff, an experienced Washington litigator best known as the final Watergate special prosecutor, began Clinton's defense on Tuesday, January 19. He immediately challenged the managers' case as "a witches brew of charges" that he proceeded to disparage. His most telling argument focused on the managers' accusation that Vernon Jordan had stepped up a job search for Lewinsky as soon as the judge in the Jones lawsuit ruled that Lewinsky could be examined. The judge's order, Ruff pointed out, was issued forty minutes after Jordan's plane had taken off for Amsterdam, rendering him unavailable to do what was charged. Complaining about "prosecutorial fudging," Ruff concluded that he was not there to defend Clinton's personal behavior but, rather, to point out that the president had not put the nation at risk. He admonished the Senate that the framers intended that impeachment would have to be found the only solution to a problem with the chief executive before it could be justified.[88]

Several hours after Ruff spoke to the Senate, Clinton appeared on the other side of the Capitol in the House chamber before a joint session of Congress to deliver his annual State of the Union address. As on the same occasion a year earlier just after the Lewinsky scandal had surfaced, his speech completely ignored the impeachment issue. Instead, he delivered an upbeat report on the nation's situation, highlighting a projected federal budget surplus that he proposed be used to strengthen the Social Security system. With overnight polls indicating that Clinton had once again attained broad support among the American people, by the next morning even an enemy such as the fundamentalist minister Reverend Pat Robertson declared impeachment to be politically dead.[89]

The Senate trial continued the next day with two of the president's defense lawyers, Greg Craig and Cheryl Mills, trying to pick apart the arguments against him. The following day, attorney David Kendall continued in the same light, before former Arkansas senator Dale Bumpers wrapped up the case. Just three weeks out of office after four terms in the Senate, Bumpers was a familiar and well-liked colleague to most members of the body. He tore into the charges against Clinton, bringing the focus back to his sexual misconduct. Oozing irony, he observed, "When you hear somebody say, 'This is not about sex,' it's about sex."[90]

When the two days set aside for senators' questions began the next day, issues of evidence and proof dominated for the first two hours. Then the senior Democrat, Senator Robert Byrd of West Virginia, whom his colleagues widely respected and deferred to on matters of constitutional interpretation, raised a central issue. His written question began by quoting from *Federalist* 65's justification of

Herblock,
Washington Post,
January 29, 1999.
© The Herb Block
Foundation.

impeachment for "the misconduct of public men or, in other words, the abuse or violation of some public trust." Byrd then queried, "Putting aside the specific legal questions concerning perjury and obstruction of justice, how does the president defend against the charge that by giving false and misleading statements under oath, such 'misconduct' abused or violated 'some public trust'?"[91]

Charles Ruff responded bluntly that Clinton's actions did not threaten the nation and did not justify overturning the results of an election in which he was chosen as president. House Manager James Rogan countered by focusing on what he characterized as Clinton's lies under oath, ridiculing the White House argument that the president had been evasive, misleading, and incomplete but not untruthful. Lying under oath, Rogan implied, was a violation of public trust and in itself sufficient for impeachment.[92]

Constrained by the procedural rules in place, Byrd did not respond to either speaker, but shortly thereafter his office issued a press release. In it Byrd announced that he planned to move for dismissal of the articles and an end to the trial. He explained that he thought Clinton had done wrong and had weakened public confidence in government. "But," he continued, "I am convinced that the necessary two-thirds for conviction are not there and that they are not likely to develop. I have also become convinced that lengthening the trial will only prolong and deepen the divisive, bitter, and polarizing effect that this sorry affair has visited upon our nation." Without saying a word in Clinton's defense, Byrd sent a powerful signal that the effort to remove the president had failed.[93]

Anticipating incorrectly that Byrd's motion would pass, Henry Hyde soon revealed the bitterness of a true believer in the cause of removing Clinton as well as in the unfairness of the assumed Senate response to the House initiative. He told the senators, "By dismissing the articles of impeachment before you have a complete trial, you are sending a terrible message to the people of the country. You are saying, I guess, perjury is okay, if it is about sex. Obstruction is okay, even though it is an effort to deny a citizen her right to a fair trial." He concluded with a rhetorical sneer reflective of long-standing House resentment of the Senate as well as his own passion for impeaching Clinton. "I know, oh do I know," he said, "what an annoyance we are in the bosom of this great body. But we are a constitutional annoyance and I remind you of that fact."[94]

The next day a far more dispassionate comment from Manager Lindsey Graham tempered Hyde's outburst and put the issues of the case that had attracted most attention in perspective. He pointed out that both the president's critics and his defenders had spoken in absolutes about whether the president had committed an impeachable offense and should be removed. Graham confessed that for him it was a close call and asked whether it was a matter upon which reasonable people could disagree. "I would be the first to admit," he said, "that the Constitution is silent on the question about whether or not every high crime has to result in removal." Either choice would have an impact on society, Graham observed, and, getting to the crux of the political dilemma facing the Senate, he concluded, "You have to consider what is best for this nation."[95]

When the trial reconvened on Monday, January 25, it soon became clear that many senators had answered to their own satisfaction Graham's question regarding the essential political judgment to be made in an impeachment trial. The Senate voted on motions scheduled before the trial began for consideration at this moment, Byrd's to dismiss and a Republican request to call witnesses. The former failed 44–56 while the latter was approved 56–44. With one exception, Democrat Russell Feingold of Wisconsin, senators divided along party lines, thus showing Democratic resistance to continuing and Republican resolve to plunge ahead. Although the two votes kept the trial going, taken together they demonstrated that eleven more senators than necessary for acquittal were ready to put an end to Clinton's prosecution. The trial would proceed even though the result was no longer in doubt.

Over the following week, House managers would depose three witnesses—Monica Lewinsky, Vernon Jordan, and White House aide Sidney Blumenthal. Both Lewinsky and Jordan calmly and confidently denied that they had done anything improper, and Blumenthal, a secondary figure, provided no useful information. Their testimony was so unhelpful to the case the managers were trying to build that the president's attorneys barely exercised their right of cross-examination. When videotaped excerpts of Lewinsky's deposition were shown to the Senate, the principal impression given was that she was a surprisingly mature woman who knew what she was doing in her relationship with the president. She was no exploited naïf. As a consequence, twenty-five Republican senators joined all forty-five Democrats in rejecting the motion to call Lewinsky for live testimony.

As the depositions and Senate proceedings ground on, a few senators on both sides continued to explore possibilities for expressing disapproval of Clinton short of impeachment. Democrat Dianne Feinstein of California, one of many senators who wanted to punish him in some fashion for what he had done, kept alive the idea of a censure of the president. Republican Susan Collins of Maine advocated an alternative solution: passage of a finding of fact, a statement of presidential offenses that would have no immediate legal consequence beyond certifying the conclusions of a Senate majority. A finding of fact could, however, be used if the president misbehaved again or if he were to be sued after leaving office. Both approaches eventually foundered on the difficulties of fashioning acceptable language and the perception that either action might set a dangerous precedent by creating a level of chastisement that could debilitate impeachment. Democrat Patrick Leahy of Vermont warned of setting "the dangerous precedent that a Senate impeachment trial could be used for the purpose of criticizing non-impeachable conduct, thereby trivializing the constitutional impeachment process and inviting future impeachments for non-impeachable offenses."[96] Republican Fred Thompson of Tennessee, respected by his colleagues on such matters because of his service as minority counsel on the Senate Watergate committee, saw the opposite danger. "We shouldn't hamper future trials by setting a floor, by saying that a future president can get away with this—lying, a cover-up. That would become part of the impeachment process," he advised.[97] Such comments helped doom both measures. Collins's plan never came to a vote, and Feinstein's, brought to the floor after the impeachment issue was decided, gained a 56–43 majority but not the two-thirds majority needed to suspend Senate rules so that a vote on it could be taken.[98]

As the trial neared its conclusion, all thirteen House managers again addressed the Senate, each in his own way calling for impeachment. Midway through their parade, Charles Ruff made the sole speech on the president's behalf, once again challenging the managers' allegations and their vision as "too dark" and "too little attuned to the needs of our democracy." He scorned the impeachment effort, saying, "I believe it to be a vision more focused on retribution, more designed to achieve partisan ends, more uncaring about the future we face together."[99] All the speakers on both sides were conscious that the patience of the Senate and the public was wearing thin, even before a gray-bearded man in the gallery stood and shouted, "Good God Almighty! Take the vote and get it over with!" before the Capitol police escorted him out.[100]

From February 9 until the morning of February 12 the Senate met behind closed doors to deliberate. Senators in turn made prepared statements assessing the evidence and the balance of factors determining their decision. As some senators released their statements and word of others leaked out, it became clear that they were as united in their distaste for Clinton's sexual conduct and attempts to conceal it as they were divided over whether it merited impeachment. Senator Phil Gramm, a Republican from Texas and a fierce Clinton critic, was probably not alone in wishing that a presidential resignation had spared the Senate as in Watergate. "The difference between Nixon and Clinton," he sneered, "is that Nixon had some shame."[101] Not spared from the need to resolve the matter, however, each senator was forced to reach a judgment on the requirements of impeachment and whether this case met them.

In a Senate chamber packed with one hundred senators, the House managers, White House attorneys, and various aides as well as galleries jammed with journalists, invited onlookers, and the public, Chief Justice Rehnquist ordered a roll call on the first article of impeachment just after noon on February 12. The perjury charge, widely viewed as the weaker article, polled guilty votes from forty-five Republicans. All forty-five Democrats and ten Republicans declared Clinton not guilty. On the second article, the obstruction of justice allegation, every Democrat again voted not guilty. This time they were joined by five Republicans, one of whom, Arlen Specter of Pennsylvania, had sought to offer a third choice drawn from Scottish law, "not proven." In the end Specter declared, "Not proven and therefore not guilty." With a 50–50 division on Article II, the supporters of impeachment were denied a majority, much less the two-thirds margin required for conviction.

The Clinton impeachment trial had at last ended thirty-six days after it officially began and more than a year after the circumstances that provoked it had come to light. As expected, it had failed to remove the president from office. It did, however, generate great partisan rancor and frustration. Democrats were left dismayed that impeachment had occurred, Republicans, that it had failed. The nation as a whole was left with a sullied president and a new view of impeachment that included a wider understanding of the constitutional mechanism and the political nature of its operation. None of these impressions were altered when, on the day before he was to leave office in January 2001, Clinton publicly acknowledged in a negotiated concession to avoid further pursuit by Robert Ray, Starr's successor as independent counsel, that in his Jones deposition "certain of my responses to questions about Ms. Lewinsky were false." He hoped, he said, his declaration would "help bring closure and finality to these matters."[102]

The Clinton impeachment put on display the no-holds-barred, go-for-the-throat, off-with-his-head political climate of the 1990s. It also showed the an-enemy-of-my-enemy-is-my-friend defensive response provoked by such vituperative partisanship. As a consequence, the battle over Clinton's impeachment widened the growing gulf between the competitors for control of American government. The zealous pursuit of partisan advantage led to unprecedented exposure of the private lives of public figures, bringing disgrace upon individuals in both parties whose personal conduct in past decades under different standards now stood revealed. The political culture of the moment also trapped many upright politicians against their will in a situation where they had to choose between excusing conduct they found appalling or contributing to the downfall of a public policy agenda they had labored to advance. In this contentious environment, impeachment proved the ultimate battleground, the arena where the stakes were the highest, the weapons most powerful, and the combat most brutal.

In an uncompromising and unforgiving political culture in which any degree of moderation was widely regarded as a weakness rather than a virtue, the Republican campaign against Clinton had gone forth without restraint. There was no William Buckley saying, "Robert Welch, you don't have a responsible case against Earl Warren," no House of Representatives concluding, "Gerald Ford, you don't have a substantial case against William O. Douglas," no Elliot Richardson or Barry Goldwater saying, "Spiro Agnew or Richard Nixon, you should resign," and no Daniel Inouye saying, "The case against Ronald Reagan should not go forward because the cost to the country would be too great." The result was a completed impeachment process that ended disastrously for all concerned.

The Clinton impeachment produced multiple victims. The most obvious was the incumbent president himself, long distracted and weakened in pursuing his policy agenda as well as personally discredited though not ultimately removed from office. A second casualty was the institution of the presidency, exposed to ridicule and diminished in the public esteem that serves as a source of its effective power. A third was the system of independent counsels created in the aftermath of Watergate to assure that federal inquiry and action against executive branch wrongdoing could take place without the interference of a self-interested administration. In the aftermath of Kenneth Starr's performance, neither party in Congress was enthusiastic about renewal of the federal statute authorizing such special prosecutors, and it was laid to rest. An attempt by Senator Lieberman, Clinton's most outspoken Democratic critic, to revive the Independent

Counsel Act in 2003 attracted only one cosponsor and went nowhere.[103] A fourth injured party was the electorate that had chosen a president and then seen him forced to devote a substantial portion of his time and energy to matters other than carrying out the tasks they expected him to perform.

The most significant long-term victim may well have been the American constitutional system of exquisitely balanced and restrained authority. The failure of the effort to remove Clinton made evident the limits of impeachment as a restraint on the presidency. His immediate successors would thus have less reason to fear constitutional sanction for abusing their office. Whether the Clinton impeachment was politically cynical or simply inept, its partisan nature and the equally partisan defense against it undermined the constitutional design of the framers. Reduced to a partisan tool, and an ineffective one at that, impeachment, at least in the short run, lost status as the last line of constitutional defense. Perhaps even more so than in the failed impeachment of Andrew Johnson 130 years earlier, a vital feature of the constitutional system of checks and balances had been weakened.

13

Impeachment as Conventional:
Expressions of Public Scorn

By the beginning of the new millennium, impeachment had moved from periphery to prominence in American political and constitutional culture. The undercurrent of discussion throughout much of his term in office about impeaching the first twenty-first-century president, George W. Bush, made this transformation manifest. Concrete experiences with executive and judicial impeachment and near impeachment during the previous forty years had contributed to an expanded awareness of the process as well as a willingness to put it in motion. Likewise, ongoing discussions of impeachment in the literature, theater, and film of the era fostered increased sensitivity to its availability for one purpose or another. Heightened consciousness of the device provided by the Constitution for remedying mistakes in the selection of federal officials had erased the notion that it was merely a "rusted blunderbuss" with no applicability to contemporary affairs.

Many individuals contributed to the attentive, if contentious, approach to impeachment that by the term of the second President Bush had replaced that dismissive 1950s judgment, but perhaps none had a greater influence than Herbert L. Block. A gifted cartoonist better known as Herblock, he had for decades provided images that translated the complexities of U.S. government into terms a vast public could grasp. His acerbic images helped shape the American public's notions as to when impeachment was or was not appropriate. Although he departed the scene early in George W. Bush's presidential tenure, his work helped build an American constitutional culture both receptive to and skeptical of appeals for impeachment.

During the last four decades of the twentieth century, newspaper editorial cartoons proved to be a powerful device for fixing ideas about impeachment in American minds. Simple but striking images augmented by cynically humorous captions rendered complex stories comprehensible, if not always undistorted, as they unfolded. Since the era of Thomas Nast in the nineteenth century, editorial cartoons had influenced the way newspaper readers perceived the political process. Focusing attention on a singular aspect of the day's news and often offering a highly charged interpretation of its meaning, cartoons offered a reductionist explanation of political life and public policy that could leave a strong impression on those who saw them and reiterated their themes in one forum or another. Impeachment, invariably a convoluted and confusing matter involving a cast of characters who could be cast as villains or victims, provided cartoonists great opportunities to practice their craft and shape popular opinion in a far-reaching and lasting way.

No editorial cartoonist during the age of impeachment had a wider audience or greater influence than Block of the *Washington Post*. Herblock, as he called himself from the time he started drawing editorial cartoons for the *Chicago Daily News* in 1929 while still a teenager, built a national reputation in the 1930s with the Scripps-Howard feature service. His 1942 wartime cartoons won him the first of his four Pulitzer Prizes. Herblock's 1946 move to the *Washington Post* was considered a major coup for a newspaper that faced bankruptcy in 1933 and that at the time of his arrival was still struggling to climb above fourth place in local circulation. For the next fifty-five years the *Post* published Herblock's cartoons several days a week and also distributed his work to dozens of other papers across the country. As much as the paper's growing staff of talented political and investigative reporters, Herblock was responsible for elevating the *Post* to the position of most widely read and respected Washington newspaper.[1] Seen nearly every day by the Washington press corps, his deft images and pointed captions interpreting the news exerted a subtle but strong influence on national political journalism.

Herblock brought with him to the *Post* a liberal sensibility developed during the Great Depression, an internationalism borne of antifascism, and an antipathy to militarism stirred by World War II. His early revulsion at the anticommunist crusade of the House Un-American Activities Committee (HUAC) led him to draw his first unflattering image of Richard Nixon in May 1948. The cartoon showed Nixon and fellow HUAC members Karl Mundt and Chairman J. Parnell Thomas burning the Statue of Liberty at the stake. Herblock also scorned the conduct of Joseph McCarthy in the years that followed. Indeed, he coined the term "McCarthyism" to label the smear tactics employed by the Wisconsin senator and the spreading shadow of fear he created. Nixon and McCarthy appeared together in numerous Herblock cartoons, unshaven, covered in dirt, and carrying buckets of tar and dripping brushes with which to smear their opponents. His memorable images from that era repeatedly featured Vice President Nixon climbing out of a gutter or sewer to appeal for support. One of these in 1958 had Nixon saying, "Of course, if I had the top job I'd act differently."[2] The cartoonist's antipathy for Nixon continued to show during the 1960 and 1968 presidential campaigns in images of a devious, dirty, unshaven, tar-carrying shyster, in one case preparing to fire a cannon labeled "Fight crime by attacking the U.S. Supreme Court."[3]

After the 1968 election Herblock famously drew a barbershop with a sign posted, "This shop gives every new president of the United States a free shave. H. Block, proprietor."[4] Nevertheless, he soon resumed criticizing Nixon. The battles over Supreme Court nominees Clement Haynsworth and G. Harrold Carswell provoked a series of cartoons questioning Nixon's motives and tactics. When the struggle ended with the president's harsh condemnation of the Senate's refusal to confirm either candidate, Herblock brought back an old image. He drew a skulking Nixon with bucket and brush having just splattered tar on the Senate's door.[5] Throughout Nixon's first term, the *Post* cartoonist continued to produce unflattering depictions of White House policies, political tactics, fund-raising practices, statements to the media, and connections between campaign contributions and lax law enforcement.[6]

As soon as the Watergate break-in occurred on June 17, 1972, even before the *Washington Post's* reporters uncovered evidence linking the burglars to the White House, Herblock started drawing the connection. On June 19 and 20 he sketched images of Nixon, Attorney General John Mitchell, and Deputy Attorney General Richard Kleindienst for the following mornings' editorial pages. In the first, as the burglars were being arrested the three stood outside the door of the Democratic National Committee asking, "Who would think of doing such a thing?" The next day they held an office door closed with the attorney general telling the others, "Remember, we don't talk till we get a lawyer." Most striking was the Herblock cartoon created on June 22 and appearing the following morning, the day on which Nixon would have the cover-up conversation recorded on the "smoking gun" tape that eventually proved fatal to his presidency. Dirty footprints, some labeled "Bugging Case" and some named for other suspect activities, led straight out of the White House.[7]

Over the months that followed, Herblock returned time and time again to the topic of the Watergate investigation as it acquired a name and gained momentum. On August 29 the *Post* published his drawing of a cauldron of scandals with Nixon urging aides, "Keep the lid on until after the election." Scenes of the president with unaccounted-for campaign funds and trying to conceal a variety of scandals dominated the cartoonist's treatment of the fall campaign.[8] Early in 1973, as most attention focused on the Watergate burglars themselves, Herblock continued to suggest that Nixon was ultimately responsible. On February 4, for instance, he showed a dark figure labeled "Administration" pushing a bewildered citizen down a stairway at the top of which was a door bearing the presidential seal. The figure was saying, "We've done everything possible to get to the bottom of this. We just don't want anyone to get to the top of it."[9]

As the probing of the White House continued, Herblock marked every revelation, administration response, and new suspicion with an unflattering editorial cartoon. His drawings repeatedly showed closets bulging with skeletons, fumes rising from overflowing garbage cans, vaults stuffed with records and money, and Nixon sweeping things under the Oval Office rug. The president correcting previous statements (often while crouching behind his desk), the Republican Party as a bewildered elephant, and a foundering ship of state also became recurrent tropes. Among the most persistent images was a rising tide of slime or water around the White House or even in the Oval Office as the president clung to his upended desk.

Herblock would regularly rough out three or four different sketches for his next cartoon and show them to *Post* reporters to confirm that he was capturing the details of the latest developments.[10] Nevertheless, some of his most striking images contained his general observations. In an April 1973 cartoon a Republican elephant with Nixon riding on its back sinks into mud labeled "The Watergate Mess" and says, "It may not be touching you, Boss, but it's getting to me."[11] In one, two months later, a White House spokesman standing before a huge, partially covered whale labeled "Nixon Scandals" says, "I am authorized to say, 'What whale?'"[12] Even readers not following each twist and turn of the story could grasp the significance of a floundering pachyderm or a stinking carcass.

In the fall of 1973 the cartoonist's attention was diverted by the investigation and resignation of Spiro Agnew, the nomination of Gerald Ford, and the growing economic crisis of high energy prices and inflation. Thereafter Nixon's efforts at tax avoidance and the example they set provided a recurrent theme. However, Herblock returned time and time again to the battle over the White House tapes. Immediately after the Saturday Night Massacre, he drew Lady Justice being mugged. The cufflinks of the unseen attacker bore the initials RN.[13] Claims of executive privilege were disparagingly portrayed as concealment, as was the revelation that some tapes were missing and one contained an eighteen-and-a-half-minute gap. Perhaps the most memorable of all the cartoons Herblock drew appeared in the *Post* on May 24, 1974, just after the release of edited tape transcripts. Nixon was shown dangling between two huge reels of tape, one bearing the words "I am" and the other "A crook," while his mouth held a piece of tape labeled "Not." The simple image brilliantly summed up the artist's view of the disparity between the truth and Nixon's claims to the contrary.[14]

As the Watergate investigation ground on, Herblock criticized its pace and congressional Republicans' continuing support of the president. On May 3 he showed Nixon lecturing a cringing GOP, "Listen, are you going to be loyal to me or that (expletive deleted) Constitution?"[15] Three weeks later, he drew the president and his lawyer in front of the White House tearing up special prosecutor and congressional subpoenas with Nixon saying, "Of course this looks bad, but it can't hurt us as much as giving them the evidence."[16] Two months later a cartoon captioned "The Other Cover-Up" depicted a Republican congressman holding a sign proclaiming, "I don't see anything," while standing before a mountain of paper labeled "evidence" with a bag over his head.[17]

Herblock applauded the Supreme Court's decision in *United States v. Nixon* by drawing the Court's facade inscribed with "Equal Justice under Law 8, Nixon Claim of Absolute Privilege 0."[18] When the House Judiciary Committee finally approved articles of impeachment, he drew a hospitalized but happy Uncle Sam taking a spoonful of medicine labeled "Impeachment Proceedings" and saying, "Gee, Doc, they told me you'd cut me to pieces."[19] By August 6 Uncle Sam was out of the hospital and determinedly using a reel of tape to pull a resisting figure out of the executive office.[20] The next day a glum congressman, head in his hand, listened to the "smoking gun" tape.[21] Finally, on August 9, Herblock drew the small hand of Nixon signing a letter of resignation being held by the large hand of Uncle Sam.[22]

In retrospect, Herblock's body of Nixon cartoons, sharp-edged as they were, could well be regarded as prescient and educational. They often tied together disparate elements of a story, linking funding to outcomes or contrasting statements and actions. Repeated revelations of administration wrongdoing gave validity to Herblock's perception of Nixon as consistently duplicitous, self-serving, and threatening to the United States. The cartoon images helped solidify public impressions that Nixon's impeachment was justified and, indeed, overdue. Herblock's cartoons would appear in histories of Watergate, and the Pulitzer Prize committee identified him specifically in its citation honoring the *Washington Post*'s Watergate coverage. The whole episode enlarged his reputation as a shrewd observer and fearless interpreter of Washington politics. Whenever impeachment arose again as a subject of public discussion over the following nearly three decades, Herblock's images would once more influence public thinking because of the stature he gained from his body of Watergate work.

Herblock did not particularly admire President Ronald Reagan or his policies. Nevertheless, the cartoonist's drawings in the 1980s seldom conveyed the venom he had regularly displayed in his treatments of Nixon. The small, crouching stature accorded Nixon and the filth that always seemed attached to him were not elements in Herblock's caricatures of Reagan. The artist most often drew Reagan as an aged cowboy or a straight-backed and clean old man in a suit, a figure of amusement rather than of unrelieved disdain.

When the Iran-Contra story began to emerge, however, Herblock conveyed his sense of its seriousness by resurrecting some of his stock Watergate images. As details became public, he again used the trope of rising water, portraying the ship of state foundering in heavy seas or rain falling on the White House. He responded to the Tower Commission Report with a reminder of Reagan's earlier public statements, drawing the White House with a sign on its fence quoting, with clever highlighting, "We did not trade WEAPONS or anything else FOR HOSTAGES."[23] In another cartoon the stench of scandal rising ominously from administration activities also reappeared, though now the fumes emanated from shredding machines rather than Nixon's garbage cans.[24]

The pervasive image of mendacity that Herblock attached so effectively to Nixon was not central to his treatment of Reagan. Instead, his *Post* cartoons suggested more gently that the president concocted a false public impression. One of Herblock's most memorable characterizations of Reagan in the spring of 1987 showed the president struggling to prop up a falling three-times-life-size cardboard representation of himself.[25] Later the cartoonist called attention to the administration's shifting story by drawing Reagan doing repeated takes of a filmed explanation of Iran-Contra. In Take 1 he is saying, "It didn't happen." In Take 2 he asserts, "It happened but I didn't know." The next panel, numbered Take 28, has the president declaring, "I might have known, but I don't remember." Take 34 follows, with Reagan saying, "I just remembered—I knew, but the laws don't apply to me." Finally, as the film crew departs, he calls out, "Wait—I just thought of something else—."[26]

In contrast to his treatment of Watergate, Herblock's Iran-Contra coverage tended to focus on the activities of presidential deputies rather than those of the chief executive himself. He repeatedly parodied Attorney General Edwin Meese, White House Chief of Staff Donald Regan, and especially National Security Adviser John Poindexter and his deputy Lieutenant Colonel Oliver North. Only occasionally did President Reagan become the focus of an Iran-Contra cartoon, and then he was more often cast as inept than malign. At the end of February 1987 Herblock drew the president and his chief of staff considering the just-issued Tower Commission Report. Regan, wearing a placard identifying him as "Chief of Chaos," says "I thought you came off pretty well" to the smiling president, whose sign is inscribed, "Out to lunch."[27]

As Iran-Contra inquiries proceeded, Herblock occasionally went beyond the image of rising waters around the White House in drawing parallels to Watergate. Whereas once he had pictured dirty footprints leading to the White House, he now showed falling dominos heading in the same direction.[28] Two weeks later he sketched a man and woman outside the White House reading a newspaper headlined "Iran-Contra Scandals" and hearing an echo of the Nixon tapes, "We could raise the money, but . . . ."[29] For the most part, however, the cartoonist's attention was drawn to Meese's ineffective investigations, Poindexter's deceptions, and North's document shredding and outrageous testimony. Reminders of who was ultimately responsible tended to be sly, as in the cartoon showing two gentlemen in easy chairs saying, "It's awful that so many people around the president did these things—who in the world hired those people?"[30]

Herblock saved his harshest portrayal of Ronald Reagan until the joint congressional hearings on Iran-Contra had concluded and the committee's report had been issued. He then drew Reagan and Meese dressed in clown costumes.[31] Three years later, when the Iran-Contra criminal trials concluded, he sketched a wall of participant portraits, seven with guilty labels on them and the other two picturing Reagan and George H. W. Bush as "What's his name" and "That other fellow."[32] Though Herblock never treated Reagan or his successor as harshly as he had Nixon, he in the end left a clear impression of two chief executives who had evaded legitimate charges of misconduct.

George H. W. Bush avoided congressional scrutiny for his role in Iran-Contra far more easily than he escaped Herblock's pen. The cartoonist kept "the other fellow" in the pictures he drew of the Iran-Contra principals. When testimony finally emerged near the end of Bush's presidency that he had been involved in Iran-Contra all along, Herblock drew a picture of a lasso descending on him as he says, "I was out of the loop."[33] Yet like Special Prosecutor Lawrence Walsh, the *Washington Post* artist treated Bush as a secondary figure, one to be disbelieved but not to be alarmed about. By the time Bush was snarled in his own statements, he was about to leave the White House and thus avoid the possibility of being impeached for perjury.

Bill Clinton was the tenth president caricatured by Herblock in his tenure at the *Washington Post* and the third to face the distinct possibility of impeachment. From the outset the cartoonist drew Clinton in a much more sympathetic manner than he had employed with Nixon, Reagan, or Bush, or, for that matter, Dwight Eisenhower, Lyndon Johnson, Gerald Ford, or Jimmy Carter. Though, like Clinton, all were skewered from time to time, only Harry Truman and John Kennedy could be fairly judged to have received as kind treatment overall.

Herblock drew Clinton as a boyish figure, an often bewildered innocent among the tough and aggressive figures of the capital. For instance, in similar 1972 and 1997 images of the two incumbent presidents traversing a muddy mess, a dirt-covered, hunched-over, hand-wringing Nixon crosses over "Nixon scandals," whereas a head-up, shoulders-back, briefcase-carrying Clinton is having his clean suit spattered from below by "charges."[34] In an even more striking contrast to his representations of Nixon's or Reagan's ships of state as foundering ocean liners, Herblock, during the impeachment trial, drew Clinton scratching his head as he sits in the bow of a rowboat named *The Impeachment Case* that is sinking from the weight of a figure in its stern labeled "Congress" saying, "Now look at the mess you've got us into."[35] Later, with the Senate trial soon to begin, a cartoon showed a bound Clinton standing by wide-eyed as a figure labeled "Congress," hopelessly tangled up in a rope dangling from a tree branch, tells a bystander identified as "U.S.," who is also entangled, "I'll have him strung up in no time."[36]

Even when registering disapproval of Clinton, Herblock displayed a lighter approach than he had used on Nixon or others. Clinton delivered his 1998 State of the Union message announcing the first balanced federal budget in nearly three decades while the Monica Lewinsky story was breaking. The cartoonist drew Clinton poised on a tightrope with a heavy volume titled "Budget" in one hand and a shapely young woman pirouetting on the other. The caption, ambiguous if not admiring, read, "Balance."[37]

Instead of focusing scorn on Clinton, Herblock made Kenneth Starr the regular object of his ridicule during the protracted investigation by the independent counsel. Early in 1997, as the long inquiry dragged on, the *Post* artist drew a man in a telephone booth saying, "Hello, Kenneth Starr hotline? I have a tip that Clinton threw his porridge down from his high chair, and—get this—he pulled the pigtail of a little girl in the first grade."[38] Months later Herblock has Starr saying, "I think I'm beginning to smell something." Starr is pictured up to his knees in mud with fumes rising about his head as he looks at a sign labeled "Reported inquiries into Clinton personal life," while behind him are a series of similar signs marked "Continued law clients," "Leaks to press," "Pepperdine U. flip-flop-floop," "Political speeches," and "Appointment to replace Fiske."[39] After Starr delivered his report to Congress on the Lewinsky affair, Herblock dusted off an old trope, though this time the can of garbage was being dumped on a surprised citizen by a filthy independent prosecutor. The cartoon's caption quoted the Marx brothers: "The garbage man is here." "Tell him we don't want any."[40]

Along with Starr, the House of Representatives attracted Herblock's repeated derision during the Clinton investigation and impeachment. He went back to an image used during Watergate of outrageous, self-serving words being added to the Constitution, only this time attributing the alterations to Congress rather than the executive.[41] After the 1998 election he drew the chairman of the Judiciary Committee, Henry Hyde, whip in hand, riding the Republican elephant with Starr clinging to him and declaring, "Onward—while we still have a working majority in Congress."[42] Later Herblock depicted Hyde bowling a bomb into the House chamber.[43] Finally, he showed Hyde saying to Starr as they looked through the fence at the still-standing White House, "There must still be some way to get him out of there."[44]

To his devoted followers, Herblock conveyed an unequivocal message that the Clinton impeachment proceedings lacked legitimacy and involved unrelenting partisanship. He did not portray Clinton or his staff as the dark characters of the Nixon and Reagan administrations. Whereas the *Post*'s editorial page fixture had at least reinforced and perhaps initially helped shape the public's belief that Nixon's removal was justified and that Reagan's actions were questionable, he repeatedly expressed doubt about the assault on Clinton. Herblock's views came through clearly in the midst of the House deliberations in late 1998. He drew a guillotine labeled "Impeachment" and had one waiting executioner ask the other, "What have we got that's more like a close shave?"[45]

Other nationally seen political cartoonists offered images that, each in its own way, paralleled Herblock's message of Nixon's menace, Reagan's and Bush's misrepresentations, and Clinton's minor sins magnified by a hostile opposition. As they turned their attention to each president in turn, Gary Trudeau's syndicated *Doonesbury* strips aimed at the baby boom generation and Jules Feiffer's sketches for various intellectual journals offered more biting humor than did Herblock, but neither Trudeau nor Feiffer addressed specific unfolding events as closely or as frequently as he did.[46] Bill Mauldin, who like Herblock had been drawing since World War II for newspaper syndication, crafted numerous disparaging Nixon cartoons, while a series of younger cartoonists weighed in on one or more of the later episodes. But only Herblock, Trudeau, and Feiffer were professionally prominent during all three late-twentieth-century presidential impeachment episodes. The *Post* artist's work provided the most pointed commentary on actual events, made the most direct comparisons among impeachments, and reached the most diverse and mass audience. His impact on the evolving culture's general sense of impeachment was certainly influential. Herblock helped embed in the American mind the notion that Nixon's conduct was repeatedly reprehensible and richly deserving of punishment, that Reagan avoided responsibility for his administration's errors as a result of being viewed as inattentive and forgetful, and that Clinton, while personally flawed, was a satisfactory chief executive victimized by excessive and relentless political opposition. Herblock's suspension of cartooning in August 2001 and his death two months later spared George W. Bush the force of his perceptions and pencil. Nevertheless, by the time of the cartoonist's demise he had helped shape a new awareness of impeachment that pervaded American thought and would plague the Bush presidency.

Looking from the millennial moment forward into the first presidency of the twenty-first century as well as backward provides insight into the changes that impeachment caused in the political culture. By the turn of the millennium the American political system had acquired considerable knowledge and experience regarding the operation of its constitutional instrument for forcing the departure of federal officials. The Congress was filled with members who had taken part in one or more impeachment proceedings. Prominent in the ranks of the incoming administration in 2001 were individuals with substantial first-hand observation of impeachment. The new president's father had been an object of suspicion during the Iran-Contra episode. His chief political adviser, Karl Rove, had taken part in the tarnished 1972 Nixon reelection campaign as the twenty-one-year-old head of the College Republicans. Vice President Richard Cheney, while a member of the House of Representatives in the 1980s, had played an important role in defusing the congressional investigation of Iran-Contra. Secretary of Defense Donald Rumsfeld had held a prominent position in the White House during the Nixon administration; Cheney had served as his aide, and both had worked in the Ford White House during the aftermath of Watergate. These and other individuals involved with the new administration had observed impeachment up close, learning how to fend it off as well as to be sensitive to its possibility.

In the same span of years, the populace had developed more far-reaching notions as to when it might be appropriate to make use of the once rarely employed constitutional device. "High crimes and misdemeanors," at one time very narrowly defined, had come to be widely applied to disapproved conduct, even if arguably sanctioned by Congress or if only by the most expansive standards related to official duties. An altered attitude toward impeachment emerged on the part of possible proponents, potential targets, and the broader political culture. While it had once been regarded as a measure of disgrace even to have one's impeachment suggested, by the turn of the twenty-first century such a circumstance had come to be considered as a brutal but almost routine part of political combat, one that would surely produce embarrassment and distraction and possibly resignation or removal but one that presidents might expect and be ready to resist.

With three of the last six presidents of the twentieth century having endured serious impeachment consideration and with a fourth conceivably vulnerable had he won reelection in 1992, dealing with the threat of constitutional removal was beginning to seem a commonplace aspect of serving in the executive office, one to be anticipated and prepared for. As a consequence, the age of impeachment served to reshape the conduct of the presidency. Gone were the days when impeachment was highly exceptional and of no concern to the resident of 1600 Pennsylvania Avenue. Those days were replaced by an era featuring a more secretive and defensive executive office.

Beginning in the 1960s with calls for removing Supreme Court justices and quickly accelerating with Watergate, familiarity with impeachment had grown markedly. Political professionals and journalists were not alone in their heightened knowledge. A wide range of those in the broader American population observed and absorbed the same notions to one degree or another. The mounting experience with impeachment that culminated in the Senate trial of Bill Clinton altered perceptions of the once-seldom-used constitutional instrument and led a growing number of American citizens to regard it as an ordinary and routine political tool. Willingness to resort to impeachment underscored the go-for-the-jugular approach to partisan competition and the cynical don't-trust-anyone political atmosphere of the era. The enlarged contemplation of impeachment in American political and popular culture both reflected and contributed to an increasingly sour civic climate.

By the early years of the twenty-first century, demands for impeachment had become a first response to unhappiness with a president's policies and judgment, rather than a last resort in dealing with serious misconduct. The Republican Party, which bore the lion's share of responsibility for shaping more-aggressive attitudes regarding the use of impeachment, had to deal with the consequences of the change it had provoked. A small but steady stream of calls for the impeachment of George W. Bush began at the outer fringes of the political spectrum during the second year of his presidency. What Nixon, Reagan, and Clinton experienced in their lame-duck second term now for the first time confronted a president in his initial term. The calls for Bush's ouster grew in intensity and spread across the growing antiwar movement as his tenure wore on. Consequently, Bush had to bear invidious comparisons to Richard Nixon and Bill Clinton that ate away at his always limited and shaky political support.

Paradoxically, the familiarity of its senior members with impeachment equipped the first post-Clinton administration to fend off a constitutional assault. At the same time, confidence in their ability to avoid impeachment fostered the hubristic belief that they could circumvent traditional constitutional constraints. The result was a presidency that asserted its authority in foreign affairs as aggressively as had Ronald Reagan and in domestic matters as expansively as had Nixon. At the same time, it became the most guarded of American presidencies, strikingly closed off from the public and its congressional representatives as well as from the media.

Anticipating a suspicious and accusatory political culture, the administration of the second George Bush adopted a defensive and secretive posture from its earliest days. Refusing from the outset to release information about its activities to either Congress or the press, surreptitiously attempting to discredit its critics, and even seeking to prevent the opening of records of preceding administrations in which its inner circle had worked, George W. Bush's White House showed a wariness built on the experiences of its senior members during the Nixon, Ford, Reagan, and previous Bush administrations. The legacy of a frequent resort to impeachment in prior decades, together with the distaste with which it came to be held by a large share of the public, not to mention the Democratic Party, was a shaping influence on the first presidency of the twenty-first century.

The example set by Republican partisans since the 1960s and particularly during the late 1990s encouraged members of both the Grand Old Party and its opponents to think of impeachment as a means of demonstrating opposition to public officials and policies of which they disapproved. Calls for impeachment no longer necessarily adhered strictly to condemnation of "high crimes and misdemeanors" but, rather, reflected broader disapproval of those targeted. In news reports, opinion polls, political rhetoric, and public discussion during the first years of the new millennium, discourse repeatedly focused on the possible impeachment of various U.S. officials.

The number of simultaneous impeachment targets was unprecedented. Throughout most of the history of the United States it had been unusual to have even one impeachment under consideration. Only with the 1980s judicial cases had more than one individual proceeding overlapped. To be discussing multiple actions at one time, as was the case by 2005, even if most cases were insubstantial, was extraordinary. These calls made evident that perspectives on impeachment had shifted to a remarkable extent. Developments of recent decades had created an attitude across the political spectrum that treated impeachment as a commonplace political device instead of the extremely unusual phenomenon it had once been.

In 2005 no serious congressional effort was underway to impeach any particular federal official, but multiple possibilities were being mentioned, and some were manifesting support. Notably, a group of advocates of what they called the "right to life," including the U.S. House of Representatives Republican majority leader, Tom DeLay, and longtime conservative activist Phyllis Schlafly, called for the mass impeachment of a group of federal judges. The impeachment demand arose from individuals and groups upset by a series of federal district and appellate court rulings that permitted the removal of artificial life support from Terri Schiavo, a Florida woman who had spent fifteen years in a persistent vegetative state following a severe stroke. A dispute between her husband, Michael Schiavo, who after a decade and a half was resigned to letting her die, and her parents, Robert and Mary Schindler, who were desperately seeking to sustain her life, led to protracted state and federal litigation, intense journalistic attention, vigorous public debate, repeated interventions by the state government, and repeated court rulings that supported her husband's decision. Eventually, in March 2005, Terri Schiavo's feeding tube was removed. With other avenues exhausted, DeLay quickly summoned the House of Representatives, then in recess, into an extraordinary Sunday session, assembled a quorum, and won adoption of a resolution requiring a Florida federal district court to review the case once more. The Senate immediately concurred, and President Bush cut short a visit to his Texas home to fly back to Washington and sign the bill the same night. The stipulated district court hearing, held the following day, led to a reaffirmation of earlier rulings, and over the next three days both the Eleventh Circuit and the U.S. Supreme Court declined to hear appeals. Terri Schiavo died less than two weeks after artificial life support was removed. An autopsy revealed that at least 40 percent of her brain had withered over the course of her long comatose existence and that there had been no possibility of her regaining normal consciousness.[47]

Each of the six different state and federal courts that ruled in the Schiavo case confirmed long-standing precedent. None took any action that challenged prevailing legal or constitutional arrangements. No allegation was ever made that even the slightest judicial corruption was involved in any decision. Nevertheless, unhappy with the outcome and unwilling to concede that neither the various judges directly involved nor the U.S. Supreme Court justices who declined to hear a final appeal had simply upheld well-established law, critics advocated wholesale impeachment of all nineteen members of the bench who had been asked to address the case. The day that Terri Schiavo died, DeLay took the House floor to advocate impeachment and declare, "The time will come for the men responsible for this to answer for their behavior. We will look at an arrogant, out-of-control judiciary that thumbs its nose at Congress and the president."[48] Since neither DeLay nor any other House member actually moved to introduce an impeachment resolution, the political posturing of the campaign was clear.

It soon became evident that advocates of impeaching the Schiavo case judges had overreached. Even proponents of the "right to life," when the issue was abortion, found the prospect of government intervention in this instance distasteful. Requiring life-sustaining procedures proved overwhelmingly unpopular when a case was considered medically hopeless and the individual had indicated to a responsible custodian his or her desire to terminate such conditions. Americans clearly did not want government intruding into the intensely personal decisions of when and how to let go of life. Efforts of state and federal legislators to craft new devices to supervise and restrict end-of-life decisions, not to mention an attempt by Florida governor Jeb Bush, the president's brother, to subject Michael Schiavo's decision to further official scrutiny, came to an abrupt end. Talk of judicial impeachments ceased just as quickly, but not before the point was underscored that impeachment had grown into a ready tool of political warfare.

Judges had been the most frequent targets of impeachment throughout the history of the United States. During the post-1960 age of impeachment but before the Schiavo episode, no fewer than eight judges, including three justices of the U.S. Supreme Court, had been proposed for impeachment. Perhaps the judicial critics of 2005 were encouraged by the fact that those eight cases had produced three resignations in addition to three convictions and removals from office. If they anticipated driving the Schiavo judges from the bench, however, they failed to note that the judges who had left the bench unwillingly in recent years, as in earlier instances in American history, had been charged with committing improper self-enriching acts. Simple unhappiness with public policy decisions had never provided sufficient cause for successful impeachment. By 2005, however, the presumed efficacy of impeachment, not a careful analysis of its history or its proper grounds, was uppermost in the minds of those seeking to remove an official who had vexed them. In the conception of impeachment that had taken root in the political culture, the appeal of an instrument to expedite removal of a no-longer-satisfactory official applied, even more than to judges, to those most visibly eligible for impeachment: chief executives.

As the Schiavo case reached its apogee, another expression of the impeachment culture was emerging. It became manifest as unhappiness with President George W. Bush's so-called war on terror accelerated. After getting off to a somewhat rocky start in public opinion polls during his first seven and a half months in office, in part because of his disputed victory in the 2000 election and also because, once in office, his primary political interest appeared to be the substantial reduction of taxes on the wealthiest Americans, the second President Bush had gained a high level of support from a traumatized public following the September 11, 2001, al Qaeda attacks on New York and Washington.[49] At first the distressed country accepted with little hesitation the facile characterization of the September 11 assault, first by journalists but almost immediately by the president as well, as the launching of a war against the United States.

This label stuck despite the fact that the onslaught had come not at the direction of a foreign state but at the hands of a small shadowy group of expatriated individuals who could justifiably have been termed international criminals. The acceptance of a loosely defined conflict with an imprecisely identified foe and vaguely expressed objectives as a war had profound constitutional implications for the United States.

The sense of peril aroused by the horrific September 11 incident far exceeded its casualty toll. The attacks represented a dreadful loss from a single event, though fewer deaths than occurred in the United States during the same year from drowning accidents.[50] Considerable time would pass before a realization would begin to ripen throughout the nation of the consequences of treating the calculated violence of a clandestine group of stateless radicals as an act of war. Doing so placed much greater constitutional power in the hands of the president than he would have been able to acquire if he was merely being asked to deal with a criminal conspiracy. During past wars presidential authority had expanded far beyond the executive's normal peacetime prerogative. The Bush administration's war footing would become its core identity. Its assertion that the nation was at war would serve as justification for claiming extraordinary constitutional authority to engage in surveillance, interrogation, and incarceration, as well as to undertake two separate overseas military offensives and spend hundreds of billions of dollars. Eventually these claims of authority would become sources of public concern that its government was off track.[51]

Weeks after the September 11 attacks and a discovery soon thereafter of anthrax spores, a potent airborne biological poison, in incoming U.S. Senate mail, Bush had no trouble gaining overwhelming congressional approval for an array of security measures restricting civil liberties, measures that had been hastily gathered into what its sponsors called the USA Patriot Act. He was also able to gain the endorsement of Congress for an invasion of Afghanistan, the alleged base of operations for al Qaeda. Warming to his new role as commander in chief, Bush declared that Afghanistan represented "still just the beginning" of a "war on terror" and that if the government of Iraq developed "weapons of mass destruction that will be used to terrorize nations, they will be held accountable." This statement, made in late November 2001, was the first public indication that the president was focusing on Iraq, a secular state against which his father had gone to war in 1991 but that thus far had not been mentioned in relation to the fundamentalist religious movement of al Qaeda. By the time Bush gave his 2002 State of the Union address the following January, he was proclaiming that the United States confronted an "axis of evil" that involved Iraq, Iran, and North Korea. This alleged source of extreme threat stretched far beyond the Muslim Middle East previously identified with al Qaeda. President Bush predicted that the increasingly vaguely defined "war on terror" would need to be an ongoing effort, keeping the nation on a war footing and with an empowered presidency long into the future.[52]

With the United States experiencing no further terrorist incidents, the anxiety that followed the September 11 attacks began to subside. Enthusiasm for the administration's early actions soon started to erode as well.[53] Doubts began to be expressed about the need for increased domestic surveillance and for incarceration without judicial hearings of individuals alleged to have links to al Qaeda, and about the administration's suggestions that Iraq constituted an additional threat. In response, the administration sounded additional warnings about al Qaeda and Iraq. Administration sources gave *New York Times* reporter Judith Miller a story about an Iraqi defector who claimed to have worked on secret biological, chemical, and nuclear weapons projects. Miller's alarming front-page account of December 20, 2001, lacked the crucial detail, not provided to her, that the informant had three days earlier failed a CIA lie detector test.[54]

During interviews through the spring of 2002 and in speeches in San Francisco and Nashville, Tennessee, in August, Vice President Richard Cheney repeatedly stressed that al Qaeda was in contact with Iraq and that "there is no doubt" that the latter was at work on weapons of mass destruction. In September 2002 the administration loosed a barrage of warnings concerning Iraq. Cheney announced that "we do know, with absolute certainty" that Iraq was acquiring equipment to enrich uranium for nuclear bomb making. National Security Adviser Condoleezza Rice used the Watergate standard for proof of an Iraqi threat as she declared, "We don't want the smoking gun to be a mushroom cloud." Defense Secretary Donald Rumsfeld and Secretary of State Colin Powell echoed the message. Bush himself firmly reiterated the claim of Iraqi nuclear weapons development in a speech to the United Nations a year and a day after the September 11 attacks.[55]

Claiming to have intelligence showing Iraq's links to al Qaeda and its imminent threat to the United States, Bush asked Congress to authorize military measures against Iraq if he determined they were necessary. Lacking any independent capacity to verify or discredit the administration's claims and facing an anxious electorate within weeks, only about a quarter of the members of Congress were prepared to refuse the president's request for authority that seemed, to all but the most skeptical, justified and within constitutional bounds. In his January 28, 2003, State of the Union address, Bush stepped up the sense of impending grave danger from "outlaw regimes that seek and possess nuclear, chemical, and biological weapons." He warned the country that Iraq held and was prepared to use all these weapons of mass destruction, weapons capable of devastating large populations in the Middle East and elsewhere.[56] Eight days thereafter, Secretary of State Powell told the United Nations that Iraq was acquiring uranium for nuclear bomb making in the African country of Niger. Six weeks later, on March 19, Bush ordered a preemptive U.S. attack on Iraq. Baghdad was soon in U.S. military hands, and on May 1 the president announced "Mission Accomplished" with great flourish from the deck of an aircraft carrier off the coast of San Diego. Nevertheless, hostilities in Iraq continued, and doubts about the administration's justification for the war began to mount.

The American occupation force in Iraq proved unable to find any sign of the weapons of mass destruction that the administration had so ominously described. Questions quickly began to arise as to whether the call for invasion had been warranted. Before long, evidence began to emerge that the administration had not been forthright in its claims. On July 6, 2003, the Sunday *New York Times* published former ambassador Joseph C. Wilson's account of his trip to Africa more than a year earlier. He had gone at the behest of the CIA to investigate allegations that Niger had been selling Iraq uranium yellowcake, the raw material for nuclear bomb making. Wilson had reported back that he had found no evidence of such transactions. Now he questioned whether there was any basis for the president's claims to the contrary in his 2003 State of the Union address.[57] Eight days later, conservative newspaper columnist Robert Novak drew further attention to the matter when, in the course of a *Washington Post* op-ed article on the matter, he exposed Wilson's wife, Valerie Plame, as a covert CIA weapons expert.[58]

In the months that followed, the administration continued to characterize the Iraq invasion as a notable achievement. The despotic government of Saddam Hussein had fallen, and steps were being taken to erect a democratic replacement. Persistent violence against U.S. occupation forces as well as ongoing sectarian conflict among Iraqi religious groups clouded this image. Nevertheless, running for reelection in 2004 as a leader who had responded effectively to terrorist threats to the United States, Bush slipped past his Democratic opponent, John Kerry. Bush's victory appeared to be a mark of marginal public approval, at least for the moment, of the actions he had taken. After the election, however, U.S. casualties in Iraq escalated, the Plame and Wilson story began to unravel, and the president's carefully crafted image started to slip noticeably.

The CIA initiated an investigation of the leak of Valerie Plame's identity, a potential felony, and the Justice Department felt compelled to join in. Recognizing that once again the integrity of an administration investigating itself for improper conduct would be questioned, Attorney General John Ashcroft turned the inquiry over to a nonpartisan career federal prosecutor, Patrick Fitzgerald of Chicago. The resulting year-and-a-half-long probe eventually led to the indictment of Vice President Cheney's chief of staff, Lewis "Scooter" Libby. Accused in 2006 of perjury and obstruction of justice for lying under oath regarding conversations with reporters about Plame, Libby was found guilty in March 2007.[59]

Libby's conviction at least partially exposed the media manipulation the administration had engaged in to justify going to war and raised doubts about the veracity and motives of his superiors. In July 2007 the president commuted Libby's sentence shortly before he was to begin a thirty-month jail term. The action appeared strikingly inconsistent with Bush's long-standing unwillingness, both as Texas governor and as president, to grant clemency to convicted felons, even in capital cases. While the commutation fell within the president's specified constitutional powers, its grant was widely perceived at the time to be a means of assuring that Libby would never testify about a White House campaign to defend its decision to invade Iraq. Several commentators compared it to the first President Bush's pardon of convicted and accused Iran-Contra participants as a self-protective tactic.[60]

An icon of the culture of impeachment stirred further doubts about the Iraq invasion. The *Washington Post*'s legendary Watergate reporter Bob Woodward published an account of the Bush administration's repeated failure to deal forthrightly with Congress and the public regarding its planning and conduct of the invasion and occupation of Iraq. Woodward, who had earlier written two favorable books on the Bush presidency after the September 11 attacks, now cast the president and his inner circle as duplicitous, dissembling, and convinced of their own superior judgment. *State of Denial: Bush at War, Part III* inevitably reminded readers of Woodward's Watergate coverage, as well as of his repeatedly demonstrated ability to penetrate the institutions of government: the Supreme Court, the Central Intelligence Agency, the Pentagon, and, especially, the White House. His refusal to identify his sources of information had been criticized but had recently acquired new luster. Mark Felt's acknowledgement that he had been Deep Throat, a secret that Woodward had protected for thirty-three years, served to enhance the reporter's stature. When Woodward reported in *State of Denial* that Bush's inner circle had ignored CIA warnings about al Qaeda before September 11, thereafter focused on Iraq early on, knowingly presented a false argument for the Iraq invasion, and then bungled the occupation, he triggered reactions and even memories of impeachment that other authors covering the same ground, some of them much earlier, lacked the capacity to stir.[61]

Concern about the Iraq War grew from doubts not only about its initiation but also about its failure to produce the quick and positive results predicted by Bush and senior members of his administration. Instead, Iraq descended into a chaos fueled by deadly religious rivalries with which the U.S. military was unprepared to cope. American casualties increased bit by bit and eventually surpassed those of September 11, 2001. The public found the death toll and the far larger number of crippling injuries alarming. Revelations proliferated of American mistreatment of Afghan and Iraqi prisoners of war, as well as of other suspected enemies in the American military detention center in Guantanamo Bay, Cuba; at various secret foreign locations to which suspects were transferred, by a process labeled "extraordinary rendition," for severe interrogation; and, most spectacularly, at the Abu Ghraib prison in Baghdad. In all these instances the Bush government appeared to be ignoring American traditions of humane treatment of military prisoners and legal principles of allowing and honoring habeas corpus petitions to either charge or release civilian captives. Furthermore, the administration was dismissing or disregarding provisions of the Geneva Conventions on treatment of military prisoners.[62]

Such disclosures were troubling in light of confirmations that the Bush administration had persuaded the American Congress and public to undertake the war on the basis of strenuously defended claims that Iraq possessed weapons of mass destruction that it, in fact, did not have. In May 2005 the London *Sunday Times* published a British intelligence officer's report to the prime minister, Tony Blair, in July 2002 that the Bush government was determined to go to war with Iraq and was taking whatever action was needed to make the case for doing so. The Downing Street Memo, as it became known, helped confirm the impression created by the Plame and Wilson incident that the Bush administration had manipulated information regarding Iraq for its own purposes. Set against the rising carnage in Iraq, such disclosures heightened anger against the Bush presidency. A June 2005 *Washington Post*/ABC News poll found that a slight majority of Americans had come to believe that the Bush administration had "intentionally misled" the nation into Iraq.[63]

Other actions of the Bush administration led to further doubts about its respect for constitutional confinements of executive authority. Bush gradually made it evident that as long as he expressed reservations about legislation at the moment he signed it into law, he did not feel bound by it. Rather, he regarded himself as a "unitary executive," ultimately the sole authority over the executive branch. The Constitution provides no evident support for this autocratic view, but that did not inhibit the Bush White House. Previous presidents had made signing statements, generally in praise of new laws. None had employed such statements as frequently as did Bush, nor had any president systematically used them to redefine the effect of statutes, as Bush did with a congressional ban on using torture in the interrogation of prisoners, a ban affirming the Geneva Conventions. The Bush signing statement totally reversed the intent of the legislation, declaring that "none of the provisions of Geneva apply to our conflict with al Qaeda in Afghanistan or elsewhere throughout the world." A study by the nonpartisan congressional Government Accounting Office made evident that on the basis of signing statements, Bush and his subordinates were simply ignoring the specific requirements of nearly one out of three pieces of legislation, 750 acts in all, adopted since he took office. Questions arose as to whether this practice amounted to an unconstitutional assertion of unlimited presidential power, subverting the authority of Congress to adopt laws and the judiciary to review their validity.[64]

Early in the Bush "war on terror," voices on the left, including one-time attorney general of the United States Ramsey Clark and two-time presidential candidate Ralph Nader, began asserting that President Bush deserved impeachment. The rapidly increasing use of instantaneous and widely distributed electronic communication over the Internet gave such claims wide circulation and impact.

Clark objected from the outset to Bush's treatment of imprisoned alleged terrorists and in 2002 launched an Internet campaign for the president's removal.[65] Commitment of the United States to the invasion of Iraq in 2003 heightened the consternation of administration critics. Nader vigorously disparaged Bush's and Cheney's conduct and in April 2004 proposed immediate removal of both for telling falsehoods to lead the country into an unconstitutional war against Iraq.[66]

The Bush administration's penchant for secrecy and its questionable conduct drew criticisms from other quarters as well. The notice it received reflected the weight that impeachment experience continued to carry in the public consciousness. One prominent veteran of the Nixon White House, John Dean, attracted considerable attention for his assessment of the Bush presidency. Dean offered a highly uncomplimentary appraisal of Bush in a slender book with the arresting title *Worse Than Watergate*. He focused on Bush's penchant, evident from the outset of his pursuit of the presidency, for shrouding his affairs in secrecy. After the September 11 attacks, Dean pointed out, Bush wasted little time before issuing Executive Order 13233 redefining the Presidential Records Act of 1978. That post-Watergate legislation declared that presidential records constituted public property to be available for inspection, unless classified, within twelve years. President Clinton had subsequently carried the new openness further, shortening the limits of security classification to twenty-five years. In contrast, the November 2001 Bush executive order gave former as well as current presidents, their families, and their vice presidents the authority to withhold records or delay their release indefinitely, in effect countermanding the original measure. The Bush administration itself proceeded to keep a tight rein on information, dispensing it only when it served White House purposes.[67]

The most egregious case of information manipulation, that relating to prewar intelligence concerning Iraq, when subsequently exposed, stirred questions by Congress and the American people about the reasons for going to war. Congressman Charles Rangel epitomized the chorus of complaint. In May 2004 he introduced a resolution in the House calling for the impeachment of Secretary of Defense Donald Rumsfeld for overseeing a preemptive invasion and an improperly conducted occupation of Iraq.[68]

By emphasizing threats to the nation and proclaiming its successes in dealing with them, the Bush administration managed to defend its conduct of the "war on terror" to an anxious public through the president's successful reelection campaign in 2004. Bush's three-million-vote victory margin over Democrat John Kerry was robust compared to his 500,000 vote deficit in the popular tally in the 2000 election, though it was the smallest victory margin for a second-term president since 1916. While no doubt preferable in his eyes to the defeats suffered by his father and other second-term aspirants Jimmy Carter and Herbert Hoover, the 2004 balloting did not produce what political veterans would call a mandate. It did, however, prove to be the high point of Bush's political fortunes.

After the 2004 election, public enthusiasm for the administration, such as it was, declined, owing in no small part to ongoing difficulties, rising casualty tolls, and an apparent stalemate in Iraq. A public opinion survey taken in June 2005 by Zogby International found 42 percent of respondents saying that if it were proven that Bush had not told the truth about the reasons for attacking Iraq, Congress should impeach him. Enthusiasm for this suggestion was greatest in the West, where 52 percent favored and only 41 percent opposed impeachment, and in the East, where the margin was 49 percent to 45 percent. In the South, by contrast, 60 percent opposed impeachment and only 34 percent supported it. Likewise, in the Midwest 52 percent opposed and 38 percent supported impeachment.[69] Nevertheless, the overall surge in willingness to consider impeachment was noteworthy.

Perhaps the most striking aspect of the Zogby opinion survey was that upwards of 90 percent of respondents had an opinion on impeachment of the incumbent president. Few (7 percent in the West, 6 percent in the East and South, and 10 percent in the Midwest) were unwilling, for whatever reason, to take a stand one way or another. These remarkable results reflected not only the partisan polarization of the moment and the deep divisions within the nation stirred by the Iraq war itself but also the nearly universal familiarity with the concept of presidential impeachment. After a year of Watergate revelations, by comparison, only 24 percent of those surveyed in a July 1973 Gallup poll believed that Nixon should be impeached and compelled to leave the presidency.[70]

After Bush entered his second term, willingness to call for his impeachment as a means of expressing general political discontent became more and more evident. On June 16, 2005, Representative John Conyers of Michigan, the ranking Democrat on the House Judiciary Committee and a veteran of the Watergate hearings, as well as of subsequent impeachment proceedings, conducted a mock impeachment inquiry. As a minority member lacking the power to convene an official House hearing, Conyers found a vacant conference room in the Rayburn House Office Building to provide a forum for a parade of speakers critical of Bush and the Iraq war. Conyers's four-hour hearing focused on the British Downing Street Memo attesting that Bush had decided to wage war on Iraq long before presenting a case for doing so to Congress and the American people.[71] Six months later Conyers proposed resolutions censuring Bush and Cheney for refusal to provide information on the initiation and conduct of the war and retaliation against war critic Joseph Wilson. Conyers would enlist eighteen cosponsors by the end of the 109th Congress.[72]

Not long after Conyers's hearing, the Bush administration also drew criticism for its woefully insufficient response to the September 2005 devastation of New Orleans by Hurricane Katrina. Among those who perceived the Bush administration as inept in its response to Katrina as well as misguided or mendacious in its continued occupation of Iraq, calls for the president's impeachment grew more common. With no simple solutions evident for either the domestic catastrophe or the unsettled situation in Iraq, impeachment became a rhetorical staple for people deeply disenchanted with their government. On September 24, 2005, at the first large antiwar demonstration in Washington, D.C., in a generation, posters and banners advocating George W. Bush's impeachment were ubiquitous. Ramsey Clark's online impeachment campaign demonstrated its durability and organization through mass-produced printed signs and T-shirts proclaiming, "Bush Lied. Thousands Died. Impeach Bush!" or "Guilty of War Crimes! Impeach Bush!" Innumerable hand-lettered placards conveyed similar messages. When Clark, one of the featured speakers at the Saturday afternoon rally immediately south of the White House, renewed his call for Bush's impeachment, his plea was met with loud and sustained applause.[73] In the search for a way out of confounding circumstances, impeachment of the president seemed to many of those present to be the equivalent of a silver bullet.

As the political mood of the country turned ever more sour, the hail of silver bullets grew thicker. Another Zogby poll in November 2005 showed that the portion of Americans willing to impeach the president if it could be demonstrated that he had deliberately misled the country into the Iraq war had risen to 53 percent. Forty-two percent opposed the idea, and only 5 percent expressed no opinion. Enthusiasm for impeachment was reported to be highest among blacks (90 percent), registered Democrats (76 percent), and Americans under the age of 30 (70 percent).[74] The poll's sponsor, a founder of an antiwar organization, After Downing Street, called the results "stunning" and launched a Web-based political action committee, ImpeachPAC, to raise campaign funds for Democratic candidates favoring impeachment.[75]

With American casualties accelerating and the course of the Iraq invasion increasingly in question, Hollywood celebrities and Democratic Party supporters as dissimilar as Michael Moore and Barbra Streisand called for Bush's impeachment on their Web sites. After the president aggressively defended the Iraq war in a 2005 Veterans Day speech and suggested that critics were "irresponsible," Democrats responded that the Bush administration had falsified intelligence to trick the country into going to war. Senator John Kerry raised the stakes, asking, "How are the same Republicans who tried to impeach a president over whether he misled a nation about an affair going to pretend it does not matter if the administration intentionally misled the country into war?" Congresswoman Zoe Lofgren of California declared, "'Lying to the Congress about a large public purpose such as Iraq' fits the constitutional test of 'high crimes and misdemeanors' better than lying about sex."[76]

Revelations in December 2005 that Bush had ignored specific statutory requirements that judicial approval be gained before conducting domestic electronic surveillance led a distressed Democratic senator, Russell Feingold of Wisconsin, to caution that the Constitution placed limits on presidential

Washington, D.C., September 24, 2005. Courtesy of Christine Worobec.

authority and that Bush was a president, not a king. When the president responded that his broad powers as commander in chief during a time of war gave him constitutional authority to ignore a congressional directive, the cries of outrage grew louder. Senator Barbara Boxer of California called attention to the remarks of Watergate veteran John Dean. In a joint appearance with Boxer in Los Angeles Dean asserted that Bush, by acknowledging that he had authorized the National Security Agency to conduct the warrantless clandestine surveillance, was the first chief executive to have willingly confessed to an impeachable offense.[77] Using the language of impeachment clearly had become as least a rhetorical means to deal with serious public policy disputes.

Throughout 2006 the rhetoric of impeachment escalated as dissatisfaction with the policies of the Bush administration continued to increase among left-leaning politically active grassroots groups. A political culture that only a few years before had experienced a substantial impeachment proceeding that appeared to grow out of partisan conflict and only late in its evolution found a specific reason for charging commission of a "high crime" did not seem daunted by uncertainty over what the specific grounds for constitutional action might be. Indeed, the desire for removal extending beyond a clear basis for it was reflected in a poster carried by a young man at a spring 2006 San Francisco demonstration. The hand-lettered placard, whose image spread over the Internet, appealed, "Will someone PLEASE give George W. Bush a blow job so we can impeach him."

As unhappiness with the Iraq War swelled, talk of impeaching Bush did so as well. Former New York representative Elizabeth Holtzman, a veteran of the House Judiciary Committee Watergate hearings, published a call for Bush's removal from office for deceiving the country into war with Iraq, authorizing illegal wiretapping of American citizens, permitting torture, leaking classified information, and demonstrating reckless indifference to human life in his handling of Iraq and the effects of Hurricane Katrina.[78] A flurry of similar books by other authors followed.[79] From the opposite end of the political spectrum, libertarian Lyndon LaRouche chipped in with appeals for the impeachment of Bush, but only after the removal of Vice President Cheney.[80] At the time they arose, none of these initiatives gained measurable support from either the general public or legislators in a position to act on them, but they served as reminders that impeachment had become an instrument of choice for challenging a president.

Calls for impeachment came mostly from outside Congress and otherwise from members of the largely powerless minority party. It is, therefore, not surprising that such appeals generated no response from a tightly disciplined Republican congressional majority firmly bound to the administration. The chairman of the House Judiciary Committee, James Sensenbrenner, a veteran of the Clinton and several judicial impeachment proceedings, gave no hint that any inquiry, much less formal hearings, would be undertaken. The committee's ranking minority member, John Conyers, spoke of impeachment but lacked any authority to propel it forward.

Interest in impeachment continued to manifest itself in various ways. The old Herblock trope of water rising at the White House reappeared. The cover of the *New Yorker* magazine's September 19, 2005, issue showed the Oval Office with water up to the president's desktop, though Bush and his inner circle of advisers appeared oblivious to their peril. During the following year, local government bodies began to adopt ordinances calling for referendums on impeachment or petitioning state legislatures to request federal action. In the fall 2006 election campaign, yard signs calling for the president's impeachment proliferated in such normally conservative communities as Kalamazoo, Michigan. Talk of impeachment no longer seemed as radical as had once been the case in American political discourse.

The November 2006 national election made evident that sentiment for impeaching George W. Bush, in itself difficult to calculate precisely, was the tip of an iceberg of citizen unhappiness with the manner in which government was being conducted. For the first time in a dozen years, the Republican Party lost it majority in both houses of Congress, surrendering control of an extraordinary six Senate seats and thirty-eight House districts. While losing seats was

Barry Blitt, *The New Yorker,* September 19, 2005. © Condé Nast Publications Inc.

customary in the sixth year of an administration, the magnitude of the Bush loss was exceptional. If the previous sixth-year balloting, the unusual 1998 election, had represented a vote against impeachment, this seemed to some observers a contrary expression by the electorate.

Following the 2006 election, the new Democratic majority of the House of Representatives chose Nancy Pelosi of San Francisco as speaker. She wasted no time demonstrating that she held to a traditional belief that impeachment was a constitutional device only to be employed in exceptional circumstances and not to be used as a routine weapon of political combat. Months earlier, while serving as House Democratic minority leader, she had indicated in a *Washington Post* interview that although a Democratic majority would investigate the administration, it would not be with the goal of impeaching the president.[81] Therefore, during her first press conference as speaker-elect, Pelosi was asked whether impeachment would be on her agenda for the new Congress. She quickly responded that it was "off the table."[82] Incoming House Judiciary Committee chair John Conyers promptly embraced Pelosi's position. Despite his past expressions of interest in examining whether Bush merited impeachment, he now indicated that the matter was not in his committee's plans.[83] Outgoing Congresswoman Cynthia McKinney of Georgia soon signaled that not all Democrats agreed with their leaders as she introduced a symbolic, if futile, impeachment resolution in the waning hours of the 109th Congress.[84]

Shortly thereafter, as Pelosi began choosing committee chairs for the new House, she declined to appoint Representative Alcee Hastings as chair of the Permanent Select Committee on Intelligence. At the moment Hastings stood next in line for the post, and colleagues considered him highly qualified. Pelosi, however, recognized Hastings's political vulnerability due to the lingering shadow of his impeachment and removal from the bench eighteen years earlier.[85] Although not willing to place him in charge of the sensitive intelligence committee, Speaker Pelosi demonstrated respect for Hastings by designating him to preside over the House in her absence during the first days of the new Democratic Congress.[86] Criticized by her party's left for declining to pursue Bush and, to a lesser degree, for bypassing Hastings, Pelosi appeared more concerned than many of her contemporaries with treating impeachment in the narrow way that the founders had intended. Whether her views would influence the culture of impeachment remained to be seen.

As the Democratically controlled 110th Congress took office in January 2007, it faced a situation reminiscent of that confronting its predecessor twenty years earlier. Both Congresses faced a president whose policies were deeply unpopular and legally suspect—in the first instance, Iran-Contra; in the second, Iraq and the "war on terror." Likewise, both confronted the question of whether to hold a president at fault, thus worthy of impeachment, for actions for which subordinates had been held accountable, criminally indicted, and subsequently convicted. In neither case was there the hard documentary basis for a charge of "high crimes and misdemeanors" provided by the "smoking gun" of criminal cover-up, or even a court record that might be used to support allegations of presidential perjury. To the contrary, the argument could be made that Congress was somewhat complicit in the actions of the executive branch. Defining a specific impeachable offense would pose a challenge.

The Reagan and Bush situations differed in that in the midst of their difficulties, Reagan remained personally popular with most Americans, while Bush did not. A Gallup poll in January 2007 placed Bush's job approval rating for the previous year at an average of 37 percent, one of the worst annual averages recorded since Gallup began taking such measures in the late 1930s.[87] The decline continued, and by July only 29 percent of a national sample of voters indicated approval of Bush's job performance.[88] Nevertheless, in both instances, Democratic leaders would conclude that an impeachment proceeding, whether as long and drawn out as Watergate or even as relatively brief as the Clinton epi-sode, would be constitutionally uncertain, politically unachievable, and more traumatic and distracting than warranted for a nation beset with serious pub-lic policy problems. The continued willingness of Speaker Pelosi and Chairman Conyers to eschew a political gesture doomed to ultimate failure led them to resist a tide of sentiment stirred by the actions of the Bush administration. They showed a respect for the strict terms of the Constitution that, in some eyes, had recently been absent in a political culture that had come to regard impeachment as an unexceptional means to attack an unpalatable foe.

Calls for the impeachment of George W. Bush, along with his subordinates Vice President Richard Cheney, Secretary of Defense Donald Rumsfeld, and Attorney General Alberto Gonzales, not to mention the earlier demands from other quar-ters for impeaching the Schiavo case judges, however unlikely any of them were to bear fruit, reflected a political and constitutional culture that had come regu-larly to advocate impeachment. As reflected in the many cartoons of Herblock on the subject, the consideration of impeachment had gradually grown wide-spread in the United States over the course of several decades. American politics had not always been so confrontational. Regular attempts to remove individuals from office in disgrace, even though sometimes justified when officials blatantly ignored constitutional limitations, deeply eroded the middle ground on which compromise could be built. The age of impeachment fostered a nastier, more belligerent, and less tolerant political atmosphere than had prevailed through most of American history. Impeachment had gone from the last means contem-plated for dealing with a public official thought to be unsatisfactory to one of the first tactics mentioned.

By the early years of the twenty-first century, proposing impeachment had become almost commonplace. A suggestion that forty years earlier could aston-ish the nation was now a conventional and familiar political proposal. The im-peachment calls spawned by the Schiavo case and the Bush presidency stand as reminders that during the last four decades of the twentieth century impeach-ment had emerged as a powerful political and constitutional tool.

The evolving culture of impeachment had less obvious but also important as-pects. The rise of a pool of Washington attorneys experienced in dealing with impeachment was significant. It meant that legal expertise was available to draw upon, whether in advancing an impeachment measure or defending against one. When, for instance, George W. Bush was choosing a new White House le-gal counsel in January 2007, he could turn to Fred F. Fielding, once John Dean's deputy in the same office and later White House legal counsel to Ronald Reagan. Fielding's background in dealing with assertions of executive privilege was un-usual, though not altogether unique. His expertise would provide needed help in fending off growing challenges to the Bush presidency.

The ongoing Internet discussion of impeaching Bush, started by Clark at VoteToImpeach, spread to other Web sites, such as ImpeachPAC and ImpeachBush in the course of a half decade. University of Illinois law professor Francis Boyle posted a draft resolution calling for Bush's impeachment on multiple grounds in January 2003. Though Boyle charged Bush with offenses questionable as "high crimes," the professor's six articles did spotlight reasons for the president's unpopularity, including domestic security practices and preparations for attacking Iraq.[89] The development of impeachment Web sites not only reflected the emergence of a new vehicle for political communication but also served as a measure, though one admittedly far from precise, of the increasing popular embrace of impeachment. A significant feature of calls for Bush's removal was their manifest hostility to Bush's public policies and their relative lack of concern for limiting complaints to what had traditionally been considered impeachable offenses.

While the Internet conveyed news of the spread of impeachment sentiment, more substantive expressions of its extent were likewise evident. In the early months of 2006 five Vermont towns adopted resolutions calling for Bush's impeachment. A year later, the number had risen to thirty-nine. By then, the Vermont Senate had adopted an impeachment resolution, though it failed a week later in the state's lower house.[90] In eight other states, eighty cities (including Detroit and San Francisco), counties, and townships had adopted various impeachment measures as well.[91] By June 2007 ten state legislatures—California, Hawaii, Illinois, Maine, Minnesota, Missouri, New Mexico, Texas, Washington, and Wisconsin—in addition to Vermont had considered though not passed resolutions petitioning Congress to take impeachment action. None of this grassroots activity had any substantive effect, but cumulatively it did reflect the spreading impeachment culture, not to mention outright hostility to Bush.[92]

On June 17, 2007, the thirty-fifth anniversary of the break-in at the Democratic National Committee offices at the Watergate complex, veteran Washington journalist Daniel Schorr, a self-described "certified entry on Nixon's enemies list," commented on National Public Radio that the Bush White House increasingly resembled its Nixon counterpart. Schorr drew parallels between the small closed circle of decision makers in the two administrations, which he acerbically termed "juntas," and referred to their similar "extralegal surveillance on a large scale" as well as to the "extraconstitutional imprisonment of those the [Bush] junta suspects." He made no prediction that impeachment awaited Bush, instead speculating that it might be thirty-five years before evidence damaging to Bush surfaced. Schorr did suggest that Americans should pay attention to a recent wave of books on Nixon and Agnew as well as the play *Frost/Nixon* being performed in New York, reminders of impeachable presidential offenses, as they contemplated the current political scene.[93]

The anniversary brought forth another Watergate veteran, Bob Woodward, who answered questions on the *Washington Post* Web site. Eight of the twenty-two queries addressed to the journalist drew comparisons between Nixon and Bush. Woodward admitted that the press in general and he personally "should have been more aggressive in looking at the run-up to the Iraq War, and specifically the alleged intelligence that Iraq had weapons of mass destruction stockpiles." He pointed out that "to answer the WMD question before the March 2003 invasion would have been a monumental task," but he ruefully acknowledged that it was "one that we should have undertaken more systematically."[94]

Less that two weeks later, Egil Krogh, one of Nixon's Plumbers, provided some related reflections to the *New York Times*. He wrote of his own folly prior to the Watergate debacle in trusting presidential assertions of constitutional authority to commit illegal acts with impunity if national security demanded it. At a time when President Bush and Vice President Cheney were boldly asserting wartime authority and "executive privilege" to refuse congressional subpoenas of documents, Krogh drew a direct connection between their behavior and Nixon's. He advised White House lawyers, "Rely on well-established legal precedent and not some hazy, loose notion of what phrases like 'national security' and 'commander in chief' could be tortured into meaning."[95]

The efforts of Schorr, Woodward, and Krogh to draw linkages between Nixon and Bush were small manifestations of the place impeachment had come to occupy in early-twenty-first-century American political culture. The attention paid to the Watergate anniversary and its contemporary parallels manifested an ongoing preoccupation with impeachment, in at least some circles. A month later, another veteran Washington journalist, Bill Moyers, observed, "Impeachment . . . the word feared and loathed by every sitting president is back. It's in the air and on your computer screen, a growing clamor aimed at both President Bush and Vice-President Cheney."[96] Patrick Leahy, the chairman of the Senate Judiciary Committee, confirmed Moyers' perception. The senator remarked, "The Bush-Cheney White House continues to place great strains on our constitutional system of checks and balances. Not since the darkest days of the Nixon administration have we seen efforts to corrupt federal law enforcement for partisan political gain and such efforts to avoid accountability."[97]

New expressions continued to surface of the public's perception that impeachment was a satisfactory way to end the term of a chief executive with whom it had grown disenchanted. While the father and son presidents were in residence at the Bush family home in Kennebunkport, Maine, in July 2007, demonstrators gathered outside carrying signs inscribed "Impeach the Son of a Bush."[98] Later in the same month Cindy Sheehan, a highly visible and vocal leader of protests against the Iraq War to which she had lost a son, vowed to run for the House against Nancy Pelosi unless the speaker reversed direction to support Bush's and Cheney's impeachments. Sheehan then led a group of antiwar activists to present to Judiciary Committee Chairman Conyers an impeachment petition with a claimed one million signatures. After listening to her presentation, Conyers explained that there simply were not the votes in Congress to accomplish what she sought; the opportunity for a democratic expression of dissatisfaction at a national election, he pointed out, was little more than a year away. An unhappy Sheehan and her companions refused to accept Conyers's assessment or leave his office. The Capitol police arrested and led away in plastic handcuffs nearly four dozen of these latest symbols of the gulf between experienced political veterans of past impeachments, who were sensitive to the specific and difficult task of finding constitutional grounds to justify removal of an executive, and a grassroots public accustomed to thinking of the process as a means of expressing impatience for the departure of executives they had come to loathe.

The calls for Bush's and Cheney's impeachment would continue. As disgust with the Bush government continued to grow among those appalled by the ongoing Iraq War as well as by increasing revelations that the administration was ignoring constitutional limitations on domestic surveillance and long-standing national commitments regarding the humane treatment of war prisoners, the chorus of calls swelled. In November 2007 Representative Dennis Kucinich of Ohio, an insurgent candidate for the 2008 Democratic presidential nomination, tried to bring before the House a resolution impeaching the vice president for "fabricating a threat of Iraqi weapons of mass destruction" to justify the country's invasion. Even the support of Republican members of Congress intent on making mischief for their partisan opponents failed to generate sufficient votes to bring Kucinich's proposal to the floor; instead it was sent to the Judiciary Committee, where Chairman Conyers was expected to keep it from emerging. With each passing month, the likelihood declined that the demands for their removal would bear fruit before Bush and Cheney left office. Nonetheless, in January 2008, 1972 Democratic presidential candidate and Watergate victim George McGovern broke a self-imposed thirty-five-year silence on impeachment to declare that the incumbents' misdeeds exceeded even those of Nixon. Bush's and Cheney's offenses in terms of war making, domestic surveillance, and violation of international agreements were so egregious, a clearly agitated McGovern insisted, as to merit their removal even at the end of their term and "signal to the American people and the world . . . support [for] the impeachment of the false prophets who have led us astray."[99]

Despite the steadily growing unpopularity of the Bush administration's actions and stubborn claims, the protracted process of impeachment investigations, hearings, and proceedings that had become so familiar and expected required more time and political support than advocates could muster. A further complication arose from the difficulty of justifying impeachment on the basis of engaging in a war or conducting surveillance that Congress had in one way or another sanctioned. Nevertheless, ongoing grassroots discussion of the possibility of removing either or both Bush and Cheney suggested that the culture of impeachment continued to thrive.

14

The Age of Impeachment: Ended or Extended?

The fingers of one hand suffice to count the individuals, all of them Democrats, who served in Congress from the first half of the 1960s, when the John Birch Society was calling for the impeachment of Chief Justice Earl Warren, through President George W. Bush's second term, when groups on the left were loudly demanding his impeachment. Three of these veteran legislators, Representative John Dingell of Michigan, Senator Robert Byrd of West Virginia, and Senator Edward Kennedy of Massachusetts, had only limited involvement in the impeachment actions that came before the bodies in which they served. Their role was confined to the rare floor votes authorizing inquiries or determining their chamber's judgment on a case. The two other members of Congress whose long tenure put them in this group of five, Representative John Conyers of Michigan and Senator Daniel Inouye of Hawaii, were, by contrast, deeply and repeatedly involved in impeachment matters.

It seems remarkable that these overlapping congressional careers, exceptionally long ones but still covering only roughly one-fifth of Congress's over-two-hundred-year history, confronted nearly half the instances of seriously contemplated impeachment that the United States has faced altogether. At no other time in the nation's history would a federal legislator of equivalent tenure have been forced to deal so many times with issues of impeachment. Even far more common legislative careers of shorter duration were likely during this era to encounter impeachment more than once, not an experience shared with many of their legion of congressional predecessors.

The frequency with which issues of impeachment arose after 1960 made those years distinctive in American political and constitutional history. The circumstances of the individual episodes varied considerably, revealing a good deal about the evolution of impeachment during this era. As the possibility or reality of an individual being subjected to impeachment occurred over and over, those repeatedly engaged in the process gained unprecedented experience. They developed insights and differences of opinion regarding the constitutional removal mechanism.

Over the course of their more than four decades in Congress, Conyers and Inouye reached different conclusions about the role of impeachment in the American constitutional system. Their views reflected the range of attitudes toward impeachment that arose within the American political culture during the era when the removal device came into play with unusual frequency. The contrasting perspectives of the two senior legislators, both widely respected by their congressional colleagues, provide a useful framework for drawing conclusions about the place of impeachment in American constitutional government.

John Conyers took a seat on the Judiciary Committee when he was first elected to the House of Representatives from a Detroit district in 1964. He rose to become the committee's ranking Democrat, and in 2007, when his party recaptured a majority position in the House for the first time in a dozen years, he became committee chair. Over his long years of service, Conyers had several opportunities to participate in impeachment deliberations. Although he did not take part in the subcommittee investigation of William O. Douglas in 1970, he was in the midst of the full committee's consideration of the Richard Nixon case in 1974. When three-member subcommittees were appointed to consider judicial cases in the 1980s, he served on the Walter Nixon panel, chaired the Alcee Hastings investigation, and served as a House manager presenting the latter case to the Senate. His judgment that Hastings deserved removal carried great weight in both the House and the Senate. He later expressed second thoughts about the Hastings case and was an outspoken opponent of Bill Clinton's impeachment.

Conyers twice took the lead in advocating presidential impeachment, first as a sponsor of the initial resolution to remove Ronald Reagan for the Grenada invasion and twenty years later as an early critic of George W. Bush's actions toward Iraq. Conyers displayed no hesitation about endorsing impeachment whenever he concluded that a federal judge or executive's official conduct had been fundamentally improper. Still, in 2007, given his new responsibilities as chair of the House Judiciary Committee, the richly experienced and politically astute congressman declined to press further for Bush's impeachment, seeing it as a doomed-to-fail distraction from other more productive investigations of the Bush Justice Department.

Daniel Inouye entered Congress six years before Conyers, initially in 1959 as the first Representative for the new state of Hawaii and four years later as a senator. His patriotic image as a recipient of the Congressional Medal of Honor for battlefield heroism during World War II made him a shrewd choice for membership on the Ervin committee investigating Watergate, although he would explain that Senate Majority Leader Mike Mansfield persuaded him to take the job on the basis that, as one of the few senators who was a lawyer but neither the chair of a committee nor a candidate for president, he could approach the investigation both knowledgeably and objectively. Finding the experience a painful, even if necessary, one that demeaned the nation in the eyes of the watching world, Inouye was decidedly unenthusiastic about proceeding with another presidential impeachment when asked to lead the Senate inquiry into the Iran-Contra affair a dozen years later or required to vote on the Clinton impeachment a decade thereafter.[1]

Reflecting on his long experience with impeachment, Inouye expressed discomfort with the high visibility and political character of the process. He would prefer a more judicial approach to the treatment of official misconduct. Unlike jurors whose anonymity is preserved to protect their futures and assure their objectivity, he observed, the legislators deciding impeachment cases are invariably well-known figures—"in fact it's our business to make ourselves well known"—whose political futures could rest on their highly visible decisions. He pointed out that impeachment involved issues of harm not merely to an individual but, rather, to the nation and perhaps the world. Nevertheless, he mused, the case is decided by men and women "politically and philosophically at times so diverse that they're from different planets. . . . And so you find the impeachment process to be—what shall I say—inadequate for the mission that it was meant to accomplish, and in fact what we need is something better than that. I don't think impeachment is the answer."[2]

Representative Conyers and Senator Inouye, though members of the same party and the same political generation, epitomize opposite poles of the impeachment debate. Conyers proposed or advanced various impeachments and even served as a House manager in a Senate impeachment trial. He accepted impeachment as a necessary aspect of governance and as the heavy artillery of political combat. By contrast, Inouye found the use of impeachment highly distasteful and worried that it undermined respect for American government, in particular the presidency but also the judiciary. Conyers and Inouye, both thoughtful men with long and varied legislative experience, together represented the wide spectrum of views regarding impeachment that emerged in the late twentieth century.

The two legislators put forward important questions about the merits of the Constitution's impeachment device that have arisen since the 1960s and deserve careful consideration. At least by implication, they pose the question of why impeachment has been proposed as often as it has during their years of congressional service. They epitomize the debate over whether impeachment is a workable system for maintaining constitutional discipline. They also broach the alternative issue of whether reliance upon such a complicated mechanism emboldens officials inclined to disregard the Constitution's fundamental restraints. Finally, they raise the question of whether repeated calls for employment of the removal device, sometimes to no effect, enhance or undermine the public's regard for its constitutional system.

By 1960 impeachment had come to be widely viewed as an unworkable constitutional anachronism, a "rusted blunderbuss" as one scholar had recently called it. Thereafter, however, desires by disparate groups to cut short the tenure of particular federal officials resurrected interest in impeachment. What began with the crusade of a fringe political group came, within less than a decade and a half, to be embraced by mainstream America as a satisfactory solution to the problem of principal government officials deemed no longer acceptable. Thereafter, the politically engaged community and even the wider public would remain conscious of impeachment and prepared to resort to it, even though deeply divided as to when it was appropriate.

Although the John Birch Society reintroduced impeachment into the active political vocabulary of the United States, its strident calls for the removal of Earl Warren did little to dispel perceptions of impeachment's ineffectiveness. But thereafter, the departure of Abe Fortas, Spiro Agnew, and Richard Nixon on the cusp of impeachment generated a new respect for the process as a means to expel sullied and no-longer-welcome constitutional officers from the highest ranks of the federal government. The fall of Fortas began with a simple partisan campaign to stall and thus defeat a recently confirmed justice's promotion to the chief justiceship. That political initiative exposed private conduct that some thought contrary to "good behavior," even if it was not shown to be illegal. The new Nixon administration used hints of impeachment to advantage in pressing for Fortas's resignation. The success of this political maneuver to alter the makeup of the Supreme Court encouraged the White House to think that impeachment could be so employed again. Ironically, however, Fortas provided a model not for the demise of his Court colleague William O. Douglas but, rather, for that of a vice president and then a president who had fallen under much darker clouds.

Often overlooked in the story of these departures from high office was the fact that voluntary resignation preempted the completion of the constitutional process designed by the Constitution's framers. When a target refused to resign and instead resisted, as did Justice Douglas, impeachment failed to go forward. The Nixon administration had thought Douglas might be driven to resign by the mere threat of impeachment, as had been the case with Fortas. The result, however, upheld the framers' intention that constitutional officials be allowed to complete their allotted term of office unless there was a high degree of consensus among the people's representatives that great offenses in the conduct of official duties, ones that clearly violated the strictures of the Constitution, had been committed. The Douglas case demonstrated the system's protections for officials against being precipitously and inappropriately expelled from office.

A series of judicial impeachments in the 1980s and early 1990s, resulting in three removals, one resignation, and one premature retirement, collectively reinforced the growing congressional and to a lesser degree public sense of impeachment's efficacy. For the first time in the era, the Senate carried the process through to a final judgment. This happened not once but three times, not only giving the upper house its first experience with impeachment in a half century but also providing repeated demonstrations that impeachment could deal with officials unwilling to resign. In the midst of these proceedings, however, a possible presidential impeachment failed to materialize when the executive stood his ground.

In the course of these episodes, the Congress learned a great deal about how to conduct impeachments. When confronted by the Fortas and Douglas cases, Congress contained only a handful of members who had served during the impeachment and trial of Halsted Ritter in 1936. By the 1990s, however, the House had carried out a variety of inquiries and voted for several impeachments, the Senate had conducted a trio of impeachment trials and prepared for others, and Congress as a whole was no longer unfamiliar with the process. Every member of Congress had at least observed impeachment proceedings, and a great many had taken part in them. The media and the public as well had grown accustomed to the terminology, the procedures, the issues, and the implications of impeachment.

Familiarity with impeachment affected the way members of Congress, journalists, and the general American public thought about its employment. Having been through multiple considerations of what constituted grounds for removal from office prior to the expiration of an official's constitutionally mandated term, some politicians and citizens embraced the notion that impeachment ought to be used, or at least threatened, more often. Presidential impeachment in particular seemed to provide a means to keep government in check. Some disagreed, but overall, impeachment became a more commonly used term in the American political lexicon and a more frequently employed instrument in the American constitutional toolbox.

Near the end of the century, various threads of the growing culture of impeachment merged. The political impulse to search for means to drive an opponent from office, first seen in the Warren, Fortas, and Douglas cases, surfaced again in the effort to impeach Bill Clinton. The constitutional debate over what constituted "high crimes and misdemeanors," thus proper grounds for removal, reemerged as well. A by-now-experienced House of Representatives overcame its most contentious and close division ever on such an issue to adopt a presidential impeachment resolution. Finally, a Senate conducting its fourth impeachment trial in a dozen years chose for the first of these times not to follow the lead of the House. By failing to produce a majority for the removal of a chief executive, the upper chamber reminded the country that impeachment itself was only one stage of the constitutional removal process and that the Senate's decision was vitally important and not necessarily an automatic confirmation of the House's action.

In the immediate aftermath of the Clinton experience, the culture of impeachment appeared to have suffered a major setback. Widespread disapproval of Clinton's personal behavior was exceeded by an even greater sense that his impeachment had been inappropriate. This verdict was evident not only in Senate voting but also in such varied measures as the 1998 congressional election returns, the continued high approval ratings for the president in public opinion polls, the congressional refusal to reauthorize the office of independent counsel, and even the less objective evidence of editorial cartoons. Soon, however, mutterings about Clinton's successor suggested that willingness to employ the constitutional removal device had not evaporated entirely.

Despite, or perhaps even because of, the outcome of the Clinton case, a sense remained that impeachment was an important constitutional tool. In part this may have been due to the view of a sizable majority of the public that Clinton, and before him Reagan, had not deserved to be driven from office when threatened with impeachment and thus that the process had worked fairly. Regard for the removal instrument was sustained by constant reminders in American language and culture that in the case of Watergate impeachment had operated as designed to eliminate an ominous threat to good government. Though not remembered as widely or as clearly as the Nixon case, the outcomes of other impeachment episodes reinforced the impression that overall the device provided a measured deliberative process that generally reached an appropriate result. After 1960, eight of the twelve instances in which Congress genuinely contemplated impeachment ended in either resignation or removal. Of the twelve federal officeholders seriously proposed for impeachment between 1960 and the turn of the millennium, only four, Warren, Douglas, Reagan, and Clinton, escaped its worst consequences.

In the late twentieth century impeachment functioned as both cause and consequence of increasingly contentious partisan conflict. Two insightful political scientists identified this as the pursuit of "politics by other means" at a time when neither electoral contests nor partisan compromises, the traditional means of setting a direction for government, functioned to resolve disputes and establish a national course. Benjamin Ginsberg and Martin Shefter observed that in an era of divided government beginning in 1968 and continuing—except for six years—until the end of the century, a time when one party controlled at least one house of Congress while the other held the White House, the tools of media revelation, institutional investigation, and judicial prosecution had supplemented and to a considerable extent supplanted the traditional competition and compromise of American politics. Ginsberg and Shefter saw the dominance of politics by other means as encompassing various attacks on congressional leaders and cabinet officers as well as chief executives. Thus, it involved more than impeachment. However, they contended, it began with Watergate, became institutionalized with post-Nixon ethics and investigatory reforms, and was fully manifested in the two-term-long challenge to Clinton.[3]

Ginsberg and Shefter, for all their insights, failed to acknowledge that the roots of the political culture they described had been planted more than a decade before Watergate. The political use of the constitutional removal device originated in the early 1960s in the crusade of a frustrated, extremely conservative minority against a leading symbol of liberal domestic reform, Chief Justice Earl Warren. The crude John Birch Society effort achieved little direct effect other than to build the organization's membership. Nevertheless, the "Impeach Earl Warren" campaign brought life to the notion that driving high officials from office before the end of their constitutional terms was a principled political undertaking. Though not directly linked to the John Birch Society effort, the more sophisticated Republican campaign to thwart and then unseat Justice Abe Fortas through congressional maneuver, persistent investigation, and ultimately the threat of impeachment earned validation when Fortas resigned. Even though the subsequent effort to impeach Justice William O. Douglas did not achieve the same success, it provided ample evidence that the Nixon administration and the Republican congressional minority had recognized early on the potential of politics by other means.

During the quarter century after 1968, when the Democrats for the most part controlled Congress but not the presidency, they displayed comparative reluctance to employ impeachment. Having dominated American national government since the 1930s, the Democrats thought of themselves as responsible for ensuring its continued functioning. They repeatedly demonstrated a reluctance to take steps they perceived as weakening federal institutions, even those temporarily controlled by officials with whom they were at odds. Consequently, House Democrats declined to consider impeachment proceedings against Vice President Spiro Agnew, even when invited to do so by Agnew himself. Democrats were notably slow to press for the impeachment of President Richard Nixon, barely suggesting it until the Saturday Night Massacre, sixteen months after the arrest of the Watergate burglars, heightened alarms throughout the country about an out-of-control presidency. Even after Nixon's shocking attack on Special Prosecutor Archibald Cox, congressional Democrats proceeded with great caution in the face of ongoing White House defiance. Only the revelation of expurgated but still damning transcripts of Nixon's conversations propelled House Judiciary Committee Democrats, along with a vital cadre of their Republican counterparts, into voting for impeachment, days before the release of the "smoking gun" tape brought a general consensus that Nixon must be removed.

Democrats displayed no partisan hesitation in dealing with judicial cases during the 1980s, but they reverted to form and once again proved unwilling to press for presidential impeachment in the Iran-Contra affair. In the face of revelations of multiple violations of the law, the Democratic stance was rooted in concern for damaging the presidency and undermining confidence in the government. Recognition of Ronald Reagan's continuing popularity and thus of the difficulty of persuading the public that he had committed "high crimes and misdemeanors" reinforced the perception that taking action would be costly. As a result, Congress managed to convey an image of tolerance for unrestrained presidential conduct of foreign affairs. Under the circumstances, the nonuse of impeachment proved to have substantial consequences in terms of the further growth of an imperial presidency.

The sharp contrast between the rival parties' attitudes toward impeachment became more apparent during the presidency of Bill Clinton. Shocked by their losses in the election of 1992, Republicans quickly turned to Watergate-inspired legal devices to deal with the unwelcome new occupant of the White House. They called for the creation of an independent counsel for an unprecedented investigation of an incumbent's prepresidential career. Unsuspecting Democrats did not oppose the request. Traditional notions of limiting concern to an official's conduct in his or her current governmental position were set aside in this manifestation of politics by other means.[4]

After the Republican Party gained control of Congress in 1994, scrutiny of the president intensified. When Independent Counsel Kenneth Starr brought a highly inflammatory report of improper conduct before the House in 1998, the Republican majority responded quickly and forcefully. Although the presidential behavior in question was arguably private rather than official, Republican enthusiasm for employing impeachment was beyond question. One presidential scholar concluded, "Either the Republicans in 1998 and 1999 were serious and lacked sufficient acumen to achieve their goals, or they were playing games with the Constitution for temporary political advantage. Either way, they discredited impeachment as a part of the constitutional system of checks and balances."[5]

The Democratic congressional leadership continued to hold to its traditional position even after the Clinton experience. Not even the demands from some partisans for the impeachment of George W. Bush and Richard Cheney altered its basic stand. A few calls for action by its most aggressive members failed to loosen the restraint of the Democrats' congressional leaders. Democratic Speaker-elect Nancy Pelosi was simply reiterating her party's long-standing position in November 2006 when she made clear that the impeachment of President George W. Bush was "off the table." Partisan distinctions between Democrats and Republicans in the contentious decades bracketing the turn of the millennium were starkly drawn in terms of their contrasting approaches to impeachment.

The United States Constitution's impeachment mechanism, indeed the nation's entire constitutional system, was constructed in a very different environment from that in which the officeholder removal device came to be frequently employed. The pace of public life when communication was governed by the range of the human voice, the capacity of the printing press, and the speed of horses was markedly slower than when it relied on high-speed travel, mass media, and instantaneous communication via the telephone and the Internet. The accelerated velocity of politics in the modern age has led, among other things, to vexation on the part of politicians and the public alike with situations not lending themselves to rapid resolution.

The slow and deliberate nature of most political change in an environment governed by the rules of an eighteenth-century Constitution is understandable. In an electronic age that pace can also sometimes prove exasperating. The framers placed their faith in representative government because they preferred to insulate policy making, its execution, and the administration of justice from the passions of the moment. They believed that they had good reasons for establishing four-year renewable terms for presidents and lifetime tenure for judges. That thinking was also reflected in the choice of renewable terms of two years for representatives and six for senators, as opposed to the shorter tenure commonplace in state legislatures of the time. The framers' ultimate commitment to democracy was tempered by their interest in executive, judicial, and even legislative insulation from the demands of constant popular approval as well as the countervailing powers granted to each branch to slow action by the others. The men who gathered in Philadelphia in 1787 could not have anticipated the unfolding of public affairs at the rate and under the incessant public scrutiny that would become feasible and common two hundred years later. Nor would they have expected the widespread longevity and good health of future generations, which would frequently allow the lifetime appointments of already mature individuals to stretch into three or four decades. Consequently, political impatience in an environment in which discontent could be magnified by rapid and universal communication was not among the framers' concerns in creating the Constitution.

In the middle of the twentieth century, the political frustration of conservatives with the seemingly endless presidency of Franklin Roosevelt led to a successful effort to amend the Constitution in order to limit future presidents to two terms. The alliance of Republicans and southern Democrats in Congress and state legislatures who brought about the Twenty-second Amendment failed to foresee that the change they wrought would reduce the effective power of all second-term presidents simply because of their inability to run for reelection. Ironically, four of the next five such chief executives shared the conservative persuasion of the amendment's creators. Those who crafted the Twenty-second Amendment also failed to anticipate that their reform would fuel impatience with lame ducks' stays in office. On the basis of their experience with Roosevelt, they had no reason to expect that every second-term president in the half century after 1960, that is, Nixon, Reagan, Clinton, and George W. Bush, would confront significant calls for their removal before their term was scheduled to end.[6]

Irritation with Supreme Court justices whose decisions were unwelcome and who might nevertheless remain on the bench for many years led likewise to interest in their earlier removal. The extraordinary 1937 Court-packing battle had demonstrated that, even with one party firmly in control of both the executive and legislative branches of the federal government, the constitutional amendment needed for overall reform of the Court could appear out of reach.[7] Consequently, the use of impeachment to rein in the high court began to acquire more appeal than at any time since the failed impeachment of Justice Samuel Chase in 1805.

Offsetting the impatience-driven rising interest in impeachment were the strict requirements of the Constitution. By its provisions, mere policy differences, no matter how severe or fundamental, were insufficient to abrogate prescribed terms of office or overturn the normal selection processes of a democratic republic. Impeachment and removal could only be carried out if a majority of the House of Representatives, in the first instance, and two-thirds of the Senate, in the second, were persuaded that the commission of treason, bribery, or other "high crimes or misdemeanors" had been demonstrated. These lofty thresholds did not dissuade an exceptional number of impeachments from being proposed during and after the 1960s, but they did limit the success of such efforts aimed at officials determined to resist being ousted.

The framers had demonstrated their original intent to distance the impeachment process from politics by defining it narrowly and in various ways distinguishing it from lesser disciplinary actions such as legislative directives, veto overrides, or resolutions of censure. Impeachable acts were limited to matters of serious illegal conduct in carrying out official government duties. The obvious aim was to curb individuals from improper use of constitutional power while at the same time assuring the continued functioning of government free from nuisance distractions by partisan opponents. Unlike ordinary personal offenses punishable by fine, imprisonment, deportation, or execution, the penalty for impeachment was restricted to the loss of office. The assignment of the chief justice of the United States to preside at a presidential trial before the Senate symbolized the intention that due deliberation of an evidentiary presentation be conducted. Substantive proof rather than political emotion was to determine an allegedly tainted official's fate.

The creators of the Constitution left vague the nature of constitutional officials' responsibility for the misdeeds of their subordinates. Constitutional officeholders were required to swear an oath that they would "to the best of [their] ability preserve, protect and defend the Constitution of the United States," but whether less-than-perfect compliance by secondary officials renders their ultimate superiors impeachable was not made altogether clear. Such an obligation scarcely presented problems for judges and justices, who bore immediate and easily traceable responsibility for their official deeds, but it did pose questions regarding the executive branch, especially as the size and complexity of the bureaucracy expanded. Was a president responsible for misdeeds carried out in his name but without his direct knowledge by countless unseen underlings in cabinet departments, administrative agencies, or even the White House staff? If so, to what extent? If not, to what consequence?

The question of what legitimately constituted an impeachable offense arose in the judicial cases of the 1960s. From that time forward, the issue has never been resolved to universal satisfaction. Since the John Birch Society's complaint against Earl Warren involved the specific nature of his rulings, it won scant support as a claim of treason, bribery, or other high crimes and misdemeanors. The subsequent Fortas and Douglas cases involved charges of improper extrajudicial conduct. Fortas's resignation and the House Judiciary Committee's decision not to proceed with an impeachment of Douglas left ultimately unsettled the core issue of whether their behavior had involved bribery or other high crimes and misdemeanors.

Neither the Agnew nor the Nixon cases resolved the question of how wide was the extent of an executive's constitutional responsibility. Agnew's offense involved no federal official other than himself. Nixon's was decidedly otherwise, but his direct involvement was unquestionably proven, demonstrated by the "smoking gun" tape's confirmation that his behavior from June 20, 1972, onward constituted personal obstruction of justice and abuse of power. His resignation cut off discussion as to whether his impeachment should rest solely on his own conduct or also upon his failure to maintain adherence to the Constitution on the part of his subordinates.

The importance of the issue of direct personal involvement came to the forefront in the Iran-Contra case. The essence of the Reagan defense against impeachment became that he was unaware of what his close subordinates were doing in his name. They in turn would eventually testify that they had not informed him of their action but had believed they were fulfilling his wishes. The decision of Congress not to pursue the case beyond the hearings in the summer of 1987 left hanging the constitutional question of whether a president could properly be impeached for misdeeds carried out by others acting in his name. In political terms, however, the lesson of the Iran-Contra episode appeared to be that, when it came to presidential impeachment, plausible evidence of disengagement trumped the burdens of the constitutional oath of office.

A rare degree of clarity in the determination of impeachable offenses appeared in the cases of judges convicted of federal crimes. Both Harry Claiborne and Walter Nixon chose to test whether conviction for bribery and tax evasion would meet the constitutional threshold. They were no doubt unhappy to learn that in the eyes of Congress it most certainly did. Contemporaneously, however, Alcee Hastings discovered that equating the outcome of a criminal prosecution with justification of impeachment was not always the standard applied. His criminal acquittal was overridden as Congress concluded that he still should be removed from office for violation of the "good behavior" judicial standard. The definition of an impeachable offense remained a political judgment. What the three judicial cases did make clearly evident at long last was that Congress had the capacity to carry through an impeachment proceeding to its prescribed conclusion.

The Clinton impeachment brought the issue of what constituted impeachable high crimes and misdemeanors once again to the fore. Advocates of his removal from office asserted that his alleged perjury in a civil suit concerned with prepresidential behavior and grand jury testimony compelled thereafter by a special prosecutor transgressed his presidential obligation. Opponents of that view held that even if the perjury allegations were true, the offense in question did not involve Clinton's official executive duties. A reasonable reading of the congressional assessment of the issue would be that the former view was embraced by a small majority of the House, while the latter position prevailed in the Senate. Although politics appeared to drive both conclusions, the result was a continuing lack of clarity and consensus as to appropriate grounds for impeachment and removal. In practical terms, however, the Clinton episode indicates that only narrowly based and substantial claims of high crimes and misdemeanors stand a good chance of achieving their ultimate objective.

The continuing absence of universal agreement throughout the American political culture as to what exactly constituted a sufficient basis for impeachment grew evident in public discourse after the turn of the millennium. The Schiavo episode made clear that unhappiness with policy outcomes still led some practitioners of politics by other means, latter-day counterparts of the John Birch Society, to advocate impeachment of officials for merely carrying out their constitutional responsibilities. The overwhelmingly negative reception of that particular proposal suggests that respect for the standard of "treason, bribery, or other high crimes and misdemeanors," strictly applied, remained intact, even if the exact definition of what constituted such acts was not always agreed upon.

In retrospect, Congress has found the easiest impeachment cases to deal with, other than the ones resolved by resignation, to be those in which the evidence of misconduct appeared to be indisputable and decidedly personal. Nixon's "smoking gun" tape persuaded all but a handful of the members of Congress that the president deserved impeachment and removal, though his resignation cost all but the members of the House Judiciary Committee their opportunity actually to cast such a vote. The verdicts in the criminal trials of Harry Claiborne, Walter Nixon, and Alcee Hastings's colleague William Borders served a similar function for the representatives and senators asked to decide the judges' fates. When, on the other hand, there was no compelling piece of condemnatory evidence at which to point, Congress preferred to embrace alternative, more benign explanations that would spare the need for a constitutional officer's removal. In essence, while more cases of bad behavior came to light in an expanded judiciary and there were more instances in which use of the impeachment tool was suggested by practitioners of politics by other means, congressional enthusiasm for casting out high-ranking officials, except in the Republican caucus of the 105th Congress, did not increase noticeably in the age of impeachment.

Among the consequences of much talk but relatively little achievement of impeachment since 1960 has been a reasonably strong, if not absolute, sense on the part of American chief executives that the odds were fairly good that they would not be prematurely cast out against their will, other than by the verdict of a national election. Presidents and vice presidents have necessarily become conscious that Congress has grown familiar with the mechanism for their removal, as well as what conduct opens the door to its use. Executive officers have been alerted that they must be careful to anticipate and avoid enabling efforts along such lines. The first president of the twenty-first century, as a result, became extraordinarily tightfisted with the records of his administration's activities. Most important and disquieting, however, presidents have seen that they can with confidence assume they will not be driven from office as a result of asserting authority exceeding previously assumed constitutional bounds of restraint.

Judicial officers have not gotten an equivalent sense of being unbound as a result of the age of impeachment. First, the number of judges losing their seats on the bench has been larger, though still tiny in an era of an expanded judiciary. Second, at least after the 1970s, the process has rested on a set of procedures designed to call questionable activities to the attention of knowledgeable peers and provide for their thorough examination. Finally, partisan motives, if not entirely absent, have appeared to be less of a factor in the initiation and decision of judicial impeachment. In all, the disciplinary effect of the possibility of impeachment has not diminished in the case of the judiciary.

For the executive branch, however, a contrary outcome may have resulted. Richard Nixon's downfall might not appear to have encouraged the expansion of presidential authority. Not only Nixon's premature departure from office but also the shadow that continued to hang over his reputation long thereafter would seem to argue to the contrary. Likewise, the adoption of the War Powers Act in 1973, the Federal Election Campaign Act Amendments, the Freedom of Information Act, and the Presidential Recordings and Materials Preservation Act in 1974, and the Independent Counsel Act in 1978 would appear to have further confined chief executives.

Yet it is important to note that as the Watergate scandal evolved, the focus of condemnation narrowed from Nixon's full range of constitutionally suspect behavior to the far more limited matter of clearly unconstitutional substantive official conduct that could be attributed to him personally. The articles of impeachment approved by the House Judiciary Committee addressed his direct abuse of power and obstruction of justice in covering up criminal acts as well as his noncompliance with subpoenas. However, Nixon's other arguably impeachable conduct escaped congressional condemnation.

Despite John Conyers's insistence that the issue be brought to a vote in 1974, twenty-six of thirty-eight House Judiciary Committee members were not willing to impeach Nixon for his unauthorized bombing of the neutral nation of Cambodia or his subsequent ground invasion of that benighted country. Articles of impeachment based on Nixon's refusal to carry out congressional directives by impounding appropriated funds, his responsibility for the illegal break-in at the office of Daniel Ellsberg's psychiatrist, and the president's income tax evasion also fell by the way, not even brought to a vote by the Judiciary Committee. Congress was not willing to use its ultimate power of sanction against unauthorized presidential military initiatives or illegal domestic surveillance, both issues that would arise again in later decades, when national security concerns were asserted.

Rather than feeling restrained in its conduct of foreign affairs by what had happened to Nixon, the Reagan administration proceeded to take actions in Central America and the Middle East that had been specifically prohibited by Congress. The Iran-Contra affair amounted to an executive branch assertion of power to conduct foreign relations in a manner that ignored congressional directives. When Congress declined to impeach the responsible chief executive, it left a further impression of its reluctance to challenge presidential initiatives abroad, even on constitutional grounds.

The full measure of this Nixon-Reagan legacy can be found in the conduct of the George W. Bush administration. Not coincidentally, Bush's closest adviser, Vice President Richard Cheney, had worked in the Nixon White House. Cheney had also served on the staff of the president who pardoned Nixon, as well as in the Republican congressional leadership during the consideration of the Iran-Contra affair, and, finally, as secretary of defense under the first President Bush, who had remained under the Iran-Contra shadow throughout his term. The second Bush administration contained other impeachment veterans as well, among them Secretary of Defense Donald Rumsfeld, a Nixon veteran; David Addington, Cheney's aide in the congressional Iran-Contra investigation; and Elliott Abrams, a key National Security Council adviser on Iraq and formerly a convicted Iran-Contra participant pardoned by the first President Bush at the end of his term. Aided in its first six years by an extraordinarily deferential Republican majority in Congress, the second Bush administration pursued an extremely aggressive foreign policy that involved a preemptive attack on Iraq of much greater scale than Nixon's on Cambodia, concealment of information of greater significance than Reagan's pertaining to Iran or the Contras, and much more extensive domestic surveillance under the claim of national security than at any time since the heyday of J. Edgar Hoover and the post–World War II anticommunist frenzy.

What had not been punished in the past appeared to be regarded as therefore permissible by an administration with members experienced in and sensitive to a series of previous presidential impeachment considerations. The latitude in the area of foreign affairs previously conceded by Congress to presidents was treated as a blank check by a White House that claimed everything it did was justified by

Herblock,
Washington Post,
April 13, 1974.
© The Herb Block
Foundation.

the needs of national security, the president's authority as commander in chief, and the confidentiality provisions of executive privilege. These rationalizations were extended to an extraordinary degree so as to include withholding from Congress information on staff conversations not even involving the president or related to national security issues. Also defended as necessary and proper were warrantless wiretapping, incarceration of citizens and noncitizens alike without habeas corpus or legal proceedings, and acts of torture short of what would "ordinarily be associated with a sufficiently serious physical condition or injury such as death, organ failure, or serious impediment of body functions."[8] If the consequence of the age of impeachment was to generate a presidential belief that whatever had not been specifically punished was therefore acceptable, then its impact had indeed been profound.

In addition to setting precedents for expanded presidential authority, the age of impeachment served to identify ways a chief executive, though not a federal judge, could frustrate even the best-justified impeachment effort. These means to stymie impeachment actions carried no absolute guarantee of success. Yet a highly centralized branch of government held advantages when dealing with a branch with widely dispersed power. Congress required substantial consensus in order to proceed and often found that difficult to achieve, given partisan divisions, ideological differences, and individual distinctions. Absent overwhelming evidence of a clear-cut misdeed, Congress not surprisingly discovered impeachment to be an uphill political struggle.

From the era of Watergate onward, presidents and their White House staffs found increasingly sophisticated ways to keep information about their activities out of view. Nixon's claim of executive privilege, though ruled by the Supreme Court not to be absolute, became an important shield. Other less formal approaches also emerged. After the relatively transparent governments of Gerald Ford and Jimmy Carter, the Reagan administration effectively disguised Nixon's blunt stonewalling while achieving the same effect. The Reagan White House graciously offered to cooperate with Iran-Contra investigations, but only did so after staff members were given enough advanced warning to allow them to destroy incriminating documents. Combined with presidential claims of lack of memory, which had a certain plausibility by the time they were made, the result was an obscured view of what was being done in and for the White House. Like many other Reagan-era practices, a nonbelligerent but nonetheless close hold on information continued during the administration of the first President Bush.

Whenever the Clinton administration was not forthcoming with records of its actions, it faced heavy criticism. Its relative openness, especially when facing clearly partisan inquiries, did not earn it any credit as probes into its inner dealings progressed. An unquenchable partisanship propelled the scrutiny of Clinton. Even Clinton's reduction of the time government documents could remain classified failed to assuage practitioners of politics by other means. Clinton's impeachment served as a reminder to his successors of the risks associated with the exposure of even seemingly innocuous information about the functioning of the White House.

The second Bush administration strove from the outset to exercise tight control over information about its inner workings. On the one hand, it aggressively pushed its own claims, asserting that they were founded on reliable evidence. On the other, it resisted revealing that evidence, as well as other documentary records of its affairs and even the prior activities of its members. Executive privilege was claimed more frequently and more vigorously than at any time since the Nixon presidency. By 2007, in fact, the White House legal counsel, Fred F. Fielding, was making the argument to Congress that past and present White House aides enjoyed the protection of executive privilege.[9] His prior service as associate legal counsel to the president under John Dean in the Nixon administration and as Reagan's legal counsel from 1981 to 1986 made him something of an authority on executive privilege. In vigorously defending Bush's claims, however, Fielding reached beyond what Congress and the Supreme Court had accepted during Watergate. Haldeman, Ehrlichman, and Dean had all famously waived executive privilege to testify during the Ervin committee hearings, and in *United States v. Nixon* the Court had determined that executive privilege could not be employed to thwart a criminal investigation. A noted historian of Watergate drew on that episode to suggest that Fielding's defense of Bush's executive privilege lacked constitutional merit. Rather, he suggested, it hinted at political desperation.[10]

The Bush White House's tight hold on information extended well beyond the long-practiced classification of national security and diplomatic material. Vice President Cheney, informed by his experience with the Watergate and Iran-Contra investigations, set from the start the Bush White House's stance of unwillingness to grant access to records. He refused requests and challenged congressional subpoenas for even as modestly revealing information as the names of individuals attending meetings to advise him on energy policy. If as a result Cheney gained an image of deviousness, he nevertheless was able to protect the administration he served.

The tactic of resisting requests and even subpoenas for information became common in Bush's administration. It certainly heeded the complaint of Iran-Contra independent counsel Lawrence Walsh that possible impeachment had been frustrated by the delay in releasing information until after Reagan and the first Bush were out of office. Those who worked in those administrations and returned to serve the younger Bush had learned to be exceptionally closemouthed. This did not protect lower-level officials when outside evidence surfaced of poor performance in dealing with Hurricane Katrina, questionable conduct in dismissing federal prosecutors on partisan grounds, or outright corruption in dealings with lobbyists. It did, however, protect the president from danger. President Bush and his inner circle had learned an important lesson: Impeachment delayed is impeachment denied.

Another insight available from past impeachments might be called the Agnew-Ford factor. This was the capacity of an incumbent vice president to discourage or encourage congressional action. If the vice president was generally regarded as offering an unpalatable alternative to the president, reluctance to consider removing the chief executive was notable. The prospect of someone succeeding to the highest executive office who had displayed deeply unattractive qualities provoked echoes of the old adage "Better the devil you know than the devil you don't." On the other hand, if the potential successor to an embattled president was comparatively appealing, the incumbent had less reason to feel secure.

Vice President Spiro Agnew's conduct in office, his lack of experience and engagement in national policy making, his divisive partisan rhetoric, his harsh and unexpected racial and ethnic pronouncements, and even his easily paro-died speaking style, all well known before his corrupt dealings with Maryland contractors came to light, made him widely unappealing as a replacement for Richard Nixon. He had come to be perceived as a political hatchet man, "Nixon's Nixon," and as lacking in reliable judgment because of his occasional criticism of the foreign policy that remained Nixon's strength. When Agnew suddenly departed and his place was taken by Ford, a man well known in Congress as moderate, gracious, and respectful of those, with the exception of William O. Douglas, with whom he differed, doubts about the negative consequences of re-moving Nixon soon began to evaporate.

The reverse of the Agnew-Ford factor appeared twenty-five years later when Vice President Al Gore presented the image of a decidedly nonthreatening, if not universally embraced, potential successor to President Bill Clinton. No abrupt change in government style or direction seemed likely to result from his ele-vation. Gore appeared closely aligned with Clinton on matters of foreign and domestic policy. He had been intimately involved in the inner workings of the White House. At the same time, he seemed an appealing contrast to Clinton in matters of personal morality. As a consequence, Gore offered Clinton no protec-tion from efforts to remove him from office.

One possibility apparently escaped the notice of the partisan pursuers of Clinton. Under the terms of the Twenty-second Amendment, by the time Clinton would have been removed from office, Gore's term as his presidential replace-ment would have been short enough to allow him to run twice for full terms in the White House as the incumbent. With such an advantage, Gore would have probably won the 2000 election easily, spent more than two full terms as presi-dent, and entirely eliminated the presidency of George W. Bush. The overlooked political lesson was to be careful of what one seeks—there may be a high price for success.

Richard Cheney was as much a participant in the Bush administration as Gore had been in its predecessor, but his image appeared closer to Agnew's. Far more experienced in national affairs than Bush and with a long-burnished im-age as a conservative stalwart, Cheney was widely perceived as a strong, even dominant, influence on his nominal superior. Cheney was perceived as a power-ful advocate for the administration's most criticized actions in tax reduction for the most wealthy, increased domestic surveillance, and, above all, the invasion of Iraq. Cheney's penchant for avoiding the public spotlight, together with the revelation that his chief of staff had leaked information intended to discredit Iraq policy critics, heightened his image as devious or worse.[11]

Cries of "Impeach Cheney First" as well as placards and buttons convey-ing the same sentiment demonstrated that at least some among the grassroots groups seeking Bush's overthrow understood the Agnew-Ford factor. They also realized that impeachment had always been directed at individuals and had never been a device for the wholesale overthrow of an administration. Whether from this awareness or from simple reaction to Cheney himself, the vice president's approval ratings fell faster and further than did Bush's. By July 2007 one national public opinion poll found that while 45 percent of the population favored impeaching Bush, 54 percent felt that way about Cheney.[12] Such polls signified that as long as Cheney remained in office, Bush enjoyed protection from impeachment.

Finally, the Nixon, Reagan, and Bush episodes all demonstrated that impeachment became more difficult when its targets could argue that Congress bore partial responsibility for the condemned behavior. Nixon's defenders successfully contended that Congress bore some responsibility for the Vietnam War on the basis of its Gulf of Tonkin Resolution, authorization of a military draft, and continued funding of the war. Thus, nearly three-fourths of the House Judiciary Committee felt they could not hold Nixon solely at fault for the Cambodian bombing and incursion. Likewise, Reagan's defenders in the Iran-Contra debate maintained that Congress's frequently changing authorizations of spending in support of the Nicaraguan Contras had sent mixed messages. They reached such a conclusion despite the fact that at the time funds were being secretly provided from Swiss bank accounts, a Boland Amendment prohibition on U.S. military assistance to the Contras was in effect. Clinton could offer no such argument, but from the outset of its troubles the second Bush administration insisted that Congress's adoption of the USA Patriot Act and the 2002 Iraq resolution authorized its actions.

Congress repeatedly hesitated to condemn an executive for acts that could be regarded as having been legislatively authorized. Such conduct would be difficult to assert as amounting to "treason, bribery, or other high crimes and misdemeanors" without indicting Congress itself. The most subtle of defenses against impeachment, the shared-responsibility argument, was also perhaps the most effective. In any case, together with other avoidance tactics, it provided presidents with a range of weapons to fend off impeachment even when the grassroots political culture expressed enthusiasm for it.

As impeachment became a familiar feature of U.S. political culture in the decades after 1960 and lessons were absorbed from the experience, multiple unintended consequences of the framers' creation emerged. The men who met in Philadelphia in the summer of 1787 had various expectations of the mechanism that they had modified from its British prototype. They assumed it would discipline federal officeholders, discourage them from exceeding the powers granted by the Constitution, and assure the populace that confidence in their government was normally warranted.

The faith of the founders might have been sorely tested had they been around to witness the age of impeachment. The slow pace of Congress in gathering information, coming to terms with its implications, and then resolving a case might well have troubled them. Certainly the architects of the U.S. system of checks and balances would have been disturbed to observe the ability of presidents to forestall congressional investigations and even use impeachment case precedents to expand claims of executive authority. They would not have been happy to see how a mechanism they had intended for a very specific and limited purpose had come to be thought of at the grassroots as an all-purpose solution to democratic discontents. The framers' greatest distress, however, would probably have arisen from witnessing how impeachment paralyzed the functioning of government for extended periods and, instead of reassuring the public about the integrity of its government, actually generated additional distrust and distaste among the sovereign people.

Whenever the issue of a presidential impeachment arose in the decades after the 1960s, the lower-level bureaucracies of the executive branch could continue to carry out their routine duties, but new initiatives from the White House proved difficult to launch or sustain. Judicial impeachment cases had not had the same paralyzing effect because only one federal justice or judge at a time was distracted from the normal routine of the bench. If necessary, the brethren of the accused could assume his obligations as they normally did following a temporary disability, a retirement, or a death. The situation of the president was quite different, however, an uncalculated price for concentrating authority in a single executive. Major policy decisions, overall budgetary and legislative planning, and foreign initiatives required his personal engagement to some degree. A president distracted by an impeachment threat found it difficult to concentrate on such matters, vital as they might be to a well-functioning government, when the chief executive's reputation, and indeed political survival, was at stake.

The amount of time Nixon spent dealing with the Watergate matter and the threat of impeachment is hard to measure precisely. It appeared to be limited in the first few months, but substantial by the spring of 1973 and all consuming over the last year of his presidency. Very little in the way of new policy initiatives, either foreign or domestic, emerged from the Nixon White House once the trial of the Watergate burglars began. The distraction to Nixon of dealing with the impeachment threat was enormous and prolonged. The cost to the nation of having a diverted chief executive for the better part of two years was incalculable.

The Reagan interruption was relatively less costly, if still expensive in terms of time expended. It could, after all, be measured in months rather than years. After the first intense phase, it appeared to be less consuming of administration energies, but that may well have been because Reagan's was a less centralized administration and all-controlling presidency than was Nixon's. The Clinton case, on the other hand, was a distraction throughout his presidency and absorbed an enormous amount of his attention in its climactic year. Tying an ambitious and imaginative president in knots for as long as they did may have represented sufficient rationalization to Clinton's partisan opponents for their immense expenditure of energy in a failed effort. Otherwise a justification is difficult to discern. The absence of a normally functioning government could be costly to the country, and it was not the only price that had to be paid.

Over the course of the age of impeachment, the confidence Americans expressed in their government declined markedly. The repeated experience of watching democratically chosen federal officials considered for impeachment was not the only reason for the slide in popular respect for government, but its importance cannot be ignored. The allegation and exposure of leaders' failings was shocking to citizens who had grown up with a combination of high regard for those who held their nation's high offices and little intimate knowledge of how they carried out their responsibilities. It scarcely mattered whether the issue was one of great consequence in terms of the corruption of the democratic electoral process or the conduct of U.S. foreign relations in a manner consistent with proclaimed national principles, or whether it was a comparatively petty financial bribe or effort to conceal sexual misconduct. The public was repeatedly forced in the age of impeachment to confront the frailties of executives and judges. At the same time, the conduct of Congress in dealing with the various cases revealed the slow-moving and partisan nature of the legislative branch. Even when the result of an impeachment case was in line with majority opinion, the impact of the episode was reduced public esteem for the institutions involved.

In light of all the negative consequences associated with the surge in impeachment, it is well to consider Daniel Inouye's desire for a better means for dealing with misbehavior in government. Voluntary resignation proved a relatively painless way of separating an official from the power of his position, but at the high cost of foregoing a full public hearing of the charges and accumulated evidence, not to mention a due process deliberation as to whether the removal of authority and loss of reputation were justified. The manner in which Abe Fortas was pressured to depart from the Supreme Court raises doubts about whether resignation best served the national interest of having clear standards of proper official conduct. The same lack of integrity that led to unconstitutional behavior in the first place was echoed in more than one officeholder's resistance to leaving until resignation provided the only alternative to full and humiliating exposure of contemptible conduct. Multiple cases demonstrate the wisdom of not relying on voluntary resignation to solve the overall problem of soiled officialdom.

A purely judicial removal procedure, as Inouye himself preferred, has its own limitations. The framers acknowledged that judges could have difficulty passing judgment on their own colleagues or on the person who had appointed them. Impaneling a jury sufficiently knowledgeable, free of bias, and undaunted by the publicity inevitably surrounding such a case would be difficult. The conduct of the Supreme Court in resolving the presidential election of 2000 created an image of judicial partisanship that, on its own, would cast a shadow over any impeachment decision rendered by a narrowly divided judiciary. These issues are overshadowed by the much more profound question of whether the complex and nuanced political decision of removing a federal judge or chief executive, however flawed, should be given to the branch of government often and accurately described as countermajoritarian.

Whatever problems exist with the current impeachment system must be weighed against the alternatives. That standard approximates Winston Churchill's assessment of democracy as the worst system of government, except for all the others. Any device for overturning the result of a democratic election or a lifetime judicial appointment made and confirmed by the people's representatives is by definition antidemocratic. Thus, the best way to keep its use in check, reserved for those occasions when it is unavoidable and absolutely necessary, is to assure that those who carry it out are themselves in a position to be held to account by the electorate they represent. One possible consequence of the age of impeachment is that a realization will emerge that, by those standards, the 1787 Constitution's impeachment device provides a reasonable, even if far from perfect, solution for an unfortunate problem: the occasional serious flaws in those chosen to lead a democratic republic.

Perhaps the age of impeachment is over, perhaps not. It is much too soon to tell whether presidents will acquire new respect for the constitutional requirements of their office, whether judges and justices will do likewise, whether partisanship will take the responsible path of resisting the inclination to pursue politics by other means, and whether calls for removal of officials, so easy and now customary to issue, will decline. Once well established, a political culture develops a certain momentum that is not easy to redirect.

In any case, the age of impeachment has had a mixed effect. The United States is undoubtedly better off for having removed Nixon, Agnew, and a couple of federal judges who were sitting in jail. On the other hand, the nation may have paid a heavy price in loss of respect for the Supreme Court and politicization of the selection of justices as a result of the campaigns to impeach Warren, Fortas, and Douglas. Certainly the Reagan and Clinton cases have sent a dangerous message to current and future presidents. Individually so different, the two cases pointed to the same conclusion: The Constitution's basic check on presidential power can be surmounted. If a chief executive retains the popularity demonstrated in the previous election with a public inattentive between the quadrennial balloting, he or she is likely to be able to break laws, bend the truth, and build an ever more powerful presidency. On the other hand, Congress can, for constitutional or merely partisan reasons, use impeachment to bring any presidency to its knees, though at the heavy cost of extended governmental paralysis.

The age of impeachment did not demonstrate a consistent ability by the U.S. Congress to restrain a president, at least one determined to extend the powers of the office and possessed of the skills to rally public support. The Constitution's creators originally intended impeachment to function as a brake on judicial misconduct and, most important, on the inevitable power-gathering tendencies of the executive office, especially in wartime. In both its successful and failed post-1960 applications, impeachment appears to have functioned more or less as the founders desired. However, the uneven record of presidential impeachment from Watergate onward has left the capacity of the constitutional removal device somewhat in doubt with regard to the executive branch. As a consequence, the founders' aspirations for impeachment to serve as an important check on executive aggrandizement have been disappointed. The weakening through overuse and misuse of a potentially effective restraint upon presidential violation of public trust would hardly please the framers of the Constitution and its impeachment device.

Notes

Preface

1. David E. Kyvig, *Repealing National Prohibition* (Chicago: University of Chicago Press, 1979); Kyvig, ed., *Law, Alcohol, and Order: Perspectives on National Prohibition* (Westport, Conn.: Greenwood, 1985).

2. David E. Kyvig, *Explicit and Authentic Acts: Amending the U.S. Constitution, 1776–1995* (Lawrence: University Press of Kansas, 1996); Kyvig, ed., *Unintended Consequences of Constitutional Amendment* (Athens: University of Georgia Press, 2000).

3. Bob Woodward, interview with author, May 19, 2005.

Introduction

1. Robert Michel, interview with author, February 1, 2005.

2. John D. O'Connor, "I'm the Guy They Called Deep Throat," *Vanity Fair,* May 31, 2005.

3. John Kass, "'Deep Throat,' Tripp Both Have Stuff of Heroes," *Chicago Tribune,* June 2, 2005.

1. Impeachment Evolves

1. Peter Charles Hoffer and N. E. H. Hull, *Impeachment in America, 1635–1805.* (New Haven, Conn.: Yale University Press, 1984).

2. U.S. Congress, House, Committee on the Judiciary, *Impeachment: Selected Materials on Procedure,* 93rd Cong., 2nd sess. (Washington, D.C.: GPO, 1974).

3. Lonnie Manes and Richard Chesteen, "The First Attempt at Presidential Impeachment: Partisan Conflict and Intra-Party Conflict at Loose," *Presidential Studies Quarterly* 10 (Winter 1980): 51–73; William H. Rehnquist, *Grand Inquests: The Historic Impeachments of Justice Samuel Chase and President Andrew Johnson* (New York: William Morrow, 1992), 258.

4. U.S. Congress, House, Committee on the Judiciary, *Impeachment: Selected Materials on Procedure,* 93rd Cong., 2nd sess. (Washington, D.C.: GPO, 1974), 881–82.

5. John W. Spanier, *The Truman-MacArthur Controversy and the Korean War* (Cambridge, Mass.: Belknap Press, 1959), 212.

6. See Merrill Jensen, *The Articles of Confederation* (Madison: University of Wisconsin Press, 1940), esp. 263–70.

7. This paragraph and those immediately following rely on Hoffer and Hull, *Impeachment in America,* chap. 1. Raoul Berger, *Impeachment: The Constitutional Problems* (Cambridge, Mass.: Harvard University Press, 1973), chap. 1, also provides useful background.

8. John B. Feerick, "Impeaching Federal Judges: A Study of the Constitutional Provisions," *Fordham Law Review* 29 (1970): 5–8.

9. Hoffer and Hull, *Impeachment in America,* 4–6.

10. Quoted in ibid, 5.

11. Ibid., 7–8.

12. Ibid., 8–21.

13. Ibid., 27–40.

14. Ibid., 41–56.

15. Ibid., 59–67.

16. Ibid., 96.

17. A good compact discussion of impeachment considerations in the 1787 Constitutional Convention can be found in Michael J. Gerhardt, *The Federal Impeachment Process: A Constitutional and Historical Analysis*, 2nd ed. (Chicago: University of Chicago Press, 2000), chap. 1.

18. Max Farrand, ed., *Records of the Federal Convention of 1787*, 3 vols. (New Haven, Conn.: Yale University Press, 1911): 1:20–22.

19. Ibid., 1:68–69.

20. Ibid., 1:85–86.

21. Ibid., 1:86–88.

22. Ibid., 1:244.

23. Hoffer and Hull, *Impeachment in America*, 98.

24. Farrand, *Records of the Federal Convention of 1787*, 1:292–93.

25. Ibid., 2:53, 64–69.

26. Ibid., 2:65.

27. Ibid., 2:65–66.

28. Ibid., 2:66.

29. Ibid., 2:69.

30. Ibid., 2:145, 154, 157, 159, 164, 172, 173.

31. Ibid., 2:185–86.

32. Ibid., 2:367.

33. Ibid., 2:427.

34. Ibid., 2:493, 497.

35. Ibid., 2:495, 498.

36. Ibid., 2:495.

37. Ibid., 2:550–51.

38. Ibid., 2:600.

39. Ibid., 2:551.

40. Ibid., 2:552–53.

41. Ibid., 2:612–13.

42. *Federalist* 65.

43. Ibid.

44. *Federalist* 66.

45. Gerhardt, *The Federal Impeachment Process*, 17–20.

46. Hoffer and Hull, *Impeachment in America*, 109–10. See also Robert A. Rutland, *The Ordeal of the Constitution: The Antifederalists and the Ratification Struggle of 1787–1788* (Norman: University of Oklahoma Press, 1965).

47. Hoffer and Hull, *Impeachment in America*, 119–45.

48. Ibid., 109–11.

49. Ibid., 146–63. See also Eleanor Bushnell, *Crimes, Follies, and Misfortunes: The Federal Impeachment Trials* (Urbana: University of Illinois Press, 1992), 25–41, and Buckner F. Melton, Jr., *The First Impeachment: The Constitution's Framers and the Case of Senator William Blount* (Macon, Ga.: Mercer University Press, 1998).

50. Hoffer and Hull, *Impeachment in America*, 207–20; Bushnell, *Crimes, Follies, and Misfortunes*, 43–55.

51. Rehnquist, *Grand Inquests*, 58–98.

52. Hoffer and Hull, *Impeachment in America*, 228–54; Bushnell, *Crimes, Follies, and Misfortunes*, 57–88; Rehnquist, *Grand Inquests*. 15–118.

53. Rehnquist, *Grand Inquests*, 106–7.

54. Ibid., 17–20.

55. Bushnell, *Crimes, Follies, and Misfortunes*, 91–113.

56. Ibid., 115–24.

57. The fullest and best modern assessment is Michael Les Benedict, *The Impeachment and Trial of Andrew Johnson* (New York: W. W. Norton, 1973). Also useful are Rehnquist, *Grand Inquests*, 199–261, and Bushnell, *Crimes, Follies, and Misfortunes*, 127–62.

58. Phillip S. Paludan, *A Covenant with Death: The Constitution, Law, and Equality in the Civil War Era* (Urbana: University of Illinois Press, 1975), 214.

59. Quoted in Benedict, *Impeachment and Trial of Andrew Johnson*, 144–45.

60. As Benedict points out in *Impeachment and Trial of Andrew Johnson*, 126–43, Democrats were even more rigidly partisan than Republicans, voting unanimously for acquittal.

61. Ibid., 143.

62. Emily Field Van Tassel and Paul Finkelman, *Impeachable Offenses: A Documentary History from 1787 to the Present* (Washington, D.C.: Congressional Quarterly, 1999), 119–23.

63. Bushnell, *Crimes, Follies, and Misfortunes*, 165–89.

64. Ibid., 191–214.

65. Ibid., 217–42; Clayton quoted at 223.

66. Van Tassel and Finkelman, *Impeachable Offenses*, 145–46.

67. Ibid., 144–52.

68. Bushnell, *Crimes, Follies, and Misfortunes*, 269–87.

69. *Ritter v. United States*, 84 Ct. Cl. 293 (1936).

2. Impeachment as Exceptional: The Case of Earl Warren

1. John Herbers, "Races Far Apart in Carolina City," *New York Times*, October 20, 1963; "Two Kinds of Publicity," *Washington Post*, March 18, 1963.

2. Bill Gold, "The District Line," *Washington Post*, March 2, 1962; Richard L. Strout, "Supreme Court Picture," *Christian Science Monitor*, June 21, 1963; Russell Baker, "Observer," *New York Times*, July 9, 1964.

3. Claude Sitton, "Warren Asks Modern View of Law," *Christian Science Monitor*, February 13, 1963; Joseph H. Baird, "South Greets Warren, *Christian Science Monitor*, February 14, 1963.

4. "Connecticut Priest Backs Warren Foes," *New York Times,* November 4, 1963; "Priest Is Censured for Warren Action," *New York Times*, November 9, 1963; "Diocese Tells Priest to End Warren Feud," *Chicago Tribune*, November 9, 1963.

5. "County Democrats Give Dentist $100," *Washington Post*, May 11, 1965.

6. "Essay Decreed for Birch Foe," *Washington Post*, November 5, 1965.

7. Clinton Rossiter, *The American Presidency* (New York: Harcourt, Brace, 1956), 53.

8. Good summaries of Earl Warren's life before joining the Supreme Court can be found in Bernard Schwartz, *Super Chief: Earl Warren and His Supreme Court—A Judicial Biography* (New York: New York University Press, 1983), chap. 1, and in greater detail in G. Edward White, *Earl Warren: A Public Life* (New York: Oxford University Press, 1982), 9–155.

9. Earl Warren to Daniel S. McHargue, May 17, 1973, Earl Warren Papers, Manuscript Division, Library of Congress, Washington, D.C.

10. Schwartz, *Super Chief,* 1–7. See also White, *Earl Warren*, 144–53.

11. Schwartz, *Super Chief*, 72–77.

12. The most detailed account of the *Brown* case remains Richard Kluger, *Simple Justice: The History of Brown v. Board of Education and Black America's Struggle for Equality* (New York: Knopf, 1976). Detail and perspective are added by more-recent studies: James Patterson, *Brown v. Board of Education: A Civil Rights Milestone and Its Troubled Legacy* (New York: Oxford University Press, 2001); Robert J. Cottrell, Raymond T. Diamond, and Leland B. Ware, *Brown v. Board of Education: Caste, Culture, and the Constitution* (Lawrence: University Press of Kansas, 2003);

and Michael J. Klarman, *From Jim Crow to Civil Rights: The Supreme Court and the Struggle for Racial Equality* (New York: Oxford University Press, 2004).

13. *Congressional Record,* 84th Cong., 2nd sess., vol. 102 (March 12, 1956): 4459–60.

14. "Georgia Chiefs Seek to Impeach Six Justices for 'High Crimes,'" *New York Times,* February 14, 1957; "'Impeachment Pushed': Georgia House Adopts Measure Aimed at Supreme Court," *New York Times,* February 19, 1957; "Vinson Disapproves Impeachment Plan," *New York Times,* February 22, 1957.

15. *New York Times,* June 25, 1956.

16. *Quinn v. United States,* 349 U.S. 155 (1955), and *Emspak v. United States,* 349 U.S. 190 (1955). See Arthur J. Sabin, *In Calmer Times: The Supreme Court and Red Monday* (Philadelphia: University of Pennsylvania Press, 1999): 124–25.

17. *Pennsylvania v. Nelson,* 350 U.S. 497 (1956).

18. Schwartz, *Super Chief,* 183.

19. *Slochower v. Board of Higher Education of New York City,* 350 U.S. 551 (1956).

20. *Schware v. Board of Bar Examiners of New Mexico,* 253 U.S. 232 (1957).

21. *Konigsberg v. State Bar of California,* 353 U.S. 253 (1957).

22. *Jencks v. United States,* 353 U.S. 657 (1957).

23. Alexander Charns, *Cloak and Gavel: FBI Wiretaps, Bugs, Informers, and the Supreme Court* (Urbana: University of Illinois Press, 1992), 8; Sabin, *In Calmer Times,* 228.

24. Lucas A. Powe, Jr., *The Warren Court and American Politics* (Cambridge, Mass.: Harvard University Press, 2000), 93. Powe provides a useful, if generally skeptical, review of the Red Monday and related cases in chapter 4.

25. *Service v. Dulles,* 354 U.S. 363 (1957); Sabin, *In Calmer Times,* 151–53.

26. *Watkins v. United States,* 354 U.S. 178 (1957); *Sweezy v. New Hampshire,* 354 U.S. 234 (1957); Sabin, *In Calmer Times,* 153–59.

27. *Yates v. United States,* 354 U.S. 298 (1957); Sabin, *In Calmer Times,* 160–70.

28. "A Day for Freedom," *New York Times,* June 18, 1957.

29. Schwartz, *Super Chief,* 283–85.

30. Ibid., 250.

31. *Cooper v. Aaron,* 358 U.S. 1 (1958).

32. *Mapp v. Ohio,* 367 U.S. 643 (1961). Also *Gideon v. Wainwright,* 372 U.S. 335 (1963); *Escobedo v. Illinois,* 378 U.S. 478 (1964); and *Miranda v. Arizona,* 384 U.S. 436 (1966).

33. *Jacobellis v. Ohio,* 378 U.S. 184 (1964).

34. *Engel v. Vitale,* 370 U.S. 421 (1962), and *Abington v. Schempp,* 374 U.S. 201 (1963).

35. *Baker v. Carr,* 369 U.S. 186 (1962); *Wesberry v. Sanders,* 376 U.S. 1 (1964); and *Reynolds v. Sims,* 377 U.S. 533 (1964).

36. *Griswold v. Connecticut,* 381 U.S. 479 (1965).

37. Hope Grey to John F. Kennedy, February 2, 1958, Prepresidential files, John F. Kennedy Papers, John F. Kennedy Presidential Library, Boston, Massachusetts.

38. John F. Kennedy to Hope Gray, February 7, 1958, Prepresidential files, Kennedy Papers.

39. Rosalie M. Gordon, *Nine Men against America: The Supreme Court and Its Attack on American Liberties* (New York: Devin-Adair, 1958).

40. Ibid., 3–7.

41. Ibid., 24, 63.

42. Ibid., 79–82.

43. Ibid., 131.

44. Ibid., 147–59.

45. Stephen J. Whitfield, *The Culture of the Cold War,* 2nd ed. (Baltimore: Johns Hopkins University Press, 1996). See also Gilbert Abcarian and Sherman M. Stanage, "Alienation and the Radical Right," *Journal of Politics* 27 (1965): 776–96.

46. Rick Perlstein, *Before the Storm: Barry Goldwater and the Unmaking of the American Consensus* (New York: Hill & Wang, 2001), 113–14.

47. Robert H. W. Welch, Jr., *May God Forgive Us* (Washington, D.C.: Regnery, 1952), and Welch, *The Life of John Birch* (Washington, D.C.: Regnery, 1954).

48. Robert H. W. Welch, Jr., *The Blue Book of the John Birch Society* (Privately printed, 1959), 181–82.

49. Robert H. W. Welch, Jr., *The Politician* (privately printed, 1963), 267.

50. Welch, *Blue Book of the John Birch Society,* 6.

51. Ibid., 24.

52. Ibid., 28–29.

53. Ibid., 53.

54. Ibid., 159.

55. Ibid., 163–74.

56. Ibid., 91.

57. Ibid., 92.

58. David Bennett, *The Party of Fear: The American Far Right from Nativism to the Militia Movement,* rev. ed. (New York: Vintage, 1995), 315–19.

59. Barbara S. Stone, "The John Birch Society: A Profile," *Journal of Politics* 36 (February 1974): 184–97. This essay drew on research for Barbara Shell Stone, "The John Birch Society of California" (Ph.D. diss., University of Southern California, 1968). See also Fred W. Grupp, Jr., "Personal Satisfaction Derived from Membership in the John Birch Society," *Western Political Quarterly* 24 (March 1971): 79–83, and Fred J. Cook, "The Ultras," *Nation* 194 (June 30, 1962), 585–89.

60. *Los Angeles Times,* March 8, 1961.

61. Robert Welch, cover letter to *Bulletin,* January 5, 1961, William F. Buckley, Jr., Papers, Yale University Library, New Haven, Connecticut.

62. Perlstein, *Before the Storm,* 118.

63. Lisa McGirr, *Suburban Warriors: The Origins of the New American Right* (Princeton, N.J.: Princeton University Press, 2001), provides a detailed picture of the postwar development of Orange County.

64. Ibid., 54–79.

65. *Chicago Daily News,* July 25 and 26, 1960; *Milwaukee Journal,* July 31, 1960; *Boston Herald,* August 28, 29, and 30, 1960.

66. John Birch Society, *Bulletin,* January 1961, Buckley Papers. See also Gene Grove, *Inside the John Birch Society* (Greenwich, Conn.: Gold Medal, 1961), 108–11.

67. Various correspondents to Perkins Bass, February–August 1961, Perkins Bass Papers, John Hay Library, Brown University, Providence, Rhode Island.

68. *Los Angeles Times,* March 5–12, 1961.

69. "Organization: The Americanists," *Time,* March 10, 1961, 21–22; Hans Engh, "The John Birch Society," *Nation,* March 11, 1961, 209–11. See also "The Eastland Imprimatur," *Nation,* April 1, 1961, 274–75; "The Nation Dissents," *Nation,* April 8, 1961, 294–95; "If Hopes Were Dupes," *Nation,* April 15, 1961, 314; Richard Armour, "The Ivan Birchkov Society," *Nation,* April 29, 1961, 370.

70. Walter Trohan, "Story behind Anti-Red John Birch Society," *Chicago Tribune,* March 30, 1961.

71. "Birch Unit Pushes Drive on Warren," *New York Times,* April 1, 1961.

72. "John Birch Society," *New Republic* 144 (April 10, 1961): 8.

73. Gerald W. Johnson, "Scalpel, Please," *New Republic* 144 (April 17, 1961): 12; Cushing Strout, "Fantasy on the Right," *New Republic* 144 (May 1, 1961): 13–115.

74. The broadside was found in the personal files of FBI director J. Edgar Hoover, who was always on the alert for possible communist infiltration of the U.S. government. Quoted in Charns, *Cloak and Gavel,* 11.

75. John Birch Society, *Bulletin*, March 1, 1961, Buckley Papers.

76. "Birch Unit Pushes Drive on Warren," *New York Times*, April 1, 1961.

77. *Los Angeles Times*, July 5, 1961.

78. John Wicklein, "Birch Society Will Offer $2,300 for Impeach-Warren Essay," *New York Times*, August 5, 1961; "An Essay Contest for the American Undergraduate," Buckley Papers.

79. Summarized letters to Robert Welch, undated, John Birch Society Papers, John Hay Library, Brown University, Providence, Rhode Island.

80. J. Allen Broyles, *The John Birch Society: Anatomy of a Protest* (Boston: Beacon Press, 1964): 116.

81. The literature on the new conservatism of the 1950s and 1960s is extensive. John P. Diggins, *Up from Communism: Conservative Odysseys in American Intellectual History* (New York: Harper & Row, 1975), and George H. Nash, *The Conservative Intellectual Movement in America since 1945* (New York: Basic Books, 1976) were pioneering efforts to examine conservative thought of the period. Among the most focused and useful works since are John A. Andrew III, *The Other Side of the Sixties: Young Americans for Freedom and the Rise of Conservative Politics* (New Brunswick, N.J.: Rutgers University Press, 1997); Mary C. Brennan, *Turning Right in the Sixties: The Conservative Capture of the GOP* (Chapel Hill: University of North Carolina Press, 1995); Jerome L Himmelstein, *To the Right: The Transformation of American Conservatism* (Berkeley: University of California Press, 1990); McGirr, *Suburban Warriors;* Perlstein, *Before the Storm;* Jonathan M. Schoenwald, *A Time for Choosing: The Rise of Modern American Conservatism* (New York: Oxford University Press, 2001); and the collection of essays edited by David Farber and Jeff Roche, *The Conservative Sixties* (New York: Peter Lang, 2003).

82. Brennan, *Turning Right in the Sixties,* esp. chap. 1.

83. John B. Judis, *William F. Buckley, Jr.: Patron Saint of the Conservatives* (New York: Simon & Schuster, 1988), and William Rusher, *The Rise of the Right* (New York: William Morrow, 1984).

84. Robert Alan Goldberg, *Barry Goldwater* (New Haven, Conn.: Yale University Press, 1995), 142–44.

85. Rusher, *Rise of the Right*, 99–112.

86. William F. Buckley, Jr., to Robert Welch, June 9, 1958, Buckley Papers.

87. Robert Welch to William F. Buckley, Jr., November 24, 1958, and Buckley to Welch, December 23, 1958, Buckley Papers.

88. Buckley to Welch, October 21, 1960, Buckley Papers.

89. William F. Buckley, Jr., to Robert Welch, April 14 and October 21, 1960, and Welch to Buckley, October 24, 1960, Buckley Papers.

90. Buckley to Welch, July 21, 1959, Buckley Papers.

91. Frank S. Meyer to William F. Buckley, March 28, 1961, Buckley Papers; Andrew, *The Other Side of the Sixties,* 102–3.

92. William F. Buckley, Jr., "The Uproar," *National Review* 10 (April 22, 1961): 241–43. For earlier drafts of the editorial, see *National Review,* March–April 1961 internal correspondence, Buckley Papers. See also, Judis, *William F. Buckley, Jr.,* 196.

93. *New York World Telegram,* April 15, 1961, clipping in Buckley Papers.

94. L. Brent Bozell, "Should We Impeach Earl Warren?" *National Review* 11 (September 9, 1961): 153–55.

95. Welch, *Blue Book of the John Birch Society,* 119–20.

96. Barry Goldwater to William F. Buckley, Jr., March 21, 1961, Buckley Papers.

97. Transcript, *Meet the Press,* November 19, 1961, Lawrence P. Spivak Papers, Manuscript Division, Library of Congress, Washington, D.C., quoted in Schoenwald, *A Time for Choosing,* 137.

98. Judis, *William F. Buckley, Jr.,* 198.

99. Goldberg, *Barry Goldwater,* 159.

100. William F. Buckley, Jr., "The Question of Robert Welch," *National Review* 12 (February 13, 1962): 83–88.

101. Ibid.

102. "Thunder on the Right," *Time*, February 16, 1962, 47–49.

103. Goldberg, *Barry Goldwater*, 159–60.

104. McGirr, *Suburban Warriors*, 120.

105. Drew Pearson, "Goldwater and His Birch Friends," *Washington Post*, November 14, 1963.

106. McGirr, *Suburban Warriors*, 111–46.

107. William F. Buckley, Jr., "The John Birch Society and the Conservative Movement," *National Review* 17 (October 19, 1965): 916.

108. Ibid.

109. Barry Goldwater, "Commentary," *National Review* 17 (October 19, 1965): 928–29.

110. Ward Just, "Birch vs. Warren," *Washington Post*, November 28, 1965.

111. "Birchers Chart Warren Attack," *New York Times*, January 12, 1967.

112. *Christian Science Monitor*, October 31, 1967.

113. Robert Welch and Medford Evans, "False Leadership: Wm. F. Buckley, Jr., and the New World Order," unpublished manuscript, John Birch Society Papers.

114. Earl Warren to Ralph M. Brown, March 26, 1963, Earl Warren Papers.

115. For examples, see Earl Warren to Robert Beresford, Santa Clara County Bar Association, April 2, 1963; Warren to M. Claiborne Mabel, January 6, 1964; Warren to Robert B. McConnell, June 16, 1965; and Executive Secretary to the Chief Justice to Jill Alexander, February 12, 1968, Warren Papers.

116. Schwartz, *Super Chief*, 281.

117. William O. Douglas, remarks at November 3, 1973, luncheon, William O. Douglas file, Harry A. Blackmun Papers, Manuscript Division, Library of Congress, Washington, D.C.

118. "Notes and Asides," *National Review* 20 (July 2, 1968): 644.

3. Impeachment as Political: The Case of Abe Fortas

1. A perceptive overview is Lucas A. Powe, Jr., *The Warren Court and American Politics* (Cambridge, Mass.: Harvard University Press, 2000). Much fuller coverage as well as wise insights can be found in Bernard Schwartz, *Super Chief: Earl Warren and His Supreme Court—A Judiciary Biography* (New York: New York University Press, 1983), and G. Edward White, *Earl Warren: A Public Life* (New York: Oxford University Press, 1982).

2. *Cooper v. Aaron*, 358 U.S. 1 (1958).

3. Most notable were *Mapp v. Ohio*, 367 U.S. 643 (1961); *Gideon v. Wainwright*, 372 U.S. 335 (1963); *Escobedo v. Illinois*, 378 U.S. 478 (1964); *Miranda v. Arizona*, 384 U.S. 436 (1966); and *Katz v. United States*, 389 U.S. 347 (1967).

4. *Engel v. Vitale*, 370 U.S. 421 (1962); *Abington v. Schempp*, 374 U.S. 203 (1963); *Jacobellis v. Ohio*, 378 U.S. 184 (1964).

5. *Baker v. Carr*, 369 U.S. 186 (1962); *Wesberry v. Sanders*, 376 U.S. 1 (1964); and *Reynolds v. Sims*, 377 U.S. 533 (1964).

6. *Griswold v. Connecticut*, 381 U.S. 479 (1965).

7. See David E. Kyvig, *Explicit and Authentic Acts: Amending the U.S. Constitution, 1776–1995* (Lawrence: University Press of Kansas, 1996).

8. See Michael J. Gerhardt, *The Federal Impeachment Process: A Constitutional and Historical Analysis*, 2nd ed. (Chicago: University of Chicago Press, 2000), 82–85.

9. The fullest treatment of Warren's retirement and what flowed from it is found in Bruce Allen Murphy, *Fortas: The Rise and Ruin of a Supreme Court Justice* (New York: William Morrow,

1988). Also valuable are Robert Shogan, *A Question of Judgment: The Fortas Case and the Struggle for the Supreme Court* (Indianapolis, Ind.: Bobbs-Merrill, 1972), and Laura Kalman, *Abe Fortas: A Biography* (New Haven, Conn.: Yale University Press, 1990).

10. An excellent account of the Johnson presidency can be found in Robert Dallek, *Flawed Giant: Lyndon Johnson and His Times, 1961–1973* (New York: Oxford University Press, 1998).

11. Schwartz, *Super Chief,* 680.

12. White, *Earl Warren,* 137–42.

13. Schwartz, *Super Chief,* 680–83.

14. "Washington Wire," *Wall Street Journal,* June 14, 1968.

15. *Congressional Record,* 90th Cong., 2nd sess., vol. 114 (Friday, June 21, 1968): S7499.

16. Robert P. Griffin, "The Senate Stands Taller: Remarks for Delivery in the U.S. Senate, October 1, 1968," unpublished manuscript, Robert P. Griffin Papers, Clarke Historical Library, Central Michigan University, Mount Pleasant, Michigan; *Los Angeles Times,* May 16, 1969.

17. For Fortas's earlier public image, see *Time,* August 6, 1965, 24.

18. Robert P. Griffin, press release, June 24, 1968, Griffin Papers.

19. Robert P. Griffin, press release, June 27, 1968, Griffin Papers.

20. "Chronology of Events Relating to Supreme Court Nominations," September 28, 1968, Griffin Papers.

21. Quoted in Murphy, *Fortas,* 299.

22. "Chronology," September 28, 1968, Griffin Papers; Lyle Denniston, "Dirksen, Griffin Feud over Top Court Nominees," *Washington Evening Star,* July 13, 1968.

23. Murphy, *Fortas,* 298.

24. Shogan, *A Question of Judgment,* 158–59; Kalman, *Abe Fortas,* 332.

25. "Chronology of Events Relating to Supreme Court Nominations," September 28, 1968, Griffin Papers; Lyle Denniston, "Dirksen, Griffin Feud Over Top Court Nominees," *Washington Evening Star,* July 13, 1968.

26. U.S. Senate, Committee on the Judiciary, *Nominations of Abe Fortas and Homer Thornberry: Hearings,* 90th Cong., 2nd sess. (Washington, D.C.: GPO, 1968).

27. Statement of Citizens for Decent Literature, Inc., July 22, 1968, and "Citizens for Decent Literature, Inc. Presents 'Target Smut,'" undated, Griffin Papers.

28. John P. McKenzie, "Fortas Berated for Two Hours," *Washington Post,* July 19, 1968; Fred P. Graham, "Fortas Is Grilled on His Non-judicial Role," *New York Times,* July 21, 1968, clippings in Griffin Papers; Strom Thurmond, constituent newsletter, July 22, 1968, Griffin Papers.

29. Robert P. Griffin, "The Fortas-Thornberry Issue," National Press Club, July 30, 1968, Fred P. Graham Papers, Manuscript Division, Library of Congress, Washington, D.C.

30. Sam J. Ervin, "Ervin Hits Judicial Activism of Justice Fortas," press release, August 21, 1968, Griffin Papers.

31. Griffin, "The Fortas-Thornberry Issue."

32. Griffin, "The Senate Stands Taller" manuscript; Cecil [Holland], memorandum, November 1, 1968, Griffin Papers.

33. Robert P. Griffin, memorandum to the chairman and members of the Committee on the Judiciary, September 9, 1968, Griffin Papers.

34. Senator Griffin on September 17 and 18 inserted feature stories from the *Detroit News, Washington Post,* and *Wall Street Journal* in the *Congressional Record* (90th Cong., 2nd sess.).

35. "$100,000 Professorship Awaiting Schlesinger," *Washington Post,* December 17, 1965.

36. For example, Ronald J. Ostrow and Robert I. Jackson, "Even Supporters Question Fortas Accepting Fee," *Los Angeles Times,* September 21, 1968.

37. Robert P. Griffin, press release, September 15, 1968, Griffin Papers.

38. Everett Dirksen, office press release, undated, Graham Papers; Fred P. Graham, "Fortas

Set Back by Dirksen Shift Opposing Cloture," *New York Times*, September 28, 1968, clipping in Griffin Papers.

39. Philip A. Hart, press release, September 20, 1968, Griffin Papers.

40. Robert P. Griffin, "The Senate Stands Taller" manuscript, Griffin Papers.

41. Abe Fortas to Lyndon Johnson, October 1, 1968, copy in Griffin Papers.

42. Kalman, *Abe Fortas*, 528–29.

43. Van den Toorn to Griffin and Cecil Holland, October 15, 1968, Griffin Papers. No book was ever published, though a partial manuscript for "The Senate Stands Taller" is among Griffin's papers.

44. "Griffin Demeans the Court," *Grand Rapids Press*, July 8, 1968, clipping in Griffin Papers.

45. "He Isn't Helping His Party," *Grand Rapids Press*, July 25, 1968, clipping in Griffin Papers.

46. "Sen. Griffin Is Waging an Unfortunate Crusade," *Detroit Free Press*, August 11, 1968, clipping in Griffin Papers.

47. "Bar Chief Backs Fortas Nomination: Sen. Griffin Lambasted," *Detroit Free Press*, August 13, 1968, clipping in Griffin Papers.

48. "The Majority Loses," *Grand Rapids Press*, October 4, 1968, clipping in Griffin Papers.

49. Shogan, *A Question of Judgment*, 158.

50. John Ehrlichman, *Witness to Power: The Nixon Years* (New York: Simon & Schuster, 1982), 113.

51. Fred P. Graham, "Dirksen Tests G.O.P. Sentiment if Johnson Nominates Goldberg," *New York Times*, December 13, 1968.

52. Drew Pearson, "Nixon Call to Warren Undercut LBJ," *Washington Post*, December 7, 1968.

53. Fred P. Graham, notes, "Interview with Chief Justice Earl Warren, 9/23/68," Graham Papers.

54. Detailed discussions of the Fortas-Wolfson relationship can be found in Murphy, *Fortas*, and Kalman, *Abe Fortas*. A more condemnatory account appears in Powe, *The Warren Court and American Politics*, 478–81.

55. Unsigned memo, September 22, 1968, Griffin Papers.

56. Kalman, *Abe Fortas*, 360.

57. Shogan, *A Question of Judgment*.

58. Kalman, *Abe Fortas*, 364; Murphy, *Fortas*, 549–59.

59. John W. Dean, *The Rehnquist Choice: The Untold Story of the Nixon Appointments That Redefined the Supreme Court* (New York: Free Press, 2001), 6.

60. Richard H. Poff, "Diary of White House Leadership Meanings—91st Congress, April 22, 1968," Robert T. Hartmann Papers, Gerald R. Ford Presidential Library, Ann Arbor, Michigan.

61. Dean, *The Rehnquist Choice*, 5–8; Shogan, *A Question of Judgment*, 230–33.

62. Quotations and information in this and subsequent paragraphs come from William Lambert, "Fortas of the Supreme Court: A Question of Ethics; The Justice and the Stock Manipulator," *Life*, May 5, 1969.

63. Kalman, *Abe Fortas*, 365.

64. Richard H. Poff, "Diary of White House Leadership Meanings—91st Congress, May 6, 1969," Ford Papers.

65. Robert Greenberg, "Fortas Story Incomplete: Sen. Griffin," *New York Post*, May 5, 1969, clipping in Griffin Papers.

66. "Foes Call for Ouster of Fortas," *Detroit Free Press*, May 6, 1969; "Justice Fortas Faces Threat of Impeachment in Congress," *Detroit Free Press*, May 8, 1968, clippings in Griffin Papers.

67. *Congressional Record*, 91st Cong., 1st sess., vol. 115 (May 8, 1969): S4853; H.R. 11109, Robert Taft, Jr., Papers, Manuscript Division, Library of Congress.

68. Robert Taft, Jr., to Gerald R. Ford, May 26,1969; Taft to Emanuel Celler, May 26, 1969; Ford to Celler, May 28, 1969; Ford to Taft, May 28, 1969; Celler to Taft, May 29, 1969; Taft to Celler, November 4, 1969; Celler to Taft, November 7, 1969; and Taft to Professor G. M. Hulley, December 5, 1969, Taft Papers.

69. Murphy, *Fortas*, 553–55: Kalman, *Abe Fortas*, 363.

70. Kalman, *Abe Fortas*, 367; Murphy, *Fortas*, 560–61.

71. "Nixon Refuses to Intercede," *New York Times*, May 7, 1969.

72. "Fortas Foe Tells of Threats," *Washington Daily News*, May 10, 1969, clipping in Griffin Papers.

73. Bob Woodward and Scott Armstrong, *The Brethren: Inside the Supreme Court* (New York: Simon & Schuster, 1979), 19; Murphy, *Fortas*, 562; Kalman, *Abe Fortas*, 368.

74. Murphy, *Fortas*, 571.

75. Ibid., 566.

76. Dean, *The Rehnquist Choice*, 11.

77. Shogan, *A Question of Judgment*, 259–60.

78. William J. Brennan, Jr., "RE: Dinner for the Chief Justice and Mrs. Warren," May 28, 1969, Hugo Black Papers, Manuscript Division, Library of Congress, Washington, D.C.

79. Hugo Black, William O. Douglas, John M. Harlan, William Brennan, Jr., Byron White, Potter Stewart, and Thurgood Marshall to Earl Warren, June 23, 1969, Black Papers.

80. Benjamin C. Bradlee, "Abe Fortas Resigns," *Washington Post*, May 16, 1969.

81. "Griffin's Principled Argument Vindicated," *Saginaw (Mich.) News*, May 20, 1969, clipping in Griffin Papers.

82. Shogan, *A Question of Judgment*, 117.

4. Impeachment as Partisan: The Case of William O. Douglas

1. Strom Thurmond, "Strom Thurmond Reports to the People," June 2, 1969, Gerald R. Ford Congressional Papers, Gerald R. Ford Presidential Library, Ann Arbor, Michigan.

2. Nadine Cohodas, *Strom Thurmond and the Politics of Southern Change* (Macon, Ga.: Mercer University Press, 1993).

3. Quoted in William O. Douglas, *The Court Years, 1939–1975* (New York: Vintage, 1981), 358.

4. Laura Kalman, *Fortas: The Rise and Ruin of a Supreme Court Justice* (New York: William Morrow, 1988), 572.

5. Robert Hartmann, interview with Armbruster, September 1, 1977, Ford Congressional Papers.

6. Bruce Allen Murphy, *Wild Bill: The Legend and Life of William O. Douglas* (New York: Random House, 2003), 400.

7. Ronald J. Ostrow, "Outside Income of Judicial Ethics Issue," *Los Angeles Times*, October 16, 1968; Philip Warren, "Probe Urged into Douglas Las Vegas Fee," *Chicago Tribune*, October 18, 1966; "Senator Urges Court Inquiry on Role of Douglas," *New York Times,* October 18, 1966.

8. Bob Woodward and Scott Armstrong, *The Brethren: Inside the Supreme Court* (New York: Simon & Schuster, 1979), 18.

9. John Dean, *The Rehnquist Choice: The Untold Story of the Nixon Appointment that Redefined the Supreme Court* (New York: Free Press, 2001), 24–25.

10. John Ehrlichman, *Witness to Power: The Nixon Years* (New York: Simon & Schuster, 1982), 116.

11. Michael Comiskey, *Seeking Justices: The Judging of Supreme Court Nominees* (Lawrence: University Press of Kansas, 2004), 12.

12. Dean, *The Rehnquist Choice,* 12–14; Ehrlichman, *Witness to Power*, 114.

13. Henry J. Abraham, *Justices and Presidents: A Political History of Appointments to the Supreme Court*, 2nd ed. (New York: Oxford University Press, 1985), 13–14, 296–98; Comiskey, *Seeking Justices*, 12.

14. Abraham, *Justices and Presidents*, 298.

15. Dean, *The Rehnquist Choice*, 14–18.

16. E. W. Kenworthy, "All but One of Eleven Senators Regarded as Undecided Vote against Haynsworth," *New York Times*, November 22, 1969.

17. Dean, *The Rehnquist Choice*, 18, 295n57.

18. Ibid., 19. For views contrary to Dean's, see Abraham, *Justices and Presidents*, 15–16, and Richard Harris, *Decision* (New York: E. P Dutton, 1971), 11–12.

19. Dean, *The Rehnquist Choice*, 19–20.

20. An insightful detailed account of the development of opposition to the Carswell nomination can be found in Harris, *Decision,* esp. 15–16, 41–44, 101, 133–36.

21. Harris, *Decision*, 200–2.

22. "Diary of White House Leadership Meetings—91st Congress, March 3, 1970," Ford Congressional Papers.

23. "Nixon Condemns Senators Who Barred Two Judges: Will Pick Non-Southerner," *New York Times*, April 10, 1970.

24. Linda Greenhouse, *Becoming Justice Blackmun: Harry Blackmun's Supreme Court Journey* (New York: Times Books, 2005), provides much insight on the Burger-Blackmun relationship and the eventual estrangement of the two justices.

25. Dean, *The Rehnquist Choice*, 19–23, provides an insider's perspective on Burger's role.

26. Richard Sachs, "Role of Vice-President Designate Gerald Ford in the Attempt to Impeach Associate Supreme Court Justice William O. Douglas," Legislative Reference Service, Library of Congress, Ford Congressional Papers.   .

27. Bernard L. Collier, "Douglas Resigns Foundation Post: Cites His Health," *New York Times,* May 24, 1969; Jerry Cohen, "Douglas Gives Up $12,000 Side Job," *Los Angeles Times*, May 24, 1969.

28. Hartmann, interview with Armbruster, September 1, 1977, Ford Congressional Papers. During his House confirmation hearings to be vice president, Ford described at length his use of Hartmann to investigate Douglas. See U.S. Congress, House of Representatives, Committee on the Judiciary, *Nomination of Gerald R. Ford to Be the Vice President of the United States: Hearings,* 93rd Cong., 1st sess. (Washington, D.C.: GPO, 1973), 614–17.

29. Ehrlichman, *Witness to Power,* 122.

30. Murphy, *Wild Bill,* 430.

31. Gerald R. Ford form letter, November 14, 1968, Ford Congressional Papers; Sachs, "Role of Ford in Attempt to Impeach Douglas."

32. Ehrlichman, *Witness to Power,* 122.

33. *New York Times*, November 11, 1969.

34. Lyle Denniston, "Lawmakers Pushing Effort to Impeach Justice Douglas," *Washington Evening Star*, December 21, 1969.

35. Marjorie Hunter, "Ford Concedes Aid of Justice Agency," *New York Times,* November 22, 1973; Hartmann, interview with Armbruster, September 1, 1977, Ford Congressional Papers; U.S. Congress, House, Committee on the Judiciary, *Nomination of Gerald R. Ford*, 613–14.

36. William O. Douglas, *Points of Rebellion* (New York: Random House, 1970), 95.

37. See, for example, "An Open Letter To:" *National Review* 22 (March 24, 1970); 293–94; Ernest Van Den Haag, "Justice Douglas' Book," *National Review* 23 (May 18, 1971): 526–28.

38. Sachs, "Role of Ford in Attempt to Impeach Douglas."

39. *Chicago Tribune*, April 12, 13, 1970.

40. Sachs, "Role of Ford in Attempt to Impeach Douglas"; Murphy, *Wild Bill*, 432.

41. U.S. Congress, House, Committee on the Judiciary, *Associate Justice William O. Douglas: First Report by the Special Subcommittee on H. Res. 920,* 91st Cong., 2nd sess. (Washington, D.C.: GPO, 1970), 27–44.

42. Several well-thumbed copies of *Evergreen* can be found in the Gerald R. Ford Papers.

43. ". . . a Descent to Politics," *New York Times*, April 17, 1970; Marjorie Hunter, "Douglas Inquiry Pressed in House," *New York Times*, April 24, 1970.

44. "The Mood Is Ugly, the Target Is Douglas," *New York Times*, April 19, 1970.

45. *Congressional Record*, 91st Cong., 2nd sess., vol. 115 (April 21, 1970).

46. Ibid.

47. Earl Warren to William O. Douglas, June 27, 1970, enclosing Paul N. McCloskey, Jr., to Warren, June 24, 1970, and *Congressional Record*, 91st Cong., 2nd sess., vol. 115 (April 21, 1970); Earl Warren Papers, Manuscript Division, Library of Congress, Washington, D.C.

48. Marjorie Hunter, "Celler Will Head Panel on Douglas," *New York Times*, April 22, 1970; Hartmann, interview with Armbruster, September 1, 1977, Ford Congressional Papers; Gerald R. Ford form letter, November 14, 1968, Ford Congressional Papers; Sachs, "Role of Ford in Attempt to Impeach Douglas."

49. Minutes, Special Subcommittee of House Judiciary Committee, June 30, 1953, Emanuel Celler Papers, Manuscript Division, Library of Congress, Washington, D.C.

50. Richard Nixon to Emanuel Celler, May 13, 1970, Celler Papers.

51. Emanuel Celler to Richard Nixon, May 21, 1970, Celler Papers.

52. Richard Nixon to Emanuel Celler, June 2, 1970, Celler Papers.

53. Douglas, *The Court Years*, 362.

54. William O. Douglas to Charles Horowitz, April 15, 1970, in *The Douglas Letters: Selections from the Private Papers of Justice William O. Douglas,* ed. Melvin I. Urofsky (Bethesda, Md.: Adler & Adler, 1987), 393.

55. Ford Congressional Papers.

56. "Impeachment Sought: Justice Douglas Hit by Texas House in Oil Lands Case," *New York Times*, January 17, 1951.

57. "Justice Douglas Accused in House: Wheeler Lists Treason among 6 Charges for Impeachment," *New York Times*, June 30, 1953.

58. Minutes, Special Subcommittee of House Judiciary Committee, June 30, 1953, Celler Papers; "Move to Impeach Douglas Quashed," *New York Times*, July 8, 1953.

59. Murphy, *Wild Bill*, 400.

60. William O. Douglas to Simon H. Rifkind, May 27, 1970, William O. Douglas Papers, Manuscripts Division, Library of Congress, Washington, D.C.

61. William O. Douglas to Simon H. Rifkind, May 25, 1970, Douglas Papers.

62. William O. Douglas, speech at dinner honoring Simon H. Rifkind, April 23, 1971, Douglas Papers.

63. William O. Douglas to Clark M. Clifford, April 16, 1970; Douglas to Ramsey Clark, April 22, 24, 27, 28, 29, and 30, May 5, 7, and 25, 1970; Simon H. Rifkind to Douglas, June 11, 1971, Douglas Papers. See also Urofsky, *The Douglas Letters*, chap. 15.

64. William O. Douglas to Emanuel Celler, April 27, 1970, Douglas Papers.

65. Quoted in "Douglas Backs Right of a Judge to Live Own Life Off Bench," *New York Times*, June 2, 1970.

66. Quoted in Murphy, *Wild Bill*, 435.

67. Howard W. Fogt, Jr., to William M. McCulloch, May 19 and 25, June 6 and 9, 1970, Celler Papers.

68. Simon H. Rifkind, "Memorandum on Impeachment of Federal Judges," April 15, 1970, Douglas Papers.

69. Simon H. Rifkind to Emanuel Celler, May 18, 1970, in U.S. Congress, House, Committee on the Judiciary, *Associate Justice William O. Douglas: First Report*, 50–53.

70. Ibid.

71. Ibid.

72. Ibid.

73. Ibid.

74. Ibid.

75. Fred Rodell, "Ford Move vs. Douglas, in Letters to the Editor of the Times," *New York Times*, April 21, 1970.

76. "Cellar Will Head Panel on Douglas," *New York Times*, April 22, 1970.

77. Fred Rodell to Gerald R. Ford, July 14, 1970, Ford Congressional Papers.

78. Gerald R. Ford to Fred Rodell, July 22, 1970, Ford Congressional Papers.

79. Fred Rodell to Gerald R. Ford, August 20, 1970, Ford Congressional Papers.

80. Gerald Ford, press release, August 9, 1970, Ford Congressional Papers; Sachs, "Role of Ford in Attempt to Impeach Douglas"; William O. Douglas to Simon H. Rifkind, September 30, 1970, Douglas Papers.

81. Bethel B. Kelley to Gerald Ford, June 23, 1970; Ford to Emanuel Celler, August 5, 1970; Gerald Ford, press release, August 9, 1970, Ford Congressional Papers. The Kelley memorandum can be found in U.S. Congress, House, Committee on the Judiciary, *Associate Justice William O. Douglas: Final Report by the Special Subcommittee on H. Res. 920,* 91st Cong., 2nd sess. (Washington, D.C.: GPO, 1970), 368–84.

82. Quoted in U.S. Congress, House, Committee on the Judiciary, *Associate Justice William O. Douglas: Final Report,* 368–84.

83. Simon H. Rifkind to Emanuel Celler, August 18, 1970, Douglas Papers, reprinted in U.S. Congress, House, Committee on the Judiciary, *Associate Justice William O. Douglas: Final Report,* 461–68.

84. George Lardner, Jr., "Ford Strides Out of Step with His Party," *Washington Post*, November 2, 1970.

85. Marjorie Hunter, "House Panel Votes against Impeaching Douglas," *New York Times*, December 4, 1970; *Chicago Tribune*, December 1 and 15, 1970.

86. William O. Douglas to Simon H. Rifkind, December 4, 1970, Douglas Papers.

87. William O. Douglas, remarks at November 3, 1973, luncheon, William O. Douglas file, Harry Blackmun Papers, Manuscript Division, Library of Congress, Washington, D.C.

88. Gerald R. Ford, press release, December 4, 1970, Ford Congressional Papers.

89. "Ford Calls Efforts to Oust Douglas Far from Finished," *New York Times*, December 5, 1970.

90. Joe B. Waggonner, Jr., Louis C. Wyman, Robert L. F. Sikes, and William L. Scott to colleagues, January 21, 1971, Ford Congressional Papers.

91. Donald S. Fraser to House colleagues, January 20, 1971, Douglas Papers.

92. Murphy, *Wild Bill*, 420–31.

93. *Griswold v. Connecticut,* 381 U.S. 479 (1965). A helpful discussion of the decision can be found in John W. Johnson, *Griswold v. Connecticut: Birth Control and the Constitutional Right of Privacy* (Lawrence: University Press of Kansas, 2005), chap. 8.

94. Detailed though not entirely harmonious accounts of the Court's deliberations in *Roe v. Wade* and *Doe v. Bolton* are found in David J. Garrow, *Liberty and Sexuality: The Right to Privacy and the Making of Roe v. Wade* (Berkeley: University of California Press, 1994), 531–33, and Greenhouse, *Becoming Justice Blackmun*, 80.

95. Garrow, *Liberty and Sexuality,* 533.

96. Woodward and Armstrong, *The Brethren,* 170–72.

97. Harry Blackmun, oral history interview with Harold Hangju Koh, p. 195, transcript in Blackmun Papers.

5. Impeachment as Discretionary: The Case of Spiro Agnew

1. Nixon's dilemma is discussed at length in Jules Witcover, *White Knight: The Rise of Spiro Agnew* (New York: Random House, 1972), 216–20.

2. A good review of Agnew's life before his vice presidency can be found in ibid., 3–215.

3. These and other Agnew remarks are reported in a detailed account of the campaign in ibid., 234–66.

4. Ibid., 279–80.

5. H. R. Haldeman, *The Haldeman Diaries: Inside the Nixon White House* (New York: G. P. Putnam's Sons, 1994), 27, 52, 53.

6. The most detailed examination of the Nixon-Agnew relationship, one making use of the Nixon tapes as well as of Witcover's own reporting for the *Washington Post*, is Jules Witcover, *Very Strange Bedfellows: The Short and Unhappy Marriage of Richard Nixon and Spiro Agnew* (New York: Public Affairs, 2007), but see also Spiro T. Agnew, *Go Quietly . . . Or Else* (New York: William Morrow, 1980), 31–38; John Ehrlichman, *Witness to Power: The Nixon Years* (New York: Simon & Schuster, 1982), 144–47; Haldeman, *The Haldeman Diaries,* 247; Witcover, *White Knight,* 421.

7. Haldeman, *The Haldeman Diaries,* 99–100.

8. Quoted in Witcover, *White Knight,* 305.

9. Quoted in ibid., 309.

10. Quoted in ibid., 334–36.

11. Haldeman, *The Haldeman Diaries,* 104–11; Witcover, *White Knight,* 310–21.

12. Witcover, *White Knight,* 324–71.

13. Haldeman, *The Haldeman Diaries,* 172.

14. Quoted in Ehrlichman, *Witness to Power,* 143.

15. Agnew, *Go Quietly,* 38–39.

16. The William F. Buckley, Jr., Papers, Yale University Library, New Haven, Connecticut, and the William A. Rusher Papers, Manuscript Division, Library of Congress, Washington, D.C., are filled with positive references to Agnew from 1969 to 1973.

17. Quoted in Witcover, *White Knight,* 310.

18. Ibid., 435–38.

19. Melvin Small, *The Presidency of Richard Nixon* (Lawrence: University Press of Kansas, 1999), 200.

20. An excellent account of the case is David Rudenstine, *The Day the Presses Stopped: A History of the Pentagon Papers Case* (Berkeley: University of California Press, 1996).

21. Charles W. Colson, *Born Again* (Old Tappen, N.J.: Chosen Books, 1976), 60; Tom Wicker, *One of Us: Richard Nixon and the American Dream* (New York: Random House, 1991), 640; H. R. Haldeman, *The Ends of Power,* with Joseph DiMona (New York: Times Books, 1978), 111; Herbert G. Klein, *Making It Perfectly Clear* (Garden City, N.Y.: Doubleday, 1980), 350.

22. William Safire, *Before the Fall: An Inside View of the Pre-Watergate White House* (Garden City, N.Y.: Doubleday, 1975), 358.

23. Rudenstine, *The Day the Presses Stopped,* 243–47.

24. The story of the dirty tricks campaigns and the Watergate affair that followed is told in detail in Stanley I. Kutler, *The Wars of Watergate: The Last Crisis of Richard Nixon* (New York: Knopf, 1990), and more briefly in Keith W. Olson, *Watergate: The Presidential Scandal That Shook America* (Lawrence: University Press of Kansas, 2003).

25. Kutler, *The Wars of Watergate,* 226.

26. John W. Dean III, *Blind Ambition* (New York: Simon & Schuster, 1976), 129.

27. "Press Conference, August 29, 1972," in *Public Papers of the Presidents of the United States: Richard Nixon, 1972,* 827–38 (Washington, D.C.: GPO, 1974); McGovern quoted in Stephen E. Ambrose, *Nixon,* 3 vols. (New York: Simon & Schuster, 1987–91), 2:602–3.

28. Kutler, *The Wars of Watergate*, 227–35.

29. The Deep Throat story was finally told in Bob Woodward, *The Secret Man: The Story of Watergate's Deep Throat* (New York: Simon & Schuster, 2005).

30. An account of the early stages of their journalistic investigation can be found in Carl Bernstein and Bob Woodward, *All the President's Men* (New York: Simon & Schuster, 1974).

31. Quoted in Kutler, *The Wars of Watergate*, 260.

32. Quoted in ibid., 315.

33. Quoted in ibid.

34. Ibid., 313–14.

35. Ibid., 327–34.

36. Ibid., 350–57.

37. Ibid., 358–63.

38. Ibid., 364–67.

39. Ibid., 371–78.

40. Haldeman, *The Haldeman Diaries*, 534; Ehrlichman, *Witness to Power*, 141–42.

41. Richard M. Cohen and Jules Witcover, *A Heartbeat Away: The Investigation and Resignation of Vice President Spiro T. Agnew* (New York: Viking, 1974), 3–6. The outlines of the case built against Agnew are confirmed by Witcover in *Crapshoot: Rolling the Dice on the Vice Presidency* (New York: Crown, 1992), 249–62, and at greater length in *Very Strange Bedfellows*.

42. Cohen and Witcover, *A Heartbeat Away*, 15–16.

43. Ibid., 81–96.

44. Ibid., 113–17.

45. Haldeman, *The Haldeman Diaries*, 630. According to Kutler, *The Wars of Watergate*, 659n6, a transcript of an April 14, 1973, conversation among Nixon, Ehrlichman, and Haldeman is in box 172 in Richard M. Nixon Papers, National Archives and Records Administration, College Park, Maryland.

46. Cohen and Witcover, *A Heartbeat Away*, 102–3.

47. Ibid., 103–9.

48. Ibid., 104–9.

49. Ibid., 125–30.

50. Ehrlichman, *Witness to Power*, 143–44.

51. "Statement by the Vice President," April 25, 1973, and May 22, 1973, press releases, Spiro T. Agnew Papers, Hornbake Library, University of Maryland, College Park, Maryland.

52. Quoted in Ehrlichman, *Witness to Power*, 143.

53. Ehrlichman, *Witness to Power*, 143.

54. George Beall to Judah Best re: Spiro T. Agnew, August 1, 1973, Agnew Papers.

55. Jerry Landnuer, "A New Watergate?" *Wall Street Journal*, August 7, 1973; Richard Cohen and Carl Bernstein, "Agnew Is Target of Kickback Probe in Baltimore, Proclaims His Innocence," *Washington Post*, August 7, 1973.

56. "Statement by the Vice President," August 6, 1973, press release, Agnew Papers; Jules Witcover, "Has 'No Expectation of Being Indicted'; Says He Won't Quit," *Washington Post*, August 9, 1973; Cohen and Witcover, *A Heartbeat Away*, 137–53.

57. Cohen and Witcover, *A Heartbeat Away*, 255.

58. Andrew Ripley, "Agnew's Aides Studying 100-Year-Old Case," *New York Times*, September 20, 1973; George Lardner, Jr., "Case of Grant's Vice President Presents Puzzle for Agnew," *Washington Post*, September 29, 1973; Glen Elsasser, "Agnew Tries to Build a Fortress of Precedents," *Chicago Tribune*, September 30, 1973; Bill Richards, "Experts Vote against Agnew's Stand," *Washington Post*, October 9, 1973.

59. John P. MacKenzie, "Agnew Probe Raises Many Questions," *Washington Post*, August 8, 1973; George Lardner, Jr., "Opinions of Experts Differ on Impeachment, Indictment,"

Washington Post, August 28, 1973; Glen Elsasser, "Kerner Studies Impeachment Issue," *Chicago Tribune*, August 31, 1973.

60. Cohen and Witcover, *A Heartbeat Away*, 144–45.

61. A detailed account of these efforts can be found in Witcover, *Very Strange Bedfellows*, 291–345.

62. Lou Cannon, "Defending Self, Agnew Says," *Washington Post*, August 9, 1973; Lou Cannon, "But 'He's Fighting for His Life,'" *Washington Post*, August 10, 1973; Spiro. T. Agnew, "Statement by the Vice President of the United States," August 21, 1973, press release, and Spiro T. Agnew to Elliot Richardson, August 21, 1973, copy released to the press, Agnew Papers.

63. Richard M. Cohen and Lou Cannon, "Agnew Lawyers Bargain on Plea," *Washington Post*, September 22, 1973; Cohen and Witcover, *A Heartbeat Away*, 190–251.

64. Cohen and Witcover, *A Heartbeat Away*, 218–19.

65. Ibid., 218–19, 250.

66. William Chapman, "House Gingerly Pokes at Impeachment," *Washington Post*, September 21, 1973.

67. Ibid.

68. Tony Mauro, "The Chairman in Winter: Peter Rodino Jr.'s Perspective on Impeachment," *American Lawyer* 26 (March 2004): 59–61.

69. Spiro T. Agnew to Carl Albert, September 25, 1973, Agnew Papers.

70. Ibid.

71. "Statement by the President," September 25, 1973, Office of the White House Press Secretary, Agnew Papers.

72. Cohen and Witcover, *A Heartbeat Away*, 256.

73. Gerald R. Ford, *A Time to Heal: The Autobiography of Gerald R. Ford* (New York: Harper & Row, 1979), 102.

74. Cohen and Witcover, *A Heartbeat Away*, 256–57.

75. Martin Waldron, "Justice Dept. Says Agnew Can, Legally, Be Indicted, with House Acting Later," *New York Times,* October 6, 1973; George Lardner, Jr., "Nixon's Immunity Backed," *Washington Post*, October 6, 1973; Cohen and Witcover, *A Heartbeat Away*, 261.

76. Spiro T. Agnew, address to National Federation of Republican Women, September 29, 1973, Agnew Papers; Cohen and Witcover, *A Heartbeat Away*, 264–69.

77. Spiro T. Agnew, address to United Republican fall dinner, October 4, 1973, Agnew Papers; Cohen and Witcover, *A Heartbeat Away*, 285–88.

78. Cohen and Witcover, *A Heartbeat Away*, 340–45.

79. Ibid., 365-68.

80. "Statement by Mr. Agnew to the Court," October 10, 1971, Agnew Papers.

81. Cohen and Witcover, *A Heartbeat Away*, 350–53.

82. Spiro T. Agnew, "Address to the American People," October 15, 1973, Agnew Papers.

83. Quoted in Cohen and Witcover, *A Heartbeat Away*, 109.

84. Joyce W. West to Spiro T. Agnew, October 15, 1973, Agnew Papers.

6. Impeachment as Essential: The Case of Richard Nixon

1. Stanley I. Kutler, *The Wars of Watergate: The Last Crisis of Richard Nixon* (New York: Knopf, 1990), 471.

2. James Reston, "The Decline of Civility," *New York Times*, April 8, 1973.

3. Howard Fields, *High Crimes and Misdemeanors: "Wherefore Richard M. Nixon . . . Warrants Impeachment"; The Dramatic Story of the Rodino Committee* (New York: W. W. Norton, 1978), 30–31, 35.

4. L. H. LaRue, *Political Discourse: A Case Study of the Watergate Affair* (Athens: University of Georgia Press, 1988), 2.

5. John Ehrlichman, *Witness to Power: The Nixon Years* (New York: Simon & Schuster, 1982), 143.

6. Spiro T. Agnew, "Address to the American People," October 15, 1973, Spiro T. Agnew Papers, Hornbake Library, University of Maryland, College Park, Maryland.

7. H. R. Haldeman, *The Haldeman Diaries: Inside the Nixon White House* (New York: G. P. Putnam's Sons, 1994), 138.

8. Spiro T. Agnew, *Go Quietly . . . Or Else* (New York: William Morrow, 1980), 34–38; Jules Witcover, *White Knight: The Rise of Spiro Agnew* (New York: Random House, 1972), 290–91, 296; Richard M. Cohen and Jules Witcover, *A Heartbeat Away: The Investigation and Resignation of Vice President Spiro T. Agnew* (New York: Viking, 1974), 145–46.

9. Agnew, *Go Quietly*, 95–97, 102–4, 190–91.

10. See David E. Kyvig, *Explicit and Authentic Acts: Amending the U.S. Constitution, 1776–1995* (Lawrence: University Press of Kansas, 1996), chap. 15.

11. See David E. Kyvig, ed., *Unintended Consequences of Constitutional Amendment* (Athens: University of Georgia Press, 2000).

12. Arlen Large, "Confirmation Hearings for Ford Look beyond the Vice Presidency," *Wall Street Journal*, November 2, 1973; Marjorie Hunter, "Ford and Albert Deal with Deep Problems," *New York Times*, November 3, 1973.

13. Quoted in U.S. Congress, Senate, Committee on Rules and Administration, *Nomination of Gerald R. Ford of Michigan to Be the Vice President of the United States: Hearings,* 93rd Cong., 1st sess. (Washington, D.C.: GPO, 1973), 4–6.

14. Quoted in ibid, 114.

15. Quoted in ibid, 124.

16. Quoted in Marjorie Hunter, "Senate Unit Backs Ford, 9 to 0," *New York Times*, November 21, 1973.

17. U.S. Congress, Senate, Committee on Rules and Administration, *Nomination of Gerald R. Ford;* Hunter, "Senate Unit Backs Ford"; Marjorie Hunter, "Ford Is Approved by Senate, 92–3," *New York Times*, November 28, 1973. A useful summary of the hearings can be found in James Cannon, *Time and Change: Gerald Ford's Appointment with History* (New York: HarperCollins, 1994), 233–51.

18. U.S. Congress, House, Committee on the Judiciary, *Nomination of Gerald R. Ford to Be the Vice President of the United States: Hearings,* 93rd Cong., 1st sess. (Washington, D.C.: GPO, 1973), 140–43, 266, 612–45.

19. U.S. Congress, House, Committee on the Judiciary, *Nomination of Gerald R. Ford,* 616–20, 645; *Chicago Tribune*, November 22, 1973; *New York Times,* November 22, 1973.

20. James M. Naughton, "A Watershed for Nixon," *New York Times*, December 7, 1973; the House hearings are summarized in Cannon, *Time and Change*, 254–57.

21. Naughton, "A Watershed for Nixon."

22. Cohen and Witcover, *A Heartbeat Away,* 272.

23. Quoted in Fields, *High Crimes and Misdemeanors,* 45.

24. George Gallup, "The Gallup Poll," *Washington Post*, November 13, 1973.

25. George Gallup, "The Gallup Poll," *Washington Post*, March 10, 1973; May 24, 1973; July 22, 1973; September 23, 1973; October 4, 1973; January 6, 1974; and July 26, 1974.

26. Smith and *Time* quoted in Kutler, *The Wars of Watergate,* 410–13; *Time,* November 12, 1973.

27. Elizabeth Drew, *Washington Journal: The Events of 1973–1974* (New York: Random House, 1974), 146.

28. U.S. Congress, House, Committee on the Judiciary, *Impeachment: Selected Materials,* 93rd Cong., 1st sess. (Washington, D.C.: GPO, 1973).

29. For a detailed history of the House impeachment, see Fields, *High Crimes and Misdemeanors.*

30. Kutler, *The Wars of Watergate*, 250–51.

31. Ken Gormley, *Archibald Cox: Conscience of a Nation* (Reading, Mass.: Addison-Wesley, 1997), 233–37, 268–70.

32. Kutler, *The Wars of Watergate*, 339.

33. Bill Clinton, *My Life* (New York: Knopf, 2004), 210–11; Hillary Rodham Clinton, *Living History* (New York: Scribner, 2003), 65–66.

34. John R. Labovitz, *Presidential Impeachment* (New Haven, Conn.: Yale University Press, 1978), 186.

35. Martin H. Belsky, interview with author, February 2, 2007.

36. Fields, *High Crimes and Misdemeanors*, 112–13.

37. Lou Cannon, "White House Feels Tide Is against Impeachment Vote," *Washington Post*, February 17, 1974.

38. Drew, *Washington Journal*, 168.

39. Cannon, "White House Feels Tide Is against Impeachment Vote."

40. U.S. Congress, House, Committee on the Judiciary, Impeachment Inquiry Staff, *Constitutional Grounds for Presidential Impeachment* (Washington, D.C.: Public Affairs Press, 1974).

41. Ibid.

42. Quoted in *Washington Post*, February 26, 1974.

43. Bill Kovach, "White House Moves to Narrow Grounds for an Impeachment," *New York Times*, March 1, 1974; Richard Lyons, "Nixon Lawyers Say Impeachment Requires an Indictable Crime," *Washington Post*, March 1, 1974.

44. Samuel Dash, *Chief Counsel: Inside the Ervin Committee—The Untold Story of Watergate* (New York: Random House, 1976), 223, 256.

45. Kutler, *The Wars of Watergate*, 444–49; Fields, *High Crimes and Misdemeanors*, 156.

46. Kutler, *The Wars of Watergate*, 449–55.

47. Ibid., 453–54.

48. Fields, *High Crimes and Misdemeanors*, 144.

49. Ibid., 157.

50. Ibid., 134–40, 157.

51. Ibid., 160–61.

52. Ibid., 201.

53. Ibid., 210–12.

54. Quoted in ibid., 215.

55. Quoted in Bob Woodward and Scott Armstrong, *The Brethren: Inside the Supreme Court* (New York: Simon & Schuster, 1979), 307.

56. Ibid., 312.

57. The William J. Brennan Papers at the Library of Congress contain a rich file on *United States v. Nixon*, including Warren Burger's first draft of an opinion, as well as memos from Brennan, Stewart, White, Douglas, Powell, and Blackmun offering substitute language for various sections of the opinion and endorsing his acceptance of their efforts to clarify and strengthen the ruling. See also Harry A. Blackmun and Thurgood Marshall Papers, Manuscript Division, Library of Congress, Washington, D.C.

58. William H. Rehnquist to Warren E. Burger, May 28, 1974, Brennan Papers.

59. Blackmun Papers; Marshall Papers; Woodward and Armstrong, *The Brethren*, 289–347.

60. *United States v. Nixon*, 418 U.S. 683 (1974).

61. U.S. Congress, House, Committee on the Judiciary, *Debate on Articles of Impeachment: Hearings*, 93rd Cong., 2nd sess. (Washington, D.C.: GPO, 1974), 5–6, 137–49. See also Donald A. Ritchie, *Reporting from Washington: The History of the Washington Press Corps* (New York: Oxford University Press, 2005), 208.

62. Kutler, *The Wars of Watergate*, 346, 531.

63. U.S. Congress, House, Committee on the Judiciary, *Debate on Articles of Impeachment,* 1–136.

64. Ibid., 19.

65. Ibid., 70. An excellent analysis of Butler's speech can be found in H. LaRue, *Political Discourse*, 142–52.

66. U.S. Congress, House, Committee on the Judiciary, *Debate on Articles of Impeachment,* 111–13.

67. Ibid., 133–34.

68. Ibid., 133–36.

69. Fields, *High Crimes and Misdemeanors*, 176–93.

70. Ibid., 206–23.

71. U.S. Congress, House, Committee on the Judiciary, *Debate on Articles of Impeachment,* 152–53.

72. Ibid., 161.

73. Ibid., 251–326; Fields, *High Crimes and Misdemeanors*, 263–69.

74. U.S. Congress, House, Committee on the Judiciary, *Debate on Articles of Impeachment,* 324–31.

75. Ibid., 334–35.

76. Fields, *High Crimes and Misdemeanors*, 275–77.

77. U.S. Congress, House, Committee on the Judiciary, *Debate on Articles of Impeachment,* 235–338.

78. Ibid., 338–447.

79. Fields, *High Crimes and Misdemeanors*, 276.

80. U.S. Congress, House, Committee on the Judiciary, *Debate on Articles of Impeachment,* 449–89.

81. Ibid., 37–39.

82. Ibid., 491–511.

83. Ibid., 492–517.

84. Ibid., 520–22.

85. Ibid., 522–59.

86. Floyd M. Riddick, interviewed by Donald A. Ritchie, September 28, 1978. United States Senate Historical Office, Washington, D.C.: Francis Valeo, impeachment file, Francis Valeo Papers, Manuscript Division, Library of Congress.

87. Robert Michel, interview with author, February 1, 2005; Fields, *High Crimes and Misdemeanors*, 285.

88. Fields, *High Crimes and Misdemeanors*, 291–92.

89. Drew, *Washington Journal*, 390; Douglas E. Kneeland, "Ford, Stumping in South, Draws Exuberant Crowds," *New York Times*, August 5, 1974; Gerald R. Ford, *A Time to Heal: The Autobiography of Gerald R. Ford* (New York: Harper & Row, 1979), 17.

90. Drew, *Washington Journal*, 398.

91. John Dean, interview with author, September 20, 2005.

92. Michel, interview with author; Robert Michel, "A Room Full of Tears," Robert Michel Papers, Dirksen Congressional Research Center, Pekin, Illinois.

7. Impeachment as Routine: Pardons, Powers, Prosecutors, and Judicial Self-Policing

1. Quoted in "Time for Healing," *Time*, August 19, 1974, 8–13.

2. Eileen Shanahan, "Nixon, Day before He Resigned, Sealed Pre-Presidential Papers for 11 Years," *New York Times*, August 18, 1974; Bob Kuttner, "Trials, Taxes Tangle Nixon's Papers," *Washington Post*, September 3, 1974.

3. Herblock cartoon, in Herbert Block, *Herblock Special Report* (New York: W. W. Norton, 1974), 254; originally published in *Washington Post,* September 12, 1974.

4. Quoted in U.S. Congress, Senate, Committee on Rules and Administration, *Nomination of Gerald R. Ford of Michigan to Be Vice President of the United States: Hearings,* 93rd Cong., 1st sess. (Washington, D.C.: GPO, 1973), 124.

5. Stanley I. Kutler, *The Wars of Watergate: The Last Crisis of Richard Nixon* (New York: Knopf, 1990), 558; "A Gallup Poll Finds 56% Want Nixon to Face Criminal Charges," *New York Times,* September 2, 1974.

6. Elizabeth Drew, *Washington Journal: The Events of 1973–1974* (New York: Random House, 1974), 396.

7. Gerald R. Ford, *A Time to Heal: The Autobiography of Gerald R. Ford* (New York: Harper & Row, 1979), 3–6. See also Ford's account of how he decided on the pardon and carried it out, pages 157–80.

8. Leonard Garment, *Crazy Rhythm: My Journey from Brooklyn, Jazz, and Wall Street to Nixon's White House, Watergate, and Beyond* (New York: Times Books, 1997), 301.

9. Ford, *A Time to Heal,* 156–61.

10. *Burdick v. U.S.,* 236 U.S. 79 (1915); Ford, *A Time to Heal,* 159–64.

11. Ford, *A Time to Heal,* 168–72.

12. Quoted in ibid., 169–70.

13. Ibid., 172–81.

14. *Washington Post,* September 1, 1974.

15. *New York Times,* September 11, 1974.

16. *Washington Post,* October 13, 1974.

17. Kutler, *The Wars of Watergate,* 569–71.

18. Arthur M. Schlesinger, Jr., *The Imperial Presidency* (Boston: Houghton Mifflin, 1973).

19. Harvey G. Zeidenstein, "The Reassertion of Congressional Power: New Curbs on the President," *Political Science Quarterly* 93(1978): 394–96.

20. Richard Madden, "Conferees Agree on Wide Reforms for U.S. Budgets," *New York Times,* June 6, 1974; "Congress Gains Wide Budget Role," *New York Times,* July 13, 1974; *Christian Science Monitor,* June 7, 1974; *Washington Post,* June 19 and 30, 1974; Melvin Small, *The Presidency of Richard Nixon* (Lawrence: University Press of Kansas, 1999), 200.

21. *New York Times,* July 27, 28, and 31, 1974; *Washington Post,* September 19, November 16 and 28, December 6, 1974.

22. *Washington Post,* April 12, 1974.

23. *New York Times,* June 29 and July 2, 1974.

24. *Washington Post,* August 4, and 9, 1974; *New York Times,* August 5, 1974.

25. *New York Times,* September 17, October 6, and October 10, 1974; *Washington Post,* September 22 and October 1, 1974.

26. Quoted in *Washington Post,* October 16, 1974.

27. *Buckley v. Valeo,* 424 U.S. 1 (1976).

28. *Washington Post,* March 21, 1974.

29. *New York Times,* March 15, 1974; *Wall Street Journal,* March 15, 1974.

30. *New York Times,* May 31, 1974.

31. Jerald F. terHorst, "Ford's Door Slammed by Nixon Holdovers," *Chicago Tribune,* November 1, 1974; *Washington Post,* August 23, September 11, and September 26, 1974.

32. *Washington Post,* October 18, 1974.

33. *Los Angeles Times,* October 21, 1974; *Washington Post,* October 21, 1974; *Chicago Tribune,* October 19, 1974.

34. James M. Naughton, "House Overrides Two Ford Vetoes by Huge Margins," *New York Times,* November 21, 1974; *Washington Post,* November 21, 22, 1974.

35. Richard D. Lyons, "Papers and Tapes Issues in Capital," *New York Times*, August 10, 1974; Shanahan, "Nixon, Day before He Resigned, Sealed Pre-Presidential Papers for 11 Years"; *Washington Post,* September 3, 1974.

36. Lyons, "Papers and Tapes Issues in Capital"; "Plan for Public Access to Nixon Papers Gains," *Washington Post,* September 17, 1974.

37. *Los Angeles Times*, October 4, 1974; "Congress Passes Nixon Tapes Bill," *New York Times,* December 10, 1974; "Ford Signs Bill on Nixon Papers," *New York Times,* December 20, 1974.

38. *Nixon v. Administrator of General Services*, 433 U.S. 425 (1977).

39. Sandra E. Richetti, "Congressional Power vis-à-vis the President and Presidential Papers," *Duquesne Law Review* 32 (1994): 782–90.

40. Kutler, *The Wars of Watergate*, 427–29.

41. Katy J. Harriger, *The Special Prosecutor in American Politics,* 2nd ed. rev. (Lawrence: University Press of Kansas, 2000), 52–54.

42. Ibid., 56–57.

43. Ibid., 57–59.

44. Ibid., 59–62.

45. *Morrison v. Olson,* 487 U.S. 654 (1988).

46. Ibid., 697–734.

47. Richard Ben-Veniste, interview with author, March 24, 2005.

48. "U.S. District Judge Is Stripped of All Duties by Judicial Panel," *New York Times*, December 29, 1965; "Oklahoma Judge Appeals to High Court," *New York Times,* January 7, 1966; "Dropped U.S. Judge Offered a Hearing by Judicial Council," *New York Times,* January 14, 1966; Fred Graham, "Can Judges Silence a Judge?" *New York Times,* January 16, 1966; *Washington Post*, January 2, 1966.

49. Quoted in Fred Graham, "Chandler Controversy Prompts Inquiry in Senate," *New York Times*, February 15, 1966.

50. Quoted in "Senate Unit Airs Unfit Judge Issue," *New York Times*, February 16, 1966.

51. *Washington Post*, December 18, 1969.

52. *Chandler v. Judicial Council,* 398 U.S. 74 (1970), 94–111.

53. Ibid., 85.

54. Ibid., 142.

55. *Washington Post*, March 20, 1970; "U.S. Judge Stephen Chandler, 89; Often Feuded with His Colleagues," *New York Times*, April 29, 1989.

56. Albin Krebs, "Kerner Resigns Seat," *New York Times*, July 25, 1974; Seth S. King, "Otto Kerner Goes to Jail Today, His Once-Shining Career at End," *New York Times*, July 29, 1974; Mary L. Volcansek, *Judicial Impeachment: None Called for Justice* (Urbana: University of Illinois Press, 1993), 8–9.

57. Patrick Donald McCalla, "Judicial Disciplining of Federal Judges Is Constitutional," *Southern California Law Review* 62 (1989): 1265–67.

58. Quoted in Volcansek, *Judicial Impeachment*, 11.

59. *Congressional Quarterly, CQ Almanac* 1980, 391; Volcansek, *Judicial Impeachment,* 12–13.

60. Lewis L. Gould, *The Modern American Presidency* (Lawrence: University Press of Kansas, 2003), 167.

61. Obituary of Gerald R. Ford, *New York Times*, December 28, 2006.

8. Impeachment as Cultural: Shaping Public Conclusions

1. Quoted by Lawrence R. Meyer, interview with author, April 6, 2006.

2. An extended examination of political journalism in 1972 can be found in Timothy Crouse, *The Boys on the Bus* (New York: Ballantine, 1973). Chapter 13 offers an assessment of how

Woodward and Bernstein's Watergate reporting fit into the larger picture. A more recent examination of political press coverage before, during, and after Watergate, Donald A. Ritchie, *Reporting from Washington: The History of the Washington Press Corps* (New York: Oxford University Press, 2005), provides additional insight, especially in chapter 10.

3. A dual biography of the two reporters that explores their lives before and after as well as during Watergate is Alicia C. Shepard, *Woodward and Bernstein: Life in the Shadow of Watergate* (Hoboken, N.J.: John Wiley, 2007).

4. Carl Bernstein and Bob Woodward, *All the President's Men* (New York: Simon & Schuster, 1974); Crouse, *The Boys on the Bus.*

5. Bernstein and Woodward, *All the President's Men.*

6. Shepard, *Woodward and Bernstein,* 115–18.

7. Ibid., 88–90.

8. Bob Woodward and Carl Bernstein, *The Final Days* (New York: Simon & Schuster, 1976). Subsequent paragraphs draw on the book.

9. Quoted in Woodward and Bernstein, *The Final Days,* 471.

10. Quoted in ibid., 497 and 508.

11. Shepard, *Woodward and Bernstein,* 115–21, 125, 130–38, 143.

12. Ibid., 141–42.

13. American Film Institute, "100 Years . . . 100 Heroes and Villains."

14. David Frost, *"I Gave Them a Sword": Behind the Scenes of the Nixon Interviews* (New York: William Morrow, 1978).

15. Ibid., 13.

16. Ibid., 14.

17. Ibid., 11–14.

18. Ibid., 15–28.

19. Ibid., 32–70; Robert Sam Anson, *Exile: The Unquiet Oblivion of Richard M. Nixon* (New York: Simon & Schuster, 1984), 153–54, 163.

20. Frost, *"I Gave Them a Sword,"* 37, 51, 54–85, and James Reston, Jr., *The Conviction of Richard Nixon: The Untold Story of the Frost/Nixon Interviews* (New York: Harmony, 2007), 23–106, provide participant accounts.

21. Anson, *Exile,* 45–53.

22. Nixon quoted in Frost, *"I Gave Them a Sword,"* 86–173; Anson, *Exile,* 159.

23. Anson, *Exile,* 137–38, 153–54, 163.

24. James Reston, Jr., interview with author, June 15, 2006; Frost, *"I Gave Them a Sword,"* 54–55.

25. Quoted in Frost, *"I Gave Them a Sword,"* 196–98.

26. Ibid., 198–203.

27. Ibid., 200–201.

28. Quoted in ibid., 217.

29. Quoted in ibid., 225.

30. Ibid., 225–26.

31. Ibid., 226–33.

32. Ibid., 237–38.

33. Reston, interview with author, June 15, 2006.

34. Frost, *"I Gave Them a Sword,"* 239–40.

35. Quoted in ibid., 241–42.

36. Quoted in ibid., 243.

37. Quoted in ibid., 244–45.

38. Quoted in ibid., 245.

39. Reston, *The Conviction of Richard Nixon,* 152–57.

40. Howard Fields, *High Crimes and Misdemeanors* (New York: W. W. Norton, 1978), 298.

41. Frost, *"I Gave Them a Sword,"* 246.

42. Quoted in ibid., 248.

43. David Greenberg, *Nixon's Shadow: The History of an Image* (New York: W. W. Norton, 2003), 213.

44. "Nixon on His Fall," *Newsweek,* June 6, 1977, 28–33.

45. Reston, interview with author, June 15, 2006. Reston said essentially the same thing in a memoir of his experience with Frost that he wrote in 1977 immediately after the broadcasts and published in 2007 as *The Conviction of Richard Nixon.*

46. Anson, *Exile,* 263–65.

47. Michael Schudson, *Watergate in American Memory: How We Remember, Forget, and Reconstruct the Past* (New York: Basic Books, 1992); Greenberg, *Nixon's Shadow.*

48. Among the most influential memoirs, since they appeared in the first five years after Nixon's resignation, were Samuel Dash, *Chief Counsel: Inside the Ervin Committee—The Untold Story of Watergate* (New York: Random House, 1976); John W. Dean III, *Blind Ambition* (New York: Simon & Schuster, 1976); Leon Jaworski, *The Right and the Power: The Prosecution of Watergate* (New York: Reader's Digest Press, 1976); Richard Ben-Veniste and George Frampton, Jr., *Stonewall: The Real Story of the Watergate Prosecution* (New York: Simon & Schuster, 1977); H. R. Haldeman, *The Ends of Power,* with Joseph DiMona (New York: Times Books, 1978); and John Sirica, *To Set the Record Straight: The Break-in, the Tapes, the Conspirators, the Pardon* (New York: W. W. Norton, 1979).

49. Victor Lasky, *It Didn't Start with Watergate* (New York: Dial, 1977); Jim Hogan, *Secret Agenda: Watergate, Deep Throat, and the CIA* (New York: Random House, 1984); and Len Colodny and Robert Gettlin, *Silent Coup: The Removal of a President* (New York: St. Martin's Press, 1991).

50. Most notable was Fawn Brodie, *Richard Nixon: The Shaping of His Character* (New York: W. W. Norton, 1981).

51. Greenberg, *Nixon's Shadow,* 203.

52. Ibid., 345.

53. Stephen E. Ambrose, *Nixon,* 3 vols. (New York: Simon & Schuster, 1987–91), 3:597, quoted in Greenberg, *Nixon's Shadow,* 329.

54. Richard Nixon, *RN: The Memoirs of Richard* Nixon (New York: Grosset & Dunlap, 1978), x.

55. Ibid., 625–46.

56. Ibid., 646.

57. Ibid., 848.

58. Ibid., 935.

59. John Herbers, "Nixon, in Memoirs, Admits Cover-Up on Watergate," *New York Times,* April 30, 1978; *Chicago Tribune,* April 30, 1978.

60. *Chicago Tribune,* May 3, 1978; Herbert Mitgang, "Nixon Book Dispute Erupts at Meeting," *New York Times,* May 28, 1978; "Don't Buy Books by Crooks?" *New York Times,* May 31, 1978.

61. Richard Nixon, *In the Arena: A Memoir of Victory, Defeat, and Renewal* (New York: Simon & Schuster, 1990), 34.

62. Ibid., 36–38.

63. Ibid., 41.

64. Ibid., 21–22.

65. Monica Crowley, *Nixon in Winter* (New York: Random House, 1998), xiii–xv.

66. Ibid., 283–317.

67. Stanley I. Kutler, *The Wars of Watergate: The Last Crisis of Richard Nixon* (New York: Knopf, 1990), 615.

68. The Criterion Collection DVD of *Secret Honor* contains commentaries by director Robert Altman, playwright Donald Freed, and actor Philip Baker Hall, from which the information in this and subsequent paragraphs is taken.

69. Quoted from Altman, Criterion Collection DVD of *Secret Honor*.

70. Oliver Stone, *Nixon,* Hollywood Pictures, 1995.

71. Ibid.

72. Andrew Fleming, *Dick,* Columbia Pictures, 1999.

73. Vincent Canby, "Of Nixon and Kissinger: What Might Have Been," *New York Times*, March 13, 1996.

74. Niels Mueller, *The Assassination of Richard Nixon*, 2004.

75. Peter Morgan, *Frost/Nixon* (London: Faber and Faber, 2006), 78.

76. Ibid., 82.

77. Paul Taylor, *Independent*, August 22, 2006; Nicholas de Jongh, *Evening Standard,* August 22, 2006; Michael Billington, *Guardian*, August 22, 2006; Benedict Nightingale, *Times* (London), August 22, 2006.

78. In addition to Nixon's, memoirs appeared from Agnew, Dean, Ehrlichman, Haldeman, Kleindienst, and lesser lights.

79. *Chicago Tribune*, January 10, 1982; *Washington Post*, February 21, 1983.

80. The classic studies are Fred I. Greenstein, *Children and Politics* (New Haven, Conn.: Yale University Press, 1965), and David Easton and Jack Dennis, *Children in the Political System: The Origins of Political Legitimacy* (New York: McGraw-Hill, 1969). See also Stanley W. Moore, Kenneth Wagner, James Lare, and D. Stephen McHargue II, "The Civic Awareness of Five and Six Year Olds," *Western Political Quarterly* 29 (September 1976): 410–24.

81. F. Christopher Arterton, "The Impact of Watergate on Children's Attitudes toward Political Authority," *Political Science Quarterly* 89 (June 1974): 269–88.

82. Ibid., 272–83.

83. F. Christopher Arterton, "Watergate and Children's Attitudes toward Political Authority Revisted" *Political Science Quarterly,* 90 (1975): 477–88.

9. Impeachment as Distasteful: The Case of Ronald Reagan

1. This account of Reagan's life before the presidency draws on Garry Wills, *Reagan's America: Innocents at Home* (Garden City, N.Y.: Doubleday, 1987); Haynes Johnson, *Sleepwalking through History: America in the Reagan Years* (New York: W. W. Norton, 1991); and Jules Tygiel, *Ronald Reagan and the Triumph of American Conservatism* (New York: Pearson, 2005).

2. Quoted in Rick Perlstein, *Before the Storm: Barry Goldwater and the Unmaking of the American Consensus* (New York: Hill & Wang, 2001), 122.

3. Ibid., 166, 350, 499–510.

4. "The President's News Conference, January 29, 1981," in *Public Papers of the Presidents of the United States: Ronald Reagan, 1981,* 55–62 (Washington, D.C.: GPO, 1982), 57.

5. "The President's News Conference, June 18, 1985," in *Public Papers of the Presidents of the United States: Ronald Reagan, 1985,* 1:778–85 (Washington, D.C.: GPO, 1988), 1:779.

6. "Move for Impeachment Is Begun by 7 in House," *New York Times*, November 11, 1983.

7. James F. Clarity and William E. Farrell, "Briefing: Reagan Impeachment Drive," *Washington Post,* December 29, 1983.

8. A detailed account of U.S.–Central American relations during the 1980s can be found in Theodore Draper, *A Very Thin Line: The Iran-Contra Affairs* (New York: Hill & Wang, 1991).

9. Johnson, *Sleepwalking through History,* 275–76.

10. Draper, *A Very Thin Line,* 17–19.

11. Quoted in ibid., 22–23.

12. Johnson, *Sleepwalking through History,* 280; Draper, *A Very Thin Line,* 25.

13. "House Passes First Foreign Aid Bill since '81," *New York Times,* August 1, 1985.

14. Jane Mayer and Doyle McManus, *Landslide: The Unmaking of the President, 1984–1988* (Boston: Houghton Mifflin, 1988), 248–49.

15. Quoted in Johnson, *Sleepwalking through History,* 281.

16. Ibid., 281–83.

17. Quoted in ibid, 283.

18. Joel Brinkley, "Nicaraguan Rebels Getting Advice from White House on Operations," *New York Times,* August 8, 1985; Gerald M. Boyd, "Role in Nicaragua Described by U.S.," *New York Times,* August 9, 1985.

19. Ronald Reagan, *The Reagan Diaries,* edited by Douglas Brinkley (New York: HarperCollins, 2007), 450.

20. Ibid., 381.

21. "Address to the Nation on the Iran Arms and Contra Aid Controversy, November 13, 1986," in *Public Papers of the Presidents of the United States: Ronald Reagan, 1986,* 2:1546–48 (Washington, D.C.: GPO, 1989).

22. Draper, *A Very Thin Line,* 482–84; "The President's News Conference, November 19, 1986," in *Public Papers of the Presidents: Ronald Reagan, 1986,* 2:1567–75; "Statement on the Iran Arms and Contra Aid Controversy, November 19, 1986," in *Public Papers of the Presidents: Ronald Reagan, 1986,* 2:1575.

23. William S. Cohen and George J. Mitchell, *Men of Zeal: A Candid Inside Story of the Iran-Contra Hearings* (New York: Viking, 1988), 221–29.

24. David Johnston, "Meese Testifies That Impeachment Was a Worry," *New York Times,* March 28, 1989. See also Lou Cannon, *President Reagan: The Role of a Lifetime* (New York: Simon & Schuster, 1991), 704.

25. Quoted in Draper, *A Very Thin Line,* 522.

26. Michael Schudson, *Watergate in American Memory: How We Remember, Forget, and Reconstruct the Past* (New York: Basic Books, 1992), 168.

27. Quoted in Lawrence E. Walsh, *Firewall: The Iran-Contra Conspiracy and Cover-up* (New York: W. W. Norton, 1997), 360.

28. Cannon, *President Reagan,* 704.

29. Quoted in Draper, *A Very Thin Line,* 552.

30. Quoted in David Hoffman and Lou Cannon, "'I'm Not Going to Back Off'; Reagan, Facing a Deepening Crisis, Expresses Defiance, Hits News Media," *Washington Post,* December 1, 1986.

31. See Raoul Berger, *Impeachment: The Constitutional Problems* (Cambridge, Mass.: Harvard University Press, 1973); Charles L. Black, *Impeachment: A Handbook* (New Haven, Conn.: Yale University Press, 1974), 46; Schudson, *Watergate in American Memory,* 177.

32. Draper, *A Very Thin Line,* 552.

33. Susan F. Basky, "Inquiry into N.S.C. Uncovering Little about Iran Deals," *New York Times,* January 18, 1987; Bob Woodward, "Iran Panel Presses to See Reagan," *Washington Post,* January 19, 1987; Susan Okie and Chris Spolar, "McFarlane Takes Drug Overdose," *Washington Post,* February 10, 1987; David Hoffman, "McFarlane Struggled to Cope with Career Dip, Friends Say," *Washington Post,* February 11, 1987; Martin Tolchin, "Friends' Views of McFarlane: Failed Himself," *New York Times,* February 11, 1987.

34. Quoted in Walsh, *Firewall,* 369; Cannon, *President Reagan,* 708–12.

35. "Fair, Respectful—and Humiliating," *New York Times,* February 27, 1987; "The Tower Report," *Washington Post,* February 27, 1987.

36. Anthony Lewis, "The Empty Chair," *New York Times,* February 27, 1987.

37. *Washington Post,* December 2, 1986.

38. Richard J. Meislin, "Poll Shows a Slight Rise in Approval for Reagan since Iran Report," *New York Times,* March 31, 1987.

39. *New York Times*, February 28, 1987; *Washington Post*, February 28, 1987.

40. Bob Woodward, interview with author, May 20, 2005; Woodward, *Shadow: Five Presidents and the Legacy of Watergate* (New York: Simon & Schuster, 1999), 151.

41. "Address to the Nation on the Iran Arms and Contra Aid Controversy, March 4, 1987," in *Public Papers of the Presidents of the United States: Ronald Reagan, 1987,* 1:208–11 (Washington, D.C.: GPO, 1989); Cannon, *President Reagan,* 733–35; see also Jane Mayer and John Walcott, "President Reagan Admits Arms for Hostages Swap by His Administration and Says It Was 'a Mistake,'" *Wall Street Journal*, March 5, 1987.

42. Gerald M. Boyd, "Top Aides Cheer Reagan's Pep Talk," *New York Times*, March 31, 1987.

43. David Hoffman, "Poll Finds Growing Majority Disbelieves Reagan on Iran," *Washington Post*, April 15, 1987.

44. Bob Woodward, "Contra Aid Findings Withheld," *Washington Post*, January 6, 1987.

45. Daniel Inouye, interview with author, March 8, 2005.

46. Ibid.

47. John Dean, interview with author, September 20, 2005.

48. Cohen and Mitchell, *Men of Zeal,* 56–57.

49. Lee Hamilton, interview with author, June 28, 2005.

50. David E. Rosenbaum, "Iran Panels to Start Immunity Process This Week," *New York Times*, February 24, 1987.

51. Arthur L. Liman and Mark A. Belnick, "Congress Had to Immunize North," *Washington Post*, July 29, 1990.

52. Richard Ben-Veniste, interview with author, March 24, 2005.

53. Daniel Schorr, interview with author, October 19, 2004.

54. Cohen and Mitchell, *Men of Zeal,* 62–129.

55. Ibid., 118–43.

56. Ibid., 147–93.

57. Ibid., 194–210.

58. Ibid., 210–20.

59. Ibid., 242–48.

60. Daniel K. Inouye and Lee. H. Hamilton, *Report of the Congressional Committees Investigating the Iran-Contra Affair*, abridged ed. (New York: Times Books, 1988), 33.

61. Ibid., 361.

62. Cohen and Mitchell, *Men of Zeal,* 45.

63. Ibid., 46–50.

64. "Iran-Contra's Unfollowed Leads," *New York Times*, May 2, 1990.

65. Richard Cheney et al., "Minority Report," in Inouye and Hamilton, *Report of the Congressional Committees Investigating the Iran-Contra Affair*, 375.

66. Christopher Lehmann-Haupt, "Books of the Times," *New York Times*, September 30, 1987.

67. Ethan Bronner, *Battle for Justice: How the Bork Nomination Shook America* (New York: W. W. Norton, 1989), esp. 317.

68. Reagan, *The Reagan Diaries*, 549.

69. Lawrence Walsh's memoir, *Firewall,* provides a detailed account of his struggles to pursue the case and the resistance he faced.

70. Ibid., 206.

71. Joe Pichirallo, "Reagan Says He Told Aides 'We Don't Break the Law,'" *Washington Post*, February 23, 1990.

72. Joe Pichirallo, "Poindexter Gets 6 Months in Prison," *Washington Post*, June 12, 1990; Walsh, *Firewall*, 222–46.

73. Walsh, *Firewall*, 317–54.

74. Ibid., 437, 441–43; Woodward, *Shadow*, 200.

75. Walsh, *Firewall*, 451–54, 488–89.

76. Woodward, *Shadow*, 197–98; Walsh, *Firewall*, 490–94.

77. "The Best Case for the Pardons," *New York Times*, December 28, 1992.

78. Ibid.; Walsh, *Firewall*, 507.

79. Quoted in Walsh, *Firewall*, 493.

80. Ibid., 493–94.

81. Ibid., 501–3.

82. Anthony Lewis, "George Milhous Bush," *New York Times*, December 28, 1992.

83. Walsh, *Firewall*, 515.

84. Lawrence E. Walsh, *Final Report of the Independent Counsel for Iran/Contra Matters*, vol. 1, *Investigations and Prosecutions* (Washington, D.C.: United States Court of Appeals for the District of Columbia Circuit, August 4, 1993).

85. Edwin Yoder, "Reagan Was Responsible," *Washington Post*, May 7, 1990.

86. Ibid.

87. Linda Greenhouse, "Law Ill-Equipped for Politics," *New York Times*, December 28, 1992.

10. Impeachment as Inexorable: The Cases of Harry Claiborne and Walter Nixon

1. This account of Claiborne's prosecution and trial is drawn from Mary L. Volcansek, *Judicial Impeachment: None Called for Justice* (Urbana: University of Illinois Press, 1993), chap. 2.

2. Quoted in Mary Thornton, "Impeached Judge Ends Testimony," *Washington Post*, September 24, 1986.

3. Two scholars who have studied the Claiborne case carefully both reached the same conclusion as the jury. See Volcansek, *Judicial Impeachment*, chap. 2, and Eleanor Bushnell, *Crimes, Follies, and Misfortunes: The Federal Impeachment Trials* (Urbana: University of Illinois Press, 1992), chap. 13.

4. *Washington Post*, May 17, 1986; *Wall Street Journal*, July 23, 1986; *New York Times*, July 24, 1986.

5. Quoted in *Washington Post*, June 3, 1986.

6. *Washington Post*, May 23, 1986.

7. *Washington Post*, June 3 and 4, 1986.

8. U.S. Congress, House, Committee on the Judiciary, Subcommittee on Courts, Civil Liberties, and the Administration of Justice, *Subcommittee Markup of House Resolution 461, Impeachment of Judge Harry E. Claiborne*, 99th Cong., 2nd sess. (Washington, D.C.: GPO, 1986), 2.

9. U.S. Congress, House, Committee on the Judiciary, Subcommittee on Courts, Civil Liberties, and the Administration of Justice, *Conduct of Harry E. Claiborne, U.S. District Judge, District of Nevada: Hearing*, 99th Cong., 2nd sess. (Washington, D.C.: GPO, 1986).

10. U.S. Congress, House, Committee on the Judiciary, Subcommittee on Courts, Civil Liberties, and the Administration of Justice, *Subcommittee Markup of House Resolution 461, Impeachment of Judge Harry E. Claiborne*.

11. Ibid.

12. *Washington Post*, July 23, 1986.

13. Volcansek, *Judicial Impeachment*, 54.

14. U.S. Congress, Senate, Impeachment Trial Committee, *Report of the Impeachment Trial Committee*, 99th Cong., 2nd sess. (Washington, D.C.: GPO, 1986), 1:18–19.

15. Ibid., 1:41–118, 463–71.

16. Ibid., 1:531–657.

17. Ibid. The transcript of Claiborne's August 1984 district court trial can be found in parts II and III of the report.

18. Ibid., 1:924–1180.

19. U.S. Congress, Senate, *Proceedings in the Impeachment Trial of Harry E. Claiborne,* 99th Cong., 2nd. sess. (Washington, D.C.: GPO, 1987), 158.

20. Ibid., 107–8.

21. Ibid., 150.

22. Ibid., 31.

23. Ibid., 301–74.

24. Ibid., 290–97.

25. Bushnell, *Crimes, Follies, and Misfortunes,* 302.

26. U.S. Congress, Senate, *Proceedings in the Impeachment Trial of Harry E. Claiborne,* 314, 328–29, 340–41, 343, 354.

27. Ibid., 303, 311, 315–16.

28. Bushnell, *Crimes, Follies, and Misfortunes,* 303–4; quoted in *Las Vegas Review Journal,* January 21, 2004.

29. Biographical information can be found in "Presentencing Report, for Judge Walter L. Nixon, Jr.," in U.S. Congress, House, Committee on the Judiciary, Subcommittee on Civil and Constitutional Rights, *Judge Walter L. Nixon, Jr., Impeachment Inquiry: Hearings,* 100th Cong., 2nd sess. (Washington, D.C.: GPO, 1988), Appendix 1.

30. Volcansek, *Judicial Impeachment,* 121; *New York Times,* May 30 and June 7, 1968.

31. This account of the investigation and trial of Walter Nixon draws on Volcansek, *Judicial Impeachment,* chap. 6, and the voluminous records of U.S. Congress, House, Committee on the Judiciary, Subcommittee on Civil and Constitutional Rights, *Judge Walter L. Nixon, Jr., Impeachment Inquiry.*

32. U.S. Congress, House, Committee on the Judiciary, Subcommittee on Civil and Constitutional Rights, *Judge Walter L. Nixon, Jr., Impeachment Inquiry,* 10–11.

33. Boyce Holleman and William B. Jeffress, Jr., "Memorandum, June 7, 1986," in U.S. Senate, Impeachment Trial Committee, *Report of the Senate Impeachment Trial Committee on the Articles against Judge Walter L. Nixon, Jr.: Hearings,* 101st Cong., 1st sess. (Washington, D.C.: GPO, 1989), 2:4B:1847–58.

34. "Presentencing Report, for Judge Walter L. Nixon, Jr.," 641.

35. Quoted in *Jackson (Miss.) Clarion Ledger,* January 21, 1988.

36. Quoted in *New York Times,* February 12, 1986.

37. H. Res. 407, *Congressional Record,* 100th Cong., 2nd sess., vol. 134: 4220.

38. U.S. Congress, House, Committee on the Judiciary, Subcommittee on Civil and Constitutional Rights, *Judge Walter L. Nixon, Jr., Impeachment Inquiry,* 2.

39. Ibid.

40. Volcansek, *Judicial Impeachment,* 146.

41. U.S. Congress, Senate, Impeachment Trial Committee, *Report on the Articles against Judge Walter L. Nixon, Jr.,* 1:9–10.

42. Ibid., 1:292–95.

43. Ibid., 1:296–99.

44. Ibid., 1:319–27.

45. Ibid., 2:2.

46. Ibid., 2:2–16.

47. Ibid., 2:3225.

48. U.S. Congress, Senate, *Proceedings of the United States Senate in the Impeachment Trial of Walter L. Nixon, Jr.,* 101st Cong., 1st sess. (Washington, D.C.: GPO, 1989): 1–359.

49. Ibid., 366–421, with the Nixon quotation at 385. See also *New York Times,* November 4, 1989.

50. U.S. Congress, Senate, *Proceedings of the United States Senate in the Impeachment Trial of Walter L. Nixon, Jr.,* 427–37.

51. Ibid., 443–65.

52. Neil A. Lewis, "Senate Conviction of U.S. Judge Is Set Aside as Unfairly Reached," *New York Times,* September 18, 1992.

53. "Supreme Court Debates Senate Trial Procedure," *New York Times,* October 15, 1992.

54. *Nixon v. United States,* 506 U.S. 224 (1993).

55. Ibid.

56. Ibid., 238.

57. *Biloxi (Miss.) Sun Herald,* August 8, 2001.

11. Impeachment as Irreversible But Not Fatal: The Case of Alcee Hastings

1. Mary L. Volcansek, *Judicial Impeachment: None Called for Justice* (Urbana: University of Illinois Press, 1993), 69–70; Alan J. Baron, "The Curious Case of Alcee Hastings," *Nova Law Review* 18 (1994–1995): 873.

2. The most detailed accounts of the case appear in U.S. Congress, House, Committee on the Judiciary, Subcommittee on Criminal Justice, *In the Matter of the Impeachment Inquiry Concerning U.S. District Judge Alcee L. Hastings: Hearings,* 100th Cong., 1st sess. (Washington, D.C.: GPO, 1987), and U.S. Congress, Senate, Impeachment Trial Committee, *Report on the Articles against Judge Alcee L. Hastings,* 101st Cong., 1st sess. (Washington, D.C.: GPO, 1989). A summary can be found in Volcansek, *Judicial Impeachment,* 70–75.

3. Volcansek, *Judicial Impeachment,* 70–83.

4. Ibid., 83–85.

5. Ibid., 84–85, 87–88.

6. Alcee L. Hastings, interview with author, February 18, 2005.

7. Volcansek, *Judicial Impeachment,* 85–87.

8. Quoted in ibid, 88.

9. Investigating Committee of the Judicial Council of the Eleventh Circuit, "In the Matter of Certain Complaints against United States District Judge Alcee L. Hastings," in U.S. Congress, House, Committee on the Judiciary, Subcommittee on Criminal Justice, *In the Matter of the Impeachment Inquiry Concerning U.S. District Judge Alcee L. Hastings: Hearings,* Appendix 1, 1–346.

10. Ibid., Appendix 1, 347–48.

11. Ibid., Appendix 1, 1–358.

12. *Report of the Proceedings of the Judicial Conference of the United States,* March 17, 1987 (Washington, D.C. 1987), 41–42.

13. Volcansek, *Judicial Impeachment,* 103.

14. Ibid., 106.

15. U.S. Congress, House, Committee on the Judiciary, *Impeachment of Judge Alcee L. Hastings: Report to Accompany H. Res. 499,* 100th Cong., 2nd sess. (Washington, D.C.: GPO, 1988), 1–12.

16. *Congressional Record,* 100th Cong., 2nd sess., vol. 134 (August 3, 1988): 20213–14.

17. Baron, "The Curious Case of Alcee Hastings," 875.

18. Alan I. Baron, interview with author, October 5, 2005.

19. A reliable guide to the entire chronology is Volcansek, *Judicial Impeachment.*

20. U.S. Congress, Senate, *Proceedings in the Impeachment Trial of Alcee L. Hastings,* 101st Cong., 1st sess. (Washington, D.C.: GPO, 1989), 13–21.

21. Ibid., 21–30.

22. Ibid., 31–46.

23. Ibid., 55–56.

24. Ibid., 45.

25. U.S. Congress, Senate, Impeachment Trial Committee, *Report on the Articles against Judge Alcee L. Hastings,* 101st Cong., 1st sess. (Washington, D.C.: GPO, 1989), pt. 2A, 2–22.

26. Ibid., pt. 2A, 532–610, quote at 569.

27. Ibid., pt. 2A, 676–741.

28. U.S. Congress, Senate, *Proceedings in the Impeachment Trial of Alcee L. Hastings,* 627–35.

29. U.S. Congress, Senate, Impeachment Trial Committee, *Report on the Articles against Judge Alcee L. Hastings,* pt. 2A, 1261–62.

30. Ibid., pt. 2A, 1156–68, 1777–83, 2300, 2408, 2531, 2535–45.

31. U.S. Congress, Senate, *Proceedings in the Impeachment Trial of Alcee L. Hastings,* 627–73.

32. Ibid., 710–14.

33. Ibid., 714–68.

34. Ibid., 758–59.

35. Ibid., 764–72, 792–97, 799.

36. Ibid., 772–74, 797–99.

37. Ibid., 759–60.

38. Ibid., 760–63.

39. Ibid., 774–75, 763–64, 775–90.

40. Ibid., 790.

41. Ibid., 790–92.

42. Baron, "The Curious Case of Alcee Hastings," 877.

43. U.S. Congress, Senate, *Proceedings in the Impeachment Trial of Alcee L. Hastings,* 15–17.

44. Ibid., 688–703.

45. Ibid., 708–9.

46. H. Res. 176 and 177, *Congressional Record,* 103rd Cong., 1st sess., vol. 139 (May 19, 1993): H2597.

47. David Johnston, "Federal Judge Is Focus of Bribe Inquiry," *New York Times,* September 27, 1990; "U.S. Judge Indicted in New Orleans Bribery Case," *New York Times,* February 9, 1991.

48. Francis Frank Marcus, "U.S. Judge Faces Bribery Trial in New Orleans," *New York Times,* June 16, 1991; Marcus, "U.S. Judge Is Convicted in New Orleans Bribe Case," *New York Times,* June 30, 1991; "U.S. Judge Is Given Prison Sentence," *New York Times,* September 7, 1991.

49. Emily Field Van Tassel, "Resignations and Removals: A History of Federal Judicial Service—and Disservice—1789–1993," *University of Pennsylvania Law Review* 142 (1993): 337–38.

50. "Judge Denies Hewlett Motion," *New York Times,* August 3, 1988; "Ruling in Case of Apple Suit," *New York Times,* September 26, 1988; *Wall Street Journal,* August 3, 17, and 19, September 26, October 26, 1988.

51. *United States v. Robert P. Aguilar,* 515 U.S. 593 (1995).

52. U.S. Department of Justice, press release, June 24, 1996.

53. Baron, "The Curious Case of Alcee Hastings," 902.

54. David Johnston, "Hastings Ousted as U.S. Judge by Senate Vote," *New York Times,* October 21, 1989.

55. Volcansek, *Judicial Impeachment,* 116.

56. Hastings, interview with author, February 18, 2005.

57. Robert Michel, interview with author, February 1, 2005.

58. Hastings, interview with author, February 18, 2005.

59. Lee Hamilton, interviews with author, November 3, 2004, and June 28, 2005; Thomas Foley, interview with author, March 14, 2005; Ray LaHood, interview with author, April 13, 2005.

60. *Washington Post,* June 15, 2006.

61. Neil Lewis, "F.B.I. Director Is Accused of Missteps in Lab Furor," *New York Times,* March 7, 1997.

62. Hastings, interview with author, February 18, 2005.

63. Quoted in *New York Times,* November 29, 2006.

64. *Congressional Record,* 110th Cong, 1st sess., vol. 153 (January 10, 2007): H255.

65. Hastings, interview with author, February 18, 2005.

12. Impeachment as Consensual: The Case of Bill Clinton

1. This section on Congress is informed by the comments of a number of members of Congress in the course of interviews with the author, including Vic Fazio, February 8, 2005; Tom Foley, March 14, 2005; Martin Frost, April 12, 2006; Lee Hamilton, November 3, 2004, and June 28, 2005; Daniel Inouye, March 8, 2005; Ray LaHood, April 13, 2005; and Robert Michel, February 1, 2005. Also of use were the congressional papers of Howard H. Baker, Emanuel Celler, Everett McKinley Dirksen, Gerald R. Ford, Robert P. Griffin, Edward Hutchinson, Robert Michel, and Robert Taft, Jr. A reflective study by two longtime congressional scholars that amplifies many of the observations I gathered is Thomas E. Mann and Norman J. Ornstein, *The Broken Branch: How Congress Is Failing America and How to Get It Back on Track* (New York: Oxford University Press, 2006).

2. O'Neill's eruption against Gingrich on May 15, 1984, was subsequently expunged at his request from the *Congressional Record* but is described in Joe Klein, *The Natural: The Misunderstood Presidency of Bill Clinton* (New York: Doubleday, 2002), 89–90.

3. Katharine Q. Seelye, "House Mutineers Tell Captain to Keep 3-Day Workweek," *New York Times,* December 4, 1998.

4. Ray LaHood, interview with author, April 13, 2005.

5. William S. Cohen and Gary Hart, *The Double Man* (New York: William Morrow, 1985); William S. Cohen and George Mitchell, *Men of Zeal: A Candid Inside Story of the Iran-Contra Hearings* (New York: Viking, 1988).

6. Karl A. Lamb, *Reasonable Disagreement: Two U.S. Senators and the Choices They Make* (New York: Garland, 1998).

7. The best source of biographical information on Bill Clinton is his autobiography *My Life* (New York: Knopf, 2004). Additional information about his political career can be found in William C. Berman, *From the Center to the Edge: The Politics and Policies of the Clinton Presidency* (Lanham, Md.: Rowman & Littlefield, 2001); Klein, *The Natural;* and John F. Harris, *The Survivor: Bill Clinton in the White House* (New York: Random House, 2005).

8. A good summary of the early months of the Clinton administration can be found in Berman, *From the Center to the Edge.*

9. A catalogue and detailed discrediting of most of the stories of Clinton's alleged sexual escapades can be found in Joe Conason and Gene Lyons, *The Hunting of the President: The Ten-Year Campaign to Destroy Bill and Hillary Clinton* (New York: St Martin's Press, 2000), 16–82.

10. Monica Crowley, *Nixon in Winter* (New York: Random House, 2008), 309–11.

11. Among the accounts of persistent efforts to turn up information in Arkansas damaging to the Clintons are James B. Stewart, *Blood Sport: The President and His Adversaries* (New York:

Simon & Schuster, 1996); Conason and Lyons, *The Hunting of the President;* and Sidney Blumenthal, *The Clinton Wars* (New York: Farrar, Straus & Giroux, 2003).

12. Observations on this political innovation and its consequences can be found in Lewis L. Gould, *The Modern American Presidency* (Lawrence: University Press of Kansas, 2003), 217–27.

13. Gwen Ifill, "Clinton Asks Reno to Name a Counsel on His Land Deals," *New York Times,* January 13, 1994; Harris, *The Survivor,* 109.

14. Stuart Taylor, Jr., "Keep the Special Counsel; Can the Executive Branch Be Trusted?" *New York Times,* June 22, 1992.

15. Quoted in *Christian Science Monitor,* October 25, 1993

16. Stephen Labaton, "Special Prosecutor to Open Office in Little Rock for Inquiry on Clintons' Land Deal," *New York Times,* January 22, 1994.

17. David Johnston, "Reno Wants to Reappoint Fiske under a New Law," *New York Times,* July 2, 1994.

18. Ibid.; Stephen Labaton, "Ruling Is Surprise," *New York Times,* August 6, 1994.

19. Stephen Labaton, "New Counsel Reveals Little of His Plans," *New York Times,* August 7, 1994.

20. Ibid.; Stephen Labaton, "New Counsel Is Being Urged Not to Start Inquiry Anew," *New York Times,* August 8, 1994; "Mr. Starr's Duty to Resign," *New York Times,* August 18, 1994; David Johnston, "Three Judges Spurn Protest on Whitewater Prosecutor," *New York Times,* August 19, 1994; Conason and Lyons, *The Hunting of the President,* 127, 135.

21. "Mr. Starr's Duty to Resign"; David Johnston, "Three Judges Spurn Protest on Whitewater Prosecutor," *New York Times,* August 19, 1994; "Judge Rules Fiske Removal Was Ethical," *New York Times,* November 3, 1994; "Judges Err on Whitewater," *New York Times,* November 9, 1994.

22. Jeffrey Toobin, *A Vast Conspiracy: The Real Story of the Sex Scandal That Nearly Brought Down a President* (New York: Random House, 1999), 80.

23. Ibid., 80, 91–92.

24. William Safire, "The Big Flinch," *New York Times,* February 20, 1997. See also Stephen Labaton, "Special Counsel Intends to Leave Whitewater Case," *New York Times,* February 18, 1997.

25. Quoted in Conason and Lyons, *The Hunting of the President,* 267.

26. Ibid., 267–68.

27. A useful summary of Starr's situation in 1997 can be found in ibid, 258–59, 264–68.

28. Quoted in David Stout, "Starr's Inquiry of President Tries Patience of Trent Lott," *New York Times,* March 7, 1997.

29. This account of the Paula Jones story was assembled from Stewart, *Blood Sport;* Conason and Lyons, *The Hunting of the President;* and Harris, *The Survivor.*

30. *Jones v. Clinton and Ferguson,* 869 F. Supp. 690 (1994).

31. Ibid., at 699.

32. *Jones v. Clinton and Ferguson,* 879 F. Supp. 86 (1995).

33. *Jones v. Clinton and Ferguson,* 72 F. 3d 1354 (1996).

34. *Clinton v. Jones,* 520 U.S. 681 (1997).

35. Quoted in Toobin, *A Vast Conspiracy,* 126; for details of the failed negotiations see also 118–28.

36. The web of anti-Clinton foundations, funders, and activists is described in Conason and Lyons, *The Hunting of the President,* esp. 268, 298–300, 349–50.

37. Toobin, *A Vast Conspiracy,* 103.

38. See Michael Isikoff's own account, *Uncovering Clinton: A Reporter's Story* (New York: Crown, 1999), as well as Conason and Lyon, *The Hunting of the President,* esp. 124, 171–72, 289–91, 349, and Toobin, *A Vast Conspiracy,* esp. 32–35, 104–8, 132–33, 154, 164.

39. Susan Schmidt and Michael Weisskopf, *Truth at Any Cost: Ken Starr and the Unmaking of Bill Clinton* (New York: HarperCollins, 2000), 263.

40. Quoted in Harris, *The Survivor*, 309.

41. Ibid., 311–14; Berman, *From the Center to the Edge,* 80–81.

42. Quoted in Harris, *The Survivor*, 340.

43. Quoted in ibid.

44. Quoted in ibid., 344.

45. A detailed account of how the report was put together can be found in Schmidt and Weisskopf, *Truth at Any Cost,* 251–56.

46. U.S. Congress, House, *Referral from Independent Counsel Kenneth W. Starr,* House Document no. 105-310 (Washington, D.C.: GPO, 1998).

47. Schmidt and Weisskopf, *Truth at Any Cost*, 252–53.

48. U.S. Congress, House, *Referral from Independent Counsel Kenneth W. Starr.*

49. Quoted in Alison Mitchell, "Feud Erupts in Congress over Details of Release," *New York Times*, September 11, 1998. See also Peter Baker, *The Breach: Inside the Impeachment and Trial of William Jefferson Clinton* (New York: Berkley, 2000), 68–82.

50. Alison Mitchell, "With Echoes of Watergate in the Air, House Members Take a Historic Vote," *New York Times,* September 12, 1998.

51. John M. Broder, "Nation Showing Its Dismay and Reluctance," *New York Times,* September 14, 1998.

52. Ibid.; Lizette Alvarez and Eric Schmitt, "Gauging a Bombardment of Opinions That Could Determine Clinton's Fate," *New York Times,* September 16, 1998.

53. Quoted in Alison Mitchell, "Next Step for Congress: Impeachment Decision," *New York Times,* September 22, 1998.

54. Ibid.

55. Richard L. Berke, "Poll Finds Clinton in Strong Rebound since Video Airing," with Janet Elder, *New York Times,* September 25, 1998.

56. "The Impeachment Picture," *New York Times,* September 30, 1998; Stephen Erlander, "Starr's Efforts to Expand Inquiry Raise Doubts, White House Says," *New York Times*, October 5, 1998; "A Debate on Allowable Lies," *New York Times*, October 6, 1998; Allison Mitchell and Lizette Alvarez, "President Urges 'Conscience' Vote on House Inquiry," *New York Times*, October 8, 1998; Baker, *The Breach*, 111–29.

57. John W. Dean, *Conservatives without Conscience* (New York: Viking, 2006), xxvii–xxxi.

58. Martin Frost, interview with author, April 12, 2006.

59. Alison Mitchell, "Inquiry Defended," and Jill Abramson, "Image Isn't Everything," *New York Times*, November 20, 1998; the scene is well described in Baker, *The Breach*, 169–74.

60. Stephen Labaton, "Whitewater Prosecutor Adding Ethics Counsel to Allay Criticism," *New York Times*, October 6, 1994. See also Anthony Lewis, "A Kangaroo Court," *New York Times*, November 17, 1998.

61. John M. Broder, "White House Voicing Hope for Censure Deal after Talks," *New York Times*, December 11, 1998; Alison Mitchell, "3 Articles Charge Perjury and Obstruction of Justice," *New York Times*, December 12, 1998.

62. Quoted in Baker, *The Breach*, 184.

63. Ibid., 188–89.

64. H. Res. 611, *Congressional Record,* 105th Cong., 2nd sess., vol. 144 (December 15, 1998): H11760. Compare this language to that used for Nixon: "In all of this, Richard M. Nixon has acted in a manner contrary to his trust as President and subversive of constitutional government, to the great prejudice of the cause of law and justice and to the manifest injury of the people of the United States. Wherefore Richard M. Nixon, by such conduct, warrants impeachment and trial and removal from office" (U.S., Congress, House, Committee on the Judiciary. *Debate on Articles of Impeachment,* 93rd Cong., 2nd sess. [Washington, D.C.: GPO, 1974] 152–53).

65. David P. Schippers, *Sell Out: The Inside Story of President Clinton's Impeachment*, with Alan P. Henry (Washington, D.C.: Regnery, 2000).

66. Mitchell, "3 Articles Charge Perjury and Obstruction of Justice."

67. Merrill McLoughlin, ed., *The Impeachment and Trial of President Clinton: The Official Transcripts, from the House Judiciary Committee Hearings to the Senate Trial* (New York: Times Books, 1999), 158–64.

68. Ray LaHood, interview with author, May 13, 2005.

69. Katharine Q. Seelye, "Livingston Urges Clinton to Follow Suit," *New York Times*, December 20, 1998; Beschloss, *The Impeachment and Trial of President Clinton*, 205.

70. LaHood, interview with author, May 13, 2005; Beschloss, *The Impeachment and Trial of President Clinton*, 205.

71. Baker, *The Breach*, 166, 227–36.

72. Richard W. Stevenson, "Republicans' Image Eroding Fast, Poll Shows," with Michael R. Kagay, *New York Times*, December 19, 1998.

73. McLoughlin, *The Impeachment and Trial of President Clinton*, 168–69.

74. Ibid., 170.

75. Ibid., 172.

76. Lee Hamilton, interview with author, June 28, 2005; Ray LaHood, interview with author, April 13, 2005; Vic Fazio, interview with author, February 8, 2005; Tom Foley, interview with author, March 14, 2005; Martin Frost, interview with author, April 12, 2006.

77. Quoted in Baker, *The Breach*, 250–51.

78. Ibid., 251–52.

79. Quoted in ibid, 254.

80. Alison Mitchell and James Dao, "First Tally Falls Short of an Ouster," *New York Times*, December 23, 1998.

81. Baker, *The Breach*, 200–3.

82. For the full argument, see Bruce Ackerman, *The Case against Lameduck Impeachment* (New York: Seven Stories Press, 1999).

83. Baker, *The Breach*, 266, 269–70.

84. Ibid., 260–78.

85. Ibid., 279–94.

86. McLoughlin, *The Impeachment and Trial of President Clinton*, 257–58.

87. Quoted in Baker, *The Breach*, 312–13.

88. R. W. Apple, Jr., "Emphatic 'Not Guilty' Opens the Case for the Defense," *New York Times*, January 20, 1999; Beschloss, *The Impeachment and Trial of President Clinton*, 278–304.

89. Francis X. Clines, "A Double-Edged Day Ends on a Note of Hopefulness," *New York Times*, January 20, 1999; Baker, *The Breach*, 317–18.

90. Quoted in "Weight of History Is 'on All of Us,' Senate Is Told by One of Its Own," *New York Times*, January 22, 1999.

91. Lizette Alvarez and Frank Bruni, "Byrd Will Offer a Motion to End Trial of Clinton," *New York Times*, January 23, 1999; Byrd quotation from Baker, *The Breach*, 334.

92. Baker, *The Breach*, 334–35.

93. Alvarez and Bruni, "Byrd Will Offer a Motion"; quoted in Baker, *The Breach*, 335.

94. Quoted in Baker, *The Breach*, 336.

95. Quoted in ibid., 342.

96. Quoted in ibid, 381.

97. Quoted in ibid., 386.

98. Ibid., 411–12.

99. Quoted in ibid., 393.

100. Ibid., 389.

101. Quoted in ibid., 397.

102. Quoted in ibid., 422.

103. S. Res. 1712, *Congressional Record*, 108th Cong., 1st sess., vol. 149 (October 3, 2003): S12338.

13. Impeachment as Conventional: Expressions of Public Scorn

1. Obituary of Herbert L. Block, *Washington Post*, October 8, 2001.

2. Herbert Block, *Herblock Special Report* (New York: W. W. Norton, 1974), 15–82.

3. Herblock, editorial cartoon, *Washington Post*, May 12, 1968.

4. Block, *Herblock Special Report*, 85.

5. Ibid., 85–94.

6. Ibid., 86–106.

7. Ibid., 108–10.

8. Ibid., 111–25.

9. Ibid., 129.

10. Author interviews with David Broder, May 27, 2006; George Lardner, Jr., May 16, 2005; Lawrence Meyer, June 27, 2006; and Bob Woodward, May 19, 2005.

11. Block, *Herblock Special Report*, 137.

12. Ibid., 149.

13. Ibid., 182.

14. Ibid., 232.

15. Ibid., 224.

16. Ibid., 229.

17. Ibid., 240.

18. Ibid., 243.

19. Ibid., 245.

20. Ibid., 246.

21. Ibid., 247.

22. Ibid., 248.

23. Herblock, editorial cartoon, *Washington Post*, March 1, 1987.

24. Herblock, editorial cartoon, *Washington Post*, June 18, 1987.

25. Herblock, editorial cartoon, *Washington Post*, March 5, 1987.

26. Herblock, editorial cartoon, *Washington Post*, May 21, 1987.

27. Herblock, editorial cartoon, *Washington Post*, February 27, 1987.

28. Herblock, editorial cartoon, *Washington Post*, May 1, 1987.

29. Herblock, editorial cartoon, *Washington Post*, May 17, 1987.

30. Herblock, editorial cartoon, *Washington Post*, June 27, 1987.

31. Herblock, editorial cartoon, *Washington Post*, February 2, 1987.

32. Herblock, editorial cartoon, *Washington Post*, April 18, 1990.

33. Herblock, editorial cartoon, *Washington Post*, October 4, 1992.

34. Compare Block, *Herblock's Special Report*, 122, with Herblock, editorial cartoon, *Washington Post*, January 22, 1998.

35. Herblock, editorial cartoon, *Washington Post*, January 29, 1999.

36. Herblock, editorial cartoon, *Washington Post*, January 8, 1999.

37. Herblock, editorial cartoon, *Washington Post*, February 4, 1998.

38. Herblock, editorial cartoon, *Washington Post*, January 29, 1997.

39. Herblock, editorial cartoon, *Washington Post*, June 26, 1997.

40. Herblock, editorial cartoon, *Washington Post*, October 14, 1998.

41. Herblock, editorial cartoon, *Washington Post*, December 16, 1998.

42. Herblock, editorial cartoon, *Washington Post,* November 19, 1998.

43. Herblock, editorial cartoon, *Washington Post*, December 12, 1998.

44. Herblock, editorial cartoon, *Washington Post*, February 3, 1999.

45. Herblock, editorial cartoon, *Washington Post*, November 27, 1998.

46. See G. B. Trudeau, *The Doonesbury Chronicles* (New York: Holt, Rinehart and Winston, 1975), and Jules Feiffer, *Feiffer on Nixon: The Cartoon Presidency* (New York: Random House, 1974).

47. The judicial proceedings are summarized in Jeffrey Toobin, *The Nine: Inside the Secret World of the Supreme Court* (New York: Doubleday, 2007), 247-48; *Washington Post*, June 16, 2005.

48. Quoted in Toobin, *The Nine*, 248.

49. The Gallup poll reported that George W. Bush enjoyed an 86 percent job approval rating in the fourth quarter of his first year as president, the three months immediately after the September 11, 2001, attacks, the highest rating for a full quarter since Harry Truman's first three months following the death of Franklin Roosevelt in 1945. This followed earlier approval ratings for Bush that started about 60 percent but fell to 51 percent just before 9/11. Gallup Poll, "Bush Averages Near-Record 86% Job Approval Rating in Fourth Quarter," January 17, 2002, http://www.galluppoll.com/.

50. Luke Mitchell, "At Issue in the 2004 Election: A Run on Terror," *Harper's,* March 2004, 79.

51. A particularly vigorous assertion of this realization is found in Joe Conason, *It Can Happen Here: Authoritarian Peril in the Age of Bush* (New York: St. Martins Press, 2007).

52. George W. Bush, "Address before a Joint Session of the Congress on the State of the Union, January 29, 2002," in *Public Papers of the Presidents of the United States: George W. Bush, 2002,* 1:129–35 (Washington, DC: GPO, 2004).

53. Richard L. Berke and Janet Elder, "Survey Shows Doubts Stirring on Terror War," *New York Times*, October 30, 2001.

54. Frank Rich, *The Greatest Story Ever Sold: The Decline and Fall of Truth from 9/11 to Katrina* (New York: Penguin, 2006), 40–41. See George W. Bush, "Address to the General Assembly of the United Nations, September 12, 2002," in *Public Papers of the Presidents of the United States: George W. Bush, 2002,* 2:1572–76.

55. Rich, *The Greatest Story Ever Sold*, 58–60.

56. George W. Bush, "Address before a Joint Session of the Congress on the State of the Union, January 28, 2003," in *Public Papers of the Presidents of the United States: George W. Bush, 2003,* 1:82–90 (Washington, DC: GPO, 2006).

57. Joseph C. Wilson, "What I Didn't Find in Africa," *New York Times*, July 6, 2003.

58. Robert D. Novak, "Mission to Niger," *Washington Post*, July 14, 2003.

59. *New York Times*, March 6, 2007.

60. *New York Times*, July 2, 3, 4, and 8, 2007.

61. Bob Woodward, *State of Denial* (New York: Simon & Schuster, 2006), pt. 3.

62. An extended account of these practices can be found in Frederick A. O. Schwartz, Jr., and Aziz Z. Huq, *Unchecked and Unbalanced: Presidential Power in a Time of Terror* (New York: New Press, 2007), esp. 65–123.

63. *Washington Post*, June 8, 2005; Rich, *The Greatest Story Ever Sold*, 177.

64. Charles Savage, "Bush Challenges Hundreds of Laws," *Boston Globe*, April 30, 2006.

65. See http://www.votetoimpeach.org.

66. Ralph Nader, "Iraq an Unconstitutional, Illegal War," press release, April 13, 2004, http://www.votenader.org/media_press/index.php?cid=15.

67. John W. Dean III, *Worse Than Watergate: The Secret Presidency of George W. Bush* (New York: Little, Brown, 2004).

68. H. Res. 629, *Congressional Record*, 108th Cong., 2nd sess., vol. 150 (May 6, 2004): H27271.

69. Zogby International Poll, June 30, 2005, http://www.zogby/com/news/ReadNews/dbm?ID=1007.

70. George H. Gallup, *The Gallup Poll: Public Opinion, 1972–1977,* 2 vols. (Wilmington, Del.: Scholarly Resources, 1978), 1:139–40.

71. *Washington Post,* June 17, 2005.

72. H. Res. 636 and 637, *Congressional Record,* 109th Cong., 1st sess., vol. 151 (December 18, 2005): H12259.

73. This account is based on the author's eyewitness observations.

74. Zogby International Poll, November 4, 2005, http://www.zogby/com/news/ReadNews/dbm?ID=1007.

75. See http://www.afterdowningstreet.org/ and http://www.impeachpac.org/.

76. Quotes from Morton M. Kondracke, "Will Democratic Charges That Bush Lied Lead to His Impeachment?" *Roll Call,* November 17, 2005.

77. Barbara Boxer, December 18, 2005, press release, http://boxer.senate.gov/news/record.cfm?id=249975.

78. Elizabeth Holtzman, *The Impeachment of George W. Bush: A Practical Guide for Concerned Citizens,* with Cynthia L. Cooper (New York: Nation Books, 2006).

79. Among them were Elizabeth De la Vega, *United States v. George W. Bush et al.* (New York: Seven Stories Press, 2006); John Nichols, *The Genius of Impeachment: The Founders' Cure for Royalism and Why It Must Be Applied to George W. Bush* (New York: New Press, 2006); Lewis Lapham, *Pretensions to Empire: Notes on the Criminal Folly of the Bush Administration* (New York: New Press, 2006); Dave Lindorff and Barbara Olshansky, *The Case for Impeachment: The Legal Argument for Removing President George W. Bush from Office* (New York: Thomas Dunne Books, 2006); Center for Constitutional Rights, *Articles of Impeachment against George W. Bush* (Hoboken, N.J.: Melville House, 2006); and Dennis Loo and Peter Phillips, eds., *Impeach the President: The Case against Bush and Cheney* (New York: Seven Stories Press, 2006).

80. "Impeach Cheney First," *Executive Intelligence Review,* January 13, 2006, http://www.larouchepub.com/other/editorials/2006/3302cheney_first.html.

81. *Washington Post,* May 12, 2006.

82. *New York Times,* November 8, 2006.

83. Ibid.

84. H. Res. 1106, *Congressional Record,* 109th Congress, 2nd sess., vol. 152 (December 8, 2006): H93171.

85. *New York Times,* November 29, 2006.

86. *Congressional Record,* 110th Cong., 1st sess., vol. 153 (January 10, 2007): H255.

87. "Bush's Job Approval Average in Last Year One of Worst," January 19, 2007, Gallup News Service, http://www.gallup.com/poll/26191/Bush-job-Approval-Average-Last-Year-One-Worst.aspx.

88. Frank Newport and Joseph Carroll, "Bush Job Approval at 29%, Lowest of His Administration," July 10, 2007, Gallup News Service, http://www.gallup.com/poll/28093/Bush-job-Approval-29-Lowest-Administration.aspx.

89. Francis A. Boyle, "Draft Impeachment Resolution against President George W. Bush," http://www.counterpunch.org/boyle01172003.html.

90. *Burlington (Vt.) Free Press,* April 20 and 26, 2007.

91. *Los Angeles Times,* July 22, 2007.

92. Drake Bennett, "The 'I' Word," *Boston Globe,* June 24, 2007.

93. Daniel Schorr, *Weekend Edition Sunday,* NPR, June 17 2007.

94. Bob Woodward, "The Watergate Legacy, 35 Years Later," http://www.washingtonpost.com, June 18, 2007.

95. *New York Times,* June 30, 2007.

96. *Bill Moyers Journal,* July 13, 2007.

97. Quoted in Klaus Marre, "Leahy Issues Subpoena for Rove," *Hill*, July 26, 2007.

98. *New York Times*, July 2, 2007.

99. Johanna Neuman, "Cheney Impeachment Resolution Sent to House Committee," *Los Angeles Times*, November 7, 2007.

100. George McGovern, "Why I Believe Bush Must Go: Nixon Was Bad, These Guys Are Worse," *Washington Post,* January 6, 2008.

14. The Age of Impeachment: Ended or Extended?

1. Daniel Inouye, interview with author, March 8, 2005.

2. Ibid.

3. Benjamin Ginsberg and Martin Shefter, *Politics by Other Means: Politicians, Prosecutors, and the Press from Watergate to Whitewater*, rev. ed. (New York: W. W. Norton, 1999), 15–44.

4. See Ginsberg and Shefter, *Politics by Other Means*, 27, 31–32, 38, 41–42, 163.

5. Lewis L. Gould, *The Modern American Presidency*. (Lawrence: University Press of Kansas, 2003), 230.

6. A detailed discussion of the Twenty-second Amendment's adoption and operation can be found in David E. Kyvig, *Explicit and Authentic Acts: Amending the U.S. Constitution, 1776–1995* (Lawrence: University Press of Kansas, 1996), 325–36.

7. Ibid., 289–307.

8. White House Office of Legal Counsel memo quoted in Frederick A. O. Schwarz, Jr., and Aziz Z. Huq, *Unchecked and Unbalanced: Presidential Power in a Time of Terror* (New York: New Press, 2007), 79. Schwarz and Huq provide a detailed account of executive assertions of authority after the 9/11 attacks.

9. *New York Times*, July 10, 2007.

10. Stanley I. Kutler, "The Executive Privilege Dodge," *Boston Globe*, March 29, 2007.

11. A detailed picture of Cheney's role in the Bush administration can be found in a series of four feature articles by Barton Gellman and Jo Becker with the umbrella title "Angler: The Cheney Vice Presidency" in the *Washington Post*, June 24–28, 2007.

12. Agence France-Presse, July 7, 2007.

Bibliography

Archives and Manuscript Collections

Agnew, Spiro T., Papers. Hornbake Library, University of Maryland, College Park, Maryland.

Baker, Howard H., Jr., Papers. Baker Center for Public Policy, University of Tennessee, Knoxville, Tennessee.

Bass, Perkins, Papers. Hall-Hoag Collection, John Hay Library, Brown University, Providence, Rhode Island.

Black, Hugo, Papers. Manuscript Division, Library of Congress, Washington, D.C.

Blackmun, Harry A., Papers. Manuscript Division, Library of Congress, Washington, D.C.

Block, Herb, Collection. Prints and Photographs Division, Library of Congress, Washington, D.C.

Bork, Robert H., Papers. Manuscript Division, Library of Congress, Washington, D.C.

Brennan, William J., Papers. Manuscript Division, Library of Congress, Washington, D.C.

Buchanan, Patrick J., Papers. In Richard M. Nixon Papers. National Archives and Records Administration, College Park, Maryland.

Buckley, William F., Jr., Papers. Yale University Library, New Haven, Connecticut.

Celler, Emanuel, Papers. Manuscript Division, Library of Congress, Washington, D.C.

Dirksen, Everett McKinley, Papers. Dirksen Congressional Center, Pekin, Illinois.

Douglas, William O., Papers. Manuscript Division, Library of Congress, Washington, D.C.

Ehrlichman, John D., Papers. In Richard M. Nixon Papers. National Archives and Records Administration, College Park, Maryland.

Ford, Gerald R., Papers. Gerald R. Ford Presidential Library, Ann Arbor, Michigan.

Frankfurter, Felix, Papers. Manuscript Division, Library of Congress, Washington, D.C.

Garment, Leonard, Papers. Manuscript Division, Library of Congress, Washington, D.C.

Graham, Fred P., Papers. Manuscript Division, Library of Congress, Washington, D.C.

Griffin, Robert P., Papers. Clarke Historical Library, Central Michigan University, Mount Pleasant, Michigan.

Haldeman, H. R., Papers. In Richard M. Nixon Papers. National Archives and Records Administration, College Park, Maryland.

Hartmann, Robert T., Papers. Gerald R. Ford Presidential Library, Ann Arbor, Michigan.

Hutchinson, Edward, Papers. Gerald R. Ford Presidential Library, Ann Arbor, Michigan.

John Birch Society Papers. John Hay Library, Brown University, Providence, Rhode Island.

Johnson, Frank M., Jr., Papers. Manuscript Division, Library of Congress, Washington, D.C.

Kennedy, John F., Papers. John F. Kennedy Presidential Library, Boston, Massachusetts.

Lardner, George, Jr., Papers. Manuscript Division, Library of Congress, Washington, D.C.

Marshall, Thurgood, Papers. Manuscript Division, Library of Congress, Washington, D.C.

Michel, Robert, Papers. Dirksen Congressional Center, Pekin, Illinois.

Nixon, Richard M., Papers. National Archives and Records Administration, College Park, Maryland.

Regan, Donald T., Papers. Manuscript Division, Library of Congress, Washington, D.C.

Rusher, William A., Papers. Manuscript Division, Library of Congress, Washington, D.C.

Sirica, John J., Papers. Manuscript Division, Library of Congress, Washington, D.C.

Spivak, Lawrence P., Papers. Manuscript Division, Library of Congress, Washington, D.C.

Taft, Robert, Jr., Papers. Manuscript Division, Library of Congress, Washington, D.C.

Valeo, Francis. Papers. Manuscript Division, Library of Congress, Washington, D.C.
Warren, Earl, Papers. Manuscript Division, Library of Congress, Washington, D.C.

Court Cases

Abington v. Schempp, 374 U.S. 203 (1963)
Baker v. Carr, 369 U.S. 186 (1962)
Buckley v. Valeo, 424 U.S. 1 (1976)
Burdick v. U.S., 236 U.S. 79 (1915)
Chandler v. Judicial Council, 398 U.S. 74 (1970)
Clinton v. Jones, 520 U.S. 681 (1997)
Cooper v. Aaron, 358 U.S. 1 (1958)
Engel v. Vitale, 370 U.S. 421 (1962)
Emspak v. United States, 349 U.S. 190 (1955)
Escobedo v. Illinois, 378 U.S. 478 (1964)
Gideon v. Wainwright, 372 U.S. 335 (1963)
Gravel v. United States, 408 U.S. 606 (1972)
Griswold v. Connecticut, 381 U.S. 479 (1965)
Jacobellis v. Ohio, 378 U.S. 184 (1964)
Jencks v. United States, 353 U.S. 657 (1957)
Jones v. Clinton and Ferguson, 879 F. Supp. 86 (1995)
Jones v. Clinton and Ferguson, 72 F. 3d 1354 (1996)
Katz v. United States, 389 U.S. 347 (1967)
Konigsberg v. State Bar of California, 353 U.S. 252 (1957)
Mapp v. Ohio, 367 U.S. 643 (1961)
Miranda v. Arizona, 384 U.S. 436 (1966)
Morrison v. Olson, 487 U.S. 654 (1988)
Nixon v. Administrator of General Services, 433 U.S. 425 (1977)
Nixon v. Fitzgerald, 457 U.S. 731 (1982)
Nixon v. United States, 506 U.S. 224 (1993)
Nixon v. Warner Communications, 435 U.S. 589 (1978)
Pennsylvania v. Nelson, 350 U.S. 497 (1956)
Powell v. McCormack, 395 U.S. 486 (1969)
Quinn v. United States, 349 U.S. 155 (1955)
Reynolds v. Sims, 377 U.S. 533 (1964)
Ritter v. United States, 84 Ct. Cl. 293 (1936)
Schware v. Board of Bar Examiners of New Mexico, 253 U.S. 332 (1957)
Service v. Dulles, 354 U.S. 363 (1957)
Slochower v. Board of Higher Education of New York City, 350 U.S. 551 (1956)
Sweezy v. New Hampshire, 354 U.S. 234 (1957)
United States v. Aguilar, 515 U.S. 593 (1995)
United States v. Brewster, 408 U.S. 501 (1972)
United States v. Nixon, 418 U.S. 683 (1974)
Watkins v. United States, 354 U.S. 178 (1957)
Wesberry v. Sanders, 376 U.S. 1 (1964)
Yates v. United States, 354 U.S. 298 (1957)

Published Documents

Brinkley, Joel, and Stephen Engelbert, eds. *Report of the Congressional Committees Investigating the Iran-Contra Affair with the Minority View*. Abridged ed. New York: Times Books, 1988.

Farrand, Max, ed. *Records of the Federal Convention of 1787.* 3 vols. New Haven, Conn.: Yale University Press, 1911.

Inouye, Daniel K., and Lee H. Hamilton. *Report of the Congressional Committees Investigating the Iran-Contra Affair.* Abridged ed. New York: Times Books, 1988.

McLoughlin, Merrill, ed. *The Impeachment and Trial of President Clinton: The Official Transcripts, from the House Judiciary Committee Hearings to the Senate Trial.* New York: Times Books, 1999.

New York Times. *The Watergate Hearings: Break-in and Cover-up: Proceedings of Senate Select Committee on Presidential Campaign Activities.* New York: Bantam, 1973.

Public Papers of the Presidents of the United States. Washington, D.C.: GPO, 1971–2006.

Report of the Proceedings of the Judicial Conference of the United States. March 17, 1987. Washington, D.C. 1987.

The Starr Report: The Independent Counsel's Complete Report to Congress on the Investigation of President Clinton. New York: Pocket Books, 1998.

Urofsky, Melvin I., ed. *The Douglas Letters: Selections from the Private Papers of Justice William O. Douglas.* Bethesda, Md.: Adler & Adler, 1987.

U.S. Congress, House. Committee on the Judiciary. *Associate Justice William O. Douglas: Final Report by the Special Subcommittee on H. Res. 920.* 91st Cong., 2nd sess. Washington, D.C.: GPO, 1970.

———. *Associate Justice William O. Douglas: First Report by the Special Subcommittee on H. Res. 920.* 91st Cong., 2nd sess. Washington, D.C.: GPO, 1970.

———. *Authorization of an Inquiry into Whether Grounds Exist for the Impeachment of William Jefferson Clinton, President of the United States.* 105th Cong., 2nd. sess. Washington, D.C.: GPO, 1998.

———. *Debate on Articles of Impeachment: Hearings.* 93rd Cong., 2nd. sess. Washington, D.C.: GPO, 1974.

———. *Impeachment: Selected Materials.* 93rd Cong., 1st sess. Washington, D.C.: GPO, 1973.

———. *Impeachment: Selected Materials on Procedure.* 93rd Cong., 2nd sess. Washington, D.C.: GPO, 1974.

———. *Impeachment Inquiry.* 93rd Cong., 2nd. sess. Washington, D.C.: GPO, 1974.

———. *Impeachment of Judge Alcee L. Hastings: Report to Accompany H. Res. 499.* 100th Cong., 2nd. sess. Washington, D.C.: GPO, 1988.

———. *Impeachment of Richard M. Nixon, President of the United States: Final Report.* With introduction by R. W. Apple, Jr. New York: Bantam, 1974.

———. *Impeachment of William Jefferson Clinton, President of the United States: Report.* 105th Cong., 2nd. sess. Washington, D.C.: GPO, 1998.

———. *Markup of House Resolution 461, Impeachment of Judge Harry E. Claiborne.* 99th Cong., 2nd sess. Washington, D.C.: GPO, 1986.

———. *Nomination of Gerald R. Ford to Be the Vice President of the United States: Hearings.* 93rd Cong., 1st sess. Washington, D.C.: GPO, 1973.

———. *Post Trial Memorandum of the House of Representatives in re Impeachment of Judge Alcee L. Hastings.* 101st. Cong., 1st. sess. Washington, D.C.: GPO, 1989.

U.S. Congress, House. Committee on the Judiciary, Impeachment Inquiry Staff. *Constitutional Grounds for Presidential Impeachment.* Washington, D.C.: Public Affairs Press, 1974.

U.S. Congress, House. Committee on the Judiciary, Special Subcommittee on H. Res. 920. *Associate Justice William O. Douglas; Final Report.* 91st. Cong., 2nd. sess. Washington, D.C.: GPO, 1970.

———. *Associate Justice William O. Douglas; First Report.* 91st. Cong., 2nd. sess. Washington, D.C.: GPO, 1970.

U.S. Congress, House. Committee on the Judiciary, Subcommittee on Civil and Constitutional Rights. *Judge Walter L. Nixon, Jr., Impeachment Inquiry: Hearings.* 100th Cong., 2nd. sess. Washington, D.C.: GPO, 1989.

U.S. Congress, House. Committee on the Judiciary, Subcommittee on Courts, Civil Liberties, and the Administration of Justice. *Conduct of Harry E. Claiborne, U.S. District Judge, District of Nevada: Hearing.* 99th Cong., 2nd sess. Washington, D.C.: GPO, 1986.

———. *Subcommittee Markup of House Resolution 461, Impeachment of Judge Harry E. Claiborne.* 99th Cong., 2nd sess. Washington, D.C.: GPO, 1986.

U.S. Congress, House. Committee on the Judiciary, Subcommittee on Criminal Justice. *Impeachment Inquiry: Hearings Pursuant to H. Res. 128, Impeaching Alcee L. Hastings, Judge of the United States District Court.* 100th Cong., 2nd. sess. Washington, D.C.: GPO, 1988.

———. *In the Matter of the Impeachment Inquiry Concerning U.S. District Judge Alcee L. Hastings: Hearings.* 100th Cong., 1st sess. Washington, D.C.: GPO, 1987.

U.S. Congress, House. *Referral from Independent Counsel Kenneth W. Starr.* House Document no. 105–310. Washington, D.C.: GPO, 1998.

U.S. Congress, Senate. *Impeachment of President William Jefferson Clinton: The Evidentiary Record.* 106th Cong., 1st sess. Washington, D.C.: GPO, 1999.

———. *Proceedings in the Impeachment Trial of Alcee L. Hastings.* 101st Cong., 1st sess. Washington, D.C.: GPO, 1989.

———. *Proceedings in the Impeachment Trial of Harry E. Claiborne.* 99th Cong., 2nd sess. Washington, D.C.: GPO, 1987.

———. *Proceedings in the Impeachment Trial of Walter L. Nixon, Jr.* 101st Cong., 1st sess. Washington, D.C.: GPO, 1989.

U.S. Congress, Senate. Committee on the Judiciary. *Nominations of Abe Fortas and Homer Thornberry: Hearings.* 90th Cong., 2nd sess. Washington, D.C.: GPO, 1968.

U.S. Congress, Senate. Committee on Rules and Administration. *Nomination of Gerald R. Ford of Michigan to Be the Vice President of the United States: Hearings.* 93rd Cong., 1st sess. Washington, D.C.: GPO, 1973.

———. *Procedure for the Impeachment Trial of United States District Judge Alcee L. Hastings in the United States Senate: Report to Accompany S. Res. 38 to Provide for the Appointment of a Committee to Receive and to Report Evidence.* 101st Cong., 1st sess. Washington, D.C.: GPO, 1989.

———. *Procedure for the Impeachment Trial of United States District Judge Alcee L. Hastings in the United States Senate: Report to Carry the Impeachment Proceedings over to the 101st Congress.* 100th Cong., 2nd sess. Washington, D.C.: GPO, 1988.

U.S. Congress, Senate. Impeachment Trial Committee. *Report of the Impeachment Trial Committee.* 4 vols. 99th Cong., 2nd sess. Washington, D.C.: GPO, 1986.

———. *Report on the Articles against Judge Alcee L. Hastings.* 101st Cong., 1st sess. Washington, D.C.: GPO, 1989.

———. *Report on the Articles against Judge Walter L. Nixon Jr.* 101st Cong., 1st sess. Washington, D.C.: GPO, 1989.

U.S. National Commission on Judicial Discipline and Removal, *Research Papers,* 2 vols. [Washington, D.C.: GPO, 1993].

Walsh, Lawrence E. *Final Report of the Independent Counsel For Iran/Contra Matters.* 3 vols. Washington, D.C.: United States Court of Appeals for the District of Columbia Circuit, 1993.

Welch, Robert H. W., Jr. *The Blue Book of the John Birch Society.* Privately printed, 1959.

———. *The Life of John Birch.* Washington, D.C.: Regnery, 1954.

———. *May God Forgive Us.* Washington, D.C.: Regnery, 1952.

———. *The Politician.* Privately printed, 1963.

Newspapers and Periodicals

Christian Science Monitor, 1960–1991

Los Angeles Times, 1960–1968

Nation, 1961–1999
National Review, 1960–2000
New Republic, 1961–1964
New York Times, 1951–2007
Wall Street Journal, 1960–1987
Washington Post, 1960–2005

Interviews

Baron, Alan I., October 5, 2005
Belsky, Martin H., February 2, 2007
Ben-Veniste, Richard, March 24, 2005
Broder, David, May 27, 2006
Bush, Frederick, January 22, 2005
Dean, John W., September 20, 2005
Fazio, Vic, February 8, 2005
Foley, Thomas, March 14, 2005
Frost, Martin, April 12, 2006
Hamilton, Lee, November 3, 2004; June 28, 2005
Hastings, Alcee, February 18, 2005
Inouye, Daniel, March 8, 2005
LaHood, Ray, April 13, 2005
Lardner, George, Jr., May 16, 2005
Meyer, Lawrence R., April 6 and June 27, 2006
Michel, Robert, February 1, 2005
Reston, James, Jr., June 15, 2006
Schorr, Daniel, October 19, 2004
Totenberg, Nina, November 17, 2004
Woodward, Bob, May 19, 2005

Oral History Transcripts

Fortas, Abe. Interviewed by Joe B. Frantz, August 14, 1969. Lyndon Baines Johnson Library Oral History Project, Austin, Texas.

Griffin, Robert P. Interviewed by Michael L. Gillette, March 2, 1979. Lyndon Baines Johnson Library Oral History Project, Austin, Texas.

Riddick, Floyd M. Interviewed by Donald A. Ritchie, September 28, 1978. United States Senate Historical Office, Washington, D.C.

Warren, Earl. Interviewed by Joe B. Frantz, September 21, 1971. Lyndon Baines Johnson Library Oral History Project, Austin, Texas.

Written Participant Memoirs

Agnew, Spiro T. *Go Quietly . . . or Else*. New York: William Morrow, 1980.

Aiken, George D. *Senate Diary: January 1972–January 1975*. Brattleboro, Vt.: Stephen Green Press, 1976.

Barr, Bob. *The Meaning of Is: The Squandered Impeachment and Wasted Legacy of William Jefferson Clinton*. Atlanta: Stroud and Hall, 2004.

Bayh, Birch. *One Heartbeat Away: Presidential Disability and Succession*. Indianapolis, Ind.: Bobbs-Merrill, 1968.

Ben-Veniste, Richard, and George Frampton, Jr. *Stonewall: The Real Story of the Watergate Prosecution*. New York: Simon & Schuster, 1977.

Bernstein, Carl, and Bob Woodward. *All the President's Men.* New York: Simon & Schuster, 1974.

Blumenthal, Sidney. *The Clinton Wars.* New York: Farrar, Straus & Giroux, 2003.

Bradlee, Benjamin C. *A Good Life: Newspapering and Other Adventures.* New York: Simon & Schuster, 1995.

Bradley, Bill. *Time Present, Time Past: A Memoir.* New York: Vintage, 1996.

Buckley, James L. *If Men Were Angels: A View from the Senate.* New York: G. P. Putnam's Sons, 1975.

Byrd, Robert C. *Losing America: Confronting a Reckless and Arrogant Presidency.* New York: W. W. Norton, 2004.

Clinton, Bill. *My Life.* New York: Knopf, 2004.

Clinton, Hillary Rodham. *Living History.* New York: Scribner, 2003.

Cohen, William S., and George Mitchell. *Men of Zeal: A Candid Inside Story of the Iran-Contra Hearings.* New York: Viking, 1988.

Colson, Charles W. *Born Again.* Old Tappen, N.J.: Chosen Books, 1976.

D'Amato, Alfonso. *Power, Pasta and Politics: The World According to Senator Al D'Amato.* New York: Hyperion, 1995.

Dash, Samuel. *Chief Counsel: Inside the Ervin Committee—The Untold Story of Watergate.* New York: Random House, 1976.

Dean, John W., III. *Blind Ambition.* New York: Simon & Schuster, 1976.

———. *Conservatives without Conscience.* New York: Viking, 2006.

———. *The Rehnquist Choice: The Untold Story of the Nixon Appointment That Redefined the Supreme Court.* New York: Free Press, 2001.

———. *Worse than Watergate: The Secret Presidency of George W. Bush.* New York: Little, Brown, 2004.

Douglas, William O. *The Court Years, 1939–1975.* New York: Vintage, 1980.

Drinan, Robert F. *God and Caesar on the Potomac: A Pilgrimage of Conscience.* Wilmington, Del.: Michael Glazer, 1985.

Ehrlichman, John. *Witness to Power: The Nixon Years.* New York: Simon & Schuster, 1982.

Ervin, Sam J., Jr. *Preserving the Constitution: The Autobiography of Senator Sam J. Ervin, Jr.* Charlottesville, Va.: Michie, 1984.

———. *The Whole Truth: The Watergate Conspiracy.* New York: Random House, 1980.

Ford, Gerald R. *A Time to Heal: The Autobiography of Gerald R. Ford.* New York: Harper & Row, 1979.

Garment, Leonard. *Crazy Rhythm: My Journey from Brooklyn, Jazz, and Wall Street to Nixon's White House, Watergate, and Beyond.* New York: Times Books, 1997.

Goldwater, Barry M. *With No Apologies: The Personal and Political Memoirs of United States Senator Barry M. Goldwater.* New York: William Morrow, 1979.

Graham, Katharine. *Personal History.* New York: Knopf, 1997.

Haldeman, H. R. *The Ends of Power.* With Joseph DiMona. New York: Times Books, 1978.

———. *The Haldeman Diaries: Inside the Nixon White House.* New York: G. P. Putnam's Sons, 1994.

Hatch, Orrin. *Square Peg: Confessions of a Citizen Senator.* New York: Basic Books, 2002.

Hatfield, Mark O. *Against the Grain: Reflections of a Rebel Republican.* As told to Diane N. Solomon. Ashland, Ore.: White Cloud Press, 2001.

———. *Between a Rock and a Hard Place.* Waco, Tex.: Word Books, 1976.

Jaworski, Leon. *The Right and the Power: The Prosecution of Watergate.* New York: Reader's Digest Press, 1976.

Jeffords, James M. *An Independent Man: Adventures of a Public Servant.* New York: Simon & Schuster, 2003.

Klein, Herbert G. *Making It Perfectly Clear*. Garden City, N.Y.: Doubleday, 1980.

Ledeen, Michael A. *Perilous Statecraft: An Insider's Account of the Iran-Contra Affair*. New York: Scribner's, 1988.

Magruder, Jeb Stuart. *An American Life: One Man's Road to Watergate*. New York: Atheneum, 1974.

McCloskey, Paul N., Jr. *Truth and Untruth: Political Deceit in America*. New York: Simon & Schuster, 1972.

Montgomery, G. V. "Sonny." *Sonny Montgomery: The Veteran's Champion*. With Michael B. Ballard and Craig S. Piper. Jackson: Mississippi State Universities Libraries/University Press of Mississippi, 2003.

Nixon, Richard M. *In the Arena: A Memoir of Victory, Defeat, and Renewal*. New York: Simon & Schuster, 1990.

———. *RN: The Memoirs of Richard Nixon*. New York: Grosset & Dunlap, 1978.

North, Oliver L. *Under Fire: An American Story*. With William Novak. New York: HarperCollins, 1991.

O'Neill, Thomas P., Jr. *Man of the House: The Life and Political Memoirs of Speaker Tip O'Neill*. With William Novak. New York: Random House, 1987.

Paley, William S. *As It Happened: A Memoir*. New York: Doubleday, 1979.

Reagan, Ronald. *An American Life*. New York: Simon & Schuster, 1990.

———. *The Reagan Diaries*. Edited by Douglas Brinkley. New York: HarperCollins, 2007.

Regan, Donald T. *For the Record: From Wall Street to Washington*. San Diego: Harcourt Brace Jovanovich, 1988.

Reston, James, Jr. *The Conviction of Richard Nixon: The Untold Story of the Frost/Nixon Interviews*. New York: Harmony, 2007.

Rudman, Warren B. *Combat: Twelve Years in the U.S. Senate*. New York: Random House, 1996.

Rusher, William. *The Making of the New Majority Party*. New York: Sheed & Ward, 1975.

———. *The Rise of the Right*. New York: William Morrow, 1984.

Safire, William. *Before the Fall: An Inside View of the Pre-Watergate White House*. Garden City, N.Y.: Doubleday, 1975.

Schieffer, Bob. *This Just In: What I Couldn't Tell You on TV.* New York: G. P. Putnam, 2003.

Schippers, David P. *Sell Out: The Inside Story of President Clinton's Impeachment*. With Alan P. Henry. Washington, D.C.: Regnery, 2000.

Schomp, Gerald. *Birchism Was My Business*. New York: Macmillan, 1970.

Schorr, Daniel. *Clearing the Air.* Boston: Houghton Mifflin, 1977.

———. *Staying Tuned: A Life in Journalism*. New York: Pocket Books, 2001.

Schroeder, Pat. *Twenty-four Years of House Work . . . and the Place Is Still a Mess: My Life in Politics*. Kansas City, Mo.: Andrews McMeel, 1998.

Schultz, George P. *Turmoil and Triumph: My Years as Secretary of State*. New York: Charles Scribner's Sons, 1993.

Simon, Paul. *P.S.: The Autobiography of Paul Simon*. Chicago: Bonus Books, 1999.

Simpson, Alan K. *Right in the Old Gazoo: A Lifetime of Scrapping with the Press*. New York: William Morrow, 1997.

Sirica, John. *To Set the Record Straight: The Break-in, the Tapes, the Conspirators, the Pardon*. New York: W. W. Norton, 1979.

Specter, Arlen. *Passion for Truth: From Finding JFK's Single Bullet to Questioning Anita Hill to Impeaching Clinton*. With Charles Robbins. New York: Perennial, 2001.

Stephanopoulos, George. *All Too Human: A Political Education*. Boston: Little, Brown, 1999.

Walsh, Lawrence E. *Firewall: The Iran-Contra Conspiracy and Cover-up*. New York: W. W. Norton, 1997.

———. *The Gift of Insecurity: A Lawyer's Life*. Chicago: American Bar Association, 2003.

Weicker, Lowell P., Jr. *Maverick: A Life in Politics*. Boston: Little, Brown, 1995.

White, F. Clifton. *Suite 3505: The Story of the Draft Goldwater Movement*. New Rochelle, N.Y.: Arlington House, 1967.

Woodward, Bob. *The Secret Man: The Story of Watergate's Deep Throat*. New York: Simon & Schuster, 2005.

Wright, Jim. *Worth It All: My War for Peace*. Washington, D.C.: Brassey's, 1993.

Zeifman, Jerry. *Without Honor: Crimes of Camelot and the Impeachment of President Nixon*. New York: Thunder's Mouth Press, 1998.

Films

All the President's Men. Directed by Alan Pakula. 1976.

The Assassination of Richard Nixon. Directed by Niels Mueller. 2004.

Dick. Directed by Andrew Fleming. 1999.

Inside Deep Throat. Directed by Fenton Bailey and Randy Barbato. 2005.

Nixon. Directed by Oliver Stone. 1995.

Secret Honor. Directed by Robert Altman. 1984.

Articles

Abcarian, Gilbert, and Sherman M. Stanage. "Alienation and the Radical Right." *Journal of Politics* 27 (1965): 776–96.

Abramowitz, Alan I. "Exploring Success and Failure in the 1998 Midterm Elections: Comparing the Influence of Swing Voters and Core Party Supporters." *PS: Political Science and Politics* 32 (1999): 60–61.

———. "Name Familiarity, Reputation, and the Incumbency Effect in a Congressional Election." *Western Political Quarterly* 28 (1975): 668–84.

Allard, Bob. "Judicial Discipline and Removal Plans: A Survey and Comparative Study." *American Judicature Society* 48 (1965): 173–76.

Amar, Akhil Reed. "Nixon's Shadow." *Minnesota Law Review* 83 (1999): 1405–20.

———. "On Impeaching Presidents." *Hofstra Law Review* 28 (1999): 291–341.

Amar, Akhil Reed, and Neal Kumar Katyal. "Executive Privileges and Immunities: The Nixon and Clinton Cases." *Harvard Law Review* 108 (1995): 701–26.

Aronowitz, Stanley. "Reactionary Moralities; Or, Why a Political Clone of the Right Had to Be Impeached." *Cultural Critique* 43 (1999): 118–32.

Arterton, F. Christopher. "The Impact of Watergate on Children's Attitudes toward Political Authority." *Political Science Quarterly* 89 (1974): 269–88.

———. "Watergate and Children's Attitudes toward Political Authority Revisited." *Political Science Quarterly* 90 (1975): 477–96.

Auslander, Rose. "Impeaching the Senate's Use of Trial Committees." *New York University Law Review* 67 (1992): 68–107.

Banner, James M., Jr. "Historians and the Impeachment Inquiry: A Brief History and Prospectus." *Reviews in American History* 4 (1976): 139–49.

Barber, James David. "The Nixon Brush with Tyranny." *Political Science Quarterly* 94 (1977): 581–605.

Baron, Alan J. "The Curious Case of Alcee Hastings." *Nova Law Review* 18 (1994–1995): 1–38.

Bell, Daniel. "Afterword (2001): From Class to Culture." In *The Radical Right*, ed. Daniel Bell, 3rd ed., 447–503. New Brunswick, N.J.: Transaction, 2003.

———. "The Dispossessed—1962." In *The Radical Right: The New American Right, Expanded and Updated,* ed. Daniel Bell, 1–38. Garden City, N.Y.: Doubleday, 1963.

Bennett, Stephen E. "Modes of Resolution of a 'Belief Dilemma' in the Ideology of the John Birch Society." *Journal of Politics* 33 (1971): 735–72.

———. "Why Young Americans Hate Politics, and What We Should Do about It." *PS: Political Science and Politics* 30 (1997): 47–53.

Bestor, Arthur. "Impeachment." *Washington Law Review* 49 (1973): 255–85.

Blackmar, Charles B. "The Impeachment Trial of Samuel Chase." *American Judicature Society* 48 (1965): 83–87.

Bloch, Susan Lee. "A Report Card on the Impeachment: Judging the Institutions That Judged President Clinton." *Law and Contemporary Problems* 63 (2000): 143–67.

Bowman, Frank O., III, and Stephen L. Sepinuck. "'High Crimes and Misdemeanors': Defining the Constitutional Limits on Presidential Impeachment." *Southern California Law Review* 72 (1999): 1517–1600.

Brennan, Timothy. "The Organizational Imaginary." *Cultural Critique* 43 (1999): 79–104.

Brown, Rebecca L. "Caging the Wolf: Seeking a Constitutional Home for the Independent Counsel." *Minnesota Law Review* 83 (1999): 1269–84.

———. "When Political Questions Affect Individual Rights: The Other *Nixon v United States.*" *Supreme Court Review,* 1993: 125–55.

Burbank, Stephen B. "Alternative Career Resolution: An Essay on the Removal of Federal Judges." *Kentucky Law Journal* 76 (1988): 643–700.

Butterfield, Alexander P., and David Thelan. "Conversation between Alexander P. Butterfield and David Thelan about the Discovery of the Watergate Tapes." *Journal of American History* 75 (1989): 1245–62.

Calabresi, Steven G. "Caesarism, Departmentalism, and Professor Paulsen." *Minnesota Law Review* 83 (1999): 1421–34.

Campbell, James E. "The Referendum That Didn't Happen: The Forecasts of the 2000 Presidential Election." *PS: Political Science and Politics* 34 (2001): 33–38.

Careley, Demetrios, Charles V. Hamilton, Alpheus T. Mason, Robert A. McCaughey, Nelson W. Polsby, Jeffrey L. Pressman, Arthur M. Schlesinger, Jr., George L. Sherry, and Tom Wicker. "American Political Institutions after Watergate—A Discussion." *Political Science Quarterly* 89 (1974): 713–49.

Casper, Gerhard. "American *Geheimniskramerei.*" *Reviews in American History* 3 (1975): 154–58.

Catz, Robert S. "Removal of Federal Judges by Imprisonment." *Rutgers Law Journal,* 18 (1986): 103–19.

Cooper, Charles J. "A Perjurer in the White House? The Constitutional Case of Perjury and Obstruction of Justice and High Crimes and Misdemeanors." *Harvard Journal of Law and Public Policy* 22 (1999): 619–46.

Cronin, Thomas E. "A Resurgent Congress and the Imperial Presidency." *Political Science Quarterly* 95 (1980): 209–37.

Dangel, Stephanie A. J. "Is Prosecution a Core Executive Function? *Morrison v. Olson* and the Framers' Intent." *Yale Law Journal* 99 (1990): 1069–88.

Daugherty, Donald A. Q. "The Separation of Powers and Abuses in Prosecutorial Discretion." *Journal of Criminal Law and Criminology* 79 (1988): 953–96.

Eagly, Alice H., and Shelly Chaiken. "Why Would Anyone Say That? Causal Attribution of Statements about the Watergate Scandal." *Sociometry* 39 (1976): 236–43.

Edwards, Drew E. "Judicial Misconduct and Politics in the Federal System: A Proposal for Revising the Judicial Councils Act." *California Law Review* 75 (1987): 1071–91.

Edwards, Harry T. "Regulating Judicial Misconduct and Divining 'Good Behavior' for Federal Judges." *Michigan Law Review* 87 (1989): 765–96.

Engh, Hans. "The John Birch Society." *Nation,* March 11, 1961, 209–10.

Feerick, John D. "Impeaching Federal Judges: A Study of the Constitutional Provisions." *Fordham Law Review* 29 (1970): 1–58.

Fenton, Paul S. "The Scope of the Impeachment Power." *Northwestern University Law Review* 65 (1970–1971): 719–58.

Finch, Gerald B. "Impeachment and the Dynamics of Public Opinion: A Comment on 'Guilty Yes, Impeachment No.'" *Political Science Quarterly* 89 (1974): 301–4.

Firmage, Edwin Brown. "The Law of Presidential Impeachment." *Utah Law Review* 1973: 681–704.

Firmage, Edwin Brown, and R. Collin Mangrum. "Removal of the President: Resignation and the Procedural Law of Impeachment." *Duke Law Journal,* 1974: 1023–1116.

Fisher, Louis. "Starr's Record as Independent Counsel." *PS: Political Science and Politics* 32 (1999): 546–49.

Fisher, Louis, and David Gray Adler. "The War Powers Resolution: Time to Say Goodbye." *Political Science Quarterly* 113 (1998): 1–20.

Fox, Brenda C. "The Justiciability of Challenges to the Senate Rules of Procedure for Impeachment Trials." *George Washington Law Review* 60 (1992): 1275–1310.

Frankel, Jack E. "Judicial Discipline and Removal." *Texas Law Review* 44 (1966): 1117–35.

———. "Removal of Judges—State and Federal." *American Judicature Society* 48 (1965): 177–82.

Franklin, Mitchell. "Romanist Infamy and the American Constitutional Conception of Impeachment." *Buffalo Law Review* 23 (1974): 313–41.

Fried, Amy, and Timothy M. Cole. "Presidential Impeachment and Institutional Dynamics in the Iran-Contra Affair and the Clinton-Lewinsky Scandal." *Congress and the Presidency* 31 (Spring 2004): 77–98.

Fry, Brian R., and John S. Stolarek. "The Impeachment Process: Predispositions and Votes." *Journal of Politics* 42 (1980): 1118–34.

Futterman, Stanley N. "The Rules of Impeachment." *University of Kansas Law Review* 24 (1974): 105–42.

Gerhardt, Michael J. "The Constitutional Limits to Impeachment and Its Alternatives." *Texas Law Review* 68 (1989): 1–104.

———. "The Historical and Constitutional Significance of the Impeachment and Trial of President Clinton." *Hofstra Law Review* 28 (1999): 349–92.

Gormley, Ken. "Impeachment and the Independent Counsel: A Dysfunctional Union." *Stanford Law Review* 51 (1999): 309–55.

Grofman, Bernard. "Richard Nixon as Pinocchio, Richard II, and Santa Claus: The Use of Allusion in Political Satire." *Journal of Politics* 51 (1989): 165–73.

Grupp, Fred W., Jr. "Personal Satisfaction Derived from Membership in the John Birch Society." *Western Political Quarterly* 24 (1971): 79–83.

Hartmann, Susan M. "In the Grip of Watergate." *Reviews in American History* 21 (1993): 710–16.

Havighurst, Harold C. "Doing Away with Presidential Impeachment: The Advantages of Parliamentary Government." *Arizona State Law Journal,* 1974: 223–37.

Heflin, Howell, "Impeaching Federal Judges: Making the Case for Change." *Trial* 71 (1990): 32–34.

———. "The Impeachment Process: Modernizing an Archaic System." *Judicature* 71 (1987): 123–25.

Hendel, Samuel, "Separation of Powers Revisited in Light of 'Watergate.'" *Western Political Quarterly* 27 (1974): 575–88.

Hersh, Seymour M. "The Iran-Contra Committees: Did They Protect Reagan?" *New York Times Magazine*, April 29, 1990.

Hershey, Marjorie Randon, and David B. Hill. "Watergate and Preadults' Attitudes toward the President." *American Journal of Political Science* 19 (1975): 703–26.

Hofstadter, Richard. "Pseudo-Conservatism Revisited: A Postscript—1962." In *The Radical Right: The New American Right, Expanded and Updated,* ed. Daniel Bell, 81–86. Garden City, N.Y.: Doubleday, 1963.

Horwitz, Leon, Barbara Green, and Hans E. Segal. "International Press Reactions to the Resignation and Pardon of Richard M. Nixon: A Content Analysis of Four Elite Newspapers." *Comparative Politics* 9 (1976): 107–23.

Hutchinson, Asa. "Did the Senate Trial Satisfy the Constitution and the Demands of Justice?" *Hofstra Law Review* 28 (1999): 393–405.

Ignagni, Joseph, and James Meernik. "Explaining Congressional Attempts to Reverse Supreme Court Decisions." *Political Science Quarterly* 47 (1994): 353–71.

Jacobs, Lawrence R., Benjamin I. Page, Melanie Burns, Gregory McAvoy, and Eric Ostermeier. "What Presidents Talk About: The Nixon Case." *Presidential Studies Quarterly* 33 (2003): 751–71.

Jacobson, Gary C. "Impeachment Politics in the 1998 Congressional Elections." *Political Science Quarterly* 114 (1999): 31–51.

Johnson, Dawn. "Executive Privilege since *United States v. Nixon:* Issues of Motivation and Accommodation." *Minnesota Law Review* 83 (1999): 1127–41.

Kagay, Michael R. "Public Opinion and Polling during Presidential Scandals and Impeachment." *Public Opinion Quarterly* 63 (1999): 449–63.

Kainec, Lisa A. "Judicial Review of Senate Impeachment Proceedings: Is a Hands Off Approach Appropriate?" *Case Western Reserve Law Review* 43 (1993): 1499–1527.

Kelly, William K. "The Constitutional Dilemma of Litigation under the Independent Counsel System." *Minnesota Law Review* 83 (1999): 1197–1259.

Kondracke, Morton M. "Will Democratic Charges That Bush Lied Lead to His Impeachment?" *Roll Call,* November 17, 2005.

Lacovara, Philip Allen. "*United States v. Nixon:* Presidential Power and Executive Privilege Twenty-five Years Later." *Minnesota Law Review* 83 (1999): 1061–67.

Ladd, Everett Carll, Jr. "The Polls: The Question of Confidence." *Public Opinion Quarterly* 40 (1976–1977): 544–52.

Lambert, William. "Fortas of the Supreme Court: A Question of Ethics; The Justice and the Stock Manipulator." *Life,* May 5, 1969.

Lang, Gladys Engel, and Kurt Lang. "Polling on Watergate: The Battle for Public Opinion." *Public Opinion Quarterly* 44 (1980): 530–47.

LaRue, L. H. "The Story about Clinton's Impeachment." *Law and Contemporary Problems* 63 (2000): 193–99.

Libernan, Lee S. "*Morrison v. Olson:* A Formalistic Perspective on Why the Court Was Wrong." *American University Law Review* 38 (1989): 313–58.

Lipset, Seymour Martin. "The Decades of the Radical Right: Coughlinites, McCarthyites, and Birchers—1962." In *The Radical Right: The New American Right, Expanded and Updated,* ed. Daniel Bell, 313–77. Garden City, N.Y.: Doubleday, 1963.

Lowi, Theodore J. Foreword to *The Politics of Scandal: Power and Process in Liberal Democracy,* ed. Andrei S. Markovitz and Mark Silverstein, vii–xii. New York: Holmes & Meier, 1988.

Luchsinger, Daniel. "Committee Impeachment Trials: The Best Solution?" *Georgetown Law Journal* 80 (1991): 163–90.

Manes, Lonnie, and Richard Chesteen. "The First Attempt at Presidential Impeachment: Partisan Conflict and Intra-Party Conflict at Loose." *Presidential Studies Quarterly* 10 (Winter 1980): 51–73.

Manning, John F. "The Independent Counsel Statute: Reading 'Good Cause' in Light of Article II." *Minnesota Law Review* 83 (1999): 1285–1335.

Marcus, Greil. "The Man from Nowhere." *Cultural Critique* 43 (1999): 1–13.

Massaro, John. "LBJ and the Fortas Nomination for Chief Justice." *Political Science Quarterly* 97 (1982–1983): 603–21.

Mauro, Tony. "The Chairman in Winter: Peter Rodino Jr.'s Perspective on Impeachment." *American Lawyer* 26 (March 2004): 59–61.

Maxman, Melissa H. "In Defense of the Constitution's Judicial Impeachment Standard." *Michigan Law Review* 86 (1987): 420–63.

McCalla, Patrick Donald. "Judicial Disciplining of Federal Judges Is Constitutional." *Southern California Law Review* 62 (1989): 1263–96.

McClain, Paula D. "Arizona 'High Noon': The Recall and Impeachment of Evan Meacham." *PS: Political Science and Politics* 21 (1988): 628–38.

McConnell, Mitch. "Reflections on the Senate's Role in the Judicial Impeachment Process and Proposals for Change." *Kentucky Law Journal* 76 (1988): 738–60.

McGeever, Patrick J. "'Guilty Yes; Impeachment No': Some Empirical Findings." *Political Science Quarterly* 89 (1974): 289–99.

McLeod, Jack M., Jane D. Brown, and Lee B. Becker. "Watergate and the 1974 Congressional Elections." *Public Opinion Quarterly* 41 (1977): 181–95.

McNeely-Johnson, K. A. "*United States v. Nixon,* Twenty Years After: The Good, the Bad, and the Ugly—An Exploration of Executive Privilege." *Northern Illinois University Law Review* 14 (1994): 251–301.

Meadow, Robert G. "Information and Maturation in Children's Evaluation of Government Leadership during Watergate." *Western Political Quarterly* 35 (1982): 539–53.

Meernik, James, and Peter Waterman. "The Myth of the Diversionary Use of Force by American Presidents." *Political Research Quarterly* 49 (1996): 573–90.

Menefee, Joan. "From the Mouths of Politicians: Representing Children in the Public Sphere." *Cultural Critique* 43 (1999): 105–17.

Miller, Arthur H. "Sex, Politics, and Public Opinion: What Political Scientists Really Learned from the Clinton-Lewinsky Scandal." *PS: Political Science and Politics* 32 (1999): 721–29.

Miroff, Bruce. "The Presidency and the Public: Leadership as Spectacle." In *The Presidency and the Political System,* ed. Michael Nelson, 4th ed., 273–96. Washington, D.C.: CQ Press, 1995.

Mitchell, Luke. "At Issue in the 2004 Election: A Run on Terror." *Harper's,* March 2004, 79.

Moore, Stanley W., Kenneth Wagner, James Lare, and D. Stephen McHargue II. "The Civic Awareness of Five and Six Year Olds." *Western Political Quarterly* 29 (1976): 410–24.

Morgan, Charles, Jr., Hope Eastman, Mary Ellen Gale, and Judith Areen. "Impeachment: An Historical Overview." *Seton Hall Law Review* 5 (1973–1974): 689–719.

Morgan, Peter W. "The Undefined Crime of Lying to Congress: Ethics Reform and the Rule of Law." *Northwestern University Law Review* 86 (1992): 177–258.

Neustadt, Richard E. "The Constraining of the President: The Presidency after Watergate." *British Journal of Political Science* 4 (1974): 383–97.

O'Connor, John D. "I'm the Guy They Called Deep Throat." *Vanity Fair,* May 31, 2005.

Oliver, Kendrick. "'Post-Industrial Society' and the Psychology of the American Far Right, 1950–74." *Journal of Contemporary History* 34 (1999): 601–18.

O'Sullivan, Julie R. "The Interaction between Impeachment and the Independent Counsel Statute." *Georgetown Law Journal* 86 (1998): 2193–2265.

Paletz, David L., Jonathan Y. Short, Helen Baker, Barbara Cookman Campbell, Richard J. Cooper, and Rochelle M. Oeslander. "Polls in the Media: Content, Credibility, and Consequences." *Public Opinion Quarterly* 44 (1980): 495–513.

Paletz, David L., and Richard J. Vinegar. "Presidents on Television: The Effects of Instant Analysis." *Public Opinion Quarterly* 41 (1977): 488–97.

Paulsen, Michael Stokes. "Nixon Now: The Courts and the Presidency after Twenty-five Years." *Minnesota Law Review* 83 (1999): 1337–1404.

Pepper, Thomas. "On the Degradation of the Political Life in a Certain Type of Object Choice Made by Men." *Cultural Critique* 43 (1999): 38–55.

Perkins, Lynette P. "Member Recruitment to a Mixed Goal Committee: The House Judiciary Committee." *Journal of Politics* 43 (1981): 348–64.

Peterson, Todd D. "The Role of the Executive Branch in the Discipline and Removal of Federal Judges." *University of Illinois Law Review,* 1993: 809–96.

Pious, Richard M. "The Paradox of Clinton Winning and the Presidency Losing." *Political Science Quarterly* 114 (1999): 569–93.

Plotke, David. "The Success and Anger of the Modern American Right." In *The Radical Right,* ed. Daniel Bell, 3rd. ed., xi–xxvi. New Brunswick, N.J.: Transaction, 2003.

Prakash, Saikrishna Bagalore. "A Critical Comment on the Constitutionality of Executive Privilege." *Minnesota Law Review* 83 (1999): 1145–89.

Rehnquist, William H. "The Impeachment Clause: A Wild Card in the Constitution." *Northwestern University Law Review* 85 (1991): 903–18.

Rezneck, Daniel A. "Is Judicial Review of Impeachment Coming?" *American Bar Association Journal* 60 (1974): 681–85.

Richetti, Sandra E. "Congressional Power vis-à-vis the President and Presidential Papers." *Duquesne Law Review* 32 (1994): 773–98.

Rieder, Jonathan. "The Rise of the Silent Majority." In *The Rise and Fall of the New Deal Order, 1930–1980,* ed. Gary Gerstle and Steve Fraser, 243–68. Princeton, N.J.: Princeton University Press, 1989.

Rieger, Carol T. "The Judicial Councils Reform and Judicial Conduct and Disability Act: Will Judges Judge Judges?" *Emory Law Journal* 37 (1988): 45–97.

Riesman, David. "The Intellectuals and the Discontented Classes: Some Further Reflections—1962." In *The Radical Right: The New American Right, Expanded and Updated,* ed. Daniel Bell, 115–34. Garden City, N.Y.: Doubleday, 1963.

Rose, Melody. "Losing Control: The Intraparty Consequences of Divided Government." *Presidential Studies Quarterly* 31 (2001): 679–98.

Rothenberg, Lawrence S., and Mitchell S. Sanders. "Lame-Duck Politics: Impending Departure and the Votes on Impeachment." *Political Research Quarterly* 53 (2000): 523–46.

Rozell, Mark. "Executive Privilege and the Modern Presidency: In Nixon's Shadow." *Minnesota Law Review* 83 (1999): 1069–1126.

Rozell, Mark, and Clyde Wilcox, "The Clinton Scandal in Retrospect." *PS: Political Science and Politics* 32 (1999): 538–40.

Rubner, Michael. "The Reagan Administration, the 1973 War Powers Resolution, and the Invasion of Grenada." *Political Science Quarterly* 100 (1986): 627–47.

Ruckman, P. S., Jr. "The Supreme Court, Critical Nominations, and the Senate Confirmation Process." *Journal of Politics* 55 (1993): 793–805.

Said, Edward. "The President and the Baseball Player." *Cultural Critique* 43 (1999): 133–38.

Schulte-Saase, Jochem. "The Quest for a Transcendent Foundation of 'The Law' in the Discourse of Impeachment." *Cultural Critique* 43 (1999): 56–78.

Schulte-Saase, Linda. "Fixing the Nation's Problems: When a Sweet Bird of Youth Crosses the Line." *Cultural Critique* 43 (1999): 13–37.

Shaney, Peter M. "Who May Discipline or Remove Federal Judges? A Constitutional Analysis." *University of Pennsylvania Law Review* 142 (1993): 142–242.

Sigelman, Lee, Christopher J. Deering, and Burdette A. Loomis. "'Wading Knee Deep in Words, Words, Words': Senatorial Rhetoric in the Johnson and Clinton Impeachment Trials." *Congress and the Presidency* 28 (2001): 119–39.

Silverstein, Mark, and Benjamin Ginsberg. "The Supreme Court and the New Politics of Judicial Power." *Political Science Quarterly* 102 (1987): 371–88.

Small, Melvin. "The New Adventures of Larry, Moe, and Curly: Oliver North's Private Enterprise." *Reviews in American History* 20 (1992): 270–75.

Smith, Alexa J. "Federal Judicial Impeachment: Defining Process Due." *Hastings Law Journal* 46 (1995): 639–74.

Smith, David Todd. "Impeachment Trial Clause—A Claim That Senate Impeachment Rule XI Violates the Impeachment Trial Clause Is a Nonjusticiable Political Question." *St. Mary's Law Journal* 25 (1994): 855–83.

Smoller, Fred. "Watergate Revisited." *PS: Political Science and Politics* 25 (1992): 225–27.

Sonner, Molly W., and Clyde Wilcox. "Forgiving and Forgetting: Public Support for Bill Clinton during the Lewinsky Scandal." *PS: Political Science and Politics* 32 (1999): 554–57.

Spitzer, Robert J. "Clinton's Impeachment Will Have Few Consequences for the Presidency." *PS: Political Science and Politics* 32 (1999): 541–45.

Stewart, David O. "Impeachment by Ignorance," *ABA Journal* 76 (1990): 52.

Stolz, Preble. "Disciplining Federal Judges: Is Impeachment Hopeless?" *California Law Review* 57 (1969): 659–70.

Stone, Barbara S. "The John Birch Society: A Profile." *Journal of Politics* 36 (February 1974): 184–97.

Strum, Philippa. "Change and Continuity on the Supreme Court: Conversations with Justice Harry A. Blackmun." *University of Richmond Law Review* 34 (March 2000): 285–304.

Stuckey, Mary E., and Shannon Warshall. "Sex, Lies, and Presidential Leadership: Interpretations of the Office." *Presidential Studies Quarterly* 30 (2000): 514–33.

Sugrue, Thomas J. "Crabgrass-Roots Politics: Race, Rights, and the Reaction against Liberalism in the Urban North, 1940–1964." *Journal of American History* 82 (1995): 551–78.

Sullivan, Terry. "Impeachment Practice in the Era of Lethal Conflict." *Congress and the Presidency* 25 (1998): 117–28.

Sunstein, Cass R. "Impeaching the President." *University of Pennsylvania Law Review* 147 (1998): 279–315.

Sussmann, Leila. "News Coverage in the Downfall of Nixon." *Contemporary Sociology* 12 (1983): 622–29.

Sweeney, J. P. "Presidential Impeachment and Judicial Review." *American University Law Review* 23 (1974): 959–93.

Thomas, Jeannie B. "Dumb Blondes, Dan Quayle, and Hillary Clinton: Gender, Sexuality, and Stupidity in Jokes." *Journal of American Folklore* 110 (1997): 277–313.

Thompson, Frank, Jr., and Daniel H. Pollitt. "Impeachment of Federal Judges: An Historical Overview." *North Carolina Law Review* 49 (1970): 87–121.

Turley, Jonathan. "Congress as Grand Jury: The Role of the House of Representatives in the Impeachment of an American President." *George Washington Law Review* 67 (1999): 735–90.

———. "Paradise Lost: The Clinton Administration and the Erosion of Executive Privilege." *Maryland Law Review* 60 (2001): 205–48.

———. "Senate Trials and Factional Disputes: Impeachment as a Madisonian Device." *Duke Law Journal* 49 (October 1999): 1–146.

Uslaner, Eric M., and Margaret Conway. "The Responsible Congressional Electorate: Watergate, the Economy, and Vote Choice in 1974." *American Political Science Review* 79 (1985): 788–803.

Van Tassel, Emily Field. "Resignations and Removals: A History of Federal Judicial Service—and Disservice—1789–1992." *University of Pennsylvania Law Review* 142 (1993): 333–408.

Viereck, Peter. "The Philosophical 'New Conservatism'—1962." In *The Radical Right: The New American Right, Expanded and Updated,* ed. Daniel Bell, 155–73. Garden City, N.Y.: Doubleday, 1963.

Walton, R. Brent. "We're No Angels: *Paula Corbin Jones v. William Jefferson Clinton.*" *Tulane Law Review* 71 (1997): 897–985.

Wayne, Stephen J. "Clinton's Legacy: The Clinton Persona." *PS: Political Science and Politics* 32 (1999): 558–64.

Weiner, Matthew Cooper. "In the Wake of Whitewater: Executive Privilege and the Institutionalized Conflict Element of Separation of Powers." *Journal of Law and Politics* 12 (1996): 775–811.

Westin, Alan F. "The John Birch Society: Radical Right and Extreme Left in the Political Context of Post World War II—1962." In *The Radical Right: The New American Right, Expanded and Updated,* ed. Daniel Bell, 201–26. Garden City, N.Y.: Doubleday, 1963.

Wright, Gerald C., Jr. "Constituency Response to Congressional Behavior: The Impact of the House Judiciary Committee Impeachment Votes." *Western Political Quarterly* 30 (1977): 401–10.

Yampert, John de, Jr. "The Death of Constitutional Law: A Critique of the *Clinton v. Jones* Decision." *Thurgood Marshall Law Review* 26 (2001): 185–203.

Yoo, John C. "The First Claim: The Burr Trial, *United States v. Nixon,* and Presidential Power." *Minnesota Law Review* 83 (1999): 1435–79.

Zeidenstein, Harvey G. "The Reassertion of Congressional Power: New Curbs on the President." *Political Science Quarterly* 93 (1978): 393–409.

Books

Abraham, Henry J. *Justices and Presidents: A Political History of Appointments to the Supreme Court.* 2nd ed. New York: Oxford University Press, 1985.

Ackerman, Bruce. *The Case against Lameduck Impeachment.* New York: Seven Stories Press, 1999.

Adams, Willi Paul. *The First American Constitutions: Republican Ideology and the Making of the State Constitutions in the Revolution Era.* Chapel Hill: University of North Carolina Press, 1980.

Adler, David Gray, and Michael A. Genovese. *The Presidency and the Law: The Clinton Legacy.* Lawrence: University Press of Kansas, 2002.

Alterman, Eric. *What Liberal Media? The Truth about Bias and the News.* New York: Basic Books, 2003.

———. *When Presidents Lie: A History of Official Deception and Its Consequences.* New York: Viking, 2004.

Ambrose, Stephen E. *Nixon.* 3 vols. New York: Simon & Schuster, 1987–91.

Anderson, Terry H. *The Movement and the Sixties: Protest in America from Greensboro to Wounded Knee.* New York: Oxford University Press, 1995.

Andrew, John A., III. *The Other Side of the Sixties: Young Americans for Freedom and the Rise of Conservative Politics.* New Brunswick, N.J.: Rutgers University Press, 1997.

———. *Power to Destroy: The Political Use of the IRS from Kennedy to Nixon.* Chicago: Ivan R. Dee, 2002.

Annis, J. Lee. *Howard Baker: Conciliator in an Age of Crisis.* Lanham, Md.: Madison Books, 1995.

Anson, Robert Sam. *Exile: The Unquiet Oblivion of Richard M. Nixon.* New York: Simon & Schuster, 1984.

Arnold, Peri. *Making the Managerial Presidency: Comprehensive Reorganization Planning, 1905–1996.* 2nd ed. Lawrence: University Press of Kansas, 1998.

Auth, Tony. *Behind the Lines.* Boston: Houghton Mifflin, 1977.

Baker, Peter. *The Breach: Inside the Impeachment and Trial of William Jefferson Clinton.* New York: Berkeley, 2000.

Bartley, Numan. *The Rise of Massive Resistance: Race and Politics in the South during the 1950s.* Baton Rouge: Louisiana State University Press, 1969.

Bartley, Numan, and Hugh D. Graham. *Southern Politics and the Second Reconstruction*. Baltimore: Johns Hopkins University Press, 1975.

Benedict, Michael Les. *The Impeachment and Trial of Andrew Johnson*. New York: W. W. Norton, 1973.

Bennett, David. *The Party of Fear: The American Far Right from Nativism to the Militia Movement*. Rev. ed. New York: Vintage, 1995.

Berger, Raoul. *Impeachment: The Constitutional Problems*. Cambridge, Mass.: Harvard University Press, 1973.

Berlant, Lauren, and Lisa Duggan, eds. *Our Monica, Ourselves: The Clinton Affair and the National Interest*. New York: New York University Press, 2001.

Berman, Larry. *Looking Back on the Reagan Presidency*. Baltimore: Johns Hopkins University Press, 1990.

Berman, William C. *America's Right Turn: From Nixon to Clinton*. 2nd ed. Baltimore: Johns Hopkins University Press, 1998.

———. *From the Center to the Edge: The Politics and Policies of the Clinton Presidency*. Lanham, Md.: Rowman & Littlefield, 2001.

Bernstein, Dennis, and Leslie Kean. *Henry Hyde's Moral Universe: Where More Than Time and Space Are Warped*. Monroe, Me: Common Courage, 1999.

Bernstein, Irving. *Guns or Butter: The Presidency of Lyndon Johnson*. New York: Oxford University Press, 1996.

Black, Charles L., Jr. *Impeachment: A Handbook*. New Haven, Conn.: Yale University Press, 1974.

Black, Earl, and Merle Black. *The Rise of Southern Republicans*. Cambridge, Mass.: Harvard University Press, 2004.

Block, Herbert. *Herblock Special Report*. New York: W. W. Norton, 1974.

Blumenthal, Sidney. *Our Long National Daydream: A Political Pageant of the Reagan Era*. New York: Harper & Row, 1988.

———. *The Rise of the Counter-Establishment: From Conservative Ideology to Political Power*. New York: Times Books, 1986.

Brands, H. W. *The Devil We Knew: America and the Cold War*. New York: Oxford University Press, 1993.

Brant, Irving. *Impeachment: Trials and Errors*. New York: Knopf, 1971.

Brauer, Carl B. *John F. Kennedy and the Second Reconstruction*. New York: Columbia University Press, 1977.

Brennan, Mary C. *Turning Right in the Sixties: The Conservative Capture of the GOP*. Chapel Hill: University of North Carolina Press, 1995.

Breslin, Jimmy. *How the Good Guys Finally Won: Notes from an Impeachment Summer*. New York: Viking, 1975.

Brick, Howard. *Age of Contradiction: American Thought and Culture in the 1960s*. Ithaca, N.Y.: Cornell University Press, 1998.

Brock, David. *Blinded by the Right: The Conscience of an Ex-Conservative*. New York: Crown, 2002.

———. *The Republican Noise Machine: Right-Wing Media and How It Corrupts Democracy*. New York: Crown, 2004.

Brodie, Fawn. *Richard Nixon: The Shaping of His Character*. New York: W. W. Norton, 1981.

Bronner, Ethan. *Battle for Justice: How the Bork Nomination Shook America*. New York: W. W. Norton, 1989.

Brownfield, Allan C. *Dossier on Douglas*. Washington, D.C.: New Majority Book Club, 1970.

Brownlee, W. Elliot, and Hugh Davis Graham, eds. *The Reagan Presidency: Pragmatic Conservatism and Its Legacies*. Lawrence: University Press of Kansas, 2003.

Broyles, J. Allen. *The John Birch Society: Anatomy of a Protest*. Boston: Beacon Press, 1964.

Bryce, James. *The American Commonwealth*. 2 vols. New York: Macmillan, 1895.

Busby, Robert. *Defending the American Presidency: Clinton and the Lewinsky Scandal*. New York: Palgrave, 2001.

———. *Reagan and the Iran-Contra Affair: The Politics of Presidential Recovery*. New York: St. Martin's Press, 1999.

Bushnell, Eleanor. *Crimes, Follies, and Misfortunes: The Federal Impeachment Trials*. Urbana: University of Illinois Press, 1992.

Cain, Edward. *They'd Rather Be Right*. New York: Macmillan, 1963.

Cannon, Lou. *The McCloskey Challenge*. New York: E. P. Dutton, 1972.

———. *President Reagan: The Role of a Lifetime*. New York: Simon & Schuster, 1991.

Carter, Dan T. *From George Wallace to Newt Gingrich: Race in the Conservative Counterrevolution, 1963–1994*. Baton Rouge: Louisiana State University Press, 1996.

———. *The Politics of Rage: George Wallace, the Origins of the New Conservatism, and the Transformation of American Politics*. New York: Simon & Schuster, 1995.

Center for Constitutional Rights. *Articles of Impeachment against George W. Bush*. Hoboken, N.J.: Melville House, 2006.

Charns, Alexander. *Cloak and Gavel: FBI Wiretaps, Bugs, Informers, and the Supreme Court*. Urbana: University of Illinois Press, 1992.

Clancy, Paul R. *Just a Country Lawyer: A Biography of Senator Sam Ervin*. Bloomington: Indiana University Press, 1974.

Clymer, Adam. *Edward M. Kennedy: A Biography*. New York: William Morrow, 1999.

Cochran, Augustus B., III. *Democracy Heading South: National Politics in the Shadow of Dixie*. Lawrence: University Press of Kansas, 2001.

Cohen, Richard M., and Jules Witcover. *A Heartbeat Away: The Investigation and Resignation of Vice President Spiro T. Agnew*. New York: Viking, 1974.

Cohodas, Nadine. *Strom Thurmond and the Politics of Southern Change*. Macon, Ga.: Mercer University Press, 1993.

Colodny Len, and Robert Gettlin. *Silent Coup: The Removal of a President*. New York: St. Martin's Press, 1991.

Comiskey, Michael. *Seeking Justices: The Judging of Supreme Court Nominees*. Lawrence: University Press of Kansas, 2004.

Conason, Joe. *It Can Happen Here: Authoritarian Perils in the Age of Bush*. New York: St. Martin's Press, 2007.

Conason, Joe, and Gene Lyons. *The Hunting of the President: The Ten-Year Campaign to Destroy Bill and Hillary Clinton*. New York: St. Martin's Press, 2000.

Cook, Fred J. *Barry Goldwater: Extremist of the Right*. New York: Grove Press, 1964.

Cottrell, Robert J., Raymond T. Diamond, and Leland B. Ware. *Brown v. Board of Education: Caste, Culture, and the Constitution*. Lawrence: University Press of Kansas, 2003.

Coulter, Ann H. *High Crimes and Misdemeanors: The Case against Bill Clinton*. Washington, D.C.: Regnery, 1998.

Cox, Gary W., and Samuel Kernell. *The Politics of Divided Government*. Boulder, Colo.: Westview Press, 1991.

Crawford, Alan. *Thunder on the Right: The "New Right" and the Politics of Resentment*. New York: Pantheon, 1980.

Crouse, Timothy. *The Boys on the Bus*. New York: Ballantine, 1973.

Crowley, Monica. *Nixon in Winter*. New York: Random House, 1998.

Dabney, Dick. *A Good Man: The Life of Sam J. Ervin*. Boston: Houghton Mifflin, 1976.

Dallek, Robert. *Flawed Giant: Lyndon Johnson and His Times, 1961–1973*. New York: Oxford University Press, 1998.

————. *Hail to the Chief: The Making and Unmaking of American Presidents*. New York: Hyperion, 1996.

————. *An Unfinished Life: John F. Kennedy, 1917–1963*. Boston: Little, Brown, 2003.

Daniel, Pete. *Lost Revolutions: The South in the 1950s*. Chapel Hill: University of North Carolina Press, 2000.

DeKoster, Lester. *The Christian and the John Birch Society*. Grand Rapids, Mich.: William B. Eerdmans, 1965.

De la Vega, Elizabeth. *United States v. George W. Bush et al*. New York: Seven Stories Press, 2006.

Denton, Robert E., Jr., and Rachel L. Holloway, eds. *Images, Scandal, and Communication Strategies of the Clinton Presidency*. Westport, Conn.: Praeger, 2003.

Dershowitz, Alan M. *Sexual McCarthyism: Clinton, Starr, and the Emerging Constitutional Crisis*. New York: Basic Books, 1998.

Diamond, Sara. *Roads to Dominion: Right-Wing Movements and Political Power in the United States*. New York: Guilford Press, 1995.

Diggins, John P. *Up from Communism: Conservative Odysseys in American Intellectual History*. New York: Harper & Row, 1975.

Douglas, William O. *Points of Rebellion*. New York: Random House, 1970.

Draper, Theodore. *A Very Thin Line: The Iran-Contra Affairs*. New York: Hill & Wang, 1991.

Drew, Elizabeth. *The Corruption of American Politics: What Went Wrong and Why*. Secaucus, N.J.: Birch Lane Press, 1999.

————. *Washington Journal: The Events of 1973–1974*. New York: Random House, 1974.

Dunne, Gerald. *Hugo Black and the Judicial Revolution*. New York: Simon & Schuster, 1977.

Easton, David, and Jack Dennis. *Children in the Political System: The Origins of Political Legitimacy*. New York: McGraw-Hill, 1969.

Ehrlich, Walter. *Presidential Impeachment: An American Dilemma*. Saint Charles, Mo.: Forum Press, 1974.

Ellers, Joseph C. *Strom Thurmond: The Public Man*. Orangeburg, S.C.: Sandlapper, 1993.

Emery, Fred. *Watergate: The Corruption of American Politics and the Fall of Richard Nixon*. London: Jonathan Cape, 1994.

Epstein, Benjamin R., and Arnold Forster. *The Radical Right: Report on the John Birch Society and Its Allies*. New York, Random House, 1967.

Farber, David, and Jeff Roche, eds. *The Conservative Sixties*. New York: Peter Lang, 2003.

Farrell, John Aloysius. *Tip O'Neill and the Democratic Century*. Boston: Little, Brown, 2001.

Feeney, Mark. *Nixon at the Movies: A Book about Belief*. Chicago: University of Chicago Press, 2004.

Feiffer, Jules. *Feiffer on Nixon: The Cartoon Presidency*. New York: Random House, 1974.

Felsenthal, Carol. *Power, Privilege, and the Post: The Katharine Graham Story*. New York: Putnam's, 1993.

Fields, Howard. *High Crimes and Misdemeanors: "Wherefore Richard M. Nixon . . . Warrants Impeachment": The Dramatic Story of the Rodino Committee*. New York: W. W. Norton, 1978.

Fiorina, Morris. *Divided Government*. New York: Macmillan, 1992.

Fleming, James S. *Window on Congress: A Congressional Biography of Barber B. Conable Jr.* Rochester, N.Y.: University of Rochester Press, 2004.

Forster, Arnold, and Benjamin R. Epstein. *Danger on the Right*. New York: Random House, 1964.

Frank, Pat, ed. *The Goldwater Cartoon Book*. Washington, D.C.: National Publishing, 1964.

Fredrickson, Kari. *The Dixiecrat Revolt and the End of the Solid South, 1932–1968*. Chapel Hill: University of North Carolina Press, 2001.

Freeman, Richard B., ed. *Graphics '75: Watergate, the Unmaking of a President*. Lexington: University of Kentucky Art Gallery, 1975.

Fried, Amy. *Muffled Echoes: Oliver North and the Politics of Public Opinion*. New York: Columbia University Press, 1997.

Frost, David. *"I Gave Them a Sword": Behind the Scenes of the Nixon Interviews*. New York: William Morrow, 1978.

Garrow, David. *Liberty and Sexuality: The Right to Privacy and the Making of Roe v. Wade*. New York: Macmillan, 1994.

Gerhardt, Michael J. *The Federal Impeachment Process: A Constitutional and Historical Analysis*. 2nd ed. Chicago: University of Chicago Press, 2000.

Ginsberg, Benjamin, and Martin Shefter. *Politics by Other Means: Politicians, Prosecutors, and the Press from Watergate to Whitewater*. New York: W. W. Norton, 1999.

Goldberg, Robert Alan. *Barry Goldwater*. New Haven, Conn.: Yale University Press, 1995.

Gordon, Rosalie M. *Nine Men against America: The Supreme Court and Its Attack on American Liberties*. New York: Devin-Adair, 1958.

Gormley, Ken. *Archibald Cox: Conscience of a Nation*. Reading, Mass.: Addison-Wesley, 1997.

Gould, Lewis L. *The Modern American Presidency*. Lawrence: University Press of Kansas, 2003.

Green, John C., Mark J. Rozell, and Clyde Wilcox, eds. *The Christian Right in American Politics: Marching to the Millennium*. Washington, D.C.: Georgetown University Press, 2003.

Greenberg, David. *Nixon's Shadow: The History of an Image*. New York: W. W. Norton, 2003.

Greenhouse, Linda. *Becoming Justice Blackmun: Harry Blackmun's Supreme Court Journey*. New York: Times Books, 2005.

Greenstein, Fred I. *Children and Politics*. New Haven, Conn.: Yale University Press, 1965.

———. *The Presidential Difference: Leadership Style from FDR to Clinton*. New York: Free Press, 2000.

Griffen, G. Edward. *The Great Prison Break: The Supreme Court Leads the Way*. Belmont, Mass.: Western Islands, 1970.

Grove, Gene. *Inside the John Birch Society*. Greenwich, Conn.: Gold Medal, 1961.

Hardisty, Jeqaan. *Mobilizing Resentment: Conservative Resurgence from the John Birch Society to the Promise Keepers*. Boston: Beacon Press, 1999.

Harriger, Katy J. *The Special Prosecutor in American Politics*. 2nd ed. rev. Lawrence: University Press of Kansas, 2000.

Harris, John F. *The Survivor: Bill Clinton in the White House*. New York: Random House, 2005.

Harris, Richard. *Decision*. New York: E. P. Dutton, 1971.

———. *Justice: The Crisis of Law, Order, and Freedom in America*. New York: E. P. Dutton, 1970.

Hayward, Steven F. *The Age of Reagan: The Fall of the Old Liberal Order, 1964–1980*. Roseville, Calif.: Forum, 2001.

Hertsgaard, Mark. *On Bended Knee: The Press and the Reagan Presidency*. New York: Farrar, Straus & Giroux, 1988.

Himmelstein, Jerome L. *To the Right: The Transformation of American Conservatism*. Berkeley: University of California Press, 1990.

Hodgson, Geoffrey. *The Gentleman from New York: Daniel Patrick Moynihan: A Biography*. Boston: Houghton Mifflin, 2000.

Hoff, Joan. *Nixon Reconsidered*. New York: Basic Books, 1994.

Hoffer, Peter Charles, and N. E. H. Hull. *Impeachment in America, 1635–1805*. New Haven, Conn.: Yale University Press, 1984.

Hogan, Jim. *Secret Agenda: Watergate, Deep Throat, and the CIA*. New York: Random House, 1984.

Holtzman, Elizabeth. *The Impeachment of George W. Bush: A Practical Guide for Concerned Citizens*. With Cynthia L. Cooper. New York: Nation Books, 2006.

Horwitz, Morton J. *The Warren Court and the Pursuit of Justice*. New York: Hill & Wang, 1998.

Irvine, Janice M. *Talk about Sex: The Battle over Sex Education in the United States*. Berkeley: University of California Press, 2002.

Isikoff, Michael. *Uncovering Clinton: A Reporter's Story*. New York: Crown, 1999.

Issacs, Arnold R. *Vietnam Shadows: The War, Its Ghosts, and Its Legacy*. Baltimore: Johns Hopkins University Press, 1997.

Isserman, Maurice, and Michael Katz. *America Divided: The Civil War of the 1960s*. New York: Oxford University Press, 2000.

Jensen, Merrill. *The Articles of Confederation*. Madison: University of Wisconsin Press, 1940.

Johnson, Haynes. *The Best of Times: America in the Clinton Years*. New York: Harcourt, 2001.

———. *Sleepwalking through History: America in the Reagan Years*. New York: W. W. Norton, 1991.

Johnson, John W. *Griswold v. Connecticut: Birth Control and the Constitutional Right of Privacy*. Lawrence: University Press of Kansas, 2005.

Judis, John B. *The Paradox of American Democracy*. New York: Pantheon, 2000.

———. *William F. Buckley, Jr.: Patron Saint of the Conservatives*. New York: Simon & Schuster, 1988.

Kalman, Laura. *Abe Fortas: A Biography*. New Haven, Conn.: Yale University Press, 1990.

Kaplan, Leonard, and Beverly I. Moran, eds. *Aftermath: The Clinton Impeachment and the Presidency in the Age of Political Spectacle*. New York: New York University Press, 2001.

Katcher, Leo. *Earl Warren: A Political Biography*. New York: McGraw-Hill, 1967.

Kazin, Michael. *The Populist Persuasion: An American History*. Ithaca, N.Y.: Cornell University Press, 1995.

Kelly, John F., and Phillip K. Wearne. *Tainting Evidence: Inside the Scandals at the FBI Crime Lab*. New York: Free Press, 1998.

Kennedy, John F. *Profiles in Courage*. New York: Harper, 1955.

Kimball, Jeffrey. *Nixon's Vietnam War*. Lawrence: University Press of Kansas, 1998.

Klarman, Michael J. *From Jim Crow to Civil Rights: The Supreme Court and the Struggle for Racial Equality*. New York: Oxford University Press, 2004.

Klatch, Rebecca E. *A Generation Divided: The New Left, the New Right, and the 1960s*. Berkeley: University of California Press, 1999.

———. *Women of the New Right*. Philadelphia: Temple University Press, 1987.

Klein, Joe. *The Natural: The Misunderstood Presidency of Bill Clinton*. New York: Doubleday, 2002.

Kluger, Richard. *Simple Justice: The History of Brown v. Board of Education and Black America's Struggle for Equality*. New York: Knopf, 1976.

Kurland, Philip B. *Politics, the Constitution, and the Warren Court*. Chicago: University of Chicago Press, 1970.

———. *Watergate and the Constitution*. Chicago: University of Chicago Press, 1978.

Kurtz, Howard. *Spin Cycle: Inside the Clinton Propaganda Machine*. New York: Free Press, 1998.

Kutler, Stanley I. *The American Inquisition: Justice and Injustice in the Cold War*. New York: Hill & Wang, 1982.

———. *The Wars of Watergate: The Last Crisis of Richard Nixon*. New York: Knopf, 1990.

Kyvig, David E. *Explicit and Authentic Acts: Amending the U.S. Constitution, 1776–1995*. Lawrence: University Press of Kansas, 1996.

———, ed. *Unintended Consequences of Constitutional Amendment*. Athens: University of Georgia Press, 2000.

Labovitz, John R. *Presidential Impeachment*. New Haven, Conn.: Yale University Press, 1978.

Lamb, Karl A. *Reasonable Disagreement: Two U.S. Senators and the Choices They Make*. New York: Garland, 1998.

Lang, Gladys Engel, and Kurt Lang. *The Battle for Public Opinion: The President, the Press, and the Polls during Watergate*. New York: Columbia University Press, 1983.

Lapham, Lewis. *Pretensions to Empire: Notes on the Criminal Folly of the Bush Administration*. New York: New Press, 2006.

LaRue, L. H. *Political Discourse: A Case Study of the Watergate Affair*. Athens: University of Georgia Press, 1988.

Lasky, Victor. *It Didn't Start with Watergate*. New York: Dial, 1977.

Leahy, Stephen M. *The Life of Milwaukee's Most Popular Politician, Clement J. Zablocki: Milwaukee Politics and Congressional Foreign Policy*. Lewiston, N.Y.: Edwin Mellen, 2002.

LeoGrande, William M. *Our Own Backyard: The United States in Central America, 1977–1992*. Chapel Hill: University of North Carolina Press, 1998.

Levy, Leonard W., and Dennis J. Mahoney, eds. *The Framing and Ratification of the Constitution*. New York: Macmillan, 1987.

Lindorff, Dave, and Barbara Olshansky. *The Case for Impeachment: The Legal Argument for Removing President George W. Bush from Office*. New York: Thomas Dunne Books, 2006.

Lipset, Seymour, and Earl Raab. *The Politics of Unreason: Right Wing Extremism in America, 1790–1970*. New York: Harper & Row, 1970.

Loo, Dennis, and Peter Phillips, eds. *Impeach the President: The Case against Bush and Cheney*. New York: Seven Stories Press, 2006.

Lott, Trent. *Leading the United States Senate*. The Leader's Lecture Series, 107th Cong., 2nd sess. Washington, D.C.: GPO, 2002.

Lowry, Rich. *Legacy: Paying the Price for the Clinton Years*. Washington, D.C.: Regnery, 2003.

Lukas, J. Anthony. *Nightmare: The Underside of the Nixon Years*. New York: Viking, 1976.

Malti-Douglas, Fedwa. *The Starr Report Disrobed*. New York: Columbia University Press, 2000.

Mander, Jerry. *The Wizard of "Is": The Story of the Impeachment of Billy Jeff Clinton and His Trailer Park Presidency*. Kearney, Neb.: Morris, 1999.

Mankiewicz, Frank. *U.S. v. Richard M. Nixon: The Final Crisis*. New York: Quadrangle, 1975.

Mann, Thomas E., and Norman J. Ornstein. *The Broken Branch: How Congress Is Falling Apart and How to Get It Back on Track*. New York: Oxford University Press, 2006.

Marshall, P. David. *Celebrity and Power: Fame in Contemporary Culture*. Minneapolis: University of Minnesota Press, 1997.

Martin, William. *With God on Our Side: The Rise of the Religious Right in America*. New York: Broadway Books, 1996.

Mayer, Jane, and Doyle McManus. *Landslide: The Unmaking of the President, 1984–1988*. Boston: Houghton Mifflin, 1988.

Mayer, Jeremy D. *Running on Race: Racial Politics in Presidential Campaigns, 1960–2000*. New York: Random House, 2002.

McDonald, Forrest. *The American Presidency: An Intellectual History*. Lawrence: University Press of Kansas, 1994.

McGirr, Lisa. *Suburban Warriors: The Origins of the New American Right*. Princeton. N.J.: Princeton University Press, 2001.

McMillen, Neil R. *The Citizens' Council: Organized Resistance to the Second Reconstruction, 1954–64*. Urbana: University of Illinois Press, 1971.

Melton, Buckner F., Jr. *The First Impeachment: The Constitution's Framers and the Case of Senator William Blount*. Macon, Ga.: Mercer University Press, 1998.

Merkel, Peter H. *A Coup Attempt in Washington?: A European Mirror on the 1998–1999 Constitutional Crisis*. New York: Palgrave, 2001.

Miles, Michael W. *The Odyssey of the American Right*. New York: Oxford University Press, 1980.

Milkis, Sidney. *The President and the Parties*. New York: Oxford University Press, 1993.

Morgan, Peter. *Frost/Nixon*. London: Faber and Faber, 2006.

Morin, Isobel V. *Impeaching the President*. Brookfield, Conn.: Millbrook Press, 1996.

Morris, Irwin L. *Votes, Money, and the Clinton Impeachment*. Boulder, Colo.: Westview Press, 2002.

Murphy, Bruce Allen. *Fortas: The Rise and Ruin of a Supreme Court Justice*. New York: William Morrow, 1988.

———. *Wild Bill: The Legend and Life of William O. Douglas*. New York: Random House, 2003.

Nash, George H. *The Conservative Intellectual Movement in America since 1945*. New York: Basic Books, 1976.

Nathan, Richard P. *The Plot That Failed: Nixon and the Administrative Presidency*. New York: Wiley, 1975.

Nelson, Michael, ed. *The Presidency and the Political System*. 6th ed. Washington, D.C.: CQ Press, 2000.

Neustadt, Richard. *Presidential Power and the Modern Presidency*. New York: Free Press, 1990.

Newton, Jim. *Justice for All: Earl Warren and the Nation He Made*. New York: Penguin, 2005.

Nichols, David K. *The Myth of the Modern Presidency*. University Park: Pennsylvania State University Press, 1994.

Nichols, John. *The Genius of Impeachment: The Founders' Cure for Royalism and Why It Must Be Applied to George W. Bush*. New York: New Press, 2006.

Nunberg, Geoffrey. *Talking Right: How Conservatives Turned Liberalism into a Tax-Raising, Latte-Drinking, Sushi-Eating, Volvo-Driving, New York Times–Reading, Body-Piercing, Hollywood-Loving, Left-Wing Freak Show*. New York: Public Affairs, 2006.

Olson, Keith W. *Watergate: The Presidential Scandal That Shook America*. Lawrence: University Press of Kansas, 2003.

O'Reilly, Kenneth. *Nixon's Piano: Presidents and Racial Politics from Washington to Clinton*. New York: Free Press, 1995.

Paludan, Phillip S. *A Covenant with Death: The Constitution, Law, and Equality in the Civil War Era*. Urbana: University of Illinois Press, 1975.

Patterson, James T. *Brown v. Board of Education: A Civil Rights Milestone and Its Troubled Legacy*. New York: Oxford University Press, 2001.

———. *Grand Expectations: The United States, 1945–1974*. New York: Oxford University Press, 1996.

———. *Restless Giant: The United States, 1974–2000*. New York: Oxford University Press, 2005.

Patterson, Thomas E. *Out of Order*. New York: Vintage, 1993.

Perlstein, Rick. *Before the Storm: Barry Goldwater and the Unmaking of the American Consensus*. New York: Hill & Wang, 2001.

Pfiffner, James P. *The Modern Presidency*. New York: St. Martin's Press, 1994.

Pollack, Jack Harrison. *Earl Warren: The Judge Who Changed America*. Englewood Cliffs, N.J.: Prentice-Hall, 1979.

Posner, Richard A. *An Affair of State: The Investigation, Impeachment, and Trial of President Clinton*. Cambridge, Mass.: Harvard University Press, 1999.

Powe, Lucas A., Jr. *The Warren Court and American Politics*. Cambridge, Mass.: Harvard University Press, 2000.

Rae, Nicol C., and Colton C. Campbell. *Impeaching Clinton: Partisan Strife on Capitol Hill*. Lawrence: University Press of Kansas, 2004.

Rakove, Jack N. *Original Meanings: Politics and Ideas in the Making of the Constitution*. New York: Knopf, 1996.

Reeves, Richard. *President Nixon: Alone in the White House*. New York: Simon & Schuster, 2001.

Rehnquist, William H. *Grand Inquests: The Historic Impeachments of Justice Samuel Chase and President Andrew Johnson*. New York: William Morrow, 1992.

Reinhard, David W. *The Republican Right since 1945*. Lexington: University Press of Kentucky, 1983.

Rich, Frank. *The Greatest Story Ever Sold: The Decline and Fall of Truth from 9/11 to Katrina*. New York: Penguin, 2006.

Ritchie, Donald A. *Reporting from Washington: The History of the Washington Press Corps*. New York: Oxford University Press, 2005.

Roderick, Lee. *Leading the Charge: Orrin Hatch and 20 Years of America*. Carson City, Nev.: Gold Leaf Press, 1994.

Rogin, Michael Paul, and John L. Shover. *Political Change in California: Critical Elections and Social Movements, 1890–1966*. Westport, Conn.: Greenwood, 1970.

Rozell, Mark J. *Executive Privilege: Presidential Power, Secrecy, and Accountability*. 2nd ed. rev. Lawrence: University Press of Kansas, 2002.

Rozell, Mark J., and Clyde Wilcox, eds. *The Clinton Scandal and the Future of American Government*. Washington, D.C.: Georgetown University Press, 2000.

Rudenstine, David. *The Day the Presses Stopped: A History of the Pentagon Papers Case*. Berkeley: University of California Press, 1996.

Rutland, Robert A. *The Ordeal of the Constitution: The Antifederalists and the Ratification Struggle of 1787–1788*. Norman: University of Oklahoma Press, 1965.

Sabin, Arthur J. *In Calmer Times: The Supreme Court and Red Monday*. Philadelphia: University of Pennsylvania Press, 1999.

Schell, Jonathan. *The Time of Illusion*. New York: Vintage, 1976.

Schickel, Richard. *Intimate Strangers: The Culture of Celebrity*. Garden City, N.Y.: Doubleday, 1985.

Schier, Steven E. *The Postmodern Presidency: Bill Clinton's Legacy in U.S. Politics*. Pittsburgh: University of Pittsburgh Press, 2000.

Schlesinger, Arthur M., Jr. *The Imperial Presidency*. Boston: Houghton Mifflin, 1973.

Schmidt, Susan, and Michael Weisskopf. *Truth at Any Cost: Ken Starr and the Unmaking of Bill Clinton*. New York: HarperCollins, 1999.

Schneider, Gregory L. *Cadres for Conservatism: Young Americans for Freedom and the Rise of the Contemporary Right*. New York: New York University Press, 1999.

Schoenwald, Jonathan M. *A Time for Choosing: The Rise of Modern American Conservatism*. New York: Oxford University Press, 2001.

Schram, Peter W., and Radford P. Wilson, eds. *American Political Parties and Constitutional Politics*. Lanham, Md.: Rowman & Littlefield, 1993.

Schudson, Michael. *Watergate in American Memory: How We Remember, Forget, and Reconstruct the Past*. New York: Basic Books, 1992.

Schwartz, Bernard. *Super Chief: Earl Warren and His Supreme Court—A Judiciary Biography*. New York: New York University Press, 1983.

Schwarz, Frederick A. O., Jr., and Aziz Z. Huq. *Unchecked and Unbalanced: Presidential Power in a Time of Terror*. New York: New Press, 2007.

Shawcross, William. *Sideshow: Kissinger, Nixon, and the Destruction of Cambodia*. Rev. ed. New York: Touchstone, 1987.

Shepard, Alicia C. *Woodward and Bernstein: Life in the Shadow of Watergate*. Hoboken, N.J.: John Wiley, 2007.

Shogan, Robert. *A Question of Judgment: The Fortas Case and the Struggle for the Supreme Court*. Indianapolis, Ind.: Bobbs-Merrill, 1972.

Simon, James F. *Independent Journey: The Life of William O. Douglas*. New York: Harper & Row, 1980.

Simpson, Michael M. *The Other Side of Impeachment: A Brief Look into an Unjust, Partisan "Railroad" of an American President*. Salem, Ore.: Winterbloom Books, 2003.

Skowronek, Stephen. *The Politics Presidents Make: Leadership from John Adams to George Bush*. Cambridge, Mass.: Harvard University Press, 1993.

Small, Melvin. *The Presidency of Richard Nixon*. Lawrence: University Press of Kansas, 1999.

Smant, Kevin J. *Principles and Heresies: Frank S. Meyer and the Shaping of the American Conservative Movement*. Wilmington, Del.: ISI Books, 2002.

Smith, Franklin B. *The Assassination of President Nixon*. Rutland, Vt.: Academy Books, 1976.

Smith, Winston, and Corelius Edward O'Connor. *A Call for the Impeachment of President Clinton*. Palm Beach, Fla.: Center for the Protection of Healthy Americans, 1996.

Snyder, K. Alan. *Mission: Impeachable*. Vienna, Va.: Allegiance, 2001.

Spanier, John W. *The Truman-MacArthur Controversy and the Korean War*. Cambridge, Mass.: Belknap Press, 1959.

Stewart, James B. *Blood Sport: The President and His Adversaries*. New York: Simon & Schuster, 1996.

Summers, Anthony. *The Arrogance of Power: The Secret World of Richard Nixon*. New York: Viking, 2000.

Thompson, Kenneth W., ed. *Papers on Presidential Disability and the Twenty-fifth Amendment by Six Medical, Legal, and Political Authorities*. Lanham, Md.: University Press of America, 1988.

Toobin, Jeffrey. *The Nine: Inside the Secret World of the Supreme Court*. New York: Doubleday, 2007.

———. *A Vast Conspiracy: The Real Story of the Sex Scandal That Nearly Brought Down a President*. New York: Random House, 1999.

Toplin, Robert Brent, ed. *Oliver Stone's U.S.A.: Film, History, and Controversy*. Lawrence: University Press of Kansas, 2003.

Trudeau, G. B. *The Doonesbury Chronicles*. New York: Holt, Rinehart and Winston, 1975.

Tygiel, Jules. *Ronald Reagan and the Triumph of American Conservatism*. New York: Pearson, 2005.

Vahan, Richard. *The Truth about the John Birch Society*. New York: Macfadden, 1961.

Van Tassel, Emily Field, and Paul Finkelman. *Impeachable Offenses: A Documentary History from 1787 to the Present*. Washington, D.C.: Congressional Quarterly, 1999.

Volcansek, Mary L. *Judicial Impeachment: None Called for Justice*. Urbana: University of Illinois Press, 1993.

Wasby, Stephen L., ed. *"He Shall Not Pass This Way Again": The Legacy of Justice William O. Douglas*. Pittsburgh: University of Pittsburgh Press, for the William O. Douglas Institute, 1990.

Weaver, John D. *Warren: The Man, the Court, the Era*. Boston: Little, Brown, 1967.

White, G. Edward. *Earl Warren: A Public Life*. New York: Oxford University Press, 1982.

White, Theodore H. *Breach of Faith: The Fall of Richard Nixon*. New York: Atheneum, 1975.

Whitfield, Stephen J. *The Culture of the Cold War*. 2nd ed. Baltimore: Johns Hopkins University Press, 1996.

Wicker, Tom. *One of Us: Richard Nixon and the American Dream*. New York: Random House, 1991.

Wills, Garry. *Reagan's America: Innocents at Home*. Garden City, N.Y.: Doubleday, 1987.

Wilson, Robert A. *Character above All: Ten Presidents from FDR to George Bush*. New York: Simon & Schuster, 1996.

Witcover, Jules. *Crapshoot: Rolling the Dice on the Vice Presidency*. New York: Crown, 1992.

———. *Very Strange Bedfellows: The Short and Unhappy Marriage of Richard Nixon and Spiro Agnew*. New York: Public Affairs, 2007.

———. *White Knight: The Rise of Spiro Agnew*. New York: Random House, 1972.

Wittes, Benjamin. *Starr: A Reassessment*. New Haven, Conn.: Yale University Press, 2002.

Wolfensberger, Donald R. *Congress and the People: Deliberative Democracy on Trial*. Washington, D.C.: Woodrow Wilson Center Press; Baltimore: Johns Hopkins University Press, 2000.

Woodward, Bob. *Shadow: Five Presidents and the Legacy of Watergate*. New York: Simon & Schuster, 1999.

———. *State of Denial*. New York: Simon & Schuster, 2006.

———. *Veil: The Secret Wars of the CIA, 1981–1987*. New York: Simon & Schuster, 1987.

Woodward, Bob, and Carl Bernstein. *The Final Days*. New York: Simon & Schuster, 1976.

Woodward, Bob, and Scott Armstrong. *The Brethren: Inside the Supreme Court*. New York: Simon & Schuster, 1979.

Woolson, Eric. *Grassley: Senator from Iowa*. Parkersburg, Iowa: Mid-Prairie Books, 1995.

Zelizer, Julian E. *On Capitol Hill: The Struggle to Reform Congress and Its Consequences, 1948–2000*. New York: Cambridge University Press, 2004.

Index